THE DICTIONARY OF INTERIOR DESIGN

THE DICTIONARY OF INTERIOR DESIGN

by MARTIN PEGLER

CROWN PUBLISHERS, INC., NEW YORK

To Suzan
for her faith and hope

To Karen, Lisa, and Adam
for their charity

INTRODUCTION

The historic and the contemporary go hand in hand in the language of design, since design is the continuous re-use and revitalizing of forms so that they always have meaning for our way of life. There is no design that cannot find its way back into history: at any moment a dormant historical motif may be given a renaissance by the *avant-garde*. This perpetual rejuvenation means that design terms and ideas survive from many sources and often have more than one interpretation. A word originally used in the French Gothic period might today be applied to a sophisticated element on a Park Avenue skyscraper. A classical architectural ornament might be used by an eighteenth-century cabinetmaker on a piece of furniture. Newly excavated classical remains might form the basis of an entirely new style.

The name of a sixteenth-century architect is given to an eighteenth-century movement in furniture and ornament as well as architecture, and then his name becomes synonymous with a classically elegant mid-twentieth-century style. A frivolous little Gothic castle built by a romantic in the late eighteenth century gives impetus to a revival of the medieval in early-nineteenth-century building and art.

New and exciting concepts are constantly being derived from old or antique motifs of designs. The "chair and a half" is really a contemporary revision of the early-eighteenth-century "drunkard's chair." The long-popular yacht chair is an only slightly altered version of the chair that satisfied many a Roman. Our present-day convertible couches are refinements of our forefathers' trundle or truckle beds. The architectural furniture and cabinets of medieval times are having a renaissance as built-ins, storage-wall units, modular furniture, etc. The stone curtain wall of the Gothic period is no different in concept from the light glass and aluminum curtain wall of today.

Architects, artists, building, ornaments, materials, fabrics, construction devices, accessories, woods, styles, periods, etc. all contribute to the language of design, a multilingual common language used by designers in many lands. You will find French, Italian, German, Spanish, Indian, and other exotic words in this dictionary. I have tried to achieve a lucid and comprehensive collection of these terms, illustrated wherever a picture helps define them, and I have endeavored to show their historical origins and the current meanings.

Martin Pegler

THE DICTIONARY OF INTERIOR DESIGN

AALTO, ALVAR (1898–1961). A Finnish architect and furniture designer. In a strong, modern, expressive style he adapted Finnish traditions and needs to modern European techniques. Aalto concerned himself with satisfying the particular requirements of a structure as in the library at Viipuri (1927–1935), now destroyed, which had excellent lighting, and the TB Sanitorium at Paimlo (1929–1933), which was specifically adapted to the patient's routine. He became famous as a furniture designer with his creations in laminated wood. Other noted works are: the Finnish pavillions at the Paris (1937) and New York (1940) Expositions, and the serpentine-shaped Baker House (1947–1948) at M.I.T. in Cambridge, Massachusetts, where he was made a professor in 1940. After World War II he was active in the reconstruction of Finland.

ABACA. The technical name for Manila hemp. This hard fiber is used for woven matting, carpeting, wall covering, and also for making rope.

ABACHI. A wood. See *Ayous*.

ABACUS. In architecture, the slab or pillow that forms the uppermost portion of the capital of a column. In some of the classic orders (Greek Ionic, Roman Doric and Tuscan), it may be square in plan with a molded lower edge. In other orders it may have concave sides with chamfered edges. The abacus in Gothic architecture is sometimes round or octagonal.

ABACUS

ABATTANT. The French term for a "drop lid" or "fall front," as in "secrétaire à abattant" (a drop-leaf secretary). A Chippendale design is illustrated.

ABATTANT

ABBEY. A monastery. A group of buildings of a religious order which is directed by an abbot or abbess. It is also called a priory. Illustrated is the Chartreuse of Villefranche de Rouergue (15th and 16th centuries).

ABOUDIKROU. An African wood that resembles mahogany and sapele. See *Sapele*.

ABRASION RESISTANCE. The degree to which a fabric, floor covering, etc., resists wearing out due to rubbing or applied friction.

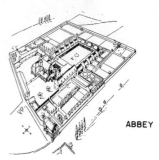

ABBEY

ABSIDIOLE

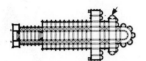

ABSIDIOLE

ABUTMENT

ABSIDIOLE. A small apse at the termination of a lateral nave or aisle in a Gothic church.

ABSTRACT ART. An art expression in which the artistic values reside in the forms and colors rather than in the reproduction or presentation of subject matter.

ABSTRACT EXPRESSIONISM. The expression of the subconscious through renderings of involuntary shapes and by the free use of color. The English counterpart is known as "action painting."

ABUTMENT. The masonry below the spring of an arch which supports the weight, and takes the downward thrust of the arch. See *Springing Line.*

ACACIA. A figured wood that varies from light brown to shades of red and green, and is similar to the American locust tree. It was used as a veneering wood in France and England during the 18th century.

ACAJOU. The French word for *Mahogany.*

ACAJOU MOUCHETÉ. A fine-quality mahogany with wavelike markings and small dark spots in the grain. The wood was popular in the late Louis XVI period, and was used for tables and commodes.

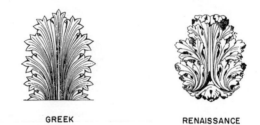

ROMAN   GREEK   RENAISSANCE

ACANTHUS

ROMANESQUE

ACANTHUS (AKANTHOS) LEAF. A carved or painted ornament that resembles the foliage or leaves of the acanthus. A classic design used by the Greeks and Romans, it appears in Gothic art and architecture, and was revived in the Renaissance. The acanthus leaf appears in the Corinthian and Composite capitals. The Greek design has pointed leaf edges, but the Roman version is rounder and broader with more vigorous curves. In Byzantine and Romanesque decoration, the acanthus is stiffer and less delicate. It becomes rounder and more bulbous in the early Gothic period, then becomes bizarre with long thistle-like foliage in the late Gothic. With the Renaissance, the acanthus and tendril motif reaches its highest degree of refinement and elegance.

ACCENT COLOR. Usually a sharp, intense color used as a contrast or pickup for a color scheme. It is used to add excitement to an overall effect.

ACCESSORIES. The small items necessary to the usefulness and comfort in a room. They are often the accents to the general color scheme. Ashtrays, vases, plants, lamps, books, etc., are usual accessories along with throw pillows, pictures, and sculpture.

ACCOTOIR

ACCOTOIR. The French word for "arm stump." It is the wood stile that extends from the frame of the chair seat up to, and supporting, the arm of the chair. Illustrated is a 17th-century Flemish Renaissance chair. See *Arm Stump.*

ACCOUDOIR. The French word for "elbow rest," "rail," or "balustrade." See *Accotoir.*

ACETATE. A generic name for a cellulose acetate fiber. Textile fibers, yarns, threads, and fabrics made from these fibers are called acetate. The fabric drapes well and dyes well, but has limitations with regard to abrasion resistance and strength of fiber.

ACETYLATION. A chemical reaction that changes cellulose linters (cotton) into cellulose acetate. This reaction improves the heat and rot resistance of the fiber yet does not adversely affect the other good properties of cotton.

ACHECH. An animal which is half lion and half bird, and appeared in ancient Egyptian art. See *Hieracosphinx.*

ACORN

ACORN. A turning that resembles the acorn (fruit of the oak tree). It was used as a finial, drop pendant, or furniture foot in the Jacobean furniture of the early 17th century in England.

ACORN CHAIR. A 17th-century Jacobean oak chair with acorn-shaped pendants decorating the cross rail of the back.

ACOUSTICAL TILE. Rectangular panels, usually 12″ x 12″, made of pulped wood, Fiberglas, compressed Styrofoam pellets, asbestos, or mixtures of the above. These tiles are used for quieting down sounds in a room (some tiles are perforated for greater sound absorption), greater insulation, or as a cosmetic over a poor ceiling. In areas where greater sound control is required, the walls may be covered with acoustical tiles. The tiles are now available in assorted colors and with various embossed patterns.

ACRILAN. A trademark for acrylic fiber composed of 85 percent or more acrylo-nitrile, a liquid derivative of natural gas and air. Acrilan fibers have stability, strength, and a luxurious wool-like feel. Fabrics made with acrilan will hold a pressed crease, and have characteristics similar to those of Orlon. Acrilan is also used as a carpeting fiber, and is manufactured by the Chemstrand Company.

ACROLITH. A classic Greek statue which had the heads, legs, and arms carved of marble, while the body, which was often sheathed in gold, was made of wood.

ACROPOLIS. The citadel of a Greek city where most of the important state and religious buildings were located. It was usually on a hill, since this had a natural defense advantage. The most famous acropolis is that in Athens.

ACROTERIA

ACROTERIA. Greek for "summit" or "extremity" (acroterion is the singular form). In classic architecture, the blocks or flat pedestals at the apex and the lowest ends of a pediment. They were often used to hold carved ornaments or statues. The term is sometimes applied to the carved ornament itself, which resembled a stylized palmette leaf. See *Akroter*.

In English and American 18th-century furniture, the acroteria refers to the end blocks of the pediment top of a secretary or bookcase, or the central block in a broken pediment which might hold an urn, vase, finial, or other ornament.

ACROTERIA

ACT OF PARLIAMENT CLOCK. A mid-18th- to early-19th-century English hanging clock with a short trunk and a large wooden dial, without a glass cover. The clock usually was painted black and accented with gold numerals. The trunk design was varied: oblong and paneled, bulbous or fiddle-shaped. The overall measurement of these clocks varied from 3'9" to 5' tall.

ADAM

ADAM BROTHERS, John (1721–1792); Robert (1728–1792); James (1730–1794); William (1739–1822). Four Scottish architect-designers who greatly influenced English interiors and furniture design during the middle and latter half of the 18th century. Robert and James were the most famous, and they designed many important buildings and interiors in a restrained, classic manner. They were very much influenced by the discoveries at Pompeii and Herculaneum, and these classic motifs appear frequently in their work: honeysuckle, swags, husks, oval paterae, flutings, wreaths of flowers festooned between rams' heads. The classic urn appears as a decoration and it was also used as a cutlery container and wine cooler. Amorini, sphinxes, and arabesques were painted on Adam furniture by such artists as Pergolesi, Zucchi, and Angelica Kauffman. The Adams also used Wedgwood medallions, which were frequently designed

ADAM

by John Flaxman, for inserts, and composition ornaments for bas relief ceilings and friezes. See *Adelphi* and *Composition Ornament*.

ADAPTATION. The changing or adjusting of a design or scale to suit another purpose. For example, oriental furniture is adapted in size and scale to conform with contemporary life, habits, and usage.

ADELPHI. Greek for "brothers." The trademark name of the Adam Brothers of England, in the latter part of the 18th century. They were architects and designers of interiors and furniture. See *Adam Brothers*.

ADLER, DANKMAR. A late-19th- early-20th-century architect who was once the engineer-contractor in partnership with Louis Sullivan. See *Sullivan, Louis*.

ADMIXTURES. Water-repellent or coloring agents which are added to mortar. Admixtures may also mean any additives which may speed up or retard the setting time of the mortar. See *Panel Wall*.

ADOBE. A Spanish word for dried brick. The term refers to the clay, as well as the sun-dried brick which is made from the clay, and is a building material in Mexico, California, Arizona, etc.

ADYTUM. Greek word for "recess." In classical architecture, the adytum was the private, inner chamber found in some Greek temples. These sanctums were reserved for the high priests, and it was from the adytum that the prophecies of the oracle were delivered.

AEDICULE. From the Latin "aedicula," a small temple. A term employed by the Romans for a niche into which a statue was placed. A pediment resting on two columns usually enveloped the opening.

AEGICRAMES. The heads or skulls of rams used as decorative elements in classic Greek and Roman sculpture.

AFARA. A wood. See *Korina* and *Limba*.

AFFLECK, THOMAS. One of the Philadelphia school of cabinetmakers of the mid-18th century in America. He was known for his highboys and lowboys, and chairs which were executed in the Georgian and early Chippendale styles.

AGATE WARE. Originally an 18th-century pottery produced by Wedgwood and others in England. The finish was made to resemble agate or quartz.

ADELPHI

AEGICRAMES

AGE OF MAHOGANY

AGE OF MAHOGANY

AGE OF OAK

AGE OF MAHOGANY. The period of interior and furniture design in England lasting from approximately 1710 to 1765. Mahogany was favored by designers and clients as well, and much of the Georgian and Chippendale type of furniture was produced in this wood. Illustrated is a Chippendale mahogany sideboard table of about 1760.

AGE OF OAK. The period of the English Renaissance (about 1500–1660) when oak was prominently used for furniture and interior paneling, wainscoting, etc. It encompasses the Tudor, Elizabethan, Jacobean, and Cromwellian periods. Illustrated is a carved oak Elizabethan bedstead of the late 16th century.

AGE OF REVIVALS

AGE OF SATINWOOD

AGE OF WALNUT

AIGRETTE

AGE OF REVIVALS. The 19th century was essentially a time of revivals of periods and styles of the past. The Classic, Renaissance, Rococo and Gothic revivals followed and overlapped one another. See *Victorian* for the various furniture style revivals. The Conservative Club in London, here shown, was built in the early 19th century and reflected the Renaissance revival.

AGE OF SATINWOOD. The elegant period in England from about 1765 to 1800, when the cabinetmakers and designers favored the light, delicate-toned satinwood for furniture. The Adam brothers used it extensively in their work as did Hepplewhite, Shearer, and Sheraton whose corner washstand of the late 18th century is illustrated. See *Satinwood*.

AGE OF WALNUT. The Restoration, Stuart, William and Mary, and Queen Anne periods in England, which ran from about 1660 to 1714. Walnut was the popular furniture and interior show wood of this time. A William and Mary walnut secretary is illustrated.

AGORA. An open-air marketplace in ancient Greece.

AIGRETTE. French for "egret," a beautifully plumed bird. The term also refers to a decorative feather or plume.

AIR BRICK. A brick perforated with holes. It allows air to enter and pass through a wall.

AIRFOAM. Goodyear's trademark name for rubber foam latex material which is used for cushions and padding.

AISLE. A passageway usually giving access to seats. In Gothic architecture: a lateral subdivision of a church which is parallel to the nave, the largest and central aisle, but is separated from it by piers or columns.

AJARCARA. A Spanish word for brickwork which has a decorative relief surface.

AJOURÉ. A design produced by piercing holes in a definite set pattern in ceramics, wood, metal, etc. It is decoratively used today on dark parchment lampshades, the pierced design having a brilliant, jewel-like effect when the lamp is lit. See *Pierced Work*.

AKANTHOS. See *Acanthus Leaf*.

AKARI LAMPS. Folding rice-paper Japanese lanterns of infinite variety, shape, and size. Many exciting lanterns were designed by Noguchi in the mid-1950's. They were based on traditional Japanese designs but were more sculptural and modern in concept.

AKO. See *Chen Chen*.

AKROTER. An ornamental finish for the apex of a gable. On ancient Greek and Roman structures, the akroter, which decorated the top angle of the pediment, was usually a variation of the palmette ornament, though griffins, figures, and other sculptured devices were used. See *Acroteria*.

AKUME. A wood. See *Bubinga*.

ALABASTER. A fine-textured, compact variety of sulfate of lime or gypsum. A milky white or semitranslucent marble-like material used for ornaments and sculpture.

ALAE. Latin for "wings." Recesses opening out from the central atrium in a classic Roman house. See *Atrium*. The word "aisle" has its origin in *alae*.

ALBERTI, LEONE BATTISTA (1404–1472). A noted Florentine architect, sculptor, painter, musician, and poet of the Italian Renaissance. Alberti wrote books on architecture, perspective, and painting which greatly influenced later craftsmen. His *De Re Aedificatoria* was the first book on architecture ever published. Besides being one of the earliest planners of St. Peter's in Rome, he also designed the Palazzo Rucellai in Florence; S. Francesco in Rimini; the upper portion of the façade of S. Maria Novella in Florence; and S. Andrea in Mantua.

ALBERTI, LEONE BATTISTA

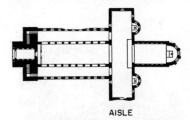

AISLE

AKANTHOS

AKROTER

ALCAZAR

ALBERTOLLI, GIOCENDO (1742–1839). An Italian Neoclassic designer of ornaments who was greatly responsible for the rise and spread of the Neoclassic style in Italy.

ALBINI, FRANCO. A 20th-century modern Italian architect and industrial designer.

ALCAZAR. A magnificent castle built in Seville, Spain, in the middle of the 14th century. It is noteworthy for its blend of Gothic and Moorish motifs.

ALCOVE

ALCOVE. A recess in a room, or a small room attached to a larger one and often designed to accommodate a bed, piano, etc. A niche for a statue, a seat. Originally a Spanish concept; a private area separated from the main room by an estrade or partition of columns. Illustrated is an Elizabethan interior of the late 16th century. An alcove is created in effect by the oriel window. The window-seat arrangement makes it a secluded area away from the main activity of the room.

ALCOVE CUPBOARD. An 18th-century English corner cupboard which was often part of the paneling of the room. See *Coin* and *Quoin*.

ALDER, RED. An American hardwood which has a maple-like figure but can be stained to imitate mahogany or walnut. Because of its strength it is often used for plywood cores. In 18th-century England, the alder wood was used for country or provincial furniture.

ALENÇON LACE

ALENÇON LACE. A decorative fabric with a solid design outlined in cord on a sheer net ground.

ALETTÉ. A small addition or wing to a building. The word also describes a door jamb.

ALEXANDRE. A 17th-century French painter of historical scenes who worked in the Gobelins factory during the period of Louis XIV.

ALMIRAH

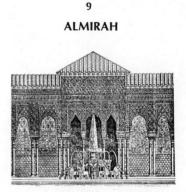

ALHAMBRA

ALHAMBRA. A citadel and palace, which is a masterpiece of 13th-century Spanish-Moslem art, near Granada in Spain. It was begun in 1248 and enlarged in 1279 and 1306. Much of the decoration is in tile and stamped plaster with exquisite geometric patterns, intricate arabesques, and Arabic characters intertwined. Some of the noteworthy parts of Alhambra are: Gate of Justice, Court of Alberia, Court of Lions, Hall of Ambassadors, Tower of Canaries, Court of Myrtles, Hall of Justice, and the many gardens, fountains, and panoramas. See *Stalactite* for the unusual ceiling treatment in the Wall of the Abencerrages. See also *Mauresque.*

ALHAMBRA VASES. Tall, amphora-shaped vases of luster earthenware done in the Hispano-Mauresque style. These vases were made in Valencia in about the 11th century, and were usually decorated with arabesques and Arabic inscriptions.

ALKORANES. The minarets on top of a mosque.

ALKORANES

ALLEGORY

ALLEGORY. A symbolic representation like the sun for Louis XIV, a dolphin for the Dauphin, or a fearless leader represented as an eagle or a lion. Illustrated is an equestrian statue of Louis XIV dressed as a Roman emperor.

ALLOY. A mixture of two or more metals to create a new metal with characteristics of the original metals but also new qualities produced by the blend. See *Bronze.*

ALLURE. The walk along the top of a medieval castle wall.

ALMENA. A Spanish term for a pinnacle or turret. It also refers to a trapezoidal type of indented battlement found in southeastern Europe.

ALMERY. Originally a cupboard set into the thickness of a wall of a medieval structure. Later the almery was a cupboard which contained the portion of food set aside for the servants and pensioners. See *Ambry.*

ALMIRAH. An Anglo-Indian term for a mobile wardrobe or cupboard.

ALLURE

ALMENA

ALMON. A Philippine wood used for veneer. Its color varies from tan to a soft reddish tone and it usually has an interrupted stripe figure. Almon is sometimes sold as white luaun.

ALMOND. A two-pointed, oval-shaped pendant of cut glass or crystal used to embellish a crystal chandelier.

ALPACA. A hard, shiny-surfaced fabric made of wool from an alpaca. The alpaca is a llama-like animal found in the mountains of Chile and Peru. Its wool is long, fine, and usually dark. The cloth may be woven completely of the alpaca wool, or mixed with sheep wool, cotton, or silk.

ALTAR. The stage or dais reserved for religious celebrations. In the classic Greek and Roman buildings, it was the stone pedestal used for sacrifices. In the medieval and Gothic church it was usually an ornately carved table used for the celebration of the Sacrament. Illustrated is the altar of St. Martin's in Cologne, a Romanesque church.

ALTAR

ALTARPIECE

ALTO-RILIEVO

ALTARPIECE. See *Reredos*. Illustrated is a German Romanesque altarpiece from the Wiesenkirche in Soest.

ALTO-RILIEVO. A high-relief sculpture. The carved area projects well out beyond the main surface of the panel, and appears almost full round. An early French Renaissance carved medallion is shown. See *Della Robbia* and *High Relief*.

ALUMINUM. An extremely light yet strong silvery blue metal which resists oxidation and tarnishing. It is as hard as zinc, yet it is malleable, can be made into threadlike wires, and is a good heat conductor. Aluminum is used for furniture frames and for decorative outdoor furniture.

AMARANTH. A wine-red or dark violet mahogany of Central and South America, especially Brazil and the Guianas. Its brilliant, exotic coloring is apt to fade when exposed to light. Amaranth is a hard strong wood and is also called violet wood, purpleheart and bois violet. It was popular during the latter part of the 18th century in France for veneering and marquetry.

AMBO. The raised rostrum or pulpit in the Romanesque and Gothic church structure. There were usually two such lecterns or pulpits in the church; one on the north side for the reading of the Epistle, and one on the south side for the Gospel. The stone-carved ambo of the 11th-century cathedral in Bitono, Italy, is shown.

AMBOYNA. A rich golden brown to orange wood, highly mottled and marked with a "bird's-eye" figure. Adam and Hepplewhite used amboyna as a furniture veneer in the second half of the 18th century in England.

AMBO

AMBRY

AMBRY. From the Latin for "chest" or "cupboard." In ecclesiastic work, the ambry or aumbry was a small cupboard used to hold the sacred vessels, books, and altar linens. It was referred to as an almery.

AMBULANTES. A French term for small, portable serving tables, tea tables, etc. This type of furniture became popular in the Louis XV period in France. See *Rafraîchissoir* and *Serviteur Fidèle*.

AMBULATORY. A walking area, like an aisle, or in a cloister. It particularly refers to the aisle around an apse in a church. The ambulatory is indicated on the plan for the Chartres Cathedral in France.

AMERICAN EAGLE PERIOD. The early part of the Federal period in America, immediately after the Revolutionary War (late 18th, early 19th century), when the eagle was a popular motif on mirrors, and was carved on the bases of couches or other furniture. The eagle also appeared on finials, standards, and the exteriors of public buildings.

AMERICAN EMPIRE MIRROR. See *Constitution Mirror*.

AMERICAN EMPIRE PERIOD. The style of furnishing and design popular in the United States from about 1820 to 1840. It was basically the French Empire style and the later Sheraton designs interpreted in crotch-grain mahogany veneers, cherrywood, curly maple, and maple. Duncan Phyfe was the leading designer of the period, and acanthus leaves, pineapples, cornucopias, and stencil gilding were important decorative motifs and techniques of the period.

AMBULATORY

AMIENS CATHEDRAL

AMERICAN INSTITUTE OF INTERIOR DESIGNERS (A.I.D.). Formerly the American Institute of Decorators. This professional organization for interior designers was founded in 1931 in Grand Rapids, Michigan. The A.I.D. has set a definition for the professional standards, education, and experience necessary for membership. The designer or decorator is "one who, by training and experience, is qualified to plan, design and execute interiors and their furnishings and to supervise the various arts and crafts essential to their completion." In addition to "financial and moral integrity and ability," it requires a "four years course at college level and three years of practical experience." The goal of the A.I.D. is to maintain a high ethical and performance level for designers in the interiors and contract field.

AMIENS CATHEDRAL. A classic example of pure and majestic French Gothic architecture. It was begun in 1220. For the plans of the Cathedral, see *Transept*.

AMILAN. A Japanese synthetic fiber of the nylon type. See *Nylon*.

AMORINI. The plural of amorino. See below.

AMORINO. The Italian word for "little love." A small cupid or cherub used as a carved or painted decoration in the Italian Renaissance period, and again in Louis XV ornament. The Adam brothers used the amorino in wall panel designs and ceiling decorations, and these elements were often painted by artists like Pergolesi and Zucchi. See *Adam Brothers*.

AMORINO

AMPHITHEATRE

AMPHITHEATRE

AMPHIPROSTYLE. A portico set at either end of a classic Greek or Roman building. The portico has pilasters for side walls, and the columns are placed in front of them.

AMPHITHEATRE or AMPHITHEATER. An oval or circular structure with seats, or steplike ledges, rising above and behind each other and surrounding a central open space, stage, or arena.

AMPHORA. A large, two-handled earthenware vase of ancient Greece. It had a narrow neck and an ovoid body.

ANAGLYPH. A type of relief sculpture or ornament which has more depth than a bas-relief, but is not as deep as a high relief. See *Mezzo-Rilievo.*

AMPHORA

ANAGLYPH

ANAGLYPHA

ANAGLYPHA. A metal urn, vase, or vessel which has raised or relief ornamentation.

ANAGLYPTA. The Greek word for "raised ornament." Raised ornaments have been made in gesso and plaster compounds. They are now being produced of rag stock which is liquefied, then poured into a form and molded. The molded pieces are then applied to walls and ceilings to simulate a carved, bas-relief effect. It is, in effect, similar to the Adam brothers' 18th-century technique of "composition ornament" or "carton-pierre." Illustrated is an Adam design for a ceiling and cornice to be executed in carton-pierre for the Duke of Richmond's home Goodwood. See *Composition Ornament.*

ANALOGOUS COLORS. Colors which are next to each other on the color wheel, i.e., orange, red-orange, red; or yellow, green-yellow, green.

ANCHOR BOLT. A long metal device used for reinforcing cornices and pinnacles to ensure greater stability.

ANCON. A Greek word for "bend." A corner of a wall. See *Ancones.*

ANCONA. An Italian word for a group of pictures or one major painting formally arranged, or a recess or niche which is architecturally framed and used for the setting of a piece of sculpture. Illustrated is an ancona with a madonna and child attributed to Michelangelo. The statue is located in the Notre-Dame of Bruges in Belgium.

ANCONES. The brackets used on either side of a door or opening which is capped with a cornice. The ancones support the cornice. See *Console.*

ANAGLYPTA

ANCONA

ANCONES

ANDIRONS

ANDROSPHINX

ANGLO-SAXON ARCHITECTURE

ANIMAL COUCHANT FOOT

ANDIRONS. A pair of upright metal supports with a transverse rod which holds the logs for burning on an open hearth. The French word for andirons is "chenets." See *Fire Dogs.*

ANDROSPHINX. In Egyptian art, a sculptured lion with a human head like the great sphinx at Giza. Illustrated is an androsphinx in the Tuileries Garden in Paris.

ANDROUET, JACQUES. See *Du Cerceau.*

ANGEL BED. An 18th-century French bed with a canopy that usually extends only partially over the bed. There are no front pillars, and the canopy is supported by back pillars or posts. The side draperies continue down to the floor and are pulled back at either side of the bed. See *Lit d'Ange.*

ANGLE IRON. A metal bar which forms a right angle or is L-shaped. Usually it is made of rolled mild steel.

ANGLO-SAXON ARCHITECTURE. The architecture of England from the settlement of the Saxons up to the time of the Norman Conquest. It is roughly the period from the 8th through the mid-11th centuries. Much of the architecture resembles the Roman prototypes that already existed in England. The tower of Earls Barton, Northamptonshire, is illustrated here.

ANGORA. A yarn made from the fleece of the angora sheep. The yarn is used in weaving mohair. See *Alpaca* and *Mohair.*

ANGUIER, GUILLAUME (1628–1708). One of the French painters employed by Le Brun at the Gobelins Factory. He created many painted interior decorations, and was also an architect. His brothers, François and Michel, were famous sculptors of the period.

ANILINE DYES. Any dyes chemically obtained from aniline or other coal-tar derivatives.

ANIMAL COUCHANT FOOT. An antique furniture leg or support sculptured to resemble an animal lying down. This motif is found in ancient Egyptian, Greek, and Roman furniture, and was successfully revived in the Empire period in the early 19th century.

ANNEALING. A method of slowly cooling off heated glass or metal to decrease the brittleness of the material.

ANNULET. A ring. One of the fillets around the lower part of the Greek Doric capital. A band of molding around a Norman column, or the ring of molding joining a group of column shafts in Gothic architecture.

ANODIZED ALUMINUM. Aluminum which has been anodized. (See *Anodizing.*) The resultant metal usually has a sheen and smooth feel.

ANODIZING. The process of coating metal with a hard, protective oxide film by means of electrochemical treatment.

ANTA. A type of projecting pier (like a pilaster) placed behind a column at the end of a side wall of a Greek temple. The base and capital differ from those of the column. "Anta" may also refer to the short wall which partially or wholly encloses the side of the portico. Illustrated is the northwest view of the Erechtheum at Athens (c. 420-393 B.C.). Note the caryatid figures at the far right of this Greek temple.

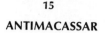

ANNULET

ANTA

ANTEFIX

ANTEFIX. An upright, conventionalized, fanlike ornament, like a spreading leaf. It was originally used in antique Greek and Roman decoration to conceal the end of a roof tile.

ANTEPAGMENTA. Molded jambs on either side of an opening or door. The overdoor and lintel moldings are called the "supercilia."

ANTEPENDIUM. A screen or hanging that covers the front of an altar.

ANTHEMION. Greek for "flower." A classic Greek and Roman decoration; a conventionalized honeysuckle or palm leaf ornament which appears to radiate from a single point. It was used to enhance cyma recta moldings. It was a popular motif during the French Empire period in the early 19th century.

ANTIMACASSAR. A mid-19th-century favorite; a crocheted or knitted doily placed over the upholstered backs of chairs and sofas to prevent them from being soiled by the macassar hair dressing used by men of the Victorian era. It became a symbol of gentility and elegance, and some are still used today. Matching doilies were often used on the arm rests.

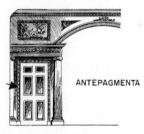

ANTEPAGMENTA

ANTHEMION

ANTIQUE. According to U.S. Customs, a work of art dating from before 1840. Antique furniture is also dated from before 1840. Carpets and rugs must have been made before 1700 to be considered antique.

ANTIQUE FINISH. A furniture-finishing technique used on wood to give it an aged look, an artificially created patina. A darker shade of paint or stain may be applied over a lighter tone, and then rubbed off; or a lighter tone may be used over the darker wood. Wood can also be "antiqued" by artificial weathering, distressing, gouging, or nicking.

APEX STONE

APEX STONE. Also called saddle stone. The uppermost stone in a gable end of a roof.

APOLLINARE IN CLASSE (SANT' APOLLINARE IN CLASSE). An early Christian church built in Ravenna in 534. It is considered one of the most nearly perfect basilicas of its time.

APOPHYGE. The slight concave curve or sweep at the top and bottom of the shaft of a column. It does not appear in the Greek Doric column. Apophyge is Greek for "a flying off."

APPOLLINARE IN CLASSE

APOTROPAIC EYE. In Greek art, the symbolic representation of an eye on the prow of a boat, on the side of a chalice, etc. It was meant to ward off evil spirits.

APOPHYGE

APOTROPAIC EYE

APPAREIL EN ÉPI

APPAREIL EN ÉPI. French term for bricks laid in a herringbone pattern.

APPARTEMENT DE PARADE. A French term for the best or showiest rooms in a home. A reception room.

APPLEWOOD. An American fruitwood used for provincial-type furniture.

APPLIED MOLDING. A geometric-shaped molding applied to the face of furniture to create a paneled effect. It was also called Jacobean ornament and was popular in the late-17th-century English cabinet and cupboard designs.

APPLIED MOLDING

APPLIQUE. A French word for a wall bracket, sconce, or candelabrum applied to a wall. See *Girandole* and *Sconce*.

APPLIQUÉ. A French term for a design or motif which is cut out and sewed or pasted onto the surface of another material as a decorative trim.

APRON. The structural part of a table directly beneath and at right angles to the top, connecting with the legs. It is often shaped, carved, or ornamented. On a chair, it is the surface below and perpendicular to the seat. The apron, frieze, or skirt on case furniture is the perpendicular face below the lowest drawer. In architecture, the protective covering over the joint where the roof and a chimney, or a dormer, meet. It is usually made of lead or zinc.

ARABESQUE (Arabian)

APPLIQUE

APRON

APSE

APSE

APSE. In architecture, the semicircular or angular extension at the east end of a Christian church. It is typical of all basilica plan (or style) churches. See *Nave* and *Transept*.

APTERAL. From the Greek, "without wings." A building with columns at its ends only, but none at its sides.

AQUARELLE. A true watercolor painting produced by using transparent colors and water. The painting surface reflects through the applied paint, and affects the tonal quality of the painting. Water colors dry very rapidly, and the technique calls for speed and dexterity.

AQUATINT. A form of intaglio etching which produces tones. It renders a transparent effect similar to that of a watercolor. It was first used by Paul Sandby, but Goya (late 18th, early 19th century) is considered the greatest aquatinter. See *Engraving*.

AQUEDUCT. A channel for conducting water from its source to the place of use. It usually refers to masonry structures like the classic Roman aqueducts, which brought water to the large cities.

AQUEDUCT

ARABESQUE (Arabian). The complicated ornamental designs based on plant growth fancifully intertwined with lines and geometric patterns used by the Moors, who were prohibited by their religion from representing animal forms.

In Greek, Roman, and Renaissance art, the arabesques are

ARABESQUE

ARAEOSTYLE

used in carvings, paintings, and inlaid work, combining plant and animal forms in complicated intertwining vertical patterns. Mohammedan arabesques are geometrical, and may go in any direction.

ARAEOSTYLE. A term used in classic architecture when the space between two columns in a Greek or Roman colonnade is equal to 3½ times the diameter of the shaft of the column.

ARAZZO. Italian for "arras" or "tapestry."

ARBOR. A framework, sometimes latticed, used as a support for vines. See *Trellis Work*.

ARBRAUM. A red ocher material sometimes used to color mahogany.

ARC DE TRIOMPHE DE L'ÉTOILE. The "Triumphal Arch" in Paris designed by Chalgrin. It was begun by Napoleon in 1806 and was finished in 1836. It is the largest structure of its kind: a single arch running through, 146′ wide, 160′ high, and 72′ deep. It was modeled after the Arch of Titus in Rome. See *Chalgrin, Jean-François*.

ARC EN ACCOLADE. An ogee arch.

ARC EN FER À CHEVAL. French for "horseshoe arch."

ARCA. A Spanish term for a storage chest of the early Renaissance period.

ARCADE. A series of adjoining arches with their supporting columns or piers.

ARCADED BACK. A furniture back with an arcade effect between the top rail and the seat. A Louis XVI motif, it was also used by Sheraton in the late 18th century in England.

ARCA

ARCADE

ARCADED BACK

ARCADED BACK

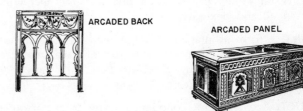
ARCADED PANEL

ARCADED PANEL. A popular motif in early English Renaissance woodwork. The field or face of a panel is ornamented with small piers supporting an arch form. It was also used as a decorative device on chests in the French Renaissance period. Illustrated is an old Jacobean carved chest with a guilloche band trim (17th century). Also see *Bedstead* for Jacobean headboard with arcaded panel.

ARC-BOUTANT. A French term for a flying buttress.

ARCEAU. French for a sculptured trefoil ornament or the curved surface of a vault or arch.

ARC–BOUTANT

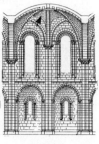
ARCEAU

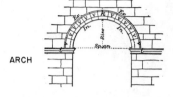
ARCH

ARCH. A curved or arced structural device spanning an opening. The arc may span the space between two walls, columns, or piers. The arc may be flattened, and may be ornamental as well as structural. The inner surface of the arch is called the "intrados." The exterior face is called the "extrados." Arches are also used as decorative features on furniture. See *Intrados, Keystone, Springer, Voussoir.*

ARCH BRICK. The wedge-shaped bricks used in the construction of an arch. See *Voussoir.*

ARCH OF CONSTANTINE. A triumphal arch built in Rome in A.D. 312. It has three archways, each ornamented with four Corinthian columns on pedestals, supporting the blocks of the entablature. A high attic is set above the entablature, and includes the statuary. The side walls of the arches are adorned with magnificent relief sculpture.

ARCH OF TITUS. One of the most effective of the Roman triumphal arches, built in Rome A.D. 81. Composite capitals adorn the engaged columns at the angles of the piers. An armed female figure and a male divinity with cornucopia are sculptured on the keystone. Beautiful, realistic reliefs are carved in the passageways: Titus in his sacred coach being crowned by victory, the horse being led by Rome, and the treasures of Jerusalem being borne on stretchers.

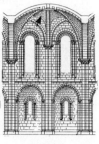
ARCH OF CONSTANTINE

ARCH OF TRIUMPH. The arch which separated the nave (body of the church) from the bema and apse (where the ceremonies were performed) in early Christian basilicas. The triangular areas formed by the arch (spandrels) were usually elaborately decorated, often with mosaic murals. The Arch of Triumph and bema of S. Prassede, which was built between 817 and 824, is illustrated. See *Arch of Titus* and *Arc de Triomphe de l'Étoile.*

ARCH RIB. The projecting band on the edge of an arch in a ceiling or an arch vaulting.

ARCH OF TRIUMPH

ARCH RIB

ARCH RIB

ARCH RIB ROOF

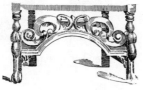

ARCHEBANE-COUCHETTE

ARCHED STRETCHER

ARCHITECTS' PERIOD

ARCH RIB ROOF. A 19th-century cast-iron girder construction technique. The roof thrust was carried down the archlike ribs. The Diana Bath in Vienna by Etzel, built in the late 19th century, is shown.

ARCHAIC. Ancient, antiquated, or primitive. Some pieces of ancient Greek furniture are illustrated.

ARCHAIC

ARCHEBANE-COUCHETTE. A 16th-century Renaissance combination coffer and bench. The slight upward projections of the sides of the chest are similar to armrests, or a headrest, should one wish to lie down.

ARCHED MOLDING. A simple, undecorated, half-round convex molding. It is sometimes used in pairs.

ARCHED MOLDING

ARCHED STRETCHER. An arc-shaped or hooped stretcher used between the legs of tables, chairs, or case furniture in the English Restoration period. It was introduced into England from Spain, where it was popular in the 17th century. See *Rising Stretchers*.

ARCHITECT. From the Greek "master builder." The designer, detailer, and often engineer of buildings and other structures.

ARCHITECTIVE FURNITURE. A contemporary group of office and residential furniture designed for the John Stuart Company in New York by Lindquist and Van der Lanken. It is basic, slablike furniture with sophisticated lines and light supports.

ARCHITECTS' PERIOD. The furniture and decoration of the 18th century in England was dominated by architects like Christopher Wren, James Gibbs, William Kent, Isaac Ware, and the Adam brothers. Their work was characterized by the use of architectural motifs and concepts in the furniture and the interior design. Marble was a popular material, and the classic orders appear over and over again. Illustrated is an Adam tripod and candleholder.

ARCHITECT'S TABLE. A combination drawing table and desk with an adjustable lid that lifted up to make an inclined surface. It was an 18th-century English innovation.

ARCHITECTURAL TERRA-COTTA. Machine-extruded or hand-molded, hard burned clay building blocks. They are usually larger than bricks and may be plain, glazed, unglazed, or decorated.

ARCHITECTURE. The art or science of building or constructing edifices of any kind for human use. John Ruskin defined it as "the art which so disposes and adorns the edifices raised by man—that the sight of them contributes to his mental health, power and pleasure." Illustrated is the 13th-century Cologne Cathedral.

ARCHITRAVE. In architecture, it corresponds to the lintel. In the classic entablature, it is the lowest of three main divisions. The architrave supports the frieze and rests directly on the column, and spans the space between columns. A molding around a door may be called an architrave molding. Illustrated is the Italian Renaissance Grimani Palace in Venice.

ARCUATE

ARCHITECT'S TABLE

ARCHITECTURE

ARCHITRAVE

ARCHIVOLT

ARCHIVOLT. The ornamentation and/or moldings on the face of an arch. It is actually an architrave molding applied to an arch. See *Architrave.*

ARCISOLIUM. A recess in a crypt or catacomb which is used as a tomb.

ARCISOLIUM

ARCO A SPRONE. Italian for "flying buttress."

ARCUATE. Arched or archlike. Illustrated is a late-17th-century English chest. Note the arched base arrangements. See *Arch.*

ARCUATE

ARCUATED ARCHITECTURE

ARENA

ARCUATED ARCHITECTURE. Architectural styles which are based on the use of the arch, like the Romanesque, Gothic, and Renaissance styles.

ARDISH. An East Indian form of decoration. Bits of colored glass were embedded in the ceiling or wall plaster to create a sparkling effect.

AREA RUG. A rug, sometimes shaped irregularly, sometimes rectangular, used to highlight one section or area of a room. It is usually patterned, more decorative and more highly colored than a "wall to wall" carpet or broadloom. The area rug is usually placed directly over wood, tiled, or ceramic floors.

AREA WALL. A brick or stone wall surrounding an area. It also refers to the retaining wall around basement windows below grade.

ARENA. The enclosed area or stage in the center of an amphitheatre. Illustrated is the plan of the Colosseum in Rome showing the arena. See *Amphitheatre*.

ARFE OR ARPHE. 15th- and 16th-century German silversmiths whose work influenced the Plateresco architectural ornament in Spain. See *Plateresco*.

ARFE

ARKWRIGHT

ARMCHAIR

ARGAND LAMP. A lamp invented in 1783 by a Swiss named Argand. The lamp had a round wick with provisions for introducing air into and around the outside of the wick. This increased the draft, and the wick produced a much brighter flame.

ARKWRIGHT. A late Gothic term for a "cabinetmaker," and his products which were usually more like carpentry than cabinetry. Illustrated is a late Gothic trestle table.

ARMADI. Italian for *Armoire*.

ARMCHAIR. A chair with armrests or arm supports as distinguished from an armless side or pull-up chair. Armchairs as we know them today were introduced into popular use in the late 17th century. See *Cacqueteuse*.

ARM PADS. The partial upholstery on the arms of a chair. They serve as padded armrests on the wood arm supports of a chair. In French they are called "manchettes."

ARM STUMP. The vertical element which supports the front part of a chair arm. It may be a turning, a carved device, or a shaped piece of wood. In French it is called *Accotoir*.

ARMARIUM. A bookcase or cupboard. Originally the armarium was a bookcase near the entrance to a church in the cloister of a monastery.

ARMOIRE. A French word for a large, movable clothes wardrobe or closet which was originally used to store armor. It is usually an important case piece of furniture. An 18th-century French Renaissance Régence armoire is illustrated. See *Lebrun, Charles,* for an illustration of a Louis XIV armoire. See *Garderobe*.

ARMOIRE À DEUX CORPS. A Renaissance cupboard of two parts. The lower part, which was formerly only a supporting base, now became enclosed and functioned as a larger cupboard, with a smaller cupboard set on top. Illustrated is a 16th-century Dutch piece. See *Beaufait*.

ARMURE. A raised satin (nonreversible) pattern on a fabric with a rep background. The pattern usually consists of small, isolated, conventional motifs arranged to form an all-over design. Originally it was a fabric woven with a small interlaced design of chain armor, and was used during the crusades (11th and 12th centuries).

ARNEBERG, ARNSTEIN. A 20th-century modern Norwegian architect. He designed one of the three main United Nations chambers in New York City in a formal Nordic style.

ARNEL. A trademark name for triacetate yarns and fibers produced by Celanese Corporation of America. It drapes well, is soft in hand, colorfast, and holds its shape.

ARQUETA. A Spanish term for a small chest, usually to hold jewels, which was kept on a table. The box was often highly ornamented.

ARRAS. Handwoven tapestry. Woven Gothic hanging, usually with figures as part of the design, and produced in Arras, France, in the 14th and 15th centuries. They had a particular texture and often had precious metals woven into the design. Illustrated is a 15th-century French interior with arras on the wall.

ARRAZZI. Italian for "arras." See above.

ARM PADS

ARM STUMP

ARMOIRE

ARMOIRE À DEUX CORPS

ARRAS

ARRIS

ARROW

ART NOUVEAU

ARTESONADO

ARRICCIATO. An Italian term for the second coat of plaster applied to a wall which will eventually have a fresco decoration. See *Fresco.*

ARRIS. In architecture, the sharp edge produced by two surfaces forming an angle. The sharp edge between two adjoining concave flutings of a column shaft.

ARROW. A slender shaft with a triangular pointed tip at one end and a "feathered" end at the back. It had been used as a decorative motif in the classic revival periods starting with Louis XVI and continuing through the Directoire, Empire, and Biedermeier periods.

ARROW SPINDLE

ARROW SPINDLE. A decorative flattened spindle with an arrow tip used in Sheraton chair backs and also in American Federal furniture. It also appeared in some American Windsor chairs.

ART MODERNE. The "modern" concept in furniture and decoration prevalent in America during the 1920's. It was not a truly contemporary style, so much as an affectation of one.

ART NOUVEAU. The "new art" that took hold in Europe and America in the 1890's. It was a style of architecture and decoration which used flat patterns of twisting, tortured plant forms based on a naturalistic concept. It was strongly influenced by Japanese and Gothic art forms. Aubrey Beardsley, the illustrator, William Morris, the designer, and James Ensor, the Belgian painter, were prime forces in this movement. Horta and Van de Velde were outstanding names in the architecture and interiors done in this style as were Charles Rennie Mackintosh in Scotland, Hector Guimard in France, and Antonio Gaudi in Spain. See *Gaudí i Cornet, Antonio,* and *Horta, Victor.*

ARTE POVERA (poor man's art). An 18th-century form of decorating furniture similar to the French "découpage." Engraved prints were hand-colored and applied to wooden furniture in imitation of the fine painted embellishments of the court furniture of the period. See *Découpage.*

ARTESONADO. Moorish woodwork or joinery usually made of Spanish cedar. The wood used for paneling, ceilings, and doors was often left in its natural state, but painted or gilded in important public buildings. Illustrated is a painted balustrade in the Spanish Gothic tower of Santo Domingo. It is very Moorish in design.

ARTIFACT. An article of great antiquity made by man, such as prehistoric carvings or clay objects.

ARTIFACTS

ARTISAN. A skilled craftsman in an art or a trade; a silversmith, cabinetmaker, weaver, etc. Illustrated is a silver gilt jug by a master craftsman, Johann Heinrich Mannlich, who worked in Augsburg, Germany, till 1718.

ARTS AND CRAFTS MOVEMENT. See *Morris, William; Pre-Raphaelite Brotherhood; and Webb, Philip Speakman.*

ARUNDEL MARBLES. A collection of Greek and Roman statues and fragments that belonged to the Earl of Arundel in England during the reign of Charles I (first half of the 17th century). Arundel was a great patron of art, and brought the symmetrical planning of the Renaissance architecture into England. Illustrated is an artist's conception of the gallery of Arundel Marbles in the Arundel mansion which was destroyed in 1678.

ARYBALLOS. A rounded or globe-shaped ancient Greek wine jar. See *Lagynos* and *Oinochoe.*

ASBESTALL. A trademark name for fire-resistant fabrics woven of asbestos and nylon yarns. It is manufactured by the United States Rubber Company.

ASBESTOS. A nonmetallic mineral fiber which is noncombustible. The fiber is woven into fabrics with other yarns, and the fabrics are flameproof.

ASBESTOS CEMENT. A fire-resistant material made of Portland cement and fibers of asbestos.

ASH. A handsomely figured blond wood with a pleasing texture. It takes dark stains well, but it is very hard and not too easy to work.

ASH, ENGLISH. A native English wood sometimes called olive burl. It has an unusual lateral grain known as "fiddleback" or "ram's horn." It was used for country-made or provincial furniture in 18th-century England. See *Olive Wood.*

ASHBEE, CHARLES ROBERT (1863–1942). An English craftsman-designer and a disciple of William Morris and the Arts and Crafts movement. He was a "medievalist" in his preferences, and in 1888 founded the Guild and School of Handicraft. His belief was that "the constructive and decorative arts are the real backbone" of any artistic culture.

ARTISAN

ARUNDEL MARBLES

ARYBALLOS

ASHLAR

ASSYRIAN

ASSYRIAN

ASTRAGAL

ASHLAR. Masonry constructed of flat, surfaced stones, with clean-cut, straight jointing.

ASPEN. An American wood of the poplar family. It is light-colored and silky-textured with light brown stripes. The crotch cut is extremely decorative. Aspen is a soft, easy-to-work-with wood, tools well, and has a natural sheen. It is similar to the European white poplar.

ASPHALT TILE. A synthetic floor covering material which is nonporous, easy to maintain, fairly fire-resistant and fade-resistant. It can be ruined by oil, paint, grease, and certain organic solvents, though a greaseproof asphalt tile is available. Asphalt tiles are affected by extreme temperature changes, becoming soft under extreme heat and brittle under extreme cold. The flooring material can be laid on wood or concrete floors, and comes in a multitude of colors and patterns, in assorted size squares or strips, and varies in thickness from $1/8''$ to $3/8''$.

ASPIDISTRA STAND. A late-19th-century jardiniere or plant stand. It was usually a tripod made of bamboo, three to four feet in height, and reinforced near the bottom with bamboo stretchers. The open top of the stand was made to receive a flowerpot, usually containing an aspidistra plant.

ASSYRIAN. An ancient civilization and art form contemporary with ancient Egypt (c. 1275–538 B.C.). Many Egyptian motifs appear ·in Assyrian works, though the winged bull, the lion, and the eagle are the most distinctive motifs. And the first true arch was developed here. Glazed tile and bricks were used in building, since stones were scarce. Illustrated is an Assyrian bas relief of King Asshurbanipal in repose. Note the furniture. See *Babylonia* and *Mesopotamia*.

ASTER CARVING. A decorative carving of three flowers which appeared on the central panel of Connecticut chests made in New England during the 17th and 18th centuries. Sunflower carvings also appeared on these chests.

ASTRAGAL. In architecture, a small torus molding which is semicircular in section. When it is decorated with beads or olive or laurel berries, it is called a barquette, chaplet, or bed molding. In furniture, the small convex molding used on the edge of an overlapping door of a cabinet, chest, secretary, etc., to keep dust out. See *Torus*.

ASTRAKHAN CLOTH. A heavy pile fabric with curled loops that simulates the caracul lambskin fur.

ASTRAL LAMP. An early-19th-century oil lamp with the burner set on a swinging tubular arm, and positioned lower than the fuel reservoir. The lamps were made of brass, cast iron, silver plate, or china, and sometimes adorned with prisms. They were usually equipped with an Argand burner. See *Argand Lamp.*

ASTYLAR. A building façade without columns or pillars. Illustrated is an Italian Renaissance design after Burckhardt.

ASYMMETRICAL. The opposite of symmetrical. Unequal. Not evenly proportioned or balanced. A favorite decorative line device of the Rococo period. See *Symmetrical.*

ATAUJIA. A Spanish term for a form of Moorish inlay work somewhat like boulle work. Gold, silver, other metals, or colored enamels were set into a metal surface. See *Boulle Work.*

ATELIER. French word for a studio or workshop, usually of a designer, artist, or artisan. Illustrated is a mid-18th-century furniture atelier.

ATRIUM

ASTYLAR

ASYMMETRICAL

ATHÉNIENNE

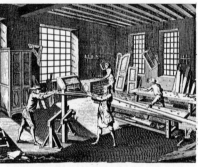

ATELIER

ATLANTES

ATHÉNIENNE. A small tripod table of the Louis XVI and Empire periods. It was sometimes used as a basin stand.

ATLANTES. Full or half male figures used in place of columns to support an entablature; or in place of furniture legs to support chests, tabletops, etc. The Atlantes are male versions of the caryatids and were popular in Renaissance architecture and interior design. See *Caryatid.*

ATRIUM. In classic Roman and contemporary architecture, the central room or courtyard of a home with a central opening in the roof. In early Christian architecture, the open space before the actual entrance to the church—an entrance hall.

ATRIUM

ATTIC

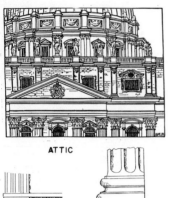

ATTIC

ATTIC BASE

ATTIC STYLE

ATTIC. An architectural order of small square pillars placed at the uppermost parts of a building by classic Athenian architects. A parapet placed on top of an entablature. In classic Roman and Renaissance architecture, a low story erected over the principal entablature, generally decorated with pilasters and a cornice, but the pilasters have neither a capital nor a base. Illustrated is the Renaissance attic of St. Peter's in Rome. An attic is also a garret or room constructed inside the roof. In certain Louis XIV chambers, the area above the entablature was called the attic.

ATTIC BASE. A scotia (concave) molding between two torus (convex) moldings. It was used as a column base in Greek and Roman Doric and Corinthian orders.

ATTIC STYLE. Relating to Athens. A pure, elegant, classic style. Illustrated is a Doric capital and entablature.

AUBERGINE. A French term for eggplant and a deep purplish color.

AUBUSSON. A rug with no pile. It is woven like a tapestry and the motifs are usually French floral and scroll designs. The name originally referred to a famous French tapestry works located in the town of Aubusson, dating back to the 15th century.

AUDITORIUM. A hall, enclosure, or theatre usually equipped with seats. A meeting place or an area for presentations which depend upon sound and acoustics for full appreciation.

AUDRAN, CLAUDE II (1639–1686). A French painter and relief carver in bronze, gold, and silver. He painted historical murals and was employed at the Gobelins works during the reign of Louis XIV.

AUDRAN, CLAUDE III (1658–1734). A French painter, decorator, and designer who created wall murals and tapestries. He made the decorations for the Luxembourg Palace in the period of the French Régence and was a teacher of Watteau.

AUDRAN, GÉRARD (1640–1703). A celebrated engraver. The third son of Claude Audran I (1597–1675).

AULA. A Roman hall. In Germany, the term is applied to a large hall or a university hall.

AUREOLE

AUREOLE. From the Latin word for "gold." A circular, elliptic, or quadrangular halo around a Christ figure, Madonna, or saint. It is also called a "mandorla" or "vesica piscis."

AUSTRIAN DRAPE. A shirred fabric treatment for windows which gives the effect of vertical rows of swags from top to bottom. The bottom edge then makes a horizontal band of semicircular scallops. It may be made to work on a pulley cord like a Roman shade, and the drape raises up in a series of poufs. See *Austrian Shade Cloth.*

AUSTRIAN SHADE CLOTH. A crinkled, woven, striped cotton fabric produced by weaving alternating groups of slack and tight warp ends. It may be made of silk, cotton, or some of the synthetic fibers. It is used for window shade fabric.

AUTHENTIC. Genuine, real, actual.

AVANTURINE LACQUER. A lacquer finish which imitates the color and sparkling quality of the mineral avanturine. It was used during the 18th century in France, sometimes for lining drawers in small chests or cabinets.

AVODIRE. An African blond wood with strong, dark brown vertical streaking and a medium hard texture. It has a pronounced mottled figure and a lustrous quality that makes it a popular veneer and modern cabinet wood.

AXMINSTER. A type of carpet. Originally the term referred to rugs woven at Axminster in England in the mid-18th century where Turkish carpets were imitated on special looms. The loom made possible an unlimited number of colors, designs, and patterns. The Axminster carpet is tightly woven and the pile is usually cut. The back of the weave is heavily ribbed.

AYACAHUITE. A satiny pinewood of Mexico and Central America with very little pine graining. It is used for furniture, and often is given a painted or lacquered finish.

AYOUS. An African west coast, creamy white to pale yellow wood similar to primavera. In veneers, the regular stripes are somewhat like mahogany. The wood is soft, lightweight, and has an even texture. It is also called abachi.

AZULEJOS. Spanish or Portuguese wall tiles decorated with sports or bullfight scenes. They were usually done in blue on white, and these tiles were used in the late Gothic period to cover the walls in place of tapestries.

BABYLONIA. The center of the ancient Mesopotamian empire which reached its cultural peak in architecture, art, and learning in about 1800 B.C. It had its renaissance under the Assyrian rule (1275–538 B.C.). The ziggurats were the major architectural accomplishments of the Babylonian rule in Mesopotamia. See *Ziggurat.*

AUSTRIAN DRAPE

B

BACCARAT. Originally a French card game. The name of a fine crystal made in France and used to decorate chandeliers and sconces, and for table service.

BACHELOR CHEST. A simple chest of drawers usually 24" to 36" wide by 30" to 36" tall. The chest may be traditional or contemporary in style, and the wood or veneer varies with the design. The bachelor chest is sometimes used in pairs, and sometimes in place of sofa tables.

BACK ARCH. A concealed arch that carries the inner part of the wall while the exterior facing material is carried by a lintel.

BACK-CUT VENEER. The wood log is sliced in a manner similar to the half-round slicing method (see *Half-Round Slicing Veneer*). The resulting veneers have a striped figure, and the sapwood is included on the edges.

BACK FILLING. In masonry, the rough masonry behind the facing material, or the filling in the extrados of an arch. When brickwork is used to fill in between studs in a frame building, it is also called "brick nogging."

BACK POST. The two rear uprights of a chair which are continuations of the rear legs. These two elements are usually connected by a top rail and may have a split between them.

BACK STOOL. An upholstered chair without arms, or literally a stool with a back. This term was used to describe the simple seats of the 15th and 16th centuries.

BACKUP. The masonry wall behind the exterior facing.

BACON CUPBOARD. A late-17th-century English cupboard for holding bacon. The cupboard was usually the back of a settle which had an ornamented drawer under the seat.

BADUEL. An early French Renaissance architect who in 1545 prepared the plans for Bournazel, one of the most beautiful, typically 16th-century French buildings.

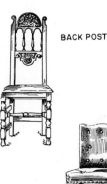

BACK POST

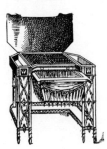

BACK STOOL

BADUEL

BAG TABLE

BAG TABLE. A small 18th- and early-19th-century worktable which is usually distinguished by the cloth bag or pouch under the one or two drawers of the table. This design was popular in England and America. See *Pouch Table*.

BAGHEERA. A fine uncut pile velvet with a roughish, crush-resistant finish.

BAGNELL. An early-18th-century Boston manufacturer of tall case clocks in the Queen Anne style. The works were of brass or wood and the cases of mahogany or maple.

BAGUETTE. A very small, convex bead molding. See *Barquette Molding*.

BAGUETTE

BAGUETTE

BAHUT

BAHUT. A large-footed chest, of the Middle Ages, which was used to hold tapestries, cushions, etc. It eventually evolved into a high cabinet. A 16th-century Italian Renaissance design is illustrated. See *Cassone*.

BAIGNEUSE. An upholstered daybed which was introduced during the French Empire period. The back piece sloped down, and it turned to form the sides; thus the arms or sides of this tublike unit angled from the back down to the front of the seat. It is similar to a *Méridienne*. See also *Grecian Sofa* and *Récamier*.

BAIL HANDLE. A handle or drawer pull which hangs downward in a reversed arch or half moon. The term usually refers to the brass drop handles introduced in the William and Mary period in England. Illustrated is a bail handle from a walnut side table of the period (late 17th century).

BAIL HANDLE

BAILEY. An open court within a medieval fortified castle. It especially refers to the space between the enclosing wall and the keep tower.

BAIZE. A wool fabric originally from Baza, Spain. It is similar to felt in feel and appearance, and can be made of wool or cotton. It is a plain, loosely woven fabric with soft twist filling yarns. The longish nap is sometimes frizzed on one side. It found great acceptance as a cover and for inserts on card tables, drawer and case linings, etc.

BAILEY

BAKED FINISH. A painted or varnished finish which has been baked at a temperature of over 150°F. This heating produces certain desired characteristics in the finish: toughness, durability, etc.

BAKELITE. A trademark name for vinyl resins manufactured by Union Carbide Corporation. It is applied to a group of thermoplastic resins and plastics used for moldings, extrusions, castings, and adhesives. It was popular at one time as a modern tabletop material.

BAKU. A lightweight, very fine, dull-finished straw fabric.

BALCONY. A platform projecting out from a wall of a building, and usually surrounded by a balustrade. Also, the upper section of an auditorium which appears as a shelflike projection over the ground floor of the hall.

BALCONY

BALDACHINO

BALDAQUIN BED

BALDACHINO. A canopy resting on columns, and usually used over altars or thrones in Italian Renaissance churches. The term was originally used to describe a fine, embroidered cloth of gold and silk which was used as a portable canopy over shrines, statues, etc., in processions. See *Canopy*.

BALDAQUIN BED. The French term for a canopy or tester bed. A late-18th-century French or English canopy or "crown" bed. The fabric canopy extended over the bed but was attached to the wall rather than supported by pillars or bedposts extending up from the four corners of the bed frame. A Sheraton design is shown.

BALINE. A plain woven, coarse fabric used for stiffening and for underwork in upholstery.

BALISTRARIA

BALISTRARIA. A loophole or small aperture in the wall of a medieval fortress. The vertical slits in this illustration are the balistrariae.

BALKENTRÄGER. German for "corbel."

BALL-AND-CLAW FOOT. A bird's or dragon's claw grasping a ball or jewel. This is believed to be an old Chinese motif symbolizing world power. It appeared in Europe in Romanesque furniture and in the Dutch designs of the 17th and 18th centuries, and was popular in Georgian England in the first half of the 18th century. A carved Queen Anne chair of the early 18th century is illustrated.

BALL AND RING. A 17th-century turning used for furniture legs, decorations, etc. The turning consists of a series of ball-like turnings separated by flattened discs or rings.

BALL-AND-STEEPLE FINIAL. A wood turning popular in 18th-century American furniture. The lowest element of the finial was a sphere surmounted by a series of rings of graduated sizes which created a tapered, steeple-like element.

BALL FLOWER. A carved Gothic ornament, circular in shape, with a three-lobed or petal effect carved in the center. The ball flower was often a carved enrichment in the hollow or convex part of a molding. It was popular during the latter part of the 13th and most of the 14th century.

BALL FOOT. A turned furniture foot of a spherical or nearly spherical shape with a narrow disc-like pad at its base. It was used extensively in 17th-century Flemish and English furniture, and is similar to a *Bun Foot.*

BALL-AND-CLAW FOOT

BALL FLOWER

BALL FOOT

BALL LEG TIP

BALL LEG TIP. A small, ball-shaped foot with a cup or ferrule, usually made of brass. It fits over the end of a chair or table leg. A French directoire chair of the early 19th century, from Malmaison, is illustrated.

BALL TURNING. See *Knob Turning.*

BALLIN, CLAUDE (1614–1678). A celebrated French metal worker of the Louis XIII and Louis XIV periods. He created many vases and urns of great beauty, including this bronze vase from the park at Versailles.

BALLIN

BALLOON

BALLOON

BALLOON BACK

BALUSTER

BAMBINO

BALLOON. The globelike element which tops a pillar or gate-post.

BALLOON BACK. The arced, or hoop-shaped chair back of the Hepplewhite period. The curved line starts in a concave form at the seat rail, then sweeps up in a bold convex arc creating a smooth loop. It is similar to the Montgolfier chair of the late 18th century in France, and was subsequently popularized during the Victorian era. See *Montgolfier Chair.*

BALLU, THÉODORE (1817–1885). French architect who worked on the construction of the church of Sainte-Clotilde and La Trinité, restored the Tour Saint-Jacques, and reconstructed (with Deperthes) the Hôtel de Ville, all in Paris.

BALUSTER. A turned spindle column that supports a railing, functions as part of a balustrade, is used as a stretcher between chair legs, or is part of a chair back. It is commonly an elongated urn or vase shape. Split or half balusters were a favorite applied ornament in the English Restoration period of furniture. A baluster is also called a banister.

BALUSTRA. A South African dense, hard wood of a light tobacco brown color.

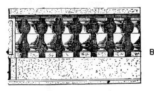

BALUSTRADE

BALUSTRADE. A continuous ornamental railing of stone, wood, or metal. It is a series of balusters topped with a rail, and serves as a decorative enclosure for balconies, terraces, stairways, etc. The balustrade was also used as a decorative motif on 18th-century English architect-designed furniture.

BAMBINO. The Christ child portrayed as an infant in swaddling clothes in sculpture and painting during the early Renaissance period.

BAMBOCCI. Plural of bambino.

BAMBOO. A woody tropical plant used for furniture and ornament. Its distinctive nodular look became very popular in Europe in the 17th and 18th centuries because of the Chinese influence and the oriental or exotic quality of bamboo. Bamboo was also artificially reproduced as a wood turning in Europe and America. See *Bamboo-turned Chair.*

BAMBOO-TURNED. Wood turnings that simulate the nodular or jointed look of natural bamboo. It was favored in the late 18th and early 19th centuries for furniture.

BAMBOO-TURNED CHAIR. A refinement and development from the spool furniture of the mid-19th century in America. It was usually made of maple or other light hardwoods, and was often gilded or painted a light, fanciful color. The turnings resemble a stylized bamboo.

BANCONE. A 15th- or 16th-century Italian writing table which consisted of a flat writing surface over two paneled drawers. A recessed section, with drawers in its end, supported the two drawers. The entire piece rested on stretcher-connected pairs of legs called "running feet." See *Runner Foot*.

BANDED COLUMN. A column which has a lower drum of a larger diameter than the shaft itself. This bottom drum may be more richly decorated than the rest of the shaft. The banded column was popular in the French Renaissance period.

BANDEROLE. A ribbon-like motif, carved or painted; often the flat part of the ribbon was filled with an inscription. A Renaissance decoration. See *Ribbon Back*.

BAMBOO-TURNED

BANDED COLUMN

BANDEROLE

BANDING

BANDING. A narrow strip of veneer used as a border or edging on tabletops, drawer fronts, etc. It was usually made of a contrasting inlay, and was popular in 18th-century furniture.

BANDY-LEGGED. A colonial American term for bowlegged or cabriole-legged furniture of England and America in the early 18th century. Illustrated is a Queen Anne marquetry settee with bandy legs and ball-and-claw feet. Note the shell carving on the knees of the cabriole legs. See *Cabriole Chair* and *Cabriole Leg*.

BANISTER. See *Baluster*. The term usually describes the split turned splats that make up a banister back chair of the late 17th century.

BANISTER BACK CHAIR. A late 17th-century English or American chair with split turned spindles or flat bars for the uprights of the chair back. A more elegant and polished variation on this type of chair back was popular in the Hepplewhite period (later 18th century). See *Bar Back*.

BANDY-LEGGED

BANISTER BACK CHAIR

BANJO CLOCK

BANJO CLOCK

BANNER SCREEN

BANJO CLOCK. A 19th-century wall clock which resembles, in contour, an inverted banjo. See *Barometer Cases*.

BANK. A long Gothic bench. See *Banquette*.

BANK

BANK OF ENGLAND CHAIR. A 19th-century English Regency chair. It is similar to a "tub chair" in that the arms start at the front post and sweep around the back in a continuous rising curve. The legs are usually cabriole, and the front edge of the seat is serpentine in form.

BANNER SCREEN. A fire screen. In the mid-18th century, the banner screen became a popular accessory, and the banner or shield was often made of tapestry or needlework. It was called, also, a "pole screen," since the screen moved up and down the pole. Some fire screens were made of carved mahogany in cheval form, with glass or silk screens.

BANQUETTE

BANQUETTE. The French term for an upholstered bench. Illustrated is an early-18th-century English example.

BANTAM WORK. A Dutch and English lacquering technique of the late 17th century. The design was usually etched into a black ground. This technique originated in Bantam in Dutch Java.

BAPTISTERY. A building, usually round or polygonal in plan, which is separated from the church proper, and contains the font used for the baptismal rite.

BAR BACK. Hepplewhite's term to describe the carved and shaped upright bars that are curved to fit the shield of an open shield back chair or sofa. A bar-backed sofa would be a three- or four-chair-back sofa.

BAR FOOT. See *Runner Foot*.

BAR BACK

BAR TRACERY. Late Gothic tracery in which the stone was cut into bars and arranged in a variety of geometric patterns. It was a refinement from "plate tracery." See *Plate Tracery* and *Tracery*.

BARBACAN or BARBICAN. A medieval tower built either as a fortification in front of the entrance to a castle yard or as a watchtower on a city wall.

BAR TRACERY

BARBACAN

BARBER'S CHAIR. An 18th-century English corner or writing chair. A headrest was sometimes perched over the semicircular top rail. Sometimes the headrest was a continuous broad splat which extended up from the seat frame and was supported by the arms on either side. See *Triangle Seat*.

BARBET, T. A 17th-century late French Renaissance designer of elegant fireplaces and mantels.

BARBIZON SCHOOL. A mid-19th-century group of landscape painters who portrayed romanticized scenes of peasant life and the countryside. Included in this school of artists were Jean-François Millet, Théodore Rousseau, and Narcisse Diaz de la Peña.

BARCELONA CHAIR. A late-17th-century and early-18th-century ladder-back type of chair of Spain. The top cross-slat was usually greatly enlarged and elaborately carved. The stretchers were ornamented with carved rosettes and chiseled grooves. Also, a contemporary 20th-century chair design by Ludwig Mies van der Rohe. The front leg curves up and back to become part of the chair back. The rear leg sweeps up and forward to support the seat. The side view is a graceful X shape. The seat and back are often tufted leather pillows.

BARCLITE. A trademark of the Barclite Corporation of America for rigid Fiberglas panels. They are translucent and patterned with embedded fabrics, foliage, etc. The panels, depending upon the gauge, can be rigid enough to be used as room dividers, sliding doors, cabinet inserts, dropped ceilings, and skylights.

BARBER'S CHAIR

BARCELONA CHAIR

BARCELONA CHAIR

BARDEAUX. French for "shingle tiles" or "weather boarding."

BARDI, LINA BO. A modern Italian born and trained architect. In 1953 she designed a plastic bowl-shaped chair that sets into a steel base, as well as a revolutionary steel and glass house in Brazil. Its cagelike interiors enclosed a garden, and the floors were paved with glass mosaic tiles.

BAREFACED TENON. A term used in the joinery of furniture and cabinets. The tenon usually has two angled edges or "shoulders." A barefaced tenon has one shoulder only.

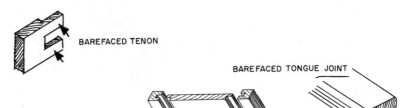

BAREFACED TENON

BAREFACED TONGUE JOINT

BAREFACED TONGUE JOINT

BAREFACED TONGUE JOINT. In furniture and cabinet joinery, a tongue, flush on only one side of a board, sets into a grooved piece of wood. This joint is also called a "groove and rabbet joint."

BARÈGE. A sheer, gauzelike fabric of wool combined with cotton, silk, or other fibers.

BARGEBOARD. The decorative woodwork that covers the joint between a gable end and the roof material of a pitched roof. The bargeboard appears under an overhanging gable. It was highly ornamented with jigsaw and cutout wood lacework at the end of the 19th and early 20th centuries.

BARJIER or BARJEER. Hepplewhite's term for an armchair or bergère. See *Bergère*.

BARLEY SUGAR TURNING. A spiral turning that resembles a twisted rope. It was much used in the mid- and late-17th century for furniture legs and stretchers. Illustrated is an upholstered chair of the Cromwellian period (mid-17th century in England).

BARGEBOARD

BARJIER

BARLEY SUGAR TURNING

BARNES, EDWARD. A contemporary architect born in Chicago in 1915. He studied at Harvard under Gropius and Breuer of Bauhaus fame, and he was greatly influenced by Le Corbusier. Barnes has designed many aircraft interiors, children's camps, etc.

BAROCCO. Italian for "baroque."

BAROCKSTIL. German for "baroque style."

BAROMETER CASES. In the 18th century, these were usually elegant mahogany cases banded with satinwood or boxwood and topped with a broken or swan's neck pediment. The dial was often surmounted by a circular mirror in a reeded frame. The "banjo" type was formed by a wide circular dial topped by a bulbous upper part. Adam and Chippendale designed many beautiful cases for this popular household accessory.

BAROQUE. French for "bizarre," "ugly," or "fantastic"; or from the Portuguese "barroco," which means a large irregular pearl. The Baroque period was a union of architecture, painting, and sculpture in the 17th and 18th centuries, to create an overwhelming and direct appeal to the senses of the beholder. It was a blend of illusionism, light and color, and movement with a new approach to classic art. The period is characterized by large-scale, bold details, sweeping curves, and a wealth of ornament. It was a period of religious emotionalism, and Bernini was one of the great architects of the period. The furniture and decoration of the Louis XIV period is also termed "baroque." Illustrated is the façade of the Church of SS. Vincent and Anastasia in Rome designed by Martino Longhi, another great designer in the baroque style. See *Bernini, Gian Lorenzo; Borromini, Francesco;* and *Jesuit Architecture.*

BAROQUE

BARQUETTE MOLDING. A small semi-circular molding ornamented with beads or olive berries. See *Astragal.*

BARQUETTE MOLDING

BARRÉ. A barred or striped effect running horizontally across knitted or woven fabric.

BARRED DOOR. Glass cabinet, secretary, and bookcase doors with wood fretwork. Because of the high cost of glass, the small precious pieces were set into the intricate, cutout, lacy wood framework. Illustrated is a Chippendale mahogany bookcase of about 1760. See *Fretwork.*

BARRED DOOR

BARREL CHAIR

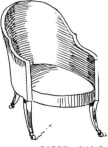

BARREL CHAIR

BARREL CHAIR. A semicircular chair, which is usually upholstered. It resembles a cylinder which has been cut in half vertically. An early-19th-century English Regency chair is illustrated.

BARREL-SHAPED SEAT. See *Garden Seat.*

BARREL VAULT. In architecture, a semicylindrical roof constructed on the principle of the arch. It is also known as a tunnel vault.

BARREL VAULT

SIR CHARLES BARRY

BARRY, SIR CHARLES (1795–1860). An architect of the Classic Revival school in England in the early 19th century. He traveled in Egypt, Greece, and Italy, and introduced into England the fashion of "astylar" façades. By omitting the columns, pilasters, and porticoes from the fronts of his buildings, Barry more truly emulated the Renaissance look. Among his noted works are: the Reform Club in London based on the Farnese Palace, the Travellers' Club in London inspired by the Pandolfini Palace in Florence, Bridgewater House in London, and the Houses of Parliament in London in conjunction with *Augustus Welby Pugin.*

BARTÉLEMY, JEAN SIMON. An 18th-century French painter and decorator of the Louis XVI period. He created a famous series of panels for Marie Antoinette's boudoir entitled "Love Assisting at the Toilet of Grace."

BARTIZAN. A hanging or projecting turret on a tower in a medieval castle or fortress. See *Bastion.*

BAS-RELIEF

BAS-RELIEF. French for "low relief." A form of sculpture in which the design is only slightly raised up from the background. It is also known as "basso relievoo" in Italian. Illustrated are bas-relief panels by Jean Goujon for the Fountain of Innocents, 1549.

BASALT. A dark green or brown stone with columnar strata which was used in Egyptian statues, like the statue of a lion carved in green basalt, here illustrated. It became a favored material in the Empire period because of the "Egyptian" quality and its rich, strong coloring.

BASALT

BASALT WARE. A black porcelain pottery invented by Josiah Wedgwood in 18th-century England.

BASE. In architecture, the series of moldings at the bottom of the shaft of a column. The spreading or gently flaring base helps to distribute the weight of the column. In sculpture, the base can be any block or molding at the bottom of a piece. In furniture, the lowest supporting part of a piece of case furniture.

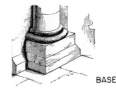

BASE

BASE WOOD. The basic construction wood or carcase of a piece of furniture which will be veneered with a more costly or more beautifully grained wood. Oak and beech are often used in European furniture. Native softwoods are used in the United States.

BASEBOARD. The horizontal board placed at the bottom of the wall and resting directly on the floor. It is usually trimmed with moldings. Illustrated is a wall area designed by Gilles Marie Oppenords, who introduced the Rococo style in France in the latter first half of the 18th century.

BASEBOARD

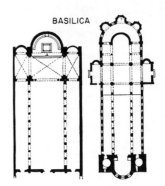

BASEMENT

BASEMENT. In classical and Renaissance architecture, a story below the main level of a building, not necessarily below ground level. Illustrated is a section of the French Renaissance Hôtel de Ville at Anvers. In contemporary usage the basement is a story partially or entirely below ground level.

BASILICA. Originally a large Roman hall or building used as an exchange or a law court, later the prototype for the early Christian church. It was a three-aisled building with the nave (central aisle) taller than the side aisles, and pierced with windows above the roof line of the side aisles. The seat of the judge was in the apse, with the altar set in front of it. The hall of a private Roman house was sometimes called a basilica. See *Arch of Triumph* and *Bema*.

BASILICA

BASILICA OF VICENZA

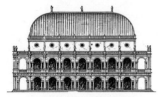

BASILICA OF VICENZA

BASIN STANDS

BASKETWEAVE

BASON STAND

BASSES

BASILICA OF VICENZA. Originally built in 1444 but enhanced with Renaissance arcades by Palladio in 1549. Twin columns support the arches of the arcade. The end bays are made narrower to suggest strength at the angles (a device used in the Parthenon). The arcades are superimposed Doric and Ionic orders, and there are circular openings in the spandrels. This grouping and combination of columns and arches is called the *Palladian Motif.*

BASIN STANDS. Small Chippendale and Hepplewhite 18th-century washstands which were designed to hold minute handbasins.

BASKET STAND. A late-18th-century two-tiered worktable. The tiers were surrounded by galleries composed of small turnings or spindles, and the entire unit rested on a tripod base. It was similar to a Canterbury and a dumbwaiter. Sheraton designed many such tables.

BASKETWEAVE. A textile which is woven with large similar-sized warps and wefts. The weft crosses over alternate warp threads, creating an effect like that of a woven reed basket. This type of weave is used to make homespun and monk's cloth. An inlay technique that simulates the woven quality of a basket.

BASON STAND. See *Basin Stand.* Illustrated is an 18th-century English design.

BASSES. The lower part of 17th-century English and French beds. The word is also used to describe the elaborate fabric treatments used to cover the basses. The fabric treatment was similar to what is today called the "dust ruffle." Illustrated is a state bed from Hampton Court Palace (late-17th-century England).

BASSET TABLE. A Queen Anne-style gaming table for the playing of five-handed basset, a popular 18th-century card game.

BASSO RELIEVO. Low-relief carving. See *Bas-Relief.*

BASSWOOD. A lightweight, light-colored wood used extensively for core stock and crossbanding in plywood panels. It does not warp readily, and it is moderately strong. Basswood is found in the northern United States and Canada and is related to the linden of Europe.

BAST FIBERS. Fibers which are obtained from stalk plants like jute, flax, and ramie. The stalks are retted (steeped in water to cause a weakening of the stalks) and decorticated (the hard outer covering removed). See *Jute* and *Ramie*.

BASTION. A medieval rampart or tower projection from the face of a fortification, usually in an irregular pentagonal plan and faced with masonry.

BASTION

BAT. In masonry, a part of a brick. A half bat is a half of a brick.

BATH. A city in England. See *Royal Crescent* and *Wood, John the Elder.*

BAT

BATHTUB. A tub, vat, or container in which a person may bathe or wash. It is usually connected to water pipes and a drain. See *Labrum.*

BATIK. A Javanese process of resist dyeing on cotton or silk. The design is waxed on the cloth, and the cloth is then dyed. The areas that have been waxed resist the stain, and the pattern appears in the background color of the fabric. The process can be repeated several times for multicolored effects. Streaked effects are obtained when the stain crawls through cracks in the wax. Batik can be imitated by machine printing.

BATISTE. A sheer, fine fabric, usually made of cotton, with a lengthwise striation. It may also be made of wool, or in silk, where it resembles "mull" and is called "batiste de soie." Batiste can also be made of rayon and decorated with woven stripes and jacquard florals.

BAT'S WING BRASSES. An early American hardware design which resembles a conventionalized silhouette of a bat's wing outstretched. The design was used on handle plates and escutcheons.

BATTEN. A long piece of sawed wood used for flooring or wainscoting, or as uprights for lathing. It is usually fastened to one or more boards as a cleat.

BATTER. A sloping or inclined face of a wall, generally used to sustain the pressure of the earth or water being withstood. It is the opposite of a corbel. The batter is also called a "relieving wall." Illustrated is the batter of the early French Renaissance Château de Blois.

BATTER

BATTING

BATTLEMENT

BAY

BAY WINDOW

BATTING. Carded cotton which is prepared in sheets or rolls and is used for stuffing and padding upholstered pieces.

BATTLEMENT. In Gothic architecture, an indented wall of a fort or a city. A crenellated parapet in which the indentations are called embrasures or crenels, and the raised portions are called the merlons.

BAUHAUS. A school of architecture, art, and design located in Weimar, Austria, and later at Dessau. During its short life (1919 to 1933) the Bauhaus declared that the artist and craftsman were inseparable, and craftsmanship was the main source of creative design. Many famous men were associated with the Bauhaus: Walter Gropius, who organized it with Lászó Moholy-Nagy, Johannes Itten, Marcel Breuer, Paul Klee, and Wassily Kandinsky.

BAY. In architecture, the space between columns or supports, or the compartment in a structure which is separated from the rest of the building by an arch, buttress, or vaulting. A bay is also called a severy.

BAY WINDOW. A window which projects outward from the perpendicular wall surface of a building. It generally starts at the ground level and continues up to the top of the building, and the window is often polygonal in shape.

BAYADÈRE. A fabric of strongly contrasting multicolored horizontal stripes. It originally referred to the garment worn by the dancing girls of India.

BAYEUX TAPESTRY

BAYEUX TAPESTRY. A French Romanesque embroidered tapestry commemorating the victory of the Normans in England.

BAYWOOD. Also called Honduras mahogany. It is lighter in color and softer than Cuban or Spanish mahogany. The fine markings of baywood make it a desirable veneering wood.

BEACH CLOTH. An imitation linen crash made of a lightweight cotton warp and mohair (or cotton) filling. The fabric is often used for draperies in casual or informal rooms.

BEAD

BEAD. A small cylindrical molding that may be carved to resemble a continuous string of pearls or beads. An *Astragal*.

BEAD AND BUTT. A panel that is set flush with the stiles and rails that make up the framework of the wall or paneled surface. A bead molding is used along the edges of the panel that butts against the stiles.

BEAD AND REEL. A decorative, half-round or bead molding with alternating circular and elongated oval shapes enriching the surface of the molding.

BEAD CURTAINS. Individual strings of beads (glass, wood, plastic, ceramic, bamboo, etc.) are joined together to form a curtain over a window, door opening, or arch, or the curtain may be used as a semitransparent divider. It was originally an Eastern or Near Eastern device but it is currently having a renaissance.

BEAD FLUSH. A small, almost circular applied molding that runs completely around a panel.

BEAK HEAD. A Norman decorative molding. The carving on this early Gothic enrichment resembles a stylized bird's head and beak.

BEAD AND BUTT

BEAD AND REEL

BEAD FLUSH

BEAM

BEAK HEAD

BEAM. A long, horizontal piece of timber or metal used to support a roof or ceiling.

BEAMED CEILING. A ceiling in which the exposed or encased beams are part of the decorative scheme.

BEARDSLEY, AUBREY. An English illustrator and "high priest" of the "Art Nouveau" period of decoration in the 1890's. He is principally known for his work in the *Yellow Book,* 1894, and his illustrations for Oscar Wilde's *Salome.* Beardsley's designs influenced the interior and furniture designs of the time. See *Art Nouveau.*

BEARER STRIP. See *Bearing Rail.*

BEARING PARTITION. In architecture, an interior wall of one story or less in height which supports a load set upon it from above, in addition to its own weight.

BEARING RAIL. The horizontal carrying member for a drawer in a table or cabinet. It is also called a "bearer strip."

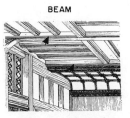

BEAMED CEILING

AUBREY BEARDSLEY

BEARING RAIL

BEAR'S-PAW FOOT

BEARING WALL. A wall which supports a vertical load in addition to its own weight.

BEAR'S-PAW FOOT. A decorative furniture foot used by the French and English designers in the late 17th and early 18th centuries. It is a carved representation of a furry paw, sometimes combined with a ball. This furniture foot was occasionally used on Chippendale-type designs.

BEAU BRUMMEL. An early-19th-century Englishman's dressing table with adjustable mirrors, drawers, shelves, candlestands, etc. It was named after the famous dandy of the time of George IV. Sheraton designed several units of this type.

BEAU BRUMMEL

BEAUFAIT

BEAUVAIS

BEAUVAIS CATHEDRAL

BEAUFAIT. The original spelling of "buffet." Illustrated is a 16th-century French buffet or cupboard. See *Buffet*.

BEAUVAIS. An art factory that specialized in textiles and tapestries, and was begun in France during the reign of Louis XIV. Boucher, during the period of Louis XV, designed many tapestries for the Beauvais looms, including the "Story of Psyche." Toward the end of the 18th century, Beauvais started to produce pile rugs. The most popular motifs used at Beauvais were love scenes and pastorals done in soft pastel colors. A Louis XV fauteuil covered in a Beauvais fabric is illustrated. See *Canapé* and *Causeuse* for other examples.

BEAUVAIS CATHEDRAL (1247–1568). The cathedral, located at Beauvais in France, is a prime example of 14th-century French Gothic architecture. It is particularly noted for its superb glass, the vaulting and the tracery of its choir, and as the highest structure in the Gothic period.

BED CHAIR. An early-18th-century Dutch innovation. It was an armed chair with a back that let down and a hidden leg that unfolded to support the lowered back. The legs and the lowered arms came together to make the center firm. The front rail was hinged so that the entire seat and back unit could come over and down. Often these "chairs" were made of nut wood or maple inlaid with tulipwood and styled with bandy (cabriole) legs and Dutch feet.

BED FRAME. In contemporary use, a steel frame which supports the spring and mattress; generally the frame is set on casters. The frame may be bolted to a headboard. See *Harvard Frame* and *Hollywood Bed*.

BED FRAME

BED JOINT

BED JOINT. A horizontal layer of mortar upon which, or into which a course of masonry or brick is set.

BED MOLDING. A small molding, or series of moldings, placed under a projection, as under the corona of a cornice. Illustrated is a late-17th-century cornice molding designed by William Penn.

BED RAILS. Strips, usually of wood, which are used to connect the headboard to the footboard, and to keep them in a vertical position. Combined with the slats, which are set at right angles to the rails, they support the spring and/or mattress.

BED STEPS. An 18th-century English and American device used for getting in and out of high beds. The steps were often incorporated into other pieces of bedroom furniture, sometimes with a chamber pot container. Illustrated is a Sheraton bed step unit which converts into a stool with an upholstered top when not in use.

BED STOCK. The actual supporting framework of certain 16th-century beds in England and on the Continent. The front posts or pillars that supported the wood tester or canopy stood free of the bed proper, and the bedstock supported the bedding. Similar to the current "bed frame."

BEDFORD CORD. A strong, durable rib-weave fabric with raised lengthwise lines produced by warpwise stuffing threads. The fabric may be made of wool, silk, cotton, rayon, or a combination of the above. This cord is used for upholstery, and is similar to piqué. The fabric was originally woven in New Bedford.

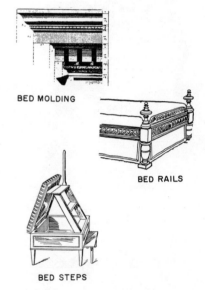

BED MOLDING

BED RAILS

BED STEPS

BEDROOM CHAIR

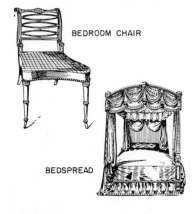

BEDROOM CHAIR

BEDSPREAD

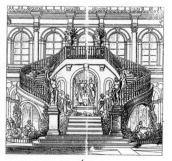

BEDSTEAD

BEDROOM CHAIR. A light frame side chair, intended for use in a bedroom. Sheraton designed this type of chair at the end of the 18th and start of the 19th centuries. Often the chair frame was made of beech, stained or japanned, and equipped with a rush seat.

BEDSIDE CUPBOARD. A small bedside unit, which usually contained a chamber pot. It was also called a "pot cupboard." An 18th-century design.

BEDSPREAD. A fabric covering for the top and sides of a bed. It can be made of a variety of fabrics and in assorted styles: a coverlet with dust ruffles, a fitted top, a loose throw which falls to the floor at the sides, etc. An early-19th-century tester bed by Sheraton is shown here.

BEDSTEAD. The supporting framework of a bed. Illustrated is an early-17th-century Jacobean oak bedstead with an arcaded head panel.

BEE. A stylized bee was the personal emblem of Napoleon I. Along with laurel wreaths, the letter N, stars, and eagles, it was a popular motif of the French Empire period (1804–1814). It has been suggested that the resemblance between the bee and the Bourbon fleur-de-lis made it possible to convert the Bourbon symbol into the Napoleonic symbol without too many drastic renovations when Bonaparte became Emperor.

BEECH. A tough, strong, pale, straight-grained wood which resembles birch and maple. Though it was used for furniture and flooring in the 17th and 18th centuries, it is mainly used today for furniture frames, rocker supports, and bent chair backs. The European beech is similar to the American beech but seasons and works better.

BEHRENS, PETER (1868–1940). A German architect who was greatly influential in the evolution of the modern architectural style. Before World War I he created utilitarian and effective factories and other structures in a simple, direct manner. Among his noted works are the workers' apartment houses in Vienna and the Abbey of St. Peter at Salzburg. He was the teacher and fountainhead for the Swiss architect Le Corbusier, and also for Walter Gropius and Ludwig Mies van der Rohe.

BEL ÉTAGE. The main story of a building, usually containing salons and reception rooms. It is most often the first story above the ground level. Illustrated is the main entrance to a French Renaissance château. See *Piano Nobile*.

BEL ÉTAGE

BELFAST ROOF. A bowstring roof. The roof is composed of a curved principal rafter and horizontal tie beams. The latter are connected by a lattice of wood strips.

BELFRY. The part of a steeple, the upper part of a structure, or the uppermost room, in which a bell is hung.

BELL (of a capital). The body of the capital between the necking and the abacus.

BELL AND TRUMPET. See *Bell Turning*.

BELL COTE. A small bell turret, either of wood or stone.

BELFRY

BELL COTE

BELL (OF A CAPITAL)

BELL SEAT. A Queen Anne chair seat with a rounded front (early-18th-century England).

BELL TOWER. See *Campanile*.

BELL TURNING. A conventionalized bell-shaped turning that was popular during the William and Mary period. The turnings were used for furniture legs and pedestal supports (late 17th century).

BELLA ROSA. A moderately hard and heavy, pink to yellowish beige wood. It is grown in the Philippines and Malaya. The graining is usually straight.

BELL SEAT

BELL TOWER

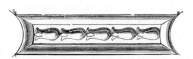
BELLFLOWER ORNAMENT

BELLFLOWER ORNAMENT. A popular 18th-century carved motif used as a furniture and interiors enrichment. The decoration is based on conventionalized bell-shaped flowers or catkins, used in a continuous chain or swag or in graduated sizes as a pendant. It is similar to the "husk" design. See *Husk Ornament*.

BELLOWS. A blowing device used to create a blast of air when it is contracted, or its area is collapsed. It is often highly decorated, carved, or embellished and used as a fireplace accessory. Illustrated is a 16th-century Venetian bellows.

BELLOWS

BELLUSCHI, PIETRO. A contemporary architect born in Ancona, Italy, in 1899 and presently a consultant on churches, shopping centers, and office buildings in the United States. He was the dean of the Department of Architecture at M.I.T. Belluschi is noted for his wood-framed and wood-clad churches and houses built in the "redwood" vernacular of the Portland, Oregon, area. These were influenced somewhat by Japanese architecture. He anticipated the sheath-type curtain wall of the Lever House with his Equitable Savings and Loan Building in Portland of 1948. The glass, mullions, and spandrel panels are all of the same plane. Among his other noted structures are: First Presbyterian Church, Cottage Grove, Oregon; First Lutheran Church, Boston, Massachusetts; and Temple Israel, Swampscott, Massachusetts.

BELOW-GRADE FLOORS. Floors set below the actual street level or ground level. The below-grade floor may be only a foot or two below the outside ground level, or one or more stories below.

BELT COURSE

BELT COURSE. A narrow horizontal course of masonry with a vertical face. It is often used in a continuous strip (under windowsills, etc.) to mark the stories on the wall or façade of the building. It is sometimes called a string or sill course. Illustrated is the Renaissance Rathaus of Lemgo. See *String Course.*

BELTER, JOHN HENRY (?   −1865). A popular New York cabinet and furniture maker of the mid-19th century. He originated and worked with laminated plywood over 100 years ago. Belter's Victorian rococo designs were constructed mainly in rosewood, oak, and walnut. His furniture usually had heavily carved and curved frames, roll moldings, and naturalistic flower details.

BELVEDERE

BELVEDERE. Italian for "beautiful view." In Italian Renaissance architecture, it referred to the uppermost story of a building which was open on several sides to allow for viewing the countryside, or to let in the cooling breezes. A lantern atop a building has also been called a belvedere. Shown here is an early English Renaissance structure by Inigo Jones.

BEMA. In early Christian churches, a raised stage or platform usually set behind the Arch of Triumph and separated from the longitudinal body of the church. In later architecture it expanded laterally into what became the transept. Illustrated is Sant'Apollinare in Classe, in Ravenna; *A* is the Arch of Triumph, *B* is the bema.

BEMA

BEMBERG. A trademark name for rayon thread and/or yarns made by a cupramonium process by American Bemberg Company.

BENCH. A long stool or rectangular seating device. It is often backless or with a low back. See *Carreau* illustration.

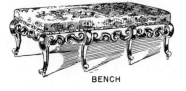
BENCH

BENCH TABLE. See *Settles*.

BENDED BACK CHAIR. See *Fiddleback Chair* and *Spoon Back*. This name is sometimes mistakenly given to a Hogarth chair because of its vase-shaped splat.

BENEMAN, GUILLAUME. An 18th- and early-19th-century French master ébéniste (cabinetmaker) for Louis XVI. He worked for Marie Antoinette at St. Cloud and later executed Percier's designs in the Empire style. Beneman's style was severely classic, and more in keeping with the Empire look. He used mahogany and elaborate gilt bronze mountings to enrich his designs.

GUILLAUME BENEMAN

BENGALINE. A heavy faille-type fabric with a fine weave and crosswise ribs. It may be woven of silk, rayon, or wool warp yarns with worsted or cotton fillings (weft yarns).

BENGE. An African wood of rich brown with tan or darker brown markings. It has a hard texture with a strong contrasting figure.

BENJAMIN, ASHER (1773–1845). American publisher of handbooks for the guidance of carpenters and builders. He was greatly responsible for the generally high level of architecture and building during the Federal period.

BENTWOOD FURNITURE. Furniture which has been made of wood that has been softened by steaming and then molded into curving forms. The term is particularly used to describe the furniture made in this manner by the Austrian, Michael Thonet, beginning in 1857. Modern contour furniture such as that created by Eames and Aalto is made in a similar fashion.

BENTWOOD ROCKER. A typical rocking chair made by Thonet (at the end of the 19th century). It has swirling bentwood arms, back, and supports. A scrolly C- and S-shape decorated unit.

BENTWOOD FURNITURE

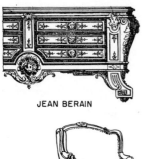

JEAN BERAIN

BERGÈRE

BERAIN, JEAN (1636–1711). A great French designer and decorator of the Louis XIV period. He designed furniture, tapestries, wood and metal accessories, and wall panels. Berain's style ranged from the Louis XIII tradition, through the chinoiserie, up to the elegance of the Régence. He is especially noted for his arabesque forms and the designs he created for Boulle's inlay technique. See *Boulle Work* and *Maître-Ébéniste*.

BERGÈRE. An all-upholstered low armchair that usually has an exposed wood frame and enclosed sides. The upholstered arms are shorter than the length of the seat, and a soft loose pillow rests on a fabric-covered seat platform. It was introduced in the Louis XV period and was also popular in the Louis XVI period. Variations of the bergère are still produced today.

BERGERIES. A popular 18th-century rural scenic design in France and England. Pastoral landscapes were peopled with rustics or elegant gentlepeople dressed as farmers and shepherdesses. Paintings were made in this style, and the popular toile de Jouy prints featured bergerie designs. See *Toile de Jouy*.

BERLAGE, HENDRIK PETRUS (1856–1934). A Dutch architect who advocated a return to simplicity of form and clarity of structure in both his architectural works and his writings. His Amsterdam Stock Exchange (1893–1903) and Diamond Workers' Union Building in Amsterdam (1899–1900) introduced a flat wall surface within a Romanesque framework. This is reminiscent of the work of H. H. Richardson. Berlage was involved in the city planning projects for The Hague (1908) and Amsterdam (1915). He won great favor with the modern architects of the "Amsterdam School," and the architects of "de Stijl" through his publications, e.g., *Bedanken über den Stil in der Baukunst* (1905).

BERNINI, GIAN (GIOVANNI) LORENZO (1598–1680). A great Italian architect and sculptor. The roots of his style were in Michelangelo, Caravaggio, and the classic forms. He used many materials together to achieve an exciting and emotional response from the viewer. Bernini did much work in and around St. Peter's and the Vatican in Rome, as well as suggested, but unused, plans for the east colonnade of the Louvre for Louis XIV. See *Baroque*.

BEVEL. The edge of a flat surface that has been cut on an angle. See *Chamfer*.

BEVEL

BEWICK, THOMAS (1753–1828). An Englishman, considered to be the "Father of Modern Wood Engravings," who introduced white line engraving. See *Engraving.*

BIBELOTS. The French term for "trinkets" or "knickknacks"; small art objects such as paintings, sculptures, snuffboxes, etc., created for personal use or as decorations. Illustrated is a gold box presented by the Empress Maria Theresa to Duke Charles of Lorraine in the latter part of the 18th century. The gold work was done by the jeweler, Franz Mach; the miniatures were painted by Antonio Bencini. See *Objet d'Art.*

BIENNAIS, MARTIN GUILLAUME

BIBLE BOX

BIBELOT

BIBLE BOX. A 17th-century carved box which contained the family Bible. The box was later made with a hinged sloping lid, which when closed served as a reading stand. The interior was sometimes fitted with compartments and small shelves. The desk was evolved from this piece of furniture. An oak piece of the early 17th century (Jacobean period) is illustrated.

BIBLIOTHÈQUE. A French term for a large bookcase or book press. Illustrated is a 19th-century bookcase by Wright and Mansfield made of juniper wood, and decorated with columns and moldings of ebony. Wedgwood plaques are set into the wood panels.

BIDET. The French for "bath." A washing unit or container usually associated with feminine hygiene.

BIEDERMEIER. A German furniture and decoration style (1815–1848). An unaristocratic, clear and simple style, mainly Empire and classic in line but rendered "homey" and "bourgeois" with painted details in black and gold made to simulate carving. The furniture was made largely of fruitwoods and mahogany, and was characterized by arches, pediments, columns, simple escutcheons, burl woods, lyres, plumes, wreathes and rounded-back chairs. The name was derived from "Papa Biedermeier," a comic symbol of homey comfort, well-being, and middle-class contentment. Biedermeier furniture was also made in Austria and Northern Italy.

BIENNAIS, MARTIN GUILLAUME. A noted 19th-century French Empire metalworker.

BIBLIOTHÈQUE

BIDET

BIEDERMEIER

BILLET

BIRD'S BEAK

BISECTED VAULT

BISCUIT TUFTING

BILBAO MIRROR. A late-18th-century mirror, often with a marble or marble and wood frame. A pair of slender columns usually appears on the vertical ends of the frame. The name was derived from Bilbao or Bilboa, where it originated.

BILDWERK. German for "sculpture."

BILLET. A type of ornament which was peculiarly Norman and consisted of short cylinders and blocks. In 18th-century furniture, inlaid billet banding was used for decoration around cabinet drawers and doors.

BIRCH. A light brown, fine grained American wood. It is strong and hard, and can take a natural finish or be stained to simulate mahogany, walnut, satinwood, and other more expensive woods. Birch is used for doors, trims, and floors as well as furniture. In quartered or flat sliced veneer, it is possible to get a curly figure. European birch is similar but less available.

BIRDCAGE CLOCK. A late-17th-century English clock made of brass with exposed pendulum and weights. An openwork clock.

BIRDCAGE SUPPORT. In early American furniture, term for the double block construction which makes it possible for a tilt-top table to rotate and tilt. It resembles the outline of a cage. In other styles (e.g. 18th-century English) the birdcage was made of turned colonnettes.

BIRD'S BEAK. In Greek classic architecture, a supporting molding which resembled the downward curve of a bird's beak. In furniture, a round V-cut on molding corners.

BIRD'S-EYE. A figuration on wood which resembles small birds' eyes. It is caused by cutting on a tangent through the indentations which sometimes appear on the annual rings of the log. This particular figuration is often noted on maple wood.

BISECTED VAULT. An arch or ceiling vault with one impost only; the crown abuts against the opposite wall. It resembles one quarter of a cylinder or half of a barrel vault.

BISCUIT. See *Bisque*.

BISCUIT TUFTING. A method of tying back upholstery and padding to create plump, square tufts on chair backs and seats. Buttons are usually sewn back taut in a regular square or diamond pattern. The excess padding is forced into the center of each square or diamond making a small "pillow." A late-19th-century German Victorian sofa is illustrated.

BISQUE. Pottery that has been fired once and has no glaze or a very thin one. At this point it is dull in color and is tan or red terra-cotta, depending upon the clay used. Bisque also refers to white, unglazed porcelain figurines and groups, made at Sèvres in France during the latter part of the 18th century.

BIZANTINO. Italian for "Byzantine."

BLACK GUM. See *Tupelo.*

BLACKWORK. A particular technique of embroidery of the English Tudor period (16th century). Patterns were picked out in black and silver thread, and these designs inspired many printed lining and wallpapers of the period. Blackwork embroidery became popular again at the end of the Elizabethan reign (after 1603).

BLACKAMOOR. A decorative statue of a Negro, usually in gaudy oriental-type costume. This was a popular motif during the Italian Renaissance and was revived in the Victorian period. The blackamoor was used as a pedestal for tables and torch holders.

BLACKWOOD. A wood similar to acacia and native to Australia and Tasmania. See *Acacia.*

BLANC DE PLOMB. French for "lead white." Some Louis XV furniture which was ordered for the Petit Trianon was originally painted white, but dust and time grayed the furniture down to "gris Trianon," a soft gray color.

BLANKET CHESTS. 17th- and 18th-century American chests which had a lidded section on top, and sometimes one or two drawers below. These units were eventually replaced by the lowboy, the highboy, and the chest of drawers. See *Connecticut Chest* and *Hadley Chest.*

BLEACHING. The process used to remove the natural and artificial impurities in fabrics, to get a pure white for even dyeing or printing. The process varies with the fiber content of the fabric. It might be bleached by exposure to air and light, by chlorine, etc. Open-textured woods can be chemically bleached to lighter tones. Blond walnut and blond mahogany are typical of bleached woods.

BLEEDING. The running off or together of excess dye from a dyed fabric during washing. In the printing of wallpaper and fabrics, the color or pigment which spreads out beyond the actual printed designs, usually into the selvage.

BLEND. A mixture of different fibers in the same yarn or fabric.

BLACKWORK

BLANKET CHEST

BLIND ARCADE

BLIND ARCADE

BLIND STORY

BLOCK FOOT

BLOCK FOOT

BLOCKFRONT

BLIND. A shade or screen device used usually over a window area to control light and air. The blind may be made of various fabrics, and work on a roller principle, or on a pull cord like a Roman shade or Austrian shade. It may also be made of slats of wood, metal, or plastic (Venetian or Boston blinds). See *Austrian Shade* and *Roman Shade*.

BLIND ARCADE. A decorative, nonstructural arcade applied to a wall surface. The arcade has no actual opening. Shown is the Romanesque church of the Trinity in Caen, France.

BLIND HEADER. In masonry, a hidden brick header inside a wall.

BLIND STITCHING. In upholstery, a method of sewing in a particular area of a couch or chair which is eventually covered and therefore impossible to reach. The hidden or blind area is therefore sewn first from the back, then the flap is put into place and finished off by sewing or tacking from the front.

BLIND STORY. See *Triforium*.

BLISTER. A wood grain effect produced by the uneven contour of the annual ring growth. It presents a bumpy, blistered figure. It is also called a "quilted figure." This particular figuration often appears in maple, cedar, poplar, and mahogany.

BLOCK FOOT. A cube-shaped foot usually used with a square, untapered leg. When the foot is tapered it is called a spade, taper, or therm foot. The block foot is also known as the "Marlborough foot," and was used by Chippendale in mid-18th-century England.

BLOCK PRINT. Fabric printed by hand, using carved wooden blocks or plates. The dye is rolled over the raised pattern on the block which is then pressed down, usually under pressure, on the fabric. If a two-color design is desired, two separate blocks are used. This technique was also used on early wallpapers and gilded leather tapestries.

BLOCKFRONT. A furniture front which is divided vertically into alternating convex and concave panels. The center panel is recessed between the two advancing side panels. This design is especially associated with John Goddard and the Newport School of 18th-century American furniture for chests, secretaries, highboys, etc. It is also called a "tub front."

BLOCKING. In masonry, the process by which two adjoining or intersecting walls, not built at the same time, are bonded by means of offsets and overhanging blocks.

BLOCKING COURSE. A course or row of masonry set over a cornice.

BLOND WOODS. Light beige-toned woods like primavera, avodire, aspen, holly, birch, and bleached mahogany and walnut. It can also refer to wood clouded with a white pigment or open grains filled in with white pigment to achieve a light look.

BLONDEL, JACQUES FRANÇOIS (1705–1774). A French architect of the period of Louis XV. He designed in a refined Rococo manner, and his interior "boiserie" is recognized by its straight, elegant, lined panels with Rococo corners and cornices.

BLUEPRINT. A positive print in white lines on a blue paper (ferroprussiate). The negative is a translucent drawing, usually of building or engineering details, plans, etc.

BLUNT ARROW LEG. The leg of an 18th-century American Windsor chair which ends in a ball-like tip. It resembles a spent practice arrow.

BOASTING. The rough shaping of a stone by a carver or sculptor before the finished sculptural or architectural details are accomplished.

BOAT BED. A bed placed in an alcove with only one long side showing. A low, massive piece popular in the French Empire and Restoration periods, and in American furniture contemporary with these periods. It is similar to the gondola or sleigh bed. The boat bed was boat-shaped and often made in light-colored woods with contrasting wood marquetry. It was often raised up on a massive, steplike base.

BOAT-SHAPED TABLE. A modern conference and dining table-top shape. The long sides of the table are shaped like parentheses (they bow out gently in the center and taper in toward the short end). The two short ends are straight. The shape is somewhat like a long oval with a flattened top and botton.

BOBBIN TURNING. Turned legs and stretchers with bobbin-like swellings that were popular in the early 17th century. In the late-18th-century Windsor chair, this type of turning was sometimes used for stretchers. A Jacobean child's chair with bobbin-turned legs is shown.

BOBBINET. A sheer, meshlike curtain fabric.

JACQUES FRANÇOIS BLONDEL

BOBBIN TURNING

BOBÈCHE

BOBÈCHE

BOFET

BOBÈCHE. A socket with a wide rim for a candle or an electric bulb. The bobèche was originally used to catch the wax drippings, but today it is used as a decorative top to a candlestick, or as a device to hook prisms and crystals onto.

BOBOTE. A tropical hardwood.

BODY. In pottery, the clay or other material from which a piece of pottery or porcelain is manufactured. It is not the glaze, which is applied later.

BODYING IN. In the wood finishing process, the filling in of the coarse grains of the wood to provide a more even finish.

BOFET. An early form of "buffet" from the original "beaufait." A 15th-century French buffet is illustrated. See *Crédence*.

BOFFET or BOFFET CHAIR. A three-legged, triangular, Scandinavian chair which was produced till the end of the 16th century. They were usually made of turnings and had carved ornaments.

BOFFRAND, GERMAIN. An 18th-century French decorator of the Louis XV style. He decorated the Palais Soubise for the Prince de Soubise.

BOG OAK. Oak which has been preserved in peat bogs to affect its color. The oak is then used for banding, paneling, and ornaments.

BOGARDUS, JAMES (1800–1874). An American architect who used iron columns to support the masonry of the outer walls and as a means of supporting the floors of a building. The first example was a five-story building. Bogardus also used prefabricated parts to construct department stores, factories, and office buildings across the United States. The Harper Brothers building is a prime example of his work, built in 1854 in Franklin Square in New York City. It appeared to have a front façade almost completely made of glass combined with iron columns and arches in the Venetian Renaissance style.

BOGEN. German for "arch."

BOGENGANG. German for "arcade."

BOIS DE BOUT. Wood which is cut across the grain, thus appearing darker.

BOIS DE FIL. See *Fil de Bois*.

BOIS (or BOISE) DE ROSE. A yellowish wood with reddish striped markings. The wood turns blond as it ages. See *Tulipwood*.

BOIS DE VIOLETTE. Also called "bois de violet" and "amaranth." See *Kingwood*.

BOISERIE. The carved woodwork and paneling of 17th- and 18th-century French interiors. The woodwork was often picked out in gilt, and could become quite elaborate as shown in this Louis XV salon. A gilt console table and mirror are to the left of the door. Note the trumeau (overdoor paneling with painting).

BOLECTION MOLDINGS. A series of rounded moldings which project far beyond the panel or wall to which they are applied. A bolection panel (illustrated) projects from the wall surface, as opposed to a "sunk" panel. See *Panel*.

BOLECTION PANEL

BOLSTER. A long, usually cylindrical, stuffed pillow or cushion that was popular in the late 18th century and early 19th century. A bolster is also an oversized pillow or back rest and may be wedge-shaped or rectangular.

BOLSTER ARM. A fat, rounded or cylindrical upholstered arm on a chair or couch which resembles a bolster. A 19th-century term

BOLTEL. In architecture, an upright, round molding. Particularly a round shaft which is part of an engaged column.

BOMBAY FURNITURE. Furniture manufactured in India after 1740 (the breakdown of the Mogul Empire). The furniture is a conglomeration of French and Portuguese styles and forms which are overlaid with typically elaborate and minute Indian carving. All this was brought about by the influence of France, England, and Holland on India at this time.

BOMBAY FURNITURE

BOISERIE

BOLSTER

BOLTEL

BOMBÉ

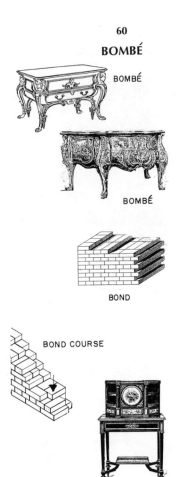

BOMBÉ

BOMBÉ

BOND

BOND COURSE

BONHEUR DU JOUR

BOMBÉ. French for "convex," "arched," or "humpbacked." A swelling or flowing curve, a surface which swells outward and then recedes. This line appears in commodes and chests at the end of the Louis XIV and the Régence periods in France, and reaches its height during the Louis XV or Rococo period. The term bombé often is given to the swollen, overblown commodes of this period. The bombé type of cabinet or drawer furniture also appears in the Venetian Rococo and Chippendale's French style. It is typical of a French base.

BONADER. Wall hangings, painted on paper or canvas, of peasant subjects. These designs were created by Swedes and Swedish Americans in the 18th century.

BOND. The arrangement of bricks, masonry, concrete blocks, etc., in a pattern that is so arranged that the vertical joints do not come out one directly beneath the other. The pattern can be made more definite by using different colored finishing bricks. See the following: *Checkerboard Bond, Common Bond, Double Stretcher Flemish Bond, Dutch Cross Bond or Dutch Bond, English Bond, English Cross Bond, Flemish Bond, Flemish Spiral Bond, Garden Wall Bond, Garden Wall Cross Bond, Running Bond, Stretcher Bond.*

BOND COURSE. The course of bricks which overlaps the bricks below.

BONHEUR DU JOUR. A small upright lady's desk with a cabinet top and drawers. The desk area was usually covered with a let-down front. A small cupboard or bookshelf was often at the rear. A popular design of the Louis XVI period. Illustrated is a design by Reisener (late-18th-century France), which has been enriched with Sèvres plaques.

BONNET TILES. The curved ceramic tiles used at the hips (corner angles) of a roof.

BONNET TILES

BONNET TOP

BONNET TOP. A rounded, bonnet-shaped top portion of a highboy, secretary, etc. The bonnet top was prevalent in 17th-century and early-18th-century English and American furniture. Also called a "hooded top."

BONNETIÈRE. An 18th-century French cabinet, usually designed tall, narrow, and deep enough to hold hats and bonnets.

BOOK BOX. See *Bible Box.*

BOOK-MATCH VENEERING. Every other sheet of veneer is turned over, as a page in a book, so that the back edge of one meets the front edge of the adjacent panel. This produces a matched joint effect.

BOOK TABLE. A rectangular, circular, or hexagonal pedestal with either exposed shelves on all sides, or doors to cover the bookshelves. An 18th-century innovation similar to the pote or pole table.

BOOKCASE. In the late 17th and early 18th centuries, the bookcase resembled the china cabinet of the times. In the mid- and late 18th century, the bookcase took on a new importance, and usually was made in two parts: a glazed door section on top of a closed cupboard. The area below had either additional shelves or drawers. The bookcase top was sometimes used with a writing desk below. Illustrated is a Sheraton-type design.

BORAX. A slang expression for cheap, commercial furniture which is usually poorly constructed, badly styled, and poorly finished.

BORDER. A continuous running motif or ornament used for banding or edging a design, fabric, or panel frame.

BORNE

BORNE. A round or oval type of French sofa with a separating pillar or rail in the center which serves as a back. This seating device was popular in public areas during the Victorian period. These upholstered poufs were usually located in the center of a room, and people sat all around on the circular seat.

BORROMINI, FRANCESCO (1599–1667). An Italian Baroque architect who introduced the undulating façade in the San Carlo alle Quattro Fontane, in Rome. It was the prototype for late-18th-century English "crescents," and appears in altered forms in contemporary architecture. The curved façade presents a picture of animation, movement, and organic growth. These same properties are seen in his St. Ivo's in Rome. It is an interpretation of inner and outer space. Illustrated is the front façade of his Church of the Four Fountains in Rome (1667).

BORROMINI, FRANCESCO

BOOK–MATCH VENEERING

BOOKCASE

BORDER

FRANCESCO BORROMINI

BOSS

BOSS

BOSS

BOSTON ROCKER

FRANÇOIS BOUCHER

BOSS. The projecting ornament which is placed at the intersections of moldings or beams. Angel heads, flowers, or foliage and animal heads are common motifs. In Gothic architecture it is often a hanging, ornamental pendant at the meeting of ribs in vaults. See *Cul-de-Lampe*. On furniture, the boss is a small oval or semicircular applied ornament found in 17th- and 18th-century English and American designs.

BOSSE. An African wood used successfully for large veneer. A uniform pink-brown color with a mottled, satiny texture. It is also called African cedar and cedar mahogany. Bosse has a cedar-like aroma when freshly cut. See *Piqua*.

BOSSE, ABRAHAM (1611–1678). A French designer, painter, and architect under Louis XIII and Louis XIV.

BOSSONA. A hard Brazilian wood with black and brown streaks on a red-brown ground. See *Gonçalo Alves*.

BOSTON ROCKER. A rocking chair, or a chair on curved supports. The wooden seat usually curves upward in the rear and dips down in front. The chair is often spindle-backed and ornamented with a painted design on the wide top rail. An early-19th-century American design.

BOTTEGA. Italian for "shop." The studio or atelier of an artist or artisan.

BOTTICELLI, SANDRO (1444–1510). An Italian Renaissance painter of classical, mythological, and religious subjects. He is noted for his "Venus Rising from the Sea."

BOTTLE END GLAZING. Glazing of cabinet doors in the 18th century that resembled bottle bottoms leaded together. A bull's-eye effect in a circular glass disk. See *Crown Glass*.

BOTTLE TURNING. A Dutch wood turning which resembles a bottle and appears in William and Mary furniture in late-17th-century England.

BOUCHER, FRANÇOIS (1703–1770). The French boudoir artist and decorator of the 18th century. Boucher specialized in voluptuous and sensuous art, and he was a favorite designer of Mme de Pompadour. In 1765, he was made Court Painter to Louis XV. Among his assignments was that of inspector at the Gobelins Factory, where his style influenced the products, including the use of an oval medallion or frame which appears on tapestries and on Sèvres china.

BOUCHER, JULES FRANÇOIS (1736–1781). The son of François Boucher, the famous painter of the Louis XV period. He painted and designed panels and interiors in keeping with the Louis XVI style. One of his chair designs is illustrated here.

BOUCHON. A cork pad covered with baize on one side and leather on the other. It was used, in the 18th century, as a removable cover over the marble top of a bouillotte table. The bouchon filled the space between the actual tabletop and the surrounding brass gallery, thus creating a level surface.

BOUCLÉ. French for "buckled" or "crinkled." A plain or twill weave with small, regularly spaced loops and flat irregular surfaces produced by using specially twisted yarns. It can be made of wool, rayon, silk, cotton, or linen, and the texture is particularly well suited to contemporary furniture upholstery.

BOUDOIR. From the French "bouder," "to pout." A woman's private apartment or room where she could go to "be alone." It was the nucleus of the court social life in the period of Louis XV. Guests were received and entertained in these feminine retreats, which were usually lavishly decorated and furnished.

BOUILLOTTE. A foot warmer used in the 18th century.

BOUILLOTTE LAMP. A late-18th-century candlestick-like lamp. It often was a three- or four-armed candlestick set into a brass galleried base, and a shallow shade, usually metal, covered and protected the flames of the candles. A decorative brass handle finial above the shade made the lamp portable. The bouillotte lamp was originally associated with the small galleried tables they were set upon. See *Bouillotte Table*.

BOUILLOTTE SHADE. A shallow, drum-shaped shade used for a lamp or candlestick. It is sometimes made of decorated metal (tôle). See *Bouillotte Lamp*.

BOUILLOTTE TABLE. An 18th-century French small circular gaming table, with a brass or bronze gallery edge. The table usually had two small drawers as well as a pair of candle slides set into the apron, below the marble top. Originally used for playing bouillotte, a card game. See *Bouchon*.

BOULARD, JEAN-BAPTISTE (1725-1789). A cabinetmaker (ébéniste) and sculptor of the Louis XVI period, noted for the magnificent bed he created for Fontainebleau.

BOULEVARD. A wide street or thoroughfare usually planted with trees and bushes. It was originally a walk on the ramparts of a fortified Gothic wall.

BOULEVARD

JULES FRANÇOIS BOUCHER

BOUDOIR

BOUILLOTE TABLE

JEAN-BAPTISTE BOULARD

ANDRÉ CHARLES BOULLE

BOULLE, ANDRÉ CHARLES (1642–1732). Boulle and his four sons were French master cabinetmakers. Boulle designed rich, ornate, massive pieces often in his own particular veneer technique of tortoiseshell and brass inlay. In 1672, Boulle was appointed head cabinetmaker to Louis XIV. Besides his noted "Boulle-work" technique, he also designed the parquet floors, mirrored walls, and inlaid panels in the Versailles Palace. His designs were opulent and full of scrolls, flowers, and arabesques. See *Boulle Work*. An armoire of Boulle work is used to illustrate *Le Brun, Charles* and *Le Roi Soleil*. Here, illustrated, is a Boulle commode in the Régence style.

BOULLE, P. Born in France in 1619. The "head cabinetmaker" to Louis XIII. See *Ébéniste*.

BOULLE WORK

BOULLE WORK. The special inlay technique of Charles André Boulle, using tortoiseshell and German silver, brass, or pewter. A sheet of metal (usually brass) and a sheet of tortoiseshell were glued together, and the design was cut out of both pieces at the same time. The piece of brass which dropped out during the cutting could then be set into the tortoiseshell, making a decorative inlay (première partie); or the tortoiseshell could be used to fill in the brass sheet (contrepartie). Boulle work is most often associated with the Louis XIV and Régence periods. See *Première Partie, Contrepartie,* and *Marquetry*.

BOURBON PERIOD

BOURBON PERIOD. The classic part of the French Renaissance period, dating from about 1589 to 1730. It encompasses the reigns of Henry IV, Louis XIII, and Louis XIV, and the Régence. Illustrated is a chair of the Louis XIII period done in the Italian style.

BOW BACK

BOW BACK. An 18th-century Windsor-type chair with the hooped or curved back continuing in its sweep down to the arms or chair seat.

BOW FRONT. A convex or "swell front" shape, typical of mid- and late-18th-century chests, commodes, sideboards, etc. This curved line was especially popular in England with Adam (illustrated) and Hepplewhite.

BOW TOP. The top rail of a chair with an unbroken curve between the uprights.

BOW FRONT

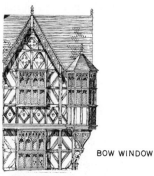

BOW WINDOW

BOW TOP

BOW WINDOW. A large projecting curved or semicircular window. Illustrated is a Tudor half-timber house with a corner bow window at the far right. See *Bay Window*.

BOWSTRING TRUSS FRAME

BOWSTRING TRUSS FRAME. A 19th-century cast-iron girder roof construction which made it possible to span great widths without using tie bars. The roof thrust was carried down to the ground. Illustrated is a railway station in Birmingham, England.

BOWTELL or BOUTELL. A round or roll molding, which was used as an enrichment on Gothic architecture.

BOWTELL

BOX BED. A bed enclosed on three sides, or sometimes a bed that folds up against the wall. In the French Gothic period, the open side was usually draped or shuttered to provide privacy and keep out the drafts. Illustrated is a 10th-century Anglo-Saxon box bed showing drapery used as a screen. See *Lit Clos.*

BOX MATCH. A veneering pattern similar to the diamond match but angled to create a series of consecutive squares radiating out from the center.

BOX BED

BOX PLEATING. A pleating technique in which fabric has been folded back on itself and then folded back again in the opposite direction creating a partially hidden panel of fabric. Similar to a *Linenfold* motif.

BOX SETTLE. A chest or box that functions as a seat and has a hinged lid that serves as the cover to the chest-seat. This piece was popular in the early English Renaissance (Tudor and Elizabethan), and also in 17th- and 18th-century Provincial American furniture.

BOX SETTLE

BOX SETTLE

BOX STRETCHER

BOXWOOD

BOX SPRING. A sleeping unit made of spiral steel springs encased in a boxlike frame. A layer of cotton felt, hair, rubberized hair, or foam is placed over the springs and tightly covered over with ticking. The unit is usually used in conjunction with a mattress, and provides the mattress with greater resiliency.

BOX STOOL. A Renaissance simple seating unit which consisted of a box with a flat hinged top that functioned as a seat.

BOX STRETCHER. A square or rectangular reinforcement at the furniture base, created by the turned or squared stretchers which are found between the legs of a table, chair, or cabinet.

BOXWOOD. A very dense, light-colored, and grained West Indian wood which is used almost entirely for inlays and small decorative articles. During the 16th century it was used as an inlay wood on walnut and oak, and in the late 18th century it was used for border edge work on satinwood pieces.

BOZZETTO. Italian for "sketch." Though it is usually applied to models for sculpture, it may also refer to painted sketches.

BOZZETTO

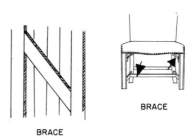

BRACE

BRACE

BRACCIO. Italian for "wing of a building."

BRACED BACK

BRACE. The part of a piece of furniture used to give added strength or rigidity. Stretchers on the legs of a piece of furniture would be considered "braces." In construction, an angled device used to transmit the weight from one part of a structure to another. It is often a piece of wood angled between two major timbers to keep them set in place and to preserve the angle they create. A reinforcement.

BRACED BACK. A term applied to a Windsor-type chair whose back is reinforced by two spindles projecting up from an extension behind the seat up to the chair rail. It is also called a "fiddle-braced back."

BRACKET. In furniture, a shaped support between the leg and the seat of a chair, or the leg and the top of a table. A bracket is also a decorative wall-hung shelf and a sconce or wall fixture. In architecture, a supporting element which projects from a wall or pier at a right angle, and helps to carry the weight of a beam or architectural member, like a cornice, etc.

BRACKET

BRACKET

BRACKET CANDLESTICK

BRACKET CANDLESTICK. A sconce or applique. A decorative wall-hung unit with a candlestick projecting forward. Illustrated is a late French Renaissance design from the Versailles Palace. See *Bronze-Doré* illustration.

BRACKET CAPITAL. In Hindu, Near-Eastern, Saracenic, and early Spanish Renaissance architecture, a capital of a column with bracket forms that make a continuing support for the lintel. Illustrated is a Persian capital found in Persepolis.

BRACKET CLOCK

BRACKET CAPITAL

BRACKET CLOCK. A small clock designed to be set on a projecting wall-hung bracket. It is a shelf clock rather than a wall-hung clock.

BRACKET CORNICE. An ornamental cornice supported by a series of brackets. An interior wooden version of a corbel table. See *Corbel Table*.

BRACKET FOOT. In cabinetry, a popular furniture leg in 18th-century English and American designs. The foot has a straight corner edge and a curved inner edge. In English furniture the leg is usually longer than it is high. It is also called a "console leg."

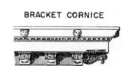

BRACKET CORNICE

BRACKET FOOT

BRAD. A small, thin nail with little or no head and usually less than one inch in length. It is often used for finishing work.

BRADSHAW, GEORGE AND WILLIAM. Cabinetmakers and upholsterers of the mid-Georgian period in England.

BRAGANZA TOE. See *Spanish Scroll Foot.*

BRAID

BRAID. A narrow strip made by intertwining several strands of silk, cotton, or other fabric. It is used as a trimming, a binding, or a finishing edge. A late-17th-century footstool is illustrated. The pillow is edged with braid.

DONATO D'ANGELO BRAMANTE

BRAMANTE, DONATO D'ANGELO (1444–1514). An Italian architect and one of the designers of St. Peter's in Rome. His proposed design for St. Peter's called for a Greek Cross, in plan, with apsidal arms and the four angles occupied by domed chapels. His plan is shown here. After his death, Rafael, Antonio San Gallo, and Michelangelo made revisions on his designs. He epitomized the high Renaissance style with his small "tempietto" in the courtyard of S. Pietro in Montorio, in Rome.

BRASS. An alloy of one part zinc and three to seven parts copper.

BRASS, ANTIQUED. Brass given an aged look through oxidation. This kind of finish can be artificially produced on new brass.

BRASS, POLISHED. Brass given a bright mirror-like finish.

BRASSES. Hardware or decorative handles, escutcheons, hinges, etc., made of brass.

BRATTISHING. A cresting like an ornamented or pierced parapet. A decorative leaf design used as a cresting device on the top of English Tudor screens or paneling. The motif is also called "Tudor Flower."

BRAZIER. A pan, on legs, which held hot embers and was used for heating. It was used up through the 19th century. The brazier is also called a brasero or brasera. A man who works in brass is called a brazier.

BRAZILWOOD. A reddish-colored wood similar to mahogany.

BREAKFAST TABLE. Chippendale's name for an elegant, small, four-legged table, often with a pierced gallery and fretwork trim. The table sometimes had a long narrow drawer.

BREAKFAST TABLE

BREAKFRONT

BREAKFRONT. A case piece of furniture whose front is formed on two or more planes; the central portion is either advanced or recessed from the two ends. It is particularly descriptive of bookcases, cabinets, and secretaries of the 18th century in England and America.

BREAKING JOINTS. Masonry units that are arranged so that continuous vertical joints do not occur in adjacent courses.

BREASTSOMMER or BRESSUMMER. A supporting beam for a wall over a wide opening. It is similar to a lintel, but the breastsommer bears the weight of the whole superstructure of a wall, not only the weight over the opening.

BREEZE BRICKS. Standard-sized bricks made of coke breeze concrete instead of baked clay. It is possible to nail or screw breeze bricks.

BRESSUMMER. See *Breastsommer*.

BREUER, MARCEL LAJOS. A 20th-century architect and designer of the Bauhaus School. He was born in Hungary in 1902 and came to America in 1937. At Harvard, he took on a teaching assignment under Walter Gropius, also of Bauhaus fame. Breuer created the "Butterfly" house in 1949 for the Museum of Modern Art in New York, which presented a vital form of split-level construction. He has also designed many beautiful residences in wood and stone based on traditional American "frame" construction. The UNESCO building in Paris was designed in collaboration with Zehrfuss and Nevri. Illustrated are the tubular metal cantilevered chairs designed by Breuer in 1925.

BREWSTER CHAIR. An early New England chair with turned spindles and a rush seat. Named after Elder Brewster. The chair usually has a double row of spindles on the back. The Brewster chair resembles Provincial Jacobean furniture and is similar to the *Carver Chair*, which, however, has horizontal rails on the back.

BREAKING JOINTS

MARCEL LAJOS BREUER

BREWSTER CHAIR

BRICK

BRICK. A hardened rectangular block of clay, dried and baked in a kiln. The brick is used as a building material, and can be stacked in a great variety of designs to create wall and floor patterns. Brick patterns are also reproduced in paper, embossed paper, plastic, vinyl, etc. The standard brick size is $8^3/_4'' \times 4^1/_4'' \times$ either 2″, $2^5/_8''$ or $2^7/_8''$. Some common types of bricks are: blue or engineering, fletton, glazed, London stock, and sand lime. There are also special facing bricks which are more interesting and colorful.

BRICK, ADOBE. Large clay bricks of varying sizes which are roughly molded and sundried.

BRICK ARCH. See *Voussoir.*

BRICK, BUILDING. Also called a common brick. Not especially textured or surfaced.

BRICK, CLINKER. A very hard burned brick.

BRICK, COMMON. See *Brick, Building.*

BRICK, ECONOMY. 4″ × 4″ × 8″, with one course laying up every 4″.

BRICK, ENGINEERED. 3.2″ × 4″ × 8″, laying up five courses in every 16″.

BRICK, FACING. Specially treated, colored or textured bricks used for exterior or decorative facing.

BRICK, FIRE. A ceramic brick which resists high temperatures.

BRICK, GAUGED. A specially dimensioned brick like an *Arch Brick* or *Voussoir.*

BRICK, NORMAN. $2^2/_3'' \times 4'' \times 12''$, laying up three courses to every 8″.

BRICK, ROMAN. 2″ × 4″ × 12″, laying up two courses in every 4″. The Roman brick is sometimes made up to 16″ long.

BRICK, SALMON. A soft, underburned, pinkish brick. It is also called a chuff or place brick.

BRICK, SCR. $2^2/_3'' \times 6'' \times 12''$, laying up three courses to 8″.

BRICK AND BRICK. A close joining of brick. Only enough mortar is used to bond the bricks and to fill in the irregularities in the bricks.

BRICK NOGGING. The use of bricks to form a partition in the space between studs. See *Back Filling.*

BRIDAL CHEST. A "hope chest." A chest to hold linens, dower, etc. See *Cassone, Connecticut Chest.* A 17th-century Flemish Renaissance bridal chest is illustrated.

BRICK NOGGING

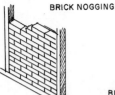

BRIDAL CHEST

BRISEAUX, CHARLES ÉTIENNE (1680–1754). A French rococo architect and interior designer. In his boiserie panels he preferred straight sides with a moderate amount of curvature on top.

BRITISH COLONIAL. The Georgian-like furniture, interiors, and architecture of the 18th century which was developed by the English Colonials in the West Indies, India, and parts of Africa. Basically, it resembled the styles current and popular in England at that time, but it was interpreted by native craftsmen in native woods with native details.

BROACH. The pyramid-shaped element which covers the triangular space left at the corner of a square tower which is surmounted by an octagonal or broach spire.

BROACH

BROACH SPIRE

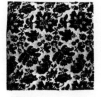

BROACH SPIRE. An octagonal spire on a square tower which has no parapet. The half pyramids which are formed by the two angles of the spire meeting the one angle of the square tower are called broaches.

BROADCLOTH. A lustrous cotton cloth with a tight, plain weave and a crosswise rib. The fabric can also be woven of wool, rayon, or silk.

BROADLOOM. A seamless carpet woven in widths of 6' or more. It is usually produced in 9', 12', 15' and 18' widths and in a variety of textures, weaves, colors, and fibers.

BROCADE. From Low Latin for "to embroider" or "to stitch." Originally a fabric of silk, satin, or velvet, variegated with gold and silver or raised and enriched with flowers, foliage, and other ornaments. The fabric resembles embroidery and is woven on a jacquard loom. The threads do not appear on the surface, but are carried across the width of the fabric on the reverse side. Brocade is much favored for drapery and upholstery in period and traditional rooms.

BROCADE, CARPET. A fabric in which the pattern is formed by heavy twisted yarn tufts on a ground of straight fiber yarns. An engraved appearance results, though the yarns are often of the same color.

BROCATELLE. Originally an imitation of Italian tooled leather. A heavy fabric which resembles damask, with a pattern which appears to be embossed. The pattern is usually a silk weave against a twill background. Also, a calcareous stone or marble having a yellow ground, flecked with white, gray, and red.

BROCATELLE

BROCATELLE VIOLETTE. The most French of all marbles. A stone or marble with a purplish undertone. It is usually richly grained and patterned.

BROCHÉ. A silk or satin ground fabric similar to brocade, with small raised floral designs made to resemble embroidery. Threads that are not used on the surface design are carried only across the width of the design on the reverse side, rather than across the entire reverse side as on brocade.

BROKEN ARCH. A curved or elliptical arch which is not completed or joined at its apex. The open center section is sometimes filled with a decorative device like an urn, finial, etc. Illustrated is a late-17th-century English china cabinet.

BROKEN ARCH

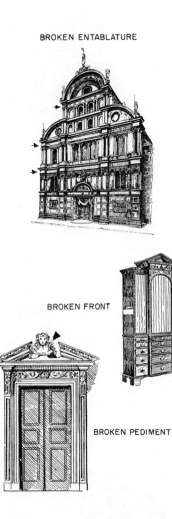

BROKEN ENTABLATURE

BROKEN FRONT

BROKEN PEDIMENT

BROKEN ENTABLATURE. An entablature which does not make a straight even projection out from the building but projects farther over the individual pilasters and columns than it does in the spaces between the pilasters or columns. Illustrated is the Renaissance Church of St. Zachary (S. Zaccaria) in Venice.

BROKEN FRONT. Like a blockfront or breakfront. The front of the piece of furniture is made up of different planes. The center section may project beyond the side sections. Illustrated is an English bookcase of the first half of the 18th century, with a typical classical pediment on top. See *Blockfront* and *Breakfront*.

BROKEN PEDIMENT. An architectural element frequently used on 18th-century English furniture on top cabinets, bookcases, curio cabinets, corner cabinets, highboys, etc. The triangular pediment is interrupted at its apex (crest), and the open central area is often filled with a decorative urn, finial, shell, etc.

BRONZE. A metal originally used for sculpture in ancient Greece and Rome as well as China and Africa. It is a compound made up mainly of copper and tin. As bronze ages and reacts with chemicals, it takes on a greenish tint and matte surface called a patina. A patina can be chemically induced. Bronze has been a popular material for cast sculpture since the 15th century. Illustrated is an ancient Pompeiian bronze figure.

BRONZE

BRONZE D'AMEUBLEMENT. Bronze furniture mounts: handles, escutcheons, drawer pulls, etc.

BRONZE-DORÉ. Gilded bronze. Illustrated is an 18th-century Italian bracket candlestick with a bronze-doré finish. See *Ormolu or Ormoulu.*

BRONZE–DORÉ

BRONZE FURNITURE. A type of metal furniture used by the ancient Greeks and Romans. The designs could be light and open since the material was so strong. In the late Renaissance and Empire period, bronze was again popular for tables, bases, etc., as well as for mounts, hardware, and trim. Illustrated is a Roman bronze lampstand found in Pompeii. See *Bronze-Doré* and *Ormolu or Ormoulu.*

BRONZE FURNITURE

BROSSE, SALOMON DE (1565–1627). The architect to Marie de Medici and the builder of the Luxembourg Palace.

BRUNELLESCHI, FILIPO (1379–1446). An Italian architect, engineer, sculptor, goldsmith, and mathematician, considered one of the first major designers of the Renaissance. He created the great dome of the Florence Cathedral ("Duomo"). It is octagonal in form, the interior brilliantly painted, and springs from the top of an octagonal drum. The dome is topped with a lantern which was added after his death, though in accord with his original design.

FILIPO BRUNELLESCHI

BRUSSELS CARPET. An uncut wool loop pile fabric woven on the Wilton loom, with a cotton back. It is also called a "round wire" carpet. The carpet is distinguished by its long pile and unusual wearing qualities.

BUBINGA. An African wood with a beautiful, purple, closely striped grain, on a pale to red-brown ground. The figure is either narrow broken stripes or mottled. This wood is also called "akume."

BUCKET ARMCHAIR. A Regency-type armchair, similar to the spoon-back chair. The arms rise in a scroll from the middle of the side rails of the seat, then form a continuous curve to create the top rail of the chair. The rounded back is often filled in with caning.

BUCKET ARMCHAIR

BUCKLAND, WILLIAM. An indentured servant, who was brought to America from England in 1755 to serve as "architect" for Gunston Hall near Mount Vernon in Virginia. This was the home of George Mason, author of the Virginia Declaration of Rights. Buckland was responsible for the exterior and interior woodwork, which is considered some of the most beautiful of the period. He also designed the exquisite woodwork in Edward Lloyd's house in Annapolis, Maryland. The Hammond-Harwood House in Annapolis is considered to be his masterpiece.

BUCKRAM. A stiffly finished, heavily sized, plain weave fabric. It is used as a stiffening for valances, etc.

BUCRANIUM. A decorative sculptured ox skull which sometimes appeared on the friezes of Roman structures.

BUCRANIUM

BUEN RETIRO. See *Capo di Monte*.

BUFFET. A cupboard or sideboard. A side table sometimes with cupboards or shelves. Early Renaissance buffets resembled medieval cupboards and were supported on bases. The entire piece was usually decorated with columns, medallions, and arabesques. Illustrated is a late-18th-century Sheraton-type buffet. See *Crédence, Desserte*.

BUFFINGTON, LEROY S. (1848–1931). American architect from Minneapolis, Minnesota, who claimed in 1880 the distinction of being the builder of the first skyscraper of skeleton construction. He patented a method of iron building construction in 1888.

BUHL WORK. The English term for *Boulle Work,* André Charles Boulle's inlay technique using brass and tortoiseshell.

BUILDING BLOCK. A hollow block made of concrete, terra cotta, or extruded burnt clay. Illustrated are late-19th-century hollow bricks.

BUILDING BOARD. Also called plasterboard. The boards are made from repulped paper, shredded wood, gypsum, and other plaster composition and then sandwiched between sheets of kraft paper. These structural boards are usually placed on lathing strips to create partitions, walls, or ceilings. The panels are usually made 4′ × 8′.

BUILT-IN FURNITURE. Elements of furnishing like cabinets, seats, beds, chests, etc., built into the room as an integral part of the interior architecture, a practice that dates from the earliest interiors. In contemporary usage, elements of furniture constructed into the actual walls, or a false wall containing cabinets, chests, bookcases, television, hi-fi, etc., designed with the aim of economy in the use of floor space. Illustrated is an early-18th-century Norse interior with built-in beds and Dutch-type chairs of the period.

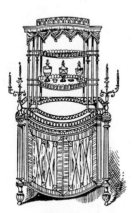
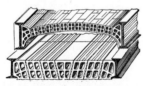

BUFFET

BUILDING BLOCK

BUILT-IN FURNITURE

BULBOUS FORM. A heavy, melon-like wood turning that was popular for furniture supports and bases during the early Renaissance in Holland, England, France, and Italy.

BULL HEADER. See *Rowlock*.

BULLANT, JEAN. A 16th-century French Renaissance architect. He succeeded Philibert Delorme (or de l'Orme) in working on the Tuileries in Paris, and he added one of the wings. Bullant also designed the small Château de Chantilly (illustrated) and Écouen (see *Château* illustration).

BULLION. See *Bull's-Eye*.

BULL'S-EYE. A circular or oval window. A circular distortion in the center of a disk of crown glass. In French it is known as "oeil-de-boeuf." See *Crown Glass*.

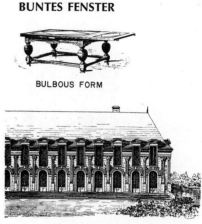

JEAN BULLANT

BULL'S-EYE

BULL'S-EYE MIRROR

BULL'S-EYE MIRROR. A round mirror, often with a convex or concave glass set in an ornamental frame. The period of decoration of the frame may vary. A *Girandole*.

BUN FOOT or Flemish Foot. A furniture support resembling a slightly flattened ball. A device used on Flemish, late French Renaissance, and English late-17th-century furniture.

BUN FOOT

BUNDLE. A unit of wallpaper, usually delivered in single, double, or triple rolls.

BUNSHAFT, GORDON. A 20th-century American architect born in Buffalo in 1909. A chief designer for Skidmore, Owings & Merrill. Bunshaft is a disciple of Ludwig Mies van der Rohe, and in his many noted works like Lever House and Manufacturers Trust Co. in New York City and the Connecticut Life Insurance Building in Hartford, Connecticut, he has attempted to create "an architectural vernacular for today."

BUNTES FENSTER. German for "stained-glass window."

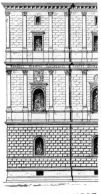

JACOB BURCKHARDT

BURCKHARDT, JACOB (1818–1897). A Swiss historian and the "discoverer" of the "Age of the Renaissance." He was the first writer in the 19th century to treat the Renaissance as a complete entity: the art, architecture, sculpture, and the social institutions of daily life. Burckhardt was the author of *Civilization of the Renaissance.* Illustrated is the Palace of the Chancellery in Rome according to Burckhardt's drawings.

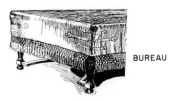

BUREAU

BUREAU. Originally the fabric used to cover a table which was to be used as a writing surface. A desk. A writing table with "pigeonhole" compartments. According to Sheraton, in late-18th-century England, "a common desk with drawers." In the 19th and 20th centuries in America, a chest of drawers used in a bedroom, or part of a bedroom suite.

BUREAU À CYLINDRE

BUREAU À CYLINDRE. French for a rolltop desk. Illustrated is the famous "bureau du roi" (king's desk) begun by Oeben and completed by Riesener. It was created for Louis XV. The rolltop desk is also called a bureau à rideau.

BUREAU À PENTE. French for a folding, slant-lid desk.

BUREAU À RIDEAU. French for a rolltop desk. See *Bureau A Cylindre.*

BUREAU BOOKCASE. A desk with a cabinet over the writing surface, according to Chippendale in 18th-century England.

BUREAU COMMODE. A Louis XIV large writing table with drawers.

BUREAU BOOKCASE

BUREAU EN DOS D'ÂNE. A Louis XV drop leaf desk which took its name from its contour. The top of the desk resembled "the back of an ass." The desk stood on tall cabriole legs with a slant-fronted unit on top. The slanted front dropped down to become a flat horizontal writing surface.

BUREAU PLAT. A flat writing table or desk. Illustrated is a Louis XVI design by Riesener with decorative hardware and mounts by Gouthière.

BUREAU PLAT

BUREAU TABLE. A kneehole table designed by Goddard of Newport, Rhode Island, in the late 18th century.

BURGOMASTER CHAIR. See *Roundabout Chair.*

BURGUNDIAN STYLE. A provincial French Renaissance furniture style of the Rhone Valley area. It was typically Renaissance in its use of architectural elements, and it was noteworthy for its massive construction and high-relief carved decoration. The two-tiered cupboard (cabinet à deux corps) with carved human or allegorical figures is typical of the Burgundian style. Hughes Sambin of Dijon, the architect, is believed to be largely responsible for the Burgundian style. In 1570 he published a book of engraved ornaments, architectural details, etc. See *Cabinet à Deux Corps* and *Sambin, Hughes*.

BURJAIR. A Chippendale term for a *Bergère*.

BURL. A growth in the bole or root of a tree. The wartlike protuberance, which is sliced to obtain veneer wood, contains dark pith centers and many undeveloped buds which produce a pitted "little eye" or "knotted effect" on the surface. The burl often appears in walnut. See *Carpathian Elm Burl*.

BURLAP. A plain weave of cotton, jute, or hemp which is coarse and loosely woven. It is used to cover springs in upholstered furniture and is also used as webbing. In informal, contemporary settings, it can be used for draperies, bedspreads, etc.

BURLING. A final checking and finishing in broadloom production. Long tufts may be clipped or hidden, sunken tufts may be straightened out, etc.

BURO TABLE. An early American (early-18th-century) term for a bureau on legs, and usually with drawers.

BURNT-OUT or ETCHED-OUT FABRIC. A fabric in which patterns are produced by chemically burning out one of the two types of yarns used in making the fabric. This technique is used in the production of brocaded velvet.

BURNT WORK. Line designs drawn on wood by means of a heated metal instrument, or shaded with hot sand.

BURR. A veneer made from transverse slices of the gnarled roots of the walnut tree. It was popular in England from the mid-17th century up to the beginning of the 18th century. See *Burl*.

BUST. A painting or sculpture of a human head and shoulders, sometimes including the chest or breast. It may be used as a freestanding piece of art, or incorporated into an architectural niche, set on a pedestal, or used as a finial in a broken pediment. Illustrated is a section of a room designed by James Paine in the mid-18th century.

BUTCHER FURNITURE. The heavy, architectural furniture produced by Duncan Phyfe after 1825. The massive scrolled quality that was characteristic of the Second or Late Empire in France. See *Second Empire or Late Empire*.

BURGUNDIAN STYLE

BUST

BUTT HINGE. A simple hinge with two leaves. When the hinge is attached to a door and a vertical frame, the pin joint is visible.

BUTT HINGE

BUTT JOINT

BUTT JOINT. The simplest and cheapest type of joint, but it will not take too much strain. One piece of wood is set perpendicular and at right angles to another piece of wood (the pieces butting up against each other). The two pieces are then glued, nailed, or screwed together.

BUTTERFLY. A popular oriental motif that also became associated with the second Empire period in France (1848-1870). Many of the symbols of the first Empire period were revived under Louis Napoleon Bonaparte, but the bee was replaced by the butterfly. It seemed better suited to the romantic and naturalistic tendencies of the period. Illustrated is a 17th-century Japanese textile.

BUTTERFLY

BUTTERFLY TABLE. A Colonial American drop-leaf table with a broad butterfly winglike bracket to support the raised leaf.

BUTTERFLY WEDGE. A double V-shaped fastener used to hold adjoining boards together. The V's connect at their points to form a butterfly shape.

BUTTERFLY TABLE

BUTTERING. In masonry, the technique of placing mortar on the stone or brick with a trowel before setting it in place.

BUTTERNUT. An American wood that is also known as "white walnut." The wood resembles black walnut in fine graining, carvability, polishability, etc., but it is lighter in color. It is hard and durable. The annual rings of the tree form a beautiful figured pattern.

BUTTRESS

BUTTRESS. In architecture, a wall or abutment which is built on the outside of a structure to support a main wall which is very high or loaded with a heavy superstructure. It is often there to resist the thrust of an arched stone roof of a building. The buttress may also be used for decorative purposes and to achieve symmetrical effects.

BUTTWOOD VENEER. In wood grains, the section of the tree toward the root where the trunk fibers swing out and produce, in cross section, a crinkly texture in addition to the long grain. It is also called a "stump grain."

BYZANTINE. Of the Byzantine Empire. Constantinople became the seat of the Roman Empire A.D. 330, and after the fall of Rome in 476, it became the seat of the Byzantine Empire until 1453. The name "Byzantine" is derived from the original town of Byzantium, which was renamed Constantinople by the Emperor Constantine. The Byzantine designs that flourished here were composed of Roman forms overlaid with Near Eastern motifs. The dome on pendentives, the rounded arch, and mosaics play an important part in Byzantine architecture. Some of the Byzantine motifs still appear in Russian and south European decoration.

CABBAGE ROSE. A flamboyant, overblown rose which was extremely popular in the Victorian era. It appeared on carpets, wallpapers, silks, and chintzes and was often combined with lovers' bowknots, doves, and cherubs.

CABINET. A general term from the French for "closet" or "receptacle." In current usage it refers to case furniture with shelves and/or cabinets, or a wooden or metal housing to contain an object (i.e., television set, radio, etc.). Illustrated is a 16th-century French Renaissance cabinet with carved door panels and architectural motifs.

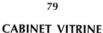

CABINET VITRINE

BYZANTINE

CABINET

CABINET À DEUX CORPS

CABINET À DEUX CORPS. A late-16th-century Renaissance case piece consisting of one cupboard or cabinet set upon a second and usually larger one. These pieces were often carved and ornamented with classic motifs, and had caryatid supports at the corners of the lower unit.

CABINET SECRÉTAIRE. A desk with a cabinet set above the writing surface. The cabinet may have glass, metal, grill, or wood-paneled doors. It was a popular innovation of the 18th century in France and England. A late-18th-century Sheraton design is illustrated.

CABINET VITRINE. A cabinet with glass doors. It is essentially a display case, and was first popularized in the late 17th and early 18th centuries when porcelain from China was rare and precious, and collections of "China" articles were worthy of display. Illustrated is an 18th-century Hepplewhite design which served as a bookcase.

CABINET SECRÉTAIRE

CABINET VITRINE

CABINETWORK

CABLE FLUTING

CABOCHON

CABRIOLE CHAIR

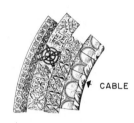

CABLE

CABINETWORK. Furniture and finished interior woodwork as opposed to construction work or rough carpentry.

CABLE. A "twisted rope" motif often used as a molding enrichment in Norman and Romanesque architecture. It is still used for wood moldings, frames, and carved furniture embellishments.

CABLE FLUTING. A semirounded molding worked into the hollowed-out channels of a column. The cables usually rise about one-third of the way up the shaft. This enrichment was originally used by the Romans in the classic times, but was greatly revitalized and emphasized in the Renaissance period in France and Italy. Illustrated is a column from the interior of Chesterfield House in London designed by Isaac Ware in the mid-18th century. Cable fluting is also called "cannelation."

CABOCHON. From the French "caboche," a hobnail. A round or oval convex polished stone. A concave or convex shape used as a carved enrichment on furniture, sometimes surrounded by ornamental leaf carvings. It is found in Rococo furniture and decoration.

CABRIOLE CHAIR. A small chair with a stuffed back made in the mid-18th century in England during Chippendale's French period. The term is an anglicized version of "cabriolet." It does not refer to the cabriole leg. See *Cabriolet* and *French Chair*.

CABRIOLE LEG. From the French "cabrioler," to leap or caper. A conventionalized animal's leg with knee, ankle, and foot adapted in wood as a furniture leg or support. It was greatly favored by designers in the late 17th and 18th centuries for French, English, Flemish, and Italian furniture. The leg curves outward toward the knee and then in and downward to the ankle, making an S shape. In the Queen Anne period the knee was often adorned with a shell. In early Georgian furniture the leg was often embellished with lion masks, satyr masks, or cabochon and leaf ornaments. The cabriole leg reached the height of refinement and ornateness during the Louis XV Rococo period, and is considered a typical Rococo feature. An 18th-century Chippendale secretary is illustrated.

CABRIOLE LEG

CABRIOLET. A small Louis XV chair with a concave back and cabriole legs. In the Louis XVI period the name was applied to a chair with an oval, hollowed-out back. The top of the frame was often decorated with a ribbon and bow as though the chair back were a frame ready to be hung. Illustrated is a Hepplewhite adaptation. A cabriolet is also a two-wheeled, one-horse carriage. See *Cabriole Chair*.

CACHE-POT. A pot made of china, wood, or porcelain, and used as a container or flowerpot holder.

CACQUETEUSE (chaise de femme). An early French Renaissance conversational chair with a high, narrow back and curved arms. A prototype for the smaller scaled "fauteuils" of the 18th century. A 16th-century French Renaissance chair is shown. See *Caqueteuse* and *Caquetoire*.

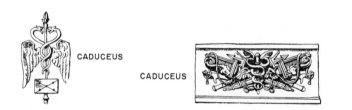

CADUCEUS

CADUCEUS

CADUCEUS. A wand or staff, entwined by two serpents, and surmounted by a pair of wings. In classic times it was the symbol for Mercury's rod. The motif appears in carved and painted form in the Louis XVI period. The caduceus is currently the symbol of the medical profession.

CAEN STONE. A yellowish limestone with wavy markings. It is used in French architecture and ornament, and is found in Caen in Normandy.

CAFÉ CURTAINS. Short curtains, usually made with a scalloped top. The top points of the scallops are hooked, clipped, or slipped over a usually decorative rod, sometimes by means of fabric loops sewn on the curtains. Café curtains are often used in pairs, one set below the other. They are used most often for an informal, country-style window treatment.

CAFFIERI, JACQUES (1678-1755). A French cabinetmaker and sculptor in bronze, who worked for Louis XV in the Rococo style.

CAFFIERI, JEAN-JACQUES (1725-1792). A great French artisan of ormolu metal mounts for Rococo furniture. He worked under Jean-François Oeben, the "king's cabinetmaker" to Louis XV.

CAFFIERI, JEAN-JACQUES

CABRIOLET

CACQUETEUSE

CAFÉ CURTAINS

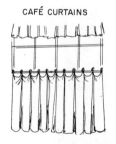

JACQUES CAFFIERI

PHILIPPE CAFFIERI

CAISSONS

CALLIGRAPHY

CAMBER

CAFFIERI, PHILIPPE (c. 1634–1716). A French sculptor in metal, wood, and marble. He was considered the greatest metal carver of his time, and he specialized in decorative furniture mounts. Caffieri worked under Le Brun at the Gobelins Factory during the reign of Louis XIV. The illustrated pedestal was designed by Boulle, the metalwork was executed by Caffieri.

CAFFOY. A rich 18th-century fabric used for hangings and draperies in state rooms.

CAISSONS. Sunken panels in a ceiling or dome. They are also called "coffers" or "lacunaria." They are found in classic Greek and Roman architecture. This same motif was simulated in wood in English Renaissance interiors, and interpreted in plaster composition or gesso in Adam brothers interiors in mid-18th-century England. This ceiling, arch, or dome enrichment is also found in French and Italian Renaissance structures, especially in domed buildings.

CALAMANDER. A wood from Ceylon used for banding and veneering in 18th-century furniture making. See *Coromandel*.

CALATHOS. The basket- or bell-shaped element which supports the acanthi of the Corinthian capital; also the name of the basket-like element on the head of a caryatid figure. See *Caryatid*.

CALCIMINE. A painting mixture often used on ceilings and as a whitewash. It is a cold-water mixture of whiting, glue, and coloring matter.

CALENDERING. A finishing process for fabrics which produces a flat, smooth, glazelike finish. The fabric is passed between hollow, heated cylinders to achieve the shiny finish.

CALICO. A plain weave, printed cotton fabric originally produced in Calicut, India. It is similar to percale.

CALLIGRAPHY. The art of free rhythmic handwriting. The brushstrokes used by the Chinese in producing their written characters. In painting, it refers to free and loose brushwork.

CAMAÏEU. French for "monochromatic." Shades and tints of a single color.

CAMBER. The slight convexing or bellying on the lower surface of a beam to accommodate for the optical illusion that the beam appears to sag in the center. This technique is also used on horizontal furniture supports. See *Entasis*.

CAMBER

CAMBRIC. A soft, white, loosely woven cotton or linen fabric originally from Cambrai, France. True linen cambric is very sheer; coarser versions are used for linings.

CAME. The soft metal strip used as the divider between adjacent pieces of glass in a stained or leaded glass window.

CAMELBACK. A chair back with a serpentine curved top rail. A late Chippendale- (illustrated) or Hepplewhite-type chair. The term may originally have been applied to the 18th-century shield-back chair.

CAMP BEDSTEAD

CAMELBACK

CAME

CAMELBACK SOFA. An upholstered couch in the mid-18th-century Chippendale tradition. The sofa back has a serpentine line which rises from the roll-over arms to a high point in the middle of the couch back.

CAMEL'S HAIR. The wool-like textured underhair of a camel. In its natural color, it varies from light tan to brownish black. The hair is soft and lustrous, and may be combined with sheep's wool. The yarn produced is sometimes used for oriental rugs.

CAMEO. A low-relief carving. A striated stone or shell which is carved in relief. Cameos were used for decoration on English furniture of the late 18th century. Illustrated is a pair of ancient Roman cameos.

CAMEO BACK. An oval-framed chair back with an upholstered oval insert. It was popular in the Louis XVI, Adam, and Sheraton styles. The cameo-back chair is similar to the Louis XV "cabriolet," and Heppelwhite's "oval-back chair." See *Le Medaillon* and *Oval Back*.

CAMERA. An arcaded or vaulted roof, or a room with a vaulted roof.

CAMLET. A rich fabric, made of camel's hair, which originated in the Orient. It was made in France in the 14th century from hair, wool, and silk, and it was used and manufactured in England in the 17th and 18th centuries.

CAMP BEDSTEAD. See *Field Bed*.

CAMELBACK SOFA

CAMEOS

CAMEO BACK

CAMPANILE

CAMPAGNOLA. The Italian term for "provincial" furniture; furniture made in the outlying districts in a simple, unsophisticated manner.

CAMPAIGN CHEST. Originally a portable chest of drawers used by officers on their campaigns. The units were reinforced with metal edges and corners to withstand the rough traveling conditions. In current usage, somewhat like a "bachelor chest," often lacquered and embellished with metal corner strips, corner pieces, and pronounced hardware. It usually sits flush on the floor.

CAMPANILE. A bell tower. The term usually refers to Italian Gothic architecture where a detached structure was built next to a church to hold the church bells. Illustrated is the noted bell tower designed by Giotto in Florence, Italy (1334-1387). The cathedral is partially visible to the right. The tower is 45' square and 275' tall, and is paneled with marble and sculptured friezes.

CANAPÉ. Originally, a 17th-century small, two-seater couch covered with a canopy. The canopy was later removed and the name applied to a small sofa. A Louis XVI canapé or sofa covered with Beauvais tapestry is here illustrated. The woodwork was carved and gilded. See *Tapet* for a 15th-century canapé.

CANAPÉ

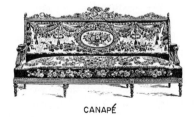

CANAPÉ

CANAPÉ À CORBEILLE. A kidney-shaped sofa. The ends curve in so that the sofa takes on the appearance of a wide topped basket. Corbeille is the French word for a wide basket or breadbasket.

CANCELLI. A Latin term from which the English "chancel" is derived. In the Early Christian churches it was the lattice or grill screen that separated the choir from the body of the church.

CANDELABRA. The plural of candelabrum. See below.

CANDELABRUM

CANDELABRUM. A branched, highly ornamental candlestick, lampstand, or hanging lighting unit or chandelier. See *Chandelier.*

CANDLE BOARD. A small shelf, under the writing surface of a desk, which slides out and is used to hold a candlestick. An 18th-century English furniture device. Illustrated is a Sheraton drawing table.

CANDLE BRACKETS. Brackets set into the base of the upper part of a secretary and meant to be used as candlesticks. Illustrated is an early-19th-century Sheraton design.

CANDLE SLIDES. See *Candle Board*.

CANDLESTAND. A light table used for candles, vases, and other small ornaments. It is usually associated with tripod-type furniture. The candlestand was made in the early Georgian period, and continued in use up through the 18th century. A Chippendale design is illustrated.

CANDLESTICK. A socketed holder made of metal, wood, china, or pottery. It can be a simple tube with an opening at one end to receive the candle and a flattened base at the other to set securely on a flat surface, or it can be elaborately decorated.

CANDLEWICK FABRIC. Fabric with a chenille effect created by applying heavy pile yarn (candlewick) loops on unbleached muslin bed sheeting. The loops are cut to simulate the fuzzy effect of a true chenille yarn. Candlewick fabrics can be used for draperies and bedspreads, and may be obtained in a variety of colors and patterns.

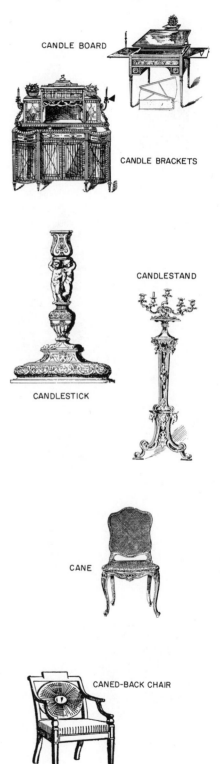

CANDLE BOARD

CANDLE BRACKETS

CANDLESTAND

CANDLESTICK

CANE

CANE. From the Latin for "reed." The stems of certain palms, grasses, or plants like bamboo and rattan. The reedlike material is plaited or woven into a mesh which is yielding, and therefore comfortable to sit on or lean back against. Cane was used as a decorative and elegant seating and chair-back material in the Louis XIV, XV, and XVI periods in France, and in the 17th- and 18-century designs in England and Holland. It is still a popular material, and is also currently used for decorative inserts in screens and case furniture.

CANE

CANED-BACK CHAIR. A popular chair back of the latter part of the 18th century. An intricately woven pattern of cane was set into a round or oval frame, which usually had an inlaid wood center. The cane appears to radiate out from the center medallion. A Sheraton design is illustrated.

CANED-BACK CHAIR

CANEPHORA

CANEPHORA

CANNELLATED

CANEPHORA. A sculptured female figure with a basket on her head. Originally it was used as a classic structural decoration somewhat like a caryatid. (See *Caryatids* and *Atlantes*.) It was used as an ornamental support for furniture and shelves in the French and Italian Renaissance.

CANNE. French for "cane" or "reed."

CANNE. French for "caned." Used, for example, in reference to a caned seat.

CANNELLATED. See *Fluting*.

CANOPY. From the Greek for "a net to keep out gnats." A covering, usually of drapery, over a piece of furniture, like the Sheraton bed illustrated. See *Canapé* and *Tester*. In architecture, a shelf, hood, or roof projecting from a building. See *Baldachino*.

CANOPY

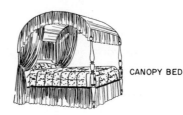

CANOPY BED

CANOPY CHAIR

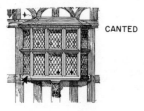

CANTED

CANOPY BED. A bed with a fabric roof over it. The canopy is often supported by four posts, one at each corner of the bed, or suspended from above. An early-19th-century American version of a Sheraton design is illustrated. See *Angel Bed, Four-poster Bedstead* and *Tent Bed*.

CANOPY CHAIR. A late-15th-, early-16th-century stately chair with a broad back that angles upward over the seat to form a projecting canopy. The design was usually heavily enriched with carved ornament. It was the probable forerunner of the smaller, wider, and more intimate 17th-century *Canapé*. See *Chayers à Dorseret*.

CANTED. Slanted or sloped; angled, beveled, or chamfered. This term is usually applied to large elements like the angles of a half-octagonal bow window.

CANTERBURY. An ornamental stand having compartments for papers, books, envelopes, etc. A sort of portable magazine rack of the 18th century. It was probably originally designed to carry trays, plates, cutlery, etc., and serve as an auxiliary piece for tea service or dining.

CANTILEVER. A projecting beam which is supported near the center and weighted at one end only. The other end extends out free and unsupported. Originally the term referred to brackets of stone, wood, or metal which projected out from a building (corbels), and supported shelves, cornices, balconies, or eaves, as seen in Gothic and early Renaissance structures. Reinforced concrete and other modern building materials and devices have made it possible to cantilever large balconies or complete sections of buildings.

CANTON CHINA. A traditional blue-and-white oriental china imported from China from the 17th century up to modern times.

CANTONE. Italian for "quoin corner."

CANTONED PIERS. Piers which are decorated with pilasters or columns at the corners or other exposed faces. A classic form of decoration which appeared in Renaissance architecture.

CANTONNIÈRE. The French word for "valance." It especially refers to the elaborate valance arrangements used on French state beds in the 16th and 17th centuries. See *Lambrequin* and *Valance*.

CAPITELLO

CANTILEVER

CANTON CHINA

CANTONED PIERS

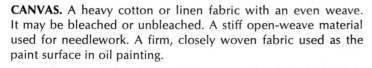
CANTONNIÈRE

CANVAS. A heavy cotton or linen fabric with an even weave. It may be bleached or unbleached. A stiff open-weave material used for needlework. A firm, closely woven fabric used as the paint surface in oil painting.

CAPITAL. The head of a column or pillar. The capital is placed directly over the shaft and immediately under the entablature. Each of the classical architectural borders has its own particular capital. The column and capital have been used as decoration and for functional supports on Renaissance and Louis XVI furniture. See *Composite Order, Corinthian Order, Doric Order, Etruscan Order,* and *Ionic Order.*

CAPITAL

CAPITELLO. Italian for "capital."

CAPO DI MONTE. A Spanish porcelain factory founded by King Charles III in 1743. In 1760, the plant was set up in Buen Retiro, and this type of porcelain is also known by that name. Figures and groupings of soft paste were made here, in typically Rococo patterns and vivid colors. Large plaques and wall brackets of Capo di Monte were used to decorate the palaces in Madrid and Aranjuez. Capo di Monte-type ware is still used today for ornamental lamps and vases.

CAPOMO. See *Satine Rubanne.*

CAPRICCIO. Italian for "caprice." A fanciful landscape composition of the 18th century.

CAPROLAN. A trademark of the Allied Chemical Corporation for nylon fibers used in making upholstery fabrics which have a high abrasion resistance. It is also used as a carpet fiber.

CAQUETEUSE. A "conversation chair" with a high wood back, and the seat sometimes arranged to turn on a pivot. It was an early French Renaissance design that was introduced into England in the 16th century. The front of the chair seat was usually wider than the back. Illustrated is a 16th-century French example. Set *Cacqueteuse.*

CAQUETOIRE. A small, light, four-legged conversation chair of the mid French Renaissance. The back of the seat is narrower than the front, and the arms are curved inward from the front to the chair back. See *Cacqueteuse.*

CARAVAGGIO, MICHELANGELO DA (1573–1610). A great realist painter of the Italian Renaissance.

CARCASE or CARCASS. The base wood framework of a piece of furniture without veneering, carving, ornament, or finish. The term usually refers to case furniture. The skeleton of an upholstered piece of furniture is called a "frame." See *Basewood.*

CARD CUT. A Chinese-style fretwork or latticework design. The pattern is carved in low relief rather than pierced or cut out. Chippendale used this type of decoration on some of his cabinets and secretaries.

CARD TABLE. A small folding table used for gaming. This type of table originated in the 17th century and was especially popular in the William and Mary and Queen Anne periods. Early card tables had depressions at the four corners of the tabletop to hold candles, and often, four additional wells or "guinea holes" for holding the money in use during the gaming. The tabletops were often covered with green baize. The styles of card tables varied with the succeeding periods. Illustrated is a Queen Anne card table with cabriole legs with

CAQUETEUSE

CAQUETOIRE

CARD CUT

CARD TABLE

shell motif on the knee. See *Dished* and *Mechanical Card Table*.

CARLIN, MARTIN. An 18th-century French master cabinet-maker to Louis XVI. He produced charming, delicate furniture in rosewood, with Sèvres porcelain inlays. Carlin was also a founder and chaser of metal furniture mounts, and one of the earliest exponents of the Classic Revival. He often used independent, or detached, balustrade columns to support the friezes of cabinets. These columns were made of wood, bronze gilt, or the two combined. Another decorative device frequently used by Carlin was the fringe of drapery pinched in with small tassels.

CARLTON TABLE. A writing table on legs with a raised back and sides, and fitted with pigeonholes, small drawers, and fittings for pens and inkwells. The desk made its appearance at the end of the 18th century in England, and was usually made of of mahogany or satinwood with inlay trim. Sheraton referred to this as a "ladies' drawing and writing table."

MARTIN CARLIN

CARLTON TABLE

CAROLEAN PERIOD

CAROLEAN PERIOD. The period in English furniture and interior design which spanned the years 1660–1688, also referred to as the Restoration, Late Stuart, or part of the Jacobean period. Illustrated is an oak chest of the period with geometric panels and lunette carving.

CAROLINGIAN. The period in architecture and art in western Europe from about the 7th to the 10th centuries. It was roughly the dynasties before, of, and after Charlemagne. See *West Work*.

CARPATHIAN ELM BURL. A decorative, light-brown to brick-red veneer wood with darker brown veins and figurations. It is often combined with walnut as a decorative accent. The wood is found in the Carpathian Mountains in Europe and also in France and England.

CARPET. In the 16th and 17th centuries, the term referred to a woven table covering. In the late 17th century, it assumed the meaning we now give it: a floor covering. See *Tapet*. Illustrated is a carpet pattern of the early-16th-century German Renaissance.

CARPET

CARREAU

CARREAU

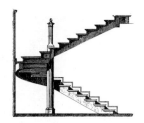

CARRIAGES

EDWARD CARTER

CARTER'S GROVE

J. CARTER

CARREAU. From the French for "square." A square tile or brick. A loose, stuffed cushion used on chairs and settles before upholstery, as known today, came into use. A squab cushion. Illustrated is a French 15th-century bench with movable backrest. See *Squab.*

CARREL. A bay or study nook which is separated from the rest of a library by an architectural screen or flanking bookcases.

CARRELAGE ENCAUSTIQUE. French for a pavement of inlaid tiles.

CARRIAGES or CARRIAGE PIECES. The supporting members for steps in stairway construction.

CARROUSEL. A triple-arched construction designed by Percier and Fontaine in the early 19th century and inspired by the Arch of Septimus Severus in Rome.

CARTAPESTA. Italian for "papier-mâché."

CARTEL (Clock). A hanging wall clock. In the Louis XV and Louis XVI periods it was often highly ornate and fanciful in design, and made of ormolu. See *Régulateur* and *Regulator.*

CARTER, EDWARD. A 17th-century English designer-architect who, with John Webb, executed many of Inigo Jones's designs. His own work was much in the style and tradition of Inigo Jones, as illustrated.

CARTER, J. A late-18th-century English designer who worked mainly in the Adam brothers tradition. He designed classic-inspired ceilings, panels, chimneypieces, gates, grates, architectural pedestals, shop fronts, and doorways.

CARTER'S GROVE. A typical Georgian house of the mid-18th century in America. It was built for Carter Burwell in James City, West Virginia, in 1751. The great central hall opened into four rooms, two of which were coupled with antechambers. The main part of the house was flanked by a kitchen and a service building (flankers). David Minitree was the builder of this brick structure done in Flemish bond.

CARTOCCIO. Italian for "cartouche" or "scroll."

CARTON-PIERRE. A Robert Adam, mid-18th-century English technique of "carved ornament" using a gesso-like composition applied to the surface of wood, panels, and ceilings. See *Anaglypta*.

CARTONNIER. A decorative 18th-century pasteboard box used to hold papers. The box was usually ornamented and lavishly decorated.

CARTONNIER

CARTOON. From the Italian "cartone," a big sheet of paper. A full-sized drawing for a painting, worked out in detail, and ready to be transferred to a wall, canvas, or panel. One of the steps in the preparation for a fresco or wall mural.

CARTOUCHE. In architecture, usually a sculptured ornament in the form of a scroll unrolled, which often appears on cornices. The cartouche is frequently used as a field for inscriptions, and as an ornamental block in the cornices of house interiors. A conventionalized shield or oval. An ornate frame.

CARTOUCHE

CARTOUCHE BACK. An upholstered chair back of a side chair or fauteuil which is scroll- or cartouche-shaped. Illustrated is a Louis XV fauteuil which is upholstered in Beauvais tapestry. The tapestry has a multicurved shield effect, and is, in turn, set into the cartouche frame of the chair.

CARVED RUG. A rug on which the pattern is created by having the pile cut at different levels. The various levels create a design in lights and shadows. A sculptured look may also be effected by eliminating some tufts, or pulling some pile yarns tightly back to create a pattern or design.

CARTOUCHE BACK

CARVER CHAIR. An early American wood-turned chair with a rush seat. A straight, square-looking chair named after a chair of that design belonging to Governor John Carver of Plymouth. The rear legs continued up to form the uprights of the back. A single row of vertical and horizontal spindles was set between the uprights. Mushroom-shaped turnings usually acted as finials on the uprights. It is closely related to the Brewster chair. See *Banister Back Chair* and *Brewster Chair*.

CARVING. A sculptured, incised, gouged, or appliquéd three-dimensional decoration or ornament. Illustrated is an early Georgian (early-18th-century) sideboard which is heavily carved and gilded.

CARVING

CARYATIDS

CARYATIDS

CASE GOODS

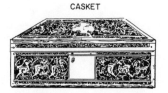

CASEMENT WINDOW

CASKET

CARYATIDS. In architecture, sculptured female figures used in place of columns or pilasters to support entablatures. The caryatid is a decorative figure used as a supporting member of a design. It appears in classic architecture and decoration, and again in the Renaissance and Empire periods. The male version of the caryatid is the Atlas. Illustrated is the Hall of the Marshal (no longer extant) in the Tuileries, Paris, as designed by Charles Percier and Pierre Fontaine in the early-19th-century Empire style. See *Canephora.* The famous "Porch of the Maidens" in the Erectheum consists of caryatid supports. See *Erectheum.*

CASCADE. See *Jabot.*

CASE GOODS. Furniture which is designed to contain or store objects: chests, cabinets, desks, bookcases, drawer units, etc. It is also called architectural furniture. A contemporary secretary-cabinet is shown here.

CASEIN PAINT. A paint which uses a casein solution instead of the usual drying oils. It is mixed with water. For interior use, the hiding property of the paint is lime, powdered chalk, and kaolin.

CASEMENT. A frame for glass that forms a window or part of one.

CASEMENT, WILLIAM. A late-18th-century English furniture designer, who contributed to the *Cabinet Makers' London Book* of prices for designs of cabinetwork.

CASEMENT CLOTH. A light-weight, usually sheer drapery cloth of silk, cotton, rayon, mohair, nylon, or mixture of the above fibers. It is used as a curtain fabric.

CASEMENT WINDOW. A side-hinged window that swings in and out, rather than one which is pushed up and down.

CASHMERE. A soft wool textile or yarn made from Indian goat hair.

CASHMERE WORK. Referring to Kashmir in India. A "mirror-mosaic" form of decoration in Indian furniture of the 18th and early 19th centuries. Small pieces of mirror were inlaid into the small, carved, geometric patterns of a panel or surface.

CASINO. An Italian word for "little house." A summerhouse or an 18th-century dancing salon.

CASKET. A box or miniature chest usually lavishly ornamented and made of wood, ivory, and precious metals. A container for trinkets, jewels, etc. A Byzantine ivory casket is illustrated.

CASO-RILIEVO. An Italian word for a relief carving in which the highest parts of the sculpture are on a level with the surface that surrounds the relief. It is also called "intaglio rilievato."

CASSAPANCA. Derived from the Italian "cassone" (chest) and "banca" (bench). A mid-Renaissance Italian, long, wooden, hinged-top chest with wooden arms and a back. It functioned as a bench as well as a chest. A prototype of the box settle. See *Box Settle*.

CASSAPANCA

CASSAWS. A late-17th-century English wallpaper which resembles a silk damask.

CASSETTE. The French word meaning "casket." It sometimes assumed monumental proportions. Illustrated is a 14th-century French wood cassette.

CASSETTE

CASSOLET or CASSOLETTE. A small box, made in a variety of shapes, for holding or burning perfumes. The term also applies to a covered urn-shaped vase sometimes with a top that reverses to become a candle holder.

CASSONE. An Italian decorated hinge-topped chest. It was usually used as a marriage chest which contained the bride's household linens. This 14th- to 16th-century chest was richly decorated and carved with gilt moldings, and often had painted front and back panels. The panels were from 4' to 6' long and about 18" in height. See *Cassapanca, Chest,* and *Marriage Chest*.

CASSONE

CASSOON

CASSOON. A sunken panel in a vault or ceiling. See *Coffered Panel*.

CAST. A reproduction, usually made of plaster of Paris, of a piece of sculpture.

CAST IRON

CAST ALUMINUM. Aluminum that has been cast in molds. Furniture which has been produced from cast aluminum components looks like cast iron, but it is much lighter and is rust-resistant.

CAST IRON. Iron which contains 3.5 percent of carbon. It was first made commercially by the Darby family in England in the early 18th century. They smelted iron ore with coke instead of charcoal. In about 1750, using coal, they turned out pig iron

CASTELLATED

CATENARY

CATENARY ARCH

of a quality they could forge into bar iron, and mass production became possible.

It was used as a roofing technique by Victor Louis in the Théâtre Français, in 1786. The wooden dome of the United States Capitol in Washington was replaced by a dome constructed of cast iron between 1855 and 1863 (see illustration). Cast iron columns appear in 1780 as structural elements. During the 19th century, it was an important building material, and became the principal means of support for early Chicago skyscrapers.

CASTELLATED. Designed with turrets and battlements like a Gothic castle.

CASTERS or CASTORS. Small wheels on swivels which are applied to legs or bases of furniture to make it movable.

CASTERS

CATACOMBS

CATACOMBS. Underground rooms used as burial tombs, especially those in Rome used by the early Christians as tombs and hiding places and for secret meetings.

CATENARY. Chainlike. A swag or festoon. See *Festoon* and *Swag*.

CATENARY ARCH. The arc or curve formed by a cord or chain of uniform density hanging freely between two points of suspension. The console with the catenary arch trim illustrated was designed by Charles Normand in the French Empire period.

CATHEDRA. The raised throne behind the altar, near the wall of the apse in an early Christian basilica. It was reserved for the bishop. The word is the Latin for bench or seat. The word "cathedral" today refers to the see or seat of the bishop, or the main church in a diocese.

CATHEDRAL CEILING. A high-pitched ceiling in a modern home. The living room in a ranch or split-level house is sometimes enhanced by the extra-high ceiling.

CATHEDRAL GLASS. A rolled glass with one surface textured partially to obscure the transparency of the glass. It may be tinted, and there are many textured patterns available.

CATHOLIKON. The central nave of a Byzantine church.

CATKINS. A decorative 18th-century motif like the bellflower or husk ornament. It was usually used as a pendant, or as a chain of stylized and graduated bell-shaped flowers. A late-18th-century Hepplewhite girondole is illustrated. See *Bell-flower Ornament* and *Husk Ornament*.

CAVO-RELIEVO

CATHOLIKON

CATKINS

CAULICOLI

CAULICOLI. The stalks that support the volutes on a classic Corinthian capital.

CAUSEUSE. A wide armchair, or a small sofa with open sides. The back and seat were often covered with Beauvais tapestry in the 17th and 18th centuries. The causeuse is similar to a marquise, love seat, or settee. Illustrated is a typical Louis XVI design covered with a Beauvais tapestry.

CAUVET, GILLES-PAUL (1731–1788). A leading French designer of interiors, furniture, and metal ornament in the Louis XVI period. His work is reminiscent of the Louis XV style.

CAVAEDIUM. An atrium in a Roman house. *I* is the impluvium, *C* is the compluvium. See *Atrium*.

CAVEA. The part of an ancient theatre that was occupied by the audience.

CAVETTO. A quarter-round, concave molding. In late-17th-century English furniture, the cavetto molding was often veneered crosswise. See *Cove*.

CAVITY WALL. Also called a "hollow wall." Two brick walls which are spaced two or three inches apart and connected to each other with metal ties or bonding bricks.

CAVO-RELIEVO. Italian for "intaglio."

CAUSEUSE

CAVAEDIUM

CAVETTO

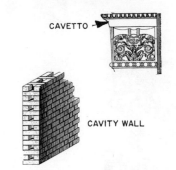

CAVITY WALL

CEDAR CHEST

CEDAR. A fragrant fine-grained wood used for chests and lining closets. Persian cedar is an eastern hardwood used for building. Cedar was a favorite wood of the Egyptians and ancient Romans.

CEDAR, RED. Not a decorative wood. It is mainly used for shingles and as a lining material.

CEDAR CHEST. A long, low chest, either made completely of, or lined only with, cedarwood. The chest is used for the storage of linens, blankets, and woolens. It can be styled to suit any period and is also often referred to as a "hope chest." Illustrated is a 15th-century carved cedar chest. See *Cassone*.

CELADON. A light-grayish sea-green color. The word is also used to describe pottery or Chinese porcelain of this pastel, sea-green color.

CELANESE. A trademark for textiles produced by the Celanese Corporation of America.

CELAPERM. A trademark name for solution-dyed acetate yarns produced by the Celanese Corporation of America.

CELATURE. A method of decorating metal surfaces by embossing or cutting into the metal.

CELATURE

CELLA

CELLA. Latin term for the inner chamber of a classic Greek or Roman temple. The god's statue usually was set in the cella, which was called the "naos" in Greek.

CELLAR. In medieval architecture, a storage room above ground level. In contemporary usage, an underground or below-grade storage area.

CELLARETTE

CELLARETTE. A portable or movable cabinet or liquor chest with a place for bottles, glasses, etc. A Sheraton design is illustrated. Also, the drawer of a sideboard fitted with divisions to hold bottles, and often lined with lead. See *Sarcophagus*.

CELLINI, BENVENUTO (1500–1571). An outstanding Italian Renaissance goldsmith, sculptor, and adventurer. A beaten silver goblet of his design is shown. See *Tazza* for another illustration of Cellini's work.

BENVENUTO CELLINI

CELLULOSE. An insoluble starchlike matter taken from plants. It is used as a basis for many synthetic materials.

CEMENT. A natural or artificial lime compound which is burnt and ground. It is used to make a mortar which will bond bricks, stones, etc.

CEMENT BLOCK. A building unit which is made of cast cement and is usually 8″ × 8″ × 16″.

CEMENT MORTAR. A mixture of cement, sand, and water used for binding bricks, stones, etc.

CENTAUR. A decorative figure with the forepart of a human male, but the body and legs of a horse. It appeared in ancient Greek mythology, and reappeared in Renaissance and later designs.

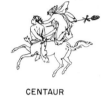

CENTAUR

CENTER or CENTERING. In masonry, a temporary timber framework upon which the masonry of an arch, or a reinforced masonry lintel, is supported till it sets and becomes rigid and self-supporting.

CENTER MATCH. Two flitches or log slices butted in the center of a single veneered panel.

CENTER OTTOMAN. See *Borne* and *Confidante*.

CENTER TABLE

CENTER OTTOMAN

CENTER TABLE. A large table which stands in the center of a hallway or large room. It is similar in use to the rectangular library table. Illustrated is an Elizabethan room with a center table. See illustration of *Venetian Gilt*.

CERAMIC. A product of baked clay. It may be pottery, tile, earthenware, etc. A 17th-century English stoneware jug is illustrated.

CERAMIC

CERAMIC COLOR GLAZE. An opaque colored glaze obtained by spraying the clay tile brick or object with a compound of metallic oxides, chemicals, and clays, and then heating the glazed unit in an oven at a high temperature. This fuses the glaze into the clay object.

CERAMIC TILE. Tiles of assorted shapes and sizes made of baked clay (glazed or unglazed). These tiles may be used to cover floors and counters, or line walls, etc. A wide range of colors is available, and a multitude of designs and patterns can be created with ceramic tiles.

CERAMIC VENEER. An architectural terra-cotta plate with large face dimensions but only 1⅛″ to 2½″ in thickness. It is actually an oversized tile applied to a brick, stone, or rough concrete surface as a facing material.

CERCEAU, JACQUES DU. A 16th-century French architect and furniture designer under Henry IV. See *Du Cerceau, Jacques Androuet.*

CERTOSINA. An Italian term for an inlay of marble, ivory, or blond woods on a darker background. It has an oriental character since it is generally set into small geometric patterns. See *Intarsia or Tarsia and Intarsi.* The name was derived from the Carthusian monks who excelled in this type of inlay work.

CHAFFEUSE. A low, fireside chair. Originally the seat was so low that the knees of a seated person were higher than his lap. It was used by nursing mothers to cradle children between their knees and body. It is also spelled "chauffeuse."

CHAIERE

CHAIERE or CHAIRE. A French Gothic term for a thronelike wood-carved chair. See *Chaire.* Illustrated is a 14th-century interior.

CHAIR. Derived from the Old French "chaiere." A seat with a back for one person. A chair usually has feet, legs, stretchers, brackets, apron, seat frame, rails, arms, splat, and top rail. Illustrated is an ancient Greek klismos.

CHAIR

CHAIR AND A HALF. An 18th-century English chair with overly generous proportions. The chair usually had wings or cheeks, and the seat was smaller than a two-seater love seat but larger than a regular upholstered chair. It is similar to the French "marquise" in proportions and was also called a *Drunkard's Chair.*

CHAIR BED. A chair or settee with a draw-out arrangement that converts into a bed. An 18th-century English innovation. See *Bed Chair.*

CHAIR RAIL. The top molding of a dado, also called a "dado cap." The chair rail is usually placed about 30″ off the ground, and the wall area below the molding is called the dado. The wood strip originally was used to protect the plaster wall from being damaged by the top rail of chairs. An 18th-century English room designed by Halfpenny is illustrated. See *Dado.*

CHAIR RAIL

CHAIR TABLE. A chair that converts into a table when the hinged back is dropped to a horizontal position. Illustrated is a 17th-century Stuart period chair. See *Table Chair.*

CHAIRE. A French term for an early Renaissance choir stall. It resembles a chest (or boxlike seat) with a tall, heavily carved back. The arms were also carved. In the Gothic period it was also called a "chayère" and its thronelike proportions made it the special seat for the lord or head of a family.

CHAIR TABLE

CHAIRE À HAUT DOSSIER

CHAIRE

CHAIRE À HAUT DOSSIER. A 16th-century French Renaissance high-back chair. It was usually ornately carved and covered in leather or tapestry.

CHAISE. French for "side chair."

CHAISE À ACCOUDOIR. See *Cockfight Chair* and *Fumeuse.*

CHAISE À BRAS. A Renaissance armchair. Illustrated is an English version from the 16th century.

CHAISE À CAPUCINE. A low slipper chair. The name is probably derived from the Capucin nuns who might have used this type of chair.

CHAISE À PORTEURS. A sedan chair. It originally was an enclosed covered chair which seated one person and was suspended between two poles. The two poles were carried by porters. Present-day variations are hooded and winged chairs that simulate the enclosed look of the chaise à porteurs. See *Sedan Chair.*

CHAISE BRISÉE. A *Chaise Longue* in two parts, one of which is the footrest. Also, a folding chair.

CHAISE LONGUE. A long chair for reclining or stretching out. A *Duchesse.* It is an upholstered chair with a very elongated seat supported by extra legs.

CHAISE À BRAS

CHAISE BRISÉE

CHAISE LONGUE

CHAITYA

CHAITYA

CHALICE

CHAITYA. An Indian temple or assembly hall. Illustrated is a section view of the Chaitya of Karu, near Poona, India.

CHALET. Originally the hut of a Swiss herdsman. The word now suggests a mountain cottage or a house built in the Swiss style.

CHALGRIN, JEAN-FRANÇOIS (1739–1811). A French architect who is best known for his design of the Arc de Triomphe de l'Étoile in Paris, France. This triumphal arch was built to commemorate Napoleon's victories, and it is located at the end of the Avenue des Champs Élysées in the center of the Place de l'Étoile. It was built between 1806 and 1836. The arch is 160' high, 150' wide, and 72' deep.

CHALICE. A cup or goblet used in church ceremony, and often made of precious metals beautifully ornamented and jeweled.

CHALLIS. A soft fabric woven of wool, silk, rayon, or cotton which usually has a small allover design, but it may be a solid-color fabric.

CHAMBER HORSE. An 18th-century English exercising mechanism designed by Sheraton. It was a bellows-like affair made up of several wooden boards separated by coils, and covered over with leather equipped with air vents. This "bellows" was set on a wood base with "arms," and a front step. The individual sat on the bellows-pillow, held onto the arms, and bounced up and down, much as one would today ride a vibrator.

CHAMBER HORSE

SIR WILLIAM CHAMBERS

CHAMBERS, SIR WILLIAM (1726–1796). An English architect who designed in the Palladian tradition during the Greek Revival period. Like Chippendale, he adapted Chinese forms to furniture. In 1759, he published *Designs of Chinese Buildings, Furniture, Dresses, Machines and Utensils*. Chambers was chief architect to George III and is still relied on in England as a leading authority on the Italian Renaissance. His *Somerset House* in London is a classic in "secular Renaissance" design.

CHAMBLIN, M. DE. Early 18th-century French Régence designer and decorator.

CHAMFER. The edge of a corner that is beveled or angled off. A splayed effect. A Chippendale press or wardrobe with chamfered edges is illustrated. See *Bevel* and *Canted*.

CHAMPLEVÉ. A type of enamelware in which the pattern is grooved out in a metal base and the grooves are then filled with colored enamels. The thin raised lines that separate the enamel color are similar to the cloisons in *Cloisonné*.

CHANCEL. The part of the church used by the clergy and the choir. It is located at the east end between the altar and the nave. The screen that separates the chancel from the body of the church is also referred to as a chancel. Illustrated is the plan of the Italian Gothic church of S. Andrea at Vercelli. The starred area is the chancel.

CHANDELIER. A hanging lighting fixture. A pendant unit with branches to hold candles or lights. It is often decorated with prisms and crystals. Crystal chandeliers were introduced into England by the French émigrés of 1685. See *Candelabra*.

CHANNELS

CHANNELS. The long, shallow, concave grooves that run vertically up and down the shaft of a column, and are separated from one another by a narrow edge called a fillet. See *Fillet* and *Fluting*. A channel is also a form of rolled steel.

CHANTILLY LACE. A bobbin lace with a delicate ground. The design is outlined by a cordonnet of thick silky threads. See *Valenciennes Lace*.

CHAPITEAU. French for "capital." Illustrated is the capital and base of a cannellated pilaster of the French Renaissance Château d'Aney le Franc.

CHAPLET. A small torus molding with a bead or berry decoration. A Byzantine capital is illustrated. See *Astragal*.

CHARCOAL. Twigs of willow that have been charred away from the air. It is mainly used for preliminary drawings on a canvas or wall, and can be readily erased.

"CHARLES OF LONDON" SOFA. A heavily upholstered, 20th-century piece that has flat, massive, low armrests. The arms barely rise above the T pillows that are set next to them. The platform is usually upholstered. The Charles of London chair, also a 20th-century innovation, has the same generally massive look.

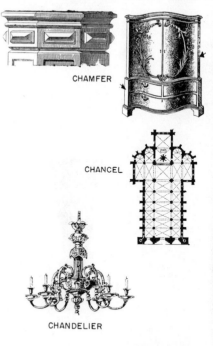

"CHARLES OF LONDON" SOFA

CHAMFER

CHANCEL

CHANDELIER

CHAPITEAU

CHAPLET

CHARLES X PERIOD. From 1824 to 1830, part of the Restoration period in France. A mixture of Louis XVI and late Empire styles and Rococo and Renaissance detail.

CHARMEUSE. A soft, silken luster produced on fine cotton-warp sateens by mercerizing and schreinering, or a satin weave fabric (of cotton, silk, or rayon) which has a matte back and a semilustrous face.

CHARTRES CATHEDRAL (1194–1260). A noted French Gothic cathedral. It is famous for its magnificent 13th-century stained-glass windows and the fine sculptured figures in the doorways of the west front and in the triple porches of the north and south transepts. From the exterior, the building presents an interesting arrangement of nine towers and flying buttresses which are three arches, one above the other. See *Ambulatory*.

CHASE. A long, recessed area in masonry, brickwork, or concrete left to accommodate service pipes.

CHASING. A method of ornamenting on any metal surface. The pattern is produced by embossing or cutting away parts of the metal. A burin or graver is also used in this technique. Chasing with a burin is also done on marquetry, on metal mounts for furniture, or on Boulle-type metal inlays. Chasing, as a form of metal enrichment, reached its peak during the 18th century in France. See *Lalonde* and *Repoussé*.

CHASING

CHÂTEAU. A French country residence, usually the country home or suburban manor of a nobleman. Illustrated is the French Renaissance Château d'Écouen by Jean Bullant.

CHÂTEAU

CHÂTEAU DE CHAMBORD

CHÂTEAU DE CHAMBORD. Built in 1526 in the Loire district of France by Pierre Nepveu. In plan this semifortress consists of a rectangle inside a rectangle. The famous double spiral staircase is another architectural feature. It is a stone cage topped with the lantern, here shown. The structure is a combination of Renaissance details and Gothic construction. The high-pitched roof, ornate dormers, and beautiful chimneys make this a typically French, Early Renaissance building.

CHEF D'OEUVRE

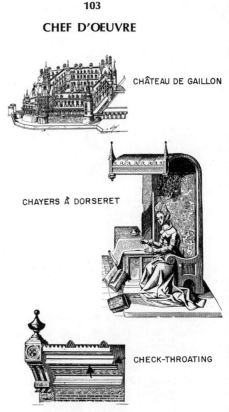

CHÂTEAU DE GAILLON

CHAYERS À DORSERET

CHECK-THROATING

CHÂTEAU DE GAILLON. Built between 1497 and 1509 by Pierre Fain for Cardinal Georges d'Amboise. It is a classic of the early French Renaissance Rouen school. It has an irregular plan, moats, drawbridges, round corner towers, turrets, high roofs, and dormers. It is a curious yet delightful blend of Renaissance details and medieval charm.

CHAUFFEUSE. A small fireside chair with a low seat of the early French Renaissance. See *Chaffeuse.*

CHAYERS À DORSERET. Late-14th- and early-15th-century Gothic canopied chairs. They were usually carved of oak or chestnut, elaborately gilded, and highlighted with color. The chayer (or chaire) was massive and thronelike. The illustrated canopied chair is a 15th-century French example. The back of the chair was lined with tapestry. See *Canopy Chair.*

CHECK-THROATING. A groove on the underside of any projecting molding which becomes a stopgap and prevents rain or water from running back onto the vertical surface of a building. See *T* on *Coping* illustration.

CHECKER. See *Chequer.* Originally the office of one of the heads of a monastery. The office usually had a checkered tabletop upon which accounts were reckoned with counters. An abbreviated form of the word "exchequer."

CHECKERBOARD BOND. In masonry, headers, only, laid one directly over the other in vertical lines. A purely ornamental arrangement, as it does not actually bond at all. See *Bond.*

CHECKERBOARD MATCH. Veneer or wood panels set so that the stripe figure is vertical in one panel and horizontal in the next. Below the vertical striped panel, a horizontal is set, and a vertical panel is set under the horizontal panel. The pattern is then repeated vertically and/or horizontally over the remaining surface to be decorated.

CHECKS. In cabinetry, small cracks which may appear in lumber which has not been dried evenly or properly. They appear perpendicular to the annual rings and radiating out from the heart of the trunk.

CHEEK. The side pieces of a dormer window. A cheek is also the side post of a gate or door.

CHEEK PIECES. The "wings" or "fins" of the tall easy chairs designed in 18th-century England. These cheeks were designed to keep draughts from the head of the person seated in the chair. See *Draught Chair, Grandfather Chair,* and *Wing Chair.*

CHEEK PIECES

CHEF D'OEUVRE. French for "masterpiece."

CHENETS

CHEQUER

CHEQUERWORK

CHEN CHEN. A pale north African wood that varies from whitish to pale gray. It is a light, soft wood that works well and has a characteristic stripe pattern. It is also called Ako and Quen Quen.

CHÊNE. French for "oak."

CHENETS. French for "andirons" or "fire dogs." See *Andirons*.

CHENILLE. From the French term for caterpillar. A woven yarn which has a pile protruding all around at right angles to the body thread. It was used for embroidery fringes and tassels. Chenille is also the name for fabrics woven from chenille yarns. The fabric has a plushlike surface. Chenille can be made of various fibers: cotton, silk, rayon, etc.

CHENILLE CARPET. A thick, soft, cut pile fabric woven on two looms, the weft loom and the chenille loom. Chenille is woven in any design, coloring, type, or surface yarn. It may be made in any shape or size up to 30' wide seamless. A variety of textural effects and thickness of pile are also available.

CHEQUER. One of the squares in a chequered or checkered pattern. An inlay design. Illustrated is chequered ashlar work from Austin Hall, Harvard University.

CHEQUERWORK. The use of stone and another contrasting material, like brick, laid in a checkerboard arrangement. Illustrated is the portal of the cloister of Lorsch in Germany.

CHERRYWOOD. A light to dark reddish grained wood resembling mahogany. It darkens with age. Cherrywood is used for small carved articles and French and American 18th-century Provincial furniture. It is also popular for inlays and marquetry. The figure varies from plain to a rich mottle. Black cherrywood is found in United States, in the Appalachians, mainly in Pennsylvania and West Virginia. French cherry is found in France and England. Wild cherry is found in England, Europe, and Asia Minor.

CHERUB. See *Amorino*. Illustrated here is a section of a Robert Adam, 18th-century English design for a pilaster.

CHERUB

CHERUB HEAD

CHERUB HEAD. A popular decorative motif which appears in Renaissance church or secular architecture. The motif was used either singly or in groups, in medallions, on corner blocks, in capitals, panels, and as furniture decoration. See *Têtes d'Anges*.

CHEVAL SCREEN

CHESS TABLE. A tabletop with a checkered pattern either painted or inlaid upon it. In medieval Europe, the tops of chests were sometimes decorated with checkerboards.

CHEST. Originally, a container or box with a hinged lid. Drawers were added to the chest in the mid-17th century, and the chest of drawers evolved. Chests in the medieval period were architectural in concept and decoration. Illustrated is a 15th-century Italian chest or cassone.

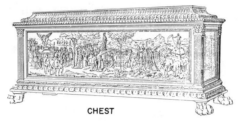

CHEST TABLE

CHEST

CHEST OF DRAWERS

CHEST OF DRAWERS. A box or chest with drawers added. Illustrated is a late-18th-century Hepplewhite design.

CHEST ON CHEST. A chest of drawers in two parts, with one set of larger drawers. It is also called a double chest.

CHESTERFIELD. An overstuffed, heavily upholstered couch or sofa. It is usually a large piece of furniture with a continuous back. The scrolled, roll-over arms are the same height as the back.

CHESTNUT. A soft wood with a coarse grain. It resembles oak, and can be used in its place when a quartered effect is not desired. Chestnut is unsuitable for fine details because the grain is coarse and it has marked annual rings. Certain cuts were used in late-18th-century England to imitate satinwood. One form of chestnut, *Wormy Chestnut,* is popular today.

CHEVAL GLASS OR MIRROR. Literally a "horse mirror," a mirror suspended between horses (see *Horse*). A mirror which is decoratively mounted so as to swing in a frame and large enough to reflect the whole figure. A full-length mirror. It was a French innovation which was introduced into England in the late 17th century. In the 18th century in England it was made in both large and small table models. The cheval mirror is also called a "swing glass" and "psyche."

CHEVAL SCREEN. A fire screen which stands on two bracketed feet. A Sheraton design is illustrated.

CHEST ON CHEST

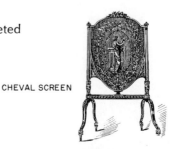

CHEVAL GLASS

CHEVAL SCREEN

CHEVET

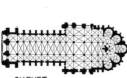

CHEVET

CHEVRON

CHIFFONNIER

CHIMERA

CHIMNEY BREAST

CHEVET. French for "head of a bed." The head of a bed, or a bolster or pillow. A bedside table or night table. In architecture, an apse. The eastern or apsidial end of a church, especially in the French Gothic style, which contains the ambulatory and surrounding chapels. The plan of the Cathedral of Rheims, illustrated, shows the apse surrounded by an ambulatory off which are the chapels.

CHEVIOT. A kind of loosely woven, rough-napped woolen cloth originally made from the wool of the cheviot sheep of the Cheviot Hills of Scotland.

CHEVRON. French for "rafter." In ornament, a zigzag design or molding. A continuous band of V's. It was frequently used in Norman and Gothic ornament, and also in the 17th century as an inlay motif. See *Churn Molding.*

CHIAROSCURO. Italian for "light-dark." The balance of light and shadow in a picture. See *Clare-Obscure* and *Grisaille.*

CHIAVE DI VOLTA. Italian for "keystone."

CHIFFON. A sheer, gauzelike silk fabric. A term used to designate the light, soft finish of a fabric like chiffon velvet.

CHIFFONNIER. A French term for a "rag-and-bone man." It was originally a general unit for collecting and containing assorted odds and ends. In the period of Louis XV, it refers to a tall chest with five drawers; however, in 19th-century England, the term is applied to a sideboard with two doors below enclosing shelves. Sometimes there were shelves at the back and top of the sideboard to hold ornaments, decorative serving pieces, etc. A Thomas Hope, early-19th-century English chiffonnier is illustrated.

CHIFFONNIÈRE. A sort of sewing table, with a three-sided gallery on top, drawers, and a shelf at the bottom, which was enclosed and used to hold balls of wool. It was a Louis XV innovation.

CHIMERA. A mythical, dragon-like animal, or composite "part human, part animal" used in decoration. The chimera was used for legs or furniture supports in the Renaissance, Empire, and later-19th-century designs.

CHIMNEY BREAST. The projecting stone or brickwork of a fireplace which is above the fireplace proper and houses the flue. The illustrated 17th-century design is from Bolsover Castle in Derbyshire, England.

CHINESE CHIPPENDALE

CHIMNEY STACK. A hollow column that carries the smoke from the chimney, up and out, through and above the roof. It was used in Gothic architecture and usually ornamented with carving. Toward the end of the 15th and the beginning of the 16th century, clustered chimneys became common, with each flue in the stack being taken up a separate shaft. In the 17th century, the chimney stack became simpler, generally a group of plain octagons or squares. By the 18th century it had ceased to be an obvious or notable architectural feature.

CHIMNEYPIECE. The ornamental structure surrounding the fireplace and the breast above it. A projecting hood, it is sometimes called the mantel. Many beautiful chimneypieces were designed and decorated by artists and architects of 18th-century England. A 16th-century French chimneypiece is illustrated. See *Mantel*.

CHINA. The European name given to porcelains imported from the Orient. A hard, translucent porcelain with a large percentage of bone ash. Illustrated is a late-17th-century Chinese vase of the K'ang Hsi period. See *Hard Paste* and *Kaolin*.

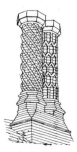

CHIMNEY STACK

CHIMNEYPIECE

CHINA

CHINA CLOSET

CHINA CLOSET or CABINET. A display cabinet, usually with glass sides and front, which was used for exhibiting china collections. A popular piece of furniture in the late 17th and early 18th centuries when Oriental china was rare, and avidly collected. The illustrated laquered design is of the William and Mary period.

CHINA SILK. A sheer, plain-weave silk fabric which is nearly transparent. It may be made of rayon combined with silk.

CHINESE BRACKET FOOT or CHINESE FOOT. A bracket-type foot with a reverse S-shape curve (cyma recta) on the face of the bracket. It is also called an ogee bracket foot. A support favored by Chippendale in the mid-18th century.

CHINESE CHIPPENDALE. A period in Chippendale's work, in the mid-18th century, when he was greatly influenced by chinoiserie, Chinese motifs, and the work of Sir William Chambers. See *Chambers, Sir William; Chinoiserie; Lacquerwork*.

CHINESE BRACKET FOOT

CHINESE CHIPPENDALE

CHINESE KEY DESIGN

CHINOISERIE

CHINESE KEY DESIGN. A continuous geometric border design, similar to the Greek key design or meander. This type of design was used by Chippendale in his fretwork and openwork grille doors for bookcases, secretaries, etc.

CHINESE ROOM. An 18th-century English fad or craze. A room in some part of the house was decorated "à la Chinoise," with imported Chinese furniture or adaptations such as Chippendale produced in his Chinese Chippendale period. China (or India or Japan) wallpaper or handpainted paper murals would usually cover the walls. Many of these wallpapers were produced in England after Chinese originals. See *Chinese Chippendale* and *Chinoiserie.*

CHINESE WALLPAPER. A wallpaper introduced into Europe in the mid-17th century under the name of "India" or "Japan" paper. It was sold in sets of 25 rolls, each 12' long and 4' wide with a studied dissimilarity of detail from panel to panel. In the mid-18th century, chinoiserie had reached the peak of its popularity, and Chinese papers were very much in vogue. Among the favorite motifs were flowering shrubs, trees, flowers, birds, and butterflies. These were later replaced with exotic landscapes and curious "oriental" figures. The authentic Chinese wallpapers were greatly imitated by French and English paper printers, and often contemporary 18th-century occidental figures are portrayed wandering through lush pseudo-oriental scenes. James Minikin of England produced wallpapers of this type.

CHINOISERIE. Chinese-type or Chinese-like decorative motifs: gay, picturesque, imaginative occidental versions of oriental designs. Particularly popular in the Louis XV period in France and the 18th-century English styles. See *Chinese Chippendale; Formal; Huet, Christophe; Singerie;* and *Venetian Chinoiserie.*

CHINTZ. From the Hindu word for "spotted." A fine cotton cloth with a printed design. The fabric is usually glazed or calendered. The design can be printed by blocks, copper plates, screens, or rollers. Unglazed chintz is called cretonne.

CHIP CARVING. A simple, low relief form of ornamentation of the 18th and early 19th centuries, on American furniture. The work was accomplished with flat chisels and semicircular gouges. In the early 17th century, chip carving was used to enrich English furniture.

CHIPPENDALE, THOMAS I. An early-18th-century English cabinetmaker, and the creator of many early Georgian pieces. He was father of Thomas II, the most famous of the three Chippendales.

CHIPPENDALE, THOMAS II (1718–1779). The noted Chippendale. An English furniture designer and cabinetmaker. His earliest work was in the refined Georgian style, and in 1754 he published the *Gentleman and Cabinet-Maker's Director*. Chippendale's designs had great beauty, and he created in a variety of styles, including the decorated Queen Anne, Chinese, and Rococo French, as well as the Gothic. He was noted for his chairs, girandoles, mirrors, frames, and assorted beds (canopy, Chinese, dome, Gothic, field, and tent). He also designed many stands, side and serving tables, and teapoys. Henry Copeland, William Ince, Thomas Johnson, Mathias Lock, Robert Manwaring, J. Mayhew, and others followed in the styles originated by Chippendale. A Chippendale Chinese sofa is illustrated.

THOMAS CHIPPENDALE

CHIPPENDALE, THOMAS III (1749-1822). The son of the noted Chippendale. He designed and executed furniture in the Regency style. He worked in partnership with Thomas Haig.

CHITON. The tunic worn by the ancient Greeks. The Doric variation was usually made of wool and was rectangular in shape. It was worn wrapped around the right side, pinned at the left shoulder, and left open on the left side. The Ionic chiton was more voluminous, made of linen or cotton, and fastened in several places to create sleeves of a sort and an interesting drapery pattern.

CHITON

CHOIR. The area of the church fitted for the singers, or more broadly, the enclosed space for all those engaged in an ecclesiastic ceremony.

CHRIST CHURCH (Old North). Built in Boston, Massachusetts, in 1723, and was the first example of the Renaissance influence in New England. The church design was based on Sir Christopher Wren's St. James's in Piccadilly, and it was devised in brick by William Price, a local printseller.

CHROMA or CHROME. The degree of intensity, brilliance, or saturation of a spectrum color. Yellow is in the center of the spectrum, and is the most brilliant, but of the palest chroma because it has the least saturation. Blue is the darkest, and has the greatest saturation. Red has a medium chroma.

CHROME PLATED. Covered with a thin deposit of chromium deposited by electrolysis which gives the underlying metal a shiny appearance and makes it corrosion-resistant.

CHROMSPUN. A trademark name for solution-dyed acetate fibers produced by Tennessee Eastman Company. Filaments are used in carpet and upholstery fabrics.

CHRYSELEPHANTINE

CHURCH-GOING CHAIR

CHURN MOLDING

CHUTE

CIEL DE LIT

CHRYSELEPHANTINE. Made of ivory and gold. Certain ancient Greek statues were so made, the exposed body, face, and hands made of ivory, and the clothing or drapery of gold.

CHUFF. A reject brick. It cannot be used for building because of inherent weaknesses.

CHURCH-GOING CHAIR. A light, portable, folding chair of the 16th and 17th centuries. It is similar to today's folding bridge chairs. The chair was made of wood, with a leather or fabric seat. The chair back was often a colonnade motif made up of spiral colonnettes.

CHURN MOLDING. The zigzag or chevron molding used to enrich Norman architecture.

CHURRIGUERA, JOSÉ (1665–1725). A Spanish architect who introduced the Baroque style into Spanish architecture. Hero-ically scaled motifs were applied onto structures rather than planned as funtioning parts of the construction. Columns and pilasters became spiral or baluster-form shafts; voluptuous volutes replaced pediments; and nudes, cherubim, plaster clouds, waterfalls, draperies and such became lost in the mélange of swirls, curves, and fantasy.

CHURRIGUERESQUE. The bold and massive Spanish Baroque style of the 17th century. The period was mainly influenced by the architect Churriguera. The Baroque period in Spain ran concurrently with the Rococo and up through the mid-18th century. There are an exuberance of color and an extravagance of ornament in this Baroque period which also had an effect on the Spanish possessions in the Americas. Examples of this style are: the west façade of the Granada Cathedral, the west façade of the Cathedral of Santiago de Compostela, and the gardens of the Palace of La Granja.

CHUTE. The French for "fall" or "tumble." The chutes were decorative bronze pieces that fitted over the exposed angles and on the legs of wood furniture pieces. The ornate plates were used to protect as well as reinforce these areas. These functional enrichments appear in 18th- and 19th-century French furniture. Many famous craftsmen like Caffieri made these chased and engraved pieces. Sometimes the chutes were finished as ormolu or as bronze-doré. Illustrated is a typical Louis XV commode. See *Sabots*.

CIBORIUM. See *Baldachino*.

CIEL DE LIT. French for a bed tester or canopy. Illustrated is an early French Renaissance bed.

CIMABUE, GIOVANNI. A 13th-century Italian painter of frescoes and designer of mosaics. He is credited with being the "father of modern painting."

CIMBORIO. The Spanish term for "lantern." A raised structure above a dome which is fenestrated to allow light into the interior of the structure below. See *Lantern*.

CINCTURE. The broad fillet located below the concave molding (congé), which is located at the bottom of the shaft of a classic order column.

CINDER BLOCK. A building unit made of cinder concrete.

CINQUECENTO. The 16th century.

CINQUEFOIL. A five-leaf clover shape; also a motif in Gothic tracery.

CINQUEFOIL

CIPRIANI, GIOVANNI BATTISTA (1727–1785). An Italian painter of the Adam period in 18th-century England. He painted many ceiling and wall panels, as well as medallion inserts for Adam furniture. Cipriani did elegant, decorative, classic pieces and many graceful arabesque panels.

CIRAGE. A monochromatic painting in yellow.

CIRCASSIAN WALNUT. A highly figured veneer wood that is produced from twisted, gnarled, and warped walnut trees grown in the dry Black Sea area of Europe.

CIRCUS. Originally a Roman racecourse.

CIRE PERDUE. French for "lost wax." A method of bronze casting in which a figure is modeled in wax and then coated with clay. The figure is heated, the melted wax runs out through holes left in the clay, and molten metal is poured into the clay shell. The final details are often worked directly on the bronze casting.

CIRE PERDUE

GIOVANNI CIMABUE   CIMBORIO

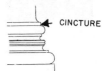

CINCTURE

GIOVANNI BATTISTA CIPRIANI

CISELÉ VELVET

CITADEL

CLAP TABLE

CLAPBOARD HOUSE

CISELÉ VELVET. A raised, cut velvet which was typical of the Renaissance in Genoa. The pattern was raised up against a flattened background.

CISELEUR. A chiseler; a craftsman who ornaments bronze and other metals by chiseling, one who does chasing. A term applied to finishers of metal mounts and chutes for 18th-century furniture. A Renaissance metal hinge is illustrated.

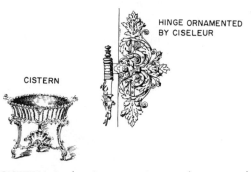

HINGE ORNAMENTED BY CISELEUR

CISTERN

CISTERN. In furniture, a wine cooler, sarcophagus, or cellarette of the latter part of the 18th century. It was most often used to keep bottles on ice, but sometimes it was used for washing up. A Chippendale cistern is illustrated. In architecture, a rectangular, metal, open-topped container for cold water. See *Cellarette, Sarcophagus,* and *Wine Cooler.*

CITADEL. A fortified structure like a stronghold or fortress.

CITRONNIER. French for lemon tree. A pale, honey-colored wood which was popular for furniture at the end of the 18th century.

CLAIRE-VOIE. French for "clerestory."

CLAP TABLE. An early 18th-century English pier or console table which usually had a pier looking glass set over it. Illustrated is a clap table designed by Thomas Johnson.

CLAPBOARD HOUSE. The typical 17th-century New England house. Clapboarding (see *Clapboard Wall* below) was originally used as a protection for half-timbered houses in late Gothic–early Renaissance England, and was brought over to the New World. The house of Parson Capen at Topsfield, Massachusetts, (1683) is a typical clapboard house.

CLAPBOARD WALL. An exterior wall facing made up of horizontal, slightly overlapping planks. A weatherboarded wall.

CLARE-OBSCURE. The 18th-century Anglicised form of the French "clair-obscur," a method of painting in lights and shades or "chiaroscuro." It is similar to *Grisaille* painting.

CLASSIC. Referring to the architecture, sculpture, arts, and literary arts of the ancient Greeks and Romans. Something with an antique source or an established degree of excellence. 18th- and 19th-century architecture and arts based on Greek and Roman elements; this style usually called Neoclassic or new classic. Illustrated is the Greek Doric order.

CLASSIC REVIVAL. The early-19th-century architectural trend in England and the Continent which stressed the revival of classic forms and motifs. Classic prototypes were reexamined and supplied inspiration for new structures. Examples of the Classic Revival are the Royal Exchange in London, the Palais de Justice in Paris, the Court Theatre in Berlin. Greek columns and porticoes were frequently used. See *Barry, Sir Charles,* and *Neo-Greek* for illustrations.

CLAVATED. Club-shaped. A type of turning used for furniture legs and stretchers on early Renaissance Spanish furniture. A Louis XIII Renaissance chair done in the Spanish style is illustrated.

CLAVECIN. See *Clavichord* and *Pianoforte*.

CLAVICEMBALO. A predecessor of the pianoforte which resembled a dulcimer with a keyboard attached to it.

CLAVICHORD. A 17th-century forerunner of the piano. A stringed instrument that was used in England during the Carolean, William and Mary, and Queen Anne periods.

CLAW-AND-BALL FOOT. See *Ball-and-Claw Foot*. Illustrated is a "roundabout" or corner chair of the late 17th century.

CLAY MORTAR MIX. A finely ground clay which is added to mortar as a plasticizer.

CLEAR CERAMIC GLAZE. A translucent tinted glaze. See *Ceramic Color Glaze*.

CLEARCOLE. A priming or sizing solution made of white lead ground in water with glue. It is used in Great Britain.

CLEAT. A wood strip fastened on a wood surface as a means of joining two adjacent surfaces, or a method of reinforcing the join. The cleat can also prevent warping. See *Butterfly Wedge*.

CLEAT

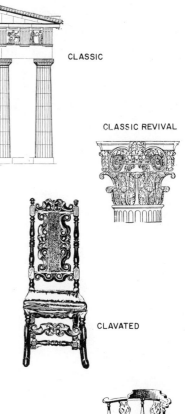

CLASSIC

CLASSIC REVIVAL

CLAVATED

CLAW-AND-BALL FOOT

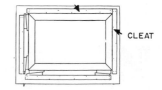

CLEAT

CLEF PENDANTE

CLEF PENDANTE. French for "boss." A hanging or projecting ornamental pendant. See *Boss*.

CLEPSYDRA. An ancient Greek time-measuring device. Time was calculated by the dropping of water through a small aperture.

CLERESTORY. A window placed near the top of a wall above an adjacent roof. Clerestory windows in the nave wall of a church are those above the roof of the side aisles. See *Basilica*.

CLERESTORY

CLOACA

CLOACA. An antique Roman sewer or drain. Illustrated is the Cloaca Maxima.

CLOCHE. A glass dome fitted over a wood base usually to protect artificial flowers, a clock, or an objet d'art from dust or harm.

CLODION, CLAUDE MICHEL (1738–1814). A French sculptor who specialized in terra-cotta figures and figurines of satyrs, nymphs, and other decorative and sensual subjects. After the French Revolution, he was able to adapt to the Roman taste, and work on the Colonne de le Grande Armée, and the Arc de Triomphe du Carrousel (1806–1809).

CLOISONNÉ

CLOISONNÉ. A type of enamelware in which delicate metal partition filaments hold and separate the assorted colored enamels in a pattern. The individual metal partitions are called cloisons. Illustrated is a section of a Japanese copper dish with cloisonné inlay.

CLOISTER. The covered passageway around an inner courtyard; sometimes the courtyard itself. A feature of Gothic architecture.

CLOISTER

CLOISTER

CLOSE CHAIR or CLOSE STOOL. An enclosed box or stool equipped with a removable chamber pot. It was in use before the toilet or water closet came into architectural being. Sheraton describes his design in his *Cabinet Dictionary* (1803) as: "made to have the appearance of a small commode, standing upon legs; when it is used the seat part presses down to a proper height by the hand, and afterward it rises by means of lead weights, hung to the seat, by lines passing over the pulleys at each end, all which are enclosed in a case."

CLOSER. The last tile or brick in a course.

CLOSER

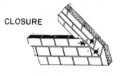
CLOSURE

CLOSURE. A cut or trimmed brick, usually ¼ or ¾ of a brick. It is used at corners to obtain proper bonding.

CLOTHESPRESS. A chest of drawers, sometimes with a cupboard set above it. The cupboard or cabinet has shelves to hold clothes. Illustrated is a Chippendale design.

CLOTHESPRESS

CLOVEN FOOT

CLOVEN FOOT. Decorative foot for a Louis XIV furniture leg. It resembles a deer's cleft hind foot. See *Pied de Biche*.

CLUB CHAIR. A large, roomy, upholstered easy chair. It may or may not be skirted, and the type of arms may vary with period or style, from high to low, from thick to thin, from all-upholstered to partially unholstered and partially framed. An oversized bergère.

CLUB FOOT. A flat, round pad ending for a cabriole leg. It was used frequently on early-18th-century English furniture. See *Dutch Foot, Pad Foot,* and *Spoon Foot.*

CLUNY LACE. See *Valenciennes Lace.*

CLUB FOOT

CLUSTERED COLUMN LEG

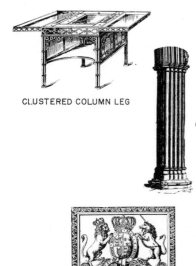

CLUSTERED COLUMN LEG

CLUSTERED COLUMN

COAT OF ARMS

COAL SCUTTLE

CLUSTERED COLUMN LEG. A furniture leg made up of several grouped or engaged turnings or columns. This type of leg was used by Chippendale and William Ince in mid-18th-century England.

CLUSTERED COLUMNS. Several columns placed together or having overlapping shafts which form a single support. A Gothic architectural motif.

COAL SCUTTLE. A box or bucket used as a coal receptacle. Sometimes made of brass and ornamented. See *Pipkins*.

COAT OF ARMS. Originally a lightweight garment, usually embroidered or decorated with heraldic emblems and worn over armor. In more recent terminology, the heraldic emblems of a family or institution. Illustrated is a design by the Adam brothers (mid-18th century) for the English royal family.

COB WALL. A wall built of "clay bat" blocks which are made of unburnt clay or chalk mixed with straw.

COBB, JOHN. An 18th-century English furniture maker and partner of William Vile. See *Vile, William*.

COBBLER'S BENCH. A shoemaker's bench with seat, last holder, and compartments for pegs, etc. It was "rustic" and usually made of pine in Colonial America. Reproductions and adaptations are made today and are used as cocktail tables in American-Provincial-type rooms.

COCHIN, CHARLES NICHOLAS (1714–1790). A French designer and engraver who opposed the rococo style and worked in the classic tradition.

COCHOIS, JEAN-BAPTISTE. A French master cabinetmaker (ébéniste) to Louis XVI. He was an inventor of dual purpose and change-about furniture: a chiffonière that converted into a night table, etc.

COCK BEADING or MOLDING. A small convex or half-round projecting molding used around the edges of drawers. See *Single Arch Molding*.

COCK BEADING

COCKADE. A ribbon rosette or badge popularized by the French Revolution. It was much in use in the French Directoire period as a decorative element.

COCKFIGHT CHAIR. A saddle-like chair with a small shelf as the top rail of the chair back. The individual straddles the chair facing the back. The top rail, usually padded, functioned as an armrest. This type of chair was used for reading, writing, and viewing sports events (like cockfighting, etc.) An 18th-century English favorite. See *Fumeuse, Ponteuse, Straddle Chair, Voyelle,* and *Voyeuse.*

COCKLESHELL. Also called the escallop or shell ornament. It was used as a carved decorative feature on furniture knees, crestings, and pendants of chairs and other furniture pieces in early-18th-century English, Louis XIV, and Louis XV period designs. See *Rococo* and *Scallop Shell.*

COCKFIGHT CHAIR

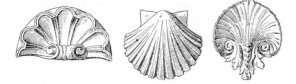

LOUIS XIV SHELL   NATURAL SHELL   LOUIS XIV SHELL

COCKTAIL TABLE. See *Coffee Table.*

COCO BOLO. A fine, uniform grain, dark brown wood with a purplish cast which takes a fine polished finish. It is found in Central America and is used for modern furniture and fancy cabinetwork.

COCO WOOD. A hard and brittle wood with purplish brown stripes on a medium dark ground. It is native to India.

CODEX. A manuscript in the form of a volume with the pages bound together. This replaced the long rolls or scrolls originally used for manuscripts. The codex appears in the early Christian period. Illustrated is a Byzantine enamel from a codex now in the Library of S. Marco in Venice.

CODEX

COFFEE TABLE. A low table, usually placed in front of a sofa or couch, and used to hold ashtrays, magazines, and refreshments. It can be styled to suit any particular period. In the 18th century, similar tables were designed as tea tables to hold tea service, cups, saucers, etc.

COFFER. See *Coffered Panel* and *Coffre.*

COFFERED PANEL. In architecture, a sunken panel in the ceiling of a vault or dome, or in the underside of a cornice. The coffer is usually ornamented and decorated. Illustrated is the Pantheon in Rome.

COFFERED PANEL

COFFRE (COFFER). A chest or strongbox used for holding valuables. It also served as a seating unit in Gothic interiors. A French Romanesque example is illustrated.

COFFRE

COGGING

COIN

COLLAR

COLOGNE CATHEDRAL

COFFRET. A small chest or coffer, often on its own stand or table.

COFFIN STOOL. A small oak four-legged stool, with stretchers, usually left undecorated. It may have been used originally to hold coffins awaiting interment.

COGGING. A form of joinery with the pieces of wood crossing each other at right angles. The lower member is grooved out so that a projection fits into a slot on the underside of the upper member.

COGSWELL. A 20th-century easy-chair with a fully upholstered back and seat, and a low upholstered platform. The sides are not enclosed. The arm stump rises from the platform and carries an overstuffed arm pad.

COIFFEUSE. A hairdressing table or makeup table of the Louis XV and Louis XVI periods. See *Poudreuse* and *Table à Coiffer.*

COIGN. See *Quoin.*

COIN. A corner cupboard. See *Encoignure* and *Quoin.* Illustrated is an American corner cupboard, circa 1800.

COLLAGE. From the French for "gluing." A picture or ornament built up with pieces of paper, cloth, and other materials which are glued or stuck on to a canvas or other surface. See *Montage.*

COLLAR. An astragal, or molding, which forms a band or ring around a furniture element like a table or chair leg.

COLLAR BEAM. A wooden tie which is fixed to the main rafters above the wall-plate level in a collar roof. See C on *Hammer-Beam Roof* illustration.

COLLAR ROOF. Roof in which wood ties are fixed to the rafters above wall-plate level. The ceiling of a room under a collar roof has two sloping surfaces which correspond to the angle of the rafters joined by a flat surface which is carried on the underside of the ties.

COLLECTION. A group of related units, or an accumulation of similar pieces like a Wedgwood collection, or a group of furniture by a particular designer, or one based on the same decorative styles or ornaments.

COLOGNE CATHEDRAL. The largest Gothic cathedral in North Europe, it was built chiefly between 1248 and 1322, and covers 91,000 square feet. Its twin towers rise 500 feet above the ground. The plan is 468' long and 275' wide and the nave is 150' high (almost as high as Beauvais). The building was completed according to the original plans between 1824 and 1880. The proportions and details are not as refined as those of the French Gothic structures.

COLONIAL AMERICA. The period in American art and architecture from 1620 up to the Revolution. It is the period of early settlement in America and blending of English, French, and Dutch influences with native provincial interpretations.

COLONNA. Italian for "column" or "pillar."

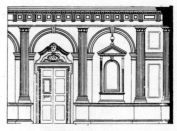

COLONIAL AMERICA

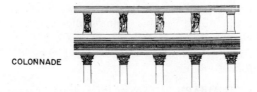

COLONNADE

COLONNADE. A row of columns supporting a single entablature. An architectural treatment for a passageway or corridor.

COLONNATO. Italian for "colonnade."

COLONNETTE. A miniature column used in architecture and also as a furniture decoration. In the Sheraton chair back here illustrated, the uprights resemble Corinthian columns. A group or cluster of colonnettes is sometimes used as a support for a pedestal table. A classic motif and a favorite of the Renaissance period.

COLONNETTE

COLORBOND. A trademark name for an oil-in-water resin pigment dyeing technique developed by Dan River Company. It makes cotton, viscose, rayon, acetate, nylon, and other synthetics or blends colorfast to sunlight, washing, dry cleaning, gases, etc.

COLORFAST. A term used to describe the ability of a fabric to retain its color when subjected to normal light, air, gas, and laundering. Little or no noticeable change of shade should take place, though it is almost impossible to produce an absolutely colorfast fabric.

COLORWAYS. The various color schemes in which a pattern or design is produced. The number of colorways refers to the number of color arrangements printed or screened on a paper, fabric, etc., of a particular design.

COLOSSEUM, ROME. Called the "Flavian Amphitheatre." This famous structure was begun A.D. 70 and completed A.D. 82. In plan, it is an ellipse, 620' × 513', and there are 80 external arcaded openings on each of the four stories. The basic construction is of concrete, tufa, and brick. Travertine blocks, set

COLUMBANI, PLACIDO

PLACIDO COLUMBANI

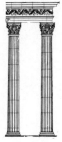

COLUMNS

COMB BACK

without mortar but cramped together, were used in the façade. The classic orders are used in a superimposed manner: Tuscan, Ionic, and Corinthian half columns on the lower stories, and Corinthian pilasters on the uppermost story. Great engineering problems were solved in this structure, and much was made possible by the invention and use of concrete. See *Roman Architecture.*

COLUMBANI, PLACIDO. An 18th-century Italian architectural designer of the Adam period. He worked with the Adam brothers in designing decorative mirror frames, and is especially noted for his chimneypieces. Columbani published *A New Book of Ornaments* in 1775, and *A Variety of Capitals, Friezes, Cornices and Chimney Pieces* in 1776. See *Crunden, John.*

COLUMBARIUM. From the Latin, "pigeon house." A small recess in the wall of a catacomb or other burial vault which will hold an urn with the ashes of the deceased. It resembles a pigeonhole.

COLUMBARIUM

COLUMN. An upright member which is taller than it is thick, and serves as a support for something resting on its top. In architecture, a shaft set on a base and topped with a capital. Illustrated is a Corinthian column from the Temple of Vesta at Tivoli. Columns are distinguished by the name of the style or period of architecture to which they belong. See *Classic.*

COMB BACK. A Windsor chair back in which the central group of spindles extends above the back proper, and is topped with an additional rail (the cresting rail). The top unit is called the comb piece since it resembles the high, Spanish-type combs that were fashionable in the 18th century. It is also called "three-back" Windsor chair.

COMMEDIA DELL'ARTE. Traditional form of Italian comedy popular with the artists and designers in the 18th century. Jacques Callot, Claude Gillot, and Antoine Watteau used scenes, costumes, and characters from the commedia dell'arte in their works.

COMMERCE TABLE. An 18th-century collapsible or folding X-shaped frame which supported an oval card-table top. It was used to play Commerce, a card game.

COMMESSO. A geometric type of mosaic work used in Italy during the Middle Ages.

COMMODE. A chest of drawers or a cabinet, usually low and squat. In about 1700, in the Louis XIV period, the term "bureau commode" was used to describe a large table with drawers. In the Regency and the Louis XV periods, the commode was often bombé in shape and it is considered the most typical piece of furniture of that time. The finer pieces showed no dividing rail or strip between the upper and lower drawer. The later units often had only two drawers. See illustration for *Chute* for a Louis XV commode. Also see *Cressent, Charles*. A commode is also a night stand, a bedside cabinet or chest. In polite usage today, a latrine, a toilet.

COMMODE CHAIR. A thronelike chair construction used to camouflage a toilet bowl. A 20th-century conceit.

COMMODE DESSERTE. A French 18th-century sideboard with a center cabinet area and open shelves on either side.

COMMODE STEP. The curved bottom step of a stairway.

COMMODES EN TOMBEAUX. Early Louis XV chests, usually designed with two small drawers on top, and two full-width drawers below. The units were heavy in appearance and the lowest drawer was only inches off the floor; the legs were that short. "Tombeau" is French for "tombstone" and these designs were massive, squat, and tombstone-like.

COMMON BOND. In masonry, several courses of stretcher bond with the sixth or eighth course made up of headers only. This provides transverse strength to the bond since the headers tie back into the next set of bricks.

COMMESSO

COMMODE

COMMODE EN TOMBEAU

COMMON RAFTER

COMMON BOND

COMMON RAFTERS. The rafters that support the roofing of a building. They slope from the top of a wall to the ridge or apex of a pitched roof. See *C.R.* in *King Post Truss* illustration.

COMMONWEALTH. The Cromwellian period in England, 1649–1660. A puritanical period of chaste, severe forms. Illustrated is the bed of Oliver Cromwell.

COMMONWEALTH

COMPANION CHAIR. Three curved upholstered chairs joined together at one point so that they appear to radiate from that central junction. Each chair is large enough to accommodate two persons. It is like a three-part *Tête-à-Tête* or *Siamoise*. The companion chair was popular in the mid and late-19th century.

COMPARTMENT. In architecture, any area enclosed or bordered by architectural elements: walls, columns, arches, etc. In furniture, a cubicle, pigeonhole, etc.

COMPASS SEAT. An early-18th-century term for a round chair seat. It was also referred to as a pincushion seat or chair.

COMPLEMENTARY COLORS. Each of the primary colors (red, yellow, and blue) has its complement, which is produced by mixing the other two. Yellow and blue make green, and green is the complement of red. Violet complements yellow, and orange complements blue.

COMPLUVIUM. The open space or center opening in the roof of a Roman atrium. See *Cavaedium*.

COMPO. See *Carton-Pierre, Composition Ornament, and Gesso.* A plaster or papier-mâché-like material molded or applied to a ceiling, panel, frame, or piece of furniture to create a bas-relief enrichment. Illustrated is a late-18th-century girandole, probably designed by Hepplewhite circa 1788, and executed on molded plaster.

COMPO

COMPOSITE ORDER. A variation of the Corinthian order. The capital resembles an Ionic volute placed above rows of Corinthian acanthus leaves. A classic Roman order.

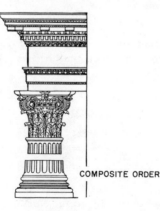

COMPOSITE ORDER

COMPOSITION. A grouping of various parts to create a unified whole.

COMPOSITION ORNAMENT. An ornament or enrichment that is made of plaster or plaster-like material. The material is cast in a mold, and then applied to a surface to make a bas-relief decoration that resembles carving. The material and resulting ornament are also called "gesso" and "yeseria." Composition ornament was introduced into England by the Adam brothers for the decoration of panels, ceilings, walls, doors, etc. See *Anaglypta, Carton-Pierre, Gesso, Papier-Mâché,* and *Pargework.*

COMPOSITION ORNAMENT

COMPOTIER. A container for stewed fruits, jellies, and jams.

CONCAVE. A sunken or caved-in line. The reverse of a convex line.

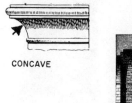

CONCAVE

CONCH. The semidome of an apse. It resembles a seashell —hence the name. Illustrated is a section of the apse of St. Jean de Noristier, a French Romanesque church.

CONCH

CONCRETE. A construction material made of cement, sand, and crushed stone, tile, or brick, mixed with water.

CONDUIT. A pipe or enclosed channel for carrying water, electrical wires, etc.

CONFESSIONAL. An 18th-century large, upholstered French wing chair. In Catholic Church architecture, a small enclosure in which the priest sits to hear the confession.

CONFIDANTE. Three seats attached in a single unit. The two end seats are usually smaller, angled, and separated from the prominent center section by arms. A Hepplewhite "centre ottoman" is illustrated.

CONFIDANTE

CONFORTABLE. An early French Renaissance all-upholstered chair. A forerunner of the bergère.

CONGÉ. A concave molding similar to a cavetto, but tangent to a plane surface. The astragal under the bell of a capital consists of bead, fillet, and congé moldings. See *Cincture.*

CONGÉ

CONOIDAL VAULT. See *Fan Vault.*

CONNECTICUT CHEST. An early American chest, with two rows of double drawers, which stands on four short legs. It was frequently decorated with split spindles, painted black, and sometimes ornamented with three carved panels (see *Aster Carving*). The Connecticut chests were often made of oak, with pine tops, backs, and bottoms.

CONSERVATORY. A greenhouse. Usually a glassed-in room in which plants and trees are grown. The room often has a glass ceiling. Also called a "jardin d'hiver." A late-19th-century favorite.

CONSOLE

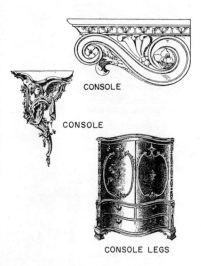

CONSOLE

CONSOLE

CONSOLE LEGS

CONSOLE SERVANTE

CONSOLE TABLE

CONSTRUCTION

CONSOLE. The French term for "bracket." A console is a bracket, usually in an S scroll or curve. It is used architecturally to support a cornice or shelf. In furniture, it is more a decorative device than a functional one. The term often applies to a console table, which is actually a shelf supported against a wall by a bracket, a leg, or a pair of legs.

CONSOLE DESSERTE. A small serving table similar to a sideboard.

CONSOLE LEGS. Scroll legs that are bracket-shaped. They are found in late-18th-century furniture and are also called "bracket feet." Illustrated is a Chippendale wardrobe.

CONSOLE MIRROR

CONSOLE MIRROR. A mirror that is set over a console or pier table. Illustrated is a German Empire console mirror and table.

CONSOLE SERVANTE. A serving table with a marble top and a shelf below, of the Louis XVI period. It is similar to the console desserte and commode desserte. A Sheraton design is illustrated.

CONSOLE TABLE. A shelflike table that is attached to a wall, and supported by a receding front leg or legs, or set on an S-shaped curved or caryatid-type bracket. It was originally popular in 18th-century France and England, and is still in use today in foyers, entries, etc. It is also called a pier table.

CONSTITUTION MIRROR. A very late-18th, early-19th-century rectangular Sheraton-type mirror frame. It was usually gilded and had a row of balls under the cornice and a painted upper panel over the mirror area. In the 19th century the painting was often of the frigate *Constitution* of the War of 1812. It was also called a "tabernacle mirror." See *Tabernacle Mirror*.

CONSTRUCTION. The assembling of the component parts into an integral unit. Illustrated is the internal construction of a couch showing the wood framework, springs, filling, and muslin.

CONTEMPORARY. A current, present-day, modern style of decoration or furniture, as opposed to "traditional," which refers to a conventional past period or antique style.

CONTOUR. The basic outline of a shape or object, disregarding painted or internal ornaments or decorations.

CONTOUR CHAIR. Any molded, shaped, or upholstered chair that conforms to the contours of the human body. Many modern pieces are designed in laminated plywood, plexiglass, aluminum, etc., by designers like Eames and Saarinen. See *Eames, Charles; Saarinen, Eero;* and *Womb Chair.*

CONTRAFFORTE. Italian for "buttress."

CONTREFORTS. French for "buttresses." Illustrated is a section of the nave of Notre-Dame de Paris showing the buttresses.

CONTREPARTIE or CONTRE BOULLE. A form of boulle marquetry in which the brass forms the groundwork. The tortoiseshell is set into it, and is therefore the less prominent material. It is the reverse form of the usual boulle work or *Première Partie.*

CONVENTIONALIZATION. The simplifying or exaggerating of natural forms to make them more acceptable and reproducible in other materials. *A* is a realistic drawing of an acanthus leaf. *B* is a conventionalized form of it.

CONVERSATION CHAIR. This term has been applied to a variety of chairs: the caqueteuse in the 16th century, the roundabout or cockfight chair in the 18th century, and the S-shaped "vis-à-vis" or "dos-à-dos" of the 19th century. Essentially, it is a comfortable chair which is not as low or as deep as an easy or lounge chair.

CONVERSATION PIECE. An informal portrait of two or more people in an appropriate setting. A family group portrait. In current usage, it refers to an oddity or unique piece of decoration in a room which may cause comment.

CONVERSATION PIT. In contemporary architecture, a sunken area in a living or family room which is surrounded by an architectural ledge. The ledge is usually covered with upholstery or pillows. The riser to the floor level, above the ledge, serves as the backrest for those seated in the pit. The unit may be rectangular, oval, or circular but the conversationalists are all facing one another.

CONVEX. A swelling or outgoing curved line or surface, as opposed to a concave line or surface. Two convex moldings are illustrated.

CONVOLUTE. A scroll or paper-roll shape.

CONVOLUTE

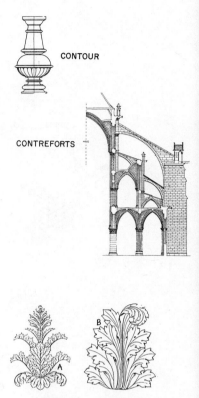

CONTOUR

CONTREFORTS

CONVENTIONALIZATION

CONVEX

CONVOLUTE

COOL COLORS. The green-yellows, greens, blue-greens, blues, blue-violets, and violets.

COORDINATED. Designed or arranged to "go together." A collection of furniture designed in the same given modules, or with the same trim and decoration, would be coordinated. Several different solid-color fabrics and a plaid consisting of all of these same colors would be a coordinated group.

COPELAND, HENRY. An 18th-century cabinetmaker of the Chippendale, and then the Adam, school. With Matthias Lock, he published *A New Book of Ornaments.*

COPE. A method of joining two molded strips at an angle. Instead of the pieces being mitered, one piece fits over the top of the other.

COPING

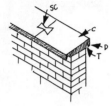

COPING. An upper course of masonry on a wall which usually overlaps the wall somewhat. It serves somewhat as a means of protection for the courses below. In the illustration, C coping, *D* drip, *T* throating, *SC* slate cramp.

COPTIC. Referring to the Copts, an early Christian group in Egypt, from the 4th to the 7th century. Their work included realistic portraits, and ended with flat decorative patterned designs.

COPTIC CLOTH. A small-patterned, plain-woven, cotton upholstery fabric which usually has a provincial or rustic appearance.

COPTIC TEXTILE. A linen fabric woven and designed in Egypt by the Coptic sect (4th to 7th centuries).

COQUILLAGE

COQUILLAGE. A French rococo shell-like pattern used with birds, flowers, masks, and other carved ornaments to decorate mirrors, frames, clocks, etc. It also appears in Chippendale's French-style furniture as a furniture enrichment.

CORBEIL or CORBEILLE. A sculptured representation of a basket of fruit or flowers.

CORBEL. In architecture, a bracket or shoulder set in a wall to carry a beam. The corbel was also adapted for use on interiors and on furniture, and was popular in Renaissance designs. See *Bracket* and *Console.*

CORBEL

CORBEL

CORBEL TABLE

CORBEL TABLE. A slab of stone or masonry which is supported by a row of corbels.

CORBELED ARCH. A span of stonework constructed by regularly advancing the successive courses from either side till the top ones nearly meet. A capstone is set in the center to close the gap. Illustrated is the early Greek Treasury of Atreus at Mycenae. Here a dome-shaped roof is achieved by the advancing in of the successive courses.

CORBIE GABLE. A gable with a stepped upper surface. It is also called a "crow-step gable" or "corbie steps."

CORBIE STEPS. See *Corbie Gable.*

CORDOVAN LEATHER. The decorated leatherwork made in the technique and style begun in Cordova, Spain, during the Middle Ages. The leather was often stamped, carved, or embossed with gilt arabesques and Moorish patterns.

CORDOVAN TAPESTRY. See *Guadamicil.*

CORDUROY. From the French, "corde du roi," the king's cord. A cotton or rayon cut pile fabric with ridges or cords in the pile which run lengthwise. The fabric has a ridged, velvet-like quality.

CORE. In cabinetry, the structural wooden body of a piece of furniture. It usually gets a veneered finish (see *Carcase or Carcass).* The central body of plywood which has crossed layers of veneer or other wood applied to either of its surfaces. This internal layer, or core, is usually made of a porous wood like poplar.

CORINTHIAN ORDER. The most slender, graceful, and elaborate of the classic architectural orders. The Romans made the height of the column equal to ten times the diameter of the shaft. The capital is enriched with rows of acanthus leaves and four volutes.

CORINTHIANESQUE. A design similar to the Corinthian order, but not an exact reproduction. Illustrated is an Italian Renaissance version of a Corinthian-type pilaster.

CORNICIONE. Italian for "entablature."

CORK TILES. Cork which has been pressed and baked into a solid, homogeneous block, and then cut into rectangular sheets or tiles. The squares may be used for flooring or wall surfacing. It is an extremely resilient material. Resin reinforced, waxed cork tile is less porous than natural cork tile, and requires less maintenance. The natural cork will stain, and because of its softness it will indent or pit. Cork can be laminated with a thin layer of vinyl or be impregnated with vinyl resins.

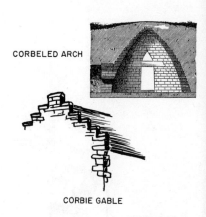

CORBELED ARCH

CORBIE GABLE

CORINTHIAN ORDER

CORINTHIANESQUE

CORLON

CORNER BLOCK

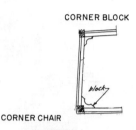

CORNER CHAIR

CORNER STILES

CORLON. A trademark name for sheet vinyl flooring with a hydrocord back, made by Armstrong. It usually comes in 6′ widths and can be used over suspended, on grade, and below grade subfloors. Corlon is available in a variety of colors, patterns, and textural effects.

CORNER BLOCK

CORNER BLOCK. In carpentry, a square block of wood used to form a junction, as between the sides and head strip of a door. In cabinetry, a triangular block used as a brace in joining legs to seat rails. A plan of a chair seat is illustrated. The chair legs are shaded.

CORNER CHAIR. See *Roundabout Chair.*

CORNER CUPBOARD. A triangular cabinet or chest originally designed by architects as an integral part of a room. In the 18th century it became a mobile piece of furniture. See *Coin* and *Encoignure.*

CORNER STILES. The corner or end vertical members in a paneled piece of furniture. A late-17th-century cabinet is illustrated.

CORNICE

CORNICE

CORNICE. The projecting top portion of a classic entablature consisting of bed fascia and crown moldings. In Renaissance-type interiors it was used on interior walls directly below the ceiling, without the frieze or architrave moldings. See *Architrave, Fascia,* and *Frieze.* Also, a decorative applied cap to a curtain or drapery arrangement on windows, canopy beds, etc. It is usually made of wood with molding trim, but it may be carved or covered with fabric. It is similar to a valance, lambrequin, or pelmet. In the mid-18th century it was called a "window mantel."

CORNISH. See *Cornice.*

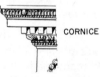

CORNUCOPIA

CORNUCOPIA. The twisting, spiraling "horn of plenty" of mythology. It is often represented with fruits and/or flowers pouring forth. As a decorative motif, it was popular in the Renaissance, Empire, and Victorian periods. Arms and legs of sofas were sometimes cornucopia-shaped in 19th-century furniture.

CORNUCOPIA SOFA. An English Regency sofa (circa 1820), with scrolled arms carved in the form of a cornucopia. The sofa back and legs repeat this motif. The foot was often a lion's paw. The cornucopia sofa also appeared in American Empire furniture.

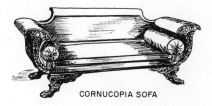

CORNUCOPIA SOFA

COROLITIC. A term used to describe something which has been decorated with sculptured branches of foliage.

COROMANDEL. Also called coromandel ebony, calamander, and Macassar ebony. A hard, dark, brown wood with black stripes. It resembles black rosewood, and was used for banding and veneering in late-18th-century furniture.

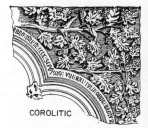

COROLITIC

COROMANDEL LACQUER. A lacquering technique originally from the Honan province in central China. It was greatly admired and used in the Louis XV period for finishing commodes and cabinets. The background was a reddish-black color which turned brown with age. The lacquer was very thick and applied in successive layers. It was possible to engrave or incise designs in the thick lacquer. Panels were decorated with figures, houses, landscapes, etc. See *Coromandel Screen.*

COROMANDEL SCREEN. A Chinese lacquered screen often decorated with an allover pattern in low relief, or executed with a landscape design. These screens were originally introduced into Europe by the East India Company in the middle of the 17th century. The finest were first made in Peking and Soochow.

CORONA. One of the moldings in a cornice, the underside of which is grooved to throw off the rain. It is the plain, undecorated feature, in classic architecture, which is supported by the lower part of the cornice, and upon which the crown molding is set.

CORONA

CORONIZED. A trademark for a heat-treating finish applied to Fiberglas cloths. The process was developed by the Owens Corning Fiberglas Corporation. It sets the weave of the fabric, and releases strains in the glass yarns. The finish gives the Fiberglas a better hand, and makes it drape better.

CORTILE. An Italian term for an inner court surrounded by an arcade.

CORTILE

COSMATI. The marble and mosaic workers of Rome from the 12th to the 14th century. They created pavements, tombs, pulpits, etc., in marble with inlays of mosaic, gilding, colored stones, and glass. By the 14th century, these workers, many of whom were from the same family, were producing sculpture. "Cosmati work" is a generic term for work in colored stone.

COSMATI WORK. See *Cosmati.*

COSTRUZIONE A SECCO. Italian for "rubblework."

COSTRUZIONE IN MATTONI. Italian for "brickwork."

COSY CORNER. An upholstered couch that fitted into the corner of a room. Forming a complete right angle, it usually had an upholstered and tufted back, and was a popular piece in the late 19th century. It was similar to the corner ottoman, and was sometimes the main furnishing of a *Turkish Corner.* The mid-20th century, sectional furniture, in a way, fulfills the same purpose: a seating unit for two or more people to sit and talk to one another.

COTELLE, JEAN (1607–1676). Ornamental painter and engraver, a pupil of Guyot and Simon Vouet.

COTTAGE ORNÉ. A French term for a pseudorustic middle-class dwelling fashionable in the 18th century.

COTTAGE PIANO. An upright piano of the 18th and early 19th centuries. It usually had a fretwork panel in front of and above the keyboard. Behind the fretwork was a pleated silk curtain.

COTTAGE-SET CURTAIN. A two-tier set of curtains usually made of a sheer or semisheer fabric. The lower tier may be pleated or shirred, and extends across the entire width of the window. The upper tier is usually ruffled along the edges, and is pulled back to either side of the window, allowing for an open center area.

COTTE, ROBERT DE (1656–1735). Cabinetmaker and designer who assumed control of the Gobelins after Mignard. He was first the pupil and later the brother-in-law of Jules-Hardouin Mansart. Cotte directed the construction of the dome of Les Invalides in Paris, built the Hôtel de Ville in Lyons, restored the choir of Notre-Dame de Paris, designed the chapel of the Château de Versailles, the Episcopal Palace at Verdun, and the Benedictine Monastery of Saint-Denis.

COTTON. A plant that produces a versatile fiber which blends well and lends its good characteristics to other fibers in a mixture. It combines with rayon, dacron, and Fortisan.

COUCH. A lounge chair used for resting, with supports and cushions at one or both ends. It was a French innovation of the early 17th century, and developed into a "daybed." In 18th-century America, couch was synonymous with daybed. In common contemporary usage, a couch is often confused with a sofa or settee.

COUCH

COUNT OF CLOTH. The number of threads per inch. The lengthwise yarns are called "ends," the crosswise yarns are called "picks." The density of a fabric may be given in "number of ends × number of picks."

COUNTER BOULLE. See *Contrepartie*.

COUNTERFLOOR. A subflooring under the main floor. It is made of battens laid on the floor joists.

COUNTERLATHING. A layer of laths laid at right angles and on top of a first layer of lath strips. A latticed effect.

COUNTERPANE. A quilt. Usually it is the exposed quilt on top of a bed. The pattern is raised or "quilted."

COUNTERSINK. A depression is made in a piece of wood so that the head of a screw, which has been inserted into it, is now flush with or below the top surface of the wood. See *Cup*.

COUNTRY CHIPPENDALE. A mid-18th-century American provincial version of Chippendale chairs, often made of pine and painted. These were simplified, but were usually very skillfully made.

COUNTRY FRENCH. A heavier, sturdier, more countrified version of the rococo style than the "French provincial" version. The "early-American" look with a French accent.

COUNTRY-MADE. Furniture or cabinets made by country or rustic cabinetmakers. The term usually implies less refined and less finished workmanship, and simplification of design.

COUPLE CLOSE ROOF. A couple roof in which the feet of the rafters are fixed to the ceiling joists. Ties are effected in this manner. See *Couple Roof*.

COUPLE ROOF. Roof in which the bottoms or feet of the rafters are fixed to the wallplate, while the tops or heads are set against the ridge piece, and no ties are used. See *Ridge*.

COUPLED COLUMNS. Columns or shafts which are grouped in pairs. In classical orders, they are usually spaced half of a diameter (of the column shaft) apart. Illustrated is a Renaissance example, the gateway to Toulouse in France.

COURSE. A horizontal row of stones, bricks, tiles, etc., that can be arranged into decorative patterns. A module of masonry.

COURSED RUBBLE. A type of masonry in which square stones of the same size are set in a horizontal row; the stones making up each separate row are the same size, but the rows are not necessarily matched in size. Illustrated is the ancient Tomb of Cyrus at Pasargadae.

COUPLED COLUMNS

COURSE

COURSED RUBBLE

COURT CUPBOARD

COURT CUPBOARD

COURT CUPBOARD. "Court" is French for short. A low cupboard mounted on legs, or a double cupboard, usually heavily carved and massive in appearance. It was originally designed to hold plate, utensils, goblets, etc. In the Tudor period it was a buffet, and probably related to the Italian and French crédence. An oak court cupboard of the Jacobean period (17th century) is illustrated. The panels are decorated with lozenge carvings.

COURTING CHAIR

COURTING CHAIR

COURTING CHAIR. An upholstered double chair or settee. It was popular in the Louis XIV period. In the Queen Anne style, the design had an open back effect, and it looked as though two chairs had been joined together with a common seat. It is also called a two-chair back settee. A forerunner of the contemporary "love seat."

COURTING MIRROR. A small 18th–19th-century mirror with a simple wood frame with insets of small pieces of glass. The pieces of glass were often painted or decorated. It may originally have been a gift presented by a swain to the girl he was courting.

COVE. A quarter-circle, concave, downward curve from the ceiling to the woodwork of a wall, or from the wall down to the floor. It is also a large concave molding often used in a cornice or under the eaves of a roof.

COVE

COVE BASE. See *Coved Skirting.*

COVE LIGHTING. A form of indirect lighting. The lighting source in the room or area is concealed from below by a recess, cove, or cornice, and the light is directed upon a reflecting surface.

COVED CUPBOARD. An early American cupboard design with a hoodlike projection on top.

COVED SKIRTING. An applied cove-shaped strip used to cover the joint of the wall and the floor. Wooden coves, rubber coves, asphalt coves, vinyl coves, etc., are used as flooring finishes between the floor and the wall.

COX, JOSEPH. A mid-18th-century American cabinetmaker and upholsterer who worked in New York City.

COYPEL, NOËL (1628–1707). A French painter and decorator. As a member of the Gobelins group, he painted furniture panels and designed tapestries. Coypel also worked on the decorations at Versailles.

CRADLE. A baby's bed usually set on a swinging device or on curved rocker supports. Many styles and variations are available.

CRAMOISY. A crimson-colored cloth used in medieval and Renaissance England.

CRAMP. A thin piece of metal with both ends turned back at right angles. The cramp is used to bind together blocks of masonry or timber.

CRANE, WALTER (1845–1915). An English craftsman-designer. A disciple of William Morris and the Arts and Crafts movement. He said, "The true root of all art lies in the handicrafts."

CRAQUELURE. The network of fine cracks on the surface of an old painting. It may be caused by shrinkages, movement of paint film, and/or varnish.

CRASH. Cotton, jute, or linen fabrics having coarse, uneven yarns and a rough texture. The fabric can be hand-blocked or printed and is used for draperies.

CRÉDENCE. A serving table and sideboard of the French Gothic period which may have evolved from a church piece. It was a chest mounted on a stand, or a display cabinet for plates, or for preparing and carving meats. See *Buffet* and *Desserte*.

CREDENZA. The Italian form of the *Crédence*.

CRÉMAILLÈRE. A swinging crane on a fireplace hearth.

CREMER. An 18th-century, French, Louis XV cabinetmaker who specialized in artificially colored marquetry work.

CREMO. An Italian marble with a creamy white ground and a network of golden veins.

CRENELLATED. An indented or notched surface. It was used as an architectural treatment on parapets and on top of castle walls during the medieval period. The term may also refer to a molding enriched with a notched-out decoration. See *Embrasure*.

CRENELLATED

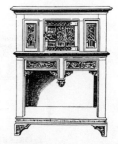

CRADLE

CRÉDENCE

CREDENZA

CRENELLATED

CRESCENT STRETCHER

CHARLES CRESSENT

CRESTING

CREPE. A large group of fabrics which are characterized by a crinkled surface obtained by hard twisting of the yarns, chemical treatment, the weave, or embossing. Crepe can be made of many natural or synthetic fibers.

CREPIDOMA. The stylobate or steps of the base of a Greek temple.

CRESCENT. A building or row of buildings built in an arc. The city of Bath, England, has a famous 18th-century crescent. See *Royal Crescent* and *Wood, John the Elder.*

CRESCENT STRETCHER. An arched or hooped stretcher, sometimes used between the legs of 18th-century furniture. It is often used as a reinforcing element on American Windsor chairs.

CRESLAN. A trademark name for an acrylic fiber manufactured by the American Cyanamid Company, which is similar to orlon and Acrilan. It is a soft, bulky fiber which has a wool-like hand. The name "Creslan" is applied to those fabrics which use the acrylic fiber and meet the performance standards set by American Cyanamid.

CRESSENT, CHARLES (1685–1768). A leading French cabinetmaker of the Régence and Louis XV periods. His designs were noted more for their ormolu trim and chased metalwork than for marquetry. Cressent was a student of Boulle, and he designed clocks and wall decorations. He used floral forms, cupids, lovers, garlands, and roses as well as monkeys and grotesques for his metal enrichments. Illustrated is a Louis XV commode attributed to Cressent. Massive gilt bronze mountings were employed.

CREST RAIL. The uppermost or top rail of a chair back. In the 16th and 17th centuries, this element was usually elaborately shaped and carved.

CREST RAIL

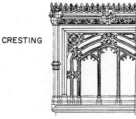

CRESTING

CRESTING. The Renaissance, elaborate carving on the top rail of a chair back or settee. The cresting was often centered on the top rail. The "crown and cherubs" was a favorite English Restoration cresting motif. In architecture, a carved, incised or perforated repeating design along the top of a wall or roof. See *Brattishing.*

CRETONNE. An unglazed chintz, printed with larger designs than usually associated with chintz. It is a common slip-covering fabric, and may be made of cotton or linen.

CREWELWORK. Embroidery done with loosely twisted worsted yarn and a large-eyed needle on unbleached cotton or linen. It was a popular fabric decoration in the 16th and 17th centuries in England. In the Jacobean period it was often used to interpret winding floral designs like the East Indian "tree of life" motif.

CRIB. An infant's bed with enclosed sides. It is usually raised off the ground on tall legs.

CRICKET. An archaic name for a low wooden footstool. An English and early American design.

CRICKET TABLE. A small, three-legged, polygonal or round-top table of the Jacobean period in England. The straight legs were supported on a triangular frame with high stretchers between the legs.

CRINOLINE STRETCHER. A common device of Chippendale's Windsor chairs. The stretcher is concave in form and separates and reinforces the two front legs. Two short arms extend from the back legs to support the crinoline stretcher. See *Crescent Stretcher.*

CRIB

CRINOLINE STRETCHER

CRIOSPHINX

CRIOSPHINX. An ancient Egyptian carved representation of an animal with a lion's body and a ram's head. See *Androsphinx* and *Sphinx.*

CROCKET. A projecting carved ornament used on the side of pinnacles and spires. The ornament is often bud- or leaf-shaped, and appears in Gothic art and architecture. In the 19th-century English Gothic revival furniture, this motif was sometimes carved on architecturally inspired cabinets, book-cases, and thronelike chair posts.

CROCKING. The tendency of excess dye to rub off a printed or dyed fabric. It is most apt to happen in deep-colored pile or napped fabrics.

CROMLECH. A circle of monoliths. See *Monolith.*

CROCKET

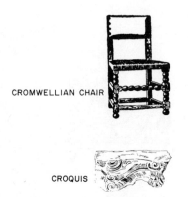

CROMWELLIAN CHAIR

CROQUIS

CROSS BANDING

CROSS BOND

CROMWELLIAN CHAIR. A severe, unadorned chair of the English Commonwealth period (1649–1660). It usually had knob or bobbin turnings, a low back, leather seat and back, and nailhead trim. The illustrated chair is an example of the Commonwealth period.

CROMWELLIAN PERIOD. See *Commonwealth.*

CROQUET CHAIR. A mid- to late-19th-century woven wicker or rattan barrel chair. The base resembles an inverted woven basket. The arms and back make a continuous line which seems partially to encircle the seated person. The back and seat are usually equipped with button-tufted upholstery. See *Peacock Chair.*

CROQUIS. A preliminary sketch or rough draft. Illustrated is a rough drawing for a Grecian-type bracket.

CROSS BANDING. A narrow band of wood veneer used as a frame or border design on a panel, door, tabletop, etc. The grain of the veneer wood of the band is at right angles to the grain of the panel itself. See *Banding.*

CROSS BOND: In masonry, alternating courses of stretchers and headers.

CROSS FIRE. A vivid, mottled effect across the grain of some mahoganies, walnuts, and satinwoods that creates a striking pattern. The effect that is created is an uneven, corrugated, transverse pattern which appears as highlights on the wood.

CROSS JOINT. See *Head Joint.*

CROSS RAIL OR MEMBER. See *Slat.* A horizontal element which joins two verticals or two sides. In a chair back, the connecting element between the back posts. An Adam armchair is shown.

CROSS RAIL

CROSS SECTION

CROSS STRETCHERS

CROSS SECTION. A view of a building or an object with an imaginary cut through it, representing a side view with the constructional elements, projections, and recesses from the straight elevation.

CROSS STRETCHERS. See *Saltire* and *X-shaped Stretchers.*

CROSS VAULT. A roof formed by two vaults intersecting at right angles.

CROTCH. The part of the tree from which the limbs and branches develop. It always produces a highly figured V grain of an extremely decorative character.

CROTCH VENEER. A thin sheet of wood cut at the crotch of the tree and used for veneering. The graining is often feather-like in appearance, or curly in effect.

CROTCHETS. Posts with forked tops. A primitive form of building structure with triangular ends. It was used by the early settlers in America to support their roofs of wattle and daub (twigs and a plaster made of mud).

CROWN. The top point of an arch. As a decorative motif, the symbol of royalty, it appears in carved, painted, and embroidered form.

CROWN BED. A simple canopy bed of the late-18th and early 19th centuries. The canopy is suspended over the bed, or extends partially out over the bed from the wall behind. See *Baldaquin Bed*.

CROWN GLASS. An early form of window glass made with a blowpipe. The glass is formed as a flat dish with a button or bull's-eye center. Illustrated is a 16th-century French interior with crown glass set into leaded windows. See *Bull's-Eye*.

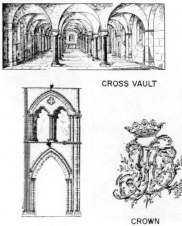

CROSS VAULT

CROWN

CROWN

CROWN GLASS

CROWN MOLDING

CROWN MOLDING. The topmost molding, particularly the fillets and cymas placed above the fascia in a classical cornice.

CROW'S BILL. A Gothic architectural enrichment like a *Bird's Beak* trim.

CROW-STEP GABLE. See *Corbie Gable*.

CRUNDEN, JOHN. An 18th-century English designer (he died in 1828), who created furniture frets, allegorical centers for ceilings, railings, and chimneypieces. In association with Thomas Milton and Placido Columbani, he prepared *A Treasury of New Designs for Chimney Pieces*. Crunden also published *Designs for Ceilings, The Carpenter's Compositions for Chinese Railings, Gates, etc.*, and *Convenient and Ornamental Architecture*.

CROW-STEP GABLE

JOHN CRUNDEN

CRYPT

CRYPT

CRYSTAL PALACE

C-SCROLL

CRYPT. From the Greek for "hidden." A subterranean chamber. Originally a cloister or burial area in early Christian churches.

CRYPTO-PORTICUS. A concealed or partially hidden colonnade or portico.

CRYSTAL. A clear, transparent quartz which resembles ice. It is usually cut and faceted to sparkle and reflect light. Crystal is often imitated in glass.

CRYSTAL PALACE. Built in London in 1851 as an exhibition hall. It covered an area of 800,000 square feet and was constructed mainly of prefabricated parts. The hall was built by Joseph Paxton, and it was based on ridge and furrow construction used in greenhouses. The entire basis of construction was the 4' sheet of glass (the largest available at the time). It was the first building of its kind and the first of such dimensions constructed of glass, iron, and timber over a framework of cast- and wrought-iron girders accurately bolted together.

C-SCROLL. An ornamental motif, painted, applied, or carved, which resembles the letter C or various combinations of the letter C. The C's may be inverted, touching back to back, top to bottom, or set askew of each other. This form of ornament is found in Spanish and French Gothic architecture and furniture. The enrichment was used extensively in the Baroque, Rococo, Queen Anne, and Chippendale periods.

CUBE FOOT

CUBE FOOT. See *Block Foot.*

CUBICULUM. A bedroom in an ancient Roman house.

CUBISM. The parent of all abstract art forms. It is the analysis of forms and their relationships to each other and space. It sometimes combines several views of the object more or less superimposed on one another, expressing the idea of the object rather than one view of it. Picasso and Braque were the main exponents of cubism.

CUCCI, DOMENICO. A great French cabinetmaker of the 17th century who designed in the Louis XIV style. He specialized in decorations of gold, bronze, colored stones, ornaments, and figures. Cucci was a rival of Boulle and Caffieri.

CUIVRE. French for "copper."

CUIVRE DORÉ. French for "gilded copper." It is also called pomponne, after the Hôtel de Pomponne, where this plated or gilded ware was originally made.

CUIVRE-JAUNE. French for "brass."

CUL-DE-LAMP. A pendant, either of wood, metal, or stone, used as a bracket for a lamp. These brackets were highly decorated with carving or painting. Illustrated is a 17th-century cul-de-lamp.

CUNEIFORM. Wedge-shaped. The wedge-shaped characters used by the Assyrians and Babylonians in writing on clay.

CUP. A metal sheath for a head of a screw in countersunk work.

CUP AND COVER TURNING. A popular Elizabethan and Jacobean turning used for furniture supports. It resembles a cup topped with a lid or an inverted saucer form. A late-16th-century Elizabethan oak four-poster bed is illustrated.

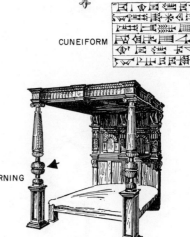

CUPID'S BOW

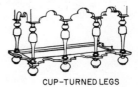

CUL-DE-LAMP

CUNEIFORM

CUP AND COVER TURNING

CUP CASTER

CUP CASTER. A brass cup with a roller below which fits onto a chair or table leg. A Sheraton book cabinet is illustrated.

CUP-TURNED LEG. The prominent cuplike feature in a turning which was popular in the late 17th and early 18th centuries. It was a development of a Portuguese bulb shape, and was also known as the bell and trumpet leg. In England the cup-turned leg is characteristic of the William and Mary style.

CUPBOARD. A storage cabinet with doors. It may be raised up on high legs, or be set low. The cabinet may have drawers or another cabinet below. The style and design varies with type and use. A 19th-century German design of late Gothic influence is illustrated.

CUPID'S BOW. A Chippendale-style top rail of a chair back which is shaped like a bow, with compound curves, and often with spiral volutes on the ends. The cupid's bow with arrows also appeared as a decorative motif in the Louis XV and Louis XVI periods.

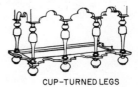

CUP-TURNED LEGS

CUPID'S BOW

CUPBOARD

CUPOLA

CUPOLA

CURRICULE CHAIR

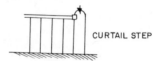

CURTAIL STEP

CURTAIN WALL

CUPOLA. A small dome-covered structure rising above the main part of a building.

CUPRAMA. A cuprammonium-type rayon fiber produced in Germany by Farbenfabriken Bayer. It has a sort of wool-like hand, resists soiling, and dyes somewhat darker than regular rayon.

CURL. The markings or "figure" of a wood. The appearance of the grain of certain woods when they are sliced against the grain.

CURLED HAIR. Animal hair used as a filler with stuffing on upholstered pieces. It is used under the muslin and the upholstery fabric, and the curled hair adds more resiliency to the stuffing. Horsehair is more desirable than the hair of hogs or cattle.

CURON. A trademark name for a multicellular plastic material. Made by the B. F. Goodrich Company, it has a fine spongelike appearance, and is produced in many colors. Curon may be use for wall or ceiling installations, and will serve as an insulating or acoustical material.

CURRICULE CHAIR. A late-18th-century, early-19th-century Sheraton-type chair with a semicircular back and splayed legs which, according to Sheraton, resembles an open carriage of the period.

CURTAIL STEP. The bottom step of a flight of stairs which has a curved end that goes partially around the newel post.

CURTAIN. A movable covering of lightweight fabrics for windows, doors, or alcoves. It was originally used to screen beds and bed areas.

CURTAIN WALL. In Gothic architecture, a nonbearing wall between columns or piers for enclosing a structure, but not supported at each story. A wall between two towers in a castle or fort. In contemporary architecture, a large surfaced façade of glass and metal. It is found in the early works of Ludwig Mies van de Rohe, Walter Gropius, Peter Behrens, and Willem Marinus Dudok. These sweeping, clean walls were made possible by advances in the metal and plastics industries in overcoming problems of waterproofing, insulation, expansion, and contraction. Lever House, in New York City, completed in 1952, has an early, dynamic example, a green glass and aluminum trim curtain wall.

CURULE CHAIR. A 17th-century chair. The arm supports and the back rails are semicircular in shape. The legs are also semicircular. The general appearance is an X created by the two intersecting S curves, or one C resting on an inverted C. A leather strip usually provides the back rest, and the seat is also a piece of leather. The design is based on a classic Roman prototype, the sella curulis of the Roman magistrate. Another version of the curule chair became popular in the early-19th-century Empire and Regency periods. A Sheraton design is illustrated. See *Dante Chair*.

CURULE CHAIR

CURULE LEGS

CURULE CHAIR

CURULE LEGS. X-shaped legs such as were used on classic Greek and Roman folding stools. They became popular again in the Renaissance period, and continued in favor up through the Regency and French Empire periods. A Chippendale design is illustrated. See *Curule Chair*.

CURVED GABLE. A triangular gabled roof made up of a series of curves and steps. This rooftop design was especially popular in the 16th and early 17th centuries in Holland, and in many 17th-century buildings in America.

CURVED GABLE

CURVILINEAR

CURVILINEAR. Created within curved or arced lines. Some Gothic tracery was curvilinear in concept. A German Rococo console table, here illustrated, shows the curvilinear line quality which was prevalent during the Rococo period.

CUSHION. A shaped, flexible bag of fabric or leather, filled with feathers or other filling materials. A pillow. Illustrated is a Louis XVI sofa with a separate cushion seat. It is added to the upholstered platform and back for extra softness and comfort.

CUSHION

CUSHIONED FRIEZE

CUSPS

CUSHIONED FRIEZE. A Rennaissance convex or cushion-shaped frieze. Sometimes used on cabinets of the late 17th and early 18th centuries. Illustrated is the top of a chest of the latter part of the 17th century.

CUSPS. The pointed endings of a trefoil or quatrefoil in Gothic architecture. The meeting points are the pendants between the arcs. Chippendale and Sheraton used cusping as a carved decorative trim on some of their chair backs. See *Quatrefoil* and *Trefoil*.

CUSSEY, DOMENICO. A French 17th-century cabinetmaker to Richelieu, the chief minister to Louis XIII.

CUT PILE. Fabric woven with an extra set of warp or filler yarns. These threads form the loop pile which is later cut. Velvet and plush are cut pile fabrics.

CUTOUT BORDERS. Wallpaper designs which are usually applied below the ceiling line or molding and used as a dado decoration, or around doors, windows, arches, etc. These designs are often architectural motifs or architectural elements combined with swags, garlands of flowers, fruits, etc., and the lower edge of the design is cut out to conform to the outline of the artwork. When the paper is applied, it appears to be part of the wall. This decorative paper is also called a "scalloped border."

CUTTING. A swatch or clipping of a piece of carpet or fabric. A small representation or sample of a larger whole.

CUVILLIÉS, FRANÇOIS DE (1698–1767). A great French furniture maker of the Louis XV period. He was an architect and engraver in the extreme Rococo style and favored the Chinese style in applied decoration.

CUVILLIÉS THE YOUNGER (Jean-François) (1731–1805). A designer of ornaments and decorations influenced by Germanic styles.

CYCLOPEAN. Masonry using large stones which are usually not hewn or squared off.

CYCLOPEAN

CYLINDER FRONT

CYLINDER FRONT. A quarter-round front of a desk or secretary which is mounted so that it can be pivoted. Illustrated is a late-18th-century Sheraton desk design.

CYLINDER TOP. A rolltop cover to a bureau or desk. It differs from the tambour top in that it does not roll up on itself. See *Gouthière, Pierre,* for an illustration of a Louis XVI cylinder secrétaire.

CYMA CURVE. An S-shaped curve.

CYMA RECTA. An S-shaped curve that starts and ends in a horizontal plane. An ogee molding.

CYLINDER TOP

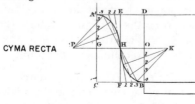

CYMA RECTA

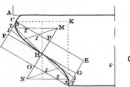

CYMA REVERSA

CYMA REVERSA. An S-shaped curve that starts and ends in a vertical plane.

CYMATIUM. A cyma molding which forms the uppermost member of a cornice.

CYMATIUM

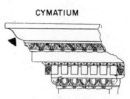

CYPRESS. A native American, light-brown wood, adapted to all types of finishes. It is generally free from warping and twisting but is considered too weak for structural timber or flooring. In the Tudor period it was used for storage chests. "Pecky cypress" is popular today for paneling and wall finishes.

CYPRESS CHESTS. Early Renaissance chests made to hold tapestries, robes, and such. Cedar was used because its aroma is repellent to moths. The cypress chest was a prototype of current cedar chests.

DACRON. A trademark name for a polyester fiber obtained from a polymer with 85 percent or more of the polyester of ethylene glycol and terephthalic acid. It makes a crisp, strong, resilient fiber. Dacron is manufactured by Dupont. Dacron combines well with cotton, linen, and wool.

DACTYLIC ALTERNATION. A style found in Byzantine and Romanesque church arcades in which two columns alternate with one pier.

DADA. French for "hobbyhorse." An antiart, antisense period of art from about 1915 to 1922 which emphasized shock rather than understanding. Marcel Duchamp was an outstanding exponent of this art form, which was a predecessor of surrealism.

D

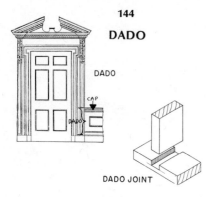

DADO

DADO

CAP

DADO

DADO JOINT

DADO. The lower portion of the wall when it is treated differently or separated from the rest of the wall by a molding strip. A wainscot. In classic styles the dado had a base, shaft, and cap molding, and it was often paneled or ornamented.

DADO CAP. The crown or cap molding of a dado. It is also called a *Chair Rail*.

DADO JOINT. A joining technique used for supporting shelving or drawer bottoms in vertical units. It is used to stiffen or reinforce the vertical member. The edge of the vertical piece of wood fits into a groove in the horizontal piece. The dado joint is also called a rabbet joint.

DAGLEY. A 17th-century French craftsman who introduced the secret of Japanese lacquer into France. The technique was used at the Gobelins and called *Vernis de Gobelins.*

DAGLIGSTUE. A Danish word for a family room, a comfortable general-purpose recreation room.

DAGOBA. A conically shaped tomb found in India.

DAGOBA

DAGOBERT CHAIR

DAGOBERT CHAIR. A famous 7th-century folding chair, originally made of gilt bronze supposedly by St. Eloi. The back and arms were added in the 12th century by Abbé Suger. It is one of the very few pieces of furniture remaining from this period.

DAGUERREOTYPE. First photographic process, invented in 1839 by Louis Daguerre. A faint image was produced which had to be viewed from an angle for clarity.

DAIS. A low raised platform usually located at the end or side of a room. Illustrated is a bench on a dais in a 10th-century interior.

DALBURGIA. "Black wood." An Indian wood used for small carved decorative elements like boxes, gong stands, etc.

DALLAGE. A French term for a pavement or floor of stone, marble, or tile.

DAIS

DAMASCENE WORK (Damascening). See *Damascus Work.*

DAMASCUS WORK. A type of metal inlay work in patterns or arabesques. The design is incised in metal and then inlaid with other metals or wires cut to fit.

DAMASK. A firm, glossy, patterned fabric with a Jacquard weave. It was introduced into Europe by Marco Polo, and named for the city of Damascus. It is similar to brocade, but it is flatter and reversible and can be in one or two color designs. On the reverse side, the pattern changes in color or may appear shiny (the pattern is matte on the face side). Damask was originally made of silk but is now woven in cotton, rayon, linen, silk, wool, or a combination of the above fibers.

DAMASSÉ. French for *Damask.*

DANCETTE. The zigzag ornament of Norman architecture. See *Zig-Zag.*

DAN-DAY CHAIR. A form of the Windsor chair produced in Suffolk in the early 19th century. It was named for its maker. Norwegian copies were made of this chair, with slight variations on the design of the underframe.

DANISH MODERN. See *Scandinavian Modern.*

DANTE CHAIR. An X-shaped chair of the Italian Renaissance period. It was usually heavily carved and upholstered in leather. The X curved up from the floor and became the arms of the chair. Variations of this design appeared in French, Spanish, English, and Teutonic early Renaissance furniture. See *Curule Chair* for another version of the X chair.

DANTESCA CHAIR. See *Dante Chair.*

DARBY AND JOAN CHAIR. A mid-18th-century English chair with a double or triple chair back and a wide seat which would accommodate several persons. A two- or three-chair-back settee named for characters in a poem, "The Joys of Love Never Forgot," published in 1735.

DARLEY, MATHIAS. An 18th-century English architect, designer, engraver, and publisher. Darley engraved plates for Chippendale's *Director* and may have assisted him with his designs. He also published *A Compleat Body of Architecture, Embellished with a Great Variety of Ornaments* and, with George Edwards, *A New Book of Chinese Designs.* See *Fire Irons* for Edwards designs.

DARLEY, MATHIAS

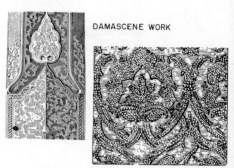

DAMASCENE WORK

DAMASK

DANCETTE

DANTE CHAIR

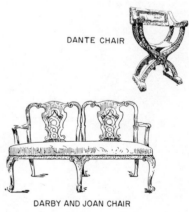

DARBY AND JOAN CHAIR

MATHIAS DARLEY

DARNICK

DAVENPORT

DAYBED

DARNICK. An 18th-century coarse damask fabric.

DAUPHINE. A matte finish, silk fabric which was popular in the late Louis XVI period.

DAVENPORT. An early-19th-century small kneehole desk with a lift top writing slope, and drawers at the side. It was named after a Captain Davenport. In contemporary usage it is an overstuffed upholstered sofa with padded arms and back. It was named after a Mr. Davenport of Boston who originally made these sofas. Illustrated is a Sheraton late-18th-century design with a loose pillow back.

DAVENPORT BED. A sofa which converts into a bed.

DAVID. See *Roentgen, David.*

DAVID, JACQUES LOUIS (1748–1825). A French painter, considered the "dictator of the Empire style." He was a classic painter, both in technique as well as in subject matter, and was Court painter to Louis XVI. David joined in the French Revolution, was a friend of Robespierre, and was imprisoned for a while. Later, he became court painter to Napoleon I. Among his works are: "Blind Belisarius Asking Alms," "Brutus," "Coronation of Napoleon," "Mme Recamier," "Death of Socrates," and "Rape of the Sabines."

DAVILIER. A 17th-century French designer and architect under Louis XIV. He created many interior detail designs.

DAVIS, ALEXANDER JACKSON. An early-19th-century American architect who in 1832 designed "Glen Ellen," the Gothic-type country estate of Robert Gilmor near Baltimore. It was equipped with oriel windows, crenellated towers, gables with crockets and finials, and a highly irregular plan.

DAVIS, JOHN. An early-18th-century American cabinetmaker who worked in Lynn, Massachusetts.

DAY, LEWIS F. (1845–1910). An English industrial designer. He was a pioneer in the modern movement, and he recognized the inevitable influence of machinery on decorative art. "Whether we like it or not, machinery and steam power, and electricity for all we know, will have something to say concerning the ornament of the future."

DAYBED. A "studio couch," rest bed, or narrow bed, placed lengthwise along a wall. It may have equally tall head and foot boards, or none at all. The daybed was introduced as a seating unit in the 17th century. It is related to chaise longues and couches. Illustrated is a caned daybed of the second half of the 17th century. The scrollwork on the stretchers and head-rails is typical of the time. See *Studio Couch.*

DE STIJL. A Dutch magazine which was published from 1917 to 1928 and fostered Mondrian and neoplasticism. Its ideas had a great influence on the architecture of Gropius and others of the Bauhaus movement, as well as German commercial art, posters, packages, etc. See *Berlage, Hendrik Petrus* and *Oud, Jacobus Johannes Pieter.*

DEAL. In the United States, southern yellow pine. In England, Scotch fir is called yellow deal. In Canada, deal refers to the northern soft pine. Deal also refers to pinewood cut into planks and the furniture made from these planks. It is also used for the carcase of veneered furniture.

DECALCOMANIA. A "transfer" form of decoration. Designs are printed on thin paper in reverse, then transferred onto a piece of furniture or decorative accessory. When the paper backing is removed, the design appears right side up. It is an inexpensive method of decorating furniture with "artwork."

DECANTER. From the French for "to pour from one vessel to another." A crystal, glass, or metal container which holds wine or other liquids. It is a serving piece. A rock crystal decanter of the French Renaissance is shown here.

DECANTER

DECASTYLE. A classic portico with ten columns.

DECEPTION BED. A concealed or partially concealed bed unit in 18th-century American cabinetwork. The term also refers to a bed which converts from a chest, chair, table, etc.

DECKLE EDGE. A rippled, irregular edge with a torn appearance. It is usually associated with the finish of handmade paper.

DÉCOR. A setting in the home or on a theatre stage. The word is usually associated with a "fashion trend" rather than a style. It suggests something gay, whimsical, fanciful, and changeable.

DECORATED PERIOD. The English Gothic architecture of the 14th century. It is noted for geometric and flowing tracery, enlarged clerestories, and star-shaped, or stellar, vaulting. It is also called the Geometrical, Curvilinear, Middle Pointed, Edwardian, and Later Plantagenet period. Illustrated is a window from the Cloisters at Westminster Abbey, A.D. 1360.

DECORATED PERIOD

DECORATED QUEEN ANNE PERIOD. The English furniture style prevalent about 1710 to 1730, also called the Early Georgian period. It was basically a continuation of the Queen Anne style with cabriole legs, claw-and-ball feet, carved and shaped splats, and more ornate and heavily carved than the previous period.

DECORATED
QUEEN ANNE PERIOD

DÉCOUPAGE. An art form created by cutting and pasting down assorted materials in interesting new patterns and arrangements. It became popular in the 18th century as the "poor man's" method of embellishing wood furniture. The technique was also employed to decorate boxes, screens, trays, etc. Découpage is similar to *Arte Povera, Collage,* and *Montage.*

DELANOIS, LOUIS (1731–1792). A French master cabinetmaker under Louis XV. He was a protégé of Mme Du Barry and designed much of the furniture at Versailles.

DELFT TILES

DELFT. The name of a city in Holland, and also the name of brilliant blue-colored, heavily glazed pottery produced in Delft. The rich blue designs are on a white field, and they are either scenic or provincial-type patterns. Ceramic tiles are also made in this particular blue and white, and they have been used to face fireplaces and walls and are also used on floors.

DELORME, PHILBERT (1515–1570). A 16th-century French architect of the mid-Renaissance period. He was the court architect under François I, Henri II, and Charles IX. Delorme was commissioned by Catherine de Médici to design the Tuileries, and it was finished by his successor, Jean Bullant. His design for a Renaissance Doric order is illustrated. See *Valois Period* for an illustration of the Tuileries.

PHILBERT DELORME

DEMARCY, GASPARD AND BALTHAZAR. 17th-century French craftsmen who worked in stucco and wood and also did metalwork. Charles Le Brun employed them during the period of Louis XIV.

DEMIDOME. A half dome topping cupboards, bookcases, and other architectural furniture of the early and mid-18th century. The demidome was often interpreted as a shell-shaped niche in Georgian furniture and interiors. Illustrated is the Lord Mayor's stall in St. Paul's Cathedral in London designed by Sir Christopher Wren at the end of the 17th century.

DEMIDOME

DEMILUNE

DEMILUNE

DEMILUNE. A half of a circle or half-round plan. A semicircular commode, console, or sideboard. A late-18th-century Sheraton design with tambour doors is illustrated. See *Doe's-Foot Leg* for a Hepplewhite demilune table.

DEMI-PATERA. A half-patera or rosette. It is often found in mid- and late-18th-century pier tables, consoles, or demilune commodes. An 18th-century Hepplewhite pier table is shown. See *Demilune*.

DEMOISELLE. See *Wig Stand*.

DEMOISELLE À ATOURNER. A Gothic wig-stand which also served as a dressing table. It was usually a round tabletop on a shaft base with a carved wooden head placed in the center to hold the wig. See *Wig Stand*.

DEMOTIC. An abridged form of hieroglyphics used by Egyptian public scribes.

DEN. A retreat or informal library. Usually a small, comfortable room equipped for the man of the house. It may also serve as a small family room or guest room.

DENIER. The size or number of filaments of silk or man-made fibers in a yarn or thread. The higher the denier, the coarser and heavier the yarn.

DENIM. A firm, heavy twill weave, cotton fabric originally called "serge de Nîmes"; hence the name. The filler yarns are usually white with colored warp yarns. The filler yarns give the fabric its traditional whitish cast.

DENTIL. One of a series of small projecting rectangular blocks in a cornice. It appears in Ionic and Corinthian cornices, and was also used as a furniture and interior detail by Adam and Hepplewhite.

DENTIL COURSE. A series of dentils in a row. Illustrated is a design for an Ionic entablature designed by the Adam brothers in the mid-18th century in England.

DERBYSHIRE CHAIR. A provincial type of Jacobean chair. The straight upright ends have inward scrolls on top. The top rail and crossrail are often arch-shaped.

DEMI-PATERA

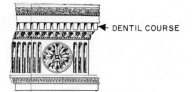

DENTIL COURSE

DERBYSHIRE CHAIR

DERIVE. Descend, be drawn (from) or based (upon). The Renaissance style was derived from those of the classic Greek and Roman periods. Illustrated is an Adam entablature based on a Greek prototype.

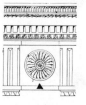

DERIVATIVE

DESK

JACOB DESMALTER

DESK. A writing surface with or without drawers and/or cabinets. See *Bureau, Cylinder Top, Drop Lid or Dropfront, Escritoire, Kneehole Desk, Pedestal Desk, Scritoire, Secrétaire,* and *Secretary.*

DESK BOX. See *Bible Box.*

DESMALTER, JACOB. An important cabinetmaker of the early 19th-century French Empire period. He executed designs created by Charles Percier. Illustrated is a piece of furniture of the type made by Desmalter in mahogany embellished with bronze and gilt.

DESORNAMENTADO. Spanish for "without ornament." A severe style of architecture and decoration developed by the Spanish Renaissance architect Juan de Herrera under Phillip II in the mid-16th century. Examples of his work are the Escorial near Madrid, and southern portion of the Alcazar in Toledo with its grand staircase enclosed under a barrel vault.

DESSERTE. A small serving table or sideboard with one or more under shelves, similar to a dumbwaiter. It appears in the Louis XVI period. See *Buffet* and *Crédence.*

DESSERTE

DEU-DARN

DEU-DARN. A two tiered *Tri-Darn* or a court cupboard without the dresser.

DIACONICON. See *Prothesis.*

DIAGONAL BOND. In brick masonry, a bonding pattern which is based on an "eye" or central core which consists of a header with a stretcher on either side, and one above and below it. In the third course up and the third course down from the central header, another header is added to the stretcher to follow the diamond pattern. The "eye" can also be a stretcher with a stretcher to either side of it. On the course above and below, a header is centered on this central stretcher. The headers are butted by stretchers.

DIAGONAL RIB

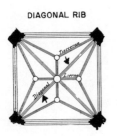

DIAGONAL RIB. In architecture, a rib which marks the intersection of two vaults.

DIAMETER. A straight line drawn through the center of a circle and touching the perimeter in two places; also, the length of such a line. In classic orders the proportions are based on the diameter of the shaft at the base of the column.

DIAMOND MATCH VENEER. Four pieces of straight-grained wood veneer are cut diagonally and are joined to meet in a central diamond shape. Increasingly larger diamond shapes emanate from the central point.

DIAMOND MATCH VENEER

DIAMOND MATCH VENEER

DIAMOND ORNAMENT

DIAMOND ORNAMENT. See *Lozenge*. A favorite late-Tudor ornament used to enrich carved chest fronts, bedsteads, cabinets, etc.

DIAPER PATTERN. An allover or repeating pattern without definite limits, applied as a decoration to a plain surface. Often the area is latticed and floral, or geometric designs are set into boxes. It is and was used on walls, wallpapers, cabinet enrichments, etc.

DIAPER PATTERN

DIASTYLE. The space between two columns in a classic arrangement equal to three or four diameters of the shaft.

DIASTYLE

DIE. The space between the cap and base of a pedestal. Also, a rectangular block on the top of a leg. Illustrated is a Sheraton furniture leg. See *Patera*.

DIE

DIFFUSING GLASS. Rolled glass, with assorted patterns or textures, which tend to cut down on the transparency of the glass.

DIMITY. A double- or multiple-thread, sheer cotton fabric usually woven in a corded, striped, or checkered pattern. It is used for bedspreads and curtains.

DINANDERIE. A 15th-century metal alloy of copper, tin, and lead. A forerunner of pewter. It was used to make ornamental figures in Dinant in Belgium. It is also called bell metal.

DIE

DIP SEAT

DION, DE, GIRDER. Named for the mid-19th-century French engineer who devised girders fit for large spans. From the study of the tensile strength of materials, he arrived at a proper form for a built-up girder capable of withstanding the various stresses·without needing tie bars. It was used in the construction of the main exhibition hall of the International Exposition in Paris in 1878.

DIORAMA. A representation of a scene showing small three-dimensional figures against an illuminated background, or a peepshow of a semitranslucent painted scene.

DIORITE. A dark-colored hard stone sometimes used in Egyptian and Assyrian sculpture.

DIP SEAT. A chair seat which is lower in the center than at the sides. It is also curved (concave) to accommodate the body of the sitter. Illustrated is a mid-18th-century Chippendale chair. See *Dropped or Dipped Seat.*

DIPTERAL. Surrounded by a double row of columns.

DIPTYCH. A small, two-panel, hinged screen, either painted or carved, which may be made of wood, metal, ivory, etc.

DIPTYCH

DIRECTORY

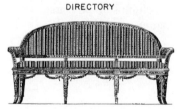

DIRECTORY

DISCHARGING ARCH

DIRECTORY. The "Directoire" period in France (1799–1804). Antique Greek and Roman decorations found even greater favor and were superimposed on the already classic lines of the Louis XVI style. The Directory period led into the Empire. See *French Directoire.*

DISCHARGING ARCH. An arch set in the body of a wall to relieve a lintel, or any of the masonry below, from the weight above.

DISHED. A term applied to the sunken areas in the top surface of card tables. The depressed areas were used to hold money or candles. A dished-top table has a raised edge or rim which gives the effect that the entire table surface is sunken.

DISHED

DISK FOOT. A small, flattened ball foot or pad on a cabriole leg in the Queen Anne style.

DISK TURNING. Flat circular turnings used to ornament furniture.

DISTANT COLORS. Spacious, receding colors. Light, airy, cool, open colors: blues, aquas, violets.

DISTEMPER. An art medium: opaque water color paints, similar to tempera, consisting of pigments, water, and white of egg, size, or emulsion of egg yolk.

DISTRESSED. Said of old pieces of wood furniture which show small scratches or holes, the result of age and use. In present-day furniture, these holes and scratches simulated in paint or spatter. "Fly-specked."

DISTYLE. A portico with two columns at one or both ends.

DIVAN. A long, armless and backless, upholstered settee. The word originally meant a Turkish or Persian court or council, or a room where such gatherings take place. The French adapted this cushion-like seat into the upholstered bench. See *Bench*. In current usage, a divan is a couch.

DIVIDER. A piece of furniture, screen, pole arrangement, etc. that separates one area of a room from the rest of the room. A divider may also artificially create an entry foyer, a dining area, a music area, etc.

DOBBY WEAVE. A cloth with a small geometric woven pattern. A special attachment is required on the loom to weave this particular fabric.

DOCUMENT BOX or DRAWER. A small vertical drawer in 18th-century English and American secretaries and cabinet desks. It is usually ornamented with colonnettes, and the document drawer is found on either side of the central compartment in the interior of the desk.

DOCUMENTARIES. Fabrics, wallpapers, etc., which are based on, or derived from, authentic period designs.

DOE'S-FOOT LEG. An elongated S-shaped leg typical of the Louis XV period. It originally terminated in a deer's cleft hoof. A Hepplewhite demilune table is illustrated.

DOG GRATE. A fireplace accessory. A movable fire grate.

DOG GRATE

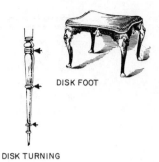

DISK FOOT

DISK TURNING

DOE'S FOOT LEG

DOG'S TOOTH

DOGLEGGED STAIRCASE. A staircase in which the outer string of the upper flight lies vertically above that of the lower flight.

DOG'S TOOTH. A form of ornamentation used in Early English Gothic architecture. It resembles a row of teeth.

DOG'S TOOTH

DOLMEN. A "stone table." An antique primitive construction used for a monument or tomb. It consisted of several large stones topped with a large stone slab.

DOLPHIN

DOLPHIN. A sea mammal, a mid-16th-century decoration and symbol for the Dauphin, eldest son of the king of France. It was also the symbol for love and swiftness. The dolphin again appears in the Louis XVI period. The dolphin here illustrated is decoratively used to form a keystone in the Fountain of Innocents in Paris, which was designed by Pierre Lescot and Jean Goujon in 1548–1549.

DOME. A spherical roof, like an inverted cup, surmounting a building. See *Cupola.*

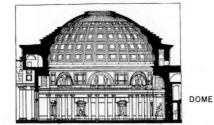

DOME

DOME BED. An 18th-century canopied bed with a dome-shaped tester. It is usually heavily draped and swagged, and was also called a "Polish Bed." A Chippendale design is illustrated.

DOME BED

DOMED TOP. See *Hooded Tops.*

DOMESTIC. Manufactured or grown in the country where the label is applied; domestic products in the United States are items produced in the United States.

DOMESTIC ORIENTAL RUG. See *Sheen Rugs.*

DOMINANT. The leading or most prominent part of a design or scheme.

DOMINO PAPERS. Marbleized squares of wallpaper, originally produced in Italy in the late 16th and early 17th centuries.

DOMINOTIERS. Producers of domino papers in France in the late 16th century.

DOMUS. Latin for "house." Usually applied to a detached residence.

DONATELLO (Donato di Niccolò di Betto Bardi) (1386–1466). A great Italian (Florentine) sculptor of the Realistic school. His work influenced the art of the 15th century, though he himself was greatly affected by antique remains in Rome. Among Donatello's most noted works are: "David," the bronze door of the Sacristy in S. Lorenzo in Florence, the equestrian monument to Gattamelata, and the carved-wood "Magdalen."

DONATELLO

DONJON. A stronghold or small castle with a round tower. The Norman round tower at Norwich in England is illustrated.

DORATURA. Italian for "gilding."

DOREUR. The French word for one who gilds or applies a gilt finish to wood, metal, etc.

DONJON

DORIC ORDER. The oldest and simplest of the Greek classic orders of architecture. In the Roman version, the column was eight times the diameter of the shaft, and the entablature was two diameters high. See *Classic* and *Diameter*.

DORIC ORDER

DORMER WINDOW. A projecting upright window which breaks the surface of a sloping roof. Illustrated is a dormer window of the French Renaissance Château de Graves.

DORURE. French for "gilding."

DOS-À-DOS. French for "back to back." A seating device which consists of two attached seats facing in opposite directions. In order to converse, the seated persons must turn around in their seats and look over their shoulders. See *Conversation Chair* and *Vis-à-Vis*.

DOSSER. A medieval or Gothic fabric hanging behind thrones or on walls behind benches, etc.

DOSSERET. In Byzantine architecture, a block above a capital of a column or a pier which gives extra support to the arch voussoirs. See *Impost*.

DORMER WINDOW

DOSSERET

DOSSIER

DOSSIER

DOSSIER PLAT

DOSSIER. French for "chair back" or "splat." A 16th-century French armchair or fauteuil (illustrated). Also a high-backed, canopied, wooden bench built into the wainscot of an English Gothic building. It was usually made to hold four, and it served as a seat for dining. In French interiors the term could also refer to the headboard or footboard of a bed.

DOSSIER PLAT. A "flat back." A French term used to describe the back of a chair. A late German Renaissance armchair is shown.

DOTTED SWISS. A crisp cotton, usually sheer, which is woven, embroidered, or printed with tiny regularly spaced dots. It is a plain weave fabric.

DOUBLE-ACTING HINGE. A special hinge which allows a door to swing 180° on its jamb.

DOUBLE BED. A standard-size double bed is usually 53" wide × 75" long. It may be made longer on special order.

DOUBLE CHAIR. See *Courting Chair.*

DOUBLE CHEST. A chest-on-chest unit. The lower chest is usually slightly wider and deeper, and the second set of drawers is set on top of it.

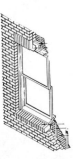

DOUBLE-HUNG SASH

DOUBLE CHEST

DOUBLE STRETCHER FLEMISH BOND

DOUBLET

DOUBLE-HUNG SASH. A standard window made up of two sliding, framed glass sections; one is lowered from the top, and the other is raised from the bottom. The raising and lowering on the frames is controlled by pulleys and weights.

DOUBLE STRETCHER FLEMISH BOND. In masonry, two stretchers alternate with a single header in a course. The header in the next course is centered over the join between the two stretchers. See *Bond, Flemish Bond,* and *Flemish Cross Bond.*

DOUBLET. In ornament, the term refers to a pair or two of the same design. Illustrated in a hanging armoire of the early French Renaissance.

DOUGLAS FIR. A very handsome, curly, grained wood that resembles white pine or soft pine. It is used extensively for plywood or laminated sheets. Douglas fir takes a natural or stained finish and is relatively inexpensive.

DOUPPIONI or DUPPION. Fabric made from silk fibers and the fibers themselves that are reeled from two silkworms that have spun a single cocoon. The yarns that are thus reeled are rough and slubby such as those found in shantung or pongee fabrics. The term may refer also to rayon or acetate fibers of a slubby, uneven texture.

DOVETAIL. In cabinetry, a type of joint used to join the front and sides of a drawer. Wedge-shaped projections on one piece of wood interlock with alternating grooves in the other piece. This produces a tight, secure joint.

DOWEL. A headless wooden peg or metal pin which is used to hold two pieces of wood together. A dowel is used in joints to prevent slipping and also to join the side rails or stretchers to the legs of chairs.

DOWEL JOINT. See *Dowel.*

DOWER CHEST. See *Cassone, Connecticut Chest,* and *Hope Chest.*

DOWN. Soft, fluffy feathers from very young birds, or from under the ordinary feathers of older birds or fowls. Down is used for stuffing pillows, cushions, and upholstered chair backs. See *Eiderdown.*

DOWNING, ANDREW JACKSON. A mid-19th-century American landscape architect and "tastemaker" of the period. He came from Newburgh, New York, and published *The Architecture of Country Houses* in 1850. The book had a great impact on the period, and the trend toward "Italian-style" villas. Downing also advocated "Gothic cottages" because they were not only "picturesque, but their floor plans are well suited to our informal world."

DRAFT. A line drawing, often geometrically or mechanically projected, of a proposed structure or design. A preliminary sketch or drawing. A smooth strip on the face of a stone made by one line of following strokes with a chisel. When stones are left with a rough face, but the edges are made smooth, the edges are called "drafted edges."

DRAGON'S CLAW FOOT. See *Ball-and-Claw Foot.* An 18th-century furniture leg ending which was a carved representation of a dragon's scaly claw, often grasping a ball or pearl.

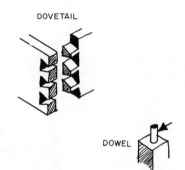

DOVETAIL

DOWEL

DRAGON'S CLAW FOOT

DRAGON'S HEAD

DRAGON'S HEAD

DRAPERY

DRAGON'S HEAD. The dragon is an oriental motif, and it is often found on heavily carved oriental furniture. It is also the symbol of Wales, and the dragon's head appears as an ornamental carved motif on English Tudor and Jacobean chests. Illustrated is an 18th-century dragon from George Edwards and Mathias Darley's *A New Book of Chinese Designs* (1754).

DRAKE FOOT. An 18th-century English furniture foot with three toes which resembles the contracted claw of a male duck.

DRAPE. A term used to describe the way a fabric hangs or falls. The ability of the fabric naturally to shape well when pleated, shirred, or pinched.

DRAPER, DOROTHY. A noted 20th-century American interior designer.

DRAPERY

DRAPERY. Fabric hangings on either side of a window, or covering a window or door, or an entire wall of windows. The fabric may be shirred, pleated, or pinched, and may be made of natural or man-made fibers. The choice of fabric, color, pattern, texture, and type of treatment depends upon the period of decoration and the general scale of the opening to be draped. The regular vertical falling drapery may be enhanced with swags, jabots, lambrequins, and cornices. Drapery may also refer to the fabric treatment on 16th-, 17th- and 18th-century beds.

DRAUGHT CHAIR

DRAUGHT CHAIR

DRAUGHT CHAIR. An 18th-century-designed upholstered winged chair with or without closed sides, which was constructed to protect one from draughts. It is similar to a *Porter Chair.*

DRAW CURTAIN. A curtain that may be drawn along a rod or rail by means of a traverse arrangement of cords and pulleys.

DRAW LEAF TABLE. See *Draw Table.*

DRAW RUNNER. A supporting device for the drop-lid or fall-front surface of a secretary or desk. It is a small strip of wood inserted into a slot immediately below the surface to be supported.

DRAW SLIP. A *Draw Runner.*

DRAW RUNNER

DRAW TABLE. A three-leaved, refectory-like table. The two end leaves rest under the center one. When these two end pieces are drawn out from under the large central table surface, the center leaf falls down into the opening thus created, and the two end leaves make a large, continuous flush surface with the central leaf. It is the forerunner of the telescope dining table. The illustrated example is of late-17th-century England and shows the Dutch influence. It is also called a "draw-leaf table."

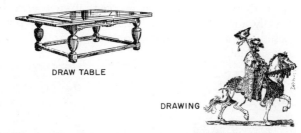

DRAW TABLE

DRAWING

DRAWING. The art of representing images, shapes, patterns, or three-dimensional elements on a two-dimensional surface.

DRAWING BOOK CHAIR BACK. A popular Sheraton design for a chair back which was widely copied by American cabinetmakers from Sheraton's book *The Cabinet-Maker and Upholsterer's Drawing Book.*

DRAWING ROOM. An abbreviated form of "withdrawing room." A comfortable sitting room to which people "withdrew" after dinner. In contemporary usage, a living room.

DRAWING BOOK CHAIR BACK

DRAWING TABLE. A late-18th-century worktable designed by Sheraton for artists or designers. The top of the table rises on a double horse and is adjustable so that the artist may stand or sit to work. A small flap draws out of the top to hold a "still life" or the small model being painted. The sliders at each end hold drawing instruments and lamps. See *Architect's Table.*

DRAWING TABLE

DRAWN WORK. An openwork pattern or design created by drawing or pulling out weft or warp threads from a fabric.

DREISCHIFFIGE KIRCHE. See *Hall Church.*

DRESS. To smooth or finish the surface of stones or to plane the surface of wood.

DRESSER. Originally a sideboard or buffet with storage space for plates, etc., or a cabinet with drawers and/or shelves. Illustrated is a Queen Anne oak dresser of the early 18th century. In contemporary usage, a long chest of drawers about 36" tall and 6' long or longer. The unit is usually part of a bedroom suite, and is designed in both traditional and modern styles.

DRESSER

DRESSING MIRROR

DRESSING MIRROR

DRESSOIR DE SALLE À MANGER

DRIP

DRIPSTONE

DRESSING MIRROR. A small, standing, portable mirror, or a mirror on a stand, sometimes with drawers, which was set on a table, low chest, or cabinet and used as an adjunct to dressing. Also called a "toilet mirror."

DRESSING ROOM. A small room or area with a closet and/or drawer space, usually adjacent to a bedroom. It sometimes has a dressing table and mirror arrangement.

DRESSING TABLE. A kneehole type of table with large and small drawers surrounding the central knee area. A mirror is usually attached to the table surface. In its present form it is based on a 19th-century innovation. For an earlier type of dressing table, see *Poudreuse*.

DRESSING TABLE

DRESSINGS

DRESSINGS. All brick and stone parts of a building other than the plain walls: e.g., columns, arches, quoins, brackets, consoles, etc. Illustrated is the central porch of the west front of Amiens Cathedral (13th-century Gothic). The moldings, colonnettes, carved figures, gargoyles, etc., are all "dressings" or trimmings.

DRESSOIR DE SALLE À MANGER. French for a dining-room dresser or buffet. A 16th-century, large dresser-top cupboard unit like this French Renaissance piece of the period of François I. See *Buffet, Crédence, Dresser,* and *Welsh Dresser*.

DRILL. A denim-like, heavy twill fabric, tough and durable.

DRINKING TABLE. See *Wine Table*.

DRIP. The portion on the front of a throating on any projection or molding which is used to prevent rain from falling on or running down the face of a building. See *Coping illustration, D*.

DRIPSTONE. The projecting molding or canopy over a door or window arch. It throws the rain off from the wall and protects the opening below from the elements. It is also called a "hood molding" or "label."

DROP FRONT. See *Drop Lid*.

DROP HANDLE. A pendant-like piece of hardware that functions as a drawer pull.

DROP LID. A top or front of a desk hinged to cover an inner compartment of drawers, boxes, pigeonholes, etc. When the front is dropped down, the inner surface of the desk front makes a flat writing surface flush with the inner compartment. There are usually drawers below the enclosed top area. See *Slope-Front Desk*.

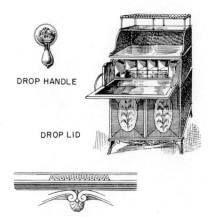

DROP HANDLE

DROP LID

DROP ORNAMENT. A carved, shaped, or pierced ornament which extends below the underframe of a chair or cabinet, but does not extend across the whole width of the underframe. When it extends across the whole length it is called an apron, front, or skirt.

DROP-LEAF TABLE. See *Flap Table*.

DROP ORNAMENT

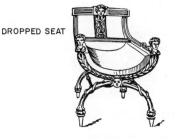

DROPPED SEAT

DROPPED OR DIPPED SEAT. A seat with a concave surface between the two side rails. A depressed center area in a chair seat, also called a "scoop seat." A late-18th-century Sheraton design is illustrated. See *Dip Seat*.

DROPS. See *Guttae*.

DRUM. A circular supporting wall for a dome.

DRUM TABLE. A round table wih a deep apron, sometimes made with drawers set in all around the apron. The table usually presents a squat, drumlike appearance.

DRUM TABLE

DRUNKARD'S CHAIR. Also called a "lover's chair." A Queen Anne period vogue which lasted through the 18th century. The seats were up to 33" wide, and allowed one person to sprawl comfortably, or two to nestle closely. In current usage it is sometimes referred to as a "chair and a half."

DRY CLEANING. A process for cleaning fabrics which are not washable. Carbon tetrachloride mineral spirits are used to remove dirt and stains. Special types of stains may require other special cleaning agents.

DRUNKARD'S CHAIR

DRY RUBBLE

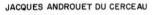

JACQUES ANDROUET DU CERCEAU

DUAL-PURPOSE UNIT

DRY RUBBLE. Roughly dressed, irregularly shaped stones set into a wall or fence without mortar.

DRY SINKS. 19th-century low kitchen cabinets usually made of pine. They were made to hold a pitcher and washbasin on the top surface, and there was usually closed cabinet space below. The top of the sink was sometimes covered with slate or marble. "Water benches" served the same purpose as the sinks.

DRYPOINT ENGRAVING. The simplest of all etching techniques. It consists of drawing with a hard steel "pencil" on a metal plate. The burr that results from scratching the surface gives the "dry point" its ability to catch the ink, and it prints with a depth which adds sharpness to the design. Not too many impressions or printings can be made from a plate. Drypoint engraving is a form of intaglio engraving.

DU CERCEAU, JACQUES ANDROUET. A 16th-century French Renaissance architect, draftsman, and furniture designer who studied in Italy under Bramante. In 1550 he published *Recueil Grave de Muebles* which set forth rules of proportion and ornamentation to be used on furniture based on antique forms. Du Cerceau originated the use of long columns, on buffets and cupboards, which rose from the base to the top of the unit. Illustrated is a bench made from a design by Du Cerceau.

DUAL BED. See *Hollywood Bed.*

DUAL-PURPOSE UNIT. Something designed to serve more than one purpose, like a convertible couch. See *Library Armchair, Library Press Bedstead,* and *Library Steps.* A Sheraton design is illustrated.

DUBOIS, JACQUES (c. 1693–1763). Cabinetmaker of the French Régence and Louis XV periods. Twisted fishtails or mermaid appendages appear in several of his pieces as terminal ends for his mounts.

DUBOIS, RENE. An 18th-century French cabinetmaker for Louis XV and Louis XVI.

DUCHESS. A one-time popular curtain fabric with an appliqué design.

DUCHESSE. A chaise longue in one piece. It is described by Sheraton as two bergères with a footstool in the middle. A Sheraton design is illustrated.

DUCHESSE

DUCHESSE BED. A canopy bed without posts. The tester is attached to the wall above the bed, and extends over the bed. The draperies from the tester are pulled back to either side of the bed, and they usually extend down to the floor. It was originally an 18th-century French design.

DUCHESSE BRISÉE. A chaise longue with a separate foot piece.

DUCHESSE LACE. See *Valenciennes Lace.*

DUCK. A tightly woven cotton or linen fabric with plain or rib weaves. It is similar to canvas, and stripes may be woven in, or painted or printed on one side.

DUCK FOOT. A webbed furniture foot of the late-17th- early-18th-centuries. It is found in Flemish and English furniture.

DUCHESSE BED

DUGOURC. An 18th-century French designer of the Louis XVI period. He was especially partial to the quiver and arrows as a decorative motif, and he faithfully produced Pompeii-inspired furniture. Dugourc was made the designer of costumes and decorations for the opera in 1784. His masterpiece was the Grand Salon à Coupola at Bagatelle.

DULCIMER. A small, stringed musical instrument of antiquity. It is triangular in shape, and the strings are struck with hammers to produce the musical notes.

DUMBWAITER. A three-tiered, tripod, circular table, dating from the 18th century. Sheraton designed many elaborate dumbwaiters with drawers, shelves, and trays. See *Rafraîchissoir.* In the Victorian period, a dumbwaiter was a lift for bringing up food from the basement kitchen to the dining room.

DUMBWAITER

DUMMY BOARD FIGURES. Also called "picture board dummies." See *Fireside Figures.*

DUNCAN PHYFE. See *Phyfe, Duncan.*

DUOMO. Any Italian cathedral.

DUPPION. See *Douppioni or Duppion.*

DUST BOTTOM OR BOARD. A thin wood separator between drawers to keep out the dust that might enter through the open spaces.

DUST RUFFLE. A shirred, pleated, or tailored fabric piece which extends, usually, from under the mattress of a bed down to the floor. It covers the legs of the bed frame, and supposedly sets up a barrier to keep the dust from getting under the bed. Examples of dust ruffles are seen from the Elizabethan period on up to the present. A mid-18th-century Chippendale bedstead is illustrated.

DUST RUFFLE

DUTCH CROSS BOND

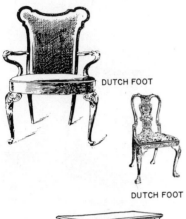

DUTCH FOOT

DUTCH FOOT

DUTCH LEG

E

EAGLE

DUTCH CROSS BOND OR DUTCH BOND. Same as *English Cross Bond.*

DUTCH DOOR. A door which is horizontally divided into an upper and lower section. Each section is independently hinged, and either or both can be opened.

DUTCH DRESSER. A hutch cabinet. A two-section unit with a closed cupboard or drawer unit, and open shelves above. See *Welsh Dresser.*

DUTCH FOOT. A pad foot or spoon foot on a cabriole furniture leg. It was especially popular in late-17th-century and early-18th-century furniture. See *Pad Foot.* See *Easy Chair* illustration.

DUTCH LEG. A wood turned leg consisting of rounded forms spaced with flattened oval discs. It usually ends in a squared-off form, and rests on a flat, oval foot.

DUTCH SETTLE. A wooden settle with a hinged tabletop surface behind. When flipped up on to the settle top, the unit becomes a table.

DWARF WALL. A partition or wall which does not extend up to the ceiling; also an interior wall between the top ceiling level and the finished roof level.

DYEING. A process for coloring yarns or fabrics with either natural or synthetic dyes. Dyes differ in their ability to resist sun fading, laundering, perspiration, etc. See *Colorfast* and *Yarn Dyed.*

DYMAXION. A term created by designer-architect-inventor Richard Buckminster Fuller for industrial designs which give maximum performance at maximum economy.

DYNEL. A synthetic fiber made from acrylonitrile and vinyl chloride. A trademark of Union Carbide Corporation. The fiber is characterized by resilience, strength, and resistance to chemicals. Dynel fibers are used in upholstery and drapery fabrics as well as for carpeting.

EAGLE. A favorite decorative motif used by the ancient Persians, Assyrians, Egyptians, and up into our present-day civilization. The Greeks considered the eagle the companion of Zeus, and the Romans used a representation of the eagle as a military standard. In ecclesiastical art, the eagle is the symbol of St. John the Evangelist. The Byzantines used a double-headed eagle, and in heraldry the eagle appears in all colors but blue. It made its appearance again in the Renaissance and

EARLY ENGLISH PERIOD

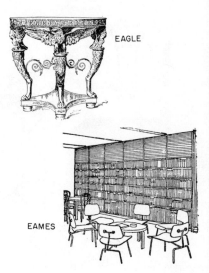

EAGLE

bloomed as a mythological symbol in 18th-century decoration. Napoleon and the Empire used the eagle to its fullest as a motif on furniture, on fabrics, in carvings, paintings, etc. The American Revolution took on the eagle as its emblem, and again it was a popular enrichment on furniture, mirror frames, fabrics, etc.

EAMES, CHARLES. A 20th-century American architect and designer. He invented a process for molding laminated plywood into compound curves, and electronically joining the plywood to other plywood or steel members with rubber discs between for resilience. Eames has produced exquisite forms and proportions, as well as the new concept of completely separating a chair's back and seat within its supporting frame. He has designed wire frame chairs for Herman Miller that can be covered with snap-on upholstery. Many of his designs are done in conjunction with his wife, Ray.

EAMES

EAMES CHAIR. See *Eames, Charles.*

EARPIECE. A scroll or volute springing from the knee of a cabriole leg and ending in the underframing of the piece of furniture. Especially popular in 18th-century English and French furniture.

EARLY AMERICAN

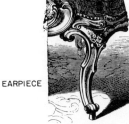

EARPIECE

EARLY AMERICAN. The period in American art, architecture, and furniture from about 1600 to about 1720. The designs are basically Jacobean, Carolean, and William and Mary, but executed simply and provincially in native woods. Dutch influences were strongly felt in areas like New York.

EARLY CHRISTIAN. See *Basilica, Byzantine,* and illustration for *Respond.*

EARLY CHRISTIAN

EARLY ENGLISH PERIOD. The earliest Gothic architecture in England, dating from 1189 to 1307. It is also known as "Lancet," "First Pointed," and "Early Plantagenet" period. The architecture is marked by tall lancet openings, projecting buttresses, pinnacles, and steep-pitched roofs. Illustrated is the transept view of Lincoln Cathedral, which was begun in 1092 and rebuilt several times. The major work, as seen today, was completed between 1185 and 1240.

EARLY ENGLISH PERIOD

EARS

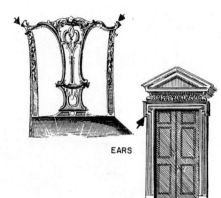

EARS

EARS. In architecture, moldings or cornices over doors or windows which overlap the uprights of the door or window frame. They were used as a cornice decoration in the 18th century in England and América. In furniture, the extended parts of the top rail beyond the upright supports of the chair back.

EARTHENWARE. Pottery made of coarse clay. It is heavy, soft, porous, and opaque like a common red flowerpot.

EASTLAKE, CHARLES L., JR. (1793–1865). An advocate of the Gothic revival in England during the 19th century. He was an architect and furniture designer who combined Gothic and Japanese ornaments, and, using machine methods, arranged to produce assorted pieces of furniture embellished with heavy hardware, metal, and tile panel inserts, etc. Cherrywood was the principal wood employed. Illustrated is a chair from Eastlake's *Hints on Household Taste.*

CHARLES L. EASTLAKE, JR.

EASY CHAIR. A roomy, comfortable, upholstered chair of any style or period, which is made for ease and relaxation. It is usually based on the bergère and wing chair. An 18th-century easy chair is shown.

EASY CHAIR

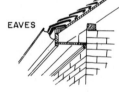

EAVES

EAVES. The lowest part of a roof which overhangs the top of a wall.

EAVES COURSE. The lowest row of tiles or slates on a roof.

ÉBÉNISTE

ÉBÉNISTE. French for "ebony worker." In the early French Renaissance (15th and 16th centuries), furniture was often made of ebony glued onto blackened pearwood for strength and size. The cabinetmakers who worked on these pieces were called "ébénistes" or "joiners and carpenters on ebony." Maître ébéniste" was the official title of the "King's cabinetmaker." Illustrated is a French cabinet of the period of Henri II (mid-16th century). See *Stabre, Laurent.*

EBONY. A tropical, hard, dense, heavy brown-black wood with a fine grain. It was popular in France during the Louis XIV period, and again in the Empire and mid-19th century. True ebony comes from Ceylon, and black ebony is found in North India and the Himalayas.

EBONY, GABOON. An African rusty brown-black wood which is expensive and available in relatively small pieces; therefore it is mainly used for veneering, musical instruments, and inlay work. See *Ebony, Macassar.*

EBONY, MACASSAR. A very hard, dense wood, with an intense, black-brown stripe on a reddish ground. It takes a brilliant polish. It is also called "coromandel." The wood is named after the seaport from where it was exported. Macassar ebony is usually figured in strong contrasting stripes.

ECCLESIASTICAL. Referring to the church, or use in the church. Illustrated is a Romanesque bishop's chair.

ECCLESIASTICAL

ECHINUS ◄

ECHINUS. An oval-shaped molding. It is part of a classical capital, and it is located between the shaft and the abacus. In furniture ornament, the egg-and-dart, egg-and-tongue, or egg-and-anchor motif carved on the ovolo molding of furniture.

ECKHARDT, ANTHONY GEORGE. An 18th-century English manufacturer of printed fabrics and wallpapers. He had a patent for printing designs on silk, cotton, muslin, calicos, and wallpaper. He worked in association with his brother Frederick, and they employed talented French designers like Boileau, Feuglet, and Joinot. The wallpaper designs were produced with wood blocks or copper plates. Often hand details were added, as well as silver and gold leaf embellishments.

ECLECTICISM. The borrowing and combining of art forms and motifs from assorted past periods and adapting them to contemporary uses. The Victorian 19th century was considered an era of eclecticism. Older patterns and styles were borrowed and adapted to the new mechanized processes of the times. Illustrated is a German mid-19th-century chair which strongly resembles Early Renaissance prototypes.

ECLECTICISM

ÉCOLE DES BEAUX ARTS. The leading French art institute of the 19th century. It tended to give greater unity and consistency to the architecture and art of France, and it had a great influence on maintaining standards of taste, refinement, and correctness of style. It also, unfortunately, negated the advancement of new ideas and styles.

ÉCRAN

ÉCRAN. A fire screen, or a small screen set on a table to shield one from the firelight. A small shade on a candlestick. Illustrated is a design by Antoine Watteau (18th-century France).

ÉCRAN À CHEVAL

ÉCRAN À CHEVAL

ÉCRAN À CHEVAL. A frame with a sliding panel, used as a fire screen. See *Banner Screen, Cheval Screen,* and *Horse Screen.*

ÉCRAN À COULISSE. A French term for a cheval or fire screen.

ÉCRAN À ÉCLISSE. See *Pole Screen.*

EDWARDIAN PERIOD. See *Decorated Period.*

EGG AND DART. A molding decoration which resembles a continuous string of egg or ovoid forms separated by dartlike or arrowhead points. "Egg and tongue" and "egg and anchor" moldings are almost identical. See *Echinus.*

EGG AND DART

EGG CRATE. A metal or plastic unit which resembles a cardboard egg separator, and is used to diffuse ceiling light. It is usually used over fluorescent light strips.

EGGSHELL FINISH. A semiflat paint. A painted finish with a soft, dull, low luster.

ÉGLOMISÉ. An art form in which the painting is done on the reverse side of glass, and often embellished with gold leaf.

ÉGOUTTOIR. A piece of French provincial furniture with open rack shelves for drying or storing dishes.

EGYPTIAN

EGYPT. The land of the Pharaohs. One of the earliest developed civilizations of the world. The art and architecture of Ancient Egypt preceded the classic Greek and Roman civilizations. From the Egyptians we inherited such motifs and decorations as the sphinx, the lotus column, lion's paw, and palmetto leaf, cross-legged chairs with leather seats, tables, stools, sarcophagi, mother-of-pearl inlays, veneering methods, etc. With Napoleon's successful campaigns in Egypt and the discovery of the Rosetta Stone at the close of the 18th century, Egyptiana became the vogue, and Egyptian-type motifs were an important part of the Empire style in the early 19th century.

EGYPTIAN

EGYPTIAN SARACENIC ARCHITECTURE. See *Tombs of the Caliphs.*

EIDERDOWN. The soft fluffy feathers obtained from large sea ducks. It is used for the luxury stuffing of pillows and cushions.

EIFFEL, ALEXANDRE GUSTAVE (1832–1923). A French engineer. See *Eiffel Tower, Magasin au Bon Marché, Marquise Vitrée,* and *Palais des Machines.* He also engineered the framework for the Statue of Liberty in New York.

EIFFEL TOWER. "The manifesto and monument of that Iron Age" (the latter half of the 19th century). It was constructed in 1889 in Paris by Alexandre Gustave Eiffel and was originally designed as a highlight of the Paris Exhibition of 1889. It is equipped with a series of elevators, the earliest ones devised for a structure of such skyscraper proportions.

EIGHT-LEGGED TABLE. An 18th-century English form of the gateleg table. It was usually made of mahogany. See *Gateleg Table* and *Thousand-Leg Table.*

EINGELEGTE ARBEIT. German for inlaid or boulle work.

ELBOW CHAIR. A chair with arms upon which one may rest one's elbows.

ELECTROPLATING. An electrical process for covering one base metal with a very thin layer of a more expensive or desirable metal.

ELGIN MARBLES

EIFFEL TOWER

EIGHT-LEGGED TABLE

ELBOW CHAIR

ELEVATION

ELEVATION. In architecture, a drawing of a flat, two-dimensional view of a room or building, usually to scale, to show relative size of architectural and decorative details. Illustrated is a side of a room drawn by Michelangelo Pergolesi, a late-18th-century English designer.

ELGIN MARBLES. The pediment and frieze sculptures of the Parthenon brought to the British Museum by Lord Elgin in the early 19th century. Illustrated is one of the carved metopes. While Ambassador from England to Turkey, Lord Elgin, with a group of architects, sculptors, and painters started excavations at the Acropolis in Athens. After much labor, effort, and money was expended he was able to get the now famous marbles to England.

ELGIN MARBLES

ELIZABETHAN

ELIZABETHAN

EMBLEM

EMBRASURE

EMBROIDERY

ELIZABETHAN. Referring to the reign of Elizabeth I of England, 1558–1603. Illustrated is the Great Bed of Ware, a state bed. Renaissance motifs are here intermingled with the remnants of the Gothic tradition. See *Chest* for an Elizabethan chest, *Center Table* for an Elizabethan interior, and *Alcove* for an Elizabethan oriel window.

ELL. See *Three-Quarter Width.*

ELLIOTT, JOHN. An 18th-century American cabinetmaker who worked in Philadelphia. He was noted for his wall mirrors and dressing cases.

ELM. A strong, tough wood which looks well when stained and polished. It is a light, brownish red with dark-brown ring marks and a strong figure. The northern elm has a finer, more uniform texture than the southern elm.

ÉMAUX DE NIELLURE. A French term for an enameling process like niello. Lines are cut into the metal and then filled with enamel.

EMBLEM. A decorative symbol or device used in heraldry. It appears in carvings, embroideries, and painted panels. Examples are Napoleon's bee and the salamander of François I.

EMBOSSED. Decorated with a raised design produced on a surface by hammering, stamping, or molding.

EMBOSSED

EMBOSSING

EMBOSSING. In fabrics, a process for pressing a design onto a fabric by passing the fabric through hot engraved rollers. A piece of embossed velvet is shown. See *Cut Pile.*

EMBRASURE. The enlargement of the aperture of a door or a window on the inside of a wall. In Gothic architecture, an opening in the wall or parapet, or the indent at the top of a battlement.

EMBROIDERY. The art of decorating a fabric with a raised design or pattern. The design is worked out with a needle and thread, either by hand or machine. The design may be of one or more colors, and a great variety of stitches or combinations of stitches may be employed. A 16th-century example of Spanish Renaissance embroidery is illustrated.

EMPAISTIC. Sculpture or structural elements made of, or covered with sheet metal which has been hammered in decorative patterns. It was a forerunner of boulle work. See *Boulle, André Charles.*

EMPIRE. The Napoleonic period in France and the great classic revival style of architecture, art, and decoration. The period roughly extends from 1804 to 1820. It is a period which combines the grandeur and martial symbols of Rome with Ancient Egyptian motifs and the elements of Greek architecture. The furniture of the period is massive, architectural in concept, and lavishly trimmed in bronze and brass on rosewood, mahogany, and ebony. Charles Percier and Pierre Fontaine were the great designers of furniture and interiors of the period, and Jacques Louis David was the major art force of the time. The style spread into England where Thomas Hope and Thomas Sheraton became leading exponents of the Empire style. Duncan Phyfe in America developed a style along the lines of the Empire, and in Germany and Austria, the Biedermeier style evolved. See *Biedermeier; David, Jacques Louis; Empire Drape; Fontaine, Pierre François Léonard; Normand, Charles P. T.;* and *Percier, Charles.*

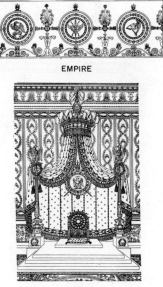

EMPIRE

EMPIRE

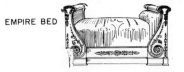

EMPIRE BED

EMPIRE BED. A typical bed of the early 19th century in France. It was low and usually set against a wall or in an alcove, with only one major side exposed. Curved sweeping ends form the headboard and footboard. The Empire bed is similar to the boat bed and the gondola bed, and was a forerunner of the American sleigh bed. Illustrated is Napoleon's bed at the Grand Trianon, Versailles.

EMPIRE DRAPE. A simple, classic drapery treatment. The fabric is caught at the top hem at equidistant points, and the valleys, formed between these points, fall freely. A formal pattern is created of fairly rigid verticals from the caught points to the floor, alternating with draped billows. It was very popular in the Empire period (early 19th century). Illustrated is a wall treatment in the Royal Palace in Venice in 1834.

EMPREINTES VELOUTÉES. French for "flocked prints" or "wallpaper." See *Flock Paper.*

EN CAS or EN CASE. A small table of the Louis XV period similar to a night table (table de chevet). It was usually marble-topped and had a drawer and a cupboard below.

EMPIRE DRAPE

EN CHARRETTE

EN RESSAUT

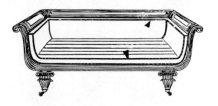

EN TABLEAU

ENAMEL

ENCARPUS

ENCOIGNURE

END TABLE

EN CHARRETTE. "Last-minute" work. Derived from the custom of 19th-century artists working on their paintings as they were being "carted" to the Beaux Arts for judgment. Doing last-minute touch-ups, etc.

EN RESSAUT. In architecture, engaged to a wall or projecting from it. Illustrated is an English corbel table of the 11th century.

EN SUITE. Of a set. See *Set*.

EN TABLEAU. An upholstery technique of the late 18th century. A sharp ridge, outlined in gimp, braid, or cord, defined the straight lines of the sofa or chair. Illustrated is a late Sheraton sofa.

EN TAILLE D'ÉPARGNE. Another (French) term for *Champlevé* enamel.

ENAMEL. A colored glaze used to decorate metal or ceramics. After firing, the paint becomes hard and permanent. It is applied to pottery or porcelain after a preliminary glaze. The piece is then fired again to fuse the enamel to the original glaze. Enamel is also a generic name for a house paint which dries with a hard, shiny surface. A 12th-century enameled reliquary is illustrated.

ENCARPUS. A fruit or flower festoon used to enhance flat surfaces. It was employed extensively in the Italian Renaissance and in the Louis XV and Louis XVI periods.

ENCLOSING WALL. An exterior, nonbearing wall in skeletal frame construction which is anchored to columns, piers, or floors, but not necessarily built between columns or piers as a curtain wall. See *Curtain Wall*.

ENCOIGNURE. A corner cabinet or table, often built in as part of the architecture of the room. See *Coin*.

ENCRIER. French for *Inkwell*.

END TABLE. A small table placed at the end of a sofa, settee, or couch, or at the side of a chair to hold a lamp, ashtray, etc. A modern device that can be styled to suit any period of furnishing. A side table. See *Side Table*.

ENDIVE MARQUETRY. A Queen Anne style of fine flowing-line marquetry similar to seaweed marquetry. The flowing lines resemble the leaves of the endive plant. See *Seaweed Marquetry*.

ENFILADE. French term for a set or suite of rooms. The term also describes a low provincial buffet with four or more cupboard doors.

ENGAGED COLUMN. A column, partially attached to a wall and projecting from it 1/3 to 3/4 of the extent of its diameter. See *Pilaster*.

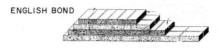

ENGLISH BOND

ENGLISH BOND. In masonry, bricks laid in alternate courses of headers and stretchers (the header is the end of the brick, the stretcher is the side of the brick). The headers are centered on the stretchers, which lie in horizontal lines.

ENGLISH CROSS BOND

ENGLISH BOND

ENGLISH CROSS BOND. A masonry method similar to English bond in that it consists of alternate courses of headers and stretchers. Instead of the stretchers lying one directly above the other in alternate courses, they break joints evenly in the successive stretcher courses. See *Bond* and *English Bond*.

ENGRAVING. A generic term covering many methods of multiplying prints. In general terms, a design is cut in a hard material such as copper, steel, or wood. The artist may incise his design; or he may cut out the areas around it, thus making a raised design. The design is inked, and impressions are taken. Some engraving techniques are: woodcut, linocut, line engraving, drypoint, etching, mezzotint, aquatint, wood engraving, intaglio engraving.

ENGRAVING ROOM. See *Print Room*.

ENRICHMENT. A painted or carved repeated design on moldings, such as the guilloche, egg and dart, honeysuckle, chevron, etc. Illustrated is a section of a French Romanesque portal showing a series of "enriched moldings."

ENROULEMENTS DÉCOUPÉS. A French term for slashed or pinked edged scrolls. A decorative carved or painted French motif of the Renaissance period. Illustrated is a panel over a doorway at St. Madou in Rouen (16th century). See *Strapwork*.

ENTABLATURE. In architecture, the upper portion of a classic order which consists of an architrave, frieze, and cornice. The entablature rests upon the column. See *Architrave, Classic,* and *Cornice*.

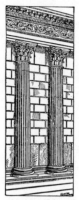

ENGAGED COLUMN

ENRICHMENT

ENTABLATURE

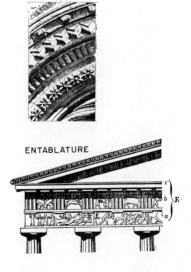

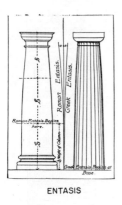

ENTASIS

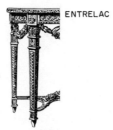

ENTRELAC

ÉPERGNE

EPISTYLE

ERECHTHEUM

ENTASIS. In architecture, a slight curve on the shaft of a column. It is limited to the upper two-thirds of the shaft, and it accommodates the optic trick which makes a column seem to bulge or buckle. The slight upper swelling makes the column appear straight-lined.

ENTRELAC. A Louis XVI decorative carved interlacing motif which is similar to a *Guilloche*.

ENTRESOL. French for "mezzanine." The low story over the ground floor or a low story between two high ones.

ENVELOPE TABLE. A square table top with four "envelope flap" hinged sections which, when flipped back, increase the tabletop surface. A late-18th-century design, also found in the Directoire period. It is often used for card table designs, and is similar in concept to the triangular *Handkerchief Table*.

ÉPERGNE. A French word for an ornamental stand with a dish on top. It may have candelabra branches extending out from the stand, below the dish, or it may have a trumpet-like container rising above the dish. The bell-like opening is used as a flower container. The épergne is usually used as a table centerpiece.

EPHEBEUM. A large gymnasium hall in a classic Roman bath.

EPINAOS. See *Posticum*.

EPISCENIUM. The proscenium and fixed set of a classic Greek theatre.

EPISTYLE. A beam that spans the space between two columns or piers, or between a column or pier and a wall. It is also called an architrave.

ÉPOQUE ROMANTIQUE. See *Romantic Epoch*.

ERECHTHEUM. A temple (420–393 B.C.) of classic Athens built by Mnesicles on a sloping site on the Acropolis. The building has no side colonnades but has three separate shrines. On the east there is an Ionic hexastyle portico, on the north there is an Ionic tetrastyle portico, and to the south there is the famous portico of Caryatid figures. The building is made of marble, and the main frieze and porticoes were of black marble decorated with white marble sculptured figures. See *Anta* for illustration. See also *Caryatid* and *Elevation*.

ESCABEAU. See *Escabelle*.

ESCABELLE. An early French Renaissance stool or chair supported on trestles. It is similar to the Italian sgabello.

ESCALLOP. See *Cockleshell* and *Scallop Shell*.

ESCRITOIRE. A French term for a small desk with drawers and compartments. A secretary.

ESCABELLE

ESCABELLE

ESCRITOIRE

ESCUTCHEON   ESCUTCHEON   ESCUTCHEON

ESCUTCHEON. A shield with a heraldic device. In hardware, a decoratively shaped plate for a keyhole, knob, pull, or doorknob backing.

ESPAGNOLETTE. A terminal ornament popular in 16th- and 17th-century French furniture. It is a female bust used as part of a support, or the ending of a volute. In the French Régence period it is a female head with a tall, stiff lace collar or ruff that gives a generally Spanish flavor. The ornate head was a popular decorative motif for wood carvings and bronze mounts.

ESPALIER. A latticework of wood upon which fruit trees and ornamental shrubs are trained to assume decorative patterns. The branches are tied and trained to grow in a set direction and make an overall preconceived pattern. The "educated," stylized trees are referred to as espalier.

ESTAGNIÉ. A French provincial open hanging shelf unit used to hold pewter utensils. The piece sometimes had a drawer under the shelves.

ESTRADE. The French version of the Spanish estrado, a drawing room. The word also refers to an elevated part of the floor or room, a platform placed at one end. It originally meant a couch or bed area in an alcove. A feature in 17th-century Spanish architecture. See *Alcove*.

ESTRON. A trademark name for a natural, uncolored acetate fiber produced by the Eastman Company. A heavy-denier yarn is especially designed for home furnishing uses.

ESPAGNOLETTE   ESPAGNOLETTE

ÉTAGÈRE

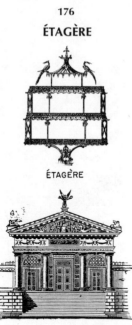

ÉTAGÈRE

ETRUSCAN ORDER

ÉTAGÈRE. Hanging or standing open shelves. A light, elegant unit for displaying books, bric-a-brac, etc. A "whatnot" unit. Illustrated is a hanging étagère designed by Chippendale. In the 19th century this same term was applied to worktables with several shelves.

ETCHING. A form of intaglio engraving. A copper plate is covered with a resinous ground impervious to acid, and the artist or etcher then draws on this surface with a needle. The plate is bathed in acid, which bites into the scratched lines, engraving the design. The design is inked and impressions are taken. Rembrandt was a famous etcher, and the 17th century was a noteworthy period in the production of etchings.

ETRUSCAN ORDER. Also called the "Tuscan order." A Roman variation of the simple Doric order. A heavy, massive column, seven diameters high. See *Diameter* and *Doric Order*.

ÉTUI. French for box or container.

EUCALYPTUS. See *Walnut, Oriental*.

EUSTYLE. The space between columns in a classic arrangement, being equal to 2¼ diameters of a column's shaft.

ÉVENTAIL. French for fan.

ÉVENTAIL

EVOLUTE

EVOLUTE. A continuous wave or Vitruvian scroll. A classic motif used in the 18th century as a decoration on bands, cornices, friezes, etc. See *Vitruvian Scroll*.

EXEDRA. A public room in a Pompeiian or Roman home. A semicircular or rectangular recess for seating. An apse or niche in a church.

EXTENSION TABLE

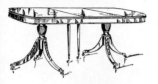

EXTENSION TABLE. A tabletop which separates in the center, and extends outward in both directions. Additional leaves are then added in the open space which has been created. Illustrated is an early-19th-century Duncan Phyfe extension table.

EXTERIOR WALL. The outside or exposed wall.

EXTRADOS. See *Arch*.

EYE. The center of an Ionic volute.

EXTRADOS

EYE

FABRILITE. A trademark name for vinyl-coated fabric and sheeting manufactured by Dupont. It is used as an upholstery material and as a durable wall covering.

FAÇADE. The principal front or face of a structure. The main view. It may also refer to the front of an architecturally designed piece of furniture. Illustrated is the front façade of Notre-Dame in Paris.

FAÇADE D'HONNEUR

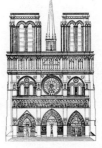

FAÇADE

FAÇADE D'HONNEUR. French for the main or front face of a building. Illustrated is the cathedral of Laon. See *Postern*.

FACCIATA. Italian for "façade" or "front."

FACE. The exposed surface of a wall or structure.

FACE BRICK. Bricks which have been selected for their better color, texture, etc., and are used to face or surface the exposed walls or fireplaces, etc. Cheaper bricks or baser materials are used behind the face brick.

FACED WALL. Wall where the facing and backing are bonded and tied together to work together under the common load.

FACETTES. The French word for the flat projections between the flutes of a column shaft.

FACETTES

FACIA. The flat vertical face in the architrave of an entablature. See *Fascia*.

FACIA

FACING. The finishing material (stone, brick, stucco, wood, etc.) which is applied to the façade of a building or wall.

FAÇONNÉ. A Jacquard type of fabric made of silk or rayon. Façonné is French for "fancy weave." A brocaded velvet.

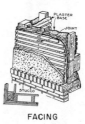

FACING

FAÏENCE. French for "pottery." Terra-cotta. A peasant type of glazed pottery originally made at Faenza, Italy. A glazed bisquit ware. It may be used as a facing for buildings or walls in the form of tiles or blocks. It is also used as a flooring material. See *Terra-Cotta.*

FAILLE. A soft, slightly glossy silk, rayon, or cotton fabric in a rib weave. The filler yarns are heavier than the warp yarns; thus they cause a flat cross-grain rib or cord.

FAKE. A counterfeit reproduction of an object made to pass as the original. It is usually artificially aged or patinaed.

FALDISTORIUM. A late Italian Renaissance curule chair which was made of wrought iron and brass, and had a leather or velvet seat. See *Curule Chair.*

FALDSTOOL. A folding or portable stool of the Gothic period.

FALEGNAMERIA. Italian for "joinery."

FALL FRONT. See *Drop Lid.* Illustrated is a Queen Anne toilet chest.

FAMILLE NOIRE, VERTE, JAUNE, ROSE, ETC. French names for Chinese pottery having a colored background. Literally it means: black family, green family, yellow family, rose family, etc.

FAN DESIGN. A semicircular, fanlike ornament used in late-18th-century furniture in England and America.

FALL FRONT

FAN DESIGN

FAN VAULTING

FAN VAULTING. Also called palm vaulting. A collection of ribs springing from a point and spreading out in a fan shape. It is peculiar to the Perpendicular Period in Gothic architecture.

FANBACK CHAIR. A chair or settee with a fanlike motif, either upright or reversed, for the chair back. Originally an 18th-century French design.

FANCY CHAIR. A Sheraton-designed small-scaled, elegant side chair. A late-18th-century favorite.

FANLIGHT. A window set above a door or entranceway. In Georgian buildings, the fanlight is often semicircular in shape, and the panes are separated by bars radiating from the center in a fanlike arrangement.

FANCY CHAIR

FANLIGHT

FARNESE PALACE. Built in Rome in 1534 by Antonio da Sangallo, it is considered to be the grandest palace of the Italian Renaissance period. The "piano nobile" (main level) has alternate triangular and segmented pediment windows. The upper story, added by Michelangelo, has columns on brackets holding up the triangular pediment. The round-headed windows beneath the pediment are a Michelangelo feature. The crowning cornice is of a magnificent scale, and it was done in the Florentine style. See *Renaissance Revival* for Sir Charles Barry's adaptation of the Farnese Palace in his Reform Club in London and *Fenestration* illustration.

FARTHINGALE CHAIR. A wide-seated chair, without arms, made to accommodate the voluminous skirts (farthingales) of the Elizabethan costume.

FAUDESTEUIL

FARNESE PALACE

FASCES

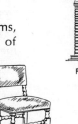

FARTHINGALE CHAIR

FASCES. A Roman symbol of power. A bundle of rods enclosing an axe. It appeared most recently as the symbol of the 20th-century Italian Fascists.

FASCIA. The projecting crown molding of a cornice. A molding with a flat vertical plane in section. Also spelled "facia."

FASCIA

FASHION. A vogue or style. A present trend or fad. Illustrated is a Chippendale bracket clock designed in the chinoiserie style popular in mid-18th-century England.

FAUDESTEUIL

FASHION

FAUDESTEUIL. A Romanesque bench or seating stool with curved X-shaped supports. This type of stool usually had a leather sling for a seat, and the piece was collapsible. In the Gothic period, the legs are fixed and the chair does not usually fold. Illustrated is a 14th-century French Gothic faudesteuil made of iron with brass finials and a leather strap for a seat. See *Pliant*.

FAUN

FAUTEUIL

FAUN. A creature from classical myth, half-man, half-goat, a decorative element in the French and Italian Renaissance period. It also appears in the Adam brothers' designs. The faun is sometimes used as a support or as an Atlas.

FAUTEUIL. French for "armchair." An upholstered armchair with open sides, and usually with upholstered arm or elbow pads. The chair was popularized in the Louis XIV period; the arms originally were placed directly over the front legs. In the Régence and Louis XV periods, the arms were set farther back, and the legs were shortened. The early Renaissance armchairs were not usually upholstered. See *Caquetoire.*

FAUTEUIL À CHÂSSIS. Armchair constructed by a French method devised in the Louis XIV period (also used to make upholstered sofas). A secondary wood framework was covered with fabric, then slipped into the prime wood frame of the piece of furniture. This technique made changes of upholstery relatively simple; the upholsterer merely put a new framed upholstered seat or back into the ornate carved frame. See *Slip Seat.*

FAUTEUIL DE BUREAU. A desk chair of the Régence and Louis XV periods in France. The chair usually had one leg centered in the front, one centered in the back, and one at either side of the seat. The curved sloping back was either caned or upholstered in leather. The fauteuil de bureau, or desk chair, was similar to the English "roundabout" chair of the 18th century.

FAUVE. French for "wild beast." An early-20th-century art movement. It was a noncoherent group of artists who used bright, strong colors, flat patterns, and wild distortions. Henri Matisse, Albert Marquet, André Derain, Maurice de Vlamenck, and Georges Rouault are grouped in this school.

FAUX ROSE. A French rosewood or Madagascar rosewood. It is a pinkish-brown wood with striped markings.

FAUX SATINE. "False satin." An amber to golden-brown cypress crotch wood found largely in the southeastern part of the United States. It is a soft, oily wood that is easy to work and is used as a decorative veneer treatment on furniture and for paneling. The wood is similar in appearance to satinwood.

FAVAS. A Louis XVI decoration which resembles a honeycomb.

FAVRILE. A late-19th-century iridescent glass, made by Louis C. Tiffany in a variety of delicate and decorative patterns, many in the Art Nouveau style.

FAY, JEAN BAPTISTE. A famous 18th-century French textile and wallpaper designer. His work captured the spirit and quality of the Louis XVI period.

FAYARD or FOYARD. French for "beech."

FEATHERED EDGE. A chamfered or beveled effect in which the edge is thinner than the thickness of the board. A thinning off of the edge of a piece of wood.

FEATHERING. Tracery, in Gothic-type architecture, formed by an arrangement of cusps and foils. It is also called foliation.

FEDERAL. An American period of architecture, art, furniture, and decoration from about 1790 to 1820. It is a classic period greatly influenced by the Adam brothers, Hepplewhite, Sheraton, and the English Regency. Duncan Phyfe is the leading American furniture designer of this period.

FEDERAL ARCHITECTURE. The architecture of America from 1790 to 1820 with considerable emphasis on the style of the Adam brothers of England. Usually the house had a flat or low-pitched roof with a balustrade over the cornice. Generally, the house was a boxlike structure on the outside, and stucco facing replaced the Georgian brick or timber façade. The main rooms sometimes were circular or elliptical in plan.

FELT. A material made by matting and interlocking, under heat and pressure, woolen and other fibers. It has no weave or pattern.

FELT BASE RUG. An inexpensive floor covering material which has an enameled design printed, and sometimes an embossed pattern pressed, on the felt-based material. It is like linoleum but not as durable, and the wearing surface does not go through to the backing.

FENDER. A low, metal guard made of iron and/or brass and used to protect the rug or floor from flying embers or sparks from the fire. A hearth or fireplace accessory.

FENESTRATION. The window and door arrangement of a building, and the relative proportions of the openings in the façade. Illustrated is the Italian Renaissance Farnese Palace in Rome.

FENÊTRE À BATTANTS. French for "French window."

FENSTER ROSE. German for "rose window."

FERROCONCRETE. See *Reinforced Concrete.*

FEATHERING

FENDER

FENESTRATION

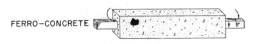

FERRO–CONCRETE

FERRULE

FESTOON

FERRONERIE VELVET. An antique Venetian velvet with a delicate wrought-iron-like pattern.

FERRULE. Formerly "verrel" from the French "virole," a metal ring holding an object fixed to the end of another. In current usage, a metal cup (usually of brass) placed on the bottom of a wood furniture leg for protection and as a reinforcing agent. The term also refers to the metal section of a paintbrush which holds the hairs or bristles to the wood stem.

FESTOON. A string or chain of any kind of material suspended between two points to form a curved or inverted arc drop. In architecture, a sculptured garland of leaves, flowers, fruits, etc., suspended between two points. A favorite Renaissance motif. In furniture, usually a carved or painted arced design of leaves, flowers, fruits, etc.

FÊTE GALANTE. A French 18th-century romantic version of a picnic with ladies and their escorts, in rich court apparel, gaily flirting and playing musical instruments and games. This theme appears in murals, tapestries, designs, and painting.

FIBER RUG. A reversible rug woven of kraft or sisal fibers, sometimes combined with wool or other fibers. These rugs come in assorted sizes, colors, patterns, and shapes for use as area rugs or to cover a complete floor.

FIBERBOARD. A pulped wood panel, usually 4' × 8', which has been compressed under great pressure to form a rigid, strong, no-grain construction unit. There are many trademarked types of pulped boards available: Masonite, Beaverboard, Homosote, etc. The materials are usually used for partitions, ceilings, and the interior construction of inexpensive furniture.

FIBERGLAS. A trademark name for fine filaments of pure glass and the textiles woven from them. The fiber is strong, soft, and pliable, and resists heat, chemicals, and soil. It is manufactured by the Owens-Corning Fiberglas Corporation. Glass fibers are also manufactured by the Pittsburgh Plate Glass Company (PPG) and Johns-Mansville Corporation (J-M).

FIDDLEBACK. A wood grain effect which has a fine, even ripple running at right angles to the direction of the grain of the wood. It is used for fiddleback veneers. This marking often appears in maple and mahogany.

FIDDLEBACK CHAIR. A Queen Anne type, American colonial chair. The back splat is shaped like a fiddle or a vase and the seat is usually made of rush. The chair has cabriole or bandy legs. A similar chair appears in Louis XV period furniture.

FIDDLEBACK CHAIR

FIDDLE BRACE BACK. See *Braced Back*.

FIDDLE-STRING BACK or STICK-BACK. A name sometimes applied to a Windsor chair or any chair which has a back made up of many rods or thin turnings which resemble the strings of a fiddle.

FIELD. In masonry, the unbroken wall area between door or window openings and corners.

FIELD or FIELDED PANEL. The surface of a panel which is on the same level as the surrounding woodwork and defined or outlined by a sunk bevel or applied molding.

FIELD BED. A small-scaled, arched canopy bed originally intended to be moved from place to place; used in the field by army officers, etc. In 18th-century design the term means a bed with smaller tester and less imposing bedposts. A Chippendale design is illustrated.

FIGURE. The highlights or cross graining in a piece of wood or veneer. The word also means patterns created by the abnormal growth of a tree. See *Burl.* The vertical graining of a piece of wood is described as the pattern.

FIL D'ARGENT. French for "silver thread." See *Fil d'Or.*

FIL DE BOIS. Veneer used in a full, uninterrupted length on a piece of furniture.

FIL DE CHYPRE. French for "Cyprus thread." See *Fil d'Or.*

FIL D'OR. French for "gold thread." A gilded silver thread originally made in Genoa and used in tapestries from the Middle Ages up to the 18th century.

FILAMENT. A term for a yarn (usually acetate, rayon, and other synthetics) made up of a number of fine continuous strands lightly twisted together. It is sold by the *Denier* size.

FILET. A square-meshed, net fabric.

FILET LACE. A type of lace in which the design is created by embroidering on net with a thread similar to that used in making the net. See *Lace.*

FILIGREE. Decorative openwork. It usually refers to fine, lace-like work done in gold or silver wire.

FILLER. Threads that run across the width of the fabric from selvage to selvage. Another term for the weft. In weaving, the filler is the thread carried by the shuttle. In woodwork, a liquid or paste composition, often pigmented, which is used to fill the pores or irregularities in coarse or open-grained woods. After using the filler, the wood can be finished and polished.

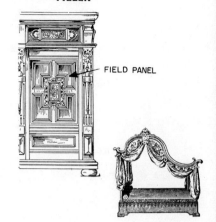

FIELD PANEL

FIELD BED

FILLET

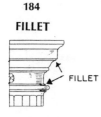

FILLET

FIN DE SIÈCLE

FINGER JOINT

FINIAL

FIRE DOGS

FIRE IRONS

FILLET. A molding with a small, flat, vertical surface in section view, usually used above and below a curved molding. The fillet is also the upright band between the flutings of a column. The term is also applied to the uppermost member of a cornice.

FILLING. The weft or woof yarns. The yarn that is used in the shuttle that moves back and forth across the lengthwise threads of a loom. Also, another term for the pick threads. The lengthwise threads are called the warp. In carpetmaking, the fillings are the threads that cross the warp and fill up the spaces between the knots or tufts. See *Pick, Weave,* and *Weft.*

FIN DE SIÈCLE. French for "end of the century." The end of the 19th century and the *Art Nouveau* style.

FINGER JOINT. A movable, interlocking joint mainly used between the movable and fixed parts of a bracket or fly rail, such as one used to support the leaves of a drop-leaf table in a horizontal position. See *Knuckle Joint.*

FINIAL. The terminating ornament on a post, pediment, or intersection. In various antique periods it has resembled a pineapple, urn, knob, or a cluster of foliage.

FINISH. In fabrics, the treatment given a fabric to produce a desired surface effect like napping, embossing, glazing, waterproofing, wrinkle resistance, etc. The finish sometimes contributes to the "feel" or "hand" of the fabric. In cabinetry, a treatment applied to wooden furniture to protect the surface, to make it more durable and resistant to stains and burns, to bring out or accentuate the natural grain of the wood, to lighten or deepen the natural color, to make a dull or glossy surface appearance, or to change the color completely by painting, lacquering, antiquing, distressing, etc.

FIR. A soft, textured wood used for commercial plywood, interior trims, etc. Not usually used for solid work in furniture.

FIRE DIVISION WALL. A wall which subdivides the building and is used to resist the spread of fire, but does not go continuously through the building as a fire wall does.

FIRE DOGS. See *Andirons.*

FIRE IRONS. Hearth accessories: the poker, tongs, and shovel used to tend a fire. Illustrated is a collection of fire irons and bellows from George Edwards and Mathias Darley's 18th-century Chinese-type ornaments.

FIRE-RETARDANT WIRED GLASS. A wire mesh, chromium-dipped to ensure clean wire and a firm adhesion and then embedded, as closely as possible, in the center of sheet glass. It is produced by a continuous rolling process, and made in many patterns, types, and finishes. The fire-retarding glass is also used as a decorative material, as on the curtain wall of the Time and Life Building in New York City.

FIRE SCREEN. An ornamental screen set in front of an open fireplace to keep the sparks from shooting or flying into the room or to provide protection from intense heat. The screen shown served the latter purpose.

FIRE SCREEN

FIRE WALL. A wall constructed of fire-retarding material which starts at the foundation and extends up to and above the roof of a building, completely dividing it; designed to hinder the spread of fire.

FIREBACKS. Metal liners or screens, often quite decorative, which were placed behind a fire in a fireplace. They served to reflect the heat back into the room and also to protect the masonry. These pieces, which were popular in the 17th and 18th centuries, were usually made of cast iron.

FIREBACKS

FIRECLAY. A clay, resistant to heat, which is used to make firebricks for lining fireplaces.

FIRESIDE CHAIR. An upholstered chair, usually skirted, with a high roll-over back which flares out as it rises up. The arms sweep away from the chair back and scroll around. The pillow seat is often T-shaped. A 20th-century design. Illustrated is a Jacobean prototype.

FIRESIDE CHAIR

FIRESIDE FIGURES. Fire screens made of wood and/or canvas, representing contemporary figures in just under life size. Often these figures were female and dressed in exotic, oriental-type costumes. The fireside figures were also called "picture board dummies" and were popular in the late 17th century.

FIRING. The heating of clay in a kiln to harden it. A term used in pottery making.

FIRST PLANTAGENET PERIOD. See *Early English Period.* Illustrated is the 13th-century Lichfield Cathedral (west front).

FIRST POINTED PERIOD. See *Early English Period.*

FIRST PLANTAGENET PERIOD

FISH TAIL. A carved detail which resembles a fish's tail which sometimes appeared on the top rail of spindled or banister-back chairs of 18th- and 19th-century American design.

FITMENTS

FITMENTS. An English expression for units (bookcases, cabinets, etc.) designed and built to fit the walls of a room. Illustrated is a mid-19th-century chimneypiece with built-in bookcases, cabinets, etc. The doors are perforated brass; the units are carved walnut with colored marble decorations.

FITTINGS. Metal hardware, mounts, escutcheons, etc.

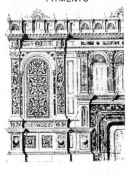

FITTINGS

FLACHBILDWERK

FLAG

FLACHBILDWERK. German for low or bas-relief work.

FLAG. A long grass which is twisted and woven into provincial-type seats. See *Rush*.

FLAGSTONE. Large, flat stones, square or irregular in shape, which are used as flooring or pavement material. Slate is often used for flagstone floors.

FLAKED. A wood figure or grain of oak which has been quarter-cut. Horizontal highlights streak across the grain of the wood. A breaking or loosening of the flake is called "broken flake."

FLAMBEAU. A flame or flaming torch used as a decorative motif. Popular in the 18th and early 19th centuries in England and France.

FLAMBEAU

FLAMBEAU

FLAMBOYANT

FLAMBOYANT. French for "flaming." The late Gothic style in French architecture (14th and 15th centuries). The window tracery was designed in conventionalized flamelike forms, reversed curved lines. See *Tracery*.

FLAME CARVING. A finial carved in a swirling, spiral effect to simulate a flame. It was used to decorate urns in the late 17th and early 18th centuries.

FLAMMENSTIL. German for "flamboyant style."

FLAME CARVING

FLÂNEUSE. From the French "flâner" which means "to lounge." A garden-type lounge chair with a footrest, it is similar to the current deck chair. The flâneuse usually had a caned seat, back, and footrest.

FLANKERS. Service houses (dependencies) which were added on to either side of the Georgian houses built in America in the mid-18th century. They were sometimes joined directly to the main block, or connected by means of arcades. Kitchens, butler's quarters, and offices were often added as flankers.

FLAP TABLE

FLAP STRAPPING. See *Strapwork*.

FLAP TABLE. An early-17th-century table with a fixed center slab and two side flaps which can be lowered by folding back the legs which support them. These legs fold back under the central table surface. The flap table is a form of gateleg or eight-legged table. An American Jacobean thousand-leg table is illustrated.

FLARE

FLARE. An outward spread, as in a chair seat which is wider at the front than at the back. Illustrated is an early-19th-century Sheraton design.

FLARE HEADER. A brick which has one end burned to a darker color than the face of the brick.

FLASHING. A material used to cover and protect joints between the roof finish and chimneys, dormers, gable walls, etc. It is usually made of lead or zinc. See *Apron.*

FLAT. A dull, nonglossy paint finish.

FLAT-CUT VENEER. A combination straight-grain and heart-figure veneer produced by slicing half of a log directly through the center or heart.

FLAT ROOF. A roof with a pitch of 20° or less.

FLAT ROOF

FLATTED

FLATTED. A term used to describe painted furniture, such as was popular in the Louis XV and Louis XVI periods.

FLATTING AGENT. A substance added to varnishes, paints, and other coating materials to reduce the gloss on the dried painted surface.

FLAX. The fiber from the inner bark of the flax plant which is used in the manufacture of linen. It is more expensive than cotton, but it is more absorbent and has a crisper, firmer hand. Flax is generally more resistant to mildew.

FLÈCHE. A thin tapering spire rising from a roof. It is usually made of wood, and sometimes covered with lead, and placed at the crossing of the nave and transepts in French Gothic churches.

FLEMISH. Referring to Flanders, the old name for the area now covered by Belgium, Holland, and parts of northern France.

FLEMISH BOND. In masonry, an arrangement of brick in which the headers and stretchers are used alternately in the same course. In the next course the arrangement is alternated so that the header is centered over the stretchers below. A single Flemish bond is used for facing only. See *Double Stretcher Flemish Bond.*

FLEMISH

FLEMISH BOND

FLEMISH BOND

FLEMISH CHAIR

FLEMISH CHAIR

FLEMISH FOOT

FLEMISH CHAIR
AND FOOT

FLEMISH SCROLL

FLEMISH CHAIR. A high-backed chair, with or without arms. The splat was a panel of cane, upholstery, laths, or balusters surmounted with an elaborate carved cresting. The legs had straight backs with bold curves in front, and they were supported by scroll feet. The stretcher consisted of two concave curves joined by a convex curve in the center. It was made in late-17th-century England. See *Flemish Scroll.*

FLEMISH CROSS BOND. In masonry, alternating Flemish and stretcher courses, with the headers in vertical lines and the stretcher courses crossed. See *Bond* and *Flemish Bond.*

FLEMISH EAR. A late French Renaissance and baroque furniture foot. It is similar to the Flemish scroll foot, except the design (the S or C) is inverted. The Flemish ear appears on some furniture of the Louis XIV period. See *Flemish Foot* and *Flemish Scroll.*

FLEMISH FOOT. A scroll-like ending to an S or C curved leg. This particular foot was popular in 17th-century styles in Flanders, England, and France.

FLEMISH SCROLL. An S or C curved ornamental form in which a scroll is broken by an angle. It was used in Flemish Renaissance furniture and also in the English Carolean and William and Mary styles.

FLEMISH SPIRAL BOND. In masonry, Flemish courses laid out so that the headers break joint over each other and form diagonal bands on the face of the wall. See *Bond* and *Flemish Bond.*

FLEUR DE LIS or FLEUR DE LYS. A decorative, conventionalized iris flower which has symbolized royalty and the French Bourbon kings.

FLUER DE LIS

FLUERETTE

FLUERETTED TREILLAGE

FLEURETTE. French for "small flower." A small flower motif carved on Louis XVI furniture and accessories.

FLEURETTED TREILLAGE. Anglicized French for "beflowered trellis." The beflowered trellis or latticework was a popular decorative motif in carved and painted form in French and German rococo and Louis XV furniture and accessories. Illustrated is the back of a sofa designed by François Peyrotte.

FLEURON. A small, flower-like decoration set on the abacus on the Corinthian capital. It appears to spring from a small bud above the middle leaf in the capital. An Italian Renaissance example is illustrated.

FLIERS. In plan, rectangular steps in staircase construction.

FLIGHT. A series of steps uninterrupted by a landing.

FLINT AND STONE WORK. A form of exterior decoration in English Gothic architecture. Stone tracery or inscriptions were set in relief in a ground of black split flint. In some late-15th-century work, the stone was sunk in about a quarter inch, and sides of the grooves were filled in with a black mortar.

FLIP TOP TABLE. A contemporary expansion table with two leaves, one set on top of the other. When the top leaf is raised and set down even with the plane of the lower leaf, the surface is doubled in area. This construction device can be used on many periods and styles of furniture. See *Chess Table* illustration.

FLITCH. Any part of the log which is sliced into veneer.

FLOATING FURNITURE. Modern furniture which is hung or suspended from the walls. The case pieces do not have legs, and are usually bracketed off stiles or upright wall standards which are bolted onto the wall.

FLOCK. Finely powdered wool or other short clipped fibers which are glued onto paper, fabric, wood, etc., to provide an allover suede or velvet finish, or applied in a design to create a cut velvet effect. See *Flocking*.

FLOCK PAPER. A wallpaper which has a velvet-like or suede surface.

FLOCKING. A technique for applying flock. Originally, the finely powdered wool was scattered over the entire surface to be decorated, but the particles adhered only to the tacky surface, or that part of the surface which was treated with glue. The rest of the flock, which did not stick to the fabric, leather, canvas, or paper, was blown or brushed off. This technique was developed during the Middle Ages, and was first applied to paper during the 17th century. Paper subjected to this treatment was called "velvet paper." The design was painted, stenciled or printed on the paper with a slow drying adhesive or varnish. When powdered color was sprinkled on in place of flock, the paper was called a "counterfeit flock." In 1634, Jérôme Lanyer was granted a patent for flocking.

FLEURON

FLITCH

FLOORCLOTH

FLOREATED

FLOWER STAND   FLOWER STAND

FLUTING

FLOORCLOTH. An early-18th-century rug made of heavy linen or canvas which was heavily sized and coated and then painted or ornamented. It was similar to *Wachstuch-tapete.*

FLOOR PLAN. See *Plan.*

FLOREATED. A term used to describe Gothic tracery and ornaments, which used floral and leaf motifs in flowing, rhythmic lines.

FLORENTINE ARCH. A Renaissance architectural feature. A semicircular arch springing directly from a column, pier, or capital, and trimmed with an architrave. The outer arch or extrados is pointed, while the inner arch or intrados is semicircular. These arches are frequently used in a series. See *Arcade.*

FLOWER STAND. See *Jardinière.* A stand for holding a plant or pot of flowers. Adam designed flower stands with sloping legs, rams' heads, and garland enrichments. A Chippendale design is illustrated.

FLUE. The enclosed portion of a chimney stack which carries the smoke up and out.

FLUORESCENT LIGHTING. A lighting device consisting of a glass tube which is coated on its inner surface with a substance that glows when a gas-conducted current is induced in the presence of mercury.

FLUSH. Said of a surface which is even, or at the same level, with its adjoining surface.

FLUSH BEAD. A molding in which the sunk bead is flush or even with the surface adjacent to it.

FLUTING. Continuous parallel hollows or channels, usually cut perpendicularly, as in a column, pilaster shaft, or furniture leg. It is like narrow concave moldings used in parallel lines. Spiral fluting is sometimes used on columns and furniture supports. Short flutings are often used on friezes as a form of ornamentation.

FLY or FLIES. The space in the theatre, above and behind the proscenium, where scenery is stored.

FLY BRACKET. A bracket, similar to a fly rail, used to support a drop-leaf on a *Pembroke* or library table. The bracket sometimes had shaped or diagonally cut ends. See *Loper.*

FLY RAIL. The folding bracket support for the flap or drop leaf of a table.

FLYING BUTTRESS. A Gothic architectural element which is a half arch that runs from a building's wall to an exterior detached stone pier. The buttress is used to carry down the internal thrust of the vaulting and resist pressure from the vaulting above. See *Buttress*.

FOAM RUBBER. A rubber material made of latex, the sap of the rubber tree, which is whipped with air to create a light, porous rubber composition. The firmness of the foam rubber depends upon the air content. Foam rubber is used for mattresses, pillows, upholstery filling, etc.

FOLLY

FLYING BUTTRESS

FOAM RUBBER

FOILS

FOILS. The small arcs which make up Gothic tracery. The foils are separated by the cusps. See *Multifoil*.

FOLD OVER. A desk or table with a "desk leaf" which folds over the upper surface. It was used in the late 18th century in France and England, and particularly by Sheraton.

FOLDING FURNITURE. Collapsible furniture which can fold into a compact unit like a folding stool, folding chair, table, bed, etc. This principle was employed by the ancient Egyptians, Greeks, and Romans, and has continued in use and popularity up to our current bridge sets. In the mid- and late 18th century, Shearer, Hepplewhite, and Sheraton designed many folding and convertible pieces of furniture (i.e., library steps).

FOLDING TABLE. An early English Renaissance multilegged table. It often had from twelve to as many as twenty legs, and the entire table could be folded to about one-third of its full size. It was the forerunner of the gateleg table, and worked on the same principle of expansion. Illustrated is a later 17th-century example (Stuart or Restoration period).

FOLIAGE. In decoration or ornament, plant and leaf forms carved, painted, or otherwise decoratively interpreted. A carved 13th-century frieze (from Notre-Dame) is illustrated.

FOLIATION. See *Feathering*.

FOLLY. A pseudoclassic or Gothic ruin specially so built to create a view or a charming effect in a garden or park. This was popular in 18th-century France. The Chippendale frame shown illustrates the classic "folly" as a decorative carved design.

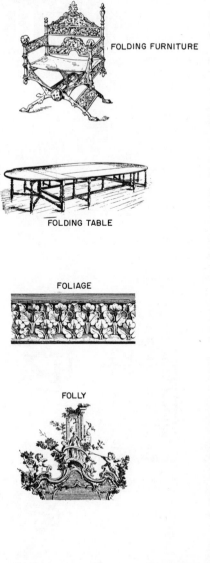

FOLDING FURNITURE

FOLDING TABLE

FOLIAGE

FOLLY

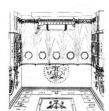

FONDEUR

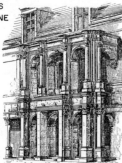

PIERRE FRANÇOIS
LÉONARD FONTAINE

FONDEUR. French for "metal caster." One who makes metal mounts, hardware, furniture embellishments, and accessories.

FONTAINE, PIERRE FRANÇOIS LÉONARD (1762–1853). A French architect-designer who, with *Charles Percier,* created the architectural and interior style known as the Empire for Napoleon at the start of the 19th century. Together they designed interiors and furniture for Malmaison, St.-Cloud, the Tuileries, and the Louvre. Their creed was: "simple lines, pure contours, correct shapes replacing . . . the curving and the irregular." See *Empire* and *Galerie d'Orléans.*

FONTAINEBLEAU. A French Renaissance château begun in the reign of François I in the early 16th century. The rooms that were created at this time had Italian Renaissance style paneling with classic order details and Vitruvian motifs. Raphael-type arabesques made of modeled plaster and fresco paintings were also used. Additions were made to the château, and variations in periods and styles of decoration are clearly discernible. The Renaissance peristyle of the château is illustrated.

FONTAINEBLEAU

FOOTBOARD. A supporting wooden piece at the lower end of the bed which connects with the two side rails. It can be an important decorative feature, carved and ornamented, or simply a horizontal rail, depending upon the style or period of the bed. In the contemporary Hollywood bed, the footboard is completely omitted.

FOOTRAIL

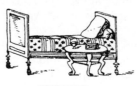

FOOTBOARD

FOOTSTOOL

FORGED

FORGED

FOOTRAIL. The lower supporting stretcher between two legs of a chair or table. An early-18th-century English chair is used to illustrate the footrail.

FOOTSTOOL. Originally an accompanying step for high throne seats and currently used as a stool or bench. A small, low hassock.

FORGED. A term applied to metals which have been heated and then hammered or beaten into a shape.

FORGED

FORM. A long, backless bench or seat of the Jacobean period, often furnished with loose pillows.

FORMAL. Regular, symmetrical, traditional in effect. Usually describes an arrangement or placement of furniture or decoration which is stately and carefully balanced. Not haphazard or whimsical. Illustrated is a late-18th-century Sheraton elevation with a chinoiserie influence.

FORMERET. In Gothic vaulting, the rib which adjoins the wall in its entire expanse. A "half rib" which is also called a "wall rib."

FORTISAN. A trademark name for a strong regenerated cellulose yarn produced by the Celanese Corporation of America. The yarn is often combined with silk, cotton, or linen to make sheer fabrics which are used for curtains. Fortisan fabrics are strong, drapable, and not much affected by changes in humidity.

FORTREL. A polyester fiber produced by Fiber Industries, Inc. It has properties similar to Dupont's Dacron: wrinkle resistance, quick drying, and good wash-and-wear performance. The trademark Fortrel may be used on those fabrics which use the polyester and meet the performance standards set by Fiber Industries.

FORTY, JEAN FRANÇOIS. An 18th-century French designer, engraver, and metal carver. He published eight volumes on design, and created some of the most beautiful metal accessories and furniture mounts of the Louis XVI period.

FORTY WINK CHAIR. See *Wing Chair.*

FORUM. The general assembling area in a Roman city, similar to the agora of a Greek city.

FOUNDATION. The base on which the walls of a structure rest. It may be made of stone, brick, or concrete.

FOUNDATION WALL. The part of a load-bearing wall below the level of the adjacent grade, or below the level of the first floor beams or joists.

FOUNTAIN. Usually a decorative, sculptured or carved unit made of marble, stone, bronze, concrete, etc., which pumps water up and out in a spouting or cascading manner. The fountain may be in a street, square, park, or garden, inside a courtyard, or in the interior of a public building or a home. It may be set in a pool area or have a small basin which catches the water. Many home-type fountains are today worked electrically with a recirculating pump arrangement. A French Renaissance fountain is illustrated.

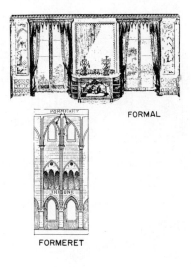

FORMAL

FORMERET

FOUNTAIN

FOUR-POSTER BEDSTEAD

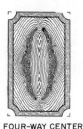

FOUR-WAY CENTER
AND BUTT MATCH

FOUR-POSTER BEDSTEAD

FOUR-POSTER BEDSTEAD. A bed with two posts in front and two in the back, or posts rising from carved or paneled foot and head boards. It sometimes was made to support a tester and drapery, or a fabric canopy. Designs vary with the changing periods and styles.

FOUR-WAY CENTER AND BUTT MATCH. A veneer like the *Diamond Match Veneer,* usually using butt, crotch, or stump veneers. This technique brings out the full interest of the graining.

FOYER. An intermediate area between the entrance and a main room of a home, apartment, or public building.

FRACTUR (or fraktur) PAINTING. Decorative birth and marriage certificates of the 18th- and 19th-century Pennsylvania Dutch.

FRAGONARD, JEAN-HONORÉ (1732–1806). A French painter and designer of the Louis XV and Louis XVI periods. He decorated many dainty boudoirs with murals and other wall decorations. Among his charming paintings are "The Swing" and "Progress of Love," which was originally created for Mme Du Barry's home. (She rejected the painting.)

FRAILERO. A Spanish Renaissance monk's chair, usually made of walnut, with plain legs and a broad front stretcher. Decorative nailheads secured the leather seat to the two side rails and the back panel between the two uprights. These were usually capped with finials. The arms were wide and simple. The frailero was probably the most typical chair of the Spanish Renaissance. See *Mission.*

FRAME. The skeleton or basic structure of a piece of furniture which will later be filled in with webbing, stuffing, muslin, upholstery, etc. The unfinished, raw basic wood framework. Illustrated is the frame of a Louis XV type of wing chair. See *Carcase or Carcass.*

FRAME

FRAME. A surrounding case or structure for the protection and enhancement of drawings, paintings, mirrors, etc. It can be carved of wood, trimmed with moldings, or embellished with gesso composition.

FRAME

FRANÇOIS I

FRANÇOIS I (1494–1547). King of France from 1515 in the early French Renaissance period. He was a great patron of the building arts and the châteaux at Chambord, Blois, and Fontainebleau were built during his reign. In his time, the flamboyant Gothic motifs were combined with the advancing Italian Renaissance style.

FRANKLIN STOVE. Originally called a "Pennsylvania stove." A combination stove and fireplace invented by Benjamin Franklin in the mid-18th century. It burned wood that was set on andirons, and it had a decorative front. Illustrated is an "improved" 19th-century version, the open-grate coal stove.

FREE FORM. An irregular, flowing abstract shape as used in modern cocktail tabletops, accent area rugs, wall decorations, etc. Free forms may also be used in plantings, gardens, etc.

FREESTANDING COLUMN. A column with clear or open space all around it. In Sheraton sofas and settees it was usually a vase-shaped extension of the front corner legs. A Sheraton type Regency chair is illustrated.

FRANKLIN STOVE

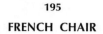

FREESTANDING COLUMN

FREESTANDING POLES. Metal or wood poles with sleeve connections to make them larger or smaller. The basic principle of the pole is the use of the pressure of the adjustable sleeve insert set in the bottom of the pole and resting on the floor, and the one set on top with its disk pressing up against the ceiling. The pole remains erect because pressure is exerted up against the ceiling and down against the floor. Modern designer George Nelson's "Omni" system is based on the use of these poles. The poles are also used for pole lights, traveling display units, etc.

FREESTONE. A stone which can be easily dressed or finished with a chisel.

FRENCH BED. An early-19th-century Empire bed with high rolling S-scrolled head and foot boards. Elegant versions were made of rosewood, had carved legs (dolphin- or cornucopia-shaped), and were splendidly embellished with ormolu designs or medallions. See *Sleigh Bed*.

FRENCH BED

FRENCH BRACKET FOOT. A bracket foot with a concave curve down the mitred edge which gives the foot a splayed effect. It is almost always combined with a valanced skirt or apron. Both the inner and outer edges of the leg are curved, giving the appearance of a stunted cabriole leg. It is also called "French foot," and was popular in 18th-century English and American furniture.

FRENCH BURL. A Persian walnut wood with an interesting curly grain favored for inserts in cabinetwork.

FRENCH CHAIR. A general name for upholstered chairs used in England in the mid-18th century. It did not apply to a particular style or decoration but to the general type of rococo chair like the bergère. A Chippendale design is illustrated.

FRENCH BRACKET FOOT

FRENCH CHAIR

FRENCH DIRECTOIRE

FRENCH DIRECTOIRE

FRENCH
EARLY RENAISSANCE

FRENCH
LATE RENAISSANCE

FRENCH LEG

FRENCH MIDDLE RENAISSANCE

FRENCH DIRECTOIRE. The period in France from 1789 to 1804. It followed the Louis XVI period and was a transitional style leading into the French Empire style. It was essentially a continuation of the classic tradition of the Louis XVI style with the addition of Revolutionary motifs: symbols of liberty, triumphal arches, liberty caps, spirit levels, pikes, oak boughs, clasped hands. Egyptian motifs were also introduced as well as martial Roman elements like spearheads, drums serving as stools, etc. The Directoire was the transition from the Greek styles of Louis XVI to the Egyptian and Roman qualities of the Empire.

FRENCH EARLY RENAISSANCE. The period from approximately 1484 to 1547, covering the reigns of Charles VIII, Louis XII, and François I. It was a transitional period which blended outgoing Gothic structural forms with the incoming Italian Renaissance architectural details and ornaments. For examples see *Château de Chambord, Château de Gaillon, François I,* and *Viart, Charles.*

FRENCH FOOT. See *French Bracket Foot.*

FRENCH HEADING. The gathering of a drapery or valance into regularly spaced folds. The folds are usually stitched in place to give a more set appearance.

FRENCH LATE RENAISSANCE. The period from approximately 1589 to 1643, covering the reigns of Henri IV and Louis XIII. The Italian Renaissance continued to dominate the architecture and decorations of the period, along with Dutch and Flemish influences. In the interiors, wall paneling became a more important wall finish, and "formality" appeared to be the keynote.

FRENCH LEG. A scrolled leg, often carved and ornamented, which was used in 17th- and early-18th-century furniture designs.

FRENCH MIDDLE RENAISSANCE. The reigns of Henri II, François II, Charles IX, and Henri III, covering the years 1547 to 1589. Catherine de Medici dominated the period, and local variations were added to the dominant use of Italian ornament and Renaissance architectural details. The Gothic forms were gradually eliminated. Illustrated is a walnut dresser of the period.

FRENCH POLISH. A high, glossy finish on wood which is obtained by adding several layers of shellac to the wood surface.

FRENCH PROVINCIAL. The term is usually associated with simplified furniture of the Louis XV or rococo style. However, plain, simple furniture was made in the provinces in all times and styles, and usually of walnut, oak, or fruitwood. Provincial furniture is simpler in line than the prevailing high fashion and rarely veneered or decorated with marquetry or ornate carving.

FRENCH PROVINCIAL

FRENCH RÉGENCE or REGENCY. The transitional period (1700 to 1730) between the grandiose formality of the Louis XIV baroque period and the frivolous, asymetrical quality of the Louis XV rococo period. Philippe, Duc d'Orléans, was Regent of France. Flat curved paneling was used for ornament with curves at the corners. Foliage and ribbon ornament was used for embellishment, and curved or cabriole legs began to replace the straight ones. Slight curves, like a crossbow, appeared on the upper parts of cabinets and bookcases. The bombé commode made its appearance at this time, and ebony was replaced as the favored wood by polished walnut, mahogany, and rosewood veneers. Illustrated is a great clock of the period made of bois de rose and bois de violette marquetry with bronze doré trim.

FRENCH REGENCE

FRENCH RESTORATION PERIOD (1830–1870). The French monarchy was restored, and the period included the reigns of Louis XVIII, Charles X, Louis-Philippe, and Napoleon III. Eclectic designs, cheaper machine production, and a general decline in taste marked this "Second Empire" period. See *Second Empire* or *Late Empire*.

FRENCH RESTORATION PERIOD

FRENCH WHORL FOOT. A furniture foot that swirled or curled forward and often rested on a shoe. It most often appeared as the termination of a cabriole leg in the Régence and Louis XV periods.

FRENCH WINDOWS. A pair of multipaned doorlike windows which extend down to the floor, and, like hinged doors, are used for access to, or egress from, a room. They usually lead out onto a terrace, a balcony or other platform; or into a garden. A Louis XV interior with French windows is illustrated.

FRENCH WINDOWS

FRESCO. The Italian for "fresh." A wall painting in a watercolor-like medium (tempera) on wet plaster. The cartoon (full-sized sketch) is applied to the plaster surface. The damp plaster is painted with pigments mixed with water or lime water. The color dries lighter and becomes integrated into the wall or ceiling itself. Frescos were made in Italy in the 14th century, and perfected in the 16th century. Raphael's decoration in the Stanza of the Vatican is a fine fresco. Illustrated is the ceiling fresco by Raphael in the Farnesina in Rome.

FRESCO

FRETWORK

FRIESIAN

◄─FRIEZE

FRIEZE DRAWER

FRESQUERA. A Spanish latticework or spindle decorated hanging food cupboard. The openwork on part of the cupboard door was for ventilation.

FRET. A border motif or geometric band of Greek origin. It is made up of interlacing and interlocking lines and forms. It is also called "Chinese key" pattern or "meander."

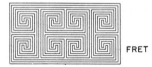

FRET

FRETWORK. Ornamental woodwork cut to represent small interlacing fillets or trellis work. It is usually made in a complicated, repeating, geometric pattern. A favored technique of Chippendale in his Chinese period (mid-18th century).

FRETWORK MIRROR. See *Silhouette Mirror*.

FRIAR'S CHAIR. See *Frailero*.

FRIESIAN. Name of a simple technique for carving with a chisel, usually used to create basic geometric forms. A popular technique in Colonial American woodwork. Also called "Frisian."

FRIESLAND. A province in the Netherlands noted for its carved furniture in the baroque style in the 17th century.

FRIEZE. In architecture, the central portion of the classic architectural entablature. It is located above the architrave and below the cornice. It usually has a flat surface which is embellished with decorative sculpture or carving. A frieze is also a painted or sculptured horizontal motif. Illustrated is the frieze and Corinthian order of the monument of Lysicrates at Athens. In furniture, the underframing of a table between the top surface and the legs. See *Apron*.

FRIEZÉ or FRISÉ. A pile fabric with uncut loops which is sometimes patterned by shearing the loops at different levels. It is usually made of wool, mohair, or heavy cotton. The term is from the French "frisé," which means curled, and the fabric was originally made in Friesland, Holland. In carpet manufacture, the name of rugs made of "hard twist," heavy, brushed wool yarns.

FRIEZE DRAWER. The top drawer of a chest which extends forward over the main body of the chest. It is usually supported by columns or pilasters. An Empire or Biedermeier early-19th-century (illustrated) design.

FUMED OAK

FRIEZE RAIL

FRIEZE RAIL. In a door made up of three horizontal rows of panels, the horizontal rail between the middle and top set of panels. Illustrated is a doorway designed by Inigo Jones (early 17th century). See also *Picture Molding or Rail.*

FRINGE. An ornamental edging used to finish or trim drapery, upholstery, etc. A continuous band or ribbon with hanging twisted threads, loops, and tassels. It may be cut, looped, tassel, or bullion fringe.

FRINGE

FRISÉ. See *Friezé or Frisé.*

FRISIAN. See *Friesian.*

FRITHSTOOL. In Gothic churches, a seat or chair carved of stone and set near the altar. It was the last and most sacred refuge for persons who sought the sanctuary of the church. "The seat of peace."

FROG. The rectangular recess on the front and back stretchers of a brick, which cuts down the weight of the brick and supplies a bed for the mortar.

FRONT. The front surface of a piece of furniture. The front may be a flat rectangle, or consist of several planes, bombé or bulging, serpentine, block or breakfront.

FRONTAL. See *Antependium.*

FRUCHTGEHÄNGE. German for a "painted or sculptured festoon of fruit."

FRUIT FESTOON. Garland of fruit, leaves, and flowers, tied with ribbons and usually draped between two rosettes to form a downward curve. It was a popular Roman motif and was greatly revived in the Renaissance periods.

FRUIT FESTOON

FRUITWOOD. Wood from fruit-bearing trees like cherry, apple, pear, etc., largely used in provincial-type furniture. It was an 18th-century favorite which is having a renaissance currently in provincial and country-style tables, chairs, commodes, chests, etc.

FRUITWOOD FINISH. A light, honey-brown finish applied to soft woods to simulate a fruitwood. The natural grain of the wood shows through this finish. The wood is often "distressed" to make it appear more "provincial" or antique.

FUMED OAK

FUMED OAK. A furniture finish of the late 19th and early 20th centuries. The oak wood was stained by ammonia fumes, and the graining became more pronounced and deeper in color. Much of the mission-style furniture was produced in fumed oak as well as late English Victorian pieces.

FUMEUSE. A smoking chair. An 18th-century variation on the voyeuse. The broad crest rail on the narrow, shaped back of the chair often had compartments to hold tobacco, pipes, flints, etc., and the person straddled the chair, facing the chair back and the equipped rail. See *Cockfight Chair.*

FUNCTIONAL FURNITURE. Utilitarian, practical furniture in which the function or use is most important, and the aesthetics is secondary.

FUR. The pelts or hairy skins of animals used for furniture and/or floor coverings.

FURRING. A method of finishing the inside of a masonry wall by either applying plaster directly to clay tiles or attaching metal or wood strips to a lathed wall. The purpose is to provide an air space for insulation, or to level the irregularities in the wall surface. It also serves to prevent the transmittance of moisture.

FUSTIAN. A sturdy cotton fabric with a suede or velvet-like pile. It is a twill weave fabric.

FUSTIC. A light yellow wood from the West Indies. In the 17th and 18th centuries it was used for marquetry and inlay work.

GABARDINE. A hard finished twill fabric with a steep diagonal effect to the twill. It can be produced of wool, cotton, rayon, or mixed fibers. The term is from the Spanish for "protection against the elements."

GABLE. The triangular space of wall enclosed at the end of a building by a sharply pitched roof.

GABLE

GABLET. A small, ornamental gable placed over a portal, buttress, tabernacle, etc.

GABOON. A soft, straight-grained wood, golden to pinkish brown in color. It is used in Europe for plywood, as well as for furniture and interior work. Gaboon is light in weight and fairly strong. It is native to the African west coast. See *Samara.*

GABRIEL, JACQUES-ANGE DE (1698–1782). French architect who became chief architect to Louis XV in 1742. He is noted for his designs for the Place de la Concorde, the Colonnades of the Rue Royale, the rebuilt central Pavillion at Versailles, and the Petit Trianon, the last-named characterized by the incoming neoclassic style. Gabriel was also responsible for the restoration of the Louvre.

GABLET

G

GADROON. From the French "godron." A series of elongated egg or ovoid forms in a parallel series or band. It is similar to a bead molding in that it projects above the surface it ornaments. When this type of decoration is used around a circular object, the oval form of ornament is called "splayed gadroon." See *Nulling*.

GADROON

GAINE. A square post or pedestal which narrows and tapers toward the bottom. The gaine may be supported by human or animal feet. It is used as a decorative support or ornament, and is often topped with a head or bust. Illustrated is a Sheraton bookcase design of the early 19th century in the Regency style. Note the use of gaines for free columns to support the frieze, and on the front ends of the base.

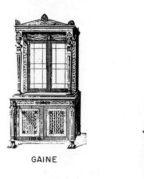

GAINE

GAINE

GALERIE DES GLACES. French for "Hall of Mirrors."

GALERIE DES MACHINES. The major exhibit hall of the Paris Exhibition of 1889. It was the climax of Eiffel's exhibit area construction. It was constructed by Contamin, and the architect was Ferdinand-Charles-Louis Dutert, and it was the largest-dimensioned gallery to that date. The skeleton consisted of twenty trusses 420 meters long, and it was enclosed by huge glass walls. The glass seemed to take in the outside and let out the inside. The girders were light, and this hall made the first major use of a steel framework.

GALERIE D'ORLÉANS. A part of the Palais Royale in Paris designed by Pierre Fontaine and built between 1829 and 1831. It was noteworthy in that wrought iron was used to construct the great glass roof.

GALLERIES

GALLERIES. The metal rods and supports at the back of sideboards of the late 18th century in England. They are also the raised metal or carved rims around tabletops or servers.

GALLERY. In architecture, a wide corridor walled in on one side only, and usually located on the upper story. The upper story of seats in a public hall or auditorium. The balcony of a theatre. In furniture, the miniature metal or wood railing along the edge of a shelf or tabletop, as in gallery-top tables.

GALLERY

GALLETING. See *Garreting*.

GALLOON or GALON. A narrow, closely woven braid used for trimming draperies and upholstery. It was frequently used in the early 18th century to finish off rough upholstery work. A lace or embroidered band with a scalloped edge on two sides is also called a galloon. See *Guimpe*.

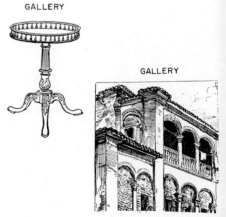

GALLERY

GAMBREL ROOF

GARDE DU VIN

GARDE-ROBE

GALVANIZED IRON. A zinc-coated iron. The coating process makes the iron rust-resistant.

GAMBREL ROOF. A double-sloped, gable-type roof with the lower slope much steeper than the upper one. A hipped roof with double slope is called a mansard roof. Illustrated is the White House Tavern in Newport, Rhode Island, built in 1673.

GAME TABLE

GAME TABLES. Tables devised for particular card games, chess, etc. It is also called a card table, or by the specific name of the game to be played like "bridge table." A Sheraton chess table is illustrated.

GARDE DU VIN. A Hepplewhite term for a "cellarette." See *Cellarette.*

GARDE-MANGER. A french term for a food cupboard; a larder or cupboard.

GARDEN APARTMENT. A multiple dwelling which is usually two stories high, and is set in a landscaped area in a suburban residential area.

GARDEN SEAT. An oriental or Chinese outdoor seat made in the shape of a small keg, barrel, or drum. Originally these pieces were carved of stone, and then they were produced in porcelain. Still later they were made with a lattice-like wooden center part but with a solid top and bottom.

GARDEN WALL BOND. In masonry, three stretchers alternate with a header in each course. In the next course up, the header falls in the center on the middle stretcher. It has longitudinal strength and sufficient transverse bonding, owing to the symmetrical placing of the headers. The bond may also be made with two stretchers (double stretcher garden wall bond) or with four or five stretchers.

GARDEN WALL CROSS BOND. In masonry, "garden wall" courses alternated with stretcher courses crossed. See *Bond* and *Garden Wall Bond.*

GARDE-ROBE. In furniture, a wardrobe or armoire. In architecture, a privy in a medieval castle. Illustrated is a 16th-century Flemish armoire or garde-robe.

GARGOYLE. In Gothic architecture, a rainspout which often was decoratively carved as a fantastic human or animal head, and ornamentally placed along the top of a parapet or roof. The term is from the Old French for "throat."

GARLAND. A wreath or circlet of leaves, flowers, and/or fruit with ribbon ties. It is used as a carved or painted decoration on furniture and in architecture. See *Garnier, Charles,* for illustration.

GARNIER, CHARLES. A 19th-century French architect who designed the Paris Opera House in 1867, and also the Casino at Monte Carlo. Illustrated is a carved panel from the attic story of the Opera House.

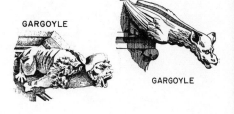

GARGOYLE

GARGOYLE

CHARLES GARNIER

GARNITURE. Any motif used for enriching a surface or area. The embellishing or decorating may be painted, carved, inlaid, applied, etc.

GARRETING. A surface finish of small stones or pebbles pressed into a mortar joint while it is still soft.

GARRETT. From the Old French for "place of refuge" or "lookout." A room constructed in the roof of a building. An attic.

GATCH. An oriental term for decorative elements made in molded plaster. See *Anaglypta* and *Carton-Pierre.*

GATELEG TABLE. A drop-leaf table with oval or rounded ends. The leaves are supported by single or double wing legs or gates. It was introduced in mid-17th-century Jacobean furniture and was popular in Colonial America. See *Eight-Legged Table, Folding Table,* and *Thousand-Leg Table.*

GAUDÍ i CORNET, ANTONIO (1852–1926). A noted Spanish architect who created unique architectural forms in keeping with the "Art-Nouveau" or "modernismo" style of the times. In some of his sculpture-type architecture he introduced color and odd bits of materials which achieved effects similar to abstract expressionism and surrealism. Gaudí was a spirited innovator, and favored the hyperbolic paraboloid form. The Expiatory Church of the Holy Family (1882–1930) represents the culmination of his techniques and ideals. Other works by Gaudí are: structures in the Park Güel, the undulating façades of the Casa Battló, and the Casa Milá.

GARNITURE

GATELEG TABLE

GAUGED ARCH

GAZEBO

GENOA VELVET

GEOMETRIC DESIGN

GEORGIAN

GAUDREAUX. An 18th-century French furniture maker in the Louis XV style. His pieces were often designed by the Slodtz brothers, and lavishly embellished with gilt bronze trim. Oval medallions with gilt bronze bas-reliefs on blue enamel grounds were sometimes used for ornamenting Gaudreaux's furniture.

GAUGE. The thickness of a material.

GAUGED ARCH. An arch composed of masonry or brick of definite sizes and shapes.

GAUZE. Thin, transparent fabrics made of a netlike or plain weave, or combination of the two. It was originated in Gaza, Palestine. Gauze can be made of silk, cotton, linen, wool, synthetic fibers, or combinations of the above. It is often used for *Glass Curtains*.

GAUZE, THEATRICAL. A semitransparent loosely woven cotton or linen fabric with a shimmering appearance.

GAZEBO. The turret on the roof of a lattice-constructed garden house. Usually the name is applied to the entire structure. An ornamental, open summerhouse.

GELÄNDER. German for "baluster."

GELOSIA. Italian for "Venetian blind." See *Jalousies.*

GENOA VELVET. A multicolored patterned velvet on a satin ground.

GEODESIC DOMES. 20th-century modern skeleton domes based on the octahedron-tetrahedron figure designed by Richard Buckminster Fuller. He has used these domes as an economic solution to mass housing problems.

GEOMETRIC DESIGNS. Designs or ornaments based on the repeated use of mechanically drawn forms like circles, squares, and triangles.

GEORGIAN. The period of the reigns of the Georges in England (1714 to the Regency, approximately 1811). The golden period of furniture design and architecture: Adam brothers, Chippendale, Shearer, Hepplewhite, Sheraton, etc. An early Georgian chair of the first part of the 18th century is illustrated. It has the typical pierced urn splat, cabriole legs with shell carvings on the knees, and ball-and-claw feet. Usually broken down into three separate periods: Early Georgian, 1714–1750; Middle Georgian, 1750–1770; and Late Georgian, 1770–1810.

GERMAN SILVER. An alloy of copper, nickel, and zinc.

GESSO. A dense and brilliant white ground with a high degree of absorbency (gypsum or chalk). It is used as a ground for tempera painting. The panels to be painted are treated with several coats of gesso and size. Also, a plaster-like composition which is molded to form a raised or bas-relief applied ornament on walls, furniture, frames, moldings, etc. This ornament is often painted and gilded. See *Anaglypta, Carton-Pierre,* and *Composition Ornament.*

GESSO

GETÄFEL EINES FUSSBODENS. German for "parquet flooring."

GETÄFELTE WANDBEKLEIDUNG. German for "wall paneling."

GEWÖLBE. German for "arch" or "vault."

GEWÖLBESTUTZ. German for "flying buttress."

GEWIRKTER TEPPICH or TAPETE. German for "tapestry" or "arras."

GHIBERTI, LORENZO (1378–1455). An Italian goldsmith and sculptor who is probably best known for the bronze doors of the Baptistry in Florence. The doors consist of twenty-eight high reliefs (the figures are in gilt against a neutral background) enclosed in Gothic frames. The subject matter was based on parts of the New Testament. He later (1423) made another set of doors with ten scenes from the Old Testament, which were much finer in handling and draftsmanship. Michelangelo called these later doors "the doors to paradise."

GIANT ORDER. Columns or pilasters which are two or more stories high. Michelangelo and other baroque architects used this design.

GIBBONS, GRINLING (1648–1721). An English master woodcarver and sculptor. He worked in close association with Sir Christopher Wren, the noted architect, and he created many famous carved trophy panels and mantels. Gibbons did much of the sculptured embellishment for the choir in St. Paul's Cathedral, as well as the dimensional foliage and festoons of the stalls. He worked mainly in limewoods, used oak for church panels and moldings, and occasionally cedar for architraves. Medallion portraits were sometimes carved of pearwood or boxwood. Gibbons sculptured realistically in high relief, with deep undercuts, and his motifs included fruit, vegetables, game, fish, leaves, and flowers created into swags, festoons, draperies, and frames.

GRINLING GIBBONS

JAMES GIBBS

JAMES GIBBS

GILDED FURNITURE

GILDING

GIBBS, JAMES (1683–1754). An English architect and furniture designer in the tradition of Sir Christopher Wren. He created, in the first part of the 18th century, many interior architectural features such as mantels as well as furniture. Gibbs is probably most known for St. Martin's-in-the-Fields in London (1721–1726), which is here illustrated. The portico is Greek in feeling, while the steeple is in the style of Wren.

GIGANTOMACHIA. A classic sculptured group, showing a combat between gods and giants.

GIGLIO. An Italian word for a decorative element similar to a fleur de lis. It is usually associated with Florence, Italy.

GIGLIO

GILDED or GILT FURNITURE. Furniture finished by gilding, an early-17th-century finish which was adopted in England during the early Queen Anne period and also in France. William Kent was a leading designer of English gilt furniture. Illustrated is a Louis XV carved gilt console table. See *Gilding*.

GILDED LEATHER. A popular treatment for leather tapestries from the 16th through the 18th centuries. The leather was sized, then covered with gold or silver leaf. Areas of the leather were then colored in lacquer. Sometimes the surface was tooled or embossed with chisels or patterned punches called "irons." Tiny roses, rosettes, squares, circles, arabesques, and heraldic motifs were popular designs. The Dutch, during the 17th century, often used colored grounds, and bronzed or gilded fruits and cherubs in bold relief. The English favored chinoiserie motifs. See *Cordovan Leather, Guadamicil,* and *Moroccan (Maroquin) Tapestries.*

GILDING. The art of ornamenting furniture, accessories, and architectural details with gold leaf or gold dust. Illustrated is a mid-18th-century gilded frame (English).

GILLINGHAM, JAMES. A Philadelphia cabinetmaker of the mid-18th century.

GILLOT, CLAUDE (1673–1722). A French painter and designer of fauns, satyrs, and grotesques during the period of Louis XIV. He was the master (teacher) of Watteau.

CLAUDE GILLOT

GILLOW, RICHARD and ROBERT. Furniture makers in the first half of the 18th century in England. Much of the furniture and cabinetwork produced by the Gillows was exported to the West Indies.

GIMP or GUIMPE. Originally a woven silk braid of assorted designs. A binding material used on the outer edges of upholstered furniture to cover fabric joins or upholstery tacks, or as an enrichment. Gimp is also used as a trim on draperies, bedspreads, etc.

GINGHAM. A lightweight, yarn-dyed, cotton material woven in checks or stripes.

GIOCONDO, FRA (1435–1515). A Renaissance architect of Verona who is noted for his Palazzo del Consiglio (1476) which is here illustrated. The arcade façade is modeled after the Hospital of the Innocents in Florence. Most noteworthy is the colored sgraffito work on the façade. See *Sgraffito*.

GIORGIONE (Giorgio da Castelfranco) (c. 1478–1510). Considered the first Venetian Renaissance painter, he was a student of Bellini. Giorgione greatly influenced the work of Titian, and some of his unfinished works were actually completed by Titian. His paintings were both secular and ecclesiastic in subject matter. Among his surviving works are: "Laura," "Tempest" (a moody landscape), and the "Castelfranco Madonna."

GIOTTO DI BONDONE (c. 1270–1337). A Florentine painter who broke with the stereotyped forms of Italo-Byzantine art. He brought humanism into his work, as well as a degree of naturalism. Giotto is also known as an architect. His "Bell Tower" (see *Campanile* for illustration) is particularly well known. He greatly influenced not only his contemporaries (the Giotteschi school of painting) but also Masaccio and Michelangelo.

GIRANDOLE. A multibranched wall sconce to hold candles, which is often mirrored. A late-17th- and 18th-century accessory and lighting device. When lit, it seemed to have the sparkle and shimmer of fireworks. In the 19th century, the term described a circular mirror, often convex, with or without a candle sconce. In American designs, the mirror was often capped with an eagle. In the mid-19th century, a girandole was a Bohemian glass, prism-hung candlestick, often used in pairs on mantels. See *Applique* and *Bull's-Eye Mirror*. It also refers to any branched candlestick.

FRA GIOCONDO

GIOTTO DI BONDONE

GIRANDOLE

GIRARDON, FRANÇOIS

GIRDER

GLASTONBURY CHAIR

GLASTONBURY CHAIR

GLAZED DOOR

GLAZING BAR

GIRARDON, FRANÇOIS (1628-1715). A French sculptor whose work was used to enhance the Louvre, Grand Trianon, and Versailles. Illustrated is a war trophy by Girardon, now in the park at Versailles.

FRANÇOIS GIRANDON

GIRDER. A heavy beam used over wide spans, and supporting small beams or concentrated weights. Illustrated is a late-19th-century interior showing iron girders and columns which were designed to support a vaulted ceiling.

GLASS BRICK. A hollow block, composed of two halves of molded soda-lime glass. The pieces are sealed together with a vacuum between, and can then be mortared together into wall units.

GLASS CURTAINS. Curtains made of sheer, semitransparent fabrics which hang against a windowpane or glass surface. They may be used with blinds or shades, or be overhung with draperies.

GLASTONBURY CHAIR. A 16th-century ecclesiastic chair with X-shaped legs and sloping arms and back.

GLAZE. In pottery, a thin coating of glass fired on pottery to give it a glossy appearance. A glaze may also be employed to color the pottery.

GLAZED CHINTZ. A chintz or plain colored fabric which is glazed or given a crisp feel and a sheen, by means of calendering or by being paraffin-treated. See *Calendering.*

GLAZED DOOR. A door made up of panes of glass framed in wood molding strips. It is similar to a French door. In furniture, cabinet, secretary, bookcase, etc., doors which are made of glass panes held together in a decorative framework of wood strips. A Chippendale mahogany bookcase is shown.

GLAZING. In fabrics, a method of giving a smooth, high-polished finish to fabrics like chintz or tarletan. The fabrics can be treated with starch, glue, shellac, or parafin, and then run between hot friction rollers. The finish will not withstand washings unless synthetic resin or something similar is baked in at high temperatures.

GLAZING BARS. The wood or metal strips which form the framework around individual panes of glass in a window.

GLOBE STAND. A favored 18th-century accessory. It was usually a carved tripod made to hold a rotating globe of the world. Smaller stands were made to stand on tables or desks, and larger units were made to stand on the floor.

GOLD LEAF

GLOBE STAND

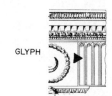

GLYPH

GLYPH. A shallow, vertical groove, cut into a flat or carved surface. A form of fluting. Glyphs are often found in classic Doric architecture. See *Triglyphs.*

GLYPTOTHECA. A Greek term for a room or building used to house or preserve sculpture.

GOBELINS. A tapestry factory started in Paris in the 16th century by a family of dyers named Gobelin. Louis XIV, in 1662, purchased the factory, and Charles Le Brun was made chief designer and director of the art-producing plant which now turned out textiles, metalwork, silverwork, wood carvings, frescoes, as well as tapestries. It was during this period that the Savonnerie rug factory was combined with the Gobelins. Among the famous artists and artisans who worked at the Manufacture Nationale des Gobelins are the following: Marc de Coomans, François Delaplanche, Laurent Guyot, Guillaume Dumée, Antoine Caron, Simon Vouet, Michel Corneille, Eustache Le Sueur, Nicolas Poussin, Philippe de Champaigne, Louis and Charles Le Brun, Antoine and Charles Coypel, Pierre Mignard, Jean-François de Troy, Louis de Boulogne, François Desportes, several members of the Audran family, and the Anguiers.

GOBELINS

GODDARD, JOHN (1724–1785). An American designer and cabinetmaker in Newport, Rhode Island. He produced, in association with his son-in-law John Townsend, a particular type of blockfront desk, secretary, and cabinet, usually with ogee bracket feet and shell ornaments. See *Blockfront.*

GODROON. See *Gadroon.*

GOING. The horizontal distance between one riser face and the next, in stairway construction.

JOHN GODDARD

GOLD LEAF. Also called mosaic gold or Dutch gold. Originally, it was made in Germany, and was an amalgam of tin and copper. The bright, shiny, thin sheet is laid over the surface which has been made tacky by a shellac, adhesive, or gold size. The sheet adheres to the sized surface. See *Gilding.*

GONDOLA BED

GOOSENECK

GOTHIC BOND

GOTHIC PERIOD

GOTHIC REVIVAL

GOLD PLATING. A process whereby particles of gold coat a baser metal unit. This is usually accomplished electrolitically.

GONCALO ALVES. Also called "bossona." A Brazilian wood with a decided black and brown streak on a red-brown ground. It is hard and horny and sometimes develops surface cracks.

GONDOLA BED. A 19th-century Empire-style bed with foot and head boards which appear to scroll or "roll over" like the ends of a gondola. Illustrated is a French Empire design. See *Boat Bed* and *Sleigh Bed*.

GONDOLA CHAIR. A low chair for a writing desk, or a sofa whose back curves downward to form the arms. The sweeping, curving line resembles an 18th-century gondola.

GOODISON, BENJAMIN. An 18th-century furniture maker to the English royalty from 1727 to 1767.

GOOSENECK. A double curved pediment popularly used in 18th-century English and American furniture. It is also referred to as "broken arch" or "swan neck."

GOOSENECK LAMP. A contemporary light fixture with a metal pipe shaft so constructed as to be flexible and bendable. It is possible to alter the direction of the beam of light by twisting the corrugated pipe right or left, up or down.

GOSTELOWE, JONATHAN (1744–1806). An American cabinet-maker who worked in Philadelphia, Pennsylvania, in the Chippendale style. He produced many fine mahogany pieces.

GOTHIC or POLISH BOND. In masonry, alternating stretchers and headers in the same course of masonry. This is a 19th-century reference to what is today called *Flemish Bond*.

GOTHIC PERIOD. The period from approximately 1150 to 1500 in Europe. It is the only European architectural style not based on classical forms, and it is an outstanding period of ecclesiastic architecture and art. This period was named by the Italians who preferred Greek and Roman architecture, and assumed that only German barbarians (the Goths) could admire such a style. The Gothic period is also referred to as the "Middle Ages."

GOTHIC REVIVAL. See *Romantic Epoch*. The renewed interest in Gothic architecture and art forms during the early 19th century in England and on the Continent. John Britton's *The Architectural Antiquities and Cathedrals of Britain* and Sir Walter Scott's novels helped foster this interest in the medieval period. Augustus Welby Pugin was the great architect and advocate of the Gothic revival in England. He erected 65

"Gothic-type" churches and decorated the interior and exterior of the Houses of Parliament, London, which was influential in popularizing this revival. Pugin was followed by Sir Gilbert Scott and Philip Hardwick, whose Hall of Lincoln's Inn is illustrated.

GOTICO. Italian for "Gothic."

GOUACHE. An opaque watercolor paint like poster paint. It dries much lighter than it appears when wet. Gouache is an art medium, as well as a technique for making studies for oil paintings. It was a popular painting technique in the 18th century. "Tempera" is the Italian term for gouache.

GOUJON, JEAN (1510–1566). A French architect and sculptor. He did reliefs in the Louvre, including some on the exterior and some figures, and the caryatids of the gallery "Salle des Caryatides." He created elongated, elegant figures, somewhat influenced by classic forms. Attributed to him is "Diana the Huntress," made for the courtyard of the Château of Diane de Poitiers. Illustrated is a bas-relief by Goujon for the Hôtel Carnavalet in Paris. See *Bas-Relief* for panels designed by Goujon for the Fountain of the Innocents in Paris.

JEAN GOUJON

GOUT CHAIR. An 18th-century chair devised for sufferers from the gout. The footstool could be pulled out from below the seat, so that the affected leg could rest on it in an extended, straight-out position. When not in use, the trundle-like footrest could be pushed back into the seat-rail.

GOUT CHAIR

PIERRE GOUTHIÈRE

GOUTHIÈRE, PIERRE (1740–1806). A notable French designer of exquisite ormolu mounts for Louis XVI period furniture. He also created mountings of great refinement and delicacy for vases of jasper, Sèvres, and oriental porcelains, as well as designs for clocks and candelabras. Illustrated is a cylinder secrétaire of the Louis XVI period with ormolu mountings by Gouthière. See *Bureau Plat*.

GOUTY STOOL. A leg rest with an adjustable top for the support of gout-afflicted legs. An 18th-century English design.

GOUTY STOOL

GOVERNOR WINTHROP DESK

GOVERNOR WINTHROP DESK

GRAFFITO WARE

GRAND MIROIR
À LA PSYCHÉ

GRANDFATHER CHAIR

GOVERNOR WINTHROP DESK. A typical fall-front desk of Colonial America (c. 1750). It was concurrent with Chippendale's designs in England. The piece has two to four graduated drawers running the width of the desk with "batwing" or "willow" brasses. The desk usually was supported by bracket feet. The interior of the desk was an arrangement of arcaded pigeonholes, with a single or double tier of small drawers beneath. The assorted governors called Winthrop, and there were several, actually lived in the 17th century, so the name is confusing.

GRADIN. See *Table à Gradin.*

GRAFFITO WARE. Heavy pottery decorated with a primitively scratched or scribed design. See *Sgraffito.*

GRAIN. In wood, the fiber lines of the wood. The figure or pattern inherent in the wood, the product of annual growth rings. The cells and pores of the tree.

GRAINED FURNITURE. Late-19th-century cheap furniture, dark in color, which was painted and artificially grained to simulate oak wood. See *Graining.*

GRAINING. A painted imitation of the grain of wood. Often the grain of an expensive or rare wood is simulated on a less expensive or plain painted surface.

GRAND MIROIR À LA PSYCHÉ. Also called a "psyche." A tall Empire pier mirror which stood on the floor and could be tilted forward or back. A German Empire version with candle brackets is illustrated. See *Pier Glasses.*

GRAND RAPIDS, MICHIGAN. A furniture manufacturing city for over a century. Popularly priced furniture is mass-produced in this area.

GRANDFATHER CHAIR. A large, roomy, upholstered chair developed from the 17th-century wing chair. It was particularly popular in the Queen Anne period.

GRANDFATHER (long case) CLOCK. A floor-standing clock with a wood case which consists of a hood, a waist, and a base. The pendulum and the weights are protected inside the clock which usually stands over six feet high. It was introduced into England after the Restoration, and became extremely popular during the 18th century.

GRANDMOTHER CLOCK. A smaller-scaled and more refined version of the grandfather clock. See *Grandfather (long case) Clock.*

GRANDFATHER CLOCK

GRANITE. The hardest and most durable of building stones. A granular crystalline rock of quartz, feldspar, and mica.

GRAPHIC ARTS. The arts of drawing, engraving, etching, block-printing, etc.

GRASS CLOTH. A wall-covering material glued onto a paper or fabric backing. It is woven of coarse vegetable fibers creating a strong horizontal effect and a nubby, irregular texture. Grass cloth may be simulated as a printed, embossed paper, cloth, or vinyl material.

GRATING. See *Grille*.

GRAY GOODS. Cloths as they come from the loom without either wet or dry finishing, before dyeing is begun. In the silk and rayon industries, this material is called "greige goods."

GREAT HALL. In the medieval castle, the large, two-storied central hall used for dining and entertainment.

GREAT MONAD or OVUM MUNDI. A circle with a horizontal S shape dividing it into two equal areas which represent the union of the basic principles: the material or feminine, and the spiritual or masculine.

GRECIAN SOFA. Another name for an Empire-style couch. Illustrated is an early-19th-century Sheraton design. The head part is higher and rolls over, as does the lower or foot end. See *Récamier*.

GRECIAN SOFA

GRECO, EL (Domenikos Theotcopoulos) (c. 1541–1614). A Greek artist who worked in Spain. His work has an ecstatic and passionate quality, and was a personal blending of the traditions of Titian, Michelangelo, Dürer, and his own Byzantine background. His very personal relation to his work and his mysticism are recorded in the elongation of the limbs, the tense figures, the sharp color contrasts, and the draperies that seem to have a movement of their own. Among his best known works are "A View of Toledo," "Martyrdom of S. Maurice and the Theman Legion," "The Disrobing of Christ," "The Assumption," and "The Burial of Count Orgaz."

GRECO-ROMAN

GRECO-ROMAN. The classic style from about 200 B.C. to A.D. 200. It is Romanized Greek forms such as were unearthed in Pompeii and Herculaneum, and it is the basis of the 18th-century classic style of the Adam brothers and the Louis XVI period.

GREEK ARCHITECTURE. See *Classic*.

GREEK ARCHITECTURE

GREEK CROSS

GREEK CROSS

GREEK CROSS. Two lines of equal length bisecting each other at their centers.

GREEK REVIVAL

GREEK KEY. A fret design. A continuous band decoration of interlacing, hooked squares.

GREEK REVIVAL. A renewed interest in Greek art and architecture in the 18th and 19th centuries. It affected the Directoire, English Regency, and Empire styles.

GREENOUGH, HORATIO (1805–1852). American sculptor who published essays in which he stated that architecture should express the use and purpose of the building. He believed that the architect should "begin from the heart, as a nucleus, and work outwards." Greenough wrote during the neo-Classic period in America, and he placed great stress on the Greek principles of beauty, proportion, and use, but did not believe in the slavish copying of Greek forms.

GREER, MICHAEL. A 20th-century interior designer.

GREIGE. A neutral grayish-beige color.

GREIGE GOODS. See *Gray Goods*.

GRENADINE. A leno weave fabric like marquisette, but finer in texture. It is either plain, or woven with dots or figures, and is made of silk and cotton, silk and wool, or all cotton.

GRENDEY, GILES (1693–1780). An English furniture maker and exporter of simple, domestic-type Georgian furniture, much of which was japanned.

GRENFELL CLOTH. A closely woven, waterproof, windproof fabric. A sturdy twill fabric.

GRESE, GRECE, GRYCE. Medieval terms for "step."

GREYWOOD. Artificially dyed English harewood, or, in America, dyed maple wood. See *Harewood*.

GRIFFIN

GRIFFIN. A decorative device. A monster with the body of a lion and the head and wings of an eagle. In antiquity, the griffin was associated with fire, and thus often appears on friezes with candelabras. In heraldry, the griffin represents wisdom and watchfulness and was popular in Gothic architecture. The Adam brothers and later Empire style used the griffin as a decorative motif.

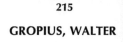

GRILLE

GRILLE. A metal, usually brass, lattice or trellis used in place of glass on cabinet doors, etc. Adam and Hepplewhite made extensive use of this textural material. Often rosettes and other ornaments were added on the intersections of the crisscrossing wires or rods. A late-18th-century Sheraton design is illustrated.

GRIS TRIANON. A soft, grayish, off-white color used for late-18th-century French painted furniture. See *Blanc de Plomb.*

GRILLE

GRISAILLE. A monochromatic painting in neutral grays or beiges only, which gives the effect of a sculptured relief panel. It was popular as a trompe l'oeil painting technique for overdoors or overmantels in the Louis XVI period. Piat Joseph Sauvage was an outstanding painter of the time in that technique. The grisaille may also serve as a first stage for an oil painting, or it may serve as a model for an engraver. Adam, Sheraton, and Hepplewhite used grisaille medallions and plaques to decorate and enhance their furniture. Angelica Kauffmann and Giovanni Battista Cipriani also painted in this style.

GRISAILLE

GROIN. The curved, sharp edge which is formed by the meeting of two vaulted surfaces.

GROIN

GROIN RIB. An exposed rib which follows the line of the groin on a vaulted surface. See *Rib.*

GROIN VAULT. A roof formed by the intersection of two barrel vaults at right angles.

GROOVE AND RABBET JOINT. See *Barefaced Tongue Joint.*

GROIN RIB

GROPIUS, WALTER. Born in 1883. A 20th-century architect and founder of the Bauhaus in Weimar. In 1925, the school was moved to Dessau. He is an educator and theoretician as well as an architect. In 1909, Gropius worked out a memorandum on standardization and mass production of small houses. He became the head of the Staatliches Bauhaus in 1919, an Academy of Art, which became the creative center of Europe at that time. It was a community of architects, painters, and craftsmen working in a new spirit in this combination school-workshop. Gropius, along with *Marcel Lajos Breuer,* is responsible for a distinct modern New England style of domestic architecture which blends white wood frames and fieldstone fireplaces with sophisticated German details of the 1920's. His great influence as an architect and educator has been in the field of medium-priced private homes. See *Behrens, Peter.*

GROIN VAULT

GROTESQUE

GUADAMICIL

GROS POINT. A coarse tapestry effect produced by using cross-stitching on net, canvas, or coarse linen. The embroidery threads are usually woolen and there are approximately twelve stitches to the lineal inch.

GROSGRAIN. Ribbed or rep silk. The cords are close together and are rounder than those of faille. It is used for draperies and ribbon decorations.

GROTESQUES (GROTTESQUES). Decorations in antiquity like sphinxes, masks, or fantastic monsters which combined human with plant and animal forms in a free manner: winged females, mermaids, etc. These classic ornaments were rediscovered in grottos, hence the name. Raphael was one of the first Renaissance artists to make use of these motifs.

GROTTO. A cave or recess, natural or artificial.

GROUND. The rough wood framing on or in a wall, upon which paneling is applied.

GROUND COLOR. The base or background color of a fabric, wallpaper, carpet, etc., upon which other colors (the top colors) are applied. In screened or printed materials, the background color is the ground color, and the design may be produced in one or more top colors.

GROUT. A liquid-like mortar or concrete which dries hard and solid, and is used as a filler or fixing agent for tiles and mosaics, and between blocks of stones, etc.

GROUTITE. A finer mortar than grout, used for small mosaic work like contemporary tabletops, plaques, decorative accessories, etc.

GRUEN, VICTOR. A 20th-century architect, who was born in Vienna in 1903. He came to the United States in 1938, and is presently the head of a firm with major production offices in Los Angeles and Detroit, as well as smaller offices in New York, Minneapolis, Miami, and San Francisco. The organization includes structural, mechanical, electrical, and civil engineers, as well as interior and graphic designers, landscape artists, etc. The Victor Gruen office has specialized in the organization and planning of large suburban shopping centers. Among its most noted examples are Northland Shopping Center in Detroit and the Palo Shopping Center in San Jose, California.

GUADAMICIL. A leather "tapestry" or decorated hanging. The technique was introduced into Europe in the 11th century by the Arabs from Morocco. It was first produced in Guadamicileria, Spain, in the 16th century. In the 17th and 18th centuries, leather tapestries were produced in France, the Netherlands, England, Germany, and Italy under such names as Cordovan or Moroccan (Maroquin) tapestries. Illustrated is an early-17th-century Spanish chair of carved walnut with embossed leather covering. See *Gilded Leather*.

GUANACASTE. A tropical hardwood. See *Kelobra*.

GUÉRIDON. A small ornamental stand or pedestal. A little round table popular in the late Queen Anne period and adopted from France, where it appeared during the reign of Louis XIII. In the Chippendale design shown, it is also used as a candlestand. See *Torchère*.

GUÉRIDON

GUÉRIDON À CRÉMAILLIÈRE. A small round table or candle-holder of the Louis XVI period. Its main feature was that it could be adjusted to various heights by means of a toothed (crémaillière) support which set into three supporting feet. The table usually was made of mahogany and had a marble top and a gilt brass gallery.

GUÉRIN, GILLES (1609–1678). A French sculptor who worked on decorative elements in the Louvre and Versailles.

GUERITE. The French word for "sentry box." A high-backed, hooded armchair which enveloped the seated person and also kept out the draughts. In the 18th century it was interpreted in wicker, and the design became a popular piece of garden furniture. Today this piece of wicker furniture is seen on the beaches of French and Italian resorts.

GUGGENHEIM MUSEUM. A modern, beehive-like, spiral, organic concrete structure designed by Frank Lloyd Wright and built in New York City to exhibit contemporary works of art.

GUILLOCHE

GUILLOCHE. A geometric classic band or border pattern of overlapping or interlacing circular forms. The circles are sometimes filled with ornamental designs. It was much used in Renaissance and Victorian Renaissance furniture and architecture.

GUIMARD, HECTOR (1867–1942). A French architect and furniture designer. Greatly influenced by Victor Horta, he became the French interpreter of the art nouveau style. One of his most noted pieces in this style is the entrance gate to the Métro stations in Paris. The cast iron has been shaped into elegant, twisted, curving, flowerlike forms. In 1938, Guimard moved to New York. See *Horta, (Baron) Victor*.

GUIMPE. See *Gimp or Guimpe*.

GUILLOCHE

GUINEA HOLES

GUINEA HOLES

GUNSTON HALL

GUINEA HOLES or POCKETS. Dished or scooped-out areas in a gaming table to hold money or chips. It was an 18th-century English device. See *Dished.*

GUMWOOD. A pink to reddish-brown wood of a heavy, strong texture. It has a wild figure with pleasing contrasts. It is possible to get a ribbon stripe veneer if the wood is quarter-cut. The heartwood, or red gum, is used for cabinetmaking, and is used architecturally inside and outside the house. The sapwood is called "sap gum" and is not as durable as the heartwood, and is used for plywood and furniture lumber, and for architectural woodwork that gets a painted finish.

GUNSTON HALL. Built in 1755, near Mount Vernon, for George Mason. The one-and-a-half-story building has a steep gabled roof with dormers and pairs of tall chimneys at either end. There is a central hall with two rooms on either side of it. William Buckland was brought from England to create and supervise the magnificent woodwork for this house. The Chippendale dining room was the first in the Colonies done in the "Chinese style." The drawing room is Palladian in concept. See *Buckland, William.*

GUSSET. A triangular insert between two pieces of fabric. This inset serves to enlarge or strengthen the whole piece.

GUTTAE. Small pendent features in classic Greek and Roman Doric cornices which resemble rows of pegs.

GUTTAE

GUTTER

GUTTER. A small trough under the eaves of a roof to carry off rainwater.

GUTTER TILE. Shaped ceramic tiles, which, when laid on a roof, form corrugated-like ridges (or gutters) which allow the rain to run down more readily.

GUTTER TILE

GYPSUM. Hydrous calcium sulfate which is used in making plaster of Paris.

GYPSUM BOARD. A wallboard material with a core of processsed gypsum rock. This is encased in a tough, heavyweight paper. The smooth paper surface can then be treated with paint, wallpaper, etc., after it has been primed with a primer sealer or varnish. The board comes in various thicknesses ($1/4''$ to $1/2''$) and can be obtained with square, tapered or beveled edges. The panels are usually 4' to 8' tall.

H HINGE. An H-shaped hinge with one upright attached to the jamb, and the other upright attached to the door. The horizontal piece works as a pivot. It is similar to an HL hinge.

H STRETCHER. A reinforcing element for chair, table, and case furniture legs. A wooden piece, or turning, connects each front leg with the leg immediately behind it. A crosspiece from one of these connecting pieces to the other forms an H. A Chinese Chippendale chair is illustrated.

HABILLÉE. An art appliqué form in which actual pieces of fabric, lace, etc., are pasted onto a picture. These textures and materials are used to represent clothing, drapery, upholstery, etc.

HACKBERRY. A native American wood which resembles the elm. Its light, natural yellowish color stains and finishes well.

HACKING. A method of laying bricks so that the bottom edge is set in from the plane surface of the wall.

HADLEY CHEST. An early American (c. 1700), New England chest on four legs. The chest had one, two, or three drawers, and would vary in height (according to the number of drawers) from 32″ to 46″. These units were decorated with simple incised carvings, and stained red, mulberry, or black. The owner's initials were often carved on the central panel. The top, body of drawers, and back were usually made of pinewood.

HAIG, THOMAS. An 18th-century English cabinetmaker, and partner of Thomas Chippendale II.

HAIRCLOTH. A stiff, wiry fabric made of cotton with a horsehair, mohair, or human hair filling, and woven plain, striped, or with small patterns. Haircloth is very durable, but is usually woven in narrow widths. It was popular for upholstery in mid-19th-century England and America and is also used today for interlining and stiffening.

HALF COLUMN. A rounded pilaster or a column partially engaged in the wall of the structure. See *Engaged Column.*

HALF-HEADED BED

HALF-HEADED BED. A bed with short posts at the four ends and no canopy.

HALF-ROUND SLICING VENEER. A method similar to the rotary method for cutting veneers from the log. The slicing goes slightly across the annual growth rings, producing a wavy look.

HALF-ROUND SLICING VENEER.

H STRETCHER

HALF COLUMN

HALF TIMBER

HALF TIMBER. A form of Gothic house construction in which the heavy beams and posts form the visible skeleton on the interior as well as the exterior of the structure. The areas between the heavy wood construction were filled with wattle and daub, plaster, stone or brick. Illustrated is a 15th-century dwelling in Rouen. See *Pane* for an illustration of a 13th-century example.

HALF TIMBER

HALF TURNING. See *Split Spindle.*

WILLIAM HALFPENNY

HALFPENNY, WILLIAM. An 18th-century English carpenter and architect who helped popularize the Chinese trend in architecture and decoration. In collaboration with his son, he published many books during the early part of the 18th century, including *The Modern Builder's Assistant* and *New Design for Chinese Temples, Triumphal Arches, Garden Seats, Railings, etc.* A pig-tailed Chinese mandarin, with umbrella, often was crowded into his ceilings, over chimneypieces, etc.

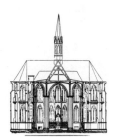

HALL CHAIR

HALFTONE. A color, in tonal value, halfway between white and black.

HALL CHAIRS. 18th-century English formal chairs, usually with decorative backs, originated by Manwaring, and also designed by Chippendale and Sheraton. A late-18th-century Sheraton design is illustrated. See *Light Chair* and *Side Chair.*

HALL CHURCH. A German Gothic form of architecture in which the nave and the aisles were of equal height. Contributing to the tall, open effect was the immense single-span roof over the nave and lofty aisles. This setup made the clerestory and triforium unnecessary. In England, the Cathedral in Bristol and the Temple Church in London were built in this style, as was the Spanish Cistercian Church in Alcobaça. The hall church is also called a "Hallenkirche," and "Dreischiffige Kirche." Illustrated is a cross section of Elisabethkirche at Marburg, a typical Hall Church.

HALL CHURCH

HALL CLOCK. See *Grandfather (long case) Clock.* A Sheraton-type case clock of the late 18th century is illustrated.

HALL CLOCK

HALL TREE. A hat and/or coat rack made of metal or wood turnings. It is a floor-standing unit with upturned arms at the top to hold hats and coats.

HALLENKIRCHE. See *Hall Church.*

HALLET, WILLIAM (1707–1781). A cabinetmaker under George II.

HALLMARK. The mark or stamp of official approval of quality that usually appears on metalwork.

HALVED JOINT. A joint formed by two pieces of wood, the end of each sunk to half its depth. They are placed at right angles to each other; thus the projection of one fits into the sinking or groove of the other. This method is referred to as "halving in."

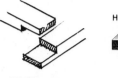
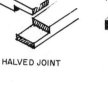

HALVED JOINT

HALVED JOINT

HAMMER BRACE. The curved vertical member which supports a hammer beam. See *B* on *Hammer-Beam Roof* illustration.

HAMMER-BEAM ROOF. A Gothic form of roof construction in which the rafters are supported by a horizontal beam which projects from the wall but does not join up with the corresponding projections from the opposite wall. The hammer beam is marked *A*.

HAMMER-BEAM ROOF

HAMMER-BEAM TRUSS

HAMMER-BEAM TRUSS. An early English Renaissance form of roof support. It was actually a Tudor arch form in wood, each end of which rested on a large wooden bracket which was usually carved.

HAMPTON COURT PALACE. A classic example of the domestic architecture of the Tudor period. It was built for Cardinal Wolsey, and the original structure, begun in 1514, was of mellow red brickwork in a diaper pattern with battlement parapets. The brickwork chimneys, the hammer-beam roof, oriel window, terra-cotta busts of the Roman emperors by Giovanni da Maiano, and the many courts are noteworthy details. Sir Christopher Wren redid the Eastern portion in the 17th century in the Renaissance style. Illustrated is the gateway of the west front.

HAMPTON COURT PALACE

HAND. The "feel" of the fabric. It refers to the resilience, flexibility, and drapability of the fabric. The finish of the goods affects the "feel." See *Finish*.

HAND BLOCKING. A method of printing a design on a piece of paper, fabric, or other surface. A design is carved or incised on a wood, linoleum, or other type of block. The flat surface is the design; the gouged-out areas will not print. Paint or dye is rolled on the surface of the block, and then pressure is exerted on the block as it makes its imprint on the surface to be decorated.

HAND PRINTS. Wallpapers, murals, fabrics, accessories, etc., which are produced by a hand-screening rather than a machine process.

HAND SCREENING. A process for applying colored decorations, designs, or artwork to paper, fabrics, vinyls, wood, or other materials. The design is prepared on one or several (depending upon the number of colors in the design) fine silk screens in wood frames. The silk is covered with a fine, non-porous film, and the film is cut away in those areas where the design will be printed. A roller or squeegee is rolled in paint, and then rolled or spread over the screen which is set down on the material that is to be printed. The paint goes through only the fine silk mesh where the film has been cut away. Each color that is to be laid down in the design requires a separate screen. Each succeeding screen, as it is laid down, must be lined up true to the previous screens so that the various colored areas set in next to one another properly, and create the intended design.

HANDKERCHIEF TABLE. A triangular table, designed to fit into the corner of a room. A second triangular top is hinged on so that when this second triangle is flipped back, a rectangular table surface results.

HANDLES. Knobs or pulls used on furniture. In the Jacobean period in England wood turnings and wrought iron were favored. Brass handles were introduced into England during the William and Mary period. In France, mounts and handles were chased and engraved and made of ormolu, and were often works of art. The ring hanging from the lion's mouth was one of Sheraton's favorite handle designs (see *Hardware*).

HANDRAIL. The top rail into which the tops of the banisters are usually set. It follows the incline of the stairs, and serves as a support for persons walking up or down the stairs.

HANGING SHELVES. Wall-attached units used for the display of books, plates, and china collections. These shelves were very popular in the late 17th and through the 18th century in France and England. Chippendale designed Chinese or Gothic types (see illustration). In the 19th-century Victorian period, many hanging "whatnots" or "knickknack" shelves were the vogue.

HANDLE

HANDLE

HANDRAIL

HANGING SHELVES

HANGINGS. Draperies on tester beds or window curtains and draperies. The term may also refer to wall tapestries or arras. The fabric embellishment may be made of damask, brocade, cotton, linen, wool, leather, etc. A 16th-century wall hanging from the Palace of Fontainebleau is illustrated. See *Arras, Guadamicil, Tapestry,* and *Wachstuch-Tapete.*

HARD CORE. A rubble filling placed under a concrete ground floor and directly over the ground. It prevents the damp or moisture from rising.

HARD PASTE. True porcelain made of kaolin or China clay.

HARDOUIN-MANSART, JULES (1646–1708). French architect who took over from Louis Le Vau the work on Versailles after 1679. He is credited with creating the Hall of Mirrors. His other works include the dome and chapel of Les Invalides, the Place Vendôme and Place des Victoires, the Grand Trianon, and Marly.

HARDOY CHAIR. A modern 20th-century version of the folding wood and canvas Italian officer's chair. The chair is made of metal (noncollapsible) and canvas and was originally manufactured and sold by Knoll Associates, Inc., in 1947. This up-to-date version was designed by Hardoy.

HARDWARE. In cabinetry, metal handles, pulls, escutcheons, hinges, decorative push plates, etc. They are also called mounts.

HARDWOOD. A general term for the lumber of broad-leafed trees, in contrast to the conifers which are termed softwoods. The name has no real connection with the hardness of the wood. The furniture hardwoods are porous, and include oak, walnut, mahogany, beech, maple, and gum.

HAREWOOD. A creamy white wood (English sycamore) which dyes a silvery gray. It has a close, curly figure and a dense grain with a tendency to lose the dye on exposure to strong light. Plain, curly, fiddleback, finger roll, or heavy crossfire figures are all possible in Harewood veneer, depending upon the slicing method. Harewood is used in cabinetwork, and will turn a grayish green when stained with oxide of iron.

HARICOT. French for "kidney bean." A crescent- or bean-shaped small Louis XV table with cabriole legs and small drawers set into the curved apron.

HARLEQUIN TABLE. A gadgety, complicated dressing-writing table, of the end of the 18th century. It was designed with hidden compartments, pigeonholes, small drawers, etc. Sheraton and Shearer both designed these pieces. See *Rachet* illustration for a lever system devised by Sheraton to raise the various surfaces and compartments.

HANGING

HARDWARE

HARLEQUIN TABLE

HARMONIUM

HARP

HARMONIUM. A small reed organ with one or two rows of keys or bellows which are controlled or pedaled by foot. A French, early-19th-century invention ascribed to Alexander Debain of Paris.

HARP. A triangular instrument played by plucking its strings; stands on a heavy base with pedals which influence the tone. An Italian Renaissance example is illustrated. In furniture, the shaped metal piece which extends up from the lamp base, and to which the lampshade is affixed. The harp is usually bowed in the center to allow the bulb to be screwed inside the socket to which the harp is attached.

HARPSICHORD. A piano-type instrument which preceded the pianoforte of the 18th century. The strings are plucked by means of quills which are attached to levers. It works on the same principle as the spinet and virginal.

HARRATEEN. An 18th-century woven curtain material.

HARRISON, PETER (1716–1775). Harrison is considered the first American architect in that he prepared sketches for others to build from. His best known works are in Newport, Rhode Island, and he made it the center of architectural art in colonial New England. Among his designs are: Redwood Library at Newport (liberally based on plates from Palladio's work, Kent's *Designs of Inigo Jones,* and Langley's *Treasury of Design*), King's Chapel, Boston (with assistance from James Gibbs's *Book of Architecture*), and his masterpiece, the Synagogue of the Congregation Jeshuat Israel (known as Touro Synagogue) which was begun in 1759 and is the oldest synagogue in the United States. See *Touro Synagogue.* Harrison was probably the American master of the British version of the Renaissance.

HARVARD CHAIR. An early American (17th-century) version of a Gothic-type three-cornered chair made of wood turnings.

HARVARD FRAME. A trademark name for a steel bed frame. See *Bed Frame.*

HARVEST TABLE. A long, narrow, drop-leaf table. The legs may be straight or turned, and the flaps have either squared ends, or they are gently rounded. The design is usually associated with 18th-century American furniture.

HASP. In a hinge lock, the hinged part which swings over the pin. In Spanish Gothic chests, the hasp was usually an ornate piece of metalwork.

HASP

HASSOCK. A heavy cushion or thick mat which is used as a footstool or ottoman.

HATCHING. In drawing, a method of shading by means of close parallel lines. "Cross-hatching" is shading produced by parallel lines drawn perpendicular to one another, and criss-crossed.

HATCHING

HAUNCH. In arch construction, the stonework between the springing line and the crown. It is here that the lateral thrust is most strongly exerted.

HAUSMALEREI. Homemade and amateurish German pottery. The pieces were partially fired, then decorated and returned to the kiln for glazing and further firing. See *Firing*.

HAUSSMANN, (BARON) GEORGES EUGÈNE (1801–1891). A noted French architect and planner who designed and laid out the plan for the main boulevards of present-day Paris. Most of his plans were executed during the reign of Napoleon III. The Boulevard Haussmann was named after him.

HAUT BOY. See *High Boy*.

HAUT RELIEF: In sculpture and ornament, high relief as opposed to bas-relief. See *High Relief*.

HAUTELISSE. The French for "high warp." A tapestry woven with an upright warp.

HEAD JOINT. In masonry, the vertical mortar joint between the ends of the masonry units. It is also called the "cross joint."

HEADBOARD. The board or panel which rises above the mattress at the head of the bed. It can be made of wood or metal, it can be upholstered or inset with cane or leather panels, etc. The headboard can be simple or ornate, modern or traditional in style, and it serves, practically, as a back support when a person is sitting up in bed. See *Footboard*.

HEADER. The end of a brick usually laid perpendicular to the face of the wall. It is used to tie two thicknesses of masonry together.

HEADER BOND. In masonry, a brick pattern made up of headers only. See *Header*.

HAUNCH

HAUT RELIEF

HEADBOARD

HEADER

HEADER BOND

HEADER COURSE. A masonry course consisting only of headers. See *Common Bond* illustration.

HEADER COURSE

HEART AND CROWN. A pierced motif carved on the cresting of a baluster chair of the late 17th century in England.

HEART-SHAPED CHAIR BACK. A typical 18th-century Hepplewhite shield chair back which resembles a heart.

HEART-SHAPED
CHAIR BACK

HEARTH

HEARTH. The brick, stone, or tile pavement beneath the opening in a chimney and inside the fireplace. It is here that the fire is made.

HELIX. A small spiral element beneath the abacus of a Corinthian capital.

HELIX

HELLENISTIC. Greek art under Alexander in the third century B.C. It is a realistic and emotional form of art with the Roman influence interpreting the Greek forms.

HELM ROOF. A roof made up of four inclining sides, all meeting at a central point on top. A gable is formed at the angle of each face.

HEMLOCK. A wood which resembles white pine. It is strong, lightweight, and easy to work.

HENRY II AND III

HENRI II and III. The rulers of France during the 16th century whose reigns form part of the mid-French-Renaissance period. The period was noteworthy for its carvings and interlaced strapwork.

HENRY II AND III

HEPPLEWHITE, GEORGE. An 18th-century English furniture designer who worked in the classic style. In 1788, he published *Cabinet-Maker and Upholsterers Guide*. His work was characterized by lightness of construction, elegant curvilinear forms, and perfection of workmanship. Hepplewhite used heart-shaped and shield chair backs carved with wheat ears, fern leaves, honeysuckle, swags, and Prince of Wales feathers. He designed japanned furniture with fruit and flowers on a black

GEORGE HEPPLEWHITE

ground, as well as satinwood and inlaid pieces. Hepplewhite favored the spade foot for his delicately grooved and fluted chair legs.

HERCULANEUM. A historic Roman city which was excavated about the middle of the 18th century, and became a source of inspiration for the classic designers of the 18th century in France and England. The influence of Herculaneum is found in the architecture and interior designs of the Adam brothers in England and is the basis of the Louis XVI style in France. Herculaneum also refers to an antique Roman-type chair designed by Sheraton in the late 18th century. Also shown is a bronze stand excavated at Herculaneum. See *Pompeii*.

HERMA. A stone pillar, usually square, which tapers downward and is topped by a bust of Hermes. The Romans used it as a boundary marker, and also as an outdoor decoration. It is similar to a *Term*. Illustrated is a Hermes figure at the Dauphine Gate of the Fontainebleau Palace.

HERMES or HERMS. See *Term*.

HERNÁNDEZ, or FERNÁNDEZ, GREGORIO (1576–1636). A Spanish sculptor of the Baroque period who was noted for his highly colored statues.

HERRERA, JUAN DE (1530–1597). A Spanish architect who was responsible for the "desornamentado" style. He worked under Phillip II, and his work was simple, severe and almost harsh in relation to the Plateresque period which preceded him and the Baroque (or Churrigueresco) which followed. Herrera was a pupil of Michelangelo. His greatest achievement is the Escorial, about 30 miles from Madrid. He also added the southern portion of the Alcazar in Toledo.

HERRINGBONE. Woodwork, brickwork, or stonework in which the material is laid at angles, so that the alternate courses point in opposite directions. Inlay, marquetry, and parquetry are sometimes done in a herringbone pattern.

HERRINGBONE MATCH. Two V-match veneer or wood panels butted together to form a series of horizontal valleys and peaks.

HETRE. French for beechwood. A popular wood for fine 18th-century chairs.

HEX SIGN. A Pennsylvania Dutch motif for good luck, or to ward off evil spirits. It is usually a variation on a circle with a six-pointed star or another geometric motif enclosed in the circle. The design was painted on barns and houses, and used decoratively on chests, furniture, etc. The hex was, and still is, usually painted in bright, pure colors.

HERCULANEUM

HERCULANEUM

HERMA

HERRINGBONE

HERRINGBONE MATCH

HIERACOSPHINX

HIEROGLYPHICS

HIGH RELIEF

HIGHBOY

HEXASTYLE. A portico with six columns.

HICKORY. A hard, tough and heavy wood of the walnut family. It is not usually used decoratively, but it is elastic and bonds easily. It is effective where thinness and strength are required, therefore it is often used for bent and molded plywood.

HIERACOSPHINX. A sculptured Egyptian lion's form with the head of a hawk.

HIERATIC. An abridged form of hieroglyphics used for religious writings. See *Demotic*.

HIEROGLYPHICS. A system of picture writing and phonetic indications used by the ancient Egyptians.

HIGH DADDY. An 18th-century American tall chest unit of six or more graduated drawers.

HIGH RELIEF. Sculpture the figures of which are carved out from the background to the extent of at least half their total mass, so that they appear almost detached or full round. See *Haut Relief*.

HIGHBOY. A tall chest of four or five drawers, on legs, with a cornice or pediment crown. It was originally mounted on a dressing table. The design was introduced from Holland into England during the William and Mary period, and was popular in America through the 18th century. Illustrated is a mid-18th-century flat-top New England highboy. The name may be derived from the French "hautbois" (high wood).

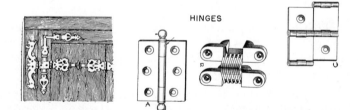

HINGES

HINGE. A metal device consisting of two plates which are joined by a pin in such a manner that they can pivot or swing.

Butt Hinge: The two plates are fixed inside the door or chest unit, and only the pivot with pin is visible. Invisible Hinge: Almost completely concealed when in use. Double-acting Hinge: Makes it possible to swing a door or panel in either direction and almost a full 360°. Sometimes hinges are very decorative, and both plates are exposed for their beauty as well as their use.

HIP. In architecture, the angle formed by the meeting of two sloping roof surfaces. In the illustration, *H.E.* is the hipped end of the hipped roof. In furniture, the "knee" of the cabriole leg and the extension above the chair rail in early-18th-century English cabriole-legged chairs were called hips.

HIP TILE. A saddle-shaped tile placed over the meeting point of two sloping roof surfaces.

HIPPED ROOF. A roof in which the end is formed by a sloping face enclosed by hips. See *Hip*.

HOCHRELIEF

HIP

HIP

HIPPED ROOF

HISPANO MAURESQUE

HISPANO MAURESQUE. Spanish art influenced by Moorish designs. It was a part of the Gothic or Medieval period in Spain, and lasted for several hundred years. The Gothic Cathedral of Toledo (1227–1493) is typical of the Moorish craftsman's influence on Spanish architecture: horseshoe arches, pierced stonework, tracery, and rich surface decoration.

HISTORIATED. Ornamented with figures, animals, etc., which are representational or symbolic. Historiated initials were a popular expression in medieval manuscripts.

HITCHCOCK, LAMBERT (1795–1852). An American designer working in Connecticut. He was the designer of the "Hitchcock chair," which was derived from the Sheraton "pillow back" or oval-turned top rail chair. The chair usually was painted black, and had a rush or cane seat, turned, splayed front legs, and gold stenciled fruit and flower decoration of the wide top rail.

HITCHCOCK CHAIRS. See *Hitchcock, Lambert*.

HL HINGE. A provincial hinge usually made of forged or wrought iron. The design resembles an uppercase I attached by a short crosspiece to an uppercase L. The hinge or pivot joint between the I and the L creates the H in the name. See *H Hinge*.

HOCHRELIEF. German for "high relief."

HISTORIATED

LAMBERT HITCHCOCK

HOCK LEG

WILLIAM HOGARTH

HOGARTH CHAIR

HOLLOW WALL

HOCK LEG. Also called "broken cabriole leg." The curve is broken below the "knee" on the inner side. The sides of the "knees" are sometimes ornamented with carved spiral scrolls called "ears." See *Cabriole Leg.*

HOFFMAN, JOSEPH (1870–1956). An Austrian decorator and architect who was the taste and pace setter for Austrian decor in the first three decades of the 20th century. The Palais Stoclet in Brussels (1905–1911) is probably his masterpiece, and in it one can see his subtle compositions which are based on simple geometric forms (rectangles and squares) with delicately handled trims. Hoffman was a student of *Otto Wagner.*

HOGARTH, WILLIAM (1697–1764). A noted painter and illustrator of the life in 18th-century England. He did many series of famous etchings. Illustrated is "Temple Bar."

HOGARTH CHAIR. A decorated Queen Anne chair with heavy "knees" and modified cabriole legs. The hoop back is usually hollow-crested and it has a pierced splat.

HOLLAND, HENRY (1740-1806). An English architect-decorator.

HOLLAND SHADE CLOTH. A plain cotton or linen cloth finished with sizing or starch and oil to make it opaque. It is used to make window shades.

HOLLOW WALL. A wall containing an air space, the facing and backing bonded together with masonry units. See *Cavity Wall.*

HOLLY, WHITE. A native American wood. The whitest and least grained wood available. It is used in marquetry, in inlays, and for stringing and banding. It turns brown with age and exposure.

HOLLYWOOD BED. A bed without a footboard. The spring and mattress are set on a metal bed-frame unit which is often equipped with casters. A headboard can be attached to the frame, or the headboard can be attached to the wall, and the frame then hooked on to it. The size of the spring and mattress may vary from twin size up to king size. Period and style are determined by the choice of headboard. See *Harvard Frame.*

HOM. The Assyrian "tree of life" pattern.

HOMESPUN. Originally a fabric loomed by hand at home, but now the name of a loose, rough fabric with a tweedy look which is obtained by using unevenly spun fibers. It may be made of cotton, rayon, or wool. It is used for curtains and upholstery.

HONEYCOMB VAULT. A brick vaulting system popular in northern German Gothic buildings. The spaces or surfaces between the ribs are folded to create a dimensional, corrugated, multipointed star pattern.

HONEYCOMBED WALL. Brick walls in which selected headers are omitted in each course to provide air circulation.

HONEYSUCKLE. A Greek decoration resembling a conventionalized fanlike arrangement of petals. It is also called "anthemion." It appears on Renaissance furniture as a carved enrichment, and Hepplewhite used it for a chair back design. Adam created a "swag" of honeysuckles to decorate panels, girandoles, furniture, etc.

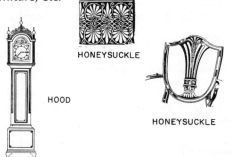

HONEYSUCKLE

HOOD

HONEYSUCKLE

HOOD. In furniture, the case enclosing the dial and works of a grandfather or long case clock. Also see *Hooded Tops.* In architecture, a sheltering overhang.

HOOD MOLD. A molding or series of moldings that form a protective "hood" over a doorway or window. See *Dripstone.* Illustrated is an English 15th-century Gothic portal.

HOODED TOPS. The rounded tops of cabinets, especially those of the early Queen Anne period (early 18th century in England). They are also called domed, curved, rounded, or semicircular tops.

HOOF FOOT. See *Cloven Foot, Does'-Foot Leg,* and *Pied de Biche.* Illustrated is a Queen Anne marquetry chair with hoof feet.

HOOKED RUG. A pile-surfaced rug made of threads or strips of cloth pushed through a canvas backing. Another kind of hooked rug is that made of braided strips of wool or other strips of cloth. The braid is shaped around and sewn together in an oval or circular shape. Color and patterns are unlimited.

HOOD MOLD

HOODED TOP

HOOF FOOT

HOOPBACK CHAIR

HOOPBACK CHAIR

THOMAS HOPE

HOOPBACK CHAIR. A chair, the uprights and top rail of whose back form a continuous curve or hoop. It appears in the Queen Anne period, and was also prominent in the Hepplewhite period.

HOPE, THOMAS (1770–1831). The leading furniture designer in the Empire style in England, which is correctly termed the English Regency period. His book of furniture designs, *Household Furniture and Interior Decorations,* published in 1807, had great influence and moderated the extravagant pseudoclassical style of the time. See *Regency (English).*

HOPE CHEST. See *Cassone* and *Cedar Chest.*

HOPPER LIGHT. The upper section of a casement window which is hinged at the bottom and opens inward.

HOPPER WINDOW. A casement window which is hinged along its bottom edge so that it opens out and backward. It is usually part of a larger window unit.

HORSE. A simple support for a trestle table. It may be an inverted V or a shaped piece as illustrated in this Tudor period table (early 16th century).

HORSE

HORSE SCREEN

HORSE SCREEN. An English term for a "cheval screen." A fire screen with two bracketed feet. A Chippendale design is illustrated. See *Cheval Screen.*

HORSEHAIR. A furniture covering woven from the hair of a horse's tail and mane. Hepplewhite used it as an upholstery material, and it was most prominent in the Victorian period. It is stiff, sturdy, and generally quite dark in color.

HORSESHOE ARCH. An arch with a curve greater than a semicircle or 180°. It was prominently used in Moorish and Spanish architecture.

HORSESHOE TABLE. A horseshoe-shaped table, about 30" wide, and popular in the late 18th century. See *Hunt Table* and *Wine Table.*

HORTA, (BARON) VICTOR (1861–1947). A Belgian architect who created in the Art Nouveau style. Two of his most noted works are the home of Baron von Eetveldes (1895) and the

HORSESHOE ARCH

"Maison du Peuple" (1896). The interior architecture, in both structures, is significant for the irregularly shaped rooms which open freely onto one another at different levels. The iron balustrades are typically Art Nouveau in their twisted, plantlike elements, as is the curving sweep of mosaic floors, plaster walls, etc. His later works are more traditional.

HOSTEL. An inn.

HÔTEL DE VILLE, BEAUGENCY. A French Renaissance municipal building of great beauty, built by Charles Viart in the mid-16th century. Viart also built the Hôtel de Ville d'Orléans in 1498. The latter was a blend of the Gothic and Renaissance, while the structure at Beaugency is in the refined Renaissance style.

HOTHOUSE. A greenhouse. See *Conservatory* and *Orangery or Orangerie.*

HOUDON, JEAN-ANTOINE (1741–1828). A great French realist sculptor who made portrait busts of many aristocrats, artists, and philosophers of Europe, as well as American statesmen. Among his noted works are: "Voltaire" (illustrated), "Franklin," "Molière," "Diderot," and "Washington."

HOUNDSTOOTH. A fabric and wallpaper design. A medium-sized broken check motif often used in tweeds.

HOURGLASS BASE. A typically Regency base for stools, benches, and sometimes chairs. The base is made up of two curved elements, one set on top of the other to create a rounded X shape. Examples of this base can be seen in earlier 18th-century stools and chairs by Chippendale, Adam, and Sheraton.

HOUSED JOINT. A socketed joint as opposed to a butt joint. One piece is grooved out to fit into the grooved part of the other. The joint illustrated is also called a "gain joint."

HOUSED JOINT

HOUSEWRIGHT. An 18th-century American term for builders of homes and public buildings. These craftsmen were not architects in the recognized sense of the word. The term was originally used by Richard Munday, who in the early 18th century was one of the foremost builders in Newport, Rhode Island (Trinity Church and Old Colony House).

HOUSSE. The French term for "slipcover."

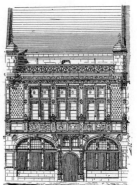

HÔTEL DE VILLE, BEAUGENCY

JEAN-ANTOINE HOUDON

HOURGLASS BASE

HUCHIERS-MENUISIERS

HUCHIERS-MENUISIERS. The French term for furniture makers of the early French Renaissance period. Literally the term means "hutch carpenters." Illustrated is a crédence of the late 16th century (period of Henri II).

HUDSON RIVER SCHOOL (1825–1870). A 19th-century American school of romantic landscape painters who glorified nature in their paintings. Washington Allston and Thomas Cole were major artists of the group, as were Frederick Edwin Church and Albert Bierstadt.

HUE. A color. A tint is a color with white added. A shade is a color with black added.

HUET, CHRISTOPHE. French artist during the reign of Louis XV. He created many chinoiserie-rococo designs: mandarins, pagodas, parasols, monkeys (singeries), ladders, and fantastic foliage.

HUET, JEAN-BAPTISTE (1745–1811). A French designer of toiles de Jouy for Christophe-Philippe Oberkampf, and wallpapers for Réveillon. His designs were full of grace, charm, animation, and a touch of humor. After the French Revolution, he created architectural and geometric backgrounds against which were set medallions, classic figures, and arabesques. These early designs were usually printed by a cylinder printing machine.

HUETEX, BLUE RIDGE. A trademark of American Saint Gobain. It is a tempered glass 5/16" thick with ceramic enamel fused to the back, and aluminum is welded to the enamel. The aluminum protects the enamel, reflects heat, and insulates. It was developed as a spandrel material, and is also used as a decorative ceiling paneling. The glass is textured on the weathering side to subdue bright reflections.

HUEWHITE. A trademark of American Saint Gobain for a translucent white, light-diffusing glass with the added strength of embedded wire mesh.

HUNG CEILING. A dropped ceiling. The ceiling is lowered by setting a new series of cross strips of wood or metal lower than the existing ceiling, then sheathing this framework with acoustic tiles, plasterboard, plastic panels, special light units, etc.

HUNT TABLE. A popular 18th-century English table, with a horseshoe-shaped top surface. The table often had drop leaves at the two ends of the horseshoe. A swinging decanter stand (which followed the inner edge) was sometimes added.

HUNTING CHAIR. An 18th-century Sheraton chair design with a special wood strip or footrest in front.

HURRICANE LAMP. A tall, glass cylinder shade set over a candlestick to protect the flame. It was introduced in the late 17th century and used through the 18th century. In current decorating, hurricane lamps are often used in pairs trimmed with prisms, and flame-shaped bulbs have replaced the candles. It is similar to the 19th-century *Girandole* or *Lustre*.

HUSHALON. A wool felt material used for wall covering. It has acoustical and thermal insulating properties and also is moth and flame proof, soil resistant, and colorfast. A trademark name.

HUSK ORNAMENT. A decorative representation of the husks of oats when ripe. The spreading of the husk into two halves makes it possible to create a chainlike pattern by having husk drooping from husk. This motif was very popular in England in the Adam and Sheraton periods. It was used as an inlay design, as a composition ornament of walls and ceilings in painted decoration, and also by Wedgwood on his jasper pottery. A section of an Adam mantel is illustrated. See *Bell-flower Ornament*.

HUSK ORNAMENT

HUTCH or HUCHE. "Huche" is Old French for "bin" or "chest." Originally a Gothic chest. In current usage, a hutch is a cabinet or cupboard placed over a buffet unit. The cupboard part may be left completely open, or have doors on two sides with an open shelving area in the middle. See *Ménagère*.

HUTCH

HUYGENS. A 17th-century Hollander who was brought to France during the reign of Louis XIV by Charles Le Brun. He was a furniture designer especially noted for his lacquerwork.

HYDRAULIC CEMENTS AND LIMES. Cements and limes which set under water.

HYDRIA. A Greek three-handled water jar.

HYPAETHRAL TEMPLE. A classic Greek temple partially open to the sky.

HYDRIA

HYPOCAUSTS. The ducts or chambers used in the ancient Roman system of heating rooms by means of hot air flues.

HYPOSTYLE. A covered hall, the roof of which rests on pillars or columns. The two central rows may be higher than those at the sides. This accomplishes what the clerestory does: allows more light into the interior. Illustrated is the early Egyptian Hypostyle Hall of Karnak.

HYPOSTYLE

HYPOTRACHELION

I BEAMS

ICONOCLASTIC MOVEMENT

ILLUMINATION

HYPOTRACHELION. The groove that encircles a Greek Doric column at the end of the shaft just below the necking.

I BEAM. A rolled steel beam shaped like a capital letter I with a pronounced top and bottom stroke.

I.M. The "inner measurement" of a unit as opposed to the O.M. or outer measurement. The I.M. of a hollow pipe is the diameter measured between opposite points on the inside surface; the O.M. is the diameter measured between opposite points on the outside surface. See *O.M.*

IAMBIC ALTERNATION. In Byzantine and Romanesque church arcades, one column alternating with one pier.

IBERIAN. Referring to the Iberian Peninsula (Spain and/or Portugal).

ICHTHUS. The Greek word for "fish." The word and the symbol were used by the early Christians to represent Jesus Christ. The initial letters of "Jesus Christ, God's Son, Saviour," in Greek, formed the word "ichthus."

ICON or IKON. Greek for "image." A religious painting of Christ, Mary, or saints painted on a panel.

ICONOCLASTIC MOVEMENT. In the early 8th century, sculptural representations of humans or animals were prohibited by the Eastern Emperor Leo III. He feared that the statues might foster paganism and idolatry. The resultant typically Byzantine and near-Eastern decoration was dependent upon floral and geometric patterns in rich color and texture.

ICONOGRAPH. A ground plan.

ICONOSTASIS. A three-doored partition which screened off the apse with the altar in the sanctuary. This was typical of most Byzantine church plans. This screen was often decorated with many tiers of icons (religious portraits). The iconostasis was a characteristic of Russian churches of the 15th and 16th centuries. This screen differs from the retable in that the latter served as a background to the services while the iconostasis shielded the people from viewing the rites which were conducted behind the screen. See *Retable*.

IDEOGRAPH. The illustration of an idea, word, or object. See *Rebus*.

ILLUMINATION. The medieval art of hand-decorating manuscripts with scrolls, arabesques, foliage, etc., in rich color and gold and silver. Religious manuscripts were often greatly enriched with colored illumination. See *Historiated*.

ILLUSIONISM. See *Trompe l'Oeil*.

IMAGINE D'ÉPINAL. A simple wood block.

IMBRICATE. To place in overlapping tiers or to give a fish-scale-like appearance. A technique used for tile roofs and also on columns, walls, etc.

IMBRICATE

IMBUYA. Brazilian walnut. The wood varies in color from olive to a deep, rich, red-brown color, and is used for veneering fine-grade furniture. It is fine-grained and moderately hard and heavy.

IMPASTO. An oil painting technique developed by Titian. Thin layers of opaque pigment and oil glazes are used to create a depth of color. When so many layers are applied as make the paint appear thick or lumpy, and the brush strokes are clearly evident, the painting is said to be "heavily impasted."

IMPERIAL HOTEL, TOKYO. A reinforced concrete, brick, and sculptured lava hotel (1916–1922) designed by Frank Lloyd Wright. The building withstood a great earthquake in the early 1920's due to its cantilever construction engineered by Wright and Paul Muellers.

IMPLUVIUM. The central area in a Roman atrium, into which the rain fell. See *Cavaedium*.

IMPOST. The member just below the springing line of an arch. It is where the arch rests.

IMPOST

IMPRESSIONISM. One of the first of the modern art movements in the 19th century. The aim was to achieve greater naturalism by analysis of tone and color, and the rendering of light on surfaces. Paint was often dabbed on in bright colors, even in the shadows. There was a lack of firm outline. Major Impressionists were: Claude Monet, Camille Pissaro, and Alfred Sisley.

IN ANTIS. Usually the term is applied to a classic Greek temple which has a portico enclosed by the extended side walls. Columns fill in between these two projecting sides.

IN SITU. Latin for "on the spot." Work done directly on the locale of the job and not made in a workshop for later installation.

INCANDESCENT LIGHT. An electric filament light. A sealed glass bulb with a filament which produces a glow and a light when an electric current passes through the filament.

INCARNADINE. A 17th-century English term to describe a light crimson to a pale fleshy pink color.

WILLIAM INCE

INCE, WILLIAM. An 18th-century English cabinetmaker, and follower of Chippendale. With Thomas Mayhew, he published *The Universal System of Household Furniture,* from 1762–1763. It contained designs for lanthorns, sideboard tables, bookcases, beds, etc. Ince used fretwork, combined with Chinese and Gothic motifs, and chair backs carved with ribbons and scrolls and patterned with brass nails. See *Mayhew, Thomas.*

INCISED. The opposite of relief carving. The pattern is produced by cutting or etching into the material. The design is engraved below the surface. See *Intaglio.*

INCISED LACQUER. Several coats of lacquer are applied to create a certain thickness. A design is then cut or carved into this thickness. This form of decoration was used on Chinese-style lacquered furniture and screens.

INCROSTARE. Italian for "inlay."

INDIA PAPERS. (Also called Japan papers.) Chinese papers that were imported into Europe in the mid-17th century by means of the Dutch, French, and English East India companies; hence the name "India papers." See *Chinese Wallpaper.*

INDIA PRINT. A printed cotton fabric with a Persian or Indian pattern hand-blocked in bright colors on a white or natural ground. It is used for draperies, bed throws, wall hangings, etc.

INDIAN RED. A soft reddish-brown or terra-cotta color. It was often used on American provincial pine furniture in the 18th century.

INDIENNE FABRICS. The French interpretation of India print cottons made during the late 17th and the 18th centuries. See *Toiles d'Indy.*

INDIRECT LIGHTING. Lighting arrangement in which the light is directed up to the ceiling or another reflective surface, from which it is bounced back to illuminate the general area. The light is not directed straight at the area below.

INDUSTRIAL DESIGNERS' INSTITUTE. A professional organization for industrial designers, but it also includes members of the "interior design" field like Jens Risom and Edward Wormley.

INGLENOOK

INGLENOOK. A wide, recessed chimney opening usually furnished with benches at either side. A Scottish term for "chimney corner."

INGRAIN. A reversible, flat woven wool, or wool and cotton, carpet made on a Jacquard loom. The ground color on one side becomes the top or design color on the reverse side. Ingrain is also a woven, multicolored fabric with a flat weave. The threads are dyed before they are woven.

INLAY. A technique in which a design is cut out of the surface to be decorated and then filled in with other contrasting materials cut to fit exactly into these openings. The contrast of color or materials creates the decoration. The inserts may be of wood veneer, metals, shells, ivory, etc. Illustrated is a Hepplewhite tabletop. See *Boulle Work, Certosina, Intarsia or Tarsia,* and *Marquetry.*

INLAY

INLAY, IMITATION. A painted decoration or decalcomania which simulates inlay work, but is recognizable by its smooth, uninterrupted surface.

INNERSPRING MATTRESS. A fairly recent (around 1924) innovation. The mattress has a center core of springs for buoyancy and resilience, with a protective pad on either side of it, sometimes made of sisal. This pad keeps the felted cotton, short-fiber cotton, curled hair, or other soft material from getting twisted in the coils. A tough fabric, like ticking, encases the whole unit. The construction, methods of tying or casing the coils, the quilting material, etc., vary with the manufacturer and with the price.

INSET PILASTER

INSET PILASTER. A flat half column set against a flush surface, usually at the front corners of a chest, cabinet, or other case piece. Illustrated is a late 16th-century chest.

INSULA. A building block surrounded on all sides by streets. A Roman urban building plan. A Latin word that means "island."

INSET PILASTER

INSULATION. The use of materials which keep in warmth, keep down sound vibration, or generally protect the structure from the outside elements. The materials may be built into the building, or added as facing materials to the inside surfaces of the rooms.

INTAGLIO. Designs cut out of a surface, leaving a relief in reverse. The finished design is below the plane which has been worked upon.

INTAGLIO ENGRAVING. Distinguished from other metal plate engraving techniques by the printing process used. The ink lies in the engraved furrows, rather than on the smooth surface. A piece of paper is dampened and laid on the plate, and both are rolled through a mangle-like heavy press. The damp paper is forced into the furrows, and picks up the ink. When the paper is dry, the engraved inked lines stand up in relief. See *Aquatint, Drypoint Engraving, Etching, Line Engraving,* and *Mezzotint.*

INTAILLE

INTARSIA

INTERCOLUMNATIONS

INTAILLE. French for "intaglio."

INTARSIA or TARSIA. Incised work which is inlaid with contrasting materials. A type of mosaic. It was used by the Italian designers in the early Renaissance period who used shell, bone, and ivory inserts. Illustrated is intarsia work from a stall in Santa Maria Novella in Florence. See *Certosina, Inlay, Intarsio,* and *Nonsuch Furniture.*

INTARSIATURA. Italian for "marquetry."

INTARSIO. Pictures executed in wood veneers and inlays. A highly sophisticated form of inlay.

INTERCOLUMNATIONS. The distance of spacing between classic columns based on the diameter of the columns' shaft. See *Araeostyle, Diastyle, Eustyle, Pycnostyle,* and *Systyle.*

INTERLACED CHAIR BACKS. An interlaced strap or ribbon-back chair similar in character to fretwork. It was used in late-18th-century French furniture, and in the Chippendale and Hepplewhite styles.

INTERLACED CHAIR BACK

INTERMEDIATE RIBS

INTERPENETRATIONS

INTERRUPTED ARCH

INTERMEDIATE RIBS. In vaulting, the added ribs between the transverse and diagonal ribs. They give extra support to the panels. The intermediate ribs are also called "tiercerons."

INTERPENETRATIONS. In Gothic vaulting, moldings intersecting each other and appearing to run through one another.

INTERRUPTED ARCH. An arched pediment top for cabinets and chests of the 18th century. The apex or top central segment of the arch is missing. See *Broken Pediment.*

INTONACO. The final layer of wet plaster upon which the fresco artist actually works. The final coat is applied to just that area which the painter will be able to cover before the plaster dries. See *Arricciato* and *Fresco.*

INTRADOS. The inner curve or surface of an arch. The soffit of an arch. See *Extrados.*

INVERTED CUP. A detail in the wood-turned shaped legs of the William and Mary period in England. The turning module resembles an inverted cup.

IONIC ORDER

INVERTED CUP

IONIC ORDER. A classical order of architecture and decoration. The spiral-shaped volute or scroll is characteristic of the capital. The Romans proportioned the columns at 9 diameters high. For an illustration of the Ionic capital, architrave, frieze, and cornice see *Zoophorus*.

IREME. Also called African teak or black afara. It is native to Ghana. A pale yellow to light brown, faintly ribbon-striped wood. It has noticeable rays and an intermediate grain.

IRIDESCENT FABRICS. Fabrics with contrasting colored warps and filling yarns. A changeable colored effect is produced, as in iridescent tafetta.

IRISH CHIPPENDALE. Mahogany furniture made in Ireland in the mid-18th century, and based on Chippendale drawings. The furniture lacked the refinement and lightness of the original Chippendale pieces. Lion masks and paw feet are often found on Irish Chippendale furniture.

IRISH POINT. A net curtain material with an appliqué design similar to *Duchess*.

IROKO. An African wood sometimes mislabeled "African oak or teak." It bleaches on exposure, though the natural color ranges from light yellow-brown to deep reddish-brown. Iroko is used as a veneer wood, and is also called kambala.

IRONWOOD. The olive wood of South America. An exceptionally hard wood. American ironwood is a brown-gray wood which is hard, heavy, and strong.

ISABELLINA. The Spanish term for the Gothic phase of minute, detailed, patterned design. The Renaissance phase was termed "plateresco." "Manuelino" is the Portuguese counterpart of "Isabellina."

ISABELLINA

ISINGLASS. Thin, translucent sheets of mica which were used for fenestration in the 18th- and 19th-century homes.

ISLON. A trademark name for an all nylon fabric with the soft look of velvet. It has body, and is drapable, soil resistant, durable, and color stable.

ISOMETRIC PROJECTION

IVORY

ISOMETRIC PROJECTION. A three-dimensional schematic view of an object. The lines are set at a 45° angle to the horizontal, and the vertical lines are projected from it in scale. The diagonal and curved lines are distorted, but the general appearance of the projection is more natural.

IUVARA (or IVARA), FILIPPO (1676?-1736). Italian architect, born in Messina, chief architect to the House of Savoy. He designed the central portion of the Royal Palace, La Granja, near Segovia in Spain.

IVORY. The tusks of elephants, which has been and is still used for decorative inlay work and carving. It is a rare material but has been imitated in plastics. Illustrated is a 15th-century French 9¹/₂"-tall statue.

IVY

IVY. A decorative leaf design. The leaf is the symbol of friendship, and was also sacred to Bacchus, and therefore appears on many ancient vases. The ivy leaf is usually broad, five-lobed, and appears at the end of long shoots in lancelike forms.

JABOT. A ruffle or frill. The cascading side pieces of a swag.

JACARANDA. See *Rosewood, Brazilian*.

JACKKNIFE SOFA BED. See *Sofa Bed*.

JACOB, FRANÇOIS HONORÉ GEORGES. A French cabinetmaker of the Louis XVI and Directoire periods. He also made and designed furniture for Napoleon.

JACOB, GEORGES. The father of the equally famous François Honoré Georges Jacob. A noted cabinetmaker of the Louis XVI period.

JACOBEAN. The period (1603–1649) in English architecture and art which extends over the reigns of James I and Charles I. It is a term which covers the merging of English Tudor designs and motifs with the Renaissance in England.

JACOBEAN ORNAMENT. Bands of molding applied to furniture in geometric patterns to create a paneled effect. This was a popular decoration on Jacobean furniture made in England in the 17th century. A table (c. 1630) is illustrated.

J

JABOT

JACOBEAN

JACOBEAN ORNAMENT

JACOBSON, ARNE. A modern Scandinavian designer of a laminated plywood-and-steel chair similar to the Eames chair. He also created the "egg" chair, which is in the tradition of Saarinen's "womb" chair.

JACQUARD. In carpeting, the pattern control on the Wilton loom. It was invented by Joseph-Marie Jacquard in Brussels, Belgium, and adapted to the Wilton loom in 1825.

JACQUARD, JOSEPH-MARIE (1752–1834). The Frenchman who, in 1801, created the Jacquard loom, which revolutionized the production of figured woven textiles. The loom made it possible to produce certain multicolored designs inexpensively. In 1825, the loom was adapted for the carpet industry.

JACQUARD WEAVE. A weave with intricate, multicolored patterns. It is produced on the type of loom created by Joseph-Marie Jacquard in the early 19th century. Damasks, tapestries, and brocades are all Jacquard weaves.

JACQUEMART AND BENARD. French wallpaper manufacturers from 1791 to 1840. They were the successors to Réveillon.

JALEE. In India, the decorated pierced marble or stone work such as was used in the Taj Mahal. Illustrated is an open-work stone window arch. See *Stone, Edward Durrel* and *United States Embassy, New Delhi.*

JALOUSIES. A French word for a louvered window, similar to Venetian blinds. A jalousied room is constructed of louvered windows or panels.

JAMB. The interior side of a door or window frame.

JAPANNING. An 18th-century finishing process. Furniture and metalwork were enameled with colored shellac, and the decoration was in relief and painted in color and gilt. The technique was an imitation of the brilliant lacquered colors of the Japanese work which was imported by the Dutch into Europe during the 17th century. See *Lacquer* and *Martin Brothers.*

JARDINIÈRE. A plant container or stand made of wood, metal, or porcelain. The jardinière reached the height of elegance during the latter part of the 18th century in France and England. A Chippendale design is illustrated.

JARDINIÈRE VELVET. A silk velvet of several depths of uncut loops set against a damask or silk background. It is usually a multicolored pattern resembling a flower arrangement against a light satin background. The velvet was originally produced in Genoa.

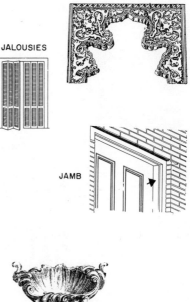

JALEE

JALOUSIES

JAMB

JARDINIÈRE

JASPÉ. In carpeting, irregular warp stripes of two hues of a color in a surface yarn, in either a patterned or plain fabric. In fabric, a streaked or mottled effect produced by an uneven dyeing of warp threads. It resembles the stone jasper.

JASPER. An opaque type of quartz, red, yellow, or brown.

JASPER WARE. An 18th-century type of hard bisquit ware (pottery) introduced by Wedgwood in England.

JEANNERET, CHARLES ÉDOUARD. See *Le Corbusier*.

JEFFERSON, THOMAS (1743–1826). The third President of the United States, and a great political philosopher. He was interested in architecture, and besides designing his own home, Monticello, he was active in the planning of Washington, D.C. Jefferson was much impressed by Roman architecture, and he designed the Capitol in Richmond, Virginia (1785–1792) based on the Maison Carrée at Nîmes (see *Maison Carrée*). The rotunda of the University of Virginia in Charlottesville, Virginia (1822–1826), was planned by Jefferson in association with Benjamin Henry Latrobe.

THOMAS JEFFERSON: MONTICELLO

JENNEY, WILLIAM LE BARON (1832–1907). American architect who is credited as the designer of the first skyscraper, a ten-story fireproof building erected on the modern principles of construction (the Home Insurance Company in Chicago, Illinois, 1883–1885).

JENNY LIND BED. A spool-turned bed named for Jenny Lind, the "Swedish Nightingale," who was visiting America at the time it was designed (1850–1852). It had a low headboard and modest bedposts.

JESTING BEAM

JERKIN HEAD GABLE. The end of a roof which is an intermediate shape between a gable and a hip. The gable rises to about halfway up to the ridge, and appears truncated, since the roof is inclined backward and up from this point onward.

JESTING BEAM. A decorative or ornamental beam, not necessarily a structural member.

JESUIT ARCHITECTURE. The Baroque style of architecture was adopted by the Jesuits as their own form of architecture. It expressed their resistance to austerity in religion. Il Gesù, the Jesuit Church in Rome, was started by Vignola in 1568, but the front façade with the typical grand scrolls by Giacomo della Porta set the style for Jesuit-Baroque churches in France, Italy, and elsewhere during the 17th and 18th centuries.

JETTY. An overhanging part of a building.

JESUIT ARCHITECTURE

JEWELING. Any small, ornamental feature carved on furniture or a building, either above or below the surface, to resemble a polished or cut jewel. Illustrated is an ornamental detail from a 16th-century English building.

JIB DOOR. A flush door which is painted or papered over to make it as inconspicuous as possible.

JIGSAW DETAIL. A cutout or fretwork design made with a jigsaw. It was used for the enhancement of buildings of the mid and late 19th century. The bargework was often made with a jigsaw. The "gingerbread" or "steamboat Gothic," late Victorian period was jigsaw work in its most aggravated form.

JIGSAW MIRROR. A type of mirror that was popular in the 18th and 19th centuries in America and England. The earlier examples were hand cut, and had detailed scrolls, while 19th-century pieces were cut on a jigsaw, one of the first of the power-operated tools. Shown here is a Queen Anne type of mirror of the early 18th century.

JOGGLE. In stonework or masonry, a joint in which the grooved part of one unit fits the projecting part of another.

JOHNSON, PHILIP. An American architect and designer born in Cleveland, Ohio, in 1906. During the 1930's he did propaganda work for modern architecture at the Museum of Modern Art, in New York City. Johnson studied architecture at Harvard in the early 1940's, and was greatly influenced by Marcel Breuer, though his style developed along the lines of Mies van der Rohe. To this classic feeling, Johnson added domes and vaulted forms (as in the Port Chester Synagogue in New York). One of his most famous buildings is his own glass home in New Canaan, Connecticut. He is able to "use the past and yet be free" to contribute to modern forms. Johnson was recently associated with Mies van der Rohe in the Seagram Building in New York City and the Four Seasons restaurant in that building. He has also worked on the new additions to the Museum of Modern Art in New York City, the Art Gallery in Utica, New York, and the New York State Theatre at the Lincoln Center in New York City.

JOHNSON, PHILIP, HIS "GLASS HOUSE," NEW CANAAN, CONNECTICUT. An all-glass house with a brick guesthouse pavilion designed by Philip Johnson. The architecture and furnishings show the influence of Mies van der Rohe's work of the 1920's. Low partitions inside the glass structure separate the work and sleeping areas from the dining and living areas. A brick cylinder, repeating the flooring material, houses the bathroom. The brick guesthouse has a noteworthy vaultlike ceiling with strip lighting which increases the sense of space.

JEWELING

JIGSAW MIRROR

THOMAS JOHNSON

JOHNSON, THOMAS. A mid-18th-century English carver of fanciful and eccentric girandoles, sconces, etc. He was a contemporary of Chippendale, and used a mixture of Gothic, Chinese, and Louis XV rococo styles.

JOHNSON ADMINISTRATION BUILDING, RACINE, WISCONSIN. It was designed by Frank Lloyd Wright in 1938. The building is a wraparound brick and glass tubular skin, with the interior space formed by piers with lily pad tops which create the ceiling. It was Wright's break from post-and-beam construction. In 1949, a laboratory tower was added which consists of floors cantilevered out from a central cylinder.

JOINER. An artisan or draftsman involved in joining woods together by means of joints, glue, nails, etc. See *Joinery*.

JOINERY. The craft of assembling woodwork by means of mortise and tenons, dovetails, tongue and grooves, dowels, etc. A dovetailed joint is illustrated. See *Dovetail, Mortise and Tenon Joint,* and *Tongue and Groove.*

JOINT. The junction at which two pieces of lumber unite to form a support or make a closure. Illustrated is a mortise and tenon joint.

JOINT STOOL. A 17th- and 18th-century simple stool made of turnings, and joined together. An oak stool of the Jacobean period (17th century) is shown.

JOINERY

JOINT

JOINT STOOL

JOIST

JOIST. A horizontal construction member used to support a floor or ceiling.

JONES, INIGO (1572–1653). A famous English Renaissance architect who introduced the classic Palladian style into England. Besides designing assorted public buildings, and the Queen's House, Greenwich, he created fanciful and imaginative masques and balls for royalty. Jones has been called the English Palladio. Illustrated is the Banquet Hall at Whitehall. See *Palladio, Andrea.*

INIGO JONES

JONES, WILLIAM. An 18th-century English architect. In 1739, he published *The Gentleman's or Builder's Companion* with plates of chimneypieces, slab tables, pier glasses, tabernacle frames, ceilings, etc.

JOUY. See *Toile de Jouy.*

JUDGE'S CHAIR. An 18th-century high-back chair. The upholstered back is raised up from the seat, and curved to cradle the head and shoulders. The upholstered arms curve around at the same level as the bottom of the chair back. The arm stumps and back chair rails are exposed. The legs are squarish, and bracket out at the seat. Box stretchers connect the four legs.

JUGENDSTIL. German for "youth style." The period contemporary with the Art Nouveau of France (1895–1912).

JUHL, FINN. A 20th-century Danish architect and furniture designer. The legs, arms, backs, etc., of his furniture designs are beautiful and subtly sculptured wood elements.

JUTE. The fibrous skin between the bark and the stalk of a tiliaceous plant grown in India. The long, tough fibers are carded and spun into strong, durable yarns that are used as stuffer warps, and binding and filling wefts. The jute yarns add strength, weight, and stiffness to carpets.

JUVARA, FILIPPO. See *Iuvara (or Ivara), Filippo.*

K.D. See *Knocked Down (K.D.).*

KAHANE, MELANIE. A contemporary 20th-century interior designer and member of the *American Institute of Interior Designers (A.I.D.).*

KAKEMONO. An unframed Chinese or Japanese painting mounted on brocade, and usually equipped with a bamboo rod, top and bottom. The painting or print is used as a wall hanging.

KAKIEMON, SAKAIDA. A 17th-century Japanese pottery artist who developed the use of colored enamel designs on porcelain. Decorations done in this manner bear the name of this artist. The pottery is also sometimes referred to as "Korean Decoration."

KAMBALA. See *Iroko.*

KAOLIN. A white clay used in making true porcelain. It is also called "china clay." Hard paste is made of this clay. See *China.*

KAPOK. Silky fibers, obtained from the seed pods of the kapok tree. It is used as a stuffing material for mattresses, cushions, etc., and is also called *Silk Floss.*

KAPPA SHELL. A trademark name for fine sheets of real ocean pearl nacre shell, which is iridescent in color. It is available in assorted sizes and thicknesses, and can be used for walls, furniture tops, lamps, lighting fixtures, screen inserts, etc. The material is similar to nacre in appearance.

K

KAS

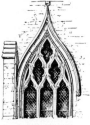

KEEL ARCH

WILLIAM KENT

KETTLE BASE

KARL JOHANS STYLE. The Empire style in Sweden (early 19th century).

KAS. Dutch term for chest or cupboard. A tall, upright cabinet, clothespress, or wardrobe. It usually had ball feet, a plain heavy cornice, and two doors that opened outward. It was the proud possession of the Dutch colonist in America. See *Armoire*.

KAUFFMANN, ANGELICA (1741–1807). A decorative painter of furniture and interiors. She was born in Switzerland, but did most of her work in England where she decorated and painted plaques, panels, and medallions for Adam, Hepplewhite, and Sheraton. See *Grisaille*.

KEEL ARCH. A curved arch that rises to a point. An ogee arch.

KEEL MOLDING. See *Ogee*.

KEEP

KEEP. The stronghold in a medieval castle.

KELOBRA. A wood native to Central America and Mexico, and primarily used as a veneer. It is a neutral brown color and is also called "guanacaste" and "genisero."

KEMP. Short, wavy, coarse wool or hair fiber, not usable for dyeing or spinning. It is often used as carpet wool.

KENT, WILLIAM (1684–1748). An English architect, furniture designer, painter, and landscape designer in the tradition of Inigo Jones. His furniture designs were in the heavy Venetian style with classical detailing, and they served as a link between the Queen Anne style and the Chippendale designs. Kent's furniture was usually produced in mahogany and gilt, and trimmed with ornately carved scrolls, swags of fruit and flowers, and often an eagle's head terminating in a scroll. In association with the Earl of Burlington, he designed the Palladian Chiswick House.

KERF. A saw cut. Several adjacent saw cuts, when made against the grain of a wood plank, sometimes make it possible to bend the wood into a curve or arc.

KETTLE BASE. A bombé base. A piece of furniture which has an outward swelling front and sides similar to a kettle. This shape appears in English and American furniture in the mid- and late-18th century. Illustrated is a unit found in Salem, Massachusetts. See *Bombé*.

KETTLE FRONT. See *Swell Front.*

KEY. A wall or ceiling surface which has been scratched or gouged so that plaster will adhere. Any roughened surface which aids in adhesion.

KEY CORNERED. A rectangular panel whose corners are broken by right angles. Paterae or rosettes are sometimes used to decorate these "opened" corners. Adam used this type of paneling, and it was also used in the Louis XVI, Directoire, and Empire periods.

KEY PATTERN. A Greek geometric band or border design. See *Fret.*

KEYING. A method of closing securely by means of interlocking. Dovetailing is one method of closing by keying. A half-lap, multiple, dovetail joint, such as is used on drawers, is illustrated.

KETTLE FRONT

KEY CORNERED

KEY PATTERN

KEYSTONE

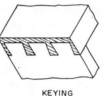

KEYING

KEYSTONE. The central wedge-shaped stone at the top of the curve of an arch. Illustrated is an arch at the Palais du Louvre in Paris. See *Voussoir.*

KICKPLATE. A plate, usually of metal or plastic, placed on the lower rail of a door to prevent the kicking or scuffing of this area.

KIDNEY DESK or TABLE. An ornamental kidney-shaped table with the concave side toward the sitter. The sitter is therefore semisurrounded by the curved front. The shape was used as a kneehole-type desk or dressing table by Sheraton and as a poudreuse in the Louis XV period. See *Writing Table* for an illustration of a Sheraton desk.

KILN-DRIED. Lumber which has been artificially dried in heated chambers, rather than air-dried in the open. In the kiln-drying method, the lumber is less subject to warping or checking since the moisture content of the wood can be more easily controlled. See *Checks.*

KING CLOSER. A brick with one header cut to half the width of the brick (one corner is removed). The other header is full width. The brick is therefore cut diagonally. See *Queen Closer.*

KIDNEY DESK

KING CLOSER

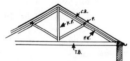

KING POST TRUSS

KINGWOOD

KNEE

KLISMOS

KING POST. The central upright post which supports the tie beam in a king-post truss.

KING-POST TRUSS. A roof whose members are joined together to form a triangular girder which supports the roofing materials and also transmits the weight vertically to the walls and/or piers. A central king post reinforces the central meeting point, and rests on the tie beam. *K.P.* is the king post. *T.B.* is the tie beam. *C.R.* is the common rafter. *P.R.* is the purlin.

KING-SIZE BED. A double bed which can be made up of two twin-sized box springs and mattresses pushed together, or one oversized spring and mattress. The bed is usually 72″ to 78″ wide by 76″ to 84″ long. The king-size bed usually has one wide headboard. Though this is a comparatively modern concept, it can be used in traditional or period rooms, depending upon the style and decoration of the headboard.

KINGWOOD. A dark, purplish-brown wood with black and golden-yellow streaks. It is a fine cabinet wood native to Sumatra and Brazil, and is also called "bois de violette." Kingwood was popular in the Louis XV and Louis XVI periods. An early Louis XVI secrétaire in kingwood and tulipwood is illustrated. It was decorated with Sèvres plaques and ormolu mounts.

KIOSK. From the French "kiosque," a small shelter or pavilion. The word is usually associated with a French newsstand or public toilet.

KITCHENETTE. A small kitchen or service area usually equipped with a stove, sink, and refrigerator.

KJAERHOLM, POUL. A modern Danish furniture designer.

KLINE. A multipurpose ancient Greek piece of furniture which served as a sofa, dining couch, and bed. It resembles an oversized bed with a sweeping curved back at one end. The front legs curved forward, and the rear legs curved out behind. The back of the unit resembles the *Klismos*.

KLISMOS. A classic Greek type of chair with a concave curved back rail and curved legs that splay out front and back. This design appears again in the Directoire, Empire, Regency, and Duncan Phyfe styles.

KLOSTERBOGEN. German for "Gothic arch."

KNEE. The upper convex curve of the cabriole leg which is sometimes embellished with carved decorations like a shell, lion's head, etc. It is also called the "hip." See *Cabriole Leg* and *Hip*.

KNEEHOLE DESK. A desk with a central open space below the writing surface for legroom. Either side of the opening is solid or filled in with drawers which may continue down to the floor. See *Reverse Serpentine* for a kneehole table by Sheraton.

KNEEHOLE PANEL. See *Modesty Panel*.

KNIFE BOX. A decorative wooden chest with vertical slots for knives. It was usually used, in pairs, on top of sideboards. It was extremely popular in 18th-century England. Chippendale and others designed beautiful inlaid knife boxes.

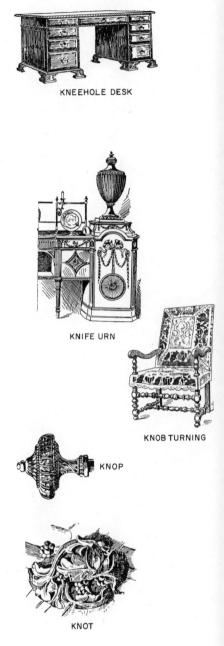

KNEEHOLE DESK

KNIFE BOX

KNIFE URNS. Ornamental vaselike forms resting on top of pedestals set at either end of an Adam-type side table. The urns were used to hold knives, forks, and spoons, or hot or iced water. These urns were later replaced by knife boxes.

KNOB TURNING. A turning resembling a series of knobs or balls, which was used for furniture legs and stretchers during the 17th century.

KNOCKED DOWN (K.D.). The practice of shipping furniture unassembled, or in several parts which must be put together at the point of use. An economy of space, labor, and shipping costs is effected when a unit is shipped "K.D."

KNOP. An archaic spelling for "knob." A handle or holding device to open doors, drawers, etc. An 18th-century Adam brass door knop is shown. The term is also used to describe a small bouquet of leaves or flowers.

KNORPELWERK. German for "rinceau" or "Renaissance scroll-work."

KNOT or KNOB. A cluster or nosegay of flowers and/or leaves used as a boss or pendant at the intersection of vaulting ribs (see *Boss*). A knot is also a dark round or oval interruption in the grain of a piece of wood. It marks where a branch grew on the tree.

KNOTTED RUG. An oriental rug weave in which the surface or pile is formed by the ends of the threads being knotted around the warps. The weft threads serve merely as binders.

KNIFE URN

KNOB TURNING

KNOP

KNOT

KNUCKLE CARVING

KRATER

KNOTTY PINE. Pinewood showing knots or dark oval shapes. The knots are often accentuated by pickling the pinewood (whiting the wood). Knotty pine is used today for Early American reproductions and for paneling informal rooms. The wood itself grows in Idaho, Washington, and Montana.

KNUBSTOL. A Norwegian provincial tree-trunk chair.

KNUCKLE CARVING. The carving which often appears on the outer edges of the arms of Chippendale chairs. It resembles the knuckles of the human hand.

KNUCKLE JOINT. The hinged joint of a drop-leaf table. The hinge functions in the same way that the knuckle joint of the finger does. See *Finger Joint* and *Pembroke Table*.

KOA. A Hawaiian showy wood used for decorative effects. It takes a fine, lustrous finish. Koa has a reddish stripe on a yellow-brown ground with a decided cross ripple or curl, which gives it a plaid effect. It is used on fine furniture, for art objects, and for musical instruments.

KODEL. The trademark name for a polyester fiber manufactured by Eastman. It is not as strong as Dacron, and has less abrasion resistance, but it dyes well, dries quickly, resists wrinkling, and is considered more stable and heat-resistant than many other polyesters.

KORAI. Votive statues of women in early Greek art. The figures were usually sculptured in heroic scale.

KOREAN DECORATION. See *Kakiemon, Sakaida.*

KORINA. A trademark name for "limba," a light, golden blond wood that resembles primavera. It is available in long, wide panels which are uniform in color and satin-like in appearance. A stripe or crossfire figured veneer is also available. Korina is also called "afara."

KOROSEAL. A trademark name for flexible synthetic fabrics or wall coverings derived from coal, limestone, and salt. Like leatherette or Naugahyde. They are produced by The B. F. Goodrich Company.

KOUROI. Early Greek life-sized statues of nude youths which were made between c. 650 B.C. and 480 B.C. These statues were probably dedicated to young athletes who won acclaim in the Olympic games.

KOYLON. The trademark name for latex-rubber foam produced by United States Rubber Company.

KRAGSTEIN. German for "bracket" or "console."

KRATER. An ancient Greek two-handled bowl used for mixing wine and water.

KREUZGEWÖLBE. German for "groined or cross vault."

KYANIZE. A process to make wood decay-resistant. The lumber is impregnated with mercuric chloride.

KYLIN. A fantastic dragon-like beast sometimes used in Chinese decorations.

KYLIX. An ancient Greek drinking cup. It is usually flat, two-handled and set on a slender foot or stem.

KYLIX

LABURNUM

KYLIN

LA GIRALDA. The tower of the Seville Cathedral which is considered one of the most beautiful structures of its kind. The name is derived from the turning figure of faith (weather vane) on top of the tower. The tower was originally built in 1159 as a minaret for the mosque that stood on that location. The belfry was added in 1568, in the Renaissance style. The total height of the tower is 275', and it is 45' square at the base.

LA GIRALDA

LABEL. See *Dripstone* and *Ribbons*.

L

LABEL

LABROUSTE, HENRI (1801–1875). A great French architect-con-structor-engineer. Though he was a student of the Académie des Beaux Arts, he rebelled against its stereotyped practices. His first major commission was a cast- and wrought-iron con-struction from the foundation to the roof, enclosed in a stone-work exterior. The Bibliothèque Nationale in Paris, in 1858, was his masterpiece. The central reading room had a light, airy feeling. The Magasin Central (stack room) consists of four stories above ground level and one below. The whole area is covered over with a glass ceiling, and the cast-iron gridiron floor plates allow daylight to penetrate into the entire stack area. The Central Reading Room is illustrated.

LABEL

LABRUM

HENRI LABROUSTE

LABRUM. A stone bath of ancient Rome.

LABURNUM. A hard, yellow to reddish-brown wood, native to southern Europe. The wood takes a fine polish, and it was used in the Queen Anne period for inlays and veneering.

254

LABYRINTH. A complicated, intricate maze. In the classic Greek period, the term referred to an edifice composed of complicated passageways which twisted, turned, and intersected one another, e.g., the Labyrinth of Crete.

LAC. A resinous material formed on trees by an insect (*Coccas lacca*). This material is treated and converted into the shellac that is used in fine varnishes.

LACE

LACE. An openwork fabric consisting of a network of threads formed into a design made by hand bobbins, needles, or hooks. Lace is also made by machine. See *Filet Lace, Nottingham Lace, Reticella,* and *Valenciennes Lace.*

LACEWOOD. An Australian decorative veneer wood with a lacy, pockmarked, flaked surface effect. It is pink to light brown in color, and has a silky sheen. Lacewood is used in small decorative areas for borders, inlays, etc.

LACING. A bonding course between brick courses of an arch, and also a course of brick in a rubble wall.

LACQUER. A colored or opaque varnish made of shellac dissolved in alcohol. Chinese and Japanese lacquer is a hard varnish made from the sap of the lacquer tree. It has a shiny, lustrous quality. See *Huygens, Japanning,* and *Vernis Martin.*

LACQUERWORK

LACQUERWORK. Articles covered with a lacquer surface on which flat or relief designs are drawn. It was a fashionable furniture finish and form of decoration in Europe from the mid-17th to the late-18th century. Illustrated is a Chinese Chippendale style four-poster bed of about 1760 which was embellished with lacquer work.

LACUNARIA

LACUNARIA. See *Caissons* and *Coffered Panel.*

LADDER-BACK

LADDER-BACK. A chair back which resembles a multirung ladder. A series of horizontal rails is contained by the two vertical chair-back stiles. These rails replace the usual vertical splat. This type of chair back is often found in provincial-type furniture. Chippendale chairs sometimes had ladder-backs. See *Slat-Back.*

LAGYNOS. A Greek oinochoe. A wine jug which has a broad bottom and a tall narrow neck as well as a loop handle. See *Aryballos* and *Oinochoe.*

LALLY COLUMN. A trade name for a supporting unit which is a cylinder of stainless steel filled with concrete.

LALONDE, RICHARD. An 18th-century French court designer of furniture and interiors in the classic Louis XVI style. Illustrated is a chased door lock by Lalonde.

LAMBELLE. A lightweight, damask, textured fabric with coarser contrasting weft threads. The warp is usually fine, mercerized threads.

LAMBREQUIN. A valance board for draperies. Usually a horizontal stiff covering for curtain or drapery headings, as well as the rods, hooks, and other hardware. It is also called a "pelmet" or "palmette." Originally the lambrequin was a fabric unit, but it was often reproduced in carved wood panels with applied moldings, or metal work decorations. See *Cantonnière* and *Pentes.*

LAMBRIS D'APPUI. A French term for paneling that reaches to waist or elbow height.

LAMBRIS DE HAUTEUR. A French term for paneling that reaches up to the cornice or picture rail.

LAMINATION. A bonding or gluing together of various layers of wood, often with a veneer on top. The assorted layers form a permanent unit. See *Plywood.* Fabric may be laminated on to other materials.

LAMPADAIRE. A classic pedestal designed to hold a lamp or candlestick. Illustrated is a Thomas Hope English Regency or Empire design.

LAMPAS. A patterned textile with two warps and two or more fillers. The pattern is always twill or plain weave, and the background is a plain or satin weave. Lampas is similar to a two-colored damask, and was extremely popular during the 18th and 19th centuries. The patterns, even today, are usually classic in style. Originally lampas was an East Indian printed silk.

LAMPSHADE. A covering or shield for a light bulb which is set on top of a lamp base. The metal frame of the shade, which is usually cylindrical, oval, or bell-shaped, is covered with silk, rayon, polyplastex, parchment, or opaque board. The shade is used to diffuse the light, cut down the glare of the bulb and/or direct the stream of light. Metal lampshades are also used. See *Bouillotte Shade, Harp,* and *Tôle Shade.*

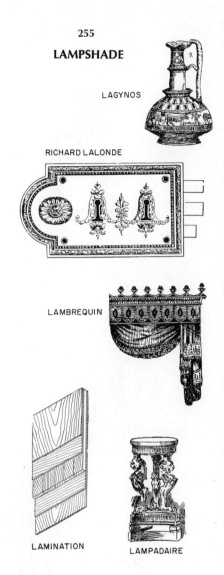

LAMPSHADE

LAGYNOS

RICHARD LALONDE

LAMBREQUIN

LAMINATION

LAMPADAIRE

LANAI

LANCASHIRE SPINDLE-BACK CHAIR

LANAI. A Hawaiian term for an outdoor patio, terrace, or veranda.

LANCASHIRE SPINDLE-BACK CHAIR. A country-style spindle-back chair of the early 18th century in England. The uprights are turnings, and they are connected with a top rail that is embellished with a shell-like ornament in the middle. Two rows of four or five spindles are contained by two horizontal rails and the top rail. The seat is made of rush, and the front stretcher is turned with a knoblike centerpiece.

LANCASTRIAN PERIOD. See *Perpendicular Style*. Illustrated is the Church of Fotheringhay, Northamptonshire, England.

LANCASTRIAN PERIOD

LANCET ARCH

LANCET PERIOD

LANCET WINDOW

BATTY LANGLEY

LANCET ARCH. A narrow pointed arch. A feature of early Gothic architecture.

LANCET PERIOD. See *Early English Period*. Illustrated is Lincoln Cathedral, showing the apse and the charter house at far right.

LANCET WINDOW. A narrow pointed window, lancet-shaped.

LANCRET, NICHOLAS (1690–1743). A French decorative painter in the style and tradition of Watteau.

LANDING. A flat platform between two flights of stairs.

LANDSCAPE. An outdoor scene or planting arrangement. A painting, mirror, or panel which is wider than it is tall.

LANGLEY, BATTY (1695–1751). An English architect and designer. He frequently used ogee or cyma curves for moldings around doors and drawers. Langley's *Gothic Architecture Improved by Rules and Proportion* helped bring in the Gothic Revival. He also compiled *Ancient Masonry,* which provided inspiration for the Colonial American 18th-century builders.

LANGLOIS, PETER. A late-18th-century French immigrant craftsman in England who worked in the technique of Boulle (inlays of brass and tortoiseshell). See *Boulle Work*.

LANNUIER, CHARLES-HONORÉ. A late-18th- and early-19th-century French cabinetmaker and designer. He worked in America in the Louis XVI classic style, and influenced the work of Duncan Phyfe.

LANTERN. In architecture, a small structure, with openings for light, placed at the very top of a dome, cupola, turret, or roof. It is often a purely decorative device. See *Château de Chambord*. In furniture, a case with a metal or wood framework furnished with panes of glass or other translucent materials. A lighted candle was originally inserted inside the framework. Today lanterns are also electrified. See *Lanthorn*.

LANTERN CLOCK. A lantern-shaped shelf clock of the late 17th century. It was usually made of brass, and was also called a "birdcage clock."

LANTERN LIGHT. A raised, vertical skylight which is set above the roof of a building. The panes of glass are vertical rather than arranged in the more usual horizontal framework.

LANTHORN. An archaic term for "lantern." Horn was used instead of glass panes in the wood or metal framework. Illustrated is a German Renaissance wrought-iron lanthorn.

LAP JOINT. Two pieces of wood with exactly grooved out areas laid one up and one down, so that they make a flush X arrangement when they are notched into each other at right angles. A form of joinery.

LAPIS LAZULI. A semiprecious, azure stone of a rich blue color. It is an aluminous mineral resembling the blue carbonate of copper. It was and is still used in inlay work and on decorative hardware.

LAQUÉ. French for "lacquered."

LARMIER. From the French "larme," a tear or drop. The drip of a cornice or the projecting eaves of the cornice of a structure.

L'ART DEL POVERO. An Italian form of *Trompe l'Oeil*.

L'ART MODERNE. A weekly periodical which was founded in Belgium by Octave Maus, Edmond Picard, and others in 1884. Its major premise was "art is the eternally spontaneous and free action of man on his environment, for the purpose of transforming it and making it conform to a new idea." The

L'ART MODERNE

LANTERN

LANTERN

LANTHORN

LAP JOINT

LASALLE, PHILIPPE DE

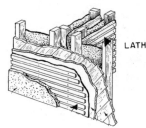

LATER PLANTAGENET PERIOD

LATIN CROSS

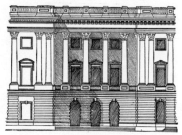

periodical was published until 1893, and brought together a group of avant-garde young Belgian artists known as "Les XX." The group included James Ensor, Ferdinand Knopff, Alfred William ("Willy") Finch, and Maus. See *Art Nouveau.*

LASALLE, PHILIPPE DE (1720–1803). A French designer and manufacturer of textiles, as well as the inventor of special weaving devices. During the Louis XVI period he was especially noted for his floral patterns and lampases. His artistry earned him the title, "the painter of textiles."

LATE POINTED PERIOD. See *Perpendicular Style.*

LATER PLANTAGENET PERIOD. See *Decorated Period.* Illustrated is a column capital from the Beverley Minster, Yorkshire, England, c. 1320.

LATEX. A product made from the sap of the rubber tree. It is a rubber coating used on carpet backings, or to hold the yarn ends of tufted fabric on to the backing. See *Foam Rubber.*

LATH. A thin strip of flat wood used for understructures or as a framework for finishing materials. Illustrated is a lath framework for stucco.

LATH

LATHE

LATHE. In cabinetry, an instrument for holding a rotating piece of wood or dowel while the wood is being curved or shaped, as e.g., a wood turning.

LATIN CROSS. A cross form with the vertical line longer than the horizontal one.

LATROBE, BENJAMIN HENRY (1766–1820). An American architect who worked in the Greek Revival style. He was greatly influenced by classic Greek and Roman architecture. Latrobe was responsible for work on the south wing of the Capitol in Washington, D.C.; the semicircular Hall of Representatives based on the monument of Lysicrates; and the Washington Treasury in 1836. In the Greek style he also designed the Second U.S. Bank in Philadelphia, Gerard College (1833), also in Philadelphia, the Washington Monument in Baltimore, and the Custom House in New York City. Latrobe also designed in the Gothic Revival style. The Cathedral in Baltimore (1805–1821) was probably the first Gothic-type structure erected in America.

LATTEN

LÂTS

LÂTS. Buddhist inscribed pillars in Indian architecture.

LATTEN. German for "laths" or "thin plates." A mixed metal of copper and zinc which resembles brass. It was used during the Gothic period for engraved panels and cast statues. Illustrated is an engraved 14th-century latten panel.

LATTICE. An openwork crisscross or fretwork made of wood laths or thin metal strips.

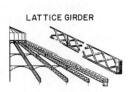

LATTICE GIRDER

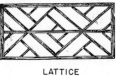

LATTICE

LATTICE GIRDER. A girder with several braces crossing over each other diagonally or in a lattice effect.

LATTICE WINDOW. A window with leaded glazing bars forming a lattice pattern. The panes are usually diamond- or lozenge-shaped.

LATTICE WINDOW

LATTICEWORK. A chair-back design by Sheraton and Manwaring which consisted of wooden or metal strips crossing over each other diagonally. This name also applies to tracery on the doors of cabinets and bookcases. Fretwork is usually much smaller in scale than latticework. See *Trelliswork*.

LAUAN. A Philippine hardwood that is reddish brown, and resembles mahogany. It is sometimes called "Philippine mahogany." A handsome ribbon figure is produced when the lauan log is quarter-sawed. See *Almon*.

LAUBGEHÄNGE. German for a "festoon of foliage."

LATTICEWORK

LATTICEWORK

LAUREL

LAUREL. An ornamental motif used as a symbol for glory. Singers and heroes in ancient times were crowned with laurels. It was used in the classic Greek and Roman periods for decoration, and also in the Louis XVI, English 18th-century, and early 19th-century European styles. Laurel was and is used as an architectural or furniture decoration on friezes, in bands, etc.

LAUREL

LAUREL WOOD. An East Indian walnut. A gray or brown, coarse-grained, hard and brittle wood which is used as a veneer on fine cabinetry. The pattern may be striped, fiddlebacked, figured, or it may have indistinct rays.

LAVABO. French for "washstand." A table and washstand, or a washbowl with a fountain, cistern, or water supply. In current wall arrangements, the lavabo often is used as a planter.

LAVORO A SBALZO. Italian for "repoussé work."

LAWN. Originally a lightweight, fine linen fabric. Currently it is also made of highly polished cotton yarn.

LAWSON COUCH. A simple, usually skirted, sofa or loveseat, with rollover arms which are usually mid-height between the seat and the top of the sofa back. A Lawson chair is similar to a couch in general line, but is wide enough to seat only one person.

LAYLIGHT. A glass or translucent panel set flush into a ceiling to admit natural or artificial light.

LAYLIGHT

LAZY SUSAN

LAZY SUSAN. A revolving tabletop or tray for serving relishes and condiments. An American adaptation of the dumbwaiter of the late 18th century in England. A Sheraton design is illustrated.

LE BRUN, CHARLES (1619–1690). Le Brun was King Louis XIV's favorite painter and decorator. He created tall, stiff, pompous, heroic-scaled furniture. Among his decorating achievements was the semicircular vaulted arch in the Hall of Mirrors (Galérie des Glaces) in Versailles, which was designed by Jules Hardouin-Mansart. Le Brun was the Director and chief designer of the Gobelins Factory which manufactured tapestries, embroideries, furniture, mosaics, bronzes, etc. He was the embodiment of the soul and spirit of the decoration of the Louis XIV period. An armoire, designed by Le Brun and executed by Charles-André Boulle, is illustrated.

LE CLERC, SÉBASTIAN (1637–1714). French engraver.

LE COMPTE, LOUIS (1639–1694). A French sculptor of the Louis XIV period. He did decorative carvings at Versailles.

CHARLES LE BRUN

LE CORBUSIER (pseudonym of Charles Édouard Jeanneret or Édouard Jeanneret-Gris). Born in Switzerland in 1887. He was an architect, painter, writer, and architectural critic. With his cousin, Pierre Jeanneret, he pioneered in the use of ferroconcrete framework to create modern, functional structures. With Amédée Ozenfant, he founded a movement for "purism in art" and wrote *Après le Cubisme* (1918) and *La Peinture Moderne* (1924). Le Corbusier also wrote *Vers une Architecture* (1923). Among his noted architectural works are the Swiss Building of la Cité Universitaire in Paris, two houses for the Werkbund Exhibition at Stuttgart (1927) and designs for the Palace of the League of Nations at Geneva (1927). He was one of the most influential architects and city planners of this century. Other works by Le Corbusier are in Russia, India, Switzerland, Brazil, Algeria, etc. Le Corbusier died in August, 1965. See *Behrens, Peter.*

LE LARGE, JEAN-BAPTISTE. A late-18th-century French furniture designer and manufacturer. He created many bergères and fauteuils for the Palais de Versailles.

LE LEU, FRANÇOIS (1729–1807). A French cabinetmaker noted for his exquisite marquetry. He worked under Jean-François Oeben at Versailles, and also created pieces for Mme Du Barry. Le Leu worked in the Louis XV and Louis XVI styles.

LE MAIRE, ELEANOR. A 20th-century designer-decorator.

LE MÉDAILLON. An oval back chair of the Louis XVI period. The chair had straight legs, and the arms were brought forward and rose directly above the front legs. See *Cameo Back* and *Oval Back.*

LE MERCIER, JACQUES (1585–1654). A 17th-century French architect who built a residence for Richelieu, which later became known as the "Palais Royale" when Richelieu presented it to King Louis XIII. He also designed many Jesuit churches. His chief remaining work is the Church of the Sorbonne, Paris (1635), which was inspired by Della Porta's designs. The dome was the model for that of the Church of the Invalides.

LE NÔTRE, ANDRÉ (1613–1700). A French architect-designer of the parks and gardens at Versailles, the Trianon, and Vaux-le-Vicomte. See *Le Vau, Louis.*

LE ROI SOLEIL. "The Sun King," sobriquet of Louis XIV of France (1643–1715) who loved pomp, splendor, and magnificence. He was a most regal and extravagent king. The flaming sunburst with radiating gilt rays appeared as a carved, painted, and embroidered decoration during this French baroque period. Illustrated is a Boulle armoire of the period.

LE ROI SOLEIL

JEAN-BAPTISTE LE LARGE

LE MÉDAILLON

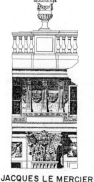

JACQUES LE MERCIER

LE ROI SOLEIL

LE ROI SOLEIL

LOUIS LE VAU

LEADED GLAZING

LEAF SCROLL FOOT

LEAFWORK

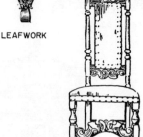

LEATHER

LE SUEUR, EUSTACHE (1617–1655). A late French Renaissance painter and decorator.

LE VASSEUR, ÉTIENNE (1721–1798). A furniture designer and cabinetmaker in the styles of Louis XV and Louis XVI. He created furniture for the Petit Trianon.

LE VAU, LOUIS (1612–1670). A French architect who began the building of Versailles for Louis XIV in 1668, which was carried on by Jules Hardouin-Mansart in 1679. He also designed the Château Vaux-le-Vicomte (1655–1661) on the outskirts of Paris for Nicholas Fouquet, the Minister of Finance to Louis XIV. The château was built on the principle of the French pavilion: in close coordination with nature. A park area, which was attached to the château, was designed by André Le Nôtre. Le Vau also designed the Collège des Quatre Nations (Institut de France) and the Church of Val-de-Grâce. Illustrated is a balustrade from Versailles.

LEAD. In masonry, the part of a wall built up and racked back on successive courses at the corner of a building. The line is attached to the lead, and the wall is built up between them. See *Racking*.

LEADED GLAZING. Windows made up of lead strips soldered together into a pattern. Small pieces of glass are set into this leaded design and held there by the lead strips. Clear, colored, patterned, or textured glass can be used. Religious and educational institutions often have leaded glass windows with pictorial representations composed of assorted colored glass. Illustrated is the leaded glazing of Little Moreton Hall in Cheshire, England.

LEAF SCROLL FOOT. A variation of the scroll foot. There is foliage carved on the face of the leg, and it sometimes hips out in front of the ankle.

LEAFWORK. Small collections of carved leaves used as decorative details on legs, splats, and cabinets during the last quarter of the 18th century in England. A Sheraton chair leg is illustrated.

LEAN-TO ROOF. A roof with one sloping side only. It is usually built flush against another building, and the roof slopes away from the other structure.

LEATHER. An upholstery material, a wall hanging, a tabletop finish, a material to cover accessories, books, etc. Usually the hide of a steer is used, and it is sliced or split five times. The three middle slices are used for upholstery. A leather-upholstered 17th-century Jacobean chair is illustrated.

LEATHERETTE (artificial leather). A nitrocellulose material with a heavy cotton backing. The top surface may be embossed or carved to simulate leather grainings. The material comes in a wide range of colors, textures, and weights, and is used for upholstery and wall covering. See *Naugahyde*.

LEAVES. Additional flat surface which can be added to extend or increase the surface of a tabletop. Some leaves are hinged to the table surface and must be raised to a horizontal position, as in the Pembroke or gateleg table. Other leaves are drawn out from beneath the table surface, as in the draw table (a late-16th-century English Renaissance table here illustrated). In other tables the framework is extended and the leaves put into the space so made. See *Draw Table, Extension Table, Folding Table, Gateleg Table,* and *Pembroke Table.*

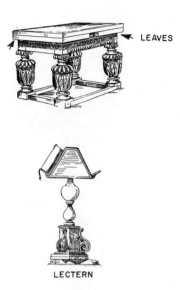

LEAVES

LECTERN. A reading desk. A carved or turned pedestal support for a Bible or a large book like a dictionary. A Hepplewhite design is illustrated.

LECTERN

LECTUS. A Roman bed or couch. The bed was sometimes equipped with a reading desk and cubicles to contain necessities.

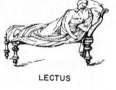

LECTUS

LEDGE

LEDGE. A simple horizontal structure, usually fixed across two vertical supports. A mantel is a ledge. Illustrated is a 15th-century early Italian Renaissance mantel.

LEG. A furniture support. The leg of a chair usually starts at the seat rail and ends in a foot. Leg designs vary with periods and styles of decoration. Illustrated are some typical turned legs of the late 17th century in England.

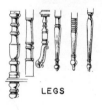

LEGS

LEKYTHOS. The Greek word for "oil flask." It is named after the shape of seed vessels. It is also spelled "lecythis."

L'ENFANT, PIERRE-CHARLES (1754–1825). A French engineer-architect who redesigned the old City Hall in New York into the First National Capitol. He created the pediment over the balcony and entrance with a crouching eagle emerging from the clouds. Thirteen stars fill the metope of the frieze, and the pilaster capitals are composed of rays and stars. L'Enfant is probably best known for his layout of Washington, D.C., which is reminiscent of Versailles; the Capitol represents the Palace, the White House is in a position similar to that of the Grand Trianon, and the Mall is the equivalent of the Park. He also laid out the gridiron of radial avenues.

LEONINE BASE

LENO WEAVE. A type of weave in which pairs of warp yarns are wound around each other between picks of filler yarns, and a net effect results.

LEONINE BASE. A table, chair, or other furniture support carved to resemble the legs and paws of a lion. Illustrated is a German 19th-century Néo-Grec wine cooler by Ruhl.

LEPAUTRE, JEAN (1617–1682). An interior designer and clockmaker for Louis XIII and Louis XIV. He published several works on decorative furniture which had a great influence on Flemish and English styles. Louis XIV named Lepautre the Royal Architect. A frieze designed by Lepautre is shown here.

JEAN LEPAUTRE

PIERRE LESCOT

LESCOT, PIERRE (1510–1578). A French Renaissance architect under François I and Henri II. He designed the original section of the present Louvre, and the façade in the cour carrée was designed in conjunction with the sculptor Jean Goujon. Illustrated is a door in the Henri II room of the Louvre.

LETTERWOOD. A wood native to Guiana which is also called "snakewood." The reddish-brown wood is distinguished by an irregular darker pattern.

LETTO. Italian for "bed." A 13th-century Gothic bed is illustrated.

LETTO CON BALDACCHINO. Italian for a "bed with a tester."

LEVER HOUSE. Located on Madison Avenue and East 53rd Street, New York City. Skidmore, Owings & Merrill were the architects, and Gordon Bunshaft was the chief designer. It is probably one of the most influential of the "curtain wall" buildings built in the 1950's. It appears as an almost all-glass structure, and is twenty-one stories high. The building is placed to one side of the site to allow for an open plaza surrounded on three sides by a single-story structure supported by stainless steel sheathed columns. The all-glass façade is tinted green, and the mullions are stainless steel.

LEWAN. In oriental houses, a room with an open side which lets out into an inner court.

LIBRARY. A reading room, sometimes equipped with bookcases on all four walls. The room usually has a desk or writing table and some comfortable chairs. It is like a den or a man's sitting room. Illustrated is an elevation of the elegant 18th-century Adam library in Syon House, Middlesex, England.

LIBRARY

LIBRARY ARMCHAIR. A late-18th-century "convertible" chair with steps under the seat. The seat flips over and becomes a small step unit.

LIBRARY CASE. A late-18th-century Hepplewhite term for a bookcase.

LIBRARY CASE

LIBRARY PRESS BEDSTEAD. A convertible bed which folded up into a cupboard, bureau, or pseudobookcase. It was popular in the 18th-century Sheraton, Shearer, and Hepplewhite periods when a sitting room would sometimes double as a bedroom.

LIBRARY STEPS. Many stepladder devices were used in the 18th century for getting at the uppermost shelves of the high built-in bookcases which often covered all the walls of the library. Illustrated is a Sheraton unit which converted into a library table, or, as shown, opened into a stepladder.

LIBRARY STEPS

LIBRARY TABLE

LIBRARY TABLE. Originally the English term for a large pedestal or kneehole desk. Presently it refers to a large table with drawers or a pedestal table. The kneehole-type desk has drawers on both sides of the opening. Illustrated is a Sheraton design for a "library table." See *Partners' Desk.*

LIEBES, DOROTHY. An outstanding 20th-century American interior and textile designer.

LIERNE. A short rib which serves to connect ridges or intermediate ribs in ceiling vaulting. It does not rise from the same spring line as the ridge rib.

LIGHT CHAIR. A lightweight, easily movable side chair. A Sheraton late-18th-century design with tapered legs and a carved vase back is shown here. See *Hall Chair* and *Side Chair.*

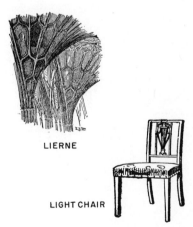

LIERNE

LIGHT CHAIR

LIGHTING LOUVERS. Plastic, metal, or glass filters set over electric bulbs to diffuse the light and soften the glare. They look like miniature circular or rectangular Venetian blinds.

LIGNEREAUX. A noted, early-19th-century French cabinetmaker of the Empire period.

LIGNUM VITAE. Wood of life. A hard, heavy, greenish-brown wood used by the Dutch and Flemish in the 17th century for linen chests and cupboards. It is very durable, oily, and waxy, and it has a fine interwoven grain texture. It is difficult to work. Lignum vitae was introduced into Europe at the beginning of the 16th century for its medicinal value.

LIGORIO, PIRRO (c. 1530–1580). Painter and architect, born in Naples. Among other works, he built the Lancellotti Palace and the Villa Pia in Rome.

LIMBA. The French name for korina wood. See *Afara* and *Korina*.

LIME. Calcium oxide which is derived from burning limestone.

LIME MORTAR. A mortar consisting of sand, water, and slaked lime. It is used to bind bricks or stone masonry.

LIMED OAK. A special finish sometimes applied to oak to give it a frosted or silvery-gray appearance. A whitish filler or paint is rubbed into the grain of the wood and then wiped off. This process tends to accentuate the grain. Woods other than oak can be limed.

LIMESTONE. A building stone, usually gray or beige, which is mainly carbonate of lime or carbonate of calcium.

LIMEWOOD. An excellent carving material favored by Grinling Gibbons in the late 17th century. It is close-grained and light in color. Illustrated is a Grinling Gibbons carving from a choir stall in St. Paul's Cathedral, London.

LIMEWOOD

LIMOSIN, LÉONARD (c. 1505–1577). A French artist who painted portraits on fine enameled copperware in Limoges.

LINDEN. A lime tree. A fine, white-grained wood, excellent for carving. Many of Grinling Gibbons' mantels and trophies were carved in linden. The American basswood is sometimes referred to as a linden. See *Gibbons, Grinling*, and *Limewood*.

LINDEN

LINE ENGRAVING. A form of intaglio engraving used for reproducing works of art. Dürer is considered one of the greatest artists to use this technique, which demands great discipline and precision. A sharp graver is used to create V-shaped furrows on a copper plate.

LINEN. A strong yarn or fabric made of smooth surfaced flax fibers. It can be woven in a plain or damask weave. There are many types of linen: Belgian, English, Irish, handwoven, hand-blocked, hand-printed, homespun, satin, etc.

LINENFOLD. A carved Gothic panel embellishment made to resemble folded linen or a scroll of linen. It was popular in England in the mid-Tudor period and was originally a Flemish motif. Another name for linenfold panels is parchment panels. See illustration for *Oak, Quartered*.

LINENFOLD

LINING. A fine line of inlaid veneer. It is the same as "stringing." Illustrated is a late-18th-century Sheraton dressing table with inlay banding around the drawers. See *Banding*. In drapery and upholstery, a fabric used to back up the fine face fabric. It gives additional weight and body to the drapery, and may also serve as an insulating agent or protect the face fabric from suns rays, etc.

LINING

LINING PAPER. An inexpensive paper which is first applied to a wall before the patterned or textured wallpaper is applied. It supplies a clean background for the wallpaper, and helps prevent cracking.

LINNELL, JOHN AND WILLIAM. 18th-century English carvers, cabinetmakers, and upholsterers. They worked in the rococo, Chinese, and classic styles.

LINOCUT or LINOLEUM CUT. A modern adaptation of the woodcut printing technique using a linoleum block. See *Woodcut*.

LINOLEUM. A manufactured floor-covering material which is cured by heating, and is therefore fairly resistant to indentation and temperature changes. The wearing surface goes right through to the backing, it is fairly resistant to grease and oil, and it has some resiliency underfoot. Linoleum will absorb moisture, therefore it is not recommended for use where there is high humidity. It is usually manufactured in 6' widths in a multitude of colors and patterns.

LINSEED OIL. An oil processed from flaxseed, and commonly used in house paints.

LINTEL. A horizontal piece of wood or stone over a door, window, or other opening to support the weight above. Illustrated is the rock-cut façade of the Egyptian tomb of Beni Hassan.

LINTEL

LINTERS. The short cotton fibers which stick to the cotton seed after the first ginning. They are used for upholstery stuffing, mattresses, and for producing cellulose sheets which are used in making rayon.

LION

LION HEAD

LION. The "king of the beasts," and always a favorite animal symbol in furniture, interiors, art, and architecture. In ancient Egypt, the lion was associated with water and was usually shown at rest, carved with a formalized rufflike mane. In the Greek and Roman periods, the lion was the symbol of the fallen hero, and was used as the guardian of gates, temples, and public buildings. Christian art used the lion to represent the Redeemer, and in medieval heraldry and even current seals, flags, shields, etc., the lion often is used as a symbol of strength, courage, and royalty.

LION HEADS

LION HEAD. A carved representation of a lion's head used on furniture and in architecture. The head served as a gargoyle on ancient classic temples, and was often used as a knocker or handle on Gothic and Renaissance doors and cabinets. It also functioned as a holder at the end of a swag or festoon. Sometimes the lion head was combined with a leg and paw, and used as part of a furniture support. Illustrated is an Empire bureau designed by Charles Percier. See *Lion Period.*

LION PERIOD

LION PERIOD. The period from 1720 to 1735 in England when it was popular to carve lions' masks on the knees of cabriole legs and the arms of chairs and settees, and the lion's paw was a carved furniture foot. The lion was the most popular motif of the period.

LION'S PAW FEET

LION'S PAW FOOT. The carved representation of a furry paw at the end of a furniture leg. This type of foot appeared in early Greek and Roman furniture, and is found in French, English, and Italian Renaissance designs. It was a prime decorating motif in 18th-century English furniture. An Italian Renaissance bed is illustrated. See *Lion Period.*

LIP MOLDING. A small convex molding found in Queen Anne and Chippendale chests and cabinets. Usually the molding was set around doors and drawers to act as a dust stop.

LIPPING. In masonry, bricks laid so that the top edge is set in from the plane surface of the wall. It is the reverse of *Hacking.*

LIP MOLDING

LISENA. An Italian word for "pilaster" in Romanesque architecture.

LISERE. A typically French fabric of the late 18th century which became popular in England. It is a silk fabric with a warp of Jacquard designs and a weft of brocaded flowers. Illustrated is a Louis XVI winged armchair upholstered in a lisere fabric.

LISERE

LISENA

LISEUSE. A Louis XVI reading table. A collapsible bookrest was set into the center top panel of the rectangular desklike table. Often several small drawers were set into the apron of the table.

LISIÈRE. The French word for "selvage"; the outer woven edge of a textile or tapestry. See *Selvage.*

LISTEL or LIST. A border fillet molding.

LIT. The French word for "bed."

LIT À LA FRANÇAISE. "French bed." A bed with a canopy over it placed sideways against a wall. A late-18th-century design. Illustrated is an early-19th-century Sheraton variation.

LIT À LA FRANÇAISE

LIT À LA POLONAISE

LIT À LA POLONAISE. "Polish bed." A late-18th-century bed with a pointed crown canopy. A Sheraton design is illustrated.

LIT À TRAVERS. A sofa bed.

LIT CANAPÉ. A sofa bed. An 18th-century Sheraton design is illustrated.

LIT CLOS. A French bed with wood panels to enclose the sleeping area. The bed was often built against the wall, and with the use of the panels it could be completely screened in. This type of bed was often found in country estates from the 17th through the 19th century. See *Built-in Furniture.*

LIT D'ANGE. "Angel bed." An 18th-century French bed with a small canopy supported by the back bedposts only. There are no front pillars, and the canopy extends only partially over the bed. A Daniel Marot design (early 18th century) is illustrated.

LIT CANAPÉ

LIT D'ANGE

LIT DE REPOS. A daybed.

LIT DE REPOS À CROSSE. A daybed with outward, rollover scrolled ends. See *Chaise Longue*.

LIT DUCHESSE. A bed of Louis XIV design with a large canopy supported by the four bedposts.

LIT EN BATEAU. A 19th-century French boat-shaped bed. It is similar to the *Sleigh Bed*.

LITHOGRAPH. A drawing or design done with a grease pencil or crayon on a special type of stone. A limited number of reproductions is possible with this technique.

LITS JUMEAUX. French for "twin beds." See *Summer Bed*.

LIVERY CUPBOARD. A 17th-century hall cupboard consisting of several open shelves for the display of plate. The lower chest or cupboard part was originally the receptacle for unused food. "Livery" is an old form of "delivery," and referred to the taking of food during the night, and therefore the livery cupboard was often found in the bedchamber. In churches, the livery cupboard was called a "dole cupboard," and it held the food which was set aside for distribution to the poor. Illustrated is a carved oak English livery cupboard originally made in 1674. The pediment top was added toward the end of the 18th century.

LIVERY CUPBOARD

LOBBY CHEST. Described by Sheraton in 1803 as a half chest of drawers about three feet tall, and with four rows of drawers. A pullout writing board sometimes was provided beneath the top surface. This small unit seemed most appropriate for small studies, lobbies, or bedchambers.

LOBE. A foil in Gothic tracery. See *Foils*.  LOBE

LOBING. See *Gadroon*.

LOCK, MATTHIAS. A mid-18th-century English designer in the rococo style. He originally worked along the lines set by Chippendale, but later switched to the more classic style of the Adam brothers. He published books on foliage, ornaments, pier frames, girandoles, shields, and sconces.

MATTHIAS LOCK

LOCK RAIL. The middle horizontal rail of a door, usually where the lock is fixed. Illustrated is a Sir Christopher Wren design executed by Grinling Gibbons.

LOCKER. In 18th- and 19th-century furniture, a small central cupboard in the interior of a writing desk or secretary. Illustrated is a Shearer writing table c. 1785.

LOCK RAIL

LOCKER

LOEWY, RAYMOND. A 20th-century American industrial and interior designer.

LOGGIA. An Italian word for a room or area with an open arcade or colonnade at one side. An arcaded gallery. Illustrated is the Loggia of the Vatican in Rome with frescoes by Raphael and Jean d'Udine.

LOIR, ALEXIS (1630–1713). A French painter and decorator of the Louis XIV period. He is noted for his decorations on furniture.

LOIR, NICHOLAS (1624–1679). A French painter, decorator, and member of the Gobelins Art Factory. He created many fine mural and tapestry designs. A ceiling design by Loir is illustrated.

LOMA-LOOM. A trademark of Burlington Industries for a carpet of wool and nylon pile with a built-in sponge rubber cushion. The cushion is an integral part of the carpet. It helps absorb shocks and friction, and gives the carpet extra resiliency.

LOGGIA

NICHOLAS LOIR

LOMBARD STYLE

LOMBARD STYLE. The Romanesque style in northern Italy.

LONG AND SHORT WORK. A Saxon method of masonry in which flat horizontal stones alternate with tall vertical ones. It was often used on the corners of walls or buildings. The tower of the Earls Barton Church in England is illustrated.

LONG CLOCK. An 18th-century hall or grandfather clock. A Chippendale design is illustrated.

LONGHENA, BALDASSARE (1604–1682). A Roman architect who practiced mainly in Venice. He is best known for his Renaissance church, *Santa Maria della Salute.*

LOOKING GLASS. See *Mirror.* A mid-18th-century Chippendale example is illustrated.

LOOP BACK. An oval chair back or a Windsor *Bow Back* without arms. A Hepplewhite design is illustrated.

LONG CLOCK

LONG AND SHORT WORK

LOOKING GLASS

LOOP BACK

LOOS, ADOLF (1870–1933). An Austrian-born architect and one of the leaders in the modern movement of the early 20th century. He recognized the impact of machinery on ornament and design and its ultimate effect on architecture. He said, "to find beauty in form instead of making it depend on ornament is the goal towards which humanity is aspiring." Of engineers, he said, "from them we receive our culture." The office building in Michaeler Platz in Vienna is probably his best-known work. His strong, austere quality had a great influence on the development of the functional style in Austria. He wrote two books, *Ins Leere Gesprochen* ("Spoken into a Void"), 1921, and *Trotzden* ("Nevertheless"), 1931.

LOOSE SEAT. See *Slip Seat.*

LOPER. The slide support under the drop front or lid of a desk. A Hepplewhite design is illustrated.

LOPER

L'ORME, PHILIBERT DE. See *Delorme, Philibert.*

LORRAIN, CLAUDE (1600-1682). A great French landscape painter of the Louis XIII and Louis XIV periods. He decorated the Chapelle des Carmes at Nancy.

LOTUS. A plant of the ancient oriental and Egyptian civilizations which was used as a decorative motif. The Egyptians used the flower form for a column capital, household utensils, and as an embellishment on their wall decorations.

LOTUS

LOTUS

LOUIS-PHILIPPE PERIOD. The period of the reign in France of Louis-Philippe, 1830–1848. The fashions and styles of the Louis XV period had a brief revival, but the work was eclectic and did not have the grace and hand workmanship of the original period.

LOUIS XIII STYLE

LOUIS XIII STYLE. See *French Late Renaissance.* Illustrated is a chair in the Louis XIII style.

LOUIS XIV (1643–1715) — THE BAROQUE STYLE. The Golden Age of the French Renaissance and the reign of the Sun. King, Louis XIV. It was a native style based on the classic orders combined with the baroque, and developed in splendor and magnificence. Rooms and furniture were enormous in scale. The ornamentation was rich and heavy, done in gilt and strong colors with sharp accents. Compass-formed curves were used to relieve the rectangular wooden wall panels.

LOUIS XV (1715–1774) — THE ROCOCO PERIOD. The reign of Louis XV in France. A period of gaiety and frivolity, effeminacy and sentimentality. The rooms and furniture were human-scaled for greater comfort, and the effect was more intimate. Curved free forms, S-shapes and asymmetry became the dominant line forms of the period. The classic orders were replaced by the exotic and Chinoiserie. Lacquered and painted furniture added to the effect of this "age of the boudoir," and Mme de Pompadour was a guiding influence of the period.

LOUIS XVI (1774–1793) — THE NEOCLASSIC STYLE. The reign of Louis XVI in France and the return to naturalism, simplicity, and reason in the decorative forms. The classic architectural forms and orders were revived, with Pompeii, Herculaneum, Greece, and the Adam brothers of England as the dominant influences. Straight lines and compass curves returned, with symmetry and a more severe classic quality.

LOUVRE (PALAIS DU)

LOUIS XIV —
THE BAROQUE STYLE

LOUIS XV —
THE ROCOCO PERIOD

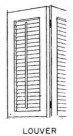

LOUIS XVI —
THE NEOCLASSIC STYLE

LOUNGE

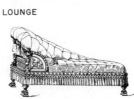

LOUNGE. A late-19th-century sofa or couch. It was often designed with one arm higher than the other, to serve as a headrest. Also, a room for relaxing or resting. A large sitting room, often in a public building.

LOUVER. An opening in a wall or ceiling, covered with slats placed at an angle.

LOUVERED DOORS. Doors with panels of overlapping horizontal slats which can be adjusted to be open, closed or in a position in between.

LOUVRE (PALAIS DU) (1546–1878). The full range of Renaissance art and architecture encompassed in one structure which was begun in the time of François I and worked on till the

LOUVER

LOVE SEAT

THE LOUVRE

reign of Napoleon III. The Louvre and the Tuileries together cover an area of over 45 acres. The original work was begun by Pierre Lescot. Jean Goujon added sculpture details to the two-story façade of Corinthian and composite pilasters and an attic story above. Jacques Du Cerceau in 1600 added a gallery. Many other noted architects worked in the Louvre: Jacques Lemercier, Louis Le Vau, Claude Perrault; and many famous artists and craftsmen worked on the magnificent interiors.

LOVE SEAT

LOVE SEAT

LOVE SEAT. An upholstered settee for two persons. It first became popular in the Louis XIV period in France and in the Queen Anne period in England. The double seat is also called a "courting chair." Illustrated is a Louis XVI love seat.

LOVER'S CHAIR. See *Drunkard's Chair*.

LOVOA. A tropical African wood that is yellow-brown to dark-brown. Though it resembles Circassian walnut, it actually belongs to the mahogany family. In the veneer, resulting from slicing a quartered log, there is a straight stripe with sharp color contrasts.

LOW–BACK CHAIR

LOW-BACK CHAIR. A mid-17th-century term for the small side chairs with backs which replaced the stools and benches in middle-class homes. The Cromwellian chair is an example of a low-back chair. The illustrated Farthingale chair is another example.

LOWBOY. A serving table or low chest of drawers. A late-17th-century English example is shown.

LOWBOY

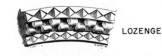

LOZENGE

LOZENGE

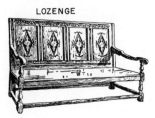

LOZENGE. A conventional diamond-shaped motif. The Normans used the diamond shape in lozenge and billet molding. A Jacobean settle with lozenge carving on the paneled back is illustrated. It is the product of the first part of the 17th century. The lozenge also appears in the Directoire period.

LUCARNE. French for a dormer window. Illustrated is an early French Renaissance example from the Château de Chambord.

LUG. A small projecting element on a building material, which makes fixing the material into place easier and the resultant setting more secure. On ceramic tiles, this projection is called a nib. It supplies an extra surface to glue or cement in place, and therefore an extra surface for adhesion.

LUMINOSITY. The quality of being capable of reflecting or giving light.

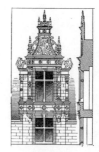

LUCARNE

LUNETTE

LUNETTE. In architecture, a semicircular window area. Also, a subsidiary vault intersecting with a main vault or dome, and, having its crown at a lower level, causing a crescent-shaped groin to be formed. The crescent shape is a lunette. A characteristic overdoor during the Italian Renaissance. In furniture, a crescent or half moon shape. It may be used in a repeated decorative band design or, as in the Jacobean period, as a carved or inlaid motif. In the 18th century, tables sometimes had lunette designs painted or inlaid on them. A Hepplewhite commode tabletop is illustrated.

LUNETTE

LUNNING, FREDERICK. A 20th-century Scandinavian furniture producer and designer.

LUREX. A trademark name for a nontarnishing, aluminum-base metallic yarn often incorporated into upholstery, drapery, or curtain fabrics. The yarn can be produced in various metallic colors. It is produced by the Dobeckmun Company.

LUSS, GERALD. A 20th-century American designer of Designs for Business Inc. He is a pioneer in space planning for offices and commercial installations. Luss has devised many modular systems for office interiors.

LUSTER. A thin metallic glaze used on pottery to produce an iridescent color. It was used on Persian ceramics, Majolica ware, and also on antique English and American ware.

LUSTRAGRAY. A trademark of American Saint Gobain for gray-tinted window glass which reduces glare by approximately 50 percent but does not obscure vision. The exterior opacity contributes to privacy, and the neutral color places no restrictions on interior decor. The glass is manufactured in assorted thicknesses.

LUSTRE. A table light or wall sconce in crystal, or enriched with crystal drops or pendants.

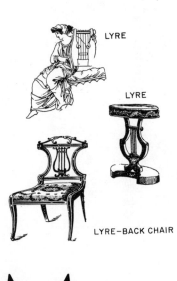

LYRE

LYRE

LYRE–BACK CHAIR

M

MACAROON

MACHICOLATIONS

LUSTRE FABRIC. In carpets, any pile-cut fabric woven with surface yarns spun from soft types of staple and chemically washed (like handwoven oriental fabrics) to give a bright sheen. The term also means a glossy finish achieved by means of heat or pressure.

LUSTRE RUGS. See *Sheen Rugs.*

LUTHERN. In a classic building, a window (bull's-eye, square, arched, or semicircular) which appeared above the cornice, vertically in line with the front exterior of the structure.

LYRE. A stringed instrument which appears in Greek decoration and was adapted in the Renaissance period. It appears in various forms in the 17th through the 19th century in France, England, and Germany. It was a popular motif in the Empire period, and a particular favorite of the 19th-century American designer Duncan Phyfe. Illustrated are a German Empire table and a classic Greek lyre.

LYRE-BACK CHAIR. A Duncan Phyfe, early-19th-century, American-style chair. The splat of the chair was an open-carved lyre design. The lyre was previously used by Adam, Sheraton, and Hepplewhite in 18th-century English furniture. A Sheraton design is illustrated.

MACAROON or MACARON. A decorative rosette-type carving used to ornament Louis XVI furniture, named after the cake called in French "macaron" and in English macaroon. It is usually an eight-petaled flower with a central bud, and resembles a cookie or patera. The macaroon usually was carved on the upper block of the chair leg or in the corners of the front seat-rail. A Louis XVI fauteuil is illustrated. See *Patera.*

MACAROON

MACHICOLATIONS. Bold projecting corbels which carry the parapet of a castle wall. The openings allowed boiling oils and other fluids to be poured through during times of warfare.

McINTYRE, SAMUEL (1757–1811). An American wood-carver of Salem, Massachusetts. He created many mantelpieces and overdoors as well as carvings on furniture. He was greatly influenced by Sheraton's later designs. Together with Duncan Phyfe, he was a leading designer of the American Federal period.

MACKINTOSH, CHARLES RENNIE (1868–1928). A Scottish artist, architect, and furniture designer who designed and created in the Art Nouveau style. The few buildings he did around the turn of the century (the Glasgow School of Art, Windy Hill in Kilmacolm, and Hill House in Helensburgh) are noted for their subtlety of proportion and lack of external decoration which appears to be derived from Scottish medieval architecture.

MADAME JUMEL CHAIR. An early-19th-century Empire chair. There are no back stiles. The top rail of the chair back curves and sweeps forward to meet the front legs. The splat (central upright of the chair back) is often lyre- or vase-shaped. It is similar to the Regency spoon-back chair. See *Spoon-Back*.

MADAME JUMEL CHAIR

(LA) MADELEINE. A church built in Paris between 1806 and 1842 in the Roman Corinthian style. Vignon was the designer of this pseudo-Roman octastyle peripteral structure. The cella is divided into three bays covered by saucer domes with openings that help illuminate the church. A dramatic set of wide sweeping stairs leads up to the church proper.

MADIO. A 16th-century Italian Renaissance sideboard.

MADOU. See *Maidou or Madou* and *Padouk*.

MAGASIN AU BON MARCHÉ. The first complete modern glass-and-iron department store with natural light throughout, built in Paris in 1876. It was designed by Louis Auguste Boileau and the engineer Alexandre Gustave Eiffel. The corner of the store is built out in a pavilion-like affair. The interior is a combination of glass skylights, aerial bridges in iron, and ornamental thin iron columns. The ground floor consists of a continuous line of show windows.

MAGNOLIA. A straight-grained and generally uniformly textured wood similar to yellow poplar, but harder and heavier. It is native to the southern part of the United States, and especially to the Appalachians.

MAHOGANY. A longtime favorite furniture and interior wood with a beautiful reddish color and a handsome grain. It works easily, is wormproof, and takes a high polish. Figured mahogany may be plain or broken stripe, mottled, fiddlebacked, or swirled. Mahogany is available in wide widths and long lengths. Among the true mahoganies are: African, Cuban, Peruvian, Brazilian, and tropical American mahogany. A mahogany wardrobe of the early Georgian period (1725) is illustrated. It was built during the "Age of Mahogany." See *Acajou, Age of Mahogany,* and *Primavera*.

MAHOGANY

MAHOGANY, HONDURAS. A yellowish-white to salmon-pink to rich golden-brown wood, figured in a rich mottle or with a straight-grained moderate crossfire. See *Baywood*.

MAHOGANY, SPANISH. One of the finest mahoganies grown. It is imported from Santo Domingo.

MAHOGANY, WHITE. See *Primavera*.

MAIDOU or MADOU. A decorative veneering wood from the East Indies and Indo-China. It is found in a long grain, or an amboyna-like, fine burled figure. The color varies from pale straw yellow to red. Padouk burl wood is sold under the name of maidou.

MAISON CARRÉE. A Roman temple in Nîmes built A.D. 14, and still in excellent condition. The temple is raised up on a high podium and is pseudoperipteral prostyle hexastyle. The Corinthian columns support a fine entablature. See *Pseudoperipteral* for an illustration of the Maison Carrée.

MAÎTRE-ÉBÉNISTE. Master cabinetmaker. A title bestowed on favored royal furniture designers and cabinetmakers by the French kings. See *Ébéniste*. Illustrated is a buffet with copper ornaments by Jean Berain (17th century).

MAÎTRE-ÉBÉNISTE

MAJOLICA

MAJOLICA. Italian and Spanish pottery coated with a tin enamel, and decorated with bright colors. The name is derived from the Island of Majorca. See *Luster*.

MAKIMONO. An oriental painting in the form of a long scroll. See *Kakemono*.

MAKORE or MAKORI. African cherrywood. It is pale pinkish brown to dark red or purplish brown in color, and has a fine, smooth-surfaced texture. Makore sometimes has a mottled figure, and it resembles American cherrywood. It is used for furniture, cabinetry, and interior finishes.

MALACHITE. A sea-green to dark green stone with intricate patterned scalloping whorls. The stone takes a high polish, and was used in ancient Egypt for amulets. In Italy, it is known as the "Peacock Stone."

MALTESE CROSS. A cross consisting of four equal arms; each is wedge-shaped, and the points meet in the center.

MAMMISI. Small Egyptian temples.

MANCHETTE. The French term for a padded arm cushion. See *Arm Pads.*

MANCHETTE

MANDORLA. Italian for "almond." An almond-shaped halo. See *Aureole.*

MANIGAULT, GABRIEL. An 18th-century architect of Charleston, South Carolina, who designed in the Federal style.

MAN-MADE FIBERS. Synthetic fibers. Manufactured fibers not of natural plant or animal origin.

MANNERISM or THE MANNERIST SCHOOL. A term coined in this century to describe the chief painting style, especially in Italy, from 1520 to 1600. It broke the rules of classic art. The human figure was set into distorted, elongated, and tortured positions with strained and bulging muscles. Compositions were strained and lopsided; perspective and scale were violently manipulated. The Mannerist artist usually used bright, harsh colors which were intended to heighten the emotional effect: reds blending into orange, and greens running into yellow. Michelangelo, Tintoretto, and El Greco are the most famous of the Mannerist artists.

MANSARD ROOF. A hipped roof with two slopes on each side. The first or lower slope is very steep, and the upper angle is less extreme. A mansard roof that is not hipped is also called a gambrel roof. The mansard roof is named for François Mansart, the late French Renaissance architect who popularized its use.

MANSARD ROOF

MANSART, FRANÇOIS (1598–1666). A noted French architect who revived the use of the steep roofs—the mansard roof. This design was originated by Lescot a century before. Mansart also designed the part of the Château de Blois that was commissioned by Gaston d'Orléans, the Château de Maisons near Paris, and the Church of the Val de Grâce in Paris.

MANSART, JULES HARDOUIN-. See *Hardouin-Mansart, Jules.*

MANSONIA. An African wood which greatly resembles walnut and has often been used as a walnut substitute in England. It is sometimes called "African black walnut." Mansonia is usually straight-grained and fine-textured. It works and glues well and also takes an excellent finish.

MANTELPIECE

MANTLESHELF

ROBERT MANWARING

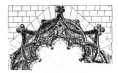

MARBLE

MANTEL. A shelf projecting above a fireplace. See *Chimney Piece* and *Ledge* for illustrations.

MANTEL

MANTELPIECE. The stonework, brickwork, or woodwork surrounding a fireplace opening. It is usually treated in a decorative manner. An 18th-century design by the English designer Abraham Swan is illustrated.

MANTELSHELF. A shelf placed over a fireplace opening. Illustrated is a late-18th-century Adam design. See *Mantel*.

MANUELINO. See *Isabellina*.

MANUELINO

MANWARING, ROBERT. An 18th-century English furniture maker and a contemporary of Chippendale. He is noted for his chairs, which are usually characterized by a small bracket between the square leg and the front seat rail, and the lattice-work splat.

MAPLE. A hard, strong, light-colored wood similar to birch. Straight-grained maple is excellent for interior finishes. Bird's-eye maple is curly-grained, swirled, blistered, and/or quilted. It is used as a decorative veneering material. Maple was used for marquetry and veneering in 17th- and 18th-century English furniture.

MAQUETTE. French for a small-scale model. See *Bozzetto*.

MARBLE. A calcerous stone of compact texture which is found in most countries. The color, pattern, and textural effects are unlimited, and the material is used architecturally and decoratively. Marble was popular for furniture decoration in the late 17th and 18th centuries in France and in the Architects' period in England. Illustrated is a marble mantelpiece designed by Robert and James Adam for the great salon of the Queen's House (mid-18th century).

MARBLING. A painted imitation of the veining and texture of marble.

MARLBOROUGH LEG

MARILLIER, CLÉMENT-PIERRE (1740–1808). A designer of flowers, trophies, and metal trimmings for furniture during the Louis XVI period. Also a notable illustrator of books.

MARLBOROUGH LEG. A straight, grooved leg with a block as a foot that was used in mid-18th-century English and American furniture. It was especially favored by Chippendale. Illustrated is an American colonial sideboard. See *Block Foot.*

MARMO. Italian for "marble."

MAROT, DANIEL. A French 17th-century designer of the Louis XIV period. Because of religious persecution, he fled from France to Holland, and then to England. There he became the chief designer to William III. In his designs he blends Louis XIV and Dutch styles. His position at court enabled him to direct a large group of refugee artisans into England. He designed mantels, sidewalls, cabinets, clocks, beds, and draperies.

DANIEL MAROT

DANIEL MAROT

MAROT, JEAN (c. 1617–1679). French architect, designer, and engraver.

MAROUFLAGE. A support or backing for a mural or second canvas or wood panel behind a painting. A reinforcing element.

MARQUEE. See *Marquise.*

MARQUETRY. The decorative pattern made by setting contrasting materials into a veneered surface. The resultant decoration is flush and level. Usually, the material that is set in is finely grained, interestingly colored woods, but tortoiseshell, horn, metal, and mother-of-pearl are also used. It was popular in the Renaissance period and also in 18th-century France and England. Marquetry can be imitated with lithographed transfers. See *Boulle Work, Inlay, Intarsia or Tarsia,* and *Parquet.*

MARQUETRY

MARQUISE. A projection or canopy over an entrance which is often decorative and made of metal and glass. It is sometimes referred to as a marquee. See *Marquise Vitrée.*

MARQUISE CHAIR

MARQUISE CHAIR

MARRIAGE CHEST

MARQUISE CHAIR. A completely upholstered small sofa, prototype of the love seat. It is comparable to an overly wide bergère. It was introduced in the Louis XV period in France, and was designed to accommodate the wide skirts and panniers of the period.

MARQUISE VITRÉE. A projecting glass canopy. It made its first major appearance as a large horizontal plane surface intersecting the vertical elements in the International Exhibition Building in Paris in 1878. It was devised by Alexandre Gustave Eiffel, and it was also used on the Magasin au Bon Marché in Paris.

MARQUISETTE. A lightweight open-mesh fabric in a leno weave. It is similar to gauze in appearance, and is made of cotton, silk, rayon, synthetics, or a combination of fibers. It is often used for glass curtains.

MARRIAGE CHEST. A cassone. An elaborately carved or painted Italian Renaissance long chest. It was used for storing household linens, etc. Illustrated is a 16th-century carved walnut cassone.

MARTHA WASHINGTON CHAIR. A Sheraton or Hepplewhite type of chair, with open arms and a high, fully upholstered back and seat. The legs were usually slender and tapered and often inlaid, though some chairs were made with turned or reeded legs.

MARTHA WASHINGTON SEWING TABLE. An oval-shaped table with deep semicircular end pockets that flank the legs of the unit. The top was hinged to allow access to the two rounded ends and the fitted central tray. The front, back, and sides of the pockets were either finely reeded to look like tambour work, or covered with pleated fabric. The legs were usually turned or reeded. This work or sewing table was a late-18th-century, early-19th-century American design.

MARTIN BROTHERS. 18th-century French artisans (Guillaume, Simon, Étienne, Julien, and Robert) who were distinguished for their lacquer finishing in the Chinese manner. Their technique, which was called Vernis Martin, employed a clear lacquer speckled with gold, and some forty other lacquers in the oriental style, but the Martin brothers were best known for their green varnish finish. Snuffboxes, furniture, and even complete rooms were finished in this technique.

MASACCIO (real name, TOMMASO GUIDI) (1401–1428). A Florentine naturalist painter who worked in an austere yet heroic style with a feeling of light, space, and depth. In his

"Madonna and Child" from the Pisa Polyptych one can see his ability to paint with realism and emotion. Masaccio's major surviving works are the frescoes in the Brancacci Chapel of the Carmelite Church in Florence. He is considered to be one of the founders of the Renaissance school of painting and ranks with Donatello (sculpture) and Filippo Brunelleschi (architecture).

MASCARON. A grotesque mask or head used as a painted or carved ornament. It is usually distinguished from a masque by being a grinning deformed caricature, distorted and sometimes terminating in foliage. The masque was a beautiful or idealized portrayal of nature. In the Gothic period, mascarons were usually caricatures. In the Renaissance and baroque styles, the mascaron was used to accentuate a keystone in an arch, or used on the backs of chairs, on carved furniture, shields, cartouches, or consoles. The illustrated design is from the Louvre in Paris. See *Grotesques (Grottesques)*.

MASCHERONE. The Italian word for a painted or carved mask or gargoyle.

MASHREBEEYAH. A latticed window. See *Moucharaby* and *Qamariyyah*.

MASCARON

MASCARON

MASCHERONE

MASHREBEEYAH

MASK STOP

MASK STOP. A 13th-century Gothic device. It was used as a decorative ending to a hood molding or dripstone. In some cases this termination resembled a human face or a caricature of a face.

MASKS. See *Masques*.

MASLAND DURAN. A trademark of Masland Duraleather Company for a vinyl fabric with an elastic backing used for upholstery. It is produced in a wide range of colors, textures, and patterns.

MASONITE. A compressed, rigid compo or building board. It may be tempered for extra strength. It is difficult to drive nails into Masonite.

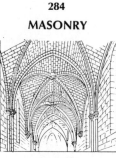

MASONRY

MASONRY. The construction of stones, tiles, bricks, etc., fitted together with mortar.

MASON'S MITRE. An angle formed, not by two moldings meeting at the mitre or angle of the corner, but by one molding turning a right-angled corner, and then butting against the second molding.

MASQUES

MASQUES

MASQUES. Exaggerated representations of the human face to suggest emotions or ideas such as those of comedy and tragedy. They were used in antique classic architecture and decoration, and were very popular during the Renaissance. Masques were often used as ornaments on the keystone of door or window arches. See *Mascarons* and *Mask Stop*. Masques were also magnificently produced entertainments with splendid costumes, scenery, floats, etc. Inigo Jones was a master designer of such masques. See *Jones, Inigo*.

MASSWERK. German for "tracery."

MASTABA. An Arabic word for "bench." The word is used to describe the mound-shaped tombs of ancient Egypt.

MASTIC. An adhesive for fixing tiles, glass, asbestos, and vinyl tiles, etc. Also a gum or resin used in the manufacturing of varnish.

MATCH BOARDS or MATCHED BOARDS. Boards which are tongued and grooved together. The joint is either beaded or chamfered.

MATELASSÉ. From the French for "padded" or "cushioned." A fabric with an embossed pattern which resembles quilting or a raised quilted design. Matelassé can be imitated by stitching or embossing.

MATTE. A dull, nonshiny finish.

MATTED. A term used to describe the rough, flat, sunk background of carving on oak furniture. This background was often pitted with small dents or gouge marks.

MATTONE. Italian for "brick."

MATTRESS. A fully filled pillow or pad which is placed over the springs or slats of a bed frame for comfort and softness. The mattress is filled with any or a combination of some of the following: down, feathers, hair, cotton batting, foam rubber, etc.

MAURESQUE. See *Moresque*. Moorish. Illustrated is the cornice impost of the central arch of the Court of Lions in the Alhambra, Granada, Spain.

MAUSOLEUM. Originally the burial tomb of the Roman Mausolus, ruler of Caria, at Halicarnassus (illustrated). The term is used now to designate a burial structure or tomb enclosure.

MAURESQUE

MAUSOLEUM

THOMAS MAYHEW

MAYHEW, THOMAS. An 18th-century English cabinetmaker who worked with William Ince. Together they published a book of designs, *The Universal System of Household Furniture*. He was a contemporary of Chippendale.

MEANDER. A decorative, geometric, repeating bank. A Greek band. See *Fret*.

MECHANICAL CARD TABLE. An early-19th-century tripod card table created by American furniture designer Duncan Phyfe. A steel rod is concealed in the turned, foliage-carved, hollow, urn-shaped support. It moves the rear legs and leaf brackets into a supporting position when the top leaf, which lies on top of the fixed leaf, is turned back to provide extra surface. The lower leaf is attached directly to the column. This table was usually made in pairs, of mahogany, and they were used as console tables when not used for gaming.

MÉDAILLIER. A French 18th-century small cabinet or display case for medals or decorations.

MÉDAILLON. See *Le Médaillon*.

MEANDER

MECHANICAL CARD TABLE

MÉDAILLON

MEDALLION

MEISSEN

JUSTE AURÈLE MEISSONIER

MEDALLION. A circular or oval frame usually with an ornamental motif enclosed.

MEDIEVAL. See *Gothic Period*. Illustrated is the interior of a 12th-century château according to Eugène Emmanuel Violet-le-Duc who was a 19th-century "Gothic" authority. See *Tapet* illustration.

MEDIEVAL

MEDIUM. The liquid or vehicle in which pigments are mixed: water, oil, wax, egg, etc. The word also refers to the actual technique of creating or rendering: oils, tempera, marble, wood, bronze, etc.

MEGALITHIC MASONRY. Prehistoric structures made up of huge stones such as those at Stonehenge.

MEGARON (plural, megara). A simple classic Greek building or residence, rectangular in plan, with a porched entrance and a gabled roof; a hall of state.

MEISSEN. A factory established at Dresden, then (1710) removed to Meissen, by Augustus, the King of Saxony. It used a process of copying Chinese porcelain credited to Johann Friedrich Böttger. The French Rococo period began to affect the designs by the middle of the 18th century, and copies of scenes by Jean Antoine Watteau and Nicolas Lancret appeared on the china. The factory produces toleware, vases, statuettes, and other decorative pieces with the trademark of crossed swords.

MEISSONIER, JUSTE (or JUST) AURÈLE (1695–1750). The "father" of the Rococo style. An Italian designer who produced a book of engravings using the shell motif which captured the fancy of the French craftsmen. They adapted and incorporated his designs into the Rococo French period woodwork (boiserie) and furniture. Meissonier became designer to Louis XV in 1725, and personally as a painter, goldsmith, architect, and interior designer carried the rococo style to its most extravagant limit. He balanced masses rather than shapes, and used asymmetrical balance as the basis of his designs.

JUSTE AURÈLE MEISSONIER

MELON BULB. A thick, bulbous turning retained from the Gothic period and used to support and embellish Elizabethan and Jacobean furniture. See *Leaves* for an illustration of a late Elizabethan draw table with melon bulb turned legs.

MELON BULB TABLE. A table of the Tudor period (early 16th-century England) with conspicuous globular turned legs. The "melon bulb" turning appeared as a support on other pieces of furniture as well. See *Melon Bulb*.

MELON TURNING. See *Cup and Cover Turning* and *Melon Bulb*.

MÉNAGÈRE. A low dresser with open shelves for crockery. The open shelves were usually equipped with racks and guardrails. It was also called a "vaisselier." See *Hutch or Huche*.

MENDLESHAM CHAIR. An early-19th-century variation of the Windsor chair made in Mendlesham, England, by Daniel Day. The back had a narrow splat and a series of turned wood balls between the straight top rail and the lower cross rail. The seat and legs were like those of the usual Windsor-type chair. See *Dan-Day Chair*.

MENUISIER. The French term for a craftsman who made chairs, beds, sofas, stools, and other pieces out of solid woods rather than of veneering. These pieces could be carved and painted and/or stained. A French Renaissance table of the mid-16th century is illustrated.

MERCERIZING. A process for treating cotton fibers or fabrics with a solution of caustic soda at a low temperature. The process makes the cotton stronger, more lustrous, more susceptible to dye, and more absorbent.

MÉRIDIENNE. A short sofa with one arm higher than the other. It was possible to recline in a half-sitting position on this particular sofa which was popular at the end of the 18th and the early 19th centuries, especially in the Empire period. A late Sheraton design is illustrated.

MERINO. A Spanish sheep and also the fine, cashmere-like wool obtained from the merino sheep.

MERISIER. The French for wild cherrywood, or a light fruitwood finish.

MERLON. Part of a Gothic battlement. One of the piers of masonry which form a battlement, and which have open spaces or crenels between them.

MESH FABRICS. Open loose-weave fabrics of any fiber content.

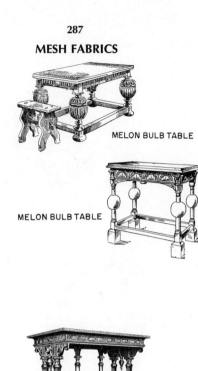

MELON BULB TABLE

MELON BULB TABLE

MENUISIER

MÉRIDIENNE

MERLON

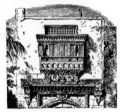

MESHERABIJEH

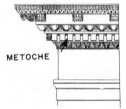

METOCHE

MESHERABIJEH. An Arabic term for a latticework window or shutters of a latticed effect.

MESOPOTAMIA. The "Cradle of Civilization." The fertile plain area around the Lower Tigris and the Lower Euphrates in western Asia. It is now known as Iraq. Early civilizations and cultures flourished in this area. The Babylonians or Chaldeans controlled Mesopotamia from 4000 to 1275 B.C. From 1275 to 538 B.C., the Assyrians ruled over Mesopotamia, and the conquering Persians held sway from 538 to 333 B.C.

MESQUITA. Spanish for "mosque."

MESSALINE. A lightweight silk satin fabric.

MÉTEZEAU, LOUIS (c. 1559–1615). French architect who worked on the Grande Galerie du Louvre and the Place Royale in Paris.

MÉTEZEAU, THIBAUT (1533–1596). The French architect to Henri III. He was the son of the architect Clément Métezeau. He was one of the original designers of the Louvre, and the Grand Mezzanine is his design.

METOCHE. The space between the dentils in the classic Ionic order.

METOPE

MEUBLE

METOPE. The space between the triglyphs in the classic Doric entablature. It is usually square (may be oblong) and is generally decorated with designs or groups of figures.

MEUBLES. French for "movable furniture" as opposed to architectural furniture or "built-ins." Illustrated is an early-19th-century French Empire chair.

MEUBLES À HAUTEUR D'APPUI. French low secretaries, cupboards, or bookcases against which one could comfortably lean or rest.

MEUBLES À TRANSFORMATIONS. Mechanically designed convertible furniture of the late Louis XV period. This trend for double-duty furniture was also prevalent in the late-18th-century English designs of Sheraton and others.

MEZZANINE. A low-ceilinged story, usually above the ground floor. An entresol.

MEZZO-RILIEVO. An Italian term for a relief sculpture which is more than a bas-relief but not as deep as high relief.

MEZZOTINT. The art reproduction process of the 18th century. It was especially popular in England where portraits by Sir Joshua Reynolds and Thomas Gainsborough were reproduced in this technique which can produce halftones and highlights. It is a form of intaglio engraving. See *Intaglio Engraving*.

MICARTA. The trademark of the United States Plywood Corporation for vinyl sheet material used for lamination onto wood or walls. It is used for tops and fronts of contemporary furniture, counters, service tables, etc. Micarta is available in a wide range of colors and patterns.

MICHELANGELO BUONARROTI (1475–1564). "The Father of Baroque." A great painter, sculptor, architect, and poet of the Renaissance. Among his many great achievements are the statues of "David," "Moses," and the "Pieta," the painted ceiling of the Sistine Chapel, and the statuary and architecture of the Medici Chapel. Illustrated is his statue of "Moses" and also the figure of "Night" from the Medici Chapel. See *Saint Peter's, Rome,* for Michelangelo's contribution to that structure, and the illustration to *Parapet Wall*.

MIDDLE AGES. See *Gothic Period*.

MIDDLE POINTED PERIOD. See *Decorated Period*.

MIGNATURES. Small-scaled sprig patterns for fabric created by Christophe-Philippe Oberkampf at his factory in Jouy during the latter part of the 18th century. This was a machine-made print with a small repeat design printed on cotton.

MIGNONNETTES. Small, sometimes egg-shaped patterns found on the background of fabrics (toiles) produced in the early 19th century. These small shapes filled the spaces between the framed or paneled elements of the design.

MILD STEEL. Steel which contains some carbon, and is not easily tempered.

MILIUM. A trademark name for a metalized fabric used for drapery linings. A metal containing a resinous binder is sprayed on the fabric to give it a silvery look. The material is characterized by a high reflectivity of high radiant heat. It is produced by Deering, Milliken, Inc.

MEZZO–RILIEVO

MICHELANGELO BUONARROTI

MICHELANGELO BUONARROTI

MILK SAFE

THOMAS MILTON

MINARET

MILK or PIE SAFES. 19th-century American cupboards that were found in Pennsylvania and the Midwest. They were the early "refrigerators." The doors had tin panels pierced in a decorative pattern to allow the air to circulate through. Illustrated is a very early 16th-century Tudor-Gothic oak cupboard, a forerunner of the milk or pie safe. Note the pierced openings used for ventilation.

MILL ENDS. Mill remnants or short ends remaining from a run of fabric.

MILLE-FLEURS. French for "thousand flowers." A 15th-century Gothic tapestry pattern which contained an overwhelming multitude of plants, leaves, and flowers.

MILTON, THOMAS. An 18th-century English designer noted for his chimneypieces. See *Crunden, John.*

MINARET. A tower on a Mohammedan mosque with one or more balconies from which the faithful are called to prayer.

MINIATURE

MIRADOR

MIROIR

MINIATURE. Any very small painting, sculpture, or objet d'art. Illustrated are two miniature portraits by Antonio Bencini (c. 1760) which were set into a golden box.

MIRADOR. A Spanish term for a balcony with a view, a loggia, or a window overlooking a vista. See *Belvedere.*

MIROIR. French for "mirror." Illustrated is a Louis XVI table mirror.

MIRROR. Looking glass. A highly polished smooth surface which reflects back an image. The earliest ones were the polished silver mirrors of ancient Egypt. Metal mirrors were also used during the Gothic period. The first silvered glass mirrors were made in Venice in the early 14th century. A Renaissance example is illustrated.

MISERERE. See *Misericord.*

MIRROR

MISERICORD. A bracket on the underside of a hinged stall seat which is arranged to support a person when standing, after the seat has been raised. It is also called a "miserere."

MISSION. A popular style of the late 19th to early 20th century based on the crude, massive furniture made by the priests and Indians for the missions in the southwest United States. The furniture was generally made of oak, with leather upholstery, and trimmed with oversized nailheads. The dark stain and massive clumsy appearance soon cost it its popularity. Gustav Stickley, who designed bungalows, also designed "mission" furniture.

MISERICORD

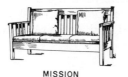

MISSION

MISSION

MISSION CHAIR. An early-20th-century cheap adaptation of the Spanish Renaissance frailero chair. See *Mission*.

MITER or MITRE. The corner junction of two pieces of wood cut at a similar angle, as in the corner of a picture frame. Usually the two pieces form a right angle.

MOBILE. A form of three-dimensional sculpture designed by the American artist, Alexander Calder. It is usually a collection of shapes connected by wires in such a manner that the entire unit can revolve and create a new arrangement of planes and solids in a three-dimensional movement.

MODEL. A three-dimensional scale representation of a building, piece of sculpture, etc.

MODERN. The architecture, furniture, and furnishings of today. A constantly changing style which is influenced by various countries, new inventions, new materials, etc. Generally, modern can be described as clean, straight lines with simple refined curves and a recognizably, functional quality. Ornament is used sparingly and is usually well integrated into the design. See *Oriental Modern, Scandinavian Modern,* and *Shaker Modern.*

MODERNE. A style of furniture which appeared after World War I (around the mid-1920's). It was based mainly on straight and angular lines with various grained woods used for contrasting effects. There was some painting and inlay work. The Bauhaus in Germany was the leading exponent of this style and introduced assorted tubular and strap metals into their

MITER

MODERNE

MODESTY PANEL

MODESTY PANEL

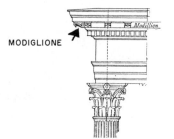

MODIGLIONE

designs. These pieces were the forerunners of our present contemporary and modern designs. A "moderne" chest is illustrated.

MODESTY PANEL. A panel of metal, wood, plastic, or cane which is set on the exposed end of a pedestal or kneehole-type contemporary desk. The seated person's knees are thus shielded from view, and the desk has a more enclosed appearance. It is also called a kneehole panel.

MODIGLIONE. Italian for a "bracket" or "corbel"; also called a "modillion."

MODILLION. The projecting decorated bracket used in a series to support the Corinthian cornice. It is one of the modillion band, and is also called a console.

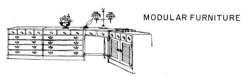

MODULAR FURNITURE

MODULAR FURNITURE. A modern concept in furniture design. Assorted correlated pieces are designed to a given set of dimensions (module) and also to fractions of that module. The assorted fractions and modules can be stacked or butted together, and units can be added or taken away as needed. Connecting devices are usually designed to combine these modular units: modular case goods, modular seating, modular lighting panels, etc. See *Module.*

MODULE. A measuring unit for an architectural order. See *Diameter.* Basic same-sized units which can be used interchangeably; they can be added to, or subtracted from. In office planning, this system makes for greater flexibility and mobility. It is possible to make adjustments and changes as new needs arise. Modules of lighting units can be of the same size as the ceiling panels, and thus interchangeable. Glass partitions, walls, doors, etc., when based on the same module, may be rearranged into spacial arrangements. Most important in a modular system are the dimensions, the detailing of the connections, and the ability to rearrange parts visually.

MOHAIR. A cloth made from the fleece of the angora goat. The fabric is now woven in combination with cotton and linen. It is a resilient fiber, and adds body to other fabrics. Mohair is also a pile fabric of cut or uncut loops similar to frieze. It is strong and durable, and was a popular upholstery fabric in 18th-century France. In England, the fabric was made of silk.

MOIRÉ. A waved or watered effect on fabric, especially rep or corded silks and synthetics. The fabric is pressed between engraved cylinders which emboss the grained design onto the material. The pattern is believed to hold better on the synthetic fabrics. See *Tabby*.

MOLDED BASE. The base of a piece of case furniture made up of molding strips or carved into a decorative molding. Illustrated is a Chippendale writing table.

MOLDED BASE

MOLDING

MOLDING or MOULDING. A shaped strip (concave, convex, half round, quarter round, ogee, cyma, etc.) used on projecting or receding features of buildings, walls, or furniture. It produces interesting patterns of light and shade. Illustrated are the moldings at the base of an ancient Roman column.

MOLESKIN. A heavy cotton fabric with a soft napped surface which is used as a lining for synthetic leathers, oilcloths, vinyls, etc.

MOMIE CLOTH. A rough, pebbly-surfaced fabric of cotton, rayon, or silk warp, usually with a woolen filling. It is used for draperies and upholstery.

MONADNOCK BLOCK. A celebrated early skyscraper in Chicago, Illinois, designed by John Root at the end of the 19th century. It was a 16-story masonry building which needed 12' walls at ground level to support the height.

MONDRIAN, PIET. A 20th-century abstract artist whose interesting designs of rectangular patterns made a great impression on the wallpaper and fabric designers of the 1940's and 1950's. In current usage his name is applied to an abstract arrangement of assorted sized rectangles used to create an allover design.

MONEL. A trademark name for a metal alloy made of nickel and copper. Its main attribute is its great resistance to corrosion.

MONEY MOTIF. A series of overlapping disks (like coins) which forms an imbricated pattern or continuous border design.

MONIAL. See *Mullion*.

MONK'S CHAIR. See *Frailero*.

MONEY MOTIF

MONK'S CLOTH. Also called friar's cloth. A heavy, coarsely woven cotton fabric. Groups of warp and weft threads are interlaced in a plain or basket weave.

MONK'S SEAT. See *Table Chair.*

MONNOYER, JEAN-BAPTISTE (1634–1699). A French decorator and painter of floral decorations in the Louis XIV period.

MONOCHROME or MONOTONE. Tints or shades of one color. A complete range of one color from very light to very dark. See *Grisaille.*

MONOLITH

MONOLITH. "One stone." An architectural structure of one solid piece. Illustrated is Stonehenge on Salisbury Plain, England. The diameter of the circle of monoliths is 100′. The circle is called a "cromlech."

MONOPTERON (or MONOPTEROS). In classic architecture, a temple which has a circular plan and a colonnade around its perimeter.

MONTAGE. The placing of one layer over another or their juxtaposition. A design created by the overlapping or superimposing of decorative elements. See *Collage.*

MONTANT. A French word for "stile," or a vertical element in a frame, door, chair, etc. See *Stile.*

MONTANT

MONTGOLFIER CHAIR. A Louis XVI chair with a balloon back designed to honor the Montgolfier brothers and their successful balloon ascension made in 1783. The slat simulates the lines of an ascension balloon. The original chair was designed by Georges Jacob, the noted French designer of the late 18th century.

MONTICELLO. Thomas Jefferson's home in Charlottesville, Virginia, from 1770 to 1809. It was designed by Jefferson and based on Palladian concepts, especially Palladio's Villa Rotonda. There are octagonal projections on either side of the domed central block. The interior is filled with many marvelous inventions and devices which are a tribute to Jefferson's ingenuity and sharp intellect.

MOORISH ARCH

MOORISH ARCH. A horseshoe arch. The curve of the arch is approximately three-quarters of a circle, and springs from the column's capitals. Illustrated is the gate of Las Palmas in Spain.

MOQUETTE. An uncut pile fabric similar to frieze, with set patterns of assorted colors. It is made of mohair and wool, or heavy cotton, and is used as an upholstery fabric. During the 16th and 17th centuries, in France, it was made of wool in multicolored designs. The Dutch version of this fabric was called "valours d'Utrecht." In France today, the term is used to describe a wool Wilton carpet. Illustrated is an early Louis XIV arch chair with moquette upholstery.

MOQUETTE

MOQUETTE

MORAND, P. DE V. A 17th-century French cabinetmaker noted for his clock cases in the Louis XIV style.

MOREEN. See *Morine.*

MORESQUE. Decoration in the Moorish style. The Moors possessed a large part of Spain during the early Gothic period, and thus greatly influenced the style of Spanish and Portuguese art, architecture, and decoration. In carpet construction, the tweed or "pepper-and-salt" effect produced by twisting two different colored yarns together in the weaving process.

MORESQUE

MORINE. A thick woolen upholstery material of the 17th and 18th centuries. Usually the warp was woolen, and the fillers were of linen, cotton, or wool. The material was either plain or figured. In the 19th century it was called "moreen."

MORNING ROOM. A sitting or writing room in English architecture with a sunny exposure, which was used for a lady's morning activities: correspondence, etc.

MOROCCAN (MAROQUIN) TAPESTRIES. Decorated leather hangings. See *Guadamicil.*

MORRIS, WILLIAM (1834–1896). An English producer and designer of wallpapers, furniture, tapestries, carpets, stained glass windows, and home accessories in the Art Nouveau style. He used dark, heavy colors, and was greatly influenced by Dante Gabriel Rossetti and Burne-Jones. Morris revolted against the eclecticism of the late 19th century. He created and designed the furnishings for his Red House at Upton in Kent, which was designed by architect Phillip Webb. Morris said, "I don't want art for a few, any more than education for a few, or freedom for a few. What business have we with art at all unless all can share it?" He attempted to bring art back to the common man, in his home and its furnishings, but unfortunately his beautiful products were too costly for the "common man." See *Pre-Raphaelite Brotherhood* and *Webb, Phillip Speakman.*

MORTAR

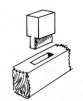

MORTISE AND TENON JOINT

MOSAIC

MOSQUE

MORRIS CHAIR. A large overstuffed 19th-century easy chair with loose cushions and an adjustable back. The seated person could lean back, after lifting the front edges of the chair's arms, and the chair back would decline into a semireclining position. It was designed by William Morris, a 19th-century architect, artist, and poet. See *Morris, William.*

MORTAR. A bonding material used in bricklaying and masonry for bedding and pointing the various members. It is usually made of cement or lime mixed with sand and water. It dries hard and firm.

MORTISE. A hole cut in a piece of wood which receives a tenon projecting from another piece of wood. It is used in cabinet joinery. See *Joinery, Mortise and Tenon Joint,* and *Tenon.*

MORTISE AND TENON JOINT. A method of joining two pieces of wood. The projecting tenon of one piece fits into the open shape (mortise) of the other. This glued joint is often used to join stretchers to leg posts or top seats to the back posts of chairs.

MORTLAKE TAPESTRIES. Early-17th-century English silk tapestries woven at Mortlake factory. They did not compare in technique or color with products of the Gobelins Factory.

MOSAIC. Small cubes (tesserae) of colored stones, marble, glass, etc., which are stuck into cement to form a pattern or design. The irregular surface quality catches light and reflects it at various angles. It was much favored as a form of decoration in the Early Christian and Byzantine churches. It is currently having a revival as a decorative art, in table and counter tops, on splashboards, etc. Illustrated are the marble mosaics of St. Mark's Church in Venice. See *Pietra Dura.*

MOSHEE. An 18th-century term for decorative borders.

MOSQUE. A Mohammedan temple of worship. It usually has a fountain for bathing, a dome or several domes, and a minaret from which to call the faithful to prayer.

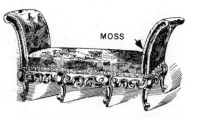

MOSS

MOSS. A chenille-like edging to a braid, used to finish and decorate pieces of upholstery and drapery. Illustrated is an early-18th-century stool or bench with rollover sides.

MOTHER-OF-PEARL. The iridescent lining of the pearl oyster and other shells. It is used for inlay work as well as small decorative items. See *Boulle Work, Intarsia or Tarsia,* and *Nacre.*

MOTIF or MOTIVE. The theme or distinctive feature of a design, period, or style. See *Lion Period* as an example. Illustrated is an early-16th-century English oak armoire with pierced work resembling the architectural tracery of the same Tudor Gothic period. The tracery motif appears in the architecture and furnishings of the period.

MOTIF

MOTTLE. A wood grain effect produced by short irregular wavy fibers lying across the face of the wood.

MOUCHARABY. A balcony with a parapet, often with machicolations which project over an entrance or a gate of a medieval structure. It was used as a defense area.

MOUCHARABY

"MOUNT AIRY"

MOUNT AIRY. A colonial mansion of the Rappahannock, in Richmond County, Virginia. It was built in 1758 for John Taylor II, and was based on the English version of Palladian design. The house is built of dark brown limestone, and it was probably originally plastered over. The plan of the estate consisted of a central block with two curving pedimented pavilions which connect two outbuildings with the main structure.

MOUNT PLEASANT. Built in 1761–1762 in Philadelphia, Pennsylvania, for John MacPherson. It was built in the tradition of the Virginia country houses with twin "flankers." It is yellow stucco framed with blocks of red brick, and has the traditional hipped roof and ballustraded deck. Twin chimneys flank either side of the house. The usual Palladian window appears over the pedimented doorway, and is itself topped with a beautifully scaled pediment. Tuscan columns flank the doorway with its Georgian fan window.

MOUNTINGS. The base and harp of an electrified lamp. See *Harp.*

MOUNTS. Ornamental and/or useful metalwork on cabinets or drawer units: handles, escutcheons, drawer pulls, etc. Cabinet hardware. Illustrated are some 18th-century brass escutcheons and handles.

MOUNTS

MOYEN ÂGE. French for "Middle Ages."

MOZARABIC. The arts and designs of Moorish Spain in which Christian and Gothic elements were also used. Illustrated is a painting on leather from the Hall of Judgment in the Alhambra.

MOZARABIC

MUDEJAR

MUDEJAR. The 13th to 17th centuries in Spain. A transitional art style in Spain in which Moorish and Christian details were often used together. It was the style of the Christianized Moor, and was superimposed first over Gothic, and later over Renaissance forms. Illustrated is the façade of the College of S. Gregorio, Valladolid (1488). It is embellished with statues, heraldic devices, canopied niches, and pinnacles. The inner courtyard (see *Plateresco*) is done in the later style.

MUFFIN STAND. A small tiered table which held plates and was used for teas and for other genteel entertaining. It was popular in 18th- and 19th-century England and America.

MULE CHEST. In Chippendale's style, a massive chest which resembles two chests set side by side and sharing a single centered bracket foot. It was a forerunner of today's double dressers. The chest often had handles on the sides, probably for moving it around. It actually evolved from the coffer or chest of the 17th century which had a drawer or two under the lid portion. Illustrated is an early-17th-century design (Jacobean).

MULE CHEST

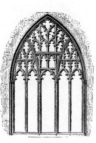

MULLION

MULLION. A slender vertical or horizontal bar between windows or glass panels.

MULTIFOIL. A pattern having many lobed forms. An arch having more than five foils or arcuate divisions. A scalloped arch.

MULTIWALL UNIT. A wall made up of two or more wythes of masonry. See *Wythe or Withe.*

MUMMY CLOTH. A silk or cotton fabric with an irregular warp figure. It has a light, fine texture.

MUNSELL SYSTEM. Albert F. Munsell's color system which designates and classifies colors, and is widely used as a standard for color and color matching. The system was published as the *Munsell Book of Color* by the Munsell Color Company, Baltimore, Maryland.

MUNTIN or MUNTING. The central vertical part of a door which divides the panels above and below the middle or lock rail. A vertical strip between two panels. The term "muntin" is also used to identify the wood strips that hold the panes of glass in a glazed door. The horizontal strip is called the "lock rail."

MULTIFOIL

MUNTIN

MURAL. Any kind of wall painting, either painted directly on the wall, or printed on paper or canvas and then applied to the wall. It is not the same as a fresco, which becomes an integral part of the structure of the wall. See *Fresco.* Illustrated is an 18th-century mural decoration designed by Giambattista Piranesi.

MURANO GLASS. Fine colored glass produced in the Murano glassworks in Venice. Much of what we today call Venetian glass is produced in Murano. A 17th-century Venetian glass ewer is illustrated.

MURILLO, BARTOLOMÉ ESTEBAN (1617–1682). A Spanish painter of religious subjects. His technique was affected by Rubens, Titian, and Velasquez. Murillo's work varied from early hard naturalism (paintings of beggar boys) to the slightly detached, slightly idealized religious paintings. He developed his figures into idealized forms with baroque, swirling draperies, and in his later years the religious image became soft, tender,

MURAL

MURANO GLASS

MURRHINE

MURRHINE

MUTULE

and touched with sentimentality. His work became the basis of a school of art that painted in his style up into the 19th century.

MURRHINE. Ancient Roman fragile and opalescent glassware.

MUSHREBEEYEH. An Arabic term for a balcony enclosed with lattice screens.

MUSHROOM TURNED KNOBS. Wooden turned knobs, with flat carved tops that resemble mushroom caps.

MUSLIN. A plain-weave fabric which may be bleached or unbleached. It is used as undercovering on upholstered pieces to tie in the stuffing and padding materials prior to putting on the final upholstery fabric. Muslin may also be dyed or printed and used for curtains, bedspreads, etc.

MUTED. Of colors, soft, restrained, dulled-down.

MUTULE. Any projection from the surface of a wall. It describes especially the square block, like the end of a beam, which appears at regular intervals above the frieze of a Doric building.

MYLAR. A trademark name for a polyester film which is made into metallic yarns. The polyester film is metalized by aluminum deposited on its surface, and then the entire fiber is sandwiched in clear film. It is usually used with Nylomar Fortisan since Mylar is a weak yarn and stretches easily. It is nontarnishing and soft in hand. Mylar is used to decorate upholstery and drapery fabrics.

MYRTLE BURL. A highly figured, very blond to golden-brown wood of widely varying designs. It is native to the western United States. The myrtle wood is hard and strong and is used for cabinetwork, inlay, and veneering.

N

N.

N.

N. Napoleon I's initial which appeared as an important decorative motif in the First French Empire style (early 19th century). The monogram was carved onto units, inlaid, painted, woven, and embroidered. Illustrated is the motif in Napoleon's throne room which was designed by Charles Percier and Pierre Fontaine.

NACRE. The lustrous, iridescent material which lines some seashells. It is mother-of-pearl, and has long been popular as an inlay material on tabletops, chair frames, cabinets, barometers, and small accessories. The Victorians found nacre irresistible as an inlay decoration on their papier-mâché trays, ornaments, and whatnots.

NAIL HEADS. Nails or brads with plain or decorated oversized heads made of brass, copper, or other metals, which are used to secure leather or fabric upholstery. They may also be used to embellish leather panels (or create a tufted effect) over wood panels and doors. The nail heads are exposed and spaced to create a definite line or pattern. This type of ornament was originally Spanish and Italian Gothic in concept. An early Italian Renaissance chair with nail-head trim is illustrated. See *Stud.*

NAIL HEADS

NAKORA. A trademark name for a Japanese blond hardwood. It is extremely light in color, and it has a definite grain pattern when rotary-cut.

NANMU. A Chinese aromatic wood which turns rich brown in color as it ages. It is also called Persian cedar.

NAOS. The chamber or "cella" of a classic Greek temple. See *Cella.*

NAP. The raised fibers on the surface of a fabric which create a downy or fuzzy appearance. The nap is not the pile of the fabric. See *Pile.* Moleskin and flannel are napped fabrics.

NARRAWOOD. A Philippine hardwood which varies from light golden tones to brown, and also from light to dark red. Narrawood may resemble mahogany or satinwood because it has ripples and also a fine mottled effect. This wood is excellent for furniture production and interior veneers.

NARTHEX. The entrance to a basilican church which is formed by a long porch set at right angles to the nave. It also appears in Byzantine-style churches like the Cathedral of San Marco in Venice. Illustrated is the plan of the original St. Peter's in Rome.

NARTHEX

NATIONAL SOCIETY OF INTERIOR DESIGNERS (N.S.I.D.). A guild of interior designers founded in 1955. It has standards similar to those of the A.I.D. (see *American Institute of Designers).* The N.S.I.D. has a broader interpretation of "professional" members who include scenic designers, landscape architects, design teachers, etc. The society also enrolls trade members, the manufacturers and suppliers to the design and decorating industry.

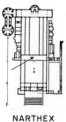

NARTHEX

NATOIRE, CHARLES-JOSEPH (1700–1777). A French painter of voluptuous nudes in the style of Boucher. Many of his paintings

NATTES

NATTES

NEBULE ORNAMENT

NEEDLEPOINT

were integrated into the decorating schemes of salons and boudoirs, set into the boiserie panels, overdoors or overmantels.

NATTES. A surface texture or decoration that resembles a plaited, basket-weave design.

NAUGAHYDE. A trademark name for vinyl upholstery and wall covering fabrics produced by the United States Rubber Company.

NAUGAWEAVE. United States Rubber's trademark name for "breathable" vinyl upholstery fabrics.

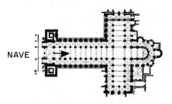

NAVE

NAVE. The main or central part of a cruciform church. It is usually flanked by aisles, and terminates in an apse. See *Apse* and *Transept.*

NEBULE ORNAMENT. A Norman form of ornament which consisted of a continuous wavy line. It was used to enrich moldings, etc.

NÉCESSAIRE. A French term for a small writing or toilet accessory case.

NECESSARY STOOL. See *Close Chair or Stool.*

NECKING. See *Collar.*

NEEDLEPOINT. An old-fashioned cross-stitch embroidery done on net, heavy canvas, or coarse linen. It resembles a coarse tapestry. From the 15th century on, it has been used as an upholstery covering for chairs, sofas, etc. A Louis XVI chair with needlepoint covering is illustrated. See *Gros Point* and *Petit Point.*

NELSON, GEORGE. A 20th-century American furniture and interior designer with a simple, direct, contemporary style. He introduced the slat bench, the adjustable headboard bed, and case furniture built on steel frames and finished in a wide range of woods or lacquered colors. Nelson is also the innovator of the "basic storage component system," OMNI office furniture composed of interchangeable parts (see *Modular Furniture),* the swaged-leg desk and chair, clocks, steel-framed chairs, elastic webbing daybeds, etc.

NEOCLASSIC. See *Neoclassicism*.

NEOCLASSICISM. A movement which originated in Rome in the mid-18th century as a reaction against the excesses of the baroque and rococo styles. The discoveries at Herculaneum and Pompeii gave impetus to this movement to return to the art and architecture of classic Greece and Rome. The Louis XVI style of France and the Adam style in England were part of this Neoclassic trend. An Adam wall candelabrum is illustrated.

NÉO-GREC. The "new Greek" style of the Louis XVI period in France influenced by the discoveries at Herculaneum and Pompeii. Greek motifs became popular for furniture and interior decorations. A Louis XVI table is illustrated. Note the caryatid-type figures used on the legs, and the classic motif on the decorative inlaid drawer fronts.

NÉO-GREEK. The American period of art and architecture (from 1815 to 1845) which was heavily flavored with classic Greek columns and entablatures.

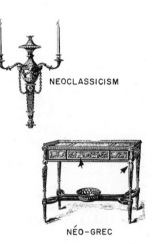

NEOCLASSICISM

NÉO-GREC

NEO-GREEK

NEPVEU, PIERRE. A French architect of the early 16th century. He designed the semifortress Château de Chambord in 1526. A plan of the château is shown here. See *Château de Chambord*.

NERVURE. In a groined vault, a secondary or side rib.

NESTED TABLES. A series of small tables, graduating in size, so that one can be set inside the other. They may serve as sofa or end tables, and they are made in a variety of styles, traditional or contemporary. See *Quartette Tables*.

NET. An open-weave, meshlike fabric used for glass curtains. It may be made of cotton, linen, rayon, or other synthetic fibers.

NET VAULT. A type of overly decorative and complicated interlocking rib vaulting peculiar to the late Gothic period in Germany and especially to the hall-type church. See *Hall Church* and *Vault*.

PIERRE NEPVEU

NEUMANN, BALTHASAR (1687–1753). A master architect of the German baroque school. He designed the Archbishop's residence at Würzburg with its noted staircase (1719), the summer castle at Werneck (1731), and the Abbey Church at Neresheim (1745).

NEUTRA, RICHARD. A 20th-century American architect born in Vienna in 1892. In the late 1920's he produced the D. R. Lovell house which was a combination of Californian "skeletal pavilions" and European cubist designs. It was made of light steel framing with balconies and horizontal strip walls cantilevered out. He believes "constructed human environment should be an entity, and not split up by specialists."

NEUTRAL. A color of no definite character or personality. A neutral color will usually blend well with most true colors. White, black, gray, and beige are neutrals.

NEW COLONIAL PERIOD or MODERN COLONIAL. An early 20th-century American-Empire-type style of furniture. The classic features were retained, but the ormolu and brass mounts were omitted. The S-shaped scroll, scroll foot, lion's paw foot, and classic columns were often in evidence. The pieces were mass-produced in Grand Rapids, Michigan; the better pieces were often made in mahogany. Illustrated is a typical china closet of the New Colonial style.

NEW COLONIAL PERIOD

NEWEL or NEWEL POST. A heavy upright post or turning at the end of a handrail of a stairway.

NIB. See *Lug*.

NEWEL POST

NICHE

NICHE

NICKING

NICHE. A recessed or hollowed-out space in a wall, usually designed to hold a statue, vase, or ornament.

NICKING. A notched or gouged ornamenting technique used on 17th-century English oak furniture.

NIELLO. A method of decorating metal surfaces by engraving lines on them. The lines are then filled with a black composition which makes the design stand out in sharp contrast.

NIELLO

NIEMEYER, OSCAR. An outstanding 20th-century South American architect who is currently designing most of the principal buildings in Brazília, the new capital of Brazil. In 1947 he served on the United Nations Design Committee in New York.

NIGHT STOOL. See *Close Chair or Stool.*

NIGHT TABLE. A bedside table, usually small, with or without a drawer or shelf. It is used to hold a lamp, ashtray, clock, etc. Sometimes small commodes are used in period rooms in place of night tables. See *Chevet.*

NIMBUS. A circular halo (a ring of gold) around a painted or carved representation of the head of Christ, the Madonna, or a saint.

NIMBUS

NINON. A smooth, very sheer, closely woven voile, usually made of rayon. It is sometimes called triple voile. Ninon is used for *Glass Curtains.*

NO-FINES. A concrete composed of cement and coarse aggregate.

NOGGING. In the construction of a partition, the placing of a horizontal piece between two vertical studs.

NOGUCHI, ISAMU. A 20th-century American sculptor-designer who has created sculptural free-form glass-topped tables which rest on intricately shaped abstract bases. He has also created a curving, armless sofa with a small backrest, as well as exquisite folding-paper "akari" lanterns. Noguchi also has designed stage sets, costumes, and landscapes for modern architectural developments.

NONBEARING. Describing a wall or partition which does not support a load or resist a force or thrust from above. It is a filler section.

NONSUCH FURNITURE. Trompe l'œil decorated furniture of the 16th and 17th centuries in England. The term refers especially to perspective views of Nonsuch Palace, which was built for Henry VIII. Designs of the palace were executed on flat-surfaced chests in inlay work. Illustrated is the Palace of Nonsuch. See *Intarsie.*

NONSUCH FURNITURE

NORMAN PERIOD. The period in England under the Norman kings, dating approximately from 1066 to 1189. The architecture

NORMAND, CHARLES is characterized by massive constructions, rough, thick-jointed masonry, rounded arches, projecting parapets carried on a corbel table, wide buttresses of slight projection, and assorted carved capitals. The prominent motifs were the chevron, star, billet, zigzag, and bird-beak moldings. The term "Romanesque" is the Continental name for Norman.

CHARLES PIERRE JOSEPH NORMAND

NORMAN PERIOD

NORMAND, CHARLES PIERRE JOSEPH (1765–1840). A noted architect and publisher of Empire style designs. He favored the Roman models as standards for his works and collections.

NORMANDY. A province of France which produced a charming, simple, country-style, 18th-century furniture. It was similar to the colonial New England designs of the same time.

NOSING

NOSING. The curved or shaped front edge of a stair tread.

NOTCHING. See *Nicking.*

NOTRE-DAME

NOTRE-DAME, PARIS. One of the oldest of the French Gothic cathedrals, which was built from 1163 to 1235. The western façade is probably the finest and most characteristic of the architecture of that period, and it was the prototype for many other cathedrals. See *Façade* for illustration. The east end (here illustrated) is noted for its slender flying buttresses, chevet chapel, gabled transepts, and the flèche (spire) which rises 300 feet above the ground. See illustration to *Contreforts.*

NOTRE-DAME

NOTTINGHAM LACE. A general name given to machine-made flat lace, particularly lace tablecloths or curtains which are made in one piece. It was originally a handmade product. See *Lace.*

NOYER. French for "walnut." Illustrated is a 16th-century French crédence made of walnut.

NUB YARN. See *Slub Yarn.*

NOYER

NULLING. A Jacobean wood-carving technique which produced an effect similar to repoussé or chased metalwork. The patterns were created by a series of small projections or recessions from the surface (like a boss or bead) of the wood.

NURSING CHAIR. An English term for a chair with a low seat. See *Chauffeuse.*

NYLON. A protein-like chemical which can be manufactured as fibers, in sheet form, or as bristles. It is tough, elastic, and strong, and it is often used in fabrics which were originally produced from silk or rayon yarns. Nylon is also used as a carpeting fiber. It provides a degree of abrasion resistance, dries quickly, and is easy to care for.

NYMPHAEUM. A classic building designed to house flowers and plants. It was usually equipped with running water and statuary, and also served as a retreat.

O.C. An abbreviation for "on center." When dimensions or measurements are given in relating one structural element to another, the distance is sometimes given from the center point of one to the center point of the other. In this case, the letters O.C. appear next to the measurement.

O.M. An abbreviation for "outside measurement." A measurement of distance between outer surfaces of a hollow object, rather than of distance between inner surfaces (inner measurement or I.M.). Outside measurement includes the thickness of the shell.

OAK. A hard, durable wood of a red or whitish color which lends itself to carving or paneling. Because it is so porous, it has to be treated with a filler before it is stained. The French and English oaks are finer-grained.

OAK, POLLARD. English brown oak which is nut-brown to deep brown in color, and spotted in black. The figure is often tortoiseshell in effect. The wood has a medium hard texture.

OAK, QUARTERED. Planks of wood sawed toward or through the center of the tree trunk, resulting in a more decorative plank or veneer. The wood has a "flake" pattern which is caused by the wide rays that reflect the light. Generally, oak is heavy, hard, and strong, and has prominent pores in spring-cut wood. A carved oak cupboard of the early 16th century is illustrated. Note the linenfold pattern carved on the panels.

OBELISK. A tall, tapering column or structure, square or rectangular in section, with a pyramid-shaped top. It is often used as a commemorative monument.

QUARTERED OAK

OBELISK

OBJET D'ART

OBVERSE

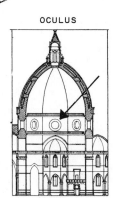

OCCASIONAL TABLE

OCULUS

OBERKAMPF, CHRISTOPHE-PHILIPPE (1738–1815). The founder of the fabric factory at Jouy near Versailles. Oberkampf was the creator of "toile de Jouy," a particular type of printed cotton fabric. See *Mignonettes, Picoté,* and *Toile de Jouy.*

OBJET D'ART. A small art object: miniature painting, sculpture, vase, snuffbox, etc. See *Bibelots.* Illustrated is a vase of the Sung dynasty.

OBLIQUE ARCH. See *Skew Arch.*

OBSCURE GLASS. A translucent, rather than a transparent, glass. It allows in light but does not permit a clear, uninterrupted view.

OBVERSE. The main face of a medal, ornament, coin, etc. The opposite side is the "reverse" side. A Roman coin is shown.

OCCASIONAL TABLE. A general term for a small odd table that can have one or several purposes: end table, sofa table, coffee table, lamp table, cocktail table, etc. The occasional table is usually a small extra table which adds to the comfort and convenience of a room. A mid-18th-century English "whatnot" table is illustrated.

OCCHIO DI BUE. Italian for "bull's-eye."

OCTASTYLE. A building or portico with eight columns.

OCULUS. A circular opening such as might appear in the opening in the crown of a dome.

ODALISQUE

ODALISQUE. A female slave or concubine in a Turkish seraglio. Because of its exotic connotation, the odalisque was a decorative motif in the erotic period of Louis XV.

ODEUM. A small ancient Greek and Roman theatre where public music and poetry competitions took place.

ODIST, J. B. C. A French 19th-century metalworker and creator of mounts for Empire furniture.

OGIVALE

JEAN FRANÇOIS OEBEN

OEBEN, JEAN FRANÇOIS. An 18th-century master cabinetmaker to King Louis XV. He trained Jean-Henri Riesener, and created many beautiful pieces which were decorated with fine marquetry work in assorted colored woods. Oeben designed furniture for the Marquise de Pompadour, who preferred simpler pieces than the then current rococo style. Illustrated is the famous desk (bureau à cylindre) created for Louis XV. It was begun by Oeben and completed by Riesener. See *Riesener, Jean-Henri.*

OECUS. Latin word for "reception room."

OEIL-DE-BOEUF. French for "bull's-eye." A round or oval window in Renaissance architecture. See *Bull's-Eye.*

OEIL-DE-BOEUF

OFFSET

OFFSET. A small projection, ledge, or lip.

OFF-WHITE. White that is tinted with a color; bluish-white, yellowish-white, etc.

OGEE. A molding made up of a concave and a convex curve. It is also called an ogive or keel molding. In architecture, an arch consisting of two opposed ogee curves meeting in a point at the top. It was popularly used in the English Decorated Gothic Period. It is also called a *Keel Arch.*

OGEE

OGEE BRACKET FOOT

OGEE BRACKET FOOT

OGEE BRACKET FOOT. See *Chinese Bracket Foot or Chinese Foot.* Illustrated is a Chippendale press.

OGIVALE. A term used to describe the Gothic architecture in France. Illustrated is Bourges Cathedral showing the flying buttresses.

OGIVALE

OIL PAINTING

OILLET

OGIVE. See *Ogee.*

OIL FINISH. A wood finish which is accomplished by repeated polishing with boiled linseed oil. A low, satin-like luster is achieved, and the wood is fairly resistant to stains from heat and water. It is currently a popular finish on walnut and teak.

OIL PAINTING. An art technique in which pigment is ground in oil and applied to a slightly absorbent surface or to a primed canvas. It is the most usual painting technique for large and important pictures. The Eycks are credited with "inventing" oil painting for pictures, though the use of oil mixtures for house and/or decorative painting dates back to antiquity. Illustrated is the "Madonna of Canon van der Paele" by Jan van Eyck.

OILED SILK. A sheer silk fabric waterproofed by being oil-soaked and then dried.

OILLET. A small opening in the wall of a medieval castle through which missiles were thrown.

OINOCHOE

OINOCHOE. A Greek wine jug. The word is from the Greek for "to pour out wine." The spout was shaped in a triangular form which made pouring easy and accurate.

OLD COLONY HOUSE, NEWPORT. Built in Rhode Island in 1739 by Richard Munday, a local builder, who also designed Trinity Church in Newport (1725), it was originally designed as a meeting hall for the Provincial Assembly. It is a beautiful brick structure with a truncated gable, and the building is capped with a gracious cupola and a balustrade. Twin chimneys flank either end of the building. A graceful balcony with a broken pediment top is perched over the main doorway.

OLIVE WOOD. A small Italian tree that, as a veneer, can be used only in small, closely matched patterns. It can also be used as a decorative inlay wood. Olive wood is a light yellow wood with greenish-yellow figures, and is somewhat like English ash.

OMBRÉ. A shaded or graduated one-color pattern, usually in a striped effect. The term is derived from the French for "shadowed." It is a range of tints to shades of a single color.

ON-THE-GLAZE. A colored design applied over glazed biscuit pottery, as in Majolica pottery.

ONION FOOT. An onion-shaped turned foot of the Early Renaissance period. It was not used very much after the William and Mary Period. Illustrated is a 17th-century Jacobean cupboard.

ONION FOOT

ONLAY. A decorative overlay or facing like a sheathing or a veneer.

ONYX. A stone or semiprecious gem, chalcedony, with two or more layers of strongly contrasting colors or marked with white and stratified with opaque and translucent lines. It is an agate stone used for cameos and inlay work.

OPALESCENT. Showing an iridescent reflection of light, opal like in its play of color; having a rainbow-like or pearly appearance.

OPEN BACK. A chair back which has an unupholstered opening between the rails and side splats, or a decorative open frame back. Illustrated is a Hepplewhite shield-back chair.

OPEN BACK

OPEN STOCK. Furniture which is regularly kept in stock and is usually available for immediate delivery. The furniture is not custom-made or specially finished. It is possible to buy parts of suites rather than complete groups.

OPEN-WELL STAIR. A stairway or two or more flights surrounding an open space.

OPERA GAUZE. See *Theatrical Gauze.*

OPISTHODOME or OPISTHODOMUS. The portico behind the naos or cella of a classic Greek temple. See *Posticum* and *Pronaos.*

GILLES MARIE OPPENORD

OPPENORD (or OPPENORT), GILLES MARIE (1672–1742). A French designer of interiors, furniture, and metalwork. He was the director of styles during the French Régence period, and was partially responsible for introducing the Rococo period. His painted panels resembled the works of Watteau and Gillot in style. See *Baseboard* for an Oppenord interior.

OPPENORD, JEAN. A 17th-century French cabinetmaker of the Louis XIV period.

OPUS ALEXANDRINUM. The mosaic work used on floors in Byzantine and Romanesque churches.

OPUS ALEXANDRINUM

OPUS FRANCIGENUM

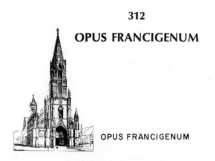

OPUS FRANCIGENUM

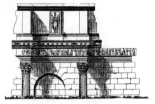

OPUS QUADRATUM

OPUS TESSELATUM

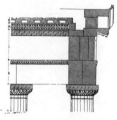

ORDERS OF ARCHITECTURE

OPUS FRANCIGENUM. "French work." A rarely used term for "Gothic architecture." German Gothic was based essentially on the French Gothic style, and the term "Opus Francigenum" is of German origin. In this way Germany acknowledged her indebtedness to French architecture. Illustrated is the Minster of Freiburg.

OPUS INCERTUM. A Roman technique for facing a concrete wall with irregularly shaped stones.

OPUS QUADRATUM. A Roman wall facing consisting of rectangular blocks of stone with or without mortar joints, and often secured with dowels or cramps. Illustrated is the Forum of Nerva, Rome.

OPUS RETICULATUM. A Roman device for facing concrete walls with diagonal lines which simulate a fishnet.

OPUS SECTILE. Roman mosaics made up of large pieces of stone or tile set into geometric patterns.

OPUS SPICATUM. A Roman method of facing a wall with stones diagonally set to form a herringbone design.

OPUS TESSELATUM. Latin term for a mosaic pavement which has tesserae laid into patterns or pictures. Tesselated pavements or floors.

OPUS TESTACEUM. Roman concrete walls faced with triangular bricks which were about 1¹/₂″ thick.

OPUS VERMICULATUM. A type of Roman mosaic work which employed diamond-shaped or long, irregularly shaped stones. It was especially adapted for pictorial designs: hair, drapery folds, features, etc.

ORANGERY or ORANGERIE. A hothouse for growing orange trees. A glassed-in house for plants.

ORCHESTRA. In the ancient Greek theatre, the space in front of the stage where the chorus sang and danced. In present-day auditoriums, the main floor which is usually pitched so that the level of the front row is just below the surface of the stage and the rows behind are placed progressively higher.

ORDERS OF ARCHITECTURE. The classic orders consisted of the pedestal, the column, and the entablature. The Greek orders were Doric, Ionic, and Corinthian. The Roman orders included the three mentioned above plus the Tuscan and the Composite. See the individual orders listed here. A Greek Doric entablature is illustrated. See *Classic* and *Vignola, Giacomo Barozzi da.*

ORGANDY (ORGANDIE). A very thin, translucent stiff and wiry cotton muslin. It can be piece-dyed or printed. Swiss organdy is chemically treated to keep its crisp, sheer finish through many launderings.

ORGANIC ARCHITECTURE. Frank Lloyd Wright's term for architecture which has been conceived as an organic whole, with the various parts relating to one another and in harmony with the environment.

ORGANZINE. A two-ply silk yarn twisted in the opposite direction from the single yarn from which it is produced.

ORIEL WINDOW. A large projecting window supported by a corbelled brick or stone construction. Illustrated is the oriel window of a German Renaissance structure. Note the corbie gabled roof. See *Alcove* for the interior view of an Elizabethan oriel window.

ORIENTAL. Far Eastern or Asiatic. Referring to things Chinese, Japanese, etc. A Chinese black lacquer panel with a raised design in gold is shown.

ORIENTAL MODERN. A popular furniture and interior trend since the mid-1950's. The basic Japanese and Chinese lines and geometric designs combine well with the low, sleek uncluttered modern concepts. Teak and bamboo are used with walnut and rosewood. Heroic bronze, brass, and pewter hardware is used for decorative accents.

ORIENTAL WALNUT. See *Oriental Wood.*

ORIENTAL WOOD. A hard-textured Australian wood of brown to pink-gray color, possibly with a pinkish cast or with pinkish streaks. It has a strong, distinctive striped figure and it is a member of the laurel family. It is also called Australian laurel, Australian walnut, and oriental walnut.

ORIENTATION. The establishment of a relationship between a structure, plot, or piece of furniture to a point of the compass, a natural landmark, or a particular wall, structure, etc.

ORLO or ORLE. A fillet or band on either the top or the bottom of the shaft of a column. It also refers to the flat plane surface between adjacent flutes or channels of columns or *Triglyphs.* The orlo is also called femor, regela, or meros.

ORLON. A Dupont trademark for an acrylic fiber with at least 85 percent acrylonitrile. The fiber adds warmth without weight, and is resistant to sun fading and some chemical reactions. Orlon has a wool-like hand, and takes a brilliant dye.

ORME. French for "elm wood."

ORIEL WINDOW

ORIEL WINDOW

ORIENTAL

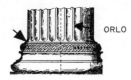
ORLO

ORMOLU

ORMOLU or ORMOULU. Gilded bronze. A bright goldlike metallic alloy with a high percentage of copper plus zinc and tin. The term may also apply to cast bronze ornaments which are hand-chased and surfaced with gilt. The making of ormolu decorations was particularly popular in France in the 17th and 18th centuries. Mounts, moldings, and medallions were used as applied decoration on furniture pieces. Illustrated is an ormolu inkstand of the Louis XV period. See *Bronze Doré*.

ORNAMENT. A decoration, trimming, enhancement, or embellishment.

ORNAMENT

OS DE MOUTON

ORNAMENTAL ENGLISH. See *Decorated Period*.

OS DE MOUTON. French for "mutton bone." A carved motif which was popular in the period of Louis XIII in France. The "mutton bone" was used for the legs and arms of chairs and sofas. The line is similar to that of a cabriole leg, but it is much heavier and stumpier in appearance.

OSNABURG. The plain coarse cotton fabric from which cretonne is produced. See *Cretonne*.

OSTWALD SYSTEM. A color system devised by Wilhelm Ostwald of Germany. See *Munsell System*.

OTTOMAN. Originally a backless, long, cushioned seat, couch, or divan. In current usage it is an oversized upholstered footrest often used and designed to relate to a club or easy chair. The contemporary use and proportion developed during the Victorian period. A late-17th-century English ottoman is illustrated. See *Hassock*. Also, a heavy corded fabric like faille, but with heavier and rounder ribs.

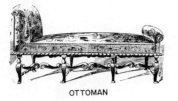

OTTOMAN

OTTOMANE. A French upholstered canapé or settee introduced in the Louis XV period. The curved enclosing side pieces are a continuation of the rounded back. It is the same as a canapé à corbeille.

OUD, JACOBUS JOHANNES PIETER (born in 1890). A Dutch architect who was the leader of the "De Stijl" group and a champion of modernism in art. In Rotterdam, where he was the city architect, he produced many housing units made of reinforced concrete in simple forms, like the workingmen's colony at Oud-Mathenesse (1921–1922); in 1926 he built another at the Hook of Holland. See *De Stijl*.

OUDRY, JEAN-BAPTISTE (1686–1755). A French court painter to Louis XV, and the superintendent of the Beauvais and Gobelin factories. He is noted for his designs for a series of tapestries based on the fables of La Fontaine, as well as for his historical and animal paintings.

OUTROUNDED CORNERS. The corners of a square or rectangular tabletop, or panel which are shaped into semicircular curves or quarter arcs. See *Segmental Cornered*.

OVAL BACK. A Hepplewhite chair back similar to French chair backs of the Louis XVI period. It is also referred to as *Le Médaillon*.

OUTROUNDED CORNERS

OVAL BACK

OVERDOOR

OVERDOOR. An architectural design set over a front entrance door. It is usually made of wood or lead mullions, and paned with glass. In the 18th century in England, these windowed transoms were greatly admired, and designers like Chippendale, Manwaring, Ince, Mayhew, as well as the Adam brothers designed many fine "overdoors." The design illustrated is by J. Carter of the Georgian 18th century. See *Fanlight*.

OVERHANGING EAVES. The lower end of a sloping roof which projects beyond the top wall of a structure and thus forms an overhang.

OVERSAILING. A continuous row of corbels which supports a load. See *Corbel Table*. The cornice of the Italian Renaissance Palazzo Riccardi is illustrated.

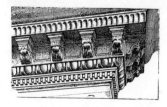

OVERHANGING EAVES

OVERSAILING

OVOLO

P

PAD FOOT

PAGODA

PAGODA

OVERSTUFFED. Describing heavily upholstered pieces of furniture, usually with concealed frames; a word often associated with plump, fluffy pillow seats and backs, and tufting.

OVOLO. A quarter-round convex molding often decorated with an *Egg and Dart* motif.

OX-EYE. A round or oval window. See *Oeil-de-Boeuf*.

OXBOW CHEST. See *Yoke-Front Chest*.

OYSTER GRAIN. A peculiarly figured walnut veneer which resembles the inside of an oyster shell. It is a busy, splotchy, swirly pattern that was popular in the Queen Anne period in England (early 18th century). See *Oystering*.

OYSTERING. The process of veneering furniture with certain burr veneers during the early 18th century. See *Burr, Oyster Grain,* and *Oysterpieces*.

OYSTERPIECES. Transverse slices through the gnarled boughs or roots of walnut and other trees.

OYSTERWOOD. See *Oystering*.

PAD FOOT. A flattened disklike foot often found under a cabriole leg. It is similar to a club foot. A late-17th-century English chair is illustrated.

PAD STONE. See *Template*.

PADOUK. A hard, firm-textured Burmese wood similar to rosewood. It is a durable wood, and varies from pinkish tones to a deep reddish brown, often with darker streaks. Padouk is a highly decorative wood. It also grows in Africa, Brazil, and the Andaman Islands and is sometimes sold under the name "madou." See *Vermilion*.

PAFRAT, JEAN. An 18th-century cabinetmaker under Louis XVI who specialized in mounting panels of old lacquerwork into small pieces of furniture.

PAGODA. A Chinese tower having several stories, each with its own upswept roof. Each succeeding roof seems to umbrella out and graduate up from the one below—the roofs get smaller as they go up. The pagoda was adapted into an 18th-century decorative element during the "chinoiserie" vogue.

PAILLON. The base coat for transparent lacquer, which is often a reflecting metallic surface or a gilded base which is then treated with transparent coloring.

PALAIS DE L'INDUSTRIE

WILLIAM PAIN

PAILOU. In Chinese architecture, a gateway which was constructed of wood (or stone in imitation of wood) with a swooping curved tile roof.

PAIN, WILLIAM. An 18th-century English architect-designer who wrote many books on architecture, including *The Practical Builder, The British Palladio, The Carpenter's Pocket Dictionary,* and *The Practical House Carpenter.* Pain designed in the classic Adam style, and his sons followed the same tradition in the homes they built in Ireland.

PAINE, JAMES (1725-1789). A classic 18th-century English architect who preceded the Adam brothers, but he later used Adam-type stucco decorations in his work. Among his most noted designs were the ceilings and chimneys for Sir Joshua Reynolds' home in Leicester Square, London. A ceiling design by Paine for Doncaster Mansion House is illustrated. See the drawing for *Bust* for a wall interior design by Paine.

JAMES PAINE

PAINTED FURNITURE. Furniture which has been finished, usually in color, with enamel, lacquer, or some other type of paint. This finish covers the natural grain and color of the wood. Painted furniture is often enhanced with gilding, line work, painted medallions, stenciling, etc. It is an ancient technique which reached its peak during the 18th century in the Venetian and French Rococo periods, and in the Adam style. A painted Adam commode is illustrated.

PAINTED FURNITURE

PAISLEY. A printed or woven fabric design which imitates an original Scottish shawl pattern created in the town of Paisley. The amoeba- and paramecium-shaped elements in the paisley design were originally Persian in concept.

PAKTONG. "White copper." A silvery alloy of copper, nickel, and zinc which was imported from China during the 18th century. It is hard and resonant, and it has been used for fire grates, fenders, fire irons, etc.

PALAESTRA. An ancient Roman wrestling school or gymnasium.

PALAIS DE L'INDUSTRIE. A structure erected in France in 1855 as an exhibition hall. It was a rectangular building with a high central aisle surrounded by a double row of galleries. The 48-meter span was the widest vaulting attempted up until that time. A tremendous amount of light came through the large glass areas set between the wrought-iron lattice girders. No tie bars were used between the round, high-swung arches over the central aisle. Large blocks of lead were used in the Gothic tradition to counteract the lateral stress. The main building was encased in heavy stone.

PALAIS DES MACHINES. See *Galerie des Machines.*

PALAMPORES. Printed East Indian cottons which were decorated with the "tree of life" motif. They were imported into England in the 17th and 18th centuries. Originally they imitated English papers, textiles, and crewel embroidery. The patterns usually contained interlacing branches and foliage with peacocks and other birds intermingled.

PALANQUIN

PALANQUIN. A covered carriage for one person which was carried on the shoulders of four persons by means of poles which projected fore and aft on both sides with the carriage suspended between the poles. It was a form of conveyance, originally oriental, that was used in 17th- and 18th-century Europe.

PALAZZO FARNESE, CAPRAROLA. An Italian Renaissance structure designed by Vignola, and completed in 1547. See *Vignola, Giacomo Barozzi da.*

PALAZZO FARNESE, CAPRAROLA

PALETTE

PALDAO. A Philippine wood of a variable tan ground with black to brown streaks. It has a hard texture and a striped or mottled figure.

PALETTE. A board or tray for mixing paint colors; also a range of colors available in fabrics, papers, carpets, etc. Illustrated is an 18th-century French Renaissance trophy panel with a palette featured.

PALISADE CONSTRUCTION. A wall construction of interlocking vertical planks of wood.

PALISANDER. The French name for East Indian rosewood. It is dark brown with a violet cast and a definite combed ˙grain stripe. The wood takes a high polish. See *Rosewood, Honduras*.

PALLADIAN. Referring to the works or designs of Andrea Palladio and the classic Roman antiques he uncovered and recorded. It is also a generic term for the 18th-century classic architecture which was influenced by his research. See the entries that follow.

PALLADIAN MOTIF. A typical architectural device designed by Palladio and illustrated in the Basilica Vicenza. Twin columns support the arches in a rhythmic arcade. See *Basilica of Vicenza*. The Palladian window is based on the same motif.

PALLADIAN

PALLADIAN MOTIF

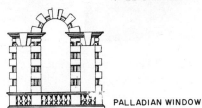

PALLADIAN WINDOW

PALLADIAN WINDOW. A three-part window design usually consisting of four pilasters or columns marking off three tall window areas. The two outer windows have a straight cornice over each, but the taller central window has an arched semi-circular cornice. The design was based on Palladio's work, and was very popular in 18th- and 19th-century architecture in England and the United States. The Palladian window was almost a trademark of the mid-18th-century New England house where it was centered to light up the stairway of the main central hallway. In the designs of William Sprat of Connecticut, it was often set over Ionic columned porticoes which decorated the main doorway, as in the Samuel Cowles House in Framington, Connecticut. The design illustrated here is by the 18th-century English designer, William Halfpenny.

ANDREA PALLADIO

PALM

PALMATED

PALLADIO, ANDREA (1518–1580). An Italian architect and excavator who, with Giacomo Barozzi da Vignola, rediscovered and standardized the proportions of the Roman architectural orders. His *I quattro libri dell' Architettura*, 1570, had great influence on contemporary architecture. Palladio also designed many buildings in the pure Italian Renaissance style: the Palazzo Thiene (1556), Palazzo Valmarana (1566), Casa del Diavolo, S. Giorgio Maggiore in Venice (1560), Villa Rotonda (Villa Capia) in Vicenza. The Basilica in Vicenza (1549) is noted for the Renaissance arcaded façade which was added by Palladio over a medieval structure. Illustrated is the Loggia del Bernardo. See *Basilica Vicenza*.

PALM. Palm leaves, branches, and the tree itself were used by early civilizations for decorative motifs. The palm was also used as a symbol of victory, triumph, and peace. The palm motif appeared in Egyptian, Greek, and Early Christian church art. Illustrated is a palm capital from an ancient Egyptian temple.

PALM VAULTING

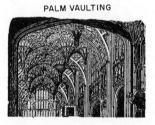

PALM VAULTING. See *Fan Vaulting*. Illustrated is the vaulting in Westminster Abbey in London. It is considered one of the most beautiful ceilings in European Gothic architecture.

PALMATED. A decorative carved band of half circles with leaf designs enclosed. It is a decoration which was typically found on the oak furniture of the Stuart period in England. Note the lower bands of decoration on this mid-17th-century oak chest with drawers, here illustrated.

PALMETTE

PALMETTE. A conventionalized fanlike branch of the palm used as a decorative motif. It is similar to the anthemion and fan motifs. The term is also used to describe a pelmet or a lambrequin.

PAMPRE. A French term for a decorative composition of grapes and vine leaves which was often used as a spiral element in the hollow areas of a twisting or twisted column.

PAMPRE

PANACHE

PANCARPI

PANE

PANACHE. The section of a groined vault which lies between two ribs.

PANCARPI. A Greek term for swags, festoons, or garlands of fruits and/or flowers. See *Encarpa*.

PANCHETTO. An Italian Renaissance wooden chair with three splayed legs and a chip carved fan back. It was much like the sgabello, but less sophisticated or finished in decoration. See *Sgabelle or Sgabello*.

PANE. A piece of glass set in a window, glazed door, etc. The term also refers to the space between two timbers in a half-timbered building.

PANEL. In drapery, a width of fabric with hemmed edges and a finished top and bottom. The actual width of a panel varies (usually 36″ to 52″), but in deciding how many panels are needed to cover a window or wall, one measures the finished pleated top. If the material is to be shirred or draped, depending upon the weight of the fabric, two or three unpleated panels usually make one finished or pleated panel. Also, a flat surface which is usually enclosed by a frame. Panels can be decorated with moldings, carvings, painting, applied fabric, wallpapers, etc.

PANEL, BOLECTION. A raised panel. The panel is above and/or in front of the frame.

PANEL, SUNK. A recessed panel. The panel is below or behind the frame or molding.

PANEL WALL. In building skeleton construction, a nonbearing wall built between columns and piers, and completely supported at each story.

PANEL

SUNK PANEL

PANEL-BACK CHAIR

PANEL-BACK CHAIR

PANNEAU

PANTILE

PAPER SCROLL

PANEL-BACK CHAIR. Also called a "wainscot chair." A massive, high-seated oak chair with heavy legs, stretchers, and a paneled back usually decorated with carving. It was an early English Renaissance design.

PANELGLAS. A trademark of the Johns-Manville Corporation for "lay-in" acoustic panels made of glass fibers. The panels (2′ × 2′ or 2′ × 4′) are mounted in simple overhead grids, and help to diffuse light as well as soak up sound.

PANETIÈRE. French for "bread box."

PANIER. French for "basket."

PANIER or PANNIER. The French word for the corbel or angled element which fills the right angle between a pilaster and the beam which rests on it.

PANNE. French for "plush." A pile fabric with a shiny or lustrous surface. The finish is produced by pressing back the pile. It is usually a silk or synthetic satin.

PANNE VELVET. A velvet with a lustrous finish produced by flattening the pile and making it all lie in the same direction.

PANNEAU. French for "panel." The term may be used to describe a panel of paper, fabric, wood, etc. Illustrated is a bas-relief sculptured wood panel for a 16th-century French Renaissance coffer.

PANTHEON. Any temple which has been consecrated to all the gods.

PANTILE. A flattened S-shaped tile made of baked clay.

PANURGE. A particular bed design of the Louis XVI period in France.

PAPELERA. A small Spanish cabinet with many compartments that held papers and writing materials. It was similar to the Vargueño, but it did not have the drop-lid front. The papelera originated in the late 16th and early 17th centuries.

PAPER SCROLL. A scroll sometimes carved on the ends of the top rails of chairs. It is a carved representation of a rolled-up sheet of paper only slightly uncurled. This motif was popular in the mid-18th century, as this Chippendale example shows. It is also called spiral whorl, spiral scroll, spiral volute, conical volute, and helicoidal volute.

PAPER STUCCO. See *Papier-mâché.*

PAPIER-MÂCHÉ

PAPIER-MÂCHÉ. A technique for making three-dimensional units. It originated in the Orient, and was revived in the mid-18th century in France. Paper is pulped and mixed with whiting and glue. This semifirm material is shaped and molded, and as it dries it becomes stronger, harder, and more durable. In France, the original artisans in this technique were the paper-hangers, and they made rococo looking glass frames, girandoles, and fancy boxes. Later, moldings and ceiling designs were made in papier-mâché or "paper stucco," as it was called in late-18th-century England where it was used as a substitute for plaster ornament. In the Victorian period, assorted pieces of furniture and accessories were made of papier-mâché, and many were painted black and inlaid with mother-of-pearl. A Victorian screen is illustrated.

PAPIER PEINT. The French term for early painted or printed wallpapers.

PAPIERS COLLÉS. A French term for a trompe l'œil technique introduced in painting by Braque in 1909, and taken up by Picasso and other cubist artists. Bits of paper, wallpaper, assorted everyday cartons and boxes, and other materials were glued on the canvas or paint boards.

PAPIERS D'ANGLETERRE. An 18th-century French term for flocked papers made in England.

PAPIERS DÉCHIRÉS. French for "tattered papers." A montage of assorted twisted, torn, and otherwise manipulated papers which are assembled on a board in semblance to reality or an abstract design. It was supposedly introduced by Picasso. See *Papiers Collés.*

PAPILLON, JEAN. A noted French wallpaper designer of the late 17th century. He was one of the first artists to specialize in wallpaper designs.

PAPYRUS. A plant used by the ancient Chinese and Egyptian civilizations. Paper was made from the plant, and the flower was used as a decorative motif in the wall paintings, architecture, and domestic arts of the ancient Egyptians.

PAPYRUS

PARACCLESION. A side chapel of a Byzantine church.

PARAKENION. A short wing which extends forth from the stage or skene of a Greek theatre.

PARAPET. A low wall, sometimes breast-high, around a tower or gallery of a Gothic structure. Illustrated is the Spanish Gothic Porte Santa Maria in Burgos.

PARAPET

PARAPET WALL

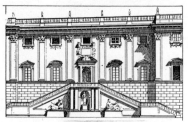

PARAPET WALL

PARCEL GILDING

PARCHMENT PANEL

PARGEWORK

PARAPET WALL. The part of the wall that extends up above the roof line. Illustrated is the Italian Renaissance Palace of the Senators in Rome, designed by Michelangelo.

PARAVENT. French for "screen." A folding screen.

PARCEL GILDING. A form of decorating in which only selected parts of a frame, carving, or surface are gilded. It was practiced in the late 17th and early 18th centuries, and it was particularly popular during the Decorated Queen Anne period as a method of decorating mirror frames. This type of gilding was often accomplished by means of stencils. Illustrated is a pair of early-18th-century frames.

PARCHMENT. A writing material of antiquity which was made by separating the inner side of a sheepskin from the outer or woolly side. The peeled skin was then treated to make the surface suitable for writing. The term also refers to the warm beige-white color of true parchment.

PARCHMENT PANEL. Another name for *Linenfold* paneling.

PARGETING. The process of using mortar to line the flue in a chimney. The term also refers to the applying of a coat of cement-mortar to the back of a facing material or the face of a backing material.

PARGETRY. See *Pargework*.

PARGEWORK. Ornamental plaster or stuccowork applied to a flat surface to create a bas-relief design. It was a late-16th-century development which attempted to emulate the ribs in a complicated fan- or star-vaulted ceiling. The oriel window in the great hall of Crosby Hall in London is illustrated. The pargework on the ceiling is a decorative effect rather than a structural rib vaulting.

PARKER, GEORGE. See *Stalker, John*.

PARLIAMENT CHAIR. An 18th-century Queen Anne side chair made of mahogany in the British colony of Bermuda. It had a high back with a shaped splat. The front legs were cabrioled with club feet.

PARLOR LAMP. A late-19th-century lamp consisting of two bulbous globes set one on top of the other with the chimney projecting up through the upper sphere. An ornate brass base commonly supported the lower globe. Both globes were usually painted or decorated with decals of lush, multicolored flowers. A Victorian design.

PARTRIDGE WOOD

PARLOR CHAIR

PARLOR or PARLOUR. From the French "parloir," a room where company is received. It is the present-day living or drawing room. In Johnson's *Dictionary* (1755) it is defined as "a room on the first floor, elegantly furnished for reception or entertainment." Illustrated is a parlor chair.

PARQUET. An inlaid wood floor, or a mosaic wood floor. A design is created on the floor by strips of wood laid out in a definite pattern. Sometimes different colored woods are used. It differs from furniture marquetry in that it specifically refers to geometric floor patterns. Illustrated is a Louis XVI salon with parquet floor.

PARQUET

PARQUETRIE or PARQUETRY. Furniture inlay work in geometric patterns like the checkerboard pattern, etc. See *Marquetry*.

PARTERRE. French term for a flat and planned garden. A garden landscaped in a formal set pattern. Also, the level space including a building site, and the part of the theatre floor behind the orchestra.

PARTHENON. It was erected in Athens on the Acropolis between 454 and 438 B.C. Ictinus and Callicrates were the architects, and Pheidias is credited as the major sculptor. The structure is surrounded by eight columns on the front entrance and seventeen on each of the sides. The Doric columns were about 6'2" in diameter at the base and 34'3" tall. The columns supported an entablature which was approximately eleven feet. Some of the finest classic Greek sculpture filled the tympana in the pediments. The Panathenaic frieze was carved along the top of the exterior of the naos wall. The sculptured metopes were done in high relief. Bright colors were originally used to decorate the sculptures in the pediments, metopes, and friezes. Many of the sculptures are today part of the Elgin Marbles in the British Museum. See *Elgin Marbles*.

PARTHENON

PARTITION. An interior wall of one story or less in height.

PARTNERS' DESK. An 18th-century, extra-wide keyhole or pedestal type of desk with drawers on both sides (not the ends) of the pedestal. It was therefore possible for two people to sit facing each other, one on either side of the desk, and for each to have his own sets of drawers. There is no front or back to the desk. The unit probably evolved from the large library tables of the early 18th century. The endpieces were usually paneled, and the desk top was often made of tooled leather. A Hepplewhite design is illustrated.

PARTNER'S DESK

PARTRIDGE WOOD. A Brazilian wood with graining which resembles partridge feathers in its red and brown coloration. It was used in the 17th century as an inlay wood.

PARTY WALL. A common wall between two structures, separating each from the other but belonging to both units.

PARVISE. An enclosed area or court in front of the west façade of a Gothic or medieval structure. The term has sometimes been incorrectly applied to a small room over a church porch.

PASSEMENTERIE. From the French "passement" which means a strip of lace. It refers to a trimming or edging of braid, gimp, beads, or cording.

PASSEPARTOUTE. From the French for "pass everywhere." The word means a mat used in framing, a gummed paper, and also a form of picture mounting. In the mounting technique, the mat and the glass are taped together along the four edges with gummed tape.

PASTE. The body of pottery. Soft paste is produced by a glass mixture, while hard paste is a mixture of kaolin and feldspar.

PASTEBOARD STUCCO. See *Papier-Mâché*.

PASTELS. Sticks of dry powdered color which are mixed with enough gum to bind the powder into a chalk. When the sticks are rubbed on paper, they disintegrate, and the colored powder remains on the paper's surface. When properly used, soft pastels can give the effect of a painting. Hard pastels are more closely related in effect to drawings. Quentin de La Tour and Jean-Baptiste Chardin were exponents of the soft pastel technique, and Edgar Degas was perhaps the greatest of the pastelists.

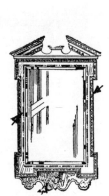

PASTIGLIA

PASTIGLIA. A bas-relief design achieved by adding successive layers of thin plaster over a surface which had been covered with a fine fabric. The final and finishing details were done with a knife, and often the design was gilded and burnished. Pastiglia was introduced in the Italian Renaissance. The term also refers to molded plaster ornaments. The Queen Anne-type mirror of the early 18th century here illustrated has applied gilded gesso work or pastiglia decorations. See *Anaglypta, Carton-Pierre,* and *Composition Ornament.*

PATERA. A round or oval disk usually decorated with a rosette or other ornament.

PATERA

PATINA or PATINE. A greenish coating on the surface of old bronze. The term now refers to the "mellowing of age" on any object or material due to age, exposure, or repeated waxings and polishings. The patina is also the gloss on woodwork. See *Bronze.*

PATIO. An inner court, open to the sky. Illustrated is a Spanish patio with Moorish horseshoe arches. See *Atrium.*

PATIO

PATTE. A French architect-designer of the 18th century who laid out plans for the city of Paris in 1748 showing the existing "places" plus the proposed "places."

PATTERN. The vertical graining of wood and veneer, as opposed to the highlights or cross grains which are called "figures." Also see *Template*.

PATTERNED ROLLED GLASS. See *Diffusing Glass*.

PAVÉ DE MOSAÏQUE. French for tesselated or mosaic pavement.

PAVEMENT. A flooring of stone, marble, or tile in a building, or the concrete or asphalt type of material used out of doors.

PAVEMENT LIGHT. A glass area set in a pavement to allow light to filter through to a basement area.

PAVILION. A separate building, yet an integral part of a large or main building. The word is ultimately derived from the Latin for "butterfly"; the pavilion was originally a tentlike affair spread out like the wings of a butterfly.

PAVILION ROOF. A low flat roof with four sides sloping inward and upward to a central point. It is similar to a hipped roof except that all four sides are hipped. See *Hip* and *Hipped Roof*.

PAVILION ROOF

PAVIMENTO DI LEGNO LUCIDO. Italian for "parquet floor."

PAVIMENTUM. Latin for "pavement." Tile, marble, stone, etc., set in cement and beaten down with a rammer to form a pavement or walk.

PAW-AND-BALL FOOT. A mid-18th-century replacement for the claw-and-ball foot. See *Ball-and-Claw Foot*.

PAW-AND-BALL FOOT

PAW FOOT

PAW FOOT. Usually a carved representation of a lion's or bear's paw, decorated with foliage, and used as a furniture foot in the late-17th- to early-18th-century French and English furniture. The illustrated foot is from a Chippendale garden seat. See *Bear's Foot*.

PAXTON, JOSEPH. A 19th-century English architect-engineer. Illustrated is the exterior view of his Crystal Palace (1851). See *Crystal Palace* for details and an interior view.

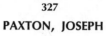

JOSEPH PAXTON

PAYSAGES or PAYSAGES-DÉCORS. An early-19th-century French term for wall murals featuring country landscapes, hunts, etc. These printed wallpaper designs were usually applied from the chair rail up to the cornice, and would form a continuous scene around the entire room. They were not "repeats" of a scene, but a series of scenes which formed a continuous panorama. The English had developed a similar art in tempera painted scenics on paper which they called "perspectives."

PEACOCK CHAIR. A large, sweeping fanback chair woven of rattan, and usually made in Hong Kong. It was originally a mid- to late-19th-century Victorian design which, with slight variations, is made today much as it was then. The chair usually has an hourglass pedestal base with supporting uprights. It is a light, lacy, openwork chair.

PEAR-DROP ORNAMENT. An ornament usually decorating the upper section of a plain frieze. In Hepplewhite and Sheraton designs it appears as a crystal-like drop at the lower points of a series of Gothic arches in relief. Illustrated is a Sheraton cornice treated with the pear-drop ornament.

PEAR-DROP ORNAMENT

PEARLING. A series of rounded forms of the same size, or graduated like a string of beads. The pearling was used as a furniture embellishment, either in straight lines, arced, or swagged. A brass 18th-century mounting with pearling decoration is illustrated.

PEARLING

PEARLS. A string of beads, either of the same size or graduated, and used as an ornamental feature on furniture or wall decor. It may be a painted or carved representation, and it is often used in a swaglike arrangement. It was popular in mid- and late-18th-century French and English designs. A design by Michelangelo Pergolesi is shown.

PEARLS

PEARWOOD. A pinkish brown, finely grained wood often used for inlay work and fine cabinetwork. It is similar to boxwood. In the 16th and 17th centuries, it was used for country-made furniture, and sometimes it was stained to simulate ebony in inlay work.

PEASANT WEAVE. See *Homespun*.

PEBBLE DASHING. Stucco or mortar which is surfaced with partially embedded pebbles.

PECAN. A South-Central United States wood of the hickory family. It resembles walnut with its strong grain pattern, and it is often used in conjunction with walnut on exposed show areas.

PÉCHÉ MORTEL. French for "deadly sin." A mid-18th-century term for a chaise longue which was sometimes made in two parts, an oversized easy chair with an upholstered stool, and joined in the middle. A Chippendale design, in one piece, is illustrated. See *Chaise Longue* and *Duchesse*.

PECKY CYPRESS. A scarred, pitted, crumbly-textured cypress wood used for interior wood paneling. It is worm-eaten in appearance, and it is structurally weak, but it has an effective look due to its uneven surface quality.

PEDESTAL. A supporting base or block for a statue, vase, etc. In architecture, it is the lowest portion of a classic order, and it consists of a base, dado, and cornice.

PEDESTAL CHAIR. A contemporary chair design which has a seat set on a single support with a flaring base. The support is usually made of metal, wood, or plastic. Sometimes the seat is molded in one with the pedestal in a continuous sculptured design.

PEDESTAL DESK. See *Kneehole Desk*.

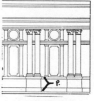

PÉCHÉ MORTEL

PEDESTAL

PEDESTAL TABLES

PEDESTAL DESK

PEDESTAL TABLE. Usually a round or oval tabletop which is supported by a single member base. This support is often a column or turning which ends in a heavy base with spreading feet. It is found in 18th-century English furniture, as illustrated, as well as in 19th-century Regency and Duncan Phyfe designs. The pedestal table is also a popular modern design with the table surface resting on a thin support which flares outward as it reaches the floor.

PEDIMENT. Originally, in Greek architecture, a triangular space at the roof line of Greek temples or other structures which was accentuated by the moldings of the entablature. The central area of the triangle was often filled with carved relief figures. Illustrated is a section of the pediment of the Pantheon in Rome. In 18th-century furniture designs, the pediment is used as a cap or finishing design for architectural case pieces, bookcases, chests, cabinets, secretaries, etc. The pediment may vary in design: swan, segmented, broken scroll, etc. A chimneypiece designed by Inigo Jones (early 17th century) is also illustrated.

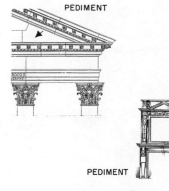

PEDIMENT

PEDIMENT

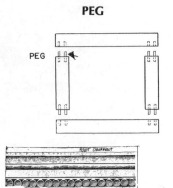

PEG

PELLET ORNAMENT

PEG. A wooden pin, dowel, or spike used for fastening or joining furniture, wood panels, floors, etc. It is used in place of a nail. A joint which is accomplished with pegs is referred to as a "doweled joint."

PEINTURES VIVANTES. French for "living pictures." A Gothic church decoration in Spain and Italy; groups of religious figures were carved in high relief, and then realistically colored. The compositions were usually framed with ornate architectural details, and illuminated by natural or artificial means.

PELLET ORNAMENT. A Norman and Gothic ornament which resembles flattened balls or disks.

PELMET. See *Lambrequin*.

PELMET

PEMBROKE TABLE

PEMBROKE TABLE. An 18th-century occasional table with two wide drop leaves, and a drawer set in the apron of the table. The drop leaves are supported by brackets set into the table frame. The central, fixed table surface is usually twice as wide as one of the drop leaves. It is believed to have been named for the tenth Earl of Pembroke. Illustrated is a Sheraton design. See *Table* illustration.

PENCIL AND PEARL

PENCIL AND PEARL. Another name for bead and reel molding. The molding consists of alternating round and elongated forms in a semicircular bead molding.

PENCIL STRIPE. A wood grain effect similar to a ribbon stripe. The stripes are much finer and much closer together. This particular type of graining is sometimes found in walnut.

PENDANT

PENDANT. A drop or hanging ornament on furniture, lighting fixtures, etc. It may be a pendant sphere, pendant finial, or pendant husk. The term may also refer to a boss or projection hanging down from a vault or ceiling. See *Boss* and *Cul-de-Lampe*.

PENDENTIVE. The triangular piece of concave masonry that transmits the weight of a circular dome to four isolated corner supports. It is shaped like part of the inside of a hemisphere. The pendentive was originated in Byzantine architecture. Illustrated is an interior view of S. Sophia in Constantinople.

PENTES

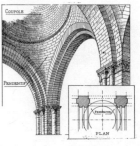

PENDENTIVE

PENDENTIVE

PENDULE. French for "clock" or "timepiece."

PENDULE À GAINE. A tall clock or grandfather clock. Illustrated is a Louis XIV design. See *Gaine.*

PENNE D'OISEAU. French for "bird's feather." A decorative, carved ornament on wooden furniture of the mid-French Renaissance Period. Illustrated is the chair back of a 16th-century fauteuil.

PENDULE À GAINE

PENNON. A streamer, ribbon, or label.

PENNSYLVANIA DUTCH. Name given to German and Swiss Mennonites who settled in Pennsylvania near York, Lancaster, and Germantown at the end of the 17th century. "Deutsch" (German) was anglicized to "Dutch," and hence the misnomer. Using simple, functional lines as a basis, they then decorated their furniture, homes, and utensils in bright, gay colors and designs. Among their favorite motifs were: circular geometric hex signs, peacocks, hearts, tulips, rosettes, roosters, hens, reindeer, and leaves. Their furniture was similar in basic construction to the 18th-century Colonial American designs.

PENNON

PENNE D'OISEAU

PENNSYLVANIA GERMAN. See *Pennsylvania Dutch.*

PENNSYLVANIA STOVE. See *Franklin Stove.*

PENT ROOF. A single angled roof. The back of a house is sometimes higher than the front so the roof slopes sharply down from the back to the front.

PENTASTYLE. A classic portico with five columns. A rare design.

PENTES. A 15th-century term for lambrequins. Ornamental draperies, valances, or scalloped fabric treatments for use on the upper part of a window, across the top of a doorway, or on mantels. See *Lambrequin.*

PENTES

PENTHOUSE

CHARLES PERCIER

PENTHOUSE. A medieval term referring to a hanging roof, or a lean-to bracketed out from a wall. In contemporary usage, a dwelling on the uppermost story of a high building, or an additional structure set on top of the roof of a tall building. The penthouse is usually set back from the main building wall allowing for a terrace or walk area.

PERBOLUS. A colonnade or enclosing wall around a sacred area in a classic structure, or the enclosure itself.

PERCALE. A medium-weight printed cotton fabric with a firm plain weave and a dull smooth finish.

PERCIER, CHARLES (1764–1834). The French architect, decorator, and furniture designer to Napoleon I. With Pierre Fontaine, he helped create the Empire style of the early 19th century. Percier worked on Malmaison, St.-Cloud, the Tuileries, and the Louvre. He designed furniture, textiles, ornaments, wallpapers, and accessories for these palaces. Illustrated is a wall decoration by Percier and Fontaine. See *Caryatid* for another example of their work. See *Empire Period.*

PERFORATED METAL. A sheet of metal with dots, dashes, or other simple designs punched out of the metal, creating a canelike or regular lattice effect.

PERGOLA. Italian for "arbor." A balcony or lattice framework covered with vines or shrubs. A latticed structure used as a summerhouse or shade area. A bower. See *Gazebo.*

PERGOLESI, MICHELANGELO. An 18th-century decorative painter, architect, and furniture designer. He worked with Robert Adam, and painted ceilings, panels, and furniture for him. Pergolesi painted his designs on a flat tint, usually pale green or yellow, rather than on the natural wood itself. See *Elevation* for his rendering of an 18th-century room.

MICHELANGELO PERGOLESI

PERIOD

PERIOD. A roughly defined time when a particular influence or style prevailed. These styles usually started before and lasted past the time of the designated period. Often there are transitional periods where the incoming and outgoing styles mix and blend. Illustrated is the Vandramin Palace in Venice. It is an example of the Early Italian Renaissance period.

PERIOD FURNITURE. Furniture of a style or period other than that of the present day. The designs do not have to be authentic reproductions of historical styles, but they should have the scale, details, or motifs of a particular period. Examples of period furniture are: Empire, Chippendale, Queen Anne, French provincial, Italian provincial. Illustrated is a late-18th-century Hepplewhite chair with a wheat-ear motif on the chair back.

PERIPTERAL. In architecture, surrounded by a row of columns. See *Parthenon* for illustration.

PERISTASIS. The space between the outer colonnade and the main room or cella of a Greek temple.

PERISTYLAR. See *Peripteral*. Having a range of columns around the exterior of a building or an interior court.

PERIOD FURNITURE

PERISTYLAR

PERISTYLIUM. The interior of a building which is surrounded by columns.

PERIWIG CHAIR. A tall-back chair of the late 17th century (William and Mary period in England) which had an elaborate pierced and/or carved cresting which accommodated and provided a setting for the elaborate wigs and headdresses of time. It was designed with turned walnut supports, and with or without arms. The back was usually caned.

PERLON. A synthetic fiber, similar to nylon, manufactured in Germany.

PEROBA. A pale rosewood of South America which is identified by its streaks. The streaks may fade under exposure to strong light.

PERPEND. The mason's abbreviation for perpendicular. The vertical lines or joints between masonry which form a running line in alternate courses.

PERPENDICULAR STYLE (1377–1485). The last phase of the Gothic period of architecture in England. It is noted for the large windowed spaces and the slender vertical lines that appear on the interiors in the tracery, and in the moldings and decoration. This particular period is also called rectilinear, late pointed, and Lancastrian.

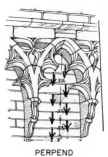

PERPEND

PERPENDICULAR STYLE

PERRAULT, CLAUDE. A 17th-century French architect noted for the east pavilion he designed for the Louvre which consisted of twenty-eight Corinthian columns. He used vermicular masonry for decorative surfacing. Perrault also collaborated with Louis Le Vau. See *Vermicular* for illustration.

PERRET, AUGUSTE (1847–1954). A famous French architect who created many noted structures in reinforced concrete. The Church at Le Raincy, near Paris (1922–1923), had low arching vaults supported by tall columns and surrounded by a continuous wall of glass resting on prefabricated concrete units. Perret also created concrete-vaulted factories and warehouses. After World War II, he helped in the rebuilding of Le Havre, Amiens, and Marseilles.

PERSANE. A French 18th-century printed fabric inspired by Persian originals. It was a pseudo-oriental fabric design.

PERSIAN CEDAR. See *Nanmu*.

PERSIANA. Venetian-blind-like elements used in Spain.

PERSIENNE. A French word for an external Venetian blind. A shutter of thin laths in a wood frame. See *Persiana*.

PERSPECTIVE. The representation of three-dimensional objects in spatial recession on a two dimensional surface. The basic assumption is that parallel lines never meet, but they appear to do so at a "vanishing point" on the horizon.

PERSPECTIVES. See *Paysages or Paysages-décors*.

PERUZZI, BALDASSARE (1481–1536). An Italian Renaissance architect who designed many famous buildings in Rome, including the Villa Farnesina, here illustrated. The Palazzo Pietro Massimi is mannerist in concept with its sweeping, convex front façade which follows the curved line of the street site. Columns and pilasters of the Doric order are used to enrich the ground level of the building.

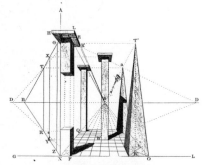

PERSPECTIVE

BALDASSARE PERUZZI

PETIT POINT

PETIT POINT. See *Needlepoint*. A finer version of needlepoint with about twenty stitches to the lineal inch. Petit-point embroidery is used for upholstery, wall hangings, and accessories. Illustrated is a Louis XIV fauteuil covered in a petit-point embroidered fabric.

PETITE COMMODE. A small table, usually with three drawers set one under the other.

PETITOT. An 18th-century French interior designer and creator of vases and urns in the pure Louis XVI style.

PETTICOAT MIRROR

PETTICOAT MIRROR. A console mirror set over a console or pier table. It was an Empire period style, and ladies could peek into the mirror to see if their petticoats were showing. See *Console Mirror.*

PETTICOAT VALANCE. A fabric valance, very full and shirred, used below the mattress on a canopy or tester bed. A dust ruffle. Illustrated is a four-poster bed of the Hepplewhite period (latter half of the 18th century). The tester has a serpentine shape.

PETTICOAT VALANCE

PEWTER. A metal alloy of tin and lead which is dull gray in appearance, and was originally used as a substitute for silver.

PFEILER. German for "pier" or "pillar."

PHILADELPHIA CHAIR. A Windsor-type chair which was manufactured in Philadelphia during the 18th century. Gilbert and Robert Gaw were important Philadelphia manufacturers of this American version of the Windsor chair. See *Windsor Chairs, American.*

PHILADELPHIA CHAIR CONSTRUCTION. A term for the construction used on Queen Anne and Chippendale chairs made in Philadelphia in the latter part of the 18th century. The side rails of the chair seat were mortised into the rear uprights of the chair.

PHILADELPHIA CHIPPENDALE. Chippendale-style furniture made of mahogany and produced in the Philadelphia area in the latter half of the 18th century. William Savery, Trotter, and John Folwell were some of the craftsmen of the period who produced Chippendale-type highboys, lowboys, and chairs rich in carved details.

PHILADELPHIA PEANUT. A bean-shaped cabochon ornament used as a decorative carved motif on 18th-century furniture made in the Philadelphia area.

DUNCAN PHYFE

PIANO NOBILE

PHILIPPINE MAHOGANY. See *Luaun*.

PHOTOMURAL. An enlarged photograph or montage of photographs used as a mural on a wall. See *Mural* and *Scenic*.

PHYFE, DUNCAN (1768–1854). A Scottish cabinetmaker who worked in America. His earliest works, while he resided in the Albany area, were in the classic Adam tradition. Today one associates Duncan Phyfe with the style of Sheraton and Hepplewhite and the Empire and Directoire styles. Phyfe personified the American Regency period. The lyre and the plume are two motifs often found in his designs. See *Mechanical Card Table* for another illustration of Phyfe's designs.

PIANO NOBILE. The principal floor or main story of a building. In Renaissance structures the grand stairway usually led up to this main floor. In France, it is sometimes called the "bel étage."

PIANO STOOL

PIANO STOOL. A round, square, or rectangular stool with a screw pivot below the seat so that it can be raised or lowered. This unit dates back to the late 18th century. A late-19th-century German piece is illustrated.

PIANOFORTE. A musical instrument invented by Cristofori in the early 18th century. It was a forerunner of the piano. To play the pianoforte one had to strike the strings.

PIAZZA. An open square surrounded by buildings. It is the Italian equivalent of the French "place." See *Place de la Concorde* and *Place Vendôme*.

PIAZZA DEL POPOLO. See *Valadier, Giuseppe*.

PICK. The single filling thread that goes completely across the loom and interlaces with the warp threads to weave a fabric. In carpet manufacturing, the weft threads (across the loom) tie in the yarn that forms the tufts and loops on the carpet's surface. The number of picks per inch indicates the closeness of the weave. In Axminister weaving the word "row" means the same as "pick." See *Count of Cloth* and *Weft*.

PICOT. A purl on lace, or a small loop woven on the edge of ribbon.

PICOTAGE. A printing technique used on toiles during the late 18th and early 19th centuries. Short metal wires were driven into the wood blocks that were used for printing, and these wires created a dotted background on the paper or fabric.

PICOTÉ. A small-scale floral pattern created by Christophe-Philippe Oberkampf at his factory in Jouy during the latter part of the 18th century. This was a short-repeat, small-scaled pattern printed on cotton. The printed motif was usually surrounded by numerous dots which softened the silhouette.

PICTURE-BOARD DUMMY. See *Fireside Figures*.

PICTURE MOLDING or RAIL. A grooved molding on a wall placed close to the ceiling line, or the lowest border of a frieze. It was originally used to suspend pictures. It is also called a "frieze rail." Illustrated is a mid-18th-century English room designed by William and John Halfpenny.

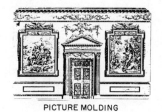
PICTURE MOLDING

"PICTURE" RUGS. A modern Scandinavian development of woven abstract "paintings" which may serve as dramatic area rugs, or may be mounted as wall decorations. They are modern floor tapestries or hand-knotted or hooked "paintings." Some of the leading artists creating these rugs today are the Danes Franka Rasmussen and Tusta Welfring, and the Swedish weaver Bittan Valberg.

PIE SAFES. See *Milk or Pie Safes*.

PIECRUST TABLE. A round pedestal table with the raised edge of the top surface carved in scallops, like the crimped edge of a pie. It was a common design in 18th-century English and American furniture, especially in Chippendale's mahogany tripod tables with carved molded rims.

PIECRUST TABLE

PIED DE BICHE. French for "hind's foot." A decorative cloven hoof-shaped foot for seating units, tables, etc. It was used in the late Renaissance periods in Italy, France, and England. Illustrated is an Italian Directory stool.

PIED DE BICHE

PIEDROIT. A French term for a small, partially embedded pier or pillar which has neither a cap nor a base. A pilaster can have a cap and/or base. See *Pier* and *Pilaster*.

PIER. An isolated, heavy, vertical masonry support like a column or pilaster, but lacking the proportions or details of either. The pier gives support to arches and beams, and it is attached to a wall at the point where a heavy load is imposed.

PIER

PIER ARCHES. Arches between the nave and the aisles in a Gothic structure.

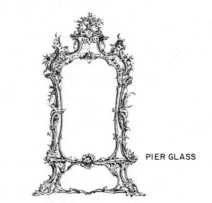

PIER ARCHES

PIER GLASS

PIER GLASS. Originally a mirror that stood on the floor against the wall. It was intended as a facing for piers or to cover the wall space between windows. The term is also used to describe wall mirrors set over console tables. A mid-18th-century design by Matthias Lock is illustrated. See *Cheval Glass or Mirror*.

PIER TABLE

PIER TABLE. A console-type table usually used in conjunction with a pier glass or mirror. It was originally intended to be used on the space (or pier) between two windows. A French Empire example is illustrated.

PIERCED SPLAT

PIERCED SPLAT. The splat or center vertical panel of a chair back that is decorated with an openwork design usually cut out with a fretsaw. An early-18th-century English chair is illustrated. See *Fretwork*.

PIERCED WORK

PIERCED WORK. Ornamental woodwork in which portions of the background are cut or chiseled out, leaving an openwork design. It is similar in appearance to fretwork. Pierced work was a popular form of decoration for chair backs, as illustrated in Chippendale's Gothic-type chair with pierced splat. Pierced work has also been used for windows, etc., in Moorish or Mohammedan architecture. It is having a renaissance in the current works of American architect Edward Durell Stone.

PIETRA DURA

PIETRA DURA or PIETRE-DURE. An Italian Renaissance mosaic inlay of marbles and assorted stones. Fine stones and marbles are inlaid or laminated into a stone base. The colors and markings are intricately used to create a pattern or picture. The pietra-dura technique was used for tabletops, cabinet embellishments, etc. A 16th-century marble inlay is illustrated. See *Intarsia or Tarsia* and *Mosaic*.

PIETRE INTARSIATE. See *Pietra Dura.*

PIGEONHOLES. Small compartments in a bureau or secretary, often found in late-17th- and 18th-century pieces. Illustrated is the interior arrangement of a secrétaire-writing table.

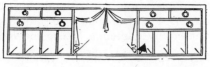

PIGEONHOLES

PIGMENT. Paint color made from natural or synthetic materials.

PILASTER. An engaged pier built as part of a wall and acting as a support for a cornice, pediment, etc. A flat-faced vertical projection from a wall, sometimes with the proportions, details, and capital and base of a classic column. Illustrated is the Italian Renaissance Cancelleria in Rome. In furniture, the pilaster is a carved representation of the architectural feature, usually at the vertical ends of a cabinet, chest, console table, etc., and it forms a support for an overhanging table surface, shelf drawer, etc.

PILASTER

PILASTRO. Italian for "column," "pier," or "pillar."

PILE. In carpet construction, the uncut loops or cut loop tufts of surface yarn that form the wearing surface of the carpet. The nap or top surface. In fabrics, see *Frieze, Plush,* and *Velvet.* In architecture, a pillar or heavy member driven into the ground as a support for the foundation of a structure. It is often made of reinforced concrete.

PILE

PILLAR. An upright member, usually a column, but it need not be cylindrical or have the proportions of a classic order. A pillar may also be a commemorative shaft. An ancient Indian pillar is illustrated.

PILLAR-AND-CLAW TABLE. A pedestal-type table of the Chippendale style with a central column-like support and terminating in splayed legs. The feet are usually carved lion or bear paws.

PILLAR

PILLAR-AND-SCROLL. A mantel clock case designed by the American clock designer Eli Terry, of Plymouth, Connecticut, in the early 19th century. It resembled the upper portion of a grandfather clock. The case had a scrolled top and skirt with columns or pillars at either side. The dial was opaque and enameled. Often a picture was painted on the glass area below the dial.

PILLOW CAPITAL

PILLOWBACK CHAIR

PILLEMENT, JEAN (1728–1808). A French painter and textile designer of the Louis XV and Louis XVI periods. He created textiles with winding stripes, interlacing ribbons, and chinoiserie patterns.

PILLOW CAPITAL. A Romanesque, simplified version of the Corinthian capital. It is simply a square block, rounded at the corners, and decorated in bas-relief sculpture. An arcade from Canterbury Cathedral in England is illustrated.

PILLOWBACK CHAIR. A variety of 19th-century Hitchcock chair with the usual rush seat, decorated or stenciled rails, and turned front legs. The distinguishing characteristic is the pillow or block in the middle of the top rail with turned decorations on either side, basically a Sheraton motif.

PILOTIS. A French word for "stilts." A modern architectural concept for building a multistoried building upon reinforced concrete columns which keep the space below the building free, open, and uncluttered. A device of the architect Le Corbusier.

PINACOTECA. The Italian word for picture gallery.

PINAKOTHEKE. Greek for "picture gallery" or a building designed to house pictures.

PINCHED TRAILING. See *Quillwork*.

PINCUSHION CHAIR. See *Compass Seat*.

PINE. The popular "early American" wood with an interesting grain. It is economical, easy to work with, and it is used for furniture as well as interior finishes.

PINE, PICKLED. An interior wall or furniture finish which is a whitish patina or rub on knotty pine. The finish probably developed from the custom of scraping paint off old English furniture. The residue paint which accented the graining gave the old furniture a mellow quality which is now emulated in new reproductions.

PINE, WHITE. Soft pine. The grain is usually uninteresting, and the wood, which is generally used for structural and finishing purposes, is often painted rather than stained.

PINE, YELLOW. Hard pine. It is stronger and heavier than white pine, and it is good for cheap flooring, trims, doors, and furniture. Yellow pine is usually painted rather than stained.

PINEAPPLE. A decorative, carved, stylized finial resembling the fruit. It was often used as a terminal piece on bedposts, newel posts, in pediments over doorways, etc. In early-19th-century America it was the symbol of wealth and prosperity.

PINNACLE. A cone-shaped or pyramidal turret used in Gothic architecture to top roofs or buttresses. The pointed termination of a spire is often decorated with *Crockets*. A pinnacle may be used decoratively as an ending or a finial at the crest or top of an architectural piece of furniture.

PINWALE. A narrow rib or ridge in a fabric, as in pinwale corduroy.

PIPING. A decorative tubular edging used to trim upholstery, draperies, etc. The tube may sometimes have a cord filler which gives the piping more roundness and a firmer appearance.

PIPKINS. An 18th-century English term for metal coal containers used at the fireside.

PISE DE TERRE

PINNACLE

PIPKIN

PIQUA. An African satin-textured wood with a uniform pinkish-brown color. See *Bosse.*

PIQUÉ. A heavy cotton fabric with raised cords running lengthwise. The name is derived from the French word for "quilted." Piqué is also called "Bedford cloth." In inlaying, gold or silver, in point or strip inlaid. The word also refers to an inlay of shell, mother-of-pearl, or ivory. This inlay technique was popular in the 17th and 18th centuries in France for decorating small accessory pieces like snuffboxes, small cabinets, jewel boxes, etc.

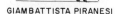

PIQUÉ

PIRANESI, GIAMBATTISTA (1720–1778). A Venetian architect-artist who made a record of Roman antiquities in a collection of magnificent etchings. His works had a great effect on the classic movement in the 18th century. A section of a room designed by Piranesi is illustrated. See *Mural.*

GIAMBATTISTA PIRANESI

PISCINA. A shallow basin in a niche near the altar in a church. Holy church vessels were washed in this basin. It also refers to the tank of a Roman bath.

PISE DE TERRE. A type of wall construction in which clay earth is rammed into shuttering, a temporary wall structure made of wood or sheet metal which is later removed. Usually, the temporary walling is filled with concrete, and when the concrete hardens, the shuttering is removed. See *Shuttering.*

PISCINA

PITCH

PITCH

PITCH. In the manufacturing of carpets, the number of warp threads per inch, measured across the width of the loom. The closer the warp threads, the finer the weave. The pitch is considered in connection with the "pick" or "rows" per inch. See *Pick*. Also, the angle or steepness of a roof's slope.

PITCHED ROOF. A roof with an angle of 20° or more from the horizontal.

PITCHED ROOF

PLACAGE. The French word for "veneering," or "plating" on metal.

PLACE DE LA CONCORDE, Paris. A large square designed by Jacques-Ange Gabriel and constructed in 1763. The place was originally known as Place Louis XV. The garden of the Tuileries, the Champs Elysées, and the Seine River make up three sides of this open area. The single boundary wall is open at the center and the Rue Royale leads from it. This place is considered one of the most beautiful in Paris.

PLACE VENDÔME. A large public square built in Paris in the early 18th century. It was designed by Jules Hardouin-Mansard.

PLAFOND

PLAFOND. French for "ceiling." A part of a 16th-century French Renaissance coffered ceiling is shown.

PLAIDS. Multicolored, checkered, or squared patterns which are created by bars of assorted colors and thicknesses crossing each other at right angles in the weaving process. This type of design may also be printed on fabric, paper, etc.

PLAIN SLICING VENEER

PLAIN SLICING VENEER. Consecutive slices cut from the half log or flitch parallel to a line through the center of the log. A variagated figure is usually produced.

PLAIN WEAVE. A basic weave in which the warp and weft are the same size, and alternate under and over each other in a regular manner. The plain weave is used to make muslin, tafetta, etc.

PLAN. The horizontal projection of any object. A drawing which shows the arrangement and horizontal measurements of a building or room. Illustrated is a typical plan for for a Romanesque church: nef=nave, T=transept, A=apse, choeur=choir, D=ambulatory, C=buttress, VB=barrel vault, VA=half vault, P=pillars, AD=double arch.

PLANCER or PLANCEER. The finished underside or soffit of a cornice.

PLANCHER. French for "floor." Also, the French word for *Plancer.*

PLANE. European sycamore wood which is used for veneers and inlays.

PLANTED MOLDING. A cut and applied molding, as distinct from a stuck molding which is formed on the surface and is an integral part of it. A late-17th-century Jacobean oak chest of drawers with planted or applied moldings is illustrated. See *Applied Molding* and *Stuck Molding.*

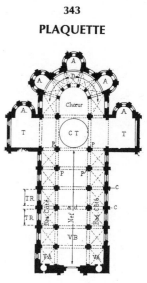

PLAN

PLAQUE

PLANTED MOLDING

PLAQUE. A plate or panel of wood, metal, glass, stone, pottery, etc., with a surface ornamentation or inscription. In furniture, an ornamental disc or plate of porcelain, lacquer, finely chased ormolu, inlay, Wedgwood, etc. It is used to enhance furniture. Illustrated is a wall plaque in the François I room at Fontainebleau, designed by Rosso in the mid-16th century. See *Cartouche.*

PLAQUE STRIÉE. A "striped plaque," usually of bronze, which appeared as a decorative banding on aprons and legs of tables and commodes in the late Louis XVI period and up through the Regency period in England.

PLAQUETTE. A rectangular or square contrasting veneer inlay in a veneer surface. The shape usually has a decorative inlaid detail like an eagle, an urn, etc. An inlaid top of a Sheraton pier table is illustrated (late 18th century).

PLAQUE STRIÉE

PLAQUETTE

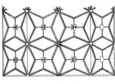

PLASTER

PLASTER. A wall and ceiling surfacing material usually made of lime, water, sand, and sometimes plaster of Paris. On occasions, hair is added to the plaster as a reinforcing agent. Illustrated is a Tudor plaster ceiling.

PLASTER OF PARIS. A composition of calcined and ground gypsum.

PLASTERBOARD. See *Building Board.*

PLASTIC. Modeled, as opposed to carved. Also, a general term for a man-made resinous material which is chemically produced. It may be molded, formed, extruded, or shaped by heat or pressure. See *Thermoplastic, Thermosetting,* and the assorted generic names for trademarked plastics.

PLAT BOND. A horizontal course of masonry in the position of an architrave (the lowest part of an entablature) or a horizontal beam.

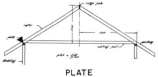

PLATE

PLATE. A beam or piece of timber laid horizontally in a wall to receive the ends of other timbers.

PLATE GLASS. Sheet metal made of selected materials. The surfaces are polished and ground.

PLATE TRACERY. In early Gothic architecture, additional light was procured for interiors by boring holes through the flat stonework. The resultant design was called plate tracery, as opposed to bar tracery. In bar tracery the stone was cut into bars and arranged into assorted geometric patterns.

PLATE TRACERY

PLATE WARMER. A metal-lined unit equipped with an iron heater which was placed in sideboards of late-18th-century English design. It later became a self-contained unit which was used on serving tables, and was similar to the current electric "hot plate."

PLATEAU. A decorative stand, set on low feet, used to raise a centerpiece above the table's surface. It was popular in the early 19th century and was often made of papier-mâché, but also of wood, brass, or glass. It is similar to a large trivet.

PLATERESCO

PLATERESCO. The period in Spanish art dating from the first half of the 16th century. The style of ornament that prevailed was an imitation of the fine details of the silversmith's art. Platero means "silversmith" in Spanish. Illustrated is the inner court of the College of San Gregorio in Valladolid, with its exuberant details, Moorish carvings, twisted columns, and three-centered arches.

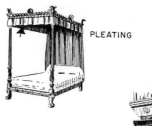

PLEATING

PLEXIFORM

PLEATING. The folding or doubling over of fabric to create a fullness below the pleats. There are various methods of pleating: pinch pleating, box pleating, accordion pleating, etc. Each technique creates a different heading effect. Pleating is more formal than shirring. Illustrated is a Chippendale four-poster with a pleated valance. See *Linenfold*.

PLEXIFORM. A surface design which resembles basket weaving or plaiting. It was often used to decorate Romanesque and Celtic architecture. See *Nattes*.

PLEXIGLAS. A trademark name for a group of plastic sheet products which are produced in a variety of sizes, colors, thicknesses, and patterns.

PLIANT. "Flexible" in French. A cross-legged folding stool, campstool, or deck chair. Illustrated is a stool of the Louis XI (Gothic) period in France. See *Faudesteuil*.

PLIANT

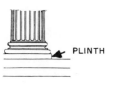

PLINTH

PLINTH. The square part of the base of a column or a pedestal piece of case furniture which is set solidly flat on the floor. It is the molded projection base of a structure or a pedestal without moldings. Illustrated is the base of an Ionic column.

PLINTH BLOCK. A small block of wood used at the bottom of a door trim. The baseboard butts against this block. Illustrated is a 17th-century doorway designed by Inigo Jones. A=the plinth of a Corinthian-type column; B=the plinth block of the door trim.

PLINTH BLOCK

PLIQUÉ À JOUR ENAMELING. A 14th-century process of enameling which created a small-scale stained-glass effect. Vitreous, translucent glass pastes were set into a fine metal network or mesh without backing.

PLISSÉ. A crinkled surface in stripes or patterns which results from a method of printing on plain-weave cotton or rayon fabrics.

PLUMWOOD. A dark red wood, like mahogany, which was used up to the 18th century.

PLUSH. A long-pile velvet. It is deeper and lusher than velvet or velour, and it may be made of silk, mohair, or synthetic fibers. Plush is used as an upholstery fabric. Velvet pile is usually less than 1/8″ thick, and plush pile is longer than 1/8″.

PLY. The number of twists, folds, or layers in yarns, papers, woods, etc.

PLYWOOD. A thick, semiporous core, on both sides of which are laminated exactly equal thin veneers, 1/16″ thick or less, with the grain of both veneers running exactly perpendicular to the grain of the core. This arrangement is called crossbanding. The finish is applied on top: a veneer with the grain running parallel with that of the core. This makes a "plaid" with all tensions pulling in different directions. This crisscross effect makes for the strength of plywood. See *Lamination*.

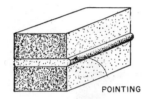

◄ PODIUM

PODIUM. A pedestal or platform. A continuous base supporting a series of columns. See *Stylobate*.

POINÇON. French for *Hallmark*.

POINT D'HONGRIE. Needlepoint with a design which vaguely resembles an irregular series of chevron forms. It is usually made of silk and used as an upholstery fabric.

POINTING

POINTING. The process of gouging out part of the mortar which was used for the bedding of bricks or masonry (up to 3/4″) and replacing it with a compound that has a greater resistance to moisture.

POISSANT, THIEBAUT (born 1605). A French architect and sculptor. His work appears in most of the palaces built and furnished for Louis XIV.

POLE PLATE. A horizontal member laid from truss to truss, and supporting the ends of the common rafters. It also forms the side of a parapet gutter.

POLE SCREEN. A fire screen. Illustrated is a Chippendale mid-18th-century design. See *Banner Screen*.

POLE TABLE. See *Pote Table*.

POLISH BED. See *Dome Bed*.

POLLARD OAK (WALNUT). Oak or walnut trees that are "polled," cut at the top to secure a bushier grain.

POLYCHROME. Multicolored. Illustrated is a multicolored ceiling of an early English Renaissance house.

POLE SCREEN

POLYCHROME

POLYETHER. See *Polyfoam* and *Polyurethane Foam.*

POLYETHYLENE. A olefin or polyolefin fiber which can be paraffin-based. It is waxy in hand, and resists dyeing, but it has excellent chemical resistance, and it resists the harmful effects of sunlight. It is lighter than water, and will therefore float.

POLYFOAM. A synthetic resin which simulates latex foam rubber. It is used for upholstery pieces, mattresses, pillow filling, etc. It is also called polyurethane foam or polyether.

POLYMER. A molecular, chainlike structure composed of monomers which are the basis of synthetic fibers like nylon, Dacron, Acrilan, Dynel, Creslan, etc.

POLYPROPYLENE. Similar to polyethylene, this is a paraffin-based fabric that is called an olefin. It is stronger, lighter, and less heat-sensitive than polyethylene, and is abrasion-resistant.

POLYURETHANE FOAM. Also called polyfoam or polyether. A synthetic resin which simulates foam rubber, and can be substituted for it. See *Foam Rubber.*

POMBALINO. A Portuguese style in mid-18th century based on the French rococo. It was named after the Marquis de Pombal who was responsible for the rebuilding of Lisbon after it was destroyed by a tidal wave in 1755. Much of the rebuilding was done in the rococo style.

POMEGRANATE. A decorative ornament based on the pomegranate fruit, which is apple-shaped and has a hard rind and a pronounced crownlike ending. It was used in classic times as a symbol for fertility.

POMMES

POMMES. French for "apples." A bellflower finial used on bedstead posts. In the late 17th century, pommes were the ornaments used by Daniel Marot to surmount the corners of his testers. See *Marot, Daniel.*

POMPEII

POMPEII. A Greco-Roman resort city which was completely covered with ashes after Mt. Vesuvius erupted in A.D. 79. In the mid-18th century, extensive excavations at Pompeii and Herculaneum uncovered great decorative works and art treasures that had a strong influence on the architectural designers of that time. These finds were a rich source of inspiration for the Adam brothers of England and the Neoclassic designers of the Louis XVI period.

POMPEII

POMPEIIAN

POMPEIIAN

POMPEIIAN. Based on motifs or designs uncovered by the excavation of Pompeii in the mid-18th century. Illustrated is a French Empire wall treatment in the Pompeiian manner.

POMPONNE. Gilded copper. See *Cuivre Doré.*

PONDEROSA PINE. A light-colored wood with soft, even texture and a faint grain pattern. It is light in weight, easy to work, and takes paint or stains well. This pine is often used as "knotty pine." It is a product of the western states of the United States.

PONGEE. A fabric of plain weave made from wild silk in its natural, beige-tan color. The fabric has an interesting slubby texture. The name is derived from the Chinese "pen chi," which means woven at home on one's own loom ("pen," own; "chi," loom). Pongee is now also produced from synthetic fibers.

PONTEUSE. A gaming chair which one straddled. The wide back rail contained compartments for chips, money, cards, etc. See *Fumeuse.*

PONTIL. An iron rod used to carry hot materials in the glass manufacturing process. In the hand-blown glass technique, the pontil is often used to support the bottom of the piece being blown.

PONTIL MARK. The mark left by the pontil after glass cools. Usually the mark appears at the bottom of handmade glass vases, pitchers, dishes, etc. The pontil mark is sometimes ground off and the bottom is polished flat, or a small dimple remains. See *Pontil.*

PONTYPOOL. An English term for a method of japanning on metal originated by Thomas Allgood at Pontypool, England, in about 1660. See *Japanning.*

POPLAR. See *Whitewood.* A very pale-colored wood with an exceptionally fine grain. It was sometimes used for paneling in the Stuart period. In the 16th and 17th centuries, poplar was used for inlay work.

POPLIN. A plain weave fabric with fine cross ribs. The warp threads are finer than the fillers. It is similar to broadcloth but it has a heavier rib.

POPPY HEAD. The decorative end of a Gothic bench. It was often carved with fleurs de lis, animals, figures, etc.

PORCELAIN. A hard, vitreous, nonporous pottery made of kaolin. Illustrated is an early-18th-century English porcelain vase. See *China, Hard Paste,* and *Kaolin.*

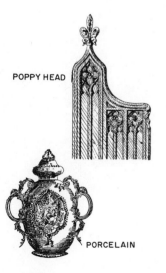

POPPY HEAD

PORCELAIN

PORCH. An exterior addition to a building. It usually forms a covered approach to a doorway. See *Portico*.

PORPHYRY. A form of marble. A rock consisting of a compact feldspathic base through which crystals of feldspar are disseminated. The crystals are lighter than the base, often white. There are red, green, and purple varieties. Porphyry is popular for architectural and ornamental use.

PORTA, GIACOMO DELLA (1541–1604). An Italian Renaissance architect. With Domenico Fontana, he completed the dome of St. Peter's in Rome, here illustrated. His façade for Il Gesù church in Rome was the forerunner of many later Jesuit-Baroque churches. See *Jesuit Architecture* and *Saint Peter's, Rome*.

GIACOMO DELLA PORTA

PORTABLE SERVER. A small, movable serving cart on casters. It can be equipped with removable trays, shelves, drawers, etc., and can be used as a bar or tea wagon.

PORTABLE SERVER

PORTAIL. French word for "portal" or "chief doorway." Illustrated is the portal of the Brussels Cathedral. See also *Façade d'Honneur*.

PORTAL. An entrance to a large, important structure.

PORTCULLIS. An open grating in the main gateway of a medieval castle, fort, or city, which could be raised or lowered like a sash window.

PORTE-COCHÈRE. French for an extension porch from a building which provided shelter for passengers alighting from carriages. A gateway for carriages leading into the courtyard of a major building. It was characteristic of French Renaissance architecture.

PORTAIL

PORTAL

PORTE SANTA MARIA. In Burgos, Spain. See *Parapet*.

PORTER CHAIR. An enclosed chair of the 18th century with a bowed top and sides, which was often set in entry halls to accommodate waiting porters or footmen and to protect them from draughts in the waiting area. See also *Sedan Chair*.

PORTICO. In architecture, an open space covered with a roof supported on columns. A porchlike structure in front of a building which is fronted with columns. See *Amphiprostyle* and *Prostyle*. Illustrated is the Doria Palace in Genoa.

PORTICO

PORTIÈRE

PORTIÈRE

PORTIÈRE. A curtain or drapery over an arch or doorway, or used in place of a door. It is a means of separating one area from another, and providing privacy. It can be used to separate an alcove from a room. Illustrated is an Empire portière from the former Palace of the Tuileries.

PORTLAND CEMENT. A synthetic cement made from lime and clay.

PORTLAND STONE

PORTLAND STONE. An English limestone which is white or creamy in color. Illustrated is a vase designed in Portland stone by James Gibbs in the early 18th century.

PORTLAND VASE. A Roman vase design of a blue-black glass with opaque white figures superimposed on the glass in a cameo carving technique. It was reproduced by Josiah Wedgwood in black porcelain in the late 18th century, as well as in some typical blue Wedgwood color schemes.

PORTUGUESE BULB

PORTRAIT

PORTRAIT. A painting or sculpture of a person. It is usually a recognizable representation.

PORTUGUESE BULB. A bulbous, knobby turning, of Portuguese origin, for furniture supports. It was used in the William and Mary style in England. The stretcher would usually connect into one of these distinctive knobs, rather than a cube shape. The stretcher itself was sometimes a bulbous prominence.

POST. A short piece of wall which is about as long as it is thick. When a post acts as a support, it is called a pedestal.

POST AND LINTEL. The basic form of construction that depends upon a horizontal member (the lintel) resting upon two uprights (the posts). Illustrated is the Arch of the Goldsmiths in Rome which shows an opening spanned by a lintel.

POST AND LINTEL

POSTERN. The back door or entrance as opposed to the portal. Illustrated is the Cathedral of Laon. For main entrance, see illustration for *Façade d'Honneur*.

POSTICUM. The space behind the inner portico or cella of a Greek temple. The open vestibule to the rear of the naos. It is also called the "epinaos." See the illustration for *Tetrastyle*.

POSTURE FURNITURE. Chairs that are designed to give proper back support, and supply correct body positions for various office duties.

POT AU FARD. French for a cosmetic jar.

POT BOARD. The lowest shelf (closest to the floor) of a dresser.

POT CUPBOARD. See *Bedside Cupboard*.

POTE TABLE. A narrow, cylindrical table which sometimes resembled the lower portion of a fluted column. The cylinder was a single pedestal either with exposed shelves on one face, or with a tambour door. An 18th-century design, it is also called a "pole table."

POUCH TABLE. A small, elegant lady's worktable of the late 18th century. It contained various fittings and a silk pouch to hold needlework. The Sheraton period combined worktables with writing tables in elaborate variations. Sheraton described a pouch table as "a table with a bag, used by ladies to work at, in which bag they deposit their fancy needlework." It is also called a *Bag Table*.

POUDRE D'ÉCAILLE. French for powdered tortoiseshell, which was the basis of a highly colored material used for finishing small wood objects.

POUDREUSE. A lady's powder or toilet table, often equipped with a mirrored lid in the center which lifts up. A Louis XV period innovation. Illustrated is a design by Roentgen.

POWDER ROOM. Originally a corner or small closet in the bedroom of an 18th-century house where one could go to have one's hair powdered. In current usage, a ladies' lavatory.

POYNTELL. A floor pattern or pavement made up of square tiles or blocks laid diagonally, or diamond shaped tiles.

PREDELLA. A footstool. Also, in Italian art, the narrow panel at the back of the altar which served as a base for the altarpiece. Often the entire grouping consisted of several small, related paintings grouped together with the major painting set above.

PREFAB. The vernacular for *Prefabricated*.

POSTERN

POUCH TABLE

POUDREUSE

PREFABRICATED. Units used in construction or decoration which are shaped, formed, and finished in a locale other than the site of construction or installation. Examples are prefabricated windows and doors made to fit doorways and frames being constructed on the site.

PREFABRICATED HOUSES. Houses which are made up of many prefinished parts that are brought to the building site, and there assembled.

PREMIÈRE PARTIE. A Boulle marquetry in which the tortoise-shell predominates and forms the groundwork for the metal inserts. See *Boulle Work* and *Contrepartie or Contre Boulle.*

PREMIÈRE PARTIE

PRE-RAPHAELITE BROTHERHOOD. During the second half of the 19th century, a group of English artists, writers, and poets who revolted against the mechanization and eclecticism of the Victorian arts and the decline of craftsmanship. Their movement started a trend back to the styles of the Italian primitives, to nature and to the handicrafts. In 1848, the Pre-Raphaelite Brotherhood was started by Dante Gabriel Rossetti, Holman Hunt, and John Everett Millais. John Ruskin was an inspiration to the group, and Edward Burne-Jones was sympathetic to their cause. The Arts and Crafts Movement, which was begun by William Morris, was an outgrowth of the Brotherhood.

PRESHRUNK. A term which is applied to fabrics which have been processed for shrinkage before being marketed. After such treatment (Sanforizing is one trademark process) there should be minimum shrinkage in future washings.

PRESS

PRESS. A cupboard or armoire in which clothes or linens were stored. In the mid and late 17th century, "press" was used to describe the case in which books were stored; it has also been used as a term for bookshelves. The press was also known as a press cupboard, great cupboard, or wainscot cupboard. A Chippendale mid-18th-century clothespress is illustrated.

PRICKET CANDLESTICK. An early form of candlestick with a spike projecting above the rim. The candle was impaled on the spike and thus held erect. Illustrated is an ancient Chinese candlestick.

PRICKET CANDLESTICK

PRIE-DIEU CHAIR. A chair designed to accommodate a person at prayer. A carved armchair with a high back, a low, hinged seat, and a receptacle for a prayer book. It is also a low chair, without arms but with a broad upholstered shelf in place of the top rail. A person kneeling in prayer can rest his or her arms on the shelflike projection.

PRIEUR. An 18th-century French designer of interiors, ornaments, arabesques, etc., during the reign of Louis XVI.

PRIMARY COLORS. The commonly accepted theory as applied to pigment as opposed to light is that red, yellow, and blue are the three basic primary colors from which all other colors can be mixed. Red and yellow make orange, blue and red produce violet, and yellow and blue form green. Black and white are not considered colors; they are neutrals. See *Secondary Colors*. In light theories, red, blue, and green are the primary colors.

PRIMAVERA. A yellow-white mahogany with a striped or cross fire figure. Mexico and Guatemala produce a similar pale yellow-brown, birch-colored wood with a mahogany grain. It is a handsome and easily worked fine cabinet wood. See *Acajou* and *Mahogany*.

PRIMING. The application of a primary or first coat of paint, primer, or sealer on a wall, piece of woodwork or furniture, floor, etc. The use of a preparatory surfacing material.

PRIMITIVE ART. Art of either deliberate or unconscious naïveté, characterized by simplicity of form and a more or less unsophisticated technique. A term applied to the art of the 15th century in Italy, to the productions of some 17th- to 19th-century American itinerant artists, and the work of such modern artists as Henri Rousseau and Grandma Moses, as well as to prehistoric art and traditional African and Australian art.

PRIMITIVE ART

PRINCE OF WALES FEATHERS. A chair-back ornament of the Hepplewhite period. It was a carved representation of the three ostrich plumes which were the badge of the Prince of Wales. See *Parlor or Parlour* for another illustration.

PRINCE OF WALES
FEATHERS

PRINCE OF WALES
FEATHERS

PRINCEWOOD. A Spanish elm imported from the West Indies. Its reddish color made it popular in late-17th-century English furniture.

PRINCIPAL RAFTER. The main rafter in a roof truss. See *P.R.* in the *King-Post Truss* illustration.

PRINT ROOMS. Prints and etchings were stylish wall decorations in mid-18th-century England. Prints were sometimes pasted directly onto the walls with ornamental paper borders around them to serve as mountings or frames. Cutout borders, frets, ribbons, and festoons of wallpaper were used to accent and dramatize wall arrangements. A room decorated in this manner was called a print or engraving room. Horace Walpole had a print room at Strawberry Hill, and Chippendale made use of this form of decoration also.

PRISCILLA CURTAIN. A curtain, usually made of a sheer fabric with a deep ruffle of the same material on three sides of each panel. Two such panels are usually set on double curtain rods, one behind the other, with the long unruffled side against the side of the window frame. The panels are then pulled back one to each side of the window, creating an overlap or crisscross effect at the window top, and tied to the window frame with loops of fabric, the tieback often being a ruffled piece of the curtain material. The ruffles cascade down from the tieback point. This curtain may also be a simple pullback curtain with the two panels meeting but not overlapping in the middle. The curtain may be sill length, three-quarter length, or floor length.

PRISMATIC GLASS. A translucent rolled glass with one smooth surface, the other surface textured with parallel prisms. Light is refracted through the glass, and the angle of refraction is determined by the way the light hits the prism.

PROFILE. The view of an object as seen from the side or in cross section.

PRONAOS. The vestibule or entry of an ancient Greek temple.

PRONG BOX. Similar to a knife box. A receptacle for table silver placed in or on an 18th-century sideboard. See *Knife Box.*

PROPORTION. The relative size of one part to the whole or to any of the other parts.

PROPYLAEA. The grand entrance or portal in Greek architecture.

PROSCENIUM. The part of the stage in front of the drop curtain. Originally, in the Greek theatre, the word meant the stage itself.

PROSCENIUM ARCH. The frame or arch that holds the drop curtain. See *Proscenium.* Illustrated is a theatre of the time of Louis XIII of France (mid-17th century).

PROSTYLE. A porch supported by a row of columns, open on three sides and surmounted by a pediment.

PROTEIN FIBERS. Synthetic fibers derived from peanuts, soybeans, caseins, cornmeal, or other protein sources.

PROFILE

PROPYLAEA

PRONG BOX

PROSCENIUM ARCH

PROTHESIS. A rectangular compartment at the eastern end of an aisle in an early Christian basilica. It was usually north of the sanctuary, and gifts were received here. The diaconicon, or vestry, was also a rectangular eastern end of an aisle, and was south of the sanctuary.

PROTHYRUM. A porch or entrance to a Roman house. See *D* in illustration of the Roman house of Pansa in Pompeii. *A* is the atrium. *E* is the entrance.

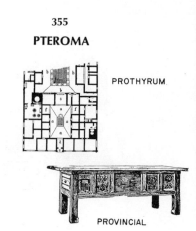

PROTHYRUM

PROVINCIAL. Of the provinces. Country-made and/or country-styled. Simple, unsophisticated, and rustic. See *French Provincial*.

PROVINCIAL FRENCH. See *French Provincial*.

PROVINCIAL

PRUD'HON, PIERRE-PAUL (1758–1823). A celebrated French painter and designer of the Empire period. He painted in the classic style, and often used allegorical or mythological subjects. Illustrated is a crib designed for the King of Rome.

PIERRE-PAUL PRUD'HON

PSEUDODIPTERAL. In classic Greek architecture, a colonnade which appears to be made up of a double row of columns, but actually has one row of columns with a wide peristyle. See *Peristylar*.

PSEUDOPERIPTERAL. A classic Roman building with half columns along the side walls. Illustrated is the Roman temple at Nîmes, the Maison Carrée.

PSEUDOPERIPTERAL

PSYCHE. An Empire-style cheval-type mirror which stood on the floor and could be tilted forward or backward. See *Cheval Glass or Mirror* and *Grand Miroir à la Psyché*. Illustrated is a psyche designed by Prud'hon for the Empress Marie-Louise. Also, an upholstered sofa, with Greek curves, of the first part of the 19th century.

PTEROMA. The open space between the columns that surround a building and the actual walls of the structure.

PSYCHE

PUCE

PUERTA DEL SOL

PUCE. From the French word for "flea." A dark brown or brownish-violet color.

PUENTE STAND. A carved trestle-type table which was designed to support the *Vargueño*.

PUERTA DEL SOL. In Toledo, Spain. It was built A.D. 1200 in the Spanish Gothic style with Moorish influences. The battlements, arches, and intersecting arcade are typically Moorish.

PUGIN, AUGUSTUS WELBY (1812–1852). English architect and writer. He was the prime architectural force in the Gothic Revival period and combined with Sir Charles Barry to design the very Gothic-inspired Houses of Parliament in London. Illustrated is a prie-dieu designed by Pugin. It was carved of oak and enriched with color and gilt. See *Barry, Sir Charles*.

AUGUSTUS WELBY PUGIN

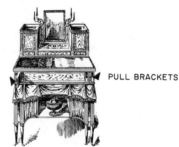
PULL BRACKETS

PULL BRACKETS. Brackets located on either side of and below a pullout writing surface of a desk or secretary. When pulled out, the brackets support the writing surface. Illustrated is an early-19th-century Sheraton design.

PULL-UP CHAIR

PULL-UP CHAIR. A small, light-scaled chair used in living rooms and bedrooms. An occasional chair which can be designed in a period or contemporary style. Illustrated is an 18th-century barrel-type pull-up chair.

PULLDOWN FRONT. A lid or covering on a secretary or bureau which, when lowered, covers the writing area and its fittings. Other types of pulldown front are cylinder, roll, and tambour fronts. A Sheraton design is illustrated.

PULLDOWN FRONT

PULLMAN KITCHEN. A narrow, shallow alcove or recess, often screened off from a living area, which is equipped with a compact arrangement of kitchen fixtures (sink, stove, refrigerator, etc.). It is sometimes one wall of a room which is camouflaged to hide its utilitarian features.

PULLS. Handles for drawers, cabinets, etc. See *Hardware*.

PULVIN. A dosseret or additional block placed over a capital in Byzantine architecture.

PULL

PULVINARIA

PULVIN

PULVINARIA. The pillow-like elements on the sides of an Ionic capital which end in the volutes. Pulvinar (the singular form) also refers to the pillow on which the statue of a god was set in the classic temples.

PULVINATED. Describing a frieze with a convex profile.

PUNCHWORK. A form of simple carved decoration. The background is stipple-textured with a fine steel punch.

PURFLED. Having a surface ornament of drapery, lacework, or embroidery or one which simulated such an effect.

PURLIN. In roof construction, a beam carried by the roof trusses, and in turn supporting the common rafters. See *P* in the *King-Post Truss* illustration.

PURLIN

PURPLE WOOD. A purplish-colored Brazilian wood which is used for inlay work. It was popular in the 18th century. Purple wood is also called violet wood. See *Amaranth*.

PUTTO. A very young boy, somewhat like a wingless cherub or cupid. It was a popular subject for decoration, painting, and sculpture in the Italian Renaissance.

PUTTO

PYCNOSTYLE. In classic architecture, intercolumnar spacing equal to one and one-half of the column's diameter.

PYLON. A high, isolated boundary marker; the flanking structure of an ancient Egyptian temple; or a compound metal support for an electric cable.

PYRAMID. A geometric solid shape, composed of four inclined triangles which meet at a point. The noted structures in ancient Egypt which are shaped like the geometric solid described above.

PYLON

PYROXYLIN. A cellulose product which, when applied to cotton or rayon fabrics, makes them stain-resistant and waterproof.

QAMARIYYAH. Arabic for a lattice window or a pierced stone or stucco opening. See *Mashrebeeyah* and *Moucharaby*.

QAMARIYYAH

QUADRA

QUADRANT BRACKETS

QUADRA. A square architectural molded frame sometimes used to accent a relief sculpture. The term also refers to the plinth block of a podium or platform.

QUADRANT BRACKETS or QUADRANTS. Quarter-circle bands of metal which are attached to the pulldown front of a secretary or bureau. When the front is down, it is supported by these bands. Illustrated is a bureau bookcase (secretary) of the Hepplewhite and Sheraton period.

QUADRATURA. A 17th- and 18th-century type of trompe l'œil mural painting. Architectural elements like columns, cornices, entablatures, cupolas, and colonnades were painted on flat walls and ceilings to create strongly foreshortened perspective views of exterior scenes. The painters who specialized in this art were called "quadraturisti" or "quadratisti."

QUADRATURE. See *Illusionism* and *Trompe l'Oeil*.

QUADRIGA. A sculptured group of a chariot and four horses. It was usually placed on top of monuments, arches, etc.

QUARREL or QUARRY. A square or diamond-shaped pane of glass. The term also refers to a square paving stone or tile.

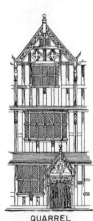

QUARREL

QUARRY ORNAMENT

QUARRY ORNAMENT. A surface treatment of crisscrossing or reticulated lines which form quadrangular or diamond-shaped spaces.

QUARTER LANDING. A square landing which makes a 45° turn in a stairway.

QUARTER LANDING

QUARTER ROUND. A convex molding which, in profile, is one quarter of a circle. See *Echinus*.

QUARTER-SLICED VENEER. A quarter of a log sliced in parallel lines at right angles to the annual growth rings. This produces striped or straight grains on the slices of veneer.

QUARTER-SLICED VENEER

QUARTETTE TABLES. A nest of four light tables which are made to be stored by nesting one inside the other. See *Nested Tables*. Sheraton was one of the originators of this device, and he called them quartetto tables.

QUATREFOIL. A four-lobed ornament, like a stylized four-leaf clover. A Gothic symbol for the cross and the four Evangelists. It was often used in Gothic window tracery and carved-wood decoration on interiors and on Gothic furniture. See *Cusps*.

QUATTROCENTO. The 15th century or the 1400's. Illustrated is a French chair of that century.

QUEEN ANNE PERIOD. The furniture and interior styles of England during the reign of Queen Anne (1702–1714). The early Queen Anne period is a continuation of the William and Mary style, while the late Queen Anne heralds the George I period. The cabriole leg with clubbed foot, shell carvings on the knees of furniture supports, and the swan's neck pediment were popular motifs of this period. The "web" or "Dutch" foot often appears in the Queen Anne style. See *Decorated Queen Anne Period*.

QUEEN CLOSER. A half width of a standard brick which is used at the end of a course next to the header which makes the corner angle of the wall. See *King Closer*.

QUEEN POST. One of the two major vertical supports in a *Queen-Post Roof*.

QUEEN-POST ROOF. A roof truss with two major vertical supports (queens) instead of a single, central, king support.

QUEEN-SIZE BED. A bed with a single mattress approximately 60" wide by 76" to 84" in length.

QUERVELLE, ANTHONY G. A 19th-century Philadelphia cabinet-maker.

QUILLING. See *Quillwork*.

QUARTETTE TABLES

QUATTROCENTO

QUATREFOIL

QUEEN ANNE PERIOD

QUEEN CLOSER

QUEEN POST

QUILLWORK. Decorative applied wavy bands of glass, especially on American and English glass. The glass is pinched as it is being applied, and thus the wavy line is formed.

QUILTED FIGURE. See *Blister.*

QUILTING. Two layers of fabric with padding between the layers, which is held in place by stitches that usually follow a definite pattern. The raised or tufted areas between the stitches give the fabric the characteristic bumpy surface associated with quilted materials. Papers and fabrics can be embossed to create a quilted effect.

QUIRK
— Sunken Fillet
—Raised Fillet

QUIRK. A sharp, incised groove in a molding. It is sometimes referred to as a "sunken fillet."

QUOIN. The corner angle of a building. Also, the brick or stone laid at the corner angle. The cornerstone may be a decorative element, as illustrated.

QUOIN

QUYSSHEN. A 16th-century term for cushion. Illustrated is a wood chair of the early French Renaissance period with the quysshen added for comfort.

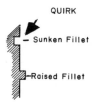
QUYSSHEN

RABBET. A continuous rectangular groove cut along the edge of a piece of wood or metal. It is usually cut to receive the edge of another piece of wood or metal, e.g., a rabbet is sometimes cut on the inner edges of a chair's seat frame to receive a slip seat.

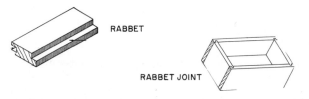
RABBET

RABBET JOINT

RABBET JOINT. In construction, a form of joinery in which a recess or groove is cut in one piece of wood to form a bed for another piece of wood. It is also called a dado joint.

RABESCO. Italian for "arabesque."

RACHET. An 18th-century term for a gearlike construction element used in English secretaries to lower the writing surface. See *Ratchet.*

R

RACHET

RACK

RACK. An angled frame or stand to hold music, books, magazines, etc. It may be a grooved frame or a stand (with or without brackets) to hold guns, cups, etc. Illustrated is a late Victorian combination bookrack and stand.

RACKING. In masonry, a method of building up the end of a wall by stepping back each course, thus making it possible to build on or against another wall without "toothing." See *Toother.*

RADIANT HEATING. A system of heating rooms by setting heat coils in the floor or walls, or both; when these areas are heated, the whole room warms up.

RAEBURN ARMCHAIR. An 18th-century English armchair with a simple upholstered rectangular back, short slim upholstered armpieces, and curved wood arm supports which sweep up and back from the front corners of the upholstered seat. The arm supports and the legs are the only exposed wood parts of the chair. The legs may be cabriole-type or straight, molded with carved or pierced brackets.

RAFFLE LEAVES

RAFFLE LEAVES. An 18th-century English term to describe ornamental foliage with serrated edges similar to the acanthus leaf. This foliage was originally found in Italian designs, and it was adapted by the English designers. Illustrated is an Adam example.

RAFRAÎCHISSOIR or SERVANTE. A small Louis XV rectangular table set on casters. This serving table was often marble-topped, with rounded corners and a drawer below. There were two shelves set between the legs, and the top was fitted with two silver-plated receptacles which could be filled with cold water to keep wine bottles chilled. Canabas designed many such tables in solid mahogany. Variations on this design also appear in the Louis XVI period. See *Dumbwaiter.*

RAFTERS. In architecture, the sloping beams that support the upper part of a roof.

RAG RUG. A rug woven of strips of rags or fabric scraps. The fabrics are sometimes plaited or braided and then sewn into a circle or oval area rug. It is made to resemble provincial Early American rugs.

RAGGLE. In masonry, a groove or channel in a mortar joint.

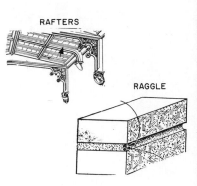

RAFTERS

RAGGLE

RAIL

RAIL. The horizontal strip of a frame or a panel. The horizontal tie bar in the framing of a piece of furniture, such as the top rail of a chair back or a stretcher rail.

RAILS

RAINCEAU

RAINCEAU. The 18th-century English spelling of "rinceau." Illustrated is an Adam design for a panel. See *Rinceau*.

RAINWATER HEAD. An iron or lead tank at the top of a pipe which acts as a funnel to receive the rainwater from a roof gutter. It is also called a cistern head.

RAKE

RAKE. An inward slant or slope from an upright, like the slope of a chair back (*R* in the illustration). An outward slope is a splay (*S* in the illustration).

RAKING CORNICE

RAKING CORNICE. In architecture, the cornice (a series of moldings) on the angled sides of a pediment.

RAMIE. A fiber, similar to flax, which is derived from a stalk plant grown in the United States and in the Orient. See *Bast Fibers*.

RAMP

RAMP. In architecture, an inclined surface which joins two different levels, or the part of a staircase handrail which rises at a sharper angle than the normal handrail. In furniture, a sharp curve ending in an angle at the end of the upright. Illustrated is an early-18th-century English Hogarth chair, in which this often appears.

RAM'S HEAD

RAM'S HEAD. A classical decorative motif. It was reintroduced in the 18th century by Robert Adam on his furniture and in his decorative accessories.

RAM'S HORN STUMP. A double curved arm support which resembles a twisted ram's horn. Illustrated is a mid-18th-century English chair.

RAM'S HORN STUMP

RANCH-STYLE HOUSE. In contemporary usage, a house built completely on one level. All the living, sleeping, and service rooms are on the ground level. The house may have a cellar or basement and a crawl-space attic.

RANDOLPH, BENJAMIN. A late-18th-century Philadelphia cabinet-maker. He designed highboys, and made chairs in the Chippendale style. See *Philadelphia Chippendale*.

RANDOM MATCH. In veneering or decorative surfacing, a casual, unmatched effect where no attempt is made at a symmetrical or repetitive pattern.

RANDOM RUBBLE. In masonry, stones of assorted shapes and sizes, roughly surfaced, which are set in not clearly defined courses.

RANDOM WIDTH. In woodworking, assorted widths of planks used vertically or horizontally to create an irregular pattern.

RANGE TABLES. A late-18th-century term for rectangular tables of the same size which could be combined to form a longer table. The outer corners of the end sections were sometimes rounded.

RANSON. An 18th-century French designer of furniture, floral decorations, and trophies in the Louis XVI style. Many beds of that period were made from his designs.

RAPHAEL (RAPHAEL SANZIO) (1483–1520). A leading artist and architect of the High Renaissance in Italy. He decorated many rooms (stanze) with frescoes and paintings for Popes Julius II and Leo X. He succeeded Bramante as the architect of St. Peter's in Rome (see plan illustrated). Among his many noted religious paintings are the Sistine Madonna, the frescoes and tapestry designs for the Farnesina in Rome, and the "Transfigurations" in the Vatican. Illustrated is his Pandolfino Palace in Florence. See *Loggia*.

RAPHAEL

RAT-CLAW FOOT. A mid- and late-18th-century English and American furniture foot which resembled the sharp spiny claws of a rodent clutching a ball.

RATCHET. A tooth or detent which is used in conjunction with a ratchet wheel for many purposes, including the raising and lowering of desk surfaces, lids, etc., on 18th-century furniture. The ratchet wheel consists of many inclined teeth around the outer rim. When the ratchet is released, it catches onto one of the angled teeth, and thus keeps the wheel from turning

RANDOM MATCH

RANDOM RUBBLE

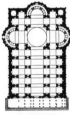

RAPHAEL

RATINÉ

any farther. This would keep a writing surface at a set angle or height. Illustrated under *Rachet* is Sheraton's ratchet mechanism for working his late-18th-century harlequin table. See *Harlequin Table*.

RATINÉ. A loose, plain-weave fabric with a nubby, uneven surface. The warp of the fabric is a special knotty yarn.

RATTAN. The long, solid, round stems of a species of palm found in India and the East. The unbranched stems are pliable and tough, and are used in wickerwork furniture. Though it does not stain readily, rattan can be lacquered.

RAYON. The trademark name for a synthetic fiber having a cellulose base. It is more lustrous, stiffer, and less expensive than silk, and may be used in combination with other synthetic or natural fibers.

RAYONNANT. The French word for "radiant" or "beaming." The name given to 13th-century French Gothic architecture which was characterized by wheel tracery and circular windows such as were used in Bourges, Amiens, and Rheims (illustrated).

RAYONNANT

READING STAND

READING STAND or READING DESK. A popular piece of furniture of the late 18th century. Hepplewhite described one of his designs as a "tripod stand having a staff slide on the stem (fixed with a screw), supporting an adjustable book holder or table."

REBATE. See *Rabbet*.

REBUS. A form of expression in which words are not spelled out in letters but are represented by pictures of objects whose names the words resemble. A picture of an eye would represent "I," and a rose could represent the act of rising.

RÉCAMIER. In furniture, a French 19th-century Directoire or Empire chaise longue named for Mme Récamier. It is a classic type of reclining couch, with one end slightly higher than the other and gracefully curved. Illustrated is an Empire or Regency version by Sheraton. The Récamier was also called a Grecian sofa.

RÉCAMIER

RECESS

RECESS. In architecture, a niche or alcove. An area set back from or into a wall. Illustrated is a recess in the 14th-century Gothic church of St. André in Bordeaux.

RECESSED STRETCH

RECESSED STRETCH. In furniture, the cross stretcher which unites with the two side stretchers rather than with the front legs. This creates a setback which allows room for the sitter's heels. See *H Stretcher, Stretcher,* and *X-shaped Stretcher.*

RÉCHAMPI. A French term for relief decoration in gilt or color, or a combination of the two. Illustrated is a Louis XIV armchair covered in tapestry, with gilded carved decoration.

RÉCHAMPI

RECLINING CHAIRS

RECTILINEAR PERIOD

RECLINING CHAIR. A mechanically operated chair which has a back that lets down and often a footrest that rises up. By dropping the back and raising the footrest, the person in the chair places himself in a horizontal position, as in a modern barber chair. A late-19th-century example is illustrated.

RECTILINEAR PERIOD. The late Gothic period in England (approximately 1377–1485). See *Perpendicular Style.* Illustrated is Westminster Hall in London, England.

RED FILLER. An early American type of furniture finish used until about 1830. It was applied on country-made pieces, and consisted of Spanish brown pigment mixed with raw linseed oil.

RED GUM. A fine-grained wood of a reddish-brown color. It is used for veneering doors, and general interior finishes. Red gum can be stained to imitate walnut, mahogany, or maple, depending upon the figure of the particular species of wood used.

REDWOOD. A handsome, uniformly red-colored wood which takes paint and stains well. Wide widths of planking are available in this wood. It is native to the western states of the United States, especially California.

REEDING. Rows of beading or semicylindrical convex moldings used in close parallel lines. When concave moldings are used it is called fluting. Illustrated is a Sheraton chair leg which is reeded.

REEDING

REFECTORY

REFECTORY

REFECTORY TABLE

REFLECTING DRESSING TABLE

REFECTORY. The dining room in a convent, monastery, institution, or school. Illustrated is an Elizabethan (1571) dining room in a charterhouse. Note the long refectory table. The oak screen in the background is typical of this period, as is the minstrel's gallery in the upper right-hand corner of the illustration.

REFECTORY TABLE. The term generally refers to a long, narrow dining table found in convents, monasteries, etc. In the early Gothic period it was a slab of wood or several fitted planks on trestles. This developed into a firm, massive table with bulbous legs, heavy stretchers, and ornate carving. Illustrated is an Italian trestle-type table.

REFLECTING DRESSING TABLE. A complex, mechanically ingenious dressing table of the mid-18th century. Illustrated is a Shearer design. See *Rudd's Dressing Table.*

RÉGENCE. See *French Régence or Regency.*

REGENCY (ENGLISH). The period in England from 1811 to 1820 when the future George IV was Regent. In furniture and interior designs, the period resembles that of the concurrent French Directoire and Empire. The period is noted for its extensive use of painted stucco and Greek, Roman, and Egyptian motifs. Thomas Hope and Sir John Soane were the leading designers. John Nash's work, especially his Brighton Pavilion, was a particularly fine achievement of the period. A Thomas Hope interior is illustrated. See *Hope, Thomas,* and *Soane, Sir John.*

REGENCY (ENGLISH)

REGLET

REGENCY (ENGLISH)

REGLET. A narrow band or fillet which separates two moldings.

REGOLO. Italian for "mullion."

REGULA. In architecture, the short band between the tenia and the guttae in a Doric entablature.

REGULA

RÉGULATEUR. A French term for a grandfather clock or a long hanging case clock. A *Regulator*.

REGULATOR. A large wall-hanging case clock. Illustrated is a mid-19th-century German example made of pearwood. See *Régulateur*.

REIGNIER WORK. Decorative inlays of colored woods similar in concept to buhl or *Boulle Work*. See *Reisner Work*.

REINFORCED BRICK MASONRY. Brick masonry with steel reinforcing bars embedded in it to help resist forces and carry loads.

REINFORCED CONCRETE. Concrete which has been strengthened with steel members or wire mesh. These are embedded in the concrete when it is being poured. This is also called ferroconcrete.

REINFORCING ROD. A metal rod or wire used in reinforcing concrete. See above illustration.

REISNER WORK. A 17th-century German ornamenting technique of inlaying colored woods similar to boulle and Reignier work.

REJA. A Spanish wrought-iron grille used to enclose a chapel or shrine.

RELIEF. A carved or applied ornament which is above the level of the general surface. It may be a high or a low relief. Illustrated is a carved running leaf pattern over the main portal of Notre-Dame in Paris.

RELIEVING ARCH. In architecture, a rough arch built over a lintel in order to distribute some of the weight which is directed on the lintel from above. It is also called a discharging arch.

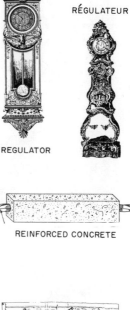

RÉGULATEUR

REGULATOR

REINFORCED CONCRETE

RELIEF

RELIEVING WALL

RELIEVING WALL. A sloping or inclined wall used to withstand the pressure of earth and/or water. A battering wall. See *Batter*. Illustrated are the ramparts of St. Malo, 15th century French Gothic.

RELIQUARY. A small container, usually of precious metals and ornamented with jewels, used to hold a sacred relic. A French Gothic design is illustrated.

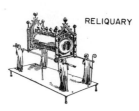

RELIQUARY

RENAISSANCE

RENAISSANCE REVIVAL

RENT TABLE

REPOUSSÉ

RERE-ARCH

RENAISSANCE. "Rebirth." The period in Europe from about the 15th century to about the end of the 17th century. Art, architecture, philosophy, and literature had a rebirth based on classic Greek and Roman models. The intellectual movement began in the 14th century with the writings of Dante, Petrarch, and Boccaccio. Vitruvius' *Treatise on Architecture,* originally written in the time of Augustus, was issued in Rome in Latin, in 1486, and translated into Italian in 1521. This became one of the bibles of Renaissance architecture. Illustrated is the Italian Renaissance Scuola di San Rocco in Venice. See *French Early Renaissance, French Late Renaissance,* and *French Middle Renaissance.*

RENAISSANCE REVIVAL. Another revival of the eclectic 19th century. The architectural designs were reminiscent of famous Renaissance structures like the Farnese Palace in Rome, St. Mark's Library in Venice, and the Pandolfini Palace in Florence. Sir Charles Barry was one of the noteworthy architect-exponents of this revival. Illustrated is his Reform Club, which was based on the aforementioned Farnese Palace. See *Farnese Palace* for illustration of the original palace.

RENT TABLE. A round or octagonal pedestal table with drawers set into the apron under the tabletop. These drawers, usually seven in number, were marked with the days of the week. This design was used in the 18th century in England by landlords for collecting and filing rents. Sheraton designed several of these tables in mahogany.

REP. A plain-weave fabric with a heavy filler thread giving the fabric a corded effect. The fabric has a definite crosswise rib. Rep can be made of most natural or synthetic fibers, and it can be used for upholstery and draperies.

REPLICA. An exact reproduction or copy.

REPOUSSÉ. Relief work on metal materials. The design is produced by hammering or pressing on the material on the reverse side so that the design appears raised on the front. See *Chasing* and *Embossed.* Illustrated is a 13th-century half-life-size head done in silver-gilt repoussé.

REPP. See *Rep.*

REPRODUCTION. A faithful copy of the form, workmanship, and ornamentation of an original. This is not an attempt at a counterfeit or a "fake."

RERE-ARCH. Rear arch. In architecture, an arch which supports the wall over the recess of a door or window. This is not an outer arch. It is also called a sconcheon or scoinson arch.

REREDOS. In architecture, the screen or wall facing set behind the altar. It is usually embellished with carving.

RÉSEAU. French for "tracery."

RESILIENCY. The natural ability of a fabric or material to spring back after being crushed or bent; the ability to resist creasing. Fabrics can be chemically treated to be made more crease-resistant.

RESPOND. In architecture, the corbel or half column which supports one end of the last arch in an arcade. Illustrated is the Basilica of Santa Agnese in Rome, an example of early Christian church architecture.

RESTORATION CHAIR. A high-backed, cane-paneled chair of the Carolean period (late 17th century in England). The legs, as well as the uprights, were usually spiral turnings. The chair often had a carved cresting representing the crown supported by cherubs and adorned with acanthus leaves and roses. The same type of design was sometimes repeated on the front stretcher.

RESTORATION PERIOD. The period from 1660 to 1688 in England. In 1660 the monarchy was restored and Charles II became king. It was also the beginning of the Age of Walnut in furniture. Though the furniture remained relatively simple and rectangular in outline, it became more ornate and decorative. This was the antithesis of the puritanical quality of the preceding Cromwellian or Commonwealth period. French and Flemish designs were popular. Illustrated is a chair made of walnut with the crown carved on the stretcher and top rail.

RESPOND

RESTORATION CHAIR

RESTORATION PERIOD

RETABLE

RETABLE or RETABLO. A short form of "retrotabulum." This is the area behind the altar in a church, usually an architectural screen decorated with sculpture, paintings, etc. The retablo in a Spanish Gothic church was particularly ornate. Illustrated is the retablo of the Cathedral of Toledo (1227–1493). The carved screen is flanked by tiers of arcaded statuary.

RETAINING WALL. A wall which holds back a mass of earth or water like a dam. It is also called a revetment.

RETAINING WALL

RETICULATED

RETICELLA. A type of lace using a combination of drawn and cut work. See *Lace*.

RETICULATED. A surface which has been decorated with a latticelike design similar to the meshes of a net.

RETROTABULUM. See *Retable or Retablo*.

RETURN

REVEAL

RETURN. A change in direction of any continuous surface. An example would be the turning of a cornice at the angle of a building and its continuance on the adjacent side of the building. This continuation would be the return. Illustrated is the 15th-century house of Jacques Coeur at Bourges.

REVEAL. In architecture, the vertical wall area which is not hidden by the frame of a window or door, and is at right angles to the wall surface.

RÉVEILLON, JEAN-BAPTISTE. A French wallpaper manufacturer of the mid-18th century. He commissioned outstanding artists like Jean-Honoré Fragonard and François Boucher to execute designs for large panel decorations. His papers had a strong Neoclassic influence, though he also produced floral and arabesque designs. The delicacy and variety of coloring used approximated to those of true mural paintings.

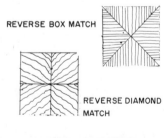

REVERSE BOX MATCH

REVERSE DIAMOND MATCH

REVERSE SERPENTINE

REVERSE BOX MATCH. A decorative veneering technique similar to a reverse diamond match, but angled to create a cross-patterned center with right-angled patterns going off in four directions.

REVERSE DIAMOND MATCH. Four wedges of wood or veneer set together to form an *X* at the center with consecutively smaller *V*'s radiating out from the center in all four directions.

REVERSE SERPENTINE. The opposite of a simple serpentine curve. The ends and center are concave while the area between is convex. Illustrated is an 18th-century Sheraton kneehole table. See *Serpentine*.

RIBBED VAULT

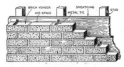

REVETMENT

REVETMENT. In architecture, a veneering, facing, or sheathing of stone or metal on a structure or architectural element for protection or adornment. This is also called a retaining wall. Illustrated is an example of brick veneering.

REZ-DE-CHAUSSÉE. French for the "ground floor" or "ground level."

RHEIMS CATHEDRAL. Built in France between 1212 and 1241 and the source of inspiration for Westminster Abbey, with its projecting transepts and chevet of five chapels. The western façade is ornately detailed and enriched with about 500 statues. The rose window is 40' in diameter. The interior is vast and open-looking with clustered piers supporting pointed arches, a tall clerestory, and the vaulting 125' off the ground. It is considered one of France's great treasurehouses of Gothic art. See illustration for *Rayonnant*.

RHEIMS CATHEDRAL

RHENISH

RHENISH. The German Romanesque style.

RIB. In architecture, a projecting band on a ceiling or vault. In the illustration, *W* is the wall rib, *D* is the diagonal rib, *C* is the cross rib. See *Groin Rib, Ribbed Vault,* and *Vault.*

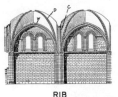

RIB

RIBBAND BACK. A Chippendale chair style. The chair back is carved to resemble a pattern of interlacing ribbons. The ribbon motif also appears in the Louis XVI style and in German rococo ornament.

RIB

RIBBAND BACK

RIBBED VAULT. A framework of arched ribs which supports light masonry. Illustrated is the vaulting in Notre-Dame in Paris.

RIBBED VAULT

RIBBON BACK

RIBBON BACK

NICHOLAS RIBBONIER

RIBBONS

RIBBON BACK. A carved chair back representing puckered ribbons tied in bows. It made a decorative splat for a chair or settee. The ribbon back was popular in the Louis XV period, and it was adapted by Chippendale and Manwaring. A Manwaring design is illustrated. See *Ribband Back*. Also, a wood grain or figure of wide, unbroken, alternating light and dark stripes. It is mainly found in quarter-sliced mahogany.

RIBBONIER, NICHOLAS. A 16th-century French Renaissance architect. Le Pailly (illustrated) and Sully are among the structures of the period that are attributed to him.

RIBBONS. Narrow widths of fabric that are used for trimming. They are manufactured in many widths, weaves, fibers, and colors. As a decorative motif, ribbons are used with foliage and flowers in garland and festoons. Ribbons are called "labels" when they bear an inscription. Antique labels are often simple and terminate in balls. Gothic labels are curled and quaint. Renaissance labels are free and elegant and are often divided at the ends like pennons. The labels of the Louis XVI period have a crinkled quality. See *Festoon* and *Pennon*.

RICHARDSON, HENRY (HOBSON). One of the first truly modern architects. His architectural career covered the years between 1865 and 1886. He was Beaux Arts trained and looked to the past for his inspirations. The "Romanesque" period inspired him to create a "flat surfaced" building with arched windows. His designs were almost contemporary in their clean lines. One classic example of his work was the Marshall Field wholesale warehouse in Chicago built in 1885, a simple, massive masonry block structure. It greatly influenced Louis Sullivan and his work on the Auditorium Building of 1887 and his later Wainwright and Guaranty buildings.

RICKRACK. A flat braid with a chevron-like design. A zigzag pattern used as an applied trimming.

RIDGE

RIDGE. In architecture, the very top meeting point of a pitched roof. The name given a roof made up of two sloping sides resting on parallel walls and meeting at a horizontal ridge. The triangular end formed below is called the gable.

RIDGE TILE. The tile which is especially shaped and designed to fit the ridge of a roof.

RIDGE TILE

JEAN–HENRI RIESENER

RIESENER, JEAN-HENRI (1735–1806). A French master cabinet-maker. He trained under Jean François Oeben during the Louis XV period, but his work had the classic look that was typical of the Louis XVI period: exquisite proportions, graceful lines, architectural motifs, and roses. Marie Antoinette favored roses. Riesener's designs included fine marquetry details in deep tones on mahogany. He also used pictorial center panels, with allover patterns on the sides of his units. Illustrated is a writing table (scritoire) designed for Marie Antoinette. See *Bureau à Cylindre*.

RIFT CUT. A method for slicing oak wood. A comb grained effect is produced by cutting perpendicularly to the medullary rays which radiate from the center of the log like wheel spokes.

RILIEVO STIACCIATO. A shallow relief which is produced by scratches and incisions. It was described by Giorgio Vasari as a "low or flattened relief."

RIM. In furniture, a border, edge, or gallery around a tabletop. It can be molded, carved, or fretted. Illustrated is a Chippendale table.

RIM

RINASCIMENTO. Italian for "Renaissance."

RINCEAU. French for "scroll ornament." Sometimes called an arabesque. It is usually a symmetrical, horizontal composition of scroll and leaf ornaments applied to a frieze, panel, or other architectural feature. It is often combined with cartouches and grotesques. A Venetian Renaissance example is shown.

RISE

RINCEAU

RISE. In architecture, the vertical distance from the springing line (starting point) to the crown (uppermost central part) of an arch.

RISER

RISING STRETCHERS

ROCAILLE

ROCAILLE

ROCOCO

RISER. In a stairway, the vertical or rising part of a step.

RISING STRETCHERS. X-shaped stretchers (the connecting cross pieces between the legs of furniture) that curve upward toward the intersection. A single stretcher that curves upward is called an arched or hooped stretcher. Rising stretchers are also called "saltires." Illustrated is an 18th-century Italian Renaissance chair.

RIYA RUG. See *Rya Rug.*

ROBBIA, DELLA. The family name for a group of Italian sculptors of the 14th and 15th centuries: Luca, Andrea, Giovanni, and Girolamo. The name is usually associated with a faïence finish, and ceramic relief round plaques or medallions with polychromed fruit and foliage garland frames surrounding, usually, a white figure on a blue ground.

ROBERT, HUBERT (1733–1808). A French painter of romantic landscapes of the Louis XVI period. Often these scenes included imaginary Roman ruins (follies). Robert created a series of six paintings for the bathroom of the Château of Bagatelle. He also designed the little "hamlet" of Normandy-like half-timber thatched cottages set around an artificial lake, where Marie Antoinette and her ladies played at being dairymaids.

ROBSJOHN-GIBBINGS, TERENCE HAROLD. A contemporary furniture and interior designer in the classic tradition: pristine simple and elegant case goods and fine lined seating units inspired by antique Greek and Roman models.

ROCAILLE. A French term for an outdoor artificial grotto decorated with odd-shaped stones and shells. The term is applied to the stone and shell decorations of the Rococo period, and it was also applied to the Louis XV period during the early 19th century.

ROCOCO. The name applied to the Louis XV period. The word is derived from rocaille (rockeries) and coquille (cockleshell). Both these motifs appeared in pottery designs of Bernard Palissy in the 16th century. Juste Aurèle Meissonier, an Italian who came to Paris in 1723, is credited with being largely responsible for developing the rococo style. He produced a book of engraved designs using the shell as a decorative motif. The period was distinguished by ornate, asymmetrical carvings and painted decorations using foliage, shells, scrolls, and fantastic whorls. Chinese or other exotic motifs were often combined with the aforementioned embellishments.

RODRIGUE VENTURA (1717–1785). A Spanish architect who worked in the Neoclassic tradition.

ROENTGEN or RÖNTGEN, DAVID (1743–1807). A great marquetry and furniture designer of the Louis XV and the Louis XVI periods. He used light, bright-toned woods as inlays in mahogany, and his marquetry work has been compared to marble mosaic work. Roentgen, also known as David, contrived numerous compartments in his cabinets and secretaries which opened and shut by means of clever mechanical devices. His furniture was produced mainly in a factory at Neuwied in Germany. Chrétien Krause and Michael Rummer are credited with doing much of the marquetry, and Johann Roetig the mechanical devices. Roentgen was patronized by Marie Antoinette. See illustration for *Poudreuse*.

ROGNON. French for "kidney." Used to describe kidney-shaped designs. Illustrated is an 18th-century Sheraton kidney-shaped kneehole desk.

ROLL. In wallpaper, 36 square feet. Wallpaper varies in width and may be 18", 22", 28", 30", or 36" wide, and the length varies, but the roll will usually average 36 square feet. Several rolls are included in a bundle or stick.

ROLL MOLDING. A round molding. In Gothic architecture it is referred to as a "bowtell."

ROGNON

ROLL MOLDING

ROLL-OVER ARMS

ROLL-OVER ARMS. Upholstered chair arms which start at the side seat rails and turn over in a full, bold sweep. They are padded scroll arms which join the chair back and thus form an enclosed seat area. They were originated in France in the early 16th century, and adapted by the English in the Restoration period (1660–1689). Illustrated is a late-17th-century English chair.

ROLLED GLASS. Glass which is extruded between two rollers in a continuous viscous strip. The strip is then passed through a heating process, and then it solidifies. A pattern may be pressed on one of the surfaces.

ROLLED STEEL SECTION. A mill-rolled steel bar which is extruded in various shapes or sections. The "I" section is the most common and is called a "rolled steel beam" (R.S.B.) or "rolled steel joint" (R.S.J.).

ROLLED STEEL SECTION

ROLLTOP DESK. See *Pulldown Front.* A late-18th-century English design is shown.

ROLLTOP DESK

ROMAN ARCHITECTURE

ROLOCK. See *Rowlock.*

ROMAN ARCHITECTURE. The architecture of the Roman republic and empire, based on the classic orders: Tuscan, Doric, Ionic, Corinthian, and Composite. The arch, vault, and dome are all prominent features in Roman architecture. Illustrated is the Colosseum in Rome which shows the three main orders (Tuscan, Ionic, and Corinthian) with Corinthian pilasters on the uppermost tier. These orders are used in a superimposed manner.

ROMAN BATH. See *Labrum* and *Thermae.*

ROMAN EAGLE

ROMAN EAGLE. A decorative motif used by many countries and for many centuries. The classic Romans used the eagle as a symbol of the deification of their emperors, and also for the standards of their armies. Napoleon I, emulating the Roman emperors, gave his armies the French eagle in 1804. The eagle appears in Louis XVI, Directoire, and Empire designs. Illustrated is an eagle from the bas-relief in Trajan's Forum, an ancient Roman edifice.

ROMAN SHADE. A window shade, which, when raised, is "accordian folded." It does not work on the usual spring roller associated with window shades. The raising and lowering is controlled by cords at one end. The shade can be made of assorted fabrics, and uses a special tape. It is a decorative shade, and is sometimes used in place of curtains for a window covering.

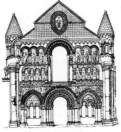

ROMANESQUE

ROMANESQUE. The period of the "Dark Ages" in Europe (about the beginning of the 9th to the end of the 12th century). It was predominantly a period of ecclesiastic arts and building. According to Sir Banister Fletcher: "Romanesque may be said to include the phases of European architecture which were based on Roman art from the departure of the Romans up to the end of the 12th century, when the pointed arch was introduced. It includes the Norman, Lombard and Byzantine periods, and was the basis for the ensuing Gothic styles." Illustrated is the church of Notre-Dame-la-Grande at Poitiers.

ROMANISCH. German for "Romanesque."

ROMANTIC EPOCH. The period of romanticized medievalism which started in France around 1830. It was an attempt at breaking away from the old classic school. Victor Hugo, with *Notre-Dame de Paris* (translated as *The Hunchback of Notre Dame*) introduced the "Gothic Revival." In the arts, the Gothic trend was picked up by Eugène Viollet-le-Duc, Théodore Ballu, and others. Illustrated is Westminster Palace (Houses of Parliament) in London, which is typical of this period.

ROMANTIC EPOCH

ROMAYNE WORK. Carved medallions, heads, or knobs used in the Jacobean and Restoration period as furniture knobs or pulls. This is also an early Renaissance motif (16th century) of classic Roman-type heads carved in medallions, and used as decorations on architectural elements.

ROMAYNE WORK

ROMNEY, GEORGE (1734–1802). An English historical and portrait painter. His works reflect the styles and taste of his period.

RONDEL. A round outline or design in a surface pattern.

RÖNTGEN, DAVID. See *Roentgen or Röntgen, David.*

ROOD. A cross, crucifix, or Christ figure, especially one which is placed at the entrance to the choir in medieval church architecture.

ROOD LOFT. A mezzanine over a rood screen.

ROOD SCREEN. In church architecture, the screen which separates the nave from the choir. Illustrated is the rood screen of the Chapelle de Pagny, France.

RONDEL

ROOD

ROOF LIGHT

ROOD SCREEN

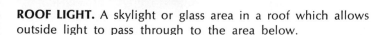

ROOF LIGHT. A skylight or glass area in a roof which allows outside light to pass through to the area below.

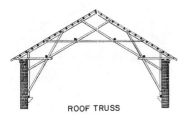

ROOF TRUSS

ROOF TRUSS. Assorted wood or metal members joined into a triangular arrangement to support the roof and its coverings, and to transmit the weight vertically down the walls or piers. See *King-Post Truss* and *Queen-Post Roof*.

ROPE BED. A bed frame with rope laced back and forth to form a spring upon which a mattress is set.

ROPE MOLDING. A half-round or quarter-round molding which is carved or embossed to resemble a rope. See *Cable Molding*.

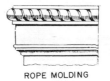

ROPE MOLDING

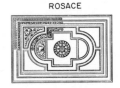

ROSACE

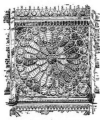

ROSE WINDOW

ROSACE. A decorative rosette or circular centerpiece in a ceiling.

ROSE WINDOW. A circular window with tracery mullions radiating like spokes of a wheel from a central point. The areas between the mullions are filled with stained or colored glass. This is principally a feature in Gothic architecture. It is also called a "wheel window."

ROSETTA STONE. A black basalt stone which was uncovered in 1798 near Rosetta in Egypt. It is inscribed with a list of honors to Ptolemy V (about 195 B.C.), made up by the Egyptian priests in recognition of his generosity to their temples. The same inscription is written in hieroglyphics, demotic, and Greek. This stone became the key to the hieroglyphic records of ancient Egypt. It was found during Napoleon's campaigns in Egypt, and deciphered by Jean François Champollion. The campaign was responsible for introducing the Egyptian motifs into the Directoire and Empire styles.

ROSETTA WOOD. An East Indian wood used by Spanish and Indian craftsmen during the 17th and 18th centuries in the Americas. It was also used for panels on some early American chests because of its brilliant red color and black graining.

ROSETTE

ROSETTES. French for "little roses." A floral decorative device, usually a circle with petals developing out from a central point. The outer contour may be round, elliptic, or square. The rosette has been a popular motif since the Gothic period. The motif was favored by Adam and Hepplewhite. See *Patera*.

ROSEWOOD, BRAZILIAN. A hard, heavy wood, mainly of a purplish-brown hue with almost black streaks. When freshly cut, the wood exudes a roselike aroma. It is also called jacaranda. It was popular during the English Empire period (19th century) for cabinets and musical instruments.

ROSEWOOD, HONDURAS. A lighter and more uniformly grained wood than Brazilian rosewood. See *Palisander.*

ROSTRUM. A raised speaker's platform. The raised tribune in the Roman Forum from which the orators spoke was called the rostra (plural of rostrum), because it was decorated with the prows of ships which were trophies of war. One of the meanings of the Latin word rostrum is "beak of a ship."

ROTARY-CUT VENEER. A slice of veneer made by cutting a log in a circular manner around the circumference. It is similar to the unwinding of a roll of paper. A bold, variegated grain is produced since the cut follows the log's annual growth rings.

ROTTENSTONE. A finely powdered soft stone (originally called Tripoli after the country of its origin). It can be used with oil to polish wood, and also for grinding and polishing sculpture, etc.

ROTUNDA. In architecture, a round building such as the Pantheon in Rome, or the main central part of a round building. A rotunda may also be a round central hall, usually surmounted with a dome, as in the Capitol in Washington, D.C. Illustrated is a section view of the early Christian church of S. Costanza in Rome.

ROUGH ARCH. An arch built of ordinary bricks instead of shaped stones or voussoirs. See *Relieving Arch.*

ROUGH CAST. A plaster made of pebbles, cement, gravel, etc., and used for the exterior surfacing of a structure.

ROTUNDA

ROUGH ARCH

ROUNDABOUT

ROUNDABOUT. A 19th-century three-seater unit. In plan, the three seats form a circle, and the three individual chair backs radiate and curve out from the central point of the circle. The seated persons must turn their heads toward the center of the circle to see and talk to the others who are seated on the same piece of furniture. See *Tête-à-Tête.*

ROUNDABOUT CHAIR

ROUNDABOUT CHAIRS

ROUNDEL

ROUNDABOUT CHAIR. This chair is usually designed to fit into a corner, the square seat diagonally set and the back extending across two adjoining sides. Thus the chair has a leg in front, one in back, and one at either side. It is sometimes referred to as a "corner" or "writing-arm chair." See *Fauteuil de Bureau.*

ROUNDEL. A round, flat form like a patera, medallion, or plaque. The term also refers to a circular disk of stained glass in a leaded window.

ROUSSEAU DE LA ROTTIÈRE, JEAN-SIMÉON (1747–c. 1822). A French designer of interiors and accessories of the Louis XVI period. He decorated the boudoir of Marie Antoinette in elegant, refined forms using golden tones. The panels ("Love Assisting at the Toilet of Grace"), which he used in this room, were done in subtle gradations of gold and silver. He also decorated the Queen's room at Versailles.

ROVANA. Dow Chemical Company's tradename for synthetic products which include Saran microtape. Rovana can be extruded as a fiber, and used in fabrics. It is flame-resistant, has excellent resistance to abrasion, and keeps its shape. It is used mainly for warp threads in drapery fabrics.

ROWLOCK. In masonry, rows of bricks laid on edge, especially for the ring of a brick arch. A rowlock course would be a row of "headers" (the small end of the brick) laid on edge. It is also called "rolok" or "bull header."

ROYAL CRESCENT. A series of thirty houses built together in the shape of an open ellipse in Bath, England, by John Wood the Younger in 1769. A broad, common lawn sloped gently down toward the town below. It was an early example of community planning and layout.

RUBBED BRICKWORK. An English Renaissance type of brickwork which used soft bricks which could be cut into exact shapes and sizes. The finely fitted bricks were rubbed down to make a smooth, even surface. Sir Christopher Wren used this technique at Hampton Court.

RUBBER TILE. A synthetic rubber floor-covering material which is made in a continuous roll or as tiles. It is nonporous and more resilient than most tiles, as well as quiet and comfortable underfoot. It remains flexible over wide temperature variations, but it is adversely affected by oil, grease, and some solvents.

RUBBLE

RUBBLE. Irregularly shaped stones set into a wall, with or without mortar.

RUBENS, PETER PAUL (1577–1640). A great Flemish painter. He also decorated the Luxembourg Palace in Paris for Marie de Medici. Illustrated is "Children Carrying Flowers" by Rubéns.

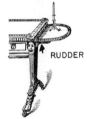

PETER PAUL RUBENS

RUDDER. A wooden support for the leaf of a drop-leaf table or shelf which resembles a ship's rudder. It is similar to a butterfly support.

RUDD'S DRESSING TABLE. A mid-18th-century English dressing table which was described by Hepplewhite as "possessing every convenience which can be wanted; or mechanism and in- genuity supply." It was named for a noted personality of the period. See *Reflecting Dressing Table* for illustration.

RUDOLPH, PAUL MARVIN. An American architect born in Ken- tucky in 1918. He is presently Chairman of the Yale University Department of Architecture. He expresses great concern for the relationship of one building to another, and like Ludwig Mies van der Rohe, he has studied the problems of reflectivity in glass façades. He has stated, "only the means change [in archi- tecture], not the end." Among his works are the Mary Cooper Jewett Arts Center at Wellesley College and the "Umbrella House" in Lido Key, Florida.

RULE JOINT. A dustproof and draftproof hinged joint on late Queen Anne furniture, screens, tabletops, etc. A hinged joint. See *Knuckle Joint*.

RULE JOINT

RUNIC KNOT. An ornamental motif of the Celtic, Scandinavian, and German Romanesque periods. It is an interlaced design using the magical symbols of ancient North European countries.

RUNIC KNOT

RUNNER. A guide strip under the center or at the sides of a drawer. A term also used to describe the curved member of a rocking chair.

RUNNER FOOT. A pair of straight legs which are connected at their base by a horizontal rail or stretcher. The legs appear to end on this crosspiece. This was a popular chair support in the Italian Renaissance period. Sometimes the ends of the crossbar were decorated with carved lion's paws.

RUNNER

RUNNER FOOT

RUNNING BOND. See *Stretcher Bond*.

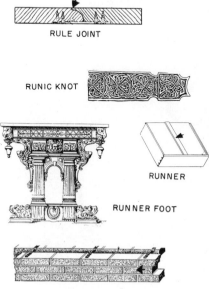

RUNNING BOND

RUNNING DOG

RUNNING DOG

RUSH SEAT

RUSTIC FURNITURE

RUSTIC STONEWORK

RUSTICATION

S-SCROLL LEGS

RUNNING DOG. A continuous scroll or wavelike design. It is also called the *Vitruvian Scroll.*

RUSH. A long grass which is twisted and woven to make seats for provincial chairs. The seats are also known as "flag seats." Rush seats have been used from earliest times, and rush has often been woven into mats. See *Flag* illustration.

RUSH SEATS. See *Rush.*

RUSKIN, JOHN. A 19th-century English writer and art critic. He felt that "ornamentation is the principal part of architecture."

RUSTIC FURNITURE. English furniture of the mid-18th century which simulated the natural growth of twigs and branches. It was gnarled, fantasy-like garden furniture. Manwaring and Chippendale (illustrated) were among those who designed pieces in this style.

RUSTIC STONEWORK. Masonry in which the face of the stone is roughened, but the block is carefully shaped, leveled, and set in straight courses. The edges are often smoothed out to emphasize the rough face of the block.

RUSTICATION. A form of masonry using stonework or bricks which have recessed or chamfered edges. A decorative, wide-jointed appearance is created. It was popular in the Baroque and Mannerist periods.

RYA RUG. A high-pile, shaggy rug. From the Scandinavian "ry" for rough or shaggy. It is an example of a Scandinavian craft which goes back to before 3000 B.C. It was originally a dowry item, and was used as a blanket for warmth. Rya rugs are used today in contemporary and provincial rooms as decorative area rugs.

S SCROLL. A popular cyma curve of the French Rococo (Louis XV) and Chippendale periods. It is sometimes used "broken" or "stepped" in the center. A Chippendale design is illustrated.

S SCROLL

S-SCROLL LEGS. A 17th-century type of furniture support of Dutch design. It was shaped and ended in an S-shaped scroll, and the element was usually heavily embellished with carving.

SAARINEN, EERO (1910–1961). A modern architect and designer who was born in Finland and arrived in America in 1923. He regarded each problem as a new and individual challenge, and he sought to answer it with a free, original form. Some of his work was in the tradition of Ludwig Mies van der Rohe. Among his works are: The General Motors Technical Center with its endless grids filled with glass, considered an "exalted" industrial product; The M.I.T. Kresge Auditorium with its three-point dome and circular brick chapel; the Georgian-like grid façade of the United States Embassy in London; Yale's Hockey Rink with its ship-turned-turtle roof; the T.W.A. Terminal at Kennedy Airport in New York City; and the giant parabola-shaped arch of the Jefferson Memorial in St. Louis, Missouri. Saarinen also designed the pedestal chair as well as other architectural furniture. He introduced the *Womb Chair* in 1946.

SAARINEN, GOTTLIEB ELIEL (1873–1950). A great Finnish-American architect and city planner. He became a resident of the United States in 1923. The railroad station in Helsinki is his most famous work in Finland. In America he designed the buildings and headed the Academy of Art at the Cranbrook Foundation. He also designed the music shed for the Berkshire Festival. In his later years, he collaborated with his son Eero. Saarinen made significant breakthroughs in home constructions. The General Motors Technical Center in Warren, Michigan (1951–1955), is one of his most noted structures.

SABER LEGS. Fine splayed legs often found on early-19th-century Sheraton "Grecian-type" chairs. The front legs flare forward, the rear legs curve out behind.

SABICU. A pink to red wood which resembles mahogany. It is hard and heavy and has a low luster. The wood is native to Cuba and Central America.

SABOT FOOT. See *Spade Foot.* An Adam chair is illustrated.

SABOTS. French for "wooden shoes." Decorative metal coverings for the feet of wood furniture. They were designed to enhance as well as protect the foot, and serve the same purpose that *Chutes* do on the angles and legs of wood furniture. These decorative metal coverings appeared in the 18th century, and were made of bronze doré, bronze, brass, etc. An 18th-century secretary by Pionniel is shown. It was made of amarynth and embellished with a Sèvres plaque.

SACK BACK. The double-bowed back of a Windsor chair.

SADDLE. See *Sill.*

SADDLE-CHECK. A bedroom easy chair of the "wing" or "forty-winks" type designed by Hepplewhite and others in the mid and late 18th century in England and America.

SABER LEGS

SABOTS

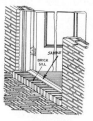

SADDLE

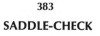

SADDLE-CHECK

SADDLE SEAT

SADDLE SEAT

SADDLEBACK ROOF

LIBRARY OF SAINT MARK

SAINT MARK'S CATHEDRAL

SADDLE SEAT. A scooped-out seat which resembles the contour of a saddle. The seat is convexed from the sides and back to a raised central ridge. It is often found in Windsor chairs with thick pine seats. A Chippendale chair is illustrated.

SADDLE STONE. See *Apex Stone.*

SADDLEBACK COPING. The uppermost course of masonry of a wall formed by a triangular brick core made up of full-sized bricks and parts of bricks.

SADDLEBACK ROOF. The roof of a tower which has a ridge and ends in gables instead of the usual pyramidal form.

SAILCLOTH. A strong, durable, firmly woven cotton canvas.

SAINT MARK, LIBRARY OF. A fine example of Venetian Renaissance architecture, built in Venice in 1536. It was designed by Jacopo Sansovino. It is arcaded with Doric columns, and the second story has Ionic columns. The deep frieze of the overly large entablature has windows separated by cherubs holding festoons of deeply carved flowers and fruit.

SAINT MARK'S CATHEDRAL. A famous cathedral built in Venice (1042-1071), strongly Byzantine in design. It was modeled after the Church of the Apostles in Constantinople. St. Mark's stands on a great marble piazza surrounded by stately arches, the Campanile, and the Palace of the Doges. The cathedral has a central dome 42' in diameter, and a dome over each arm of the cross. The interior is a blaze of colored marbles and brilliant glass mosaics that tell the story of the Creation, the Fall of man, his redemption, and the miracles of Christ. The exterior (the west façade is illustrated) has gold mosaic panels in the tympana and spandrels of the semicircular arches, and is constructed of marble and alabaster.

SAINT PAUL'S CATHEDRAL. Situated in London, this is the largest Protestant cathedral in the world. It was designed by Sir Christopher Wren in the "Italian Renaissance" style. It was begun in 1675 (the old church was destroyed in the great fire of 1666) and completed in 1710. The edifice was built of Portland stone, and Corinthian and Composite orders were used on the structure. The great dome stands on a circular drum which rises twenty feet above the roof of the Cathedral and it is topped with a lantern which is enriched with columns and crowned with a ball and cross. Illustrated is a Grinling Gibbons carved panel from the choir stalls.

SAINT PAUL'S CATHEDRAL

SALEMBIER

SAINT PETER'S

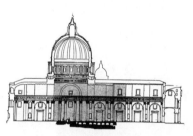

SAINT PETER'S

SAINT PETER'S, ROME. c. 1502–1626. Probably the most important building of the Italian Renaissance. The original design was by Bramante (Donato d'Agnolo): a Greek cross plan and a dome fashioned after that of the Pantheon with a peristyle and lantern added. Raphael succeeded him, and suggested a Latin cross plan. Baldassare Peruzzi was the next architect, and he reverted to the Greek cross plan. Michelangelo, at the age of seventy-two, finally took over in 1546. He used the Greek cross plan, strengthened the piers of the dome, and redesigned the chapels and the apses. He planned the great drum and dome, but he died before the dome was started. From his models, the dome was completed by Giacomo della Porta and Domenico Fontana. In 1564, Giacomo da Vignola added the side cupolas. The nave was lengthened into a Latin cross, and the façade was added by Carlo Maderna. Giovanni Bernini added the 650-foot-wide entrance piazza with 284 columns forming the four Tuscan colonnades. The famous dome has an internal diameter of 137$\frac{1}{2}$' and and it is almost 450' from the ground to the external top. The exterior is made of travertine stone, and it is adorned with Corinthian pilasters. The entablature and attic are carried around the entire structure. See *Attic* for illustration.

The Vatican, which is attached to the Cathedral, is 1,151

SAINT PETER'S

long by 767' wide, and it has eight grand staircases, twenty courts, and about 11,000 rooms. The Vatican is decorated with a great treasury of paintings and sculpture, as well as magnificent frescoes by some of the greatest artists of the period. Illustrated are the dome and a cross section of the Cathedral.

SALEM ROCKER. An early-19th-century New England rocking chair with a heavy scrolled seat, top rail, and arms. The spindle back is usually straight and not as high as that of a Boston rocker.

SALEMBIER. A French 18th-century designer in the Louis XVI style. He designed overly ornate small furniture.

SALON. A great apartment in a large house or palace. It was the room that was used for entertaining and conversing, and was the center of cultural and political society from the late 18th through the 19th centuries. Many salons were made famous by the hostesses who presided over them. Illustrated is a Louis XVI salon.

SALON

SALT GLAZE. A surfacing of thin glass for pottery or brick which is produced by throwing salt into the oven while the firing process is taking place. The glass finish is produced by the thermochemical reaction of silicates of the clay body with the vapors of the salt or chemicals.

SALTBOX HOUSE

SALTBOX HOUSE. A New England 17th- and 18th-century type of building. The second story overhung the ground floor in the front. The roof usually swept down in the rear to cover the rooms on the ground level, which extended out beyond the house proper.

SALTIRE. An X-shaped stretcher of Italian origin, used to reinforce the legs of tables, chairs, etc. See *Rising Stretchers* and *Stretcher*.

SALTIRE

SAMARA. A trademark name for a reddish-brown hardwood from French Equatorial Africa. It is rotary-cut, and usually has a large swirled grain pattern. It is also called gaboon wood.

HUGUES SAMBIN

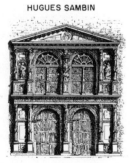

SAMBIN, HUGUES (c. 1520–1600). A French architect, furniture designer, cabinetmaker, and engraver. He worked in the tradition of the Italian Renaissance, and in 1572 he published a book of designs which featured rich French Renaissance or Burgundian forms with Italian overtones. Illustrated is the portal to Saint-Michel at Dijon, where he made use of a series of concentric arches which were typically Gothic. He used the human figure and other carved motifs for his heavily embellished furniture designs.

SAMITE. A heavy silk fabric of the Middle Ages which was usually interwoven with gold and heavily embroidered. It was used mainly for upholstery and garments.

SAMPLER. A needlework exercise performed by a child or novice in sewing or embroidery. It was especially in vogue during the 18th and 19th centuries. The sampler usually showed an alphabet or a quotation which was embroidered in a variety of stitches and colors.

SAND SHAKING. A 17th-century Dutch technique for deepening or shading the color of pieces of wood inlay by dipping them into hot sand.

SANDALWOOD. An East Indian and Pacific islands hard, yellow, close-grained wood used for ornamental objects and inlays rather than actual furniture. Illustrated is a late-18th-century door panel carved out of sandalwood, from Travancore, India.

SANDALWOOD

SANDBLASTING. A method of cleaning or polishing stone surfaces by a bombardment of sand particles propelled by jets of steam or air. It is also a technique for cutting or engraving glass or crystal in a similar manner. The blasted area is usually cloudy and gray and not as smooth to the touch as polished glass.

SANDSTONE. A natural stone which consists mainly of sand cemented together with silicic acid. Small amounts of oxide of lime, carbonate of lime, etc., are found in sandstone.

SANGUINE. From "sanguin," the French for "bloody." A reddish-brown or terra-cotta color chalk which is used for drawing. Many Renaissance drawings or studies for paintings were executed in this soft, pastel-like technique.

SANSOVINO, JACOPO (1486–1570). A Venetian architect and sculptor who designed the Library of St. Mark in Venice, the statues of Mars and Neptune for the Doge's Palace, the Zecca Mint, and the Palazzo Corner della Ca' Grande. Illustrated is part of the tomb of a prelate in the Church of Santa Maria de Popolo created by Sansovino.

JACOPO SANSOVINO

SANTA MARIA DELLA SALUTE. Church in Venice designed (1632) by Baldassare Longhena in the Italian Renaissance style. It is octagonal in plan, with a central area 65' in diameter with Corinthian columns set in the angles. The circular dome is set on a high drum, and is connected to the outer walls by means of scrolled buttresses.

SAPELE or SAPELI. An African wood which resembles mahogany in color and texture, but is more evenly striped and harder,

SANTA MARIA DELLA SALUTE

SAPPANWOOD

SARACENIC

SARACENIC

SARCOPHAGUS

SARCOPHAGUS

SASH WINDOW

heavier, and tougher than African mahogany. Sapele is usually dark red-brown in color. It is also called tiama.

SAPPANWOOD. A wood which closely resembles brazilwood, and is native to Java, Ceylon, and India. Sappanwood was used for furniture that was produced in the Dutch colonies during the 17th and 18th centuries. The furniture was based on models and designs supplied by the Dutch.

SARACENIC. Showing a Mohammedan influence. The Mohammedan Saracens (Moors) greatly influenced Spanish arts and architecture from the 8th century on, when they swept from Morocco into Spain. Saracenic Spanish arts are also called Moorish. The Saracenic motifs were chiefly abstract geometric and interlaced patterns. The Moors introduced the horseshoe arch into Europe.

SARAN. A term for the plastic vinylidine chloride from which multifilaments are extruded for use in tough, heavy-duty fabrics. It is a Dow Chemical compound product. Saran is stiff, sunlight- and weather-resistant, and excellent for outdoor use (outdoor upholstery, auto upholstery, etc.).

SARAZIN, JACQUES (1590–1660). A French sculptor of decorative elements during the reign of Louis XIV.

SARCOPHAGUS. A stone coffin originated by the ancients. Illustrated is the sarcophagus of Napoleon I in Les Invalides. In the 18th century, a wine cooler usually made of mahogany with a lead liner, and often part of a sideboard. It was also called a "cellarette" or "garde du vin."

SARKING. A lining layer under the roofing material of a pitched roof.

SASH BAR. The strip of wood or metal which subdivides the panes of glass in the frame of a window. See *Mullion* and *Tracery*.

SASH WINDOW. Usually a double-hung window which is opened and shut by raising or lowering one of the windows.

SATEEN or SATINE. A cotton fabric with a satin weave. It has a lustrous face and a dull back, and it is commonly used as a lining material for draperies, etc.

SATIN. A fabric which was originally made of silk and imported from China. It was known as "Zaytūn," after the Chinese seaport. It is a basic weave, and the face of the fabric is smooth and glossy while the back is dull. The fabric is stronger when the silk fibers are blended with linen or cotton wefts. There are many types of satins. See *Satin: Antique, Charmeuse, Hammered, Ribbed,* and *Slipper.*

SATIN, ANTIQUE. A rich, heavy fabric with a dull, uneven texture. It is used for upholstery, drapery, etc. It may be made of silk, cotton, rayon, silk and cotton, etc. See *Satin.*

SATIN, CHARMEUSE. A satin fabric with an organzine warp and a spun silk weft.

SATIN, HAMMERED. A satin fabric which has been treated to have a textured surface effect similar to that of beaten or hammered metal.

SATIN, RIBBED. Bengaline or faille fabric woven with satin face ribs which gives the fabric a lustrous unbroken surface. It can also be given a moiré finish. See *Moiré.*

SATIN, SLIPPER. A heavyweight fabric of silk or synthetic fibers with a cotton back. Originally the material was used to make slippers in the 18th and 19th centuries. It is currently used as an upholstery and drapery fabric.

SATIN FINISH. A smooth, low-luster finish on fabric, paper, paint, etc.

SATINE. See *Sateen or Satine.*

SATINE RUBANNE. Satin ribbon. A straight-grained, strong, durable South African wood which has ribbon-like markings. It is used for inlays and decorative banding, and it is also called "capomo."

SATINWOOD. A highly figured, close-grained, hard, durable wood which is native to Ceylon and the East Indies. It is light yellow to golden brown in color with a lustrous satin-like quality. It was a favorite wood in the Louis XV and Louis XVI periods, and it was also favored by Adam, Chippendale, and Sheraton for inlay and veneering. Hepplewhite used satinwood as a background for painted medallions. A Robert Adam sideboard of the mid-18th century is illustrated. It was made of mahogany with satinwood inlays. Note the knife urns. Also see *Age of Satinwood* and *Seddon, George.*

SATINWOOD

SATYR MASK

PIAT JOSEPH SAUVAGE

SAVONAROLA CHAIRS

SATYR MASK. Germanic motif which reached the height of its popularity in England from 1730 to 1740. The ornament was carved on the knees of furniture legs, and it was also used decoratively on other areas. The satyr was originally a classic motif. It also appears in French and Italian Renaissance designs.

SÄULE. German for "column" or "pillar."

SÄULENHALLE. German for "colonnade" or "portico."

SÄULENKNAUF. German for "capital."

SAULNIER, JULES. A French 19th-century architect who was noted for his chocolate factory constructed in 1871–1872 at Noisiel-sur-Marne near Paris. It was the first true skeleton-type building. The structure rested on four piers set in the Marne River, and was erected on four hollow square-sectioned iron girders. The iron skeleton was designed to carry the whole weight, with the hollow brick used merely as filling. Diagonal iron stiffeners were used for reinforcement.

SAUNIER, CLAUDE CHARLES. An 18th-century French master ébéniste (cabinetmaker) who worked for Louis XV and Louis XVI. His marquetry work was in the style of Jean François Oeben.

SAUSAGE TURNING. A wood turning which resembled links of sausages, and was typical of German Renaissance turnings. The same type of turning appeared in 19th-century American furniture.

SAUVAGE, PIAT JOSEPH. An 18th-century French painter of the Louis XVI period. He created trompe l'oeil paintings which simulated sculptured bas-reliefs. These monochromatic paintings (grisailles) were used on overdoors, overmantels, etc. See *Grisaille.*

WILLIAM SAVERY

SAVERY, WILLIAM (1721–1787). A Philadelphia cabinetmaker who worked in the ornamental Chippendale style. His highboys and lowboys are considered among the finest produced in Colonial America.

SAVONAROLA CHAIR. An early Italian Renaissance X-shaped chair. The seat was often made of interlaced strips of wood, and the back was usually carved or decorated with inlay work. The chair was named for the martyred Italian monk Girolamo Savonarola (1452–1498).

SAVONNERIE. A famous rug and tapestry factory in France, founded in 1604. The name also applies to high-pile, hand-woven rugs which were produced in this factory. They were often decorated with pastel floral and scroll designs. Illustrated is a carpet design by Robert de Cotte prepared in the early 18th century for the Savonnerie Factory.

SAWBUCK TABLE. A 17th-century simple tabletop which rested on X-shaped trestles or two-legged standards. It was also called a trestle table, and appeared in Europe and America.

SCAFFOLDING. A temporary skeletal framework built around a structure or object, or on one side of it. It provides a means of working on the outside of a building, or inside a large unplatformed area. The word also means a framework around a piece of sculpture.

SCAGLIOLA. An imitation of marble made of gypsum or plaster of Paris, chips of marble, and coloring matter. It was invented in Italy in the 17th century. Scagliola was used to make chimneypieces in the 18th century in England, and the Adam brothers used this technique on their interiors. Illustrated is an 18th-century scagliola chimneypiece designed by Thomas Milton.

SAVONNERIE

SCAGLIOLA

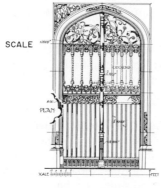

SCALE

SCALE. The dimensions of a unit of furniture in relation to the height and width of the area in which it is to be placed. The relationship between one piece of furniture and another in size and proportion. In a scale drawing, the drawing is proportionately reduced or enlarged in relation to a given ratio, for example, 1/4″ = 1′.

SCALING. An architectural surface finish which resembles the scales of a fish. It is a technique used by architects and designers to fill in the background of small panels. See *Imbricate*.

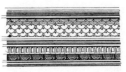

SCALING

SCALLOP SHELL

SCALLOP SHELL

SCALLOP SHELL. A shell motif used as a decoration. It was very popular in the late Renaissance, Louis XIV, Louis XV, Queen Anne, and Georgian periods. It was often found on Goddard 18th-century kneehole desks and cabriole-legged highboys (see *Goddard, John*). It is a semicircular shell with ridges radiating from a point at the center bottom. The shell as a motif often appears on the knees of cabriole legs, on aprons, on crests of furniture, and also as a hood on architectural pieces of case goods. A Queen Anne chair is illustrated.

SCALLOP SHELL

SCALLOPED ARCH

SCALLOPED EDGE

SCALLOPED ARCH. An arch having more than five foils. It is a design usually associated with Moorish architecture.

SCALLOPED BORDERS. See *Cutout Borders*.

SCALLOPED EDGE. An edge or border that has been marked or cut into segments of a circle. An outer perimeter which resembles the wavy, fluted contour of a scallop shell.

SCALPTURATUM OPUS

SCALPTURATUM OPUS. A Latin term for a technique of inlaying colored marble. It was introduced into Italy in the first century B.C.

SCANALATO. Italian for "fluting."

SCANDINAVIAN MODERN

SCANDINAVIAN MODERN. A simple, chaste, refined, up-to-date version of the traditional Empire style. It was introduced in the 1930's as Swedish or Danish Modern. The furniture has a sculptured quality with gracefully tapered legs and gently curved arms and backs. Walnut and teak are the woods most often used in interpreting this style. There is an almost complete lack of applied decorative elements; the hardware is chaste and simple.

SCANUM. A bench of ancient Rome.

SCARAMOUCHE. A decorative representation of a buffoon or clown of 17th- and 18th-century Italian comedy. The figure was usually represented in black with a black cape and hat and a grotesque mask. It was a decorative element in 18th-century English, French, and Italian designs.

SCANUM

SCARF JOINT. In cabinetry, two beveled edges laid one over the other to form a continuous level plane. An overlapping joint.

SCATTER RUG. A small area rug used as an accent on the floor. Scatter rugs are often used at the bedside, in entries and hallways, etc. They come in various sizes, shapes, colors, and patterns. The fiber content may range from wool through nylon, Acrilan, and cotton, to sisal. See *Area Rug*.

SCENIC. A wallpaper mural usually made up of three or four panels that create a continuous scene, vista, or design. It may be printed in a variety of colors on any number of background papers, vinyls, or cloths.

SCHLUSS. German for the keystone of an arch or vault.

SCHOOL. A group of artists, architects, etc., whose work shows similar characteristics owing to the influence of an individual master, region, or body of theory; the art of a country. See *Hudson River School*.

SCHWIBBOGEN. German for a "flying buttress" or "pier arch."

SCISSORS CHAIR. A folding X-shaped chair. It was used in ancient Egyptian, classic Greek, and Roman times, and was the prototype of the Dante and Savonarola chairs. Illustrated is an ancient Greek example. See *Dante Chair, Savonarola Chair,* and illustration for *Early French Renaissance*.

SCISSORS CHAIR

SCOINSON ARCH. See *Rere-Arch*.

SCONCE. An ornamental wall bracket used to hold candles or electric bulbs. The word derives ultimately from "abscondere," Latin for "to hide"; originally a sconce was a shield or protection for a flame, or a lantern to protect a light. See *Applique* and *Girandole*.

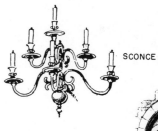

SCONCE

SCONCHEON ARCH. See *Rere-Arch*.

SCOOP SEAT

SCONCHEON ARCH

SCOOP SEAT. A slightly concave seat which is dipped to accommodate the contour of a seated person. It is found in classic chairs, and reappears in the late 18th century in Sheraton's work (illustrated) and the Empire style. A variation appears in present-day contour and molded plywood chairs. It is also called a "drop seat."

SCOTCH BOND. A brick pattern like the English *Garden Wall Bond.*

SCOTCHGARD. A trademark name for a fluorochemical process which is applied to fabrics to make them more resistant to stains from dirt, water, or oil. The process allows the fabric to breathe and does not impair the "hand" or color of the fabric. Scotchgard is produced by the Perma Dry Company, Inc.

SCOTIA. A concave molding which resembles the S curve made by two connecting curves of different radii.

SCOTIA

SIR GEORGE GILBERT SCOTT

SCOTT, SIR GEORGE GILBERT (1811–1878). An English architect who greatly favored the "Gothic" style which was having a revival in England at that time. Scott originally designed some British Government offices in Whitehall, London, in the French Gothic style. After many changes and much pressure exerted by Lord Palmerston, Scott gave the design an Italian Renaissance type of façade which was "beautifully got up in outline."

SCRATCH CARVING. A simple country-style carving done with a V-shaped chisel.

SCRATCH COAT. A rough first coat of plaster which is scratched and scored before the plaster is thoroughly dry. The finish, or smooth coat will adhere better to this coarse wall texture.

SCREED. The guide band which is applied to a surface before the application of plaster, the final layer of a concrete floor, or the finishing material of a roof (tile, asphalt, etc.).

SCREEN. A separating device. A divider. A partition or enclosure of wood, metal, or stone which can be decorative, functional, or both. See illustration for *Rood.* See also *Papier-Mâché* for an illustration of a Victorian design.

SCREEN TABLE

SCREEN TABLE. A late-18th-century Sheraton design for a lady's desk with a screen set behind the desk surface. It permitted the lady to work near a fire and yet be protected from flying embers, etc. The screen let down into a slot opening, making a level surface when it was not in use. A drawer was placed below the slider.

SCREW STAIR. A spiral staircase that twists around a slender pole.

SCRIBANNE. An imposing desk-cupboard of the Louis XIV period.

SCRIBE. In carpentry, to fit one material to another, as the side of a shaped wooden strip to an uneven wall surface. The strip has to be shaped to fit the irregular surface contour of the wall.

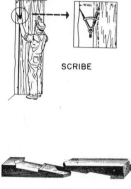

SCRIBE

SCRIBE MOLDING. A small pliable strip of wood used to cover up an irregular joint or crack.

SCRIBING. A technique of fitting frames, moldings, etc., onto irregular surfaces. The unit to be applied must be cut and shaped to fit these irregularities.

SCRIBING

SCRIM. A lightweight, open-weave, coarse cotton fabric similar to marquisette. It is usually white, cream, or ecru, and it is used for needlework. Sometimes the scrim can have larger openings ($\frac{1}{4}'' \times \frac{1}{4}''$) and be heavily sized. A form of scrim is also used to cover and hold the joints between plasterboards before plastering.

SCRINIUM. A round box of the classic Roman period which was used to hold the "books" of the time. Such boxes were generally made of beechwood, and they could be locked or sealed when necessary. The books were actually sewn in scroll form and carried about in the scrinium. A scrinium, as illustrated, would be a library case, or a collection of scrolls.

SCRINIUM

 SCRITOIRE

SCRITOIRE. French for "writing table." See *Secretary* and *Riesner, Jean-Henri* for an illustration.

SCROLL

SCROLL

SCROLL FOOT

SCROLL PEDIMENT

SCROLLED TOP MIRROR

SCROWLED CHAIR

SCRUTOIRE

SCROLL. An S or C curved design. An artistic invention in ornamentation used with acanthus leaves, laurel, oak, ivy, and wheat. A spiraling and convoluting line, like a rolled piece of paper, makes the scroll.

SCROLL BED. See *Gondola Bed* and *Sleigh Bed*.

SCROLL FOOT. A flattened scroll at the end of a cabriole leg. It originated in the Louis XIV period, and appears in England in the William and Mary and Chippendale periods.

SCROLL MOLDING

SCROLL MOLDING. A molding which resembles a curled piece of paper. It was popular in English Gothic architecture.

SCROLL PEDIMENT. A broken pediment with each half in a reverse curve ending in a scroll at the outside ends. The open center area usually is trimmed with a finial or ornament. See *Broken Pediment* and *Finial*.

SCROLLED TOP MIRROR. A Chippendale-type design found in America in the mid-18th century. It is similar to a silhouette or fretwork mirror, but is usually characterized by a broken pediment with a centered carved ornament. The mirror was often made of mahogany with gilt decoration.

SCROLLWORK. Ornate, lacelike wood cutouts made with a jigsaw. It was a popular decoration in the Steamboat Gothic period in the 19th-century United States. See *Jigsaw Detail*.

SCROWLED CHAIR. An English chair of the mid-16th to the mid-17th centuries with a heavy, high, panel back. It usually had a heavy top rail and cresting which was partly supported by brackets attached to the upper sides of the stiles. The chair had flat-shaped arms attached to the front supports, baluster legs, and low-placed stretchers. See *Wainscot Chair*.

SCRUTOIRE. A writing desk. Often a slope-top desk which has a lid that opens to form a horizontal writing surface.

SCULPTURE. The art of creating forms and decorations in three dimensions or in relief. Carving is the process of freeing the form from the material. Modeling is the building up of the form from some plastic material like clay or plasteline. Both are techniques of sculpture. Carving is usually done in wood, stone, or marble. Modeling is done in clay or wax, and then cast in plaster or metal, usually bronze. Illustrated is the head of the famous French Gothic statue "Le beau Dieu" of the Amiens Cathedral (13th century).

SCULPTURE

SCULPTURED RUG. See *Carved Rug.*

SCUTCHEON. See *Escutcheon.*

SEAGRAM BUILDING. A 42-story skyscraper in New York City designed by Ludwig Mies van der Rohe and Philip Cortelyou Johnson. Made of glass and bronze mullions, spandrels and windows, it is a clean rectangular shape with a modular construction. The curtain wall is accented by gray tinted glass and granite panels. The interior lobby walls are faced with travertine. At night, the building is lighted in accord with a preconceived architectural scheme.

SCUTCHEON

SEAM. The joint made by two surfaces meeting: the butt or overlap of two pieces of wallpaper, the sewed line of two pieces of fabric in a drapery, the hairline between two joined pieces of wood or pieces of veneer.

SEASONED LUMBER. Green wood that has been dried in the air or in a kiln to improve its durability for furniture construction, and to control warping and checking. See *Kiln-dried.*

SEAWEED MARQUETRY. A popular form of ornament during the William and Mary and the Queen Anne periods in England. It was an inlay of various woods in an arabesque pattern of small leaves and seaweed forms, also called "endive." The concept and design were probably based on the look of Boulle work. Illustrated is a Queen Anne press of the early 18th century.

SEAWEED MARQUETRY

SECESSION MOVEMENT. See *Sezession.*

SECOND EMPIRE or LATE EMPIRE. The period in France, approximately between 1852 and 1871, which produced massive scrolled and rollover-type furniture which blended the Empire with Louis XV motifs rather than classic elements. In America, Duncan Phyfe produced ungainly "butcher furniture" in this style.

SECRÉTAIRE

SECONDARY COLORS. Colors produced by mixing any two of the three primary colors. Red combined with yellow produces orange. Blue and yellow make green, and blue mixed with red will form a violet color. Therefore the three secondary colors are orange, green, and violet.

SECRÉTAIRE. French for "desk." See *Gouthière* and *Kingwood* for illustrations. See *Secretary*.

SECRÉTAIRE À ABATTANT. A drop-lid desk. See *Scrutoire* and *Secretary* illustration.

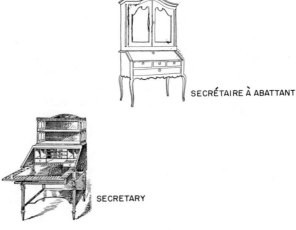

SECRÉTAIRE À ABATTANT

SECRETARY

SECRETARY. A desk surface with a space for writing appliances which is combined with a drawer base below and a bookcase cabinet above. In the 17th century, it was essentially a "bureau" (a writing table on a chest of drawers with a hinged desk arrangement equipped with brass quadrants). During the 18th century, the bookcase or shelf units were added over the desk surface. See *Bureau, Scritoire,* and *Scrutoire.* A Sheraton design is illustrated. See *Trelliswork* for another illustration.

SECTION

SECTION. In architecture, a vertically sliced view through a building, molding, etc. This view gives a clear impression of the silhouette as well as the internal construction of the object. The section view can also give vertical dimensions.

SECTIONAL FURNITURE

SECTIONAL FURNITURE. Upholstered or case furniture made in modules or small units which can be pulled together in a variety of ways to make larger units, units that turn corners, etc. The term usually refers to a sectional couch which is composed of two, three, or more parts, one of which is usually a curved or angled corner piece. It is possible with this type of modular furniture to have a continuous couch on two adjacent walls. Each part of the sectional couch can be a completely finished piece that may be used individually.

SECTROID. The curved or bent surface between the groins in a vaulted ceiling. See *Panache*.

SEDAN CHAIR. An 18th-century enclosed chair which was a form of transportation. It was usually carried by four men, and it originated in Sedan, France, in the 17th century. The sedan chair was popular in England in the 17th and 18th centuries. The French name for this chair is "chaise à porteur." See *Palanquin.*

SEDDON, GEORGE (1727–1801). An English cabinetmaker, furniture designer, and upholsterer. He worked with his sons George and Thomas, and his son-in-law Thomas Shakleton. Seddon made rich, elegant pieces and favored satinwood. Illustrated is a satinwood dressing table made by the firm of Seddon and Shakleton at the end of the 18th century.

SEDDON AND SHAKLETON. Late-18th-century English cabinet-makers who made fine carved and painted furniture in the Sheraton, Louis XVI, and Directoire or Regency styles. Much of Seddon's work has been attributed to Sheraton. The firm made many of the furnishings used by King George IV at Windsor Castle. For illustrations see *Satinwood* and *Seddon, George.*

SEDIA. The Italian word for "chair." Illustrated is an early-19th-century Italian Directoire chair designed by Guiseppe Soli.

SEDILLIA. Traditionally, the seats for the clergy along the south wall of the sanctuary of a church.

SEGMENTAL ARCH. An arch shaped as part of a circle but less than a semicircle. It has a curve that is less than half a circle. An elliptical arch.

SEGMENTAL CORNERS. The corners of a rectangular panel that are broken into curves. The cutout corners are frequently decorated with patera or rosettes. This type of ornament was often used by the Adam brothers in their designs for ceilings, walls, and doors. Illustrated is a Hepplewhite sideboard which has segmental corners on the doors and panels. See *Patera.*

SEGMENTAL CORNERS

SECTROID

SEDAN CHAIR

GEORGE SEDDON

SEDIA

SEGMENTAL ARCH

SEGMENTAL CORNERS

SEGMENTAL FRONT

SEIGNORIAL CHAIR

SERPENTINE

SERRATED EDGE

SEGMENTAL FRONT. See *Bow Front* and *Swell Front*. A Sheraton pier table is illustrated.

SEIGNORIAL CHAIR. A chair of state which in the Gothic and Renaissance periods was usually high-backed and had solid arm supports and a solid base. The chair was often canopied and elaborately carved. Less imposing versions were used for the master of the manor or castle. Illustrated is the Coronation chair from Westminster Abbey in England. See *Canopy Chair*.

SELVAGE or SELVEDGE. The reinforced up-and-down outer edges of a fabric. It is also the unpatterned or unprinted margin of wallpaper (on either side of the design) which is usually imprinted with the name, number, manufacturer's name, and joining and repeat instructions.

SEMAINIER. A tall bedroom chest with seven drawers, introduced in the Louis XV period. The seven drawers were originally one for each day of the week. It was similar to a chiffonier, which is wider and does not have a specified number of drawers.

SEMÉ. The French for "sown." A minute floral motif scattered over the background of a brocaded fabric. In the Louis XVI period, tiny rosebuds were often found within or around satin and faille stripes woven on the fabric.

SEPIA PRINT. A print of a reddish-brown tint. Sepia is a brownish pigment which was originally made from the cuttle-fish.

SERAGLIO. An enclosed or protected area in a house. A harem in a Turkish palace.

SERIOGRAPHS. Silk-screened prints in the field of graphic arts. See *Silk-screened*.

SERPENTINE. Snakelike. The juxtaposition of a concave and a convex form to create a sinuous line. Two connected cyma curves. Usually the center curve is convex and prominent. When the center curve is concave and receding, the line is called a reverse serpentine. The serpentine line was used in Louis XV commodes, and also in 18th-century English cupboards, desks, and chests. A Hepplewhite table is illustrated.

SERRATED EDGE. A zigzag, toothed, or dentil edge. A series of inverted V's in a continuous band.

SERRE-PAPIERS. See *Table à Gradin*.

SERRURERIE. The French term for "wrought iron." Illustrated is a Renaissance well. See *Wrought Iron.*

SERVANTE. See *Rafraîchissoir (or Servante).*

SERVANTE

SETTEE

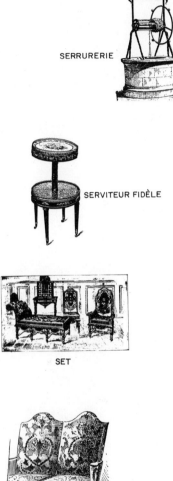

SERRURERIE

SERVITEUR FIDÈLE

SET

SETTEE

SERVER or SERVING TABLE. An auxiliary piece of furniture in a dining room, which is used to hold or contain dishes, glassware, silver, napery, bottles, etc. It usually has drawers, and it may also contain cabinet space. The larger units are similar to buffets, and the smaller pieces are like rafraîchissoirs, servantes, or dumbwaiters. The top surface is used to hold food, platters, and service pieces which will be used at the dining table.

SERVITEUR FIDÈLE. From the French, literally, "loyal servant." The French version of a dumbwaiter; a multitiered table. Illustrated is a Louis XVI design by Martin Carlin. See *Dumbwaiter* and *Rafraîchissoir.*

SET. A matched group of furniture coordinated to be used together, like a headboard, night tables, dresser, and chest of drawers all made in the same decorative style, ornamented in the same manner, finished in the same color, and intended to be used together. The group might also be called a "suite." Illustrated is a matched set of carved and gilt upholstered furniture of the period of Charles II of England (second half of the 17th century).

SET or SETT. A small rectangular wood or stone paving block.

SETTEE. A seating device which developed from the settle. A long seat with a carved or upholstered back, arms, and a soft seat. It was originally designed to hold two or more persons, and settees usually matched the individual chairs of the period in contour and chair-back decoration. They were often described as two-, three-, or four-chair-back settees. A front leg was provided between each chair back, therefore a three-chair-back settee would have four legs in front to delineate the three seats. It was popular in the late 17th and early 18th centuries.

SETTLE

SETTLES. Benches, usually of oak, for two or more persons. A settle was usually provided with a high back and arms, and sometimes there were "ears" or "wings" at either end. It was, originally, a popular seating device in the Middle Ages, often carved, paneled, and richly decorated. A settle with a hinged seat over a chest is called a "box settle." A canopied settle was called a "canapé." Illustrated is an English carved oak settle of the second half of the 17th century (the reign of Charles II).

SEVERN BRIDGE (1775–1779). A bold single-arch bridge with a span of 100$^1/_2$' and a rise of 45', and made of five cast-iron ribs. It was the first cast-iron bridge erected, and it crossed the Severn River in England. The bridge was designed and executed by John Wilkinson and Abraham Darby III of the Darby Ironworks family.

SEVERY. In architecture, a bay or compartment in a vaulted roof. Illustrated is a section of the Notre-Dame Cathedral in Paris.

SEVERY

SEVERY

SÈVRES

SÈVRES. A porcelain factory at Sèvres near Paris which was founded in 1756. Mme de Pompadour obtained royal patronage for this ceramic factory during the reign of Louis XV. Here were produced magnificent vases and plaques for furniture and table inserts. The term "Sèvres" is also used to identify the products of the factory, including the vases and urns of a special rose color, as well as King's blue. Illustrated is a Sèvres vase from the Grand Trianon. See *Kingwood* for an illustration of Sèvres plaques used as a furniture embellishment.

SEWING TABLE. A popular small working table of the mid and late 18th century. The table was usually equipped with drawers, trays, spool racks, and a cloth bag below for sewing materials. Sheraton (illustrated), Hepplewhite, and others designed many such pieces, which were also called "pouch tables." French Louis XVI and Empire designs were also created to satisfy this need.

SEWING TABLE

SEYMOUR, JOHN. An 18th-century American cabinetmaker who worked in Boston.

SEZESSION. A series of artistic revolutions which occurred in Germany and Austria during the last decade of the 19th century. The avant-garde artists left the old academic societies, and organized exhibitions of their own progressive new Impressionist or Art Nouveau styles. The three major eruptions took place in Munich in 1892, in Vienna in 1897, and in Berlin in 1899. See *Art Nouveau*.

SFUMATO. The Italian word for "smoky." In painting it refers to the blurring or hazing of the outline of an object so that it tends to blend in with the background. Leonardo da Vinci was a leading painter who used this technique.

SGABELLE or SGABELLO. A small 16th-century Italian Renaissance chair which is usually identified by its carved back splat, octagonal seat and carved trestle supports instead of legs.

SGABELLE

SGRAFFITO (GRAFFITO). Italian for "scratcher." A decorative technique of 16th-century Italy, in which tinted plaster was covered by white plaster (or vice versa). The top layer was "scratched" or cut into in a decorative pattern to reveal the color of the bottom layer; thus the pattern appeared in the color of the bottom layer. Arabesques were popular designs executed in this technique. Illustrated is a sgraffito panel from the Palazzo Montargo in Florence. See *Giocondo, Fra*.

SGRAFFITO

SGRAFFITO

SHADE. A color with black added as opposed to a tint, which is a color with white added. The term also is used to describe a protection or covering: lampshade, window shade, etc. See *Lampshade* and *Window Shade*.

SHADE CLOTH. See *Holland Shade Cloth*.

SHAFT. The central portion of a column or pilaster. The area between the capital and the base.

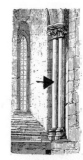

SHAFT

SHAGREEN. The untanned skins of horses, mules, or sharks which were finished with a granular surface and dyed green. It was sometimes used for covering small pieces of furniture in the 18th century.

SHAKE. A rough split-wood shingle much favored in the western part of the United States.

SHAKER

SHAVING MIRROR

SHAVING TABLE

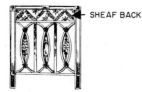

SHEAF BACK

THOMAS SHEARER

SHAKER. A religious sect in America at the end of the 18th century and early 19th century who preferred simple, plain, functional furniture devoid of "wicked decorations." The line of their designs is almost 20th-century modern in its clean straight line and the concept of built-ins.

SHAKER MODERN. A simple, chaste, up-to-date version of early-19th-century Shaker furniture. Clean, straight-lined, gentle tapers and the pegging and dovetailing details are the visible embellishments. Maple, cherry, and other fruitwoods are often used and given an oil finish.

SHANTUNG. A heavy grade of pongee originally made in Shantung, China. It is usually manufactured of wild silk, cotton, or a combination of the two. See *Pongee*.

SHAVING MIRROR. A popular device of the 18th century. A swing tilt mirror, often fitted with drawers below to hold razors, jewelry, etc., the unit could be set on top of a chest. A Sheraton design is illustrated. See *Standing Mirror*.

SHAVING TABLE. A clever, complicated, and involved dressing-shaving table of the Chippendale period (illustrated). It was often equipped with hinged side table surfaces, a basin area, a spring-up mirror, and drawers, compartments, etc. It is also called a "reflecting dressing table."

SHAW, NORMAN. A 19th-century English architect who designed domestic architecture in a romantic "Queen Anne" style based on the *Stick Style* construction. He introduced new freedom in the interior space arrangements, with reception rooms opening from a wide living hall.

SHEAF BACK. A delicate late-18th-century French chair back design resembling a bundle of stylized wheat which fanned out to meet the top rail. These chairs usually had rush or cane seats. The design was similar to the Hepplewhite chair backs of the same time.

SHEARER, THOMAS. An 18th-century English cabinetmaker and designer and contemporary of Sheraton. Shearer was influenced by Hepplewhite's work. In 1788 he published a book of designs, and he is credited with designing the sideboard as it is known today. Illustrated is part of one of his sideboard designs and a demilune buffet. See *Table* for another illustration of his work. See *Hepplewhite, George*.

THOMAS SHEARER

SHEEN RUGS. Also called "lustre rugs" or "domestic-Oriental rugs." A shine is chemically produced on these usually inexpensive rugs.

SHEER. Usually used to describe lightweight, gauzy, transparent fabrics like china silk, marquisette, net, maline, etc. These "sheers" may be woven of natural or synthetic fibers.

SHEET GLASS. Glass formed in long, ribbon-like strips, and then cut into sheets.

SHELDON'S TAPESTRIES. Tapestries which were produced in the time of Elizabeth I by Flemish weavers working in England under the supervision of William Sheldon.

SHELF. A horizontally fixed platform of wood, glass, or other rigid material. It can be set onto a wall or in a cupboard, bookcase, dresser, etc. The shelf is usually meant to hold books, china, bibelots, etc. Chippendale designed many elegant hanging shelf units, some with glass doors, others carved or inlaid. Illustrated is a 17th-century carved oak German buffet unit. Note the stepped shelves between the lower closed cabinet and the open cupboard above.

SHELF

SHELL. In architecture or furniture construction, the framework or basic construction. The unadorned, unsheathed unit. See also *Cockleshell*, *Rocaille*, and *Scallop Shell*.

SHELL

SHELL

SHELLAC. A natural resin which is soluble in alcohol. When applied to wood, it produces a shiny surface. Shellac is often used as a prime coat on unfinished wood pieces. It acts as a sealer.

SHERATON, THOMAS (1751–1806). The last of the great 18th-century furniture designers. He published *The Cabinet-Maker and Upholsterer's Drawing Book* from 1791 to 1794. Sheraton was greatly influenced by Hepplewhite and Chippendale, but even more so by the Louis XVI style in France. He used satinwood veneers, straight lines, and inlays rather than painted decorations, and there was an overall elegance, grace, and refinement in his early and middle years. In his later works, he tried to introduce an extravagant and sometimes aggravated version of the French Empire style. Urns, rosettes, festoons, scrolls, and pendant flowers were some of the decorative motifs favored by Sheraton.

THOMAS SHERATON

SHEVERET

SHEVERET

SHEVERET. An elegant drawing-room writing table with a small shelf in back for books. The front portion of the top was hinged so it could be turned over, and the front legs pulled out to support it, thus forming a writing surface. It was originally a Louis XVI design which was Anglicized at the end of the 18th century. Illustrated is a late-18th-century Sheraton variation. Books were meant to be kept on the upper back part of the unit. The writing surface falls over like a card table, and it is supported by the drawer in the frame rather than the legs.

SHIELD BACKS

SHIELD BACK. The shape of a chair back popularized by Hepplewhite in the mid-18th century in England. The chair back resembles a shield-shaped frame with a tapered point at the center bottom. The frame would sometimes have a carved splat representing the feathers of the Prince of Wales, or a sheaf of wheat. See *Prince of Wales Feathers* for illustration.

SHIKI. In fabric, a heavy silk or rayon rep made with irregular-sized filling threads. In wallpaper, a paper-backed fabric with silk threads on the face which simulates the actual shiki silk, or an embossed paper which simulates the texture of the fabric.

SHINGLE STYLE. A domestic architectural innovation of about 1870 which was based on the Queen Anne *Stick Style* of Norman Shaw of England, and on Japanese forms. •Buildings were sheathed in shingles (cedar boards) over a wood frame in curved and straight sweeps. Ground-floor space plans became more open, and porches or piazzas became noticeable external features.

SHINGLES

SHINGLES. Thin wood tiles, usually of cedar, which are used for facing outer walls, roofs, etc. These overlapping plaques are also produced today in synthetic materials.

SHINTO TEMPLES. Japanese temples devoted to the observances of the Shinto religion.

SHIRRING. A gathered effect of fabric drawn on a thread or a rod; many small folds result. An *Austrian Drape* is a fine example of a controlled shirred effect.

SHISH. A fretted wooden lattice in Egyptian architecture. See *Moucharaby* and *Qamariyyah*.

SHOE or SHOE PIECE. The part of the back seat rail of a chair that projects out to support the bottom of the splat. It is often found on brace-back Windsor chairs (see illustration). The shoe also refers to the disk often found under the foot of a furniture leg. A ferrule. A mid-17th-century Jacobean stool is illustrated.

SHUTTER

SHOE

SHOJI. A Japanese-type simple geometric frame which is sub-divided into smaller rectangular panels. The framework is usually composed of narrow black lacquered wood strips, and the open rectangular spaces are filled in with translucent materials like rice paper, polyplastex, plastics, fabrics, etc. The shoji panels are used as screens, dividers, doors that slide behind one another on a track (Japanese style), or as window coverings.

SHOJI

SHORING

SHORING. A temporary wooden framework used to support a building which is being repaired or an unstable wall.

SHOT. In carpet construction, the relationship of weft threads (across the loom) to the tufts or loops of surface yarn. A "two shot" means two weft threads between each row of surface tufts. The larger the number, the more material, and the closer the carpet construction, and therefore the stronger the weave.

SHOULDERED ARCH. An arch with a rectangular lintel which is supported by shaped corbels. The curved inner edges of the corbels create the archlike effect.

SHOVED JOINTS. In masonry, vertical joints made by mortar troweled on the ends of bricks (buttering), the bricks then being shoved next to those bricks that are already laid.

SHOVED JOINTS

SHOW WOOD. The exposed, finished wood on upholstered furniture like legs, frames, etc. Illustrated is a Louis XVI armchair.

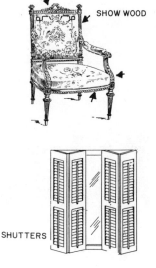
SHOW WOOD

SHUTTER. An internal or external covering for a window made of wood or metal. It may be a flat, paneled, louvered, or fabric covered frame. The shutter has been used as a window treatment on the insides of houses. External shutters are used to protect the windows and cut down on drafts.

SHUTTERS

SHUTTERING

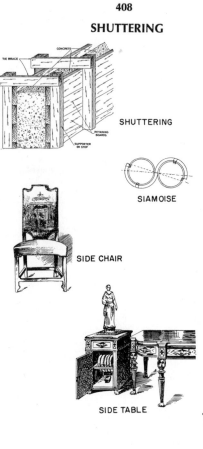

SHUTTERING

SIAMOISE

SIDE CHAIR

SIDE TABLE

SHUTTERING. The use of temporary walls of wood or metal to enclose poured concrete. These temporary pieces are removed after the concrete sets.

SIAMOISE. An S-shaped two-seater of the mid-19th century. It may be an upholstered sofa or a double armchair. When seated, two persons are facing in opposite directions and they must look over their shoulders in order to converse with each other. See plan view illustration. This design was named after the Siamese twins, Chang and Eng, who created a sensation at that time. This type of seating unit is also called a "Tête-à-Tête." See the illustration for *Tête-à-Tête.*

SIDE CHAIR. A term used to distinguish the armless chair from the armchair. The side or armless chairs were evolved in the 17th century when they replaced the stools and benches which were provided for persons other than nobility or the heads of families. See *Hall Chair* and *Light Chair.*

SIDE TABLE. Originally an ornate serving table which was often combined with pedestals (as in the Adam designs) to form sideboards. William Kent, in the 18th century, designed many magnificently carved and decorated tables, and often they were topped with marble. Illustrated is an early-19th century Duncan Phyfe design. See *Satinwood* for an illustration of an Adam sideboard with side tables.

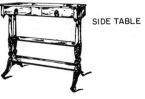

SIDE TABLE

SIDEBOARD

SIDEBOARD. As it is known today, this is an auxiliary case piece in the dining room, and it consists of drawers and cupboards that hold the items needed to furnish the dining table. Its present form was evolved by Shearer and perfected by Hepplewhite and Sheraton in the late 18th century. See *Satinwood* for an illustration of an Adam design which was a forerunner of the current design. Also see *Buffet, Crédence,* and *Credenza.*

SIÈGE EPISCOPAL. A metal church stool.

SILHOUETTE. The outline of an object. A profile or outline drawing, the outline completely filled in with a single color. Illustrated is a silhouette of a German Romanesque molding and also an elevation view of the same molding.

SILHOUETTE

SILHOUETTE MIRROR. A scrolled mahogany mirror frame of the Chippendale period. The frame was usually carved and/or gilded. A decorative ornament was often applied to the cresting. It was also called a "fretwork mirror."

SILK. A natural fiber extruded from the silkworm as it spins its cocoon. The name is probably derived from that given to the people in the part of China where silk was first known. Silk may be used as a fiber by itself, or blended with other natural or synthetic fibers. It has a fine hand, drapes beautifully, and takes a brilliant dye.

SILK FLOSS. The tangled waste fibers of silk. The term is often misused to describe kapok, an upholstery filling.

SILHOUETTE MIRROR

SILK-SCREENED. Originally an old Chinese method of hand-printing colors through stencil-like designs on screens made of fine silk tautly stretched on rigid wooden frames. As in lithography, wood blocks, and etchings, each color requires a separate screen with only that part of the design which is to appear in that particular color drawn on the screen. For more details see *Hand Screening*. Seriographs are silk-screened "fine-art" prints usually created in a limited number from a set of screens.

SILL. In construction, a horizontal strip forming the bottom of a structure; most usually, the board at the bottom of a window frame. A door sill is called a "saddle."

SILL COURSE. See *Belt Course*.

SILOE, DIEGO DE (1495–1563). A Spanish early Renaissance architect. The Cathedral of Granada and the "golden staircase" of the Burgos Cathedral are among his most noted works.

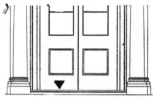

SILL

SILVERING GLASS. A late-17th-century process for making looking glass. A sheet of tin was laid on a backing and covered with a layer of quicksilver and then with a piece of glass. Pressure was applied to fix the quicksilver to the glass. The silvering was easily injured.

SILVESTRE, ISRAËL (1621–1691). A great engraver of the Louis XIV period.

SINGERIE. A "monkey trick." A decorative motif which employed the monkey as an ornament or an element in a mural, fabric, or wallpaper design. The monkey was often combined with chinoiseries in gay, delicate designs. The murals were often used to decorate dadoes and cornices. Singerie was

SINGLE ARCH MOLDING

SINGLE ARCH MOLDING

SKELETON CONSTRUCTION

SKEW ARCH

popular in France and England during the 18th century because it was considered an exotic and oriental motif. See *Huet, Christophe.*

SINGLE ARCH MOLDING. A small half-round molding strip used around drawers in case furniture of the William and Mary period in England. Illustrated is a dressing table of this time. See *Cock Beading.*

SINGLE BED. A bed that is usually 39″ wide by 78″ to 84″ long. Some single beds may be as narrow as 30″, 33″, or 36″. Two standard-size twin beds can be used together to make a king-size bed.

SINGLE GATE TABLE. A drop-leaf table with only one leaf, which can be raised to a horizontal plane by extending the one "gate" or supporting member. It is also called a "tuckaway table."

SISAL. A hard fiber, larger and stiffer than jute, flax, or hemp. It is used to make summer carpets, hard floor mats, etc.

SIX-LEGGED HIGHBOY. A highboy design which was peculiar to the William and Mary period in England. See *Highboy.*

SIZE. A gelatin-like solution used for stiffening textiles and glazing papers. Sizing is also used to prime coat a wall before painting or papering it. A new paper or paint holds better on a wall that has been treated with sizing. See *Buckram.*

SKEIN DYED YARN. Surface yarn that is spun from white wool or worsted staple, and then dyed in skein form by immersion in kettles or vats.

SKELETON CONSTRUCTION. A building construction made up of posts and beams assembled before the nonbearing walls are put in. This type of construction is usually accomplished in steel. See *Half Timber.*

SKETCH. A rough draft for a composition or a design. A trial run by the artist. A preliminary attempt which may later serve as reference material. A pictorial note or memo.

SKEW ARCH. An arch where the axis is not at right angles to the face of the arch. The courses that make up the arch are not parallel with the axis, but at right angles to the face. The resultant arch is inclined inward toward the horizon.

SKEW BACK. In arch construction, the part of the wall which supports the springing of an arch. See *Skew Arch.*

SKIRT or SKIRTING PIECE. The wood strip or panel, usually shaped, below the sill, shelf, tabletop, etc. It is also called the apron or frieze. A skirt may also refer to a fabric valance around the base of an upholstered chair, couch, etc. It hides the legs and wood construction of the seat. The skirt may be pleated, shirred, or tailored (fitted and plain). See *Apron.*

SKIRTING. A molded strip which covers the joint where the wall and the floor meet. It is often made of wood, but it can be made of vinyl, tile, rubber, etc. Illustrated is a carved skirting designed by Sir Christopher Wren, and executed by Grinling Gibbons in the late 17th century. See *Coved Skirting.*

SKYLOFT. The trademark name for Enkas air-bulked filament rayon yarn. It is being experimented with in the carpet industry.

SLAKED LIME. A mixture of quicklime and water.

SLAT. A horizontal bar connecting the upright members of a chair back. It is sometimes used as a single feature, or it may be used to hold the vertical splat. The top rail is considered a slat. The slat is also called a "horizontal splat." Also, a thin, narrow piece of wood like a lath, of one of the many metal or wood strips in a Venetian blind. In the illustration the sheathing is made up of slats.

SLEEPER WALL

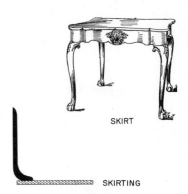

SKIRT

SKIRTING

SLAT

SLAT

SLAT-BACK

SLAT-BACK. A chair back which has several horizontal rails or crossbars. Chippendale and Sheraton (illustrated) designed more formal versions of this country-style chair. The slat-back was popular in Early American furniture. See *Ladderback.*

SLATE. A clayish stone which readily splits into plates or tiles. Slate is used as a roofing material, usually set in an overlapping manner, and it is also used for flooring and pavements.

SLEEPER WALL. A brick wall which is constructed like a *Honeycombed Wall,* and carries the ground floor joints.

SLATE

SLEEPY HOLLOW CHAIR

SLEIGH BED

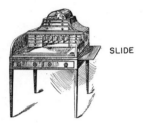

SLIDE

SLIP COVER

SLEEPY HOLLOW CHAIR. A mid-19th-century American chair which is upholstered and has a curved back and low, comfortable arms. The seat is usually scooped out. The Sleepy Hollow chair is typical of the Louis XV influence on Victorian design.

SLEIGH BED. A 19th-century American adaptation of the Empire scrolled-end bed. The resemblance of these scrolled or roll-over elements to the front and back ends of a sleigh gave the bed its name. Illustrated is an early-20th-century New Colonial style variation called a "scroll bed."

SLEY. A term used to specify the number of warp threads or ends per inch of woven fabric.

SLIDE. The pullout shelf of a desk, secretary, or serving table. Illustrated is a Shearer, mid-18th-century writing table.

SLING CHAIR. A twentieth-century canvas (or leather) and metal rod chair. The wrought-iron base is shaped like two bent butterfly paper clips with two peaks in the front and two higher peaks in the back. The canvas cover or sling has four pockets which fit over these peaks (they are similar to the corners on fitted bed sheets). The sling makes a concave sweep from the back peaks to the front peaks. The individual can sit with his legs between the two low peaks, or he may straddle the two low peaks. This unit is also called a "butterfly chair." See *Hardoy Chair*.

SLIP. Clay and water which have been mixed to a creamlike consistency; it is then applied to pottery to produce a glaze or colored effect.

SLIP COVER. A removable fitted cover made to protect the original upholstery fabric, or to cover worn upholstery, or as a "color lift" for a new season. The cover may be made of cotton, linen, chintz, silk, or synthetics. The idea of slip covering became popular in the Louis XV period.

SLIP MATCH. A veneering pattern which is created by joining the veneer sheets side by side so that the figure is repeated over and over in a continuous manner.

SLIP MATCH

SLIP SEAT **SLIP SEAT.** A seat which can be lifted out from the frame of a chair and be readily re-covered. See *Fauteuil à Châssis*.

SNAKE FOOT

SLIPPER CHAIR. Any short-legged upholstered chair with a very low seat. The seat is usually only 12″ to 14″ off the ground. A regular seat height is about 18″.

SLIPPER FOOT. A club foot with a more pointed and protruding toe. It was a popular furniture foot in the Queen Anne period in England.

SLODTZ BROTHERS. Five master furniture designers of the 18th century. Three of them worked for Louis XV of France in the rococo style. They were Antoine Sébastien (c. 1695–1754), Paul Ambroise (1702–1758), and René Michel or Michel-Ange (1705–1764).

SLOPE-FRONT DESK. A drop-front or drop-lid desk. The desk surface slants upward and backward when closed, thus creating a sloped or angled front. It appeared in 18th-century English and American designs. Illustrated is a Sheraton design. See *Drop Lid*.

SLUB YARN. A yarn with a thickness caused by wrapping or twisting one yarn around another several times. This irregularly thickened yarn adds a distinctive quality when woven into a fabric. Slub yarn is also called "nub yarn" and "thick-and-thin yarn."

SLUSHED JOINTS. In masonry, vertical or head joints made by "throwing in" with the edge of the trowel between bricks that are already laid.

SMALL CHAIR. An armless chair. A side chair. Illustrated is a Hepplewhite oval-back chair of the late 18th century.

SMITH, GEORGE. A late-18th- early-19th-century English cabinetmaker and furniture designer. He published a book on household furniture showing the then prevalent Regency style. Smith worked with Thomas Hope, and in 1808 was made Upholder Extraordinary to H.R.H. the Prince of Wales. His work showed his strong preference for things French.

SNAKE FOOT. A furniture foot carved to resemble a snake's head. It is actually a club foot with an elongated toe like a slipper foot, and it is found in 18th-century English and American furniture. A Hepplewhite bookstand is illustrated. Also, a yellow-brown or red-brown wood with dark spots and markings. It was popular for inlay work in the latter part of the 18th century.

SLIPPER FOOT

SLOPE-FRONT DESK

SMALL CHAIR

SNAKE FOOT

SNAP TABLE

SIR JOHN SOANE

SNAP TABLE. A small tripod table with a hinged top held in a horizontal position by a spring catch. It is also called a "tip-up table," and was designed in the mid-18th century in England and America.

SNAPPED HEADER. A half of a brick laid so that its end, or face forms part of the wall's surface.

SOANE, SIR JOHN (1753–1837). A English architect, and one of the group chiefly responsible for introducing classic Greek architecture into England. He studied in Rome, and found inspiration in the temples of the Caesars, which were built in the Greek style. Soane's Bank of England (1795–1827) is based on the Temple of Vesta at Tivoli. See *Temple of Vesta* for a comparison.

SOCKETING. A cheap method of joinery. The end of one piece of wood is shaped to wedge tightly into a cavity cut in a second piece, like a chair leg pegged into the round cavity on the bottom of a wood seat of a kitchen chair.

SOCLE. A plain, unmolded square pedestal for a statue or superstructure. A word also used to describe the base of case furniture.

SOCLE

SOFA

SOFA. An upholstered daybed or couch, sometimes with two arms and a back. From the Arabic word "suffah." The sofa appeared in France in the Louis XIV period. A Louis XVI sofa is illustrated.

SOFA BED. A sofa whose back drops down and becomes parallel with the seat. This increases the seat area, and makes a sleeping surface about 43" to 49" wide. This type of unit is also called a "jackknife sofa bed."

SOFA SLEEPER. A convertible sofa with a concealed sleeper unit (mattress, etc.) beneath the seat. This type of sofa may be designed in a traditional or modern style, and it may vary in size from a love seat (48" sleeping area) to a standard 7' or longer couch which usually opens to a 54" or 60" sleeping surface.

SOFA TABLE. An oblong table with flaps at the short ends which are supported by hinged brackets. It is similar to a Pembroke table. The drawers are in the longer side of the table frame. This particular type of table appeared at the end of the 18th century. A Sheraton design, c. 1804, is illustrated.

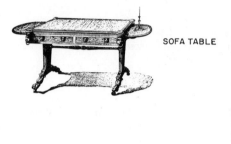

SOFA TABLE

SOFA TABLE

SOFFIT

SOFFIT. The underside of an architectural member, or its ceiling. The underside of an arch, cornice, beam, or lintel.

SOFT PASTE. A base for ceramics that lacks the whiteness and hardness of true porcelain, which is made of kaolin. See *Hard Paste*.

SOFTWOOD. See *Hardwood*.

SOHIER, HECTOR. An early French Renaissance architect of the 16th century. The châteaux of Chanteloup and Lasson have been attributed to him as well as the addition to St.-Pierre at Caen, which blends admirably with the original Gothic structure. The apsidial chapels of St.-Pierre are illustrated. St.-Pierre's beautiful spire was completely destroyed by bombs in World War II.

HECTOR SOHIER

SOLAR LAMP. A mid-19th-century fuel-burning lamp based on Argand's lamp. The fuel supply was set under the burner. The lamp usually consisted of a metal or marble column topped with a large globe. Prisms were frequently used to decorate the base of the globe. See *Argand Lamp* and *Astral Lamp*.

SOLARIUM. A room or porch enclosed with large areas of glass to allow in the sun's rays and light.

SOLDIER. In masonry, a brick laid on its end so that it appears vertical in the bond.

SOLDIER

SOLDIER ARCH. A flat arch made up of bricks that are laid on edge. It is often used as a facing for a lintel-type construction (over window and door openings).

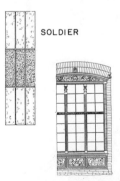

SOLDIER ARCH

SOLID MASONRY WALL

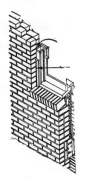

SOLID MASONRY WALL

SOMERSET HOUSE

SOLID MASONRY WALL. A wall made up of several thicknesses of masonry with mortar filling between the layers. No air or hollow spaces are left.

SOMERSET HOUSE. Designed by Sir William Chambers and built between 1776 and 1786, this is a classic example of "secular Renaissance" in London. The buildings extend from the Strand to the Victoria Embankment. In the center is a 150' square open courtyard surrounded by state offices. See *Chambers, Sir William.*

SOMMER or SUMMER. The main beam in a partition or in floor construction.

SOMNOE. A night table.

SONORA. A Philippine yellow-white to pale brown, heavy hardwood with a medium-fine texture.

SOSTEGNO. Italian for "buttress."

SOUTACHE. A narrow, rounded braid with a herringbone effect used as a trimming or edging material.

SPACKLING. A plaster or putty-like substance which is used to fill up holes or correct surface imperfections in a piece of wood or on a wall, ceiling, etc. When the spackle has dried, the excess material is sanded off, and the smooth surface is ready for the finishing coat.

SPADE FOOT. A rectangular, tapered foot often found in Hepplewhite designs and also in Sheraton's work (illustrated). It is separated from the rest of the leg by a slight projection. See *Sabot Foot* (illustration), *Taper Leg, Therm Leg,* and *Thimble Foot.*

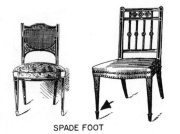

SPADE FOOT

SPALLIÈRE. A decorative painting on a chair back. The stenciled top rail of a Hitchcock chair.

SPAN. The open or clear space between two supporting elements. The space between two columns, piers, etc. The space covered by an arch. Illustrated is Belvedere, Queen Anne's summer residence in Prague. It is an example of German Renaissance architecture.

SPAN

SPAN ROOF. A roof consisting of two sloping sides meeting at a ridge.

SPANDREL. In furniture, a triangular piece spanning the space between a vertical support and a horizontal piece or rail. In architecture, the triangular surface between the spring of an arch and its square frame.

SPAN ROOF

SPANDREL

SPANDREL

SPANDREL WALL

SPANDREL WALL. In architecture, the part of the curtain wall above the top of the window of one story and the bottom of the windowsill of the story above. This area may consist of several courses of masonry, or it may be glass, metal, plastic, or combination spandrel panels such as are used in modern curtain wall constructions.

SPANDRIL STEPS. Steps, the treads of which are triangular in shape.

SPANISH CHAIR. A late-16th-century English chair with a high upholstered back and seat. The top rail or cresting was usually ornate and richly carved. Illustrated is a Spanish Renaissance chair which was a prototype for the English model described above. Note the Spanish foot and the giant nailhead trim.

SPANISH SCROLL FOOT. A hooflike, grooved and flared foot which ends in an inward curving scroll. It was introduced from Portugal during the Restoration period and used in 18th-century English and American furniture. It was also called a "Braganza toe." Illustrated is a late-17th-century cane chair with Spanish scroll feet.

SPARVER. A canopy or tester over a bed. A Sheraton camp bed is illustrated.

SPÄTBAROK. German for "late baroque."

SPÄTGOTIK. German for the late German or flamboyant Gothic period.

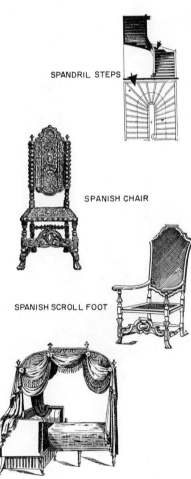

SPANDRIL STEPS

SPANISH CHAIR

SPANISH SCROLL FOOT

SPARVER

SPECIFICATIONS

SPECIFICATIONS

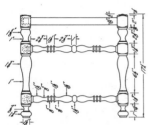

SPHINX

SPHINX

SPINDLE

SPECIFICATIONS. The exact details, measurements, materials, etc., that are stipulated for a given project, job, or construction.

SPECTRAL COLORS. Colors produced by a beam of white light as it is refracted through a prism. They are usually called violet, indigo, blue, green, yellow, orange, and red.

SPHINX. A mythical monster that combines a human head and woman's bust with the body of a lion. It was originally an ancient Egyptian motif. In the Roman era, wings were added to the sphinx. During the Renaissance, Adam, Empire, and Regency periods the sphinx was used as a carved or painted decoration. It was particularly popular as a furniture support during the Empire and Regency periods when things Egyptian were mixed with classic Greek and Roman motifs.

SPIDER-LEG TABLE. An 18th-century English drop-leaf table of Sheraton design with eight thin legs. It was actually a variation on the gateleg or eight-leg table. See *Eight-legged Table* and *Gateleg Table*.

SPINDLE. A long, slender rod often ornamented with turned moldings or swellings. A balustered effect. In architecture, a small twisted pillar. A Sheraton chair is shown.

SPINDLE AND BEAD

SPINDLED PANELS

SPINDLE AND BEAD. An ornamental molding resembling a string of sausage-like members separated by round or elliptical beads.

SPINDLED PANELS. Interior shutters made of spindles (delicate turnings) common in Spanish architecture as a window treatment.

SPINET. From the Italian spinetta which means "little thorn." A musical instrument of the 16th to 18th centuries. It was superseded by the harpsichord. The strings were plucked in the same way as they were on the harpsichord. The case was usually highly embellished with paintings, gilding, carvings, and inlays. An 18th-century French spinet is illustrated. In contemporary usage, a small upright piano. It is usually about 4' tall by 5' wide and 2' deep, with a standard keyboard.

SPINET

SPIRAL. A curve that winds around a fixed point and does not backtrack on itself. Each whorl is a complete turn of the curve around the axis, and it may be on one plane, or in an ascending or conical shape like a shell. The spiral is the basis for the volutes of classic capitals (illustrated), scrolls, or twisted rope turnings.

SPIRAL

SPIRAL LEG. A leg resembling a twisted rope, or a support with a winding descending flute or groove. It was originally of Portuguese and Indian origin, and became popular in England during the Restoration. A Sheraton, late-18th-century furniture leg is illustrated. See *Barley Sugar Turning*.

SPIRAL LEG

SPIRAL STAIRCASE. A stairway that winds around a central shaft as it rises from one level to another. Illustrated is a 19th-century cast-iron spiral staircase. It is also called a "winding staircase." See *Winding Staircase*.

SPIRAL STAIRCASE

SPIRAL WHORL. See *Paper Scroll*.

SPIRE. The pointed termination of a structure; usually conical or pyramidal in form.

SPLAD

SPIRE

SPLAD. An 18th-century English spelling of "splat." Illustrated is a mid-18th-century Chippendale chair. See *Splat*.

SPLAT

SPLAT. The central, upright wood panel of a chair back. This element may be carved, vase- or fiddle-shaped, embellished with carving and marquetry, or decorated with fretwork, pierced designs, or tracery. It is the back rest of the chair back.

SPLAY. A bevel or chamfer. A surface that is spread out or set at a slant. A large chamfer or diagonal surface formed by cutting away an angle of a wall. "Splay" is actually a shortened form of "display."

SPLAY

SPLAY LEG

SPLAY LEG

SPLINE

SPLIT SPINDLE

SPLIT SPINDLE

SPOON BACK

SPLAY LEG. A leg which angles or flares out from a chair, table, chest, etc. Illustrated are an ancient Greek klismos and a mid-19th-century Biedermeier table.

SPLAY LEG

SPLINE. In cabinetry, a method of strengthening a joint by means of a small strip of wood inserted between and projecting into the two pieces of wood that form the joint. Illustrated is a spline miter joint.

SPLIT SPINDLE. An applied ornament of 17th-century English and American furniture. A spindle (a delicate, slender turning) was cut in half lengthwise, thus creating two half-round moldings. It was applied to cabinets, cupboards, etc., and in Jacobean furniture the split spindles were used for chair backs with the smooth cut side toward the sitter's back.

SPLIT-LEVEL HOUSE. In contemporary usage, a house built on a series of levels rather than complete stories. The main level usually has the living and dining rooms, the kitchen, and sometimes a study. Several steps up from this level are the sleeping quarters, while several steps down one usually finds the utilities, recreation or family room, maid's quarters, storage, etc.

SPLOCKET. See *Sprocket.*

SPOOL FURNITURE. Turned furniture which was mass-produced in the United States in the mid-18th century. These chairs, tables, bedposts, etc., are distinguished by turnings which resemble a string of spools or buttons. The turnings were often made of pine, and stained to resemble mahogany. The better pieces were made of maple, cherry, or walnut. See *Jenny Lind Bed.*

SPOON BACK. A high chair back which is shaped to fit or conform to the curvature of the human back. The back gently slopes backward as it goes up, and it is slightly concave. This design was introduced by the Dutch, and appeared in England during the period of William and Mary. It became more popular in the Queen Anne period, and faded out with the Chippendale style.

SPOON-BACK CHAIR. An early-19th-century Regency and Biedermeier chair with a curved wood back. The low-set arms rise from the seat above the front legs, and make a continuous and rising sweep up to form the top rail. The center splat is plain, or it may be urn- or vase-shaped. The spoon-back is similar to the American Empire chair called the "Mme Jumel."

SPOON FOOT. A club or Dutch foot. The foot of a cabriole leg which flares and spreads out at the base; usually it is set on a pad. It was a popular furniture foot in the Queen Anne period.

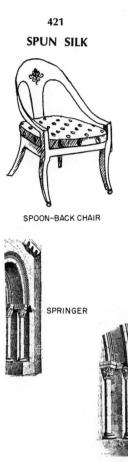

SPOON-BACK CHAIR

SPOON FOOT

SPRINGER. In the construction of an arch, the stone supporting the beginning of the arc. It is part of the abutment.

SPRINGER

SPRINGING LINE. In the construction of an arch, the top of the abutment from which the curve of the arch rises. It is the starting point of an arch.

SPRINGING POINT. See *Springing Line*.

SPRINGS. Flat, zigzag, or coiled constructions of high-quality steel which add to the resiliency of upholstered furniture or beds when used under the mattress.

SPRINGS

SPRINGING LINE

SPROCKET. The short rafter which is set at the bottom of a common rafter, and at a lesser pitch. It tends to create a curve at the bottom of the roof. It is also called a "splocket." A sprocket is also a strip of wood nailed to the foot of a rafter and overhanging the wall. The projecting eaves of the roof are formed this way.

SPROCKET

SPRUCE. A type of pine closely related to fir. It is a soft, light, strong, and straight-grained wood used for interior and exterior work.

SPUN SILK. Silk yarn which is made from waste fibers and damaged or pierced cocoons. It is heavier and less lustrous than first-grade silk.

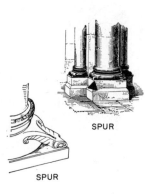

SPUR

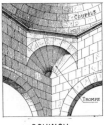

SPUR

SPUR. The triangular filler between the round shaft and the square base of a Gothic column. A filler might be a spray of foliage, a tongue, or a grotesque.

SPUR STONE. A stone specially shaped and set in the corner of a structure to prevent injury to the corner from passing traffic.

SQUAB. A loose, stuffed cushion used for seats of chairs, settees, and long stools. Squabs were replaced by upholstered seats toward the end of the 17th century, but they are still used on luxurious armchairs and sofas. Illustrated is an ancient Pompeiian chair with footstool.

SQUAB

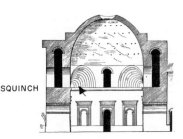

SQUINCH

SQUINCH

SQUINCH. A series of stepped, arched lintels built across the interior angle of two walls. It is used as a support for one side of an octagonal spire rising from a rectangular tower, or it may fill in the corner created by setting a round dome on a square wall. In furniture, a corner cupboard. See *Coin* and *Encoignure*.

STABRE, LAURENT. A noted cabinetmaker, "joiner and carpenter in ebony" to Louis XIII in the 17th century. At this time ebony was often glued onto blackened pearwood to obtain added strength or size.

STAINED GLASS

STAINED GLASS. Designs or pictures made of colored glass and held together by strips of lead which also form the outlines of the design. It was a Byzantine invention, but became a distinctly medieval art form. The colored glass is made by adding metallic oxides to molten glass (pot metal) or by fusing colored glass on plain glass (flashing).

STAINLESS STEEL. A steel alloy which is a bright silvery color, and is resistant to tarnish, rust, and corrosion.

STALACTITE WORK. Small vertical, polygonal, or curved niches rising and projecting in rows above one another to create a stalactite-like formation. Illustrated is the Hall of the Abencerrages in the Alhambra. This type of ornament was also used to create Moorish-type capitals.

STALKER, JOHN. With George Parker, published *A Treatise of Japanning and Varnishing* in 1688. Japanning was of great interest to the English, even at this early date.

STANCHION. A vertical, metal member (usually a rolled-steel joist) which supports a load carried onto it by a beam.

STAND. A framework, small table, or lowboy upon which chests, cabinets, drawers, basins, and such were placed. Daniel Marot, Grinling Gibbons, and William Kent carved many magnificent gilded stands in the 17th and 18th centuries.

STANDARD-SIZE BED. A double bed which is usually 53″–54″ wide by 75″ long.

STANDING MIRROR. An oval, shield-shaped, or rectangular mirror set on a chest or table. It was usually equipped with a drawer. An 18th-century design, it was also called a "shaving mirror."

STANZA. The Italian word for "room."

STAR BURST. A five-pointed star with raylike emanations. A decorative painted or carved motif.

STAR MOLDING. A decorative sculptured molding with a star motif. It was popular in Romanesque architecture.

STAINED GLASS

STALACTITE WORK

STANDING MIRROR

STAR MOLDING

STEAMBOAT GOTHIC. The ornate, overembellished woodwork, turnings, balls, finials, gables, bargeboards, and "gingerbread" that was troweled over the wood and shingle structures built in America at the end of the 19th century. The inspiration for this extravagant use of jigsaw "lace" was the "floating palaces" on the Mississippi in the middle of the 19th century.

STEEL ENGRAVING. An art reproduction technique which was introduced in the second quarter of the 19th century. A microscopic film of steel is deposited on the softer copper plate by means of electrolysis. The hard steel plate makes it possible to print large editions without destroying the fine details of the plate.

STEEL FURNITURE. This was produced in very limited quantities in the 17th and 18th centuries in Europe by gunsmiths and ironworkers. Most of the known designs are of the Directoire or Early Empire style and were created for Napoleon's campaigns, in which the strong and easily transportable folding chairs and collapsible tables, beds, and desks were particularly useful. The designs were often embellished with bronze doré rosettes and medallions as well as chiseled and chased details.

STEEPLE

STEEPLE. A tall structure surmounting a church or public edifice. This superstructure is usually equipped with bells, and topped with a spire.

STELA or STELE. A stone slab or pillar used as a commemorative or grave marker in ancient Greece.

STELA

STELLAR VAULTING

STELLAR VAULTING. Vaulting which achieves a starlike pattern by the arrangement of the intermediate and lierne ribs. A section of Canterbury Cathedral is shown. See *Lierne* and *Vault*.

STENCIL

STENCIL. A pattern made by brushing or wiping ink or paint over a sheet of metal or paper in which the required design has been cut. The paint will go through only the cut-out areas. The design can be reproduced many times over on walls, ceilings, furniture, floors, etc. In the 19th century, it was used in place of wallpaper as a method of getting an allover design on walls. The top rails of Hitchcock chairs were usually stenciled in gold.

STEPPED CURVE

STEPPED CURVE. In furniture, a sudden break or stop in the direction of a curve, or the junction of a curve with a straight line. This stepped curve was used in the uprights of the Queen Anne and Early Georgian periods. It appears in a modified form in the Hepplewhite chair back illustrated here.

STEREOBATE. The basement or foundation of a building. The word also means a continuous pedestal under a plain wall. Illustrated is the mid-15th-century Italian Renaissance Palazzo Ricardi in Florence.

STEREOCHROMY. A technique of painting on stone or marble with pigments in water glass.

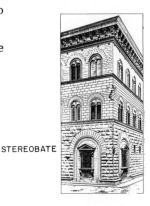

STEREOBATE

STERLING

STERLING. A term applied to silverware, jewelry, etc., which is made of silver that is at least 92½ percent pure.

STICK STYLE. A romantic 19th-century English style of architecture with "emphasis given to structural and visual multiplication of the framing sticks." It is a variation on the half-timber house, with the wood strips forming the major pattern and decoration since they are left completely exposed.

STICK TABLE. A combination pedestal table and lamp. The lamp base is usually a turning or column which appears to be a continuation of the table support, and it extends up through the table surface. A lampshade is set atop this "stick" or base. The stick table has been interpreted in most traditional styles as well as modern designs.

STICK-BACK. The back of a Windsor chair which is made up of many rods or spindles. These elements are called "sticks" or "fiddle strings."

STILE. In architecture, the margin or space between panels or architectural elements, usually the vertical pieces only. The horizontal bands are referred to as rails. In furniture, the vertical strips of the frame of a panel or case piece of furniture. The word also refers to the outer uprights of some panel-back chairs.

STILL LIFE. A painting or representation which is usually devoid of human figures; usually an arrangement of flowers, fruit, books, musical instruments, vases, etc. In certain periods a still life has included the trophies of the hunt.

STILTED ARCH. An arch that springs from above the impost. This springing line and the impost are part of the same vertical wall.

STICK-BACK

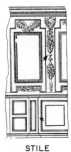

STILE

STILE

STILTED ARCH

STINKWOOD. A South African wood which has a distinctly unpleasant odor when it is freshly cut. It resembles walnut, and has a reddish cast. Stinkwood was used in the 17th and 18th centuries by the native craftsmen of the Dutch East India Company at the Cape of Good Hope to reproduce Dutch furniture designs.

STIPPLE or CRAYON ENGRAVING. A combination of etching and intaglio engraving that was especially popular in the 18th century for reproducing portrait drawings of famous personalities. The stippling consisted of making dots over a grounded plate with the point of an etching needle. See *Intaglio* and *Intaglio Engraving.*

STIPPLING. A painting technique for surfacing a wall or object with a multitude of tiny dots, spots, or blobs. It can be accomplished with the stiff bristles of a brush, a fine sponge, crumpled tissue paper, etc.

STITCHED UP

STITCHED UP. A French upholstery technique of the 17th century. The upholstery of the seat is drawn over the seat rails and attached to the rails underneath the chair. Illustrated is a Louis XIV chair. See *Stuffover Seat.*

STOA. A colonnade around an agora (an ancient Greek marketplace). A detached colonnade or portico. See *Colonnade.*

STOCK DYEING. The dyeing of a fiber before it is spun into thread or yarn.

STOEP. The Dutch word for *Veranda (Verandah).*

STONE, EDWARD DURREL. An American architect born in 1902 in Fayettesville, Arkansas. He has designed many important buildings in and out of the United States. The pierced screen and deep eaves are a sort of trademark of his current work. Stone has made excellent use of pierced concrete and clay tiles, as well as pierced metal façades. Among his noteworthy buildings are: Hotel El Panama in Panama City, the Phoenicia Hotel in Beirut, the United States Embassy in New Delhi, the American Pavilion at the Brussels World's Fair of 1958, the Social Security Hospital in Lima, Peru, as well as the Radio City Music Hall in New York City. He collaborated with Philip Goodwin in 1939 on the New York City Museum of Modern Art. See *United States Embassy, New Delhi.*

NICHOLAS STONE

STONE, NICHOLAS (1586–1647). An English stone carver who produced many of Inigo Jones's designs for fireplaces, mantels, etc. In 1626, he was appointed Master Mason to Charles I. Stone worked in marble, alabaster, touchstone, and Portland stone.

Some of his work was inlaid with other colored marbles (intarsia) or embellished with chased brass mounts. The gateway to St. Mary's Church at Oxford is one of his finest works.

STONEWARE. A heavy, opaque, nonporous, nonabsorbent pottery made from siliceous paste. Illustrated is an early-17th-century jug made in Germany.

STONEWARE

STOOL. A backless and armless seat which was replaced by small or side chairs in the 17th century. A stool is now used as a small decorative seat, or a very low design will serve as a footrest. See *Piano Stool.*

STOOL

STOPPED CHANNEL FLUTING

STOPPED CHANNEL FLUTING. A series of equidistant concave flutes with straight or rounded ends. Originally this was a decoration on classic architecture. In the 18th century it was used as a frieze decoration on cabinets and furniture.

STORAGE WALL

STORAGE WALL. A series of modular units which can be set up in a variety of combinations as a wall, or against one. This 20th-century invention was introduced by George Nelson and Henry Wright in 1945, as a space-saving answer to storage problems for apartment dwellers. It was later refined into a collection of units produced by Herman Miller in the form of a "basic storage component" system. There are currently many variations and systems available, from wall-hung to self-standing, and from modern styles to medieval and Spanish-inspired units.

STORY or STOREY. The space between two floors or between the top floor and the roof.

STORY POST. A weight-carrying post that extends through the story.

STRADDLE CHAIR. A chair one straddles or sits spread-legged across. See *Cockfight Chair* and *Voyelle.*

STORY

STRAIGHT STAIR. An unbroken, uninterrupted flight of stairs.

STRAIGHT STAIR

STRAINING

STRAINING

STRAINING. An early-17th-century technique of tightly stretching and gluing the upholstery fabric to the whole of the woodwork, as in the stately beds designed by Daniel Marot in the William and Mary period. Illustrated is a late-17th-century state bed from Knole Park in England. Note the tester. The fabric has been pulled taut and sharp across the wood framing.

STRAPWORK

STRAPWORK

STRAPWORK

STRAPWORK. A carved wooden arabesque pattern having a flat stem of a scroll in section and/or an ornament which resembles a pattern cut from a sheet of leather. An interlaced pattern which resembles a crisscross folded or plaited design which might be created from strips of leather. Elizabethan and Jacobean carved-wood decorated panels with ribbon-like bands in repeating and interlacing designs. In the Chippendale period, flat and sometimes elaborately carved strapwork was used for the splats of chairs. See *Enroulements Découpés* and *Ribband Back*.

STRAW CHAIRS. Originally provincial chairs with rush or woven straw seats. They were adapted to more formal and decorative uses in the 17th and 18th centuries.

STRAW CHAIR

STRAW MARQUETRY. An Eastern or Oriental technique which was used in France in the 17th century. Two layers of flattened and tinted straw were placed one on top of the other and cut through together, as in marquetry, and the cutout shapes were applied to wooden or papier-mâché objects. Some straw designs were executed like mosaics, others were engraved, and in some extraordinary units minute pieces of straw were built up into low-relief decorations.

STRAWBERRY HILL. Built by Horace Walpole at Twickenham, England, in the mid-18th century. It gave impetus to the Gothic revival, and was filled with fan-ribbed vaulting, tracery patterns, and details from medieval tombs.

STRETCHER

STRETCHER. The crosspiece which connects, braces, and strengthens the legs of tables, chairs, chests, etc. Illustrated is a 17-century English chair. See *Arched Stretcher*, *Rising Stretchers*, *Saltire*, and *X-shaped Stretcher*.

STRETCHER

STRETCHER BOND. In masonry, a method of bricklaying with only the stretchers showing. The stretchers in the succeeding courses appear to overlap one another, and the vertical joints fall in alternate courses instead of one directly under the other. The overlap may be only ¼ of the brick in length. See *Bond*.

STRETCHER COURSE. See *Stretchers*.

STRETCHERS. In masonry, the two surfaces of a brick bounded by the longest and the shortest sides, rather than the short end, which is called the header. A stretcher course is one which is composed only of stretchers laid in a continuous row.

STRIÉ. A fabric with an uneven color or streaked effect which is produced by using warp threads of varying tones. It is possible in this manner to produce a two-toned effect in tafetta, satin, or corded upholstery fabrics. See *Jaspé*.

STRIGES. The vertical fluting on a classical column. See *Fluting*.

STRING. In stair construction, the angled member into which the treads and risers are fixed.

STRETCHERS

STRETCHER BOND

STRING

STRING COURSE. A molding or projecting horizontal motif which runs along the face of a building to mark the division of stories or to emphasize the horizontal line in the design of a building. See *Strozzi Palace*.

STRINGING. A narrow band or strip of contrasting veneer used as a decorative border. It is the same as "lining."

STRING COURSE

STRINGING

STRIPPED JOINT. In masonry, a neat, raked joint between bricks. The mortar is recessed from the face of the wall so that the bricks are sharply defined and contoured in the bond pattern.

STRIX. A channel or groove in a fluted column. See *Fluting*.

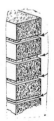

STRIPPED JOINT

STROZZI PALACE

STRUCTURAL CLAY TILE

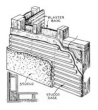

STUCCO

STROZZI PALACE. Built in Florence (1489), this is one of the famous palaces of the Italian Renaissance. It was begun by Benedetto da Maiano and completed by Il Cronaca (Antonio Pollaiuolo). The main façade is astylar (without columns), and the rusticated walls have the stories emphasized by molded string courses. The horizontal effect is further enhanced by the great crowning cornice which projects over seven feet from the face of the building. The arched windows, the angle lanterns, and the link-holders are noteworthy features on the façade.

STRUCK JOINT. In masonry, a slight compression in the mortar joint made by the trowel. The angled slope that is thus formed helps to carry off the water.

STRUCK JOINT

STRUCTURAL CLAY TILE. A hollow masonry unit with parallel air cells. It may be made of burned clay, shale, fire clay, or mixtures of the above.

STRUT. A horizontal building construction member which is set between two verticals (or vice versa) to hold them apart. A chair or table stretcher acts as a strut.

STUART STYLE. The architecture of England from the reign of Charles I into that of William and Mary (approximately 1625–1690). Illustrated is the original design for Whitehall Palace by Inigo Jones. See *Jones, Inigo,* and *Wren, Sir Christopher.*

STUART STYLE

STUBWASSER, JOHANN HEINRICH (1740–1829). An 18th-century German craftsman who in 1758 originated a method of lacquering furniture and small objects. He produced snuff-boxes, cofferets, and small pieces of furniture in wood and papier-mâché which were lacquered and decorated by fine artists.

STUCCO. A plaster or cement used for interior or exterior walls. It can be decoratively textured and/or coated. The surfacing material can be tinted. See *Composition* and *Gesso.*

STUCK MOLDING. A molding forming part of the surface it adorns rather than one applied to the surface and not an integral part of the unit. Illustrated is a 15th-century English oak buffet. See *Planted Molding*.

STUCK MOLDING

STUD. A wooden post, usually 2″ × 4″, which is used to form the skeleton of a wall or partition. The posts support the joists, and receive the lath or sheet material which finishes the wall. A stud is also a copper, brass, or gilt nailhead used for decorative purposes on chests, cabinets, door panels, etc., or for securing leather or fabric to chairs, panels, chests, cabinets, etc. Originally nailheads served a functional rather than a decorative purpose, but the heads became more ornate and larger, and eventually a form of repetitive embellishment. This form of decoration was introduced in Spain, Portugal, and Italy in the Middle Ages and in the 17th century was used in France and England. Illustrated is a chair of the Louis XIII period.

STUD

STUD

STUDENT LAMP. A late-19th-century brass lamp with the fuel reservoir higher than the burner; it is similar to the astral lamp. The chimney, which was set around the projecting burner, was partially covered by a tole shade which directed the light downward. The lampstand itself sometimes had a ring on top to make the lamp portable. Completely electrified versions of the student lamp are available today.

STUDIO COUCH. A seating device which converts into a sleeping unit by means of removable cushions or bolsters and retractable springs. An informal bed unit. A studio couch with an auxiliary set of spring and mattress kept, trundle-bed fashion, under the main spring and mattress converts into two twin beds.

STUDY. In art, a drawing or painting of a detail which is made to be studied and perhaps used as part of a larger composition. In interior design, a library or den. Usually it is a room with a desk, comfortable chairs, and bookshelves. A retreat. Illustrated is a Renaissance-style study.

STUDY

STUFFER. In carpet construction, a strong, coarse fiber like jute which runs lengthwise on the loom and is woven in with the weft and warp threads. It adds a thick protective backing to the finished carpet.

STUFFOVER SEAT. The fixed seat of a chair upholstered by drawing the fabric or leather over the seat rails and securing it with nails along the underneath surface of the rails. The join is finished off with a galloon or brass molding. Illustrated is a late-17th-century English chair. See *Stitched Up*.

STUFFOVER SEAT

STUMP

STUMP BEDSTEAD

STUMP FOOT

STYLE

STUMP. See *Buttwood Veneer.*

STUMP BEDSTEAD. A bedstead without posts. A medieval example is illustrated.

STUMP FOOT. A furniture leg that goes directly down to the floor without any special foot, pad or disk.

STUMPWORK. A relief effect in embroidery created by stitching with wool or silk threads over padding. It is a quilting or trapunto effect which was in vogue during the late Tudor and Jacobean periods.

STYLE. The characteristics of a design. The motifs, techniques, and materials typical of a certain period of time or of a particular designer. Illustrated is an example of the French Empire style. The design is by Charles Percier and Pierre Fontaine, the style setters of the Empire period.

STYLE OGIVALE

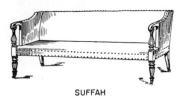

STYLOBATE

SUFFAH

STYLE OGIVALE. French for the Gothic period or style. Illustrated is the Church of St. Ouen at Rouen.

STYLOBATE. The stone blocks or steps of a Greek temple upon which the columns rest. A basement or platform upon which columns are placed to raise them above the level of the ground or floor. A continuous unbroken pedestal for a range of columns, an arcade, etc.

SUFFAH. The Arabic word from which "sofa" is derived. It is defined as "a place or couch for reclining before the doors of Eastern houses." Illustrated is a Sheraton-style sofa.

SUGAR PINE (WHITE PINE). A product of California and southern Oregon, which ranges in color from creamy white to pale brown faintly tinged with pink. It has little flecks and intermittent lines of a darker shade running parallel with the grain. The knots of the sugar pine have a purplish band around their edges. It is a close-grained wood that works well and holds a shape.

SUGI FINISH. A Japanese wood-finishing technique. The surface is charred and then rubbed with a wire brush to create a driftwood effect.

SUITE. See *Set.*

SULLIVAN, LOUIS (1856–1924). The "father" and first truly creative genius of modern American architecture. He evolved the skyscraper design, and combined new technical means with aesthetic ideals. In 1873 he worked for William Le Baron Jenney, who was later to build the first all-steel-frame building. In 1881, Sullivan became a partner of Dankmar Adler, who was the engineer-constructer of the partnership. They completed the Auditorium Building in Chicago in 1889; the structure was an opera house combined with an office block. This was the last of his "masonry" period. The Wainwright Building in St. Louis in 1891 and the Bayard Building in New York City in 1898 are early attempts by Sullivan at steel-frame structures which widely influenced American architecture. The Carson, Pirie & Scott Department Store in Chicago (1899–1904) was a tremendous step forward in "cage" construction, and even today it has a fresh, modern look with the horizontal emphasis in its façade which reflects the framework of the building. In his book *Ornament in Architecture* in 1892, he stated, "Ornament is mentally a luxury, not a necessary."

SUMMER BEAM. From the French "sommier," a rafter. A large horizontal timber used as a bearing beam. It usually spans the width of a room. In the Colonial American home, the beam ran from the central stone chimney to a post.

SUMMER BED. A Sheraton twin bed design which consisted of two single four-poster beds, separated by a space between the beds but connected at the cornice which ran straight across the two beds.

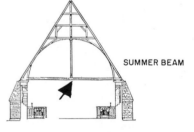

SUMMER BEAM

SUNBURST

SUMMER BED

SUNBURST. An ornamental motif, carved, painted, or inlaid with straight or jagged rays radiating from a central point. It was associated with the style of Louis XIV, "the Sun King." Illustrated is a Chippendale chair back.

SUNK PANEL

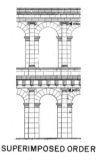

SUPERIMPOSED ORDER

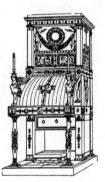

SUPPORTING COLUMN

SUNDERLAND BRIDGE. Built in Sunderland, England, over the Wear River (1793–1796), this bridge was a daring construction feat of its time. It had a single arch with a span of 236', and each of the six ribs which formed the arch was composed of 105 cast-iron panels. The original design was conceived by the British-born American political pamphleteer Thomas Paine, but the construction work was credited to Rowland Burdon.

SUNFAST. Describes a dyed fabric which does not fade appreciably under normal exposure to sunlight.

SUNK PANEL. See *Panel*.

SUNK TOP

SUNK TOP. A table surface which is set below an edge or rim, as in gallery tables. See *Gallery* and *Piecrust Table*.

SUPERIMPOSED ORDER. Each successive story of a colonnaded building having its columns, pilasters, or anta treated with a different classic order. Doric is usually on the lowest level, Ionic on the second, and Corinthian on the third story. The Romans used this device in decorating the Colosseum in Rome, and it was reintroduced in the Renaissance period. Illustrated is a section of the Roman theatre of Marcellus, which has a combination of Doric and Ionic orders.

SUPERMULLIONS

SUPERMULLIONS. The upright bars or mullions above the starting point of the foliation of a Gothic tracery window.

SUPERSTRUCTURE. An additional structure on top of a building. See the illustration for *Skeleton Construction*.

SUPPORTING COLUMN. A column at a front corner of a cabinet or chest which supports an overhanging frieze drawer. This motif is usually associated with Empire, Regency, and Biedermeier styles. Illustrated is an Empire secretary.

SURAH. A soft silk fabric, usually twill woven in a plaid design. It can be made from synthetics or a combination of fibers.

SURBASE MOLDING. In architecture, the series of moldings which form the cornice of a pedestal. In cabinetry, the pedestal of a piece of furniture treated with a carved, inlaid, or otherwise decorated molding. The pedestal is often treated with drawers.

SURBASED

SUSPENSION TRUSS FRAME

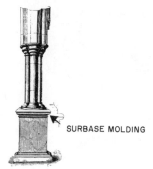

SURBASE MOLDING

SURBASED. Describes an arch or vault in which the height of the curve above the impost is less than half of its span. It is the opposite of *Surmounted*.

SURMOUNTED

SURMOUNTED. Describes an arch or vault in which the height of the curve above the level of the impost is more than one half of its span. See *Surbased*.

SURREALISM. A 20th-century school of art which had its ancestry in the weird and fantastic works of Hieronymus Bosch, Francisco Goya, Guiseppe Arcimboldo, Odilon Redon, and Henry Fuseli. It was also influenced by the nihilism of Dada and certain aspects of early-20th-century Cubism. The word was first coined in France and it was defined by André Breton as "pure psychic *automatism*, by which it is intended to express verbally, in writing or in any other way, the true process of thought. It is a dictation of thought, free from the exercise of reason, and every aesthetic or moral preoccupation." Some of today's leading surrealist artists are Salvador Dali, the late Paul Klee, Giorgio di Chirico, and Pablo Picasso.

SUSPENSION BRIDGE. The first successful suspension bridge was designed by Marc Seguin in 1824 to span the Rhone near Tournon. He used wire cables, and the success of this design made new, light, elegant constructions possible.

SUSPENSION TRUSS FRAME. A 19th-century cast-iron roof construction which made use of tie bars.

SUSPENSION TRUSS FRAME

SWAG

SWAG

ABRAHAM SWAN

SWAG. Cloth draped in a looped garland effect. A carved or painted decoration in a pendant curve. The swag may be a festoon or a garland of fruit, flowers, leaves, or ribbons. See *Festoon.*

SWAG LIGHT. A lamp or light fixture which is hooked into the ceiling with the electric cord, usually decorated with a metal chain, swagged from the hanging point to the nearest wall, and then down to the floor outlet where it is plugged in. This is a method of getting overhead light without installing electrical outlets or boxes in the ceiling.

SWAN, ABRAHAM. An early-18th-century English cabinetmaker who was noted for his mantels, doors, window trims, and staircases. In 1745 he published *The British Architect, or the Builder's Treasury of Staircases* with simple, understandable methods of drawing the classic orders. It was a source of inspiration and instruction for the Colonial American builders in the 18th century.

SWAN BED. A French Empire bed with carved swans on either side of the headboard. The front or footboard consisted of a pair of cornucopia-type legs, and usually a carved fruit arrangement. The entire bed was raised up from the floor on a heavily carved base or dais.

SWAN NECK. A general term for moldings or members with an ogee curve, as in the shape of a curved handrail ending.

SWAN NECK

SWAN NECK PEDIMENT

SWAN NECK PEDIMENT. A broken pediment in which the raking lines are composed of two opposed S curves. The upper ends are scrolled over with paterae on their faces. The pediment usually has a small central pedestal which is sometimes topped with an ornamental feature like a vase or pineapple. An 18th-century Chippendale design is illustrated. This motif was also popular in the earlier Queen Anne period.

SWASTIKA. A cross composed of four equal L-shaped arms at right angles to each other. It is an ancient symbol of good luck. It was often used in the classic Greek and Roman times as part of a fret or Greek key design. Illustrated is an ancient Pompeiian frieze.

SWASTIKA

SWATCH. A small sample of cloth or material which is also called a clipping or cutting. It is usually used as a specimen to give information about the color, pattern, and texture of a fabric.

SWEDE CLOTH. A napped fabric that resembles suede leather.

SWEDISH MODERN. A contemporary style of furniture and furnishing. It features simple, clean lines, light woods, and a lack of carved, applied, or painted decoration. Simple curves, a sculptural use of the wooden elements, and refined tapered legs add to the classic beauty of this style. See *Scandinavian Modern.*

SWEEP FRONT. A piece of furniture with a flat, bowed, or slightly curved front. Illustrated is a plan view of a Hepplewhite commode tabletop.

SWELL FRONT. A cabinet, credenza, chest of drawers, etc., with a segmental or bow front. Illustrated is a Sheraton dressing table. See *Bow Front.*

SWEEP FRONT

SWING GLASS

SWELL FRONT

SWING GLASS. See *Cheval Glass or Mirror.*

SWING-LEG TABLE. A hinged rail with a single leg which sweeps out to a right angle and supports a dropped leaf which is raised parallel with the floor. It is similar to a gate-leg table. See *Flap Table, Eight-legged Table, Gate-Leg Table, Thousand-legged Table,* and *Tuckaway Table.*

SWIRL. A wood grain effect which usually appears around knots or crotches. It is an irregular eddying grain.

SWISS. A very fine sheer cotton fabric which was first made in Switzerland. It may be plain, embroidered, or patterned with dots (dotted Swiss). It is often used for glass curtains.

SWIVEL. A revolving mechanism below the seat of a chair or below the surface of a tabletop, as in lazy Susans or dumb-waiters. It is possible to swing the seat or table surface around in a wide arc, sometimes a full 360°. The swivel is also used for desk chairs, piano stools, television bases, etc. See *Lazy Susan.* Illustrated is a German revolving armchair c. 1870.

SWIVEL

SYMBOL

SYMMETRICAL

SYCAMORE, ENGLISH. A white to light brown wood which is heavy, tough, and strong. It is usually used for finishing work. When it is stained with oxide of iron it becomes a greenish-gray color. It was popular as a veneering wood in the late 18th century. Sycamore is also called *Harewood*.

SYLMERIZED. A chemical treatment for fabrics to make them stain-resistant. The process does not affect the color, feel, or hand of the fabric.

SYMBOL. In furniture and interior decoration, a pictorial representation of an intangible, i.e., of an idea, quality, virtue, group, or trade. A decorative grouping of typical tools and instruments which represents a concept such as art, science, music, astronomy. The symbol is used as a carved, painted, and appliquéd decoration. See *Palette* and *Trophy*.

SYMMETRICAL. Used to describe a balance of mirror images: two units of exactly equal shape, size, mass, etc., set on either side of a central point or line and at equal distance from it.

SYMOND, JAMES. An early-18th-century American cabinet-maker in Salem, Massachusetts.

SYNTHETIC RESINS. Chemical compounds used in finishing textiles to give the fabric desired properties: resiliency, hand, fade-resistance. Synthetic resins are also used on coated plastic fabrics.

SYNTHETICS. Man-made fabric fibers, carpet fibers, etc. Materials which are produced chemically rather than from natural growth or development. New materials can be made from such natural elements as cotton, wood pulp, coal, etc., combined with chemicals, tars, resins, etc.

SYSTYLE. In classic architecture, intercolumnar spaces which are equal to two diameters of the column's shaft.

T-PILLOW. A seat pillow for a chair or sofa which is wider in front than at the back because the arms of the upholstered unit do not extend to the front of the seat. The two rectangular projections of the pillow (the crosspiece of the *T*) fill up the space between the end of the armpiece and the front of the chair or sofa seat. A sofa with two pillows will have only one projection or ear on each pillow.

TAAS. A pagoda.

TABARET. A stout, satin-striped silk fabric used for upholstery.

TABBY. A watered silk or moiréd effect on fabric. Also the name of an 18th-century English wallpaper ground. See *Moiré*. A term for a compound of seashells, partly crushed and partly

T-PILLOW

TAAS

burned to make a lime for binding. This material was also called Spanish concrete. It was a major building material in Charleston, South Carolina, in the 18th century, where the name "tabby" was coined.

TABERNACLE. In Gothic furniture, the openwork decoration of canopied niches. In the Renaissance period, the frame which encloses a niche which holds a statue or other ornament. Illustrated is a section of the south porch of the Gothic Chartres Cathedral.

TABERNACLE

TABERNACLE

TABERNACLE FRAME

TABERNACLE FRAME. The entire trim or decoration of a door, window, niche, or chimney which consists of columns or pilasters with an entablature and pediment over them. It is an early-18th-century term defined by Robert Adam in his *Works of Architecture.*

TABERNACLE MIRROR. See *Constitution Mirror.*

TABERRAY. See *Tabaret.*

TABLE. Before the mid-16th century, the term applied to an index, pocketbook, or tablet. In the 14th century, it referred to religious carvings and paintings in churches. In current usage, a flat, horizontal surface, raised up on legs, trestles, or on a pedestal. The size and shape are determined by the use to which the table will be put. Illustrated is a late-18th-century English Pembroke table by Shearer.

TABLE

TABLE À COIFFER

TABLE À COIFFER. A dressing table, introduced in the period of Louis XV. Usually the center sliding panel contained a mirror with a drawer below. Deep wells on either side contained cosmetic containers, washbasins, etc. The table was also called a "coiffeuse" or "poudreuse."

TABLE À ÉCRAN. A table with a sliding screen. See *Screen Table.*

TABLE À GRADIN

TABLE À GRADIN

TABLE À MILIEU

TABLE CHAIR

TABLE À GRADIN. A tiered desk of the 18th century. A second tier of boxes and/or compartments was set on the flat writing surface. It was similar to a *Bonheur du Jour*.

TABLE À JEU. A gaming or card table.

TABLE À JEU

TABLE À L'ANGLAISE. An extension-type dining table of the Louis XVI period.

TABLE À L'ARCHITECTE. A table with a hinged top. See *Architect's Table*.

TABLE À MILIEU. A *Center Table*. Illustrated is an early-19th-century English Regency design.

TABLE À OUVRAGE. A worktable. The name was usually applied to a small table with an undershelf or drawer. The drawer was often equipped with spaces for writing materials. Illustrated is a French Empire version. See *Pouch Table* and *Worktable*.

TABLE À OUVRAGE

TABLE À ROGNON

TABLE À ROGNON. A kidney-shaped table. This particular shape was especially popular in the Louis XV period. See *Kidney Desk or Table*.

TABLE CHAIR. An armchair or settle of the 16th and 17th centuries which had a hinged tabletop for a back. When the back was swung up and lowered over the arms, the table came into being. Illustrated is an oak chair of the Jacobean period. A drawer was placed below the seat.

TABLE DE CHEVET. A night table which was probably originated in the period of Louis XV. See *Chevet*.

TABLE DE DAME. A lady's small dressing or powder table of the 18th century. It was especially popular in the Louis XV period. See *Poudreuse*.

TABLE JARDINIÈRE. A table with a sunken well in the surface to hold a plant container. The earliest tables were sometimes decorated with Sèvres plaques.

TABLEAUX. French for pictures, paintings, or scenes. Illustrated is a painted window of the 13th century in Chartres Cathedral.

TABLEAU

TABLEAUX TENTURES. A set of wallpaper panels which, when put up together, makes one large panoramic scene or a series of coordinated scenes. A wallpaper mural of many panels. It was popular in the early 19th century.

TABLET CHAIR. A chair with a wide flat arm which serves as a shelf or writing surface. It appeared on 18th-century American Windsor chairs, and a popular early-20th-century version appeared in many schoolrooms. The design is also called a "writing armchair."

TABLET CHAIR

TABONUCO. A light-colored, beautifully grained, West Indian hardwood.

TABOURET. A low upholstered sitting stool. In the 17th century, in France, it was a distinguished seat for a lady of the court to sit on before the King and Queen. It was also used in the court of Queen Anne. In the 18th century, the tabouret was replaced by the side chair. A tabouret may also be an unupholstered stool which can function as a stand or table.

TABOURET

TAFFETA. A plain, basic weave, as well as the crisp fabric produced with this weave. The warp and weft threads are of equal size, and the resulting fabric is smooth on both sides with a lustrous surface. It is named for the Persian fabric "taftah." Taffeta may also be woven in such a manner as to produce a changeable, iridescent effect. It is also called "taffety."

TAFFETA, ANTIQUE. A stiff, plain-weave fabric made of duppion to simulate 18th-century taffeta. See *Douppioni or Duppion*.

TAFFETA, FAILLE. Taffeta woven with a pronounced crosswise rib.

TAFFETA, MOIRÉ. Rayon or silk taffeta with a watered or moiré effect. See *Moiré*.

TAFFETA, PAPER. A lightweight taffeta which has been treated to produce a crisp, paper-like finish.

TAFFETA, TISSUE. A very lightweight, semitransparent fabric.

TAILLE-DOUCE. French for "line engraving." See *Engraving.*

TAILPIECE. A projection on the back of the seat of certain Windsor chairs which receives the spindle braces.

TAJ MAHAL

TAJ MAHAL. A royal mausoleum (A.D. 1630) in Agra, India, made of white marble. It stands on a 313'-square platform which is 18' high. The central dome of the unit is 80' high by 58' in diameter. The dome is capped by an outer dome 200' above the platform. The interior is illuminated by pierced marble screens on the upper story. The marble is inlaid with semiprecious stones in scroll, frets, and wreaths. The entire unit is one of perfect symmetry.

TALIESIN. The late Frank Lloyd Wright's summer home in Taliesin, Wisconsin. The first house was designed in 1914, and the second house burned down in the early 1920's. In 1925, the present structure was started in wood and local stone. The building is composed of low-slung lines which appear to be growing out of the surrounding terrain.

TALL CASE CLOCK

TALIESIN WEST. The Frank Lloyd Wright home built in 1938 at Scottsdale, Arizona. It is an abstract creation of wood, stone, and canvas based on Ocotillo Camp, which was built in 1927 near Chandler, Arizona.

TALL CASE CLOCK. See *Grandfather (long case) Clock.*

TALLBOY. One chest of drawers set on top of another larger chest. This piece of furniture was introduced at the end of the 17th century. Illustrated is a design by Ware. See *Chest on Chest* and *Highboy.*

TALON-AND-BALL FOOT. See *Claw-and-Ball Foot.* Illustrated is a Hogarth chair of the Queen Anne period.

TALLBOY

TALON—AND—BALL FOOT

TAMBOUR

TAMBOUR. French for "drum," or "drum-shaped." A flexible rollover top, or rolltop desk or table. Small molding strips or reeds are transversely glued onto a heavy canvas backing, the ends of which fit into grooves on the inner sides of the piece of furniture. It may also be used as a vertical rolling or sliding door on a cabinet, chest, etc. A Hepplewhite desk is illustrated. See *Demilune* illustration.

TAMBOUR CURTAIN. Panels·of fine sheer cotton fabric (batiste, muslin, or lawn) which usually have embroidered borders or allover patterns.

TAMBOUR EMBROIDERY. A chain-stitch form of embroidery which is done on special tambour frames. At present it is a machine technique which is made to resemble the handmade product. It is used to decorate fine lawn, batiste, and muslin fabric panels that are used as curtains. See *Tambour Curtain*.

TAMO. Japanese ash. A figured blond wood with patterns that may vary: fiddleback, mottle, swirls, and "peanut-shell" figures. Tamo bends easily, glues well, and takes a beautiful finish.

TANGUILE. A Philippine dark, red-brown hardwood similar to *Lauaun*. It is sometimes marketed as Philippine maghogany.

TAPA CLOTH. A fiber cloth made in the South Seas, and usually block printed in bright, allover, native designs. The printing is accomplished with vegetable and animal dyes. The fibers that are used are usually derived from the bark of the mulberry.

TAPER LEG. A straight, rectangular furniture leg which tapers and thins down evenly as it approaches the bottom or foot. A Hepplewhite chair is illustrated. See *Therm Foot*.

TAPER LEG

TAPESTRY. From the French "tapisser," to line. A handwoven fabric with a ribbed surface like rep. The design is woven in during the manufacturing process, making it an essential part of the fabric structure. Pictorial tapestries were originally made of wool accented with silk and metallic threads, and they were used to line the cold, draughty walls of medieval castles and fortresses. A handmade tapestry is reversible if the loose threads are snipped off. At the end of the 19th century, there was a revival of this art in England under the guidance of William Morris. The earliest wallpapers in England were referred to as "paper tapestries." Illustrated is a 16th-century wall tapestry from the Fontainebleau Palace. See *Arras* and *Mortlake Tapestries*.

TAPESTRY

TAPESTRY CARPET. Carpet made with an uncut pile fabric woven on a velvet loom; often referred to as a hooked-type carpet. Special textured effects can be achieved on the tapestry carpet.

TAPET. A late-Gothic, early-Renaissance term for a carpet. At that time, a carpet meant a table covering. Illustrated is the interior of a late-14th- early-15th-century French château (after Viollet-le-Duc). Note the carpet (tapet), the built-in furniture, canapés, woodwork, and fireplace.

TAPET

444

TAPISSERIES

TARSIA

TAVERN TABLE

TAPISSERIES. French for "tapestries" or "arras."

TARLATAN. A stiff, gauzelike fabric.

TARSIA. See *Intarsia or Tarsia.*

TASLAN. A trademark name for Dupont's textured air-bulked yarn.

TASSEL. A pendent ornament; usually twisted threads around a roundish core with a thick fringe of the twisted threads falling below the core. The tassel can be applied to the corners of pillows on upholstery pieces, along the edges of draperies, on cornices, etc.

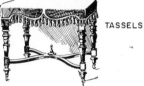

TASSELS

TATAMI. A natural straw matting woven in uneven rows. Tatami mats are often bound in black tape and used by Japanese architects, arranged in certain patterns, for wall coverings as well as floor coverings. The texture of the tatami mat has been reproduced in vinyl.

TAUPE. French for "mole" or "moleskin." A dark, brownish, gray-purple color.

TAVERN TABLE. A simple, leafless table of the 17th and 18th centuries, somewhat like a refectory table. The term is also used for a stretcher or turned table. Illustrated is a German Renaissance example.

TAZZA. An Italian term for a large ornamented cup or a footed tray. Illustrated is an Italian Renaissance design credited to Benvenuto Cellini.

TEA CADDY

TAZZA

TEA CADDY. A tea chest of elegant design made of wood, china, earthenware, pewter, or silver. In 18th-century England, these pieces were designed by the leading decorators and designers, and they were considered an important household item. A Chippendale design is illustrated.

TEAK. A light tobacco-brown wood with fine black streaks. The blackish cast that is often associated with teak is a stain. Teak is important in tropical countries where exposure to moisture, heat, and insect attacks are important factors in furniture construction. The wood has a rippled or mottled figure, and the color becomes deeper with age. Teak is native to India, Burma, Java, and the Malay Peninsula.

TEAKETTLE STAND. In the Chippendale period (mid-18th century), a small tripod table with a central column support and a gallery around the edge of the table surface.

TEAPOY. The Hindustani word for "tripod." A small, low table, most usually a tripod but sometimes four-legged. It was popularly used in the 18th century. The teapoy was actually a large tea chest on legs, with a lift-up top under which the tea caddies were kept.

TEARDROP BRASSES. Teardrop-shaped pendants or drops which are used as pulls or handles on drawers, doors, etc. Drawer pulls.

TELAMONES. Male caryatids. This is the Roman term for "Atlantes." See *Atlantes* and *Caryatids*.

TEMPER. In masonry, to add water to clay, plaster, or mortar, and mix the solution to the proper consistency for use.

TEMPERA. A common painting technique up to the 16th century. Powdered color is mixed with fresh egg yokes, thinned with water, and then applied to a panel which has been well prepared with gesso. It dries quickly, during which the color lightens; it is a tough and permanent finish. Tempera is much like the current gouache technique. See *Gesso* and *Gouache*. Illustrated is a German mid-14th-century tempera painting on a panel.

TEMPLATE. A block at the top of a wall or pier, which supports the ends of the joists or roof trusses. It is used as a load distributor, and is also called a "padstone."

TEMPLE OF VESTA. Built in the Greek style at Tivoli in the time of Augustus Caesar (27 B.C.–A.D. 14). It is a circular structure with a peristyle of eighteen Corinthian columns, and it was the inspiration for Soane's Bank of England at the end of the 18th century. See *Soane, Sir John*.

TEMPLET. A pattern for a construction or decoration. A contour drawing of the exact shape and size.

TEMPORA. A trademark name for a nonwoven, feltlike wooden upholstery and drapery fabric.

TEAKETTLE STAND

TEARDROP BRASSES

TELAMONES

TEMPERA

TEMPLE OF VESTA

TENIA

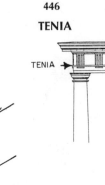

TENIA

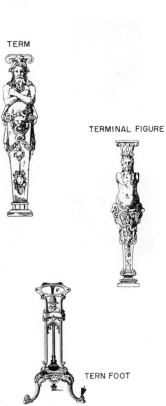

TENON

TENIA. The flat band at the top of a Doric architrave upon which the triglyphs rest.

TENON. In carpentry, a projection at the end of a piece of wood which is shaped to fit into a special opening (a mortise) of a corresponding shape in another piece of wood. It is used in joinery. See *Mortise and Tenon Joint.*

TENSILE STRENGTH. The ability of a material to resist breaking under stress.

TENT BED. An 18th-century variation of the camp or field bed. A four-poster with a tester that resembles a tent top. A Chippendale design is illustrated. See *Field Bed.*

TENT BED

TERM

TERMINAL FIGURE

TERN FOOT

TENTURE. The French term for tapestry, wall hanging, colored wallpapers, or a set or series of tapestries on one particular subject.

TERM. A pedestal which usually tapers toward the base; sometimes not only the pedestal but also the bust that stands on it. A term is also identified as a "terminus," a pilaster-like support which resembles an inverted obelisk. It was used by the Romans as a land marker. The term was used as a decorative device in the Renaissance period, and especially in the French rococo period.

TERMINAL FIGURES. Human figures, natural or grotesque, often carved in high relief, and used to embellish prominent features on furniture or architectural structures. See *Term.* See illustration for *Torso.*

TERMINUS. See *Term.*

TERN FOOT. Triple scrolled foot. Illustrated is a mid-18th-century Chippendale design.

TERRACE. A raised, out-of-doors area, usually surrounded by a balustrade or low fence. The term may also refer to a continuous row of houses.

TERRA COTTA. Italian for "baked earth." Clay fashioned into ornaments, vessels, tiles, etc., and then baked. The finished pieces vary in color from a gray brown to a brick red. The clay may be colored with paint or a baked-on glaze. Terra cotta baked in molds can be used as a facing material for buildings, flooring, etc. Illustrated is a German Renaissance terra-cotta plaque.

TERRAZZO. A concrete made up of small pieces of crushed marble and cement. It is used for pavements, floors, and walls, and is sometimes accented with metal feature strips. The color will vary with that of the crushed marble used.

TERRE-CUITE. See *Faïence* and *Terra-cotta*.

TERRY, ELI. An early-19th-century American clockmaker. See *Pillar-and-Scroll*.

TERTIARY COLORS. Colors produced by mixing a primary color with an adjacent secondary color: red and orange produce a red-orange. See *Primary Colors* and *Secondary Colors*.

TESSELLATED. Describes a surface, e.g., a wall, treated with a mosaic design composed of small cubes (tesserae) of stone, glass, marble, etc. A Pompeiian tessellated wall decoration is illustrated.

TESTALIN, LOUIS.

TERRA COTTA

TESSELLATED

TESSERAE

TESSERAE. Little cubes of glass, marble, stone, ceramic, etc., used in mosaic designs. See *Tessellated*.

TESTALIN, LOUIS. A 17th-century French portrait painter and tapestry designer at the Gobelins Factory.

LOUIS TESTALIN

TESTER

TESTER

TÊTE-À-TÊTE

TÊTE D'ANGE

TEXTILE

TESTER. A canopy on a four-post or draped bed, from the French term "testière," which means "headpiece." Originally the tester was a flat wooden canopy, paneled and carved, and used as a roof for four-post Tudor and Stuart bedsteads. This was replaced by a wooden framework heavily draped and swathed with valances, until, in the mid-18th century, it became a small wood cornice with a fabric valance and curtains.

TÊTE DE NÈGRE. French for "Negro's head." A dark blackish-brown color.

TÊTE-À-TÊTE. An S-curved sofa for two, also called a Siamoise. A 19th-century design in which the seated persons sit shoulder to shoulder but facing in opposite directions. See *Siamoise*.

TÊTE D'ANGE

TÊTES D'ANGES. Angels' heads with wings. Decorative sculptured devices sometimes set in medallions or rondels or on top of pilasters. The motif was used in Renaissance architecture and furniture, and also in the late 18th century in France and England.

TETRASTYLE. A classic building style with a four-column portico.

TETRASTYLE

TEXTILE BLOCK. A means of construction used by Frank Lloyd Wright on his "California Houses" in the 1920's. He used pre-cast patterned or pierced concrete blocks with vertical and horizontal metal rods running through them. The hollow spaces were filled with cement. The Millard House in Pasadena, California, which was built in 1923, is a classic example of textile block construction.

TEXTILES. Fabrics. Woven or unwoven materials which are used for upholstery, drapery, wall coverings, etc. They may be made of natural fibers (wool, silk, cotton, linen), synthetics (rayon, nylon, dacron, etc.), or combinations of natural and synthetic fibers. Illustrated is an Italian version of a Louis XVI style of drapery treatment.

TEXTOLITE. A trademark name for a plastic material manufactured by General Electric. It is produced in a wide range of colors, patterns, and textural effects. Textolite is easy to clean, resists stains and scratches, and is used for laminating onto table and counter tops, walls, etc.

TEXTURAL DESIGN. In fabrics and carpets, a design created in the texture of the weave rather than by the use of colored patterns.

TEXTURE. The feel and appearance of the surface of a material or fabric, e.g., smooth, rough, pebbly. Texture can also refer to the "grain" in wood. See *Embossed*.

THATCH. A roof covering of straw or reeds.

THATCH

THEATRICAL GAUZE. A plain-weave, open, lightweight cotton or linen fabric. Usually this semisheer fabric is stiffened with size to give it body. The gauze is produced in a wide range of color and in wide widths. It is also called "opera gauze," and is mainly used for glass curtains.

THERM FOOT. A rectangular, tapering foot for a chair, table, or cabinet leg. It is also called a spade foot, and was favored by mid- and late-18th-century designers like the Adam brothers, Hepplewhite, and Shearer.

THERM LEG. A four-sided tapering leg. A favorite furniture support of Hepplewhite (illustrated) and other mid- to late-18th-century English designers. The leg could be simple or highly decorated with carving or inlay work. See *Taper Leg*.

THERM FOOT

THERM LEG

THERMAE. Roman baths. Shown is the plan of the Baths of Caracalla in Rome which were 730' long by 380' wide. They contained a swimming pool, hot baths, dressing rooms, gymnasiums, and other athletic halls as well as a large domed solarium.

THERMAE

THERMOPANE. A trademark name for a double glass insulating pane used on doors and windows.

THERMOPLASTIC. Describes plastic materials and synthetic resins that soften at high temperatures.

THERMOSETTING. Describes plastics and synthetic resins that harden and set at high temperatures. The opposite of thermoplastic.

THIMBLE FOOT. A spade or sabot foot, but one that is usually turned rather than rectangular. See *Sabot Foot* and *Spade Foot*.

THIMBLE FOOT

THIRTEEN-STATE TRACERY. A late-18th-century fretwork or tracery made up of thirteen elements. The idea was originally Chinese, and the concept of the original thirteen states was superimposed on the established design. It was used to decorate the glass panels of secretaries and bookcases of the late 18th century.

THIRTEEN-STATE TRACERY

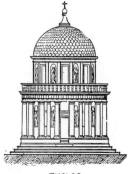

THOLOS

THOLOS. Greek for the cupola or dome of a circular building, or the building itself. Illustrated is the Italian Renaissance Tempietto designed by Bramante (Donato d'Agnolo) in the courtyard of St. Peter's in Montorio. See *Rotunda*.

THOMIRE, PIERRE PHILIPPE (1751–1843). A French Empire metal chaser and engraver who specialized in making plaques with figures in low relief, which were applied to furniture. Besides these gods, goddesses, and caryatids, he created gilt bronze mountings which were sometimes credited to his contemporary, Pierre Gouthière. Thomire was a student of the sculptor Jean Antoine Houdon.

THONET, MICHAEL. See *Bentwood Furniture*.

THORNTON, WILLIAM. A late-18th- early-19th-century American architect who prepared the first plans for the Capitol in Washington, D.C. Though he never formally studied architecture, at the age of twenty-eight he prepared a winning design for a Philadelphia library. It is believed that he "borrowed" the high central dome and the balancing wings of the Capitol from Étienne Sulpice Hallet, a French professional architect who had also entered the Capitol competition. The great rotunda was Thornton's invention, and it greatly satisfied George Washington's concept of "grandeur and simplicity." Though Thornton won the competition, Hallet was appointed superintendent of the construction. Thornton also went on to design Tudor Place in Georgetown (completed in 1815) for Washington's step-granddaughter, Mary Parke Custis. It was designed in the English Regency style. The Octagon, the Washington, D.C., town house of John Tayloe, was designed by Thornton.

THOROUGHGOOD (Adam) HOUSE. Built in 1636 in Princess Anne County, Virginia, this is believed to be the oldest Anglo-Saxon-constructed house in America. It is a four-room house with two rooms on each floor. Flemish bonding was used on the brick front, and the other sides were bricked in the English bond pattern.

THOUSAND-LEGGED TABLE. A variation of the gateleg table which dates back to the first half of the 17th century. It had a central drawer, two extra swinging legs which folded in under the braces of the tabletop, and two leaves that dropped down. When the table was fully opened, it could be as much as five feet in diameter. See *Eight-legged Table* and *Gateleg Table*.

THREE-BACK WINDSOR CHAIR. See *Comb Back*.

THREE-QUARTER WIDTH. A term in carpet construction. One quarter of a yard or 9" is a unit of loom width, and a standard carpet is "three-quarters" or 27" wide. In Europe "three-quarters" is referred to as an "ell."

THROATING. See *Check Throating*.

THRUST. The outward force exerted by an arch or vault. The stress which acts between two contiguous bodies when each is pushing the other from itself. The flying buttress was evolved to meet the thrust of the main vault at its points of concentration.

THRU-VU VERTICAL BLINDS. Vertical strip blinds used over windows and made of lightweight metal or fabric. The blinds are used to control light and air much as the traditional horizontal "Venetian" blinds do. These blinds were originally designed by George Nelson and Henry Wright. The concept has since been imitated, adapted, and improved under other trademark names. Vertical blinds are sometimes called "Boston" blinds.

THUMB MOLDING. A convex molding with a flattened curve. It is also referred to as "lip molding."

THUYA. A hard, dark, red-brown wood which is native to North Africa and usually has a bird's-eye figure. The wood takes a high polish, and is used for cabinetwork. Thuya was used by the ancient Greeks and Chinese, and it was also a popular veneer wood in 18th-century England.

TIAMA. See *Sapele or Sapeli*.

THOUSAND-LEGGED TABLE

THRUST

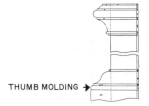

THUMB MOLDING ➔

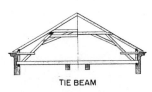

TIE BEAM

TIEBACK

TIERCERON

TILE

TILL

TICKING. A closely woven cotton fabric with a twill or satin weave. It is most usually woven with stripes, but it may also be printed. Ticking is a sturdy fabric for mattress covers, and also a decorative fabric for drapery, upholstery, and wall covering. The fine striped quality of ticking has been reproduced on wallpaper.

TIE BEAM. A horizontal beam which connects the rafters, and and keeps them from spreading. The tie beam is used in truss construction to counteract the outward thrust of the slanting members.

TIEBACK. A fabric sash or cord with tassels, or a decorative metal, glass, or wood hook, rosette, or bar to hold back a drape. When the drape is tied back to the sides (or one side only) of an opening, a decorative swelling of fabric appears above the tiebacks, and the fabric below cascades down, usually to the floor.

TIEPOLO, GIOVANNI BATTISTA (1696–1770). An outstanding Venetian artist, designer, and decorator of the 18th century. He painted many wall frescoes and ornate ceilings which were filled with light, brilliant color, and remarkable perspective and foreshortening. His ceilings often were filled with sunny skies, clouds, cherubs, and classical gods and goddesses. He personified the Venetian Rococo period, though he also worked in Würzburg (the royal palace) and Madrid.

TIER. See *Wythe or Withe.*

TIER TABLE. A small round table consisting of two or more surfaces or shelves set one over the other with the largest one at the bottom. A serving table. See *Serviteur Fidèle.*

TIERCERON. See *Intermediate Ribs.*

TIGERWOOD. Also called "African walnut" and "Nigerian golden walnut." A West African wood of a grayish-brown to golden-brown color, accented with black streaks and a definite ribbon stripe. It is used for cabinetry and paneling.

TILE. A thin slab of baked clay used for a roof covering material. The tile may be glazed and/or ornamented, and also used for walls, floors, counters, etc. Illustrated are two methods of tiling a roof: *A* uses a single tile, *B* uses a double tile.

TILL. A small drawer or compartment in a table, desk, chest, etc., for money, jewelry, or special papers. The till is often equipped with secret springs or locks.

TILTING FILLET. A triangular piece of wood laid under the lowest course of slates or tiles on a roof to give the roof an extra pitch.

TILT-TOP. A pedestal table with a hinged top which can be dropped vertically when not in use, or raised to a horizontal position when it is to be used. See *Snap Table*.

TINT. A color with white added, which in effect lightens or pales down the color to a pastel. It is the opposite of "shade," which is a color with black added.

TINTORETTO, IL (Jacopo Robusti) (1518–1594). A Venetian painter who created great emotional effects by the play of light and shadow in his paintings. His most noted works are in the Scuola di S. Rocco in Venice: the 12' tall "Life of the Virgin," in the lower hall, and the 16' "Life of Christ," in the upper hall. Scenes of the Passion are found in other rooms.

TIP-UP TABLE. A double-leaved table which folds like a book (the hinged leaves hang down on either side of a central spine). It is similar to a *Snap Table* or *Tilt-Top* table.

TIRETTES. The French term for "extensions" or pullout leaves or slides which provide a larger table surface.

TISSUES. Semisheer, crisp fabrics made of silk or synthetic yarns.

TITIAN (TIZIANO VECELLIO) (1477–1576). A Venetian painter with the sensuous quality of the Renaissance, who was influenced by the work of Giorgione (Giorgio Barbarelli). In his later years he developed a free, almost impressionistic style, in which form was rendered in patches of color rather than contours. Among his famous works are: "The Assumption of the Virgin" in S. Nicolò dei Frari Church in Venice, the "Pesaro Altar," "Portrait of Pope Pau III and His Farnese Grandsons," and many portraits of notables of the day.

TODDY TABLE. A small table of the Georgian period in England. A Hepplewhite design is illustrated. See *Urn Stands*.

TOILE. French for a linen- or canvas-like cloth. A fabric for painting, or a painting or picture. A fabric with pictures printed all over it. See *Toile de Jouy*.

TOILE DE JOUY. Originally a hand-blocked cotton or linen fabric with pastoral scenes printed all over, in one color, on a white or natural background. The printed fabrics, called "indiennes," were produced in a factory which was started and operated by Christophe-Philippe Oberkampf at Jouy, near Versailles, in the mid-18th century. Oberkampf designed pictorial groups in large repeats in one color (red, blue, green, or eggplant), and printed them on natural cream-colored cotton. They showed groups of peasants or aristocrats dressed in their different costumes and engaged in their everyday activities, as

TILT-TOP

TIRETTE

TODDY TABLE

TOILES D'INDY

TOILET MIRROR

TOILET TABLE

TOMBS OF THE CALIPHS

TONDO

well as bourgeois scenes, fables, and historical scenes. Later, discoveries at Pompeii and changes in the French government influenced Oberkampf's designs, as did the ornamental motifs of Napoleon's designers Charles Percier and Pierre Fontaine. All the original Jouy prints were marked "Bon-Teint" on the selvage, which means "fast dye."

TOILES D'INDY. Printed cottons and linens with floral or pictorial designs which were imported into France during the late 17th century from India and Persia. See *Indienne Fabrics*.

TOILET MIRROR. A cheval-type mirror with dressing table compartments. Illustrated is a Sheraton design. The toilet mirror is also called a dressing mirror.

TOILET TABLE. See *Dressing Table*.

TÔLE. French for sheet iron. Objects made of sheet metal or tin and ornamented with painted or enameled patterns. 18th-century lamps, boxes, trays, etc., were often made of tôle.

TÔLE SHADE. A lampshade made of sheet metal. It is often decorated with painted or decal artwork. This type of shade is usually associated with Early American, early 19th century, and provincial lamp designs. See *Bouillotte Shade*.

TOMBS OF THE CALIPHS. Located in Cairo, Egypt, these tombs are fine examples of Egyptian-Saracenic architecture. The Mosque of the Sultan Berkook, built in 1384, is one of this group. It is famous for the graceful domes over the tomb chambers, and the soaring minarets.

TONAL VALUE. The relative strength of a color in contrast to black and white.

TONDINO. Italian for "circular molding." See *Tondo*.

TONDO. A circular picture. This shape was popular in Italy in the mid-15th century. A painted circular panel by François Boucher is shown.

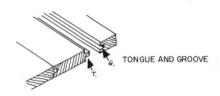

TONGUE AND GROOVE

TONGUE AND GROOVE. A type of joinery in which a long, narrow, straight projection (the tongue) fits into a corresponding groove in the adjacent piece. *T* is the tongue, *G* is the groove. See *Joinery*.

TONTINE. A trademark name for Dupont's washable window shade fabric.

TOOTHER. A masonry projection from one end of a wall against which another wall is to be built.

TOOTHING. A form of masonry for constructing a temporary end wall against which another wall will eventually be built; the end stretcher of every alternate course juts out beyond the end stretcher of the intervening courses.

TOP COLOR. In printed or screened fabrics, papers, etc., the color or colors that are applied over the basic or ground color of the material. The design or decoration is produced in the top colors. See *Ground Color*.

TOP RAIL. A horizontal bar or rail which connects the uprights of a chair back, and supports the cresting, if any. It is also called the "cresting rail." In some historical periods, the top rail appears to be a continuation of the uprights in that it is a curve, serpentine or bow-shaped. The term "top rail" also refers to the top horizontal member of a door.

TOP RAIL

TOPE

TOPES. Artificially created mounds of earth in Indian architecture. Illustrated is the Great Tope of Sanchi which is 135' in diameter and 60' high. The dome is built of brick and clay, faced with hewn stones that are coated with stucco. The topes were built to contain the sacred relics of Buddha.

TOPIARY ART. The clipping and shaping of plants, shrubs, and trees into formal or fanciful shapes: geometric, bird, or animal forms. Topiary trees have been featured in formal gardens from the 16th century to the present.

TORCH. A flambeau. A flaming brand. A Roman motif which reappeared in the Renaissance, Directoire, and Empire periods.

TORCHÈRE. Originally, a small table designed to hold a candlestick, candelabrum, or other light-giving object. The table surface was usually mounted on a pillar or light framework, and often embellished with carvings and gilt. It was originally a French design of the Louis XV period. In current terminology, a standing floor lamp, usually with an inverted bowl shade which casts the light upward toward the ceiling. Illustrated is a Chippendale design. The torchère was also called a *Guéridon*.

TORSADE. A molding with a twisted ropelike or cable design. See *Cable*.

TORCH

TORCHÈRE

TORSADE

TORSO

TORSO

TORSO. The trunk of the human body. Illustrated is a drawing by Hans Holbein of Erasmus with his hand resting on a sculptured torso and head.

TORTOISESHELL. The back plates of a sea turtle which are flattened out and joined together under heat and pressure. Tortoiseshell was used in antiquity as a veneering material for furniture. It again became popular, thanks to Charles-André Boulle and his inlay technique, during the period of Louis XIV. It is usually a mottled brown, gold, and black material which is semitranslucent. See *Boulle Work*.

TORUS. In architecture, a convex, semicircular molding, often found at the base of a column. A Roman example is illustrated.

TORUS ➤

TOUCHSTONE

TOUCHSTONE. A black marble from Namur, Belgium. It was used on chimneypieces and mantels in the late 16th and early 17th centuries. Nicholas Stone often used touchstone in his work. See *Stone, Nicholas*.

TOURO SYNAGOGUE. Built in Newport, Rhode Island, 1759–1763, by Peter Harrison. It is considered one of the most beautiful ecclesiastical interiors of the American Colonial period. The arched, two-storied, galleried hall is reminiscent of Inigo Jones's banquet hall at Whitehall Palace. The altarpiece is based on a design in Batty Langley's *Treasury of Design*.

TOWEL HORSE or TOWEL RAIL. A slight wood frame with several crossbars used to hold towels. It usually stood on two or more legs. The towel horse was in vogue in England in the mid-18th century.

TOWNSEND, JOB. An 18th-century American cabinetmaker. He is considered to have been the dean of the Newport furniture makers.

TOWNSEND, JOHN. An 18th-century American cabinetmaker who worked in and around Newport, Rhode Island.

JOB TOWNSEND

TRABEATED CONSTRUCTION. A form of construction in which the supporting members are the post and lintel rather than the arch.

TRABEATED CONSTRUCTION

TRABEAZIONE. Italian for "entablature."

TRACERY

TRACERY. Originally the stone mullions in Gothic windows. A decorative form composed of circles, with arcs formed by the intersection of circles. Thus every line is either a circle or the broken arc of a circle, and the composition of these elements makes for intricate patterns. See *Bar Tracery* and *Plate Tracery*. In the Chippendale Gothic period, tracery appears in chair backs, door panels, etc.

TRACHELION. The neck of a Greek Doric column, between the annulets and the hypotrachelion. In the illustration, *A* is the annulets, *T* is the trachelion, and *H* is the hypotrachelion.

TRACHELION

TRADITIONAL

TRADITIONAL. In interior decoration, a term usually applied to a style of a bygone age in contrast to a contemporary or modern style.

TRAFORO. Italian for "tracery" or "fretwork."

TRANSEPT. In church architecture, the part that crosses the nave at right angles near the apse of the building. The plan of Amiens Cathedral is given here.

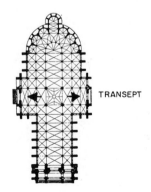

TRANSEPT

TRANSITIONAL

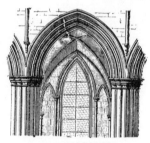

TRANSOM

TRANSFER PRINTING. A method of applying one-color designs to pottery. The pattern is printed on paper by means of a copperplate engraving, and it is then transferred to the pottery like a decal. See *Decalcomania*.

TRANSITIONAL. Describes a style which combines elements already established with those of a newly appearing style. An example would be the French Régence, which was a transition from the Louis XIV style to the Louis XV style. See *French Régence or Regency*. Illustrated is a mural design by Oppenord, a Régence designer.

TRANSLUCENT. A material (fabric, glass, etc.) which allows light to pass through, but diffuses it so that objects cannot be seen clearly. See *Obscure Glass*.

TRANSOM. The upper part of a window, or the window over a doorway. It usually is constructed to allow in air as well as light.

TRANSVERSE RIBS. In arch vaulting, the main ribs which mark or delineate the contour of a vault.

TRAPUNTO

TRANSVERSE RIBS

TRAPUNTO. A type of quilting which gives a raised relief effect to a stitched design. The design is usually outlined with single stitches, and then filled from behind. Trapunto is often used to embellish the pillow backs of upholstered pieces.

TRAVERTINE. A cream-colored, onyx-like stone which is usually pockmarked or full of irregularly shaped depressions. The material is currently being reproduced as a vinyl floor-covering design.

TRAY TABLE. A collapsible stand which, when opened, supports a tray. The tray serves as a table surface.

TRAYLE. A running vine with grape clusters and leaves which appeared as a decorative element in the architecture and designs of Tudor England. It is also called a *Vinette*.

TRAY-TOP TABLE. A small table with a low gallery or skirting around three or all four sides. This design was popular in the mid- to late-18th century. A Sheraton design is illustrated.

TRAYLE

TRAY-TOP TABLE

TREAD. In stair construction, the flat, horizontal part of the step between two risers. See *Riser* illustration where arrow points to the tread.

TREAUMAU. A noted embroiderer of the Louis XV and Louis XVI periods. He created and executed beautiful designs for pillows and chair and sofa cushions. Among his most ambitious works were the "Four Seasons" and the "Four Elements" embroidered on the cushions of the two carriages which were sent to Marie Antoinette in 1770.

TRECENTO. The thirteen hundreds or the 14th century. Illustrated is a 14th-century English folding chair.

"TREE OF LIFE" PATTERN. A tree or vine with branches, leaves, flowers, and small animals. It was originated by the ancient Assyrians and was used as a decorative motif by the Persians, Indians, and English Renaissance craftsmen. See *Hom* and *Palampores.*

TREFOIL. A three-lobed, clover-like ornament often associated with Gothic tracery and decoration. The three arcs are separated by the cusps. The trefoil was the Gothic symbol for the Holy Trinity.

TRELLISWORK. A crossbarred or lattice effect in wood. A pierced or fretted woodwork design with a reticulated appearance. Adam, Chippendale, and others used brass trelliswork for inserts in bookcase doors. Illustrated is a Sheraton "gentleman's secretary."

TRENAILS. Literally "tree nails" or wooden pegs which have been rounded and tapered to a point. They were used in the construction of finer 18th-century pieces.

TRENCHER. A large wooden serving platter or, originally, a slice of bread upon which food was placed.

TRESTLE. A supporting frame. The term is derived from the Old French "trestel," a beam. In the Tudor period, large boards were supported by these trestles to form trestle tables.

TRESTLE TABLE. See *Sawbuck Table.* For illustration, see *Arkwright.*

TRIANGLE SEAT. Sometimes called a corner seat or a boffet or buffet chair. The latter was a Scandinavian design which was made in England in the early 17th century. Triangular chairs were also made in the Queen Anne period and afterward, with splats on the two sides under the semicircular arm and backrest which encircled the two sides of the triangle. See *Barber's Chair.*

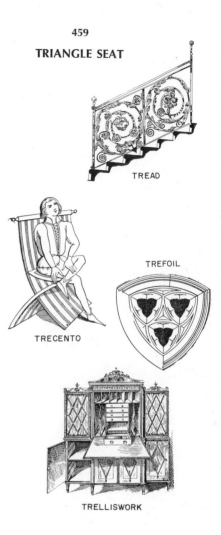

TRIANGLE SEAT

TREAD

TREFOIL

TRECENTO

TRELLISWORK

TRIBUNE GALLERY. In early Christian basilicas, as well as some Romanesque and early Gothic churches, an upper story over an aisle which usually opened onto the nave in arches. The triforium replaced the tribune gallery in later Gothic churches. See *Triforium*.

TRICLINIUM. A Roman dining room.

TRICOT. An inexpensive tapestry fabric the underside of which is different from the top side. It is usually made of cotton or rayon.

TRICOTEUSE. A small sewing table or worktable, usually with a gallery around the top. The table often had several shelves under the top surface. This type of unit appeared in the Louis XVI period, and continued through the Directoire and on into the 19th century. See *Pouch Table* and *Worktable*.

TRICTRAC TABLE. A backgammon table. It was a popular gaming table of the Régence, Louis XV, and Louis XVI periods. In the Louis XVI period, they were made of mahogany with removable tabletops. Sometimes, one side of this removable top was covered with leather and the reverse side was covered in baize. See *Baize*. The top was removed to reveal the interior of the table, a gaming area with a backgammon board, sockets for candles, and small drawers or compartments for dice and counters.

TRI-DARN. A Welsh court cupboard of the 16th century. It had two tiers of cupboards, and above them was an open, spindle-sided dresser. See *Deu-Darn*.

TRIFID

TRIFID. A three-toed furniture foot of the 18th century which was used in England and America. See *Tern Foot*.

TRIFOIL. A form of tracery consisting of three lobes or arcs. See *Trefoil*.

TRIFOIL

TRIFORIUM ►

TRIFORIUM. The upper story over the aisle of a cathedral. It is set between the sloping roof over the aisle and the vaulting over the nave. It was usually arched or arcaded. The triforium is also called a "blind story." See *Blind Story* illustration.

TRIGLYPHS. In the Doric entablature, the triple upright grooves channeled in the spaces between the metopes. The triglyphs and metopes together form the frieze.

TRIGLYPHS

TRILOK. A trademark name for corrugated, three-dimensional fabrics made of monofilament yarns. It is a durable, serviceable fabric used for upholstery in homes, autos, and public areas. It is patented by the United States Rubber Company.

TRIM. A term usually applied to the woodwork of rooms that are designed in a traditional style. Dadoes, wainscots, paneling, cornices, coves, chair rails, picture moldings, window and door moldings are all considered trims. Marble or stonework as on mantels could also be considered trim. On the exterior of a building, shutters, flower boxes, door and window moldings, cornices, etc., are trims. Illustrated is an early-18th-century wall design by Isaac Ware.

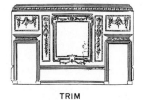

TRIM

TRIMMER ARCH. Usually a brickwork arch with a low rise which is used for supporting a fireplace hearth.

TRIPOD STAND. A small table with a flat or gallery top surface which rests on a column-like shaft. The shaft ends in a triple spread-legged support. It was a favorite little table of the 18th century in England and America. Illustrated is a Chippendale design.

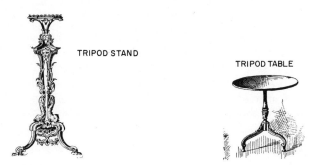

TRIPOD STAND

TRIPOD TABLE

TRIPOD TABLE. A pedestal table supported by three outward-curving legs. Adam and Chippendale designed many such tripod tables.

TRIPTYCH. Any three-panel or three-fold picture, screen, or mirror. A word originally applied to three-panel religious paintings used on altars.

TRIQUETRA. An ornamental interlaced pattern which consists of three pointed lobes.

TRIPTYCH

TRIVET. A small, openwork, three-legged frame, made in several metals and shapes, originally hung on the bars of a grate to keep a kettle or dish hot. Today, the word usually means a three-legged stand which raises a hot container off the surface of a table or server. A larger trivet is called a "footman." Trivets became fashionable in the mid-18th century.

TROMPE L'OEIL

TROPHY

TRUMEAU

TRUMEAU MIRROR

TRUSS

TROMPE L'OEIL. French for "deceive the eye." It is the technique of using such pictorial elements as perspective, foreshortening, shadows, etc., in rendering objects in paint or inlay so that they appear to be actually three-dimensional or real. The Italian form of trompe l'oeil is called "quadrature."

TROPHY. Tokens of victory. A decorative painted, carved, or inlaid arrangement of symbols of battle, weapons, horns, banners, spears, shields, laurel leaves, etc., which was set on a panel or a pilaster. Renaissance artists' trophies were executed in intarsia, woven fabrics, and tapestries. Other types of trophies were also developed: musical instruments, flowers, fruit, fish, animals, and professional symbols. See *Gibbons, Grinling,* and *Symbol.*

TRUCKLE BED. see *Trundle Bed or Truckle Bed.*

TRUMEAU. The French word for "pier" or the wall between windows. The overmantel or overdoor paneling which was usually filled with mirrors or paintings. The paintings were often made to look like relief sculpture in the 18th century. See *Grisaille.* The trumeau was part of the exquisite "boiserie" of the Louis XV and Louis XVI periods. See *Boiserie.*

TRUMEAU MIRROR. A framed mirror of the late 18th century. It was usually a tall rectangular mirror set into an overmantel. A characteristic element of the mirror is the scene painted in the upper section. In some cases, it was replaced by a carved panel. The decoration was usually more pronounced than the mirror. Illustrated is a mid-18th-century chimneypiece designed by Thomas Johnson of England with a trumeau mirror set above the mantel. See *Constitution Mirror.*

TRUMPET TURNING. A turning with a flaring end that resembles the bell of a trumpet. It was a 17th-century motif.

TRUNDLE BED or TRUCKLE BED. A trundle is a roller or caster, and the trundle or rollaway bed was originally a Gothic design. It was a small-scaled bed on casters for children or servants, which was rolled under a full-size bed when not in use. It was often used in Colonial and early American homes. In current usage, a pullout bed on casters somewhat smaller than the bed under which it is set. It is similar to a hideaway bed.

TRUSS. A combination of structural members so arranged as to form an unyielding frame which will support, without intermediate supports, a large span. See *Hammerbeam Roof, King-Post Roof,* and *Queen-Post Roof.* In furniture construction, a bracket, console, or corbel.

TUB CHAIR. A late-18th-century English easy chair with a rounded back and wide wings. It is similar to a barrel chair, but is wider, taller, and more enveloping. A Sheraton design is illustrated. In the Regency period (early 19th century) the design changed, and it more closely resembled the spoon-back chair except that, instead of having a splat, the entire back was enclosed with cane or upholstery.

TUB FRONT. See *Blockfront*.

TUB SOFA. A fully upholstered French design. The ends sweep around in curves, and they are provided with arm pads or manchettes. The persons seated at either end of this couch are slightly turned toward each other. It is similar to a kidney-shaped couch.

TUCKAWAY TABLE. An 18th-century American folding table with crossed or scissored legs. The top leaves dropped close together, and it became a compact storable unit. It was a fore-runner of the contemporary snack table.

TUDOR ARCH. A four-centered, flat-pointed arch, characteristic of the English Gothic and early Renaissance period.

TUDOR FLOWER. See *Brattishing*.

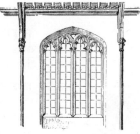

TUDOR ARCH

TUB CHAIR

TUDOR PERIOD

TUDOR PERIOD. The reign of the Tudor family in England from Henry VII through the reign of Elizabeth I (1485-1603). It was a transitional period in architecture and decoration from the late Gothic to the Renaissance. The period was essentially one of secular building which combined elements of the late Gothic perpendicular with Norman castellated motifs.

TUDOR ROSE. An English Renaissance decorative motif which consisted of a conventionalized five-petal rose with a smaller rose set in its center. It was the royal emblem of England, and symbolized the marriage of Henry VII of Lancaster (the red rose) to Elizabeth of York (the white rose).

TUDOR ROSE

TUDOR ROSE

TUFA. A lightweight volcanic stone, or a rock of a rough, irregular, cellular structure. It may also be formed as a calcareous deposit from water. The ancient Romans used tufa to make concrete.

TUFFT, THOMAS. A late-18th-century American cabinetmaker of Philadelphia. He is most noted for his simple lowboys.

TUFT. In carpet construction, a single yarn in a surface pile of a carpet. The tuft or yarn is produced by twisting together the fiber strands.

TUFTING

TUFTING. An upholstery technique. The covering fabric and the padding are tied back in a definite pattern, creating little "pillows" between the depressions. The tieback process is usually accomplished with self-covered buttons. Tufting makes the upholstery fabric conform to the curves of the unit. It is often used on leather (or imitation leather) pieces where the material is not as easily worked as most upholstery fabrics. An early-18th-century English armchair is illustrated. Tufting reached the peak of its popularity during the opulent, "overstuffed" Victorian period. Also, a new form of carpet construction. The pile yarns are sewn onto a wide fabric by means of multineedled machines. A heavy jute or canvas backing is used. The yarn ends of the tufted fabric are usually applied to the backing with latex.

TULIPWOOD. A small Brazilian tree which produces a yellowish wood with red and purple stripes. It is a member of the rosewood family, and the wood is used mainly for inlays and banding. See *Bois (or Boise) de Rose* and illustration for *Kingwood.*

TUNBRIDGE WARE. A kind of veneer which was made at Tunbridge Wells in England. It resembled minute mosaic work.

Many small rods or dowels of wood were arranged in a design, and they were then glued in place (like so many pieces of spaghetti glued together vertically). This cluster of rods was then thinly sliced, horizontally, through the collection of rods, and the design appeared on each fine, sectional slice of veneer.

TUNNEL VAULT. See *Barrel Vault*.

TUPELO. A gumwood of a light gray color which has a tendency toward warping unless it is properly dried. The wood will take a mahogany or walnut stain. Tupelo is often used for inexpensive furniture, interior trims, and in plywood construction.

TURKEY ROCKER. An overstuffed, liberally tufted easy chair set on a spring base. It was popular at the end of the 19th century.

TURKEY WORK. An oriental type of fabric or rug, or an imitation of it. Worsted yarns were pulled through a coarse, open-textured cloth, then knotted and cut. The patterns were usually executed in bright colors, and the fabric was used to cover the backs and seats of chairs after the mid-17th century.

TURKISH CORNER. An exuberant, overstuffed, overdecorated, overpillowed, and overcanopied area in a late Victorian home. It was an attempted re-creation of the informal, luxurious, exotic East in this already ornate and heavily patterned period. The corner was usually equipped with a large daybed, sometimes with a canopy, myriad bright cushions, Indian carved tables and stands, incense burners, vases with peacock feathers, water pipes, pictures, trophies, and an occasional animal skin.

TURNER, JOSEPH MALLORD WILLIAM (1775-1851). A noted English landscape painter and water colorist.

TURNING. An ornamental or structural member of furniture produced by rotating a wood dowel on a lathe, and shaping the dowel with cutting tools into a series of nodules, swellings, disks, etc. See *Spindle*.

TURNING

TURNIP DOME. A dome or cupola most often appearing in Russian, Near Eastern, and Arabic architecture and ornament. It resembles an inverted turnip, bulbous and overlapping the turrent or drum below, and tapering to a graceful point above. Illustrated is a group of turnip cupolas of a Russian church.

TURNIP DOME

TURNIP FOOT. A variation on the ball foot. The general appearance is that of an inverted turnip with a flattened end. A collar usually separated the ball from the floor. It was a 17th-century design.

TURPENTINE. A resinous fluid used as a solvent and dryer in paint mixing.

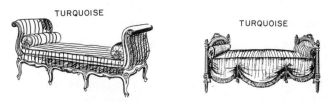

TURQUOISE

TURQUOISE

TURRET

TUSCAN

TURQUOISE. From the Old French for "Turkish." A type of daybed or settee which was introduced in the Louis XV period, and based on the oriental divan. The piece had a mattress-like cushion, no back, and equally high ends or side pieces. The daybed was usually placed with the long end against the wall, and two bolsters were set against the wall for additional comfort. Round bolsters were placed next to the rising end panels. The design was a forerunner of today's studio bed with bolster back. See *Divan* and *Studio Couch*.

TURRET. A small tower positioned above a larger one or on a building. Illustrated is the west front of the Bayeux Cathedral.

TUSCAN. See *Etruscan Order*. A Roman variation of the Doric order. See *Doric Order*.

TUSSAH SILK. Silk made from the cocoons of wild silkworms. It is usually light brown in color, and is used for weaving pongee, shiki, and shantung. It is coarse, strong, slubby, and uneven in texture.

TUXEDO SOFA. A clean-lined, simple, upholstered sofa with thin sides that flare out slightly. The upholstered sides are the same height as the sofa back, and thus a continuous line is created. The sofa can be finished with or without a skirt.

TWEED. A rough-surfaced material with a homespun effect. The yarn is usually dyed before weaving, and it is often woven in two or more colors to obtain some sort of pattern: plaid, check, or herringbone.

TWILL. A basic weave, and also the fabric produced by this weave. It has a distinct diagonal line owing to the weft yarn passing over one or more warp yarns, then under two or more. The herringbone is a variation on this weave.

TWINING STEM MOLDING. A molding which simulates a stylized tendril wound around a stem.

TWIN-SIZE BED. A standard twin-size bed is 39" wide by 75" long. Two twin-size springs may be used with one large headboard to make a unit about the size of a *King-Size Bed*.

TWIST CARPET. A floor covering made of uncut pile. Yarns of different colors are often twisted together to form the pile loops.

TWIST TURNING. A spiral turning used in France and Holland in the late 16th and early 17th centuries. It was introduced into England in the mid-17th century, and used during the Restoration period for legs, uprights, etc. Illustrated is a chair of the Louis XIII period. See *Spiral Leg*.

TWIST TURNING

TWISTED COLUMN. A decorative column which appears to be twisted around its vertical axis. It was popular in the French Renaissance period and also in the 19th century. The twisted column is also referred to as a "wreathed column."

TWO-CHAIR-BACK SETTEE. See *Courting Chair*. Illustrated is a late-17th-century English design.

TWISTED COLUMN

TWO-CHAIR-BACK SETTEE

TYMPANUM

TYMPANUM. The triangular surface of a pediment bounded by the lower molding and the sloping sides.

UMBRELLA SETUP. An architectural firm which consists of architects, engineers, landscape and interior designers, plus various other specialists. The concern is in this way able to provide a complete design coverage for a structure, internally as well as externally.

UNDERBRACING. The arrangement of stretchers, braces, or spandrels under chairs, tables, and chests. These elements are used to reinforce and strengthen the units. See *Stretcher*.

UNDERBRACING

UNDERFRAME. The part of furniture which is supported by the legs or feet, and carries the superstructure. As an example: the frame under a tabletop, or the frame under a chair seat

UNDERFRAME

UNDERGLAZE COLOR

which is called the seat frame or the seat rails. The underframe may often be painted or carved or decorated with an apron, pendants, etc. Illustrated is an early-17-century Jacobean design. See *Apron* and *Skirt or Skirting Piece.*

UNDERGLAZE COLOR. A mineral pigment used for pottery decoration. It is applied before the glazing, and it resists the high temperature of the firing process.

UNDERPINNING. The addition of supports to the foundation of a building because of a weakness in the original foundation, or because of structural changes being made adjacent to or below the structure.

UNICORN. A single-horned mythological animal that looks somewhat like a white horse with a long gold horn sticking up from its forehead.

UNIDURE. A trademark name for a permanent, wrinkle-resistant finish which is applied to spun rayon and blended fabrics. It is patented by The United Piece Dye Works.

UNITED STATES EMBASSY, NEW DELHI. Designed by Edward D. Stone, and made of reinforced concrete with an outer row of gilded steel columns. The building has a double roof, a pierced tile screen wall, and an inner water court with poetic suspended strings of aluminum disks. Cars are parked below the building, since the whole structure is raised on a rectangular platform.

UNIVERSAL JOINT. A joint which allows one or both of the connected units movement in all directions.

UNIVERSAL TABLE

UNIVERSAL TABLE. A Sheraton design of the late 18th century. The table could be used as a dining table, or be converted into a breakfast table or used to store condiments, tea, sugar, etc. The table was usually made of mahogany, and equipped with two leaves which slipped under the main table surface. A drawer, set at one side, was fitted with twelve storage bins plus a writing shelf. It was an all-purpose table.

UPHOLDER. An 18th-century term for an upholsterer.

UPHOLSTERY. The act of stuffing, padding, and covering chairs, sofas, etc., and also the materials used in this operation. Leather, velvet, petit point, gros point, tapestry, brocade, damask, brocatelle, horsehair, and Naugahyde have been and are still used as upholstery fabrics. Illustrated is a 17th-century upholstered English armchair.

UPHOLSTERY

UPRIGHTS. In chair construction, the outer vertical rails or stiles that extend up from the back legs of the chair and support the chair back. These vertical members are braced and connected by the top rail. The uprights can be turned, straight, or shaped, depending upon the period and the style of the furniture. Uprights do not appear in the oval, shield, and heartback chairs of Hepplewhite and Adam. A Sheraton design is illustrated.

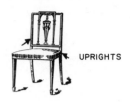

UPRIGHTS

UPSON BOARD. See *Fiberboard*.

URAEUS. A serpent used as the symbol of royalty in ancient Egyptian art and decoration.

URN. A large decorative container of wood, metal, pottery, etc. In furniture, a large wooden vaselike container which was usually set on a pedestal on either side of a side table. This was characteristic of the 18th-century Adam designs and also of Hepplewhite's work (see illustration). Urns were also used as decorative turnings at the cross points of stretchers in 16th- and 17th-century furniture designs. The urn and the vase were very often set on the central pedestal in a "broken" or "swan's neck" pediment. See *Knife Urns* and *Vase*.

URN

URN STANDS. Small tables designed to hold silver or Sheffield plate urns. They were often provided with a pullout shelf to hold a teapot or coffeepot. These stands made their appearance in the 18th century, and Chippendale designed many fanciful urn stands.

URN STAND

URN-SHAPED SPLAT. A wood chair back, cut out and shaped like a vase or urn. It was a popular decorative device in 18th-century English and American furniture. The urn was sometimes pierced for an openwork or lattice effect. Illustrated is an 18th-century Queen Anne chair with cabriole legs, claw-and-ball feet, and an urn-shaped splat.

UTRECHT VELVET. A mohair velvet with a pattern created by pressing down some of the pile under pressure. The pile which has not been pressed down has the usual soft velvet or plush touch.

URN-SHAPED SPLAT

VAISSELIER. An 18th-century French dining-room cabinet or dresser with shelves. See *Ménagère*.

VALADIER, GIUSEPPE (1762–1839). The first Italian architect to carry out a city planning scheme which blended the natural surroundings with the architecture. The Piazza del Popolo in Rome, designed by Valadier, was originally the main entrance

V

VALANCE

VALLEY

to Rome. It consisted of parks, terraces, and several levels. Along with the existing structures, several residential units were added around the Piazza. The various levels were coordinated into a single composition.

VALANCE. A decorative finishing device over the top portion of draperies. It may be made of fabric, wood, mirror, etc., and it can also be designed to go over window frames, doorways, or the hangings of the tester of a bed. See *Cantonnière, Lambrequin,* and *Pentes.*

VALENCIENNES LACE. An elaborate bobbin-made lace pattern in which the ornament and fabric are of identical thread. This method is similar in technique to those used to make Cluny, Duchesse, and Chantilly lace.

VALLEY. The interior angle formed by the meeting of two adjacent roof surfaces.

VALLEY TILE. A slightly concave tile, specially shaped to fit the angles of the roof valleys which are created at the meeting of two neighboring roofs.

VALOIS PERIOD

VALOIS PERIOD. The Renaissance period in French architecture which dates from about 1483 to 1589. It was composed of the reigns of Charles VIII, Louis XII, François I, Henri II, Henri III, and Charles IX. Illustrated is the central part of the Palace of the Tuileries (1564) which was designed by Philibert Delorme. It has since been destroyed.

VALUES. The gradations of tone from light to dark on a solid object under the play of light.

VAN CLEVE, CORNIELLE (1645–1732). A Flemish artist who worked as a sculptor in France. His media were wood, metal, and marble.

VAN DE VELDE, HENRI. A 19th-century Belgian artist turned architect, who campaigned for "l'art moderne" in Belgium, France, and Germany. He was impressed with the importance of machinery and its ultimate effect on the design and orna-

SIR JOHN VANBRUGH

menting of architecture. He was greatly influenced by John Ruskin and William Morris.

VANBRUGH, SIR JOHN (1664–1726). An architect and designer of furniture in the 18th century. He was the architect of Castle Howard and Blenheim Castle. Vanbrugh was also a scenic designer, and often his façade designs were too complicated and ornamented to be truly classic. He did not adhere closely to the Palladian concepts introduced by Inigo Jones. Illustrated is a portion of a chimneypiece designed by Vanbrugh for Castle Howard.

VANE. A weathercock.

VANITORIES. Modern dressing tables or dressing surfaces which surround the washbasin in contemporary bathrooms. The surfaces are usually marble, tile, formica, or other washable material. Drawers are sometimes set into the apron of the vanitory, and there is sometimes a cabinet set under the sink area.

VARGUEÑO. A Spanish cabinet and desk with a drop lid. It was introduced during the Plateresco period (16th and 17th centuries). The unit was a movable piece with the interior subdivided into many drawers and compartments. Vargueños were originally made of walnut, and later they were made in mahogany. The drop-lid front was either elaborately carved or inlaid with lacy pierced metal mounts, velvet panels, nacre, etc. The hardware was often very large, elaborate, and gilded.

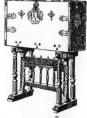

VARGUEÑO

VARNISH. A medium which is applied to woodwork to create a glossy, transparent, washable surface. It is usually made of shellac and alcohol. In the 16th and 17th centuries, an oil varnish that sank into the woodwork was used. In the early 18th century, lac dissolved in wine spirits was used. *Vernis Martin* became a popular finish in Europe in the mid-18th century. See *Lacquer*.

VASE. A decorative vessel or urn. A shaped container made of precious metals, bronze, brass, porcelain, china, glass, etc. The vase was a popular decorative motif in the 18th century. A fiddleback was also called a "vase-shaped" chair back. Illustrated is an Italian Renaissance faïence vase from the town Savona, Italy. See *Urn*.

VASE

VASE-SHAPED SPLAT. An urn-shaped splat which appears in the center of a chair back, under the top rail and between the uprights. It is similar to the fiddleback. Illustrated is a mid-18th-century Chippendale chair.

VASE-SHAPED SPLAT

VAULT

VAT DYE. A dyeing process that gives fabric a permanent fast color. Each fiber of the fabric has the vat colors chemically induced and fixed into it. The fastness of the color will vary from color to color, and this process is used mainly for cotton, rayon, linen, and some blended fibers. It is not used for silks, vinyls, nylons, polyesters, and glass fibers.

VATICAN. See *Saint Peter's, Rome.*

VAULT. A roof constructed on the principle of the arch. The word also means an underground room or burial place. See *Groin Vault* and *Ribbed Vault.*

VAULTING POST

VAULTING POST. A small engaged shaft that supports the ribs of a vault, generally a boltel (a round molding) which rests on a corbel.

VAUXHALL. The location of the noted mirror and glass factory established near London, England, in 1670 by the Duke of Buckingham.

VAUX-LE-VICOMTE. A 17th-century French château. See *Le Vau, Louis.*

VEDUTA. The Italian word for "view." A painting or drawing of a place, town, or vista. Giambattista Piranesi was an outstanding "vedutiste," witness his "Views of Rome."

VEDUTA

VEILLEUSE. From the French word for "watcher," or one who sits up to watch or look after. It was a chaise longue of the Louis XV period.

VELARE. Italian for a glaze or a thin coat of color.

VELARIUM. A great awning usually spread over part of an amphitheatre.

VEILLEUSE

VELÁZQUEZ DE SILVA, DIEGO (1599-1660). The court painter to Philip IV of Spain. His works showed his interest in naturalistic renderings in strong lights and shadows. Velázquez did many royal portraits in a sharp, realistic style. "Las Meninas," painted in 1656, is most noteworthy for the treatment of the Infanta Margareta Teresa, her ladies-in-waiting, and dwarfs.

The painting blends realism, atmosphere, and a feeling for character interpretation. Among his other works are "The Fraga Philip" (1644), "Aesop" and "Menippus" (in these two paintings he was intrigued by wrinkles, rags, and the representation of old age), "Forge of Vulcan," "Los Borrachos," and "Joseph's Coat Brought to Jacob."

VELLUM. An ancient writing material made from the skin of a calf, lamb, or kid. The skin was treated with lime. Today the term is used to describe a parchment-like paper. See *Parchment.*

VELON. A trademark of the Firestone Plastics Company for extruded plastic filaments used in making fabrics and webbing. The word is also used for a plastic upholstery fabric available in a wide range of colors, textures, patterns, and weights.

VELOUR. French for a velvet fabric. A soft, closely woven, smooth fabric with a short thick pile.

VELOURS-DE-GÊNES. A silk velvet made originally in Genoa. It usually has an allover pattern. See *Genoa Velvet.*

VELOURS D'UTRECHT. A 17th-century wool-velvet produced in Utrecht, Holland. See *Moquette* and *Utrecht Velvet.*

VELOURS–DE–GÊNES

VELVET

VELVET. A fabric with a thick short pile, less than ⅛" on the top surface, and a plain back. True velvet is made with two warps, one of which loops over a wire which later cuts the loop into pile. Velvet can be plain, striped, or figured, and can be made of wool, silk, cotton, nylon, etc., fibers.

VELVET, BROCADED. Velvet on which a pattern is created by removing part of the pile by means of heat and chemicals. It is also called "façonné."

VELVET, CHIFFON. A lightweight, soft velvet with a cut pile. It has a closer weave than transparent velvet.

VELVET, CISELÉ. A velvet with a pattern created by the contrast between the cut and uncut loops.

VELVET, LYONS. A stiff, erect, thick pile velvet usually made of silk, with a cotton or rayon back.

VELVET, NACRÉ. Velvet which has one color for the backing and another for the pile, thus creating an iridescent, pearly appearance.

VELVET, TRANSPARENT. Lightweight, soft, draping velvet which is made of silk or rayon with rayon pile.

VELVET CARPET. Plain velvet; a cut pile fabric woven on the velvet loom. It is the simplest form of carpet construction. Figured velvet is a cut pile fabric woven with wool or worsted surface yarns. All the pattern colors have been drum-dyed before being placed on the loom. Bladed pile wires form the surface texture as they do in plain velvet.

VELVET PAPER. See *Flock Paper.*

VELVETEEN. "Cotton velvet." It is woven like a sateen with weft threads floated loosely over the warp. It must be sheared to produce a fine, close pile. Velveteen is used as an upholstery and drapery fabric.

VENEER

VENEER. Usually slices of wood between 1/16" and 1/32" in thickness which are cut or sliced through the cross or vertical section of a log or flitch. These thin, continuous slices are fairly identical as to grain and figure, and can be matched in various ways to create interesting surface patterns. These veneers are applied over a sturdy backing or core of a coarser, less decorative wood. The finished effect of veneered furniture or walls is that the area has been completely constructed of a finely grained or interestingly colored wood. During the 16th century in Southern Europe, veneers were cut by hand to 1/10" in thickness. In the reign of William and Mary (the end of the 17th century in England), burr walnut veneers were applied over oak. Chippendale, Sheraton, and Hepplewhite used mahogany and satinwoods as veneers, as well as in solid construction. Illustrated is a veneered Hepplewhite bureau bookcase.

VENEER MATCHING. See *Book-Match Veneering, Box Match, Center Match, Checkerboard Match, Diamond Match Veneer, Four-Way Center and Butt Match, Herringbone Match, Random Match, Reverse Box Match, Reverse Diamond Match, Slip Match, Vertical Butt and Horizonal Book-Leaf Match.* and *V-Match.*

VENETIAN

VENETIAN. Describes the arts, architecture, and crafts of Venice, a seaport city, once a major trading center. In the early Renaissance, there was a blending here of European and Eastern motifs. Italian rococo is sometimes referred to as "Venetian" because of the flamboyant, fanciful, and ornamental quality of

VENETIAN

VENETIAN

the Venetian designs of the mid-18th century. The furniture was often elaborately painted, japanned, and/or gilded, and exaggerated bombés were prevalent.

VENETIAN BLINDS. Window coverings or shades made up of many horizontal wooden or metal slats strung together on tapes. These blinds may be raised or lowered as a unit, or the slats can be angled up or down to ensure privacy, at the same time allowing air and some light to seep in.

VENETIAN CHINOISERIE. The rococo furniture of the 18th century which was produced in Venice; it was based on the Louis XV style. The Venetians added to this an embossed quality, and satin lacquer finishes of oriental design. Though chinoiserie was adopted throughout Europe, Venice, with her advantage of direct trade with the Orient, created many of the finest orientally inspired designs in the 18th century.

VENETIAN DOOR. A door with glass side panels incorporated into the door frame.

VENETIAN FURNITURE. Late Italian Renaissance furniture, highly ornate and extravagantly curved and carved. It is a blend of the grandiose baroque, the frivolous rococo, and the exotic oriental. Illustrated is a wood frame of the period. See *Venetian* and *Venetian Chinoiserie*.

VENETIAN FURNITURE

VENETIAN GILT

VENETIAN GOLD or GILT. A gilt finish developed by the early Italian Renaissance craftsmen of Venice and Florence. Gold leaf was applied over a red paint preparation, and then burnished. Some of the red undercoat came through to add more brilliance and richness to the finish. Illustrated is a 16th-century carved center table finished with Venetian gilt.

VENETIAN SHUTTER. A louvered shutter.

VENETIAN WINDOW. A three-panel glazed window with one large central panel and two narrow side panels.

VERANDA or VERANDAH. A long, covered porch, usually built against one side of a building.

VERDIGRIS. A grayed blue-green coating or patina that forms on metals like copper, brass, and bronze. The term also refers to the color as a finish for wrought-iron furniture.

VERDITER PAPER. From the French "verd de terre," green of the earth. The term was applied to 18th-century English wallpapers which were printed in cool bluish-green colors made from chalk and precipitated copper.

VERDURE TAPESTRY. A leafy tapestry design featuring forests, bushes, trees, and meadows with only an occasional bird, animal, or figure.

VEREL. A trademark name of the Tennessee Eastman Company for a modified acrylic fiber which has a soft hand and drapes well. It rates high in its resistance to abrasion and the effects of sunlight. Verel is used in carpeting, for fire-resistant drapery, and for synthetic fur fabrics. It is similar to *Dynel*.

VERGE. The part of the roof that slightly overhangs the wall surface at the gable end. It is often finished with an ornamental board called a verge or bargeboard.

VERGE

VERGE BOARD. See *Bargeboard*.

VERMEIL. A French term for "silver gilt." Illustrated is a French 18th-century candelabrum which was originally executed in silver and then washed in gilt. Silver-plated.

VERMEIL

VERMICULAR

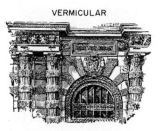

VERMICULAR. Stonework which is marked with squiggly, wormlike lines. An irregular textured design carved on the facing material of Renaissance buildings.

VERMILION. Also called "padouk." A highly decorative Indian wood with a brilliant red-orange hue on a pinkish ground. Also a pigment of the same color. See *Padouk*.

VERNIS DE GOBELINS. A Japanese lacquering process introduced into France and the Gobelins Factory by Dagley in the late 17th century.

VERNIS MARTIN. A lacquer finish invented by the Martin brothers during the reign of Louis XV. It was an imitation of Chinese and Japanese relief work rendered in lacquer. Illustrated is a Louis XV commode decorated in Vernis Martin with ormolu mounts. See *Martin Brothers.*

VERRIER. A glassware cabinet or a glass showcase with shelves. See *Vitrine.*

VERRIÈRE. French for "stained-glass window."

VERRIO, ANTONIO (c. 1639–1707). An Italian artist who painted great allegorical scenes at Hampton Court Palace under the supervision of Sir Christopher Wren. He produced overwhelming, giant-size compositions of gods, goddesses, nymphs, cupids, satyrs, etc.

VERNIS MARTIN

ANTONIO VERRIO

VERSAILLES

VERSAILLES. A palace compound erected for Louis XIV in the latter part of the 17th century by Louis Le Vau and Jules Hardouin-Mansart. It was an attempt at creating a new way of living unrestricted by the usual city limitations. The area was designed to be enveloped by and be a part of nature: parks, lakes, canals, etc. It was originally begun as a hunting lodge for Louis XIII. Versailles consists of two long wings which continue with the U of the central block, thus making an open construction. The palace is linked in a straight line to the Tuileries in Paris via the Champs-Elysées, and even the highway was integrated into the overall design. Illustrated is a vase in Versailles Park.

VERTICAL BUTT AND HORIZONTAL BOOK-LEAF MATCH. Small pieces of veneer (from a small log) are matched in two directions, vertically and horizontally. A series of rectangles which create a butt design vertically also form a book-leaf match horizontally.

VERZIERUNG. German for "decoration," "ornament," or "tracery."

VESICA PISCIS. A pointed oval shape. An almond-shaped halo. See *Aureole.*

VESICA PISCIS

VESTAL LAMP

VESTAL LAMP

CHARLES VIART

VICTORIAN CLASSIC

VICTORIAN GOTHIC

VICTORIAN JACOBEAN

VESTAL LAMP. A mid- to late-19th-century paraffin lamp which resembled an antique oil lamp set on a base and stand. The burner was raised above the fuel supply, and covered with a chimney and a glass shade. It somewhat resembles a *Student Lamp.*

VESTIBULE. An entrance hall or waiting room.

VIADUCT. A series of arches built across a gorge or waterway to serve as a road or railway surface.

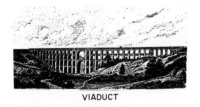

VIADUCT

VIART, CHARLES. One of the noted early French Renaissance architects of the 16th century. In his designs, he blended the medieval with the Renaissance. He designed the Ducal Palace at Nancy (illustrated) and the Hôtel de Ville in Orléans and in Beaugency. See *Hôtel de Ville, Beaugency.*

VICRTEX. A trademark name for electronically fused vinyl sheeting for upholstery or wall covering. It is produced by L. E. Carpenter and Company.

VICTORIAN. Pertaining to the reign of Queen Victoria of England (1837–1901). See the following Victorian periods.

VICTORIAN CLASSIC. A revitalization of the Louis XVI designs in Europe and America in the 1860's. The furniture had simple, delicate lines with restrained decorations. Illustrated is a Victorian classic table.

VICTORIAN GOTHIC. American and English furniture design from 1830 to its peak in 1840, after which it continued for another twenty or thirty years. The designs were light and small in scale, but decorated with Gothic-type pointed arches and tracery. Illustrated is a cabinet in the medieval style by John Gregory Crace of London, c. 1850.

VICTORIAN JACOBEAN. An unimportant furniture style of the 1870's which was characterized by strapwork, interlaced flat bands of carving, and the use of myriad small spindle turnings. Illustrated is a dining room designed in 1870.

VICTORIAN ORIENTAL. The latter part of the 19th century brought a revived interest in Chinese and Japanese art. Lacquered pieces and Chinese-type fretwork appeared in Victorian designs, as well as bamboo and bamboo-like turnings and moldings. Oriental prints also had an effect on the Art Nouveau which was then entering the design field. See *Turkish Corner*.

VICTORIAN RENAISSANCE. The period from 1850 to about 1860 when the Italian Renaissance became the source of inspiration for the eclectic Victorian furniture makers. The pieces were massive and heavy in scale, with moldings, carvings, and marble lavishly applied. The classic motifs that were used were ponderous and overly embellished. Illustrated is a carved ebony bedstead c. 1850, designed by M. Roulé of Antwerp.

VICTORIAN ROCOCO. A popular furniture style from about 1840 to 1860. It was also called the "French style" since it was adapted from the Louis XV rococo style. The designs were full of curves, scrolls, and heavy carvings of birds, flowers, and fruits. The designs were often executed in rosewood, mahogany, and black walnut. Marble was freely employed for tabletops, ledges, etc. John Belter of New York is probably the most famous American designer of this particular Victorian style. See *Belter, John Henry*.

VIEIL. From the French for "old" or "old-fashioned." The name of a silk brocade.

VIGNETTES. From the French, "small vines." In Gothic ornament, a leaf and tendril decoration. A vignette is also an ornamental motif, pattern, or design which is centered on a large field, and not confined by a border or edge. The design fades subtly into the background, and the entire composition has an unfinished quality.

VIGNOLA, GIACOMO BAROZZI DA (1507–1573). An Italian architect who, from the careful study of antique examples, formulated a set of rules and diameters for reproducing the classic Roman orders. He used half of the lower diameter of a column shaft as his unit of measure or module. His rules and proportions are still used as a guide, open to interpretation and revisions for particular requirements. He based his original theories on the works of the Roman, Vitruvius. While in France, Vignola was influenced by the French Renaissance of François I. Among his architectural achievements are the Villa of Pope Julius in Rome (1550), Palazzo Farnese, Caprarola (1547) (see illustration), and S. Andrea in Rome (1555). His

VICTORIAN ORIENTAL

VICTORIAN RENAISSANCE

VIGNETTES

GIACOMO BAROZZI DA VIGNOLA

VILLA

VINE

Church of Il Gesù in Rome was the model for many Jesuit churches in the 17th and 18th centuries. The façade was completed by Giacomo della Porta.

VILE, WILLIAM. An 18th-century furniture maker to George III. He was a partner of John Cobb, and he designed in the rococo style.

VILLA. A house on a country or suburban estate. Illustrated is the Villa Pia built in the gardens of the Vatican by Pirro Ligorio in the 16th century. It is a lovely example of Italian Renaissance architecture.

VINCI, LEONARDO DA (1452–1519). One of the great "universal" men of the Renaissance. A creative painter, sculptor, architect, scientist, engineer, writer, and musician. Among his best known works are "Mona Lisa" and "The Last Supper."

VINE. A popular motif in classical and medieval ornament. In antiquity it was associated with grapes, wine, and the god Bacchus. Ivy leaves were often combined with the vine. In the Middle Ages, the vine was used in ecclesiastical art, combined with ears of corn, to symbolize Christ. Illustrated is a 16th-century wood carving.

VINETTE

VINETTE. A continuous ornamental band of leaves and tendrils.

VINYL ASBESTOS TILE. A vinyl tile which is similar to asphalt tile and has excellent wearing qualities. It is resistant to grease, oil, and mild acids. Vinyl asbestos is much less expensive than homogeneous vinyl tile, but it is not as resilient nor as quiet underfoot. It is easy to maintain, and wears well under most normal circumstances.

VINYL FABRICS. Textiles fused or coated with vinyl plastic. In the coated types, the vinyl is opaque, and the surface is printed or embossed.

VINYL TILE. A nonporous, homogeneous flooring material resembling rubber tile. It has excellent wear resistance, and it is comfortable to walk on. Vinyl resists oil and grease, moisture and mild acids, and is very resilient. Laminated or backed vinyl is not as expensive as homogeneous vinyl, and though it has many of the advantages of vinyl it does not wear as well and it indents more easily. Vinyl is produced in a great range of brilliant and pastel colors, in a wide selection of patterns, textures, gauges, and tile sizes.

VIOLET WOOD. See *Amaranth*.

VIOLLET-LE-DUC, EUGÈNE EMMANUEL (1814–1879). A 19th-century French architect, archeologist, and writer who is noted for his dictionary of architecture. He was much enamoured with the Gothic period, and he engaged in restoring important buildings like the Notre-Dame in Paris. He also designed the central spire and the great altar of this classic Gothic building. Illustrated is a medieval bed and bedroom of the 14th and 15th centuries after research by Viollet-le-Duc.

EUGÈNE EMMANUEL VIOLLET-LE DUC

VIRGINAL. A spinet. An instrument which was popular with young maidens in the 16th and 17th centuries, hence the name. See *Harpsichord* and *Spinet*.

VIS-À-VIS. A 19th-century S-shaped two-seater. The two seats faced in opposite directions, but they were attached in the middle. This design was also called a *Dos-à-Dos, Siamoise,* and *Tête-à-Tête*.

VISCOSE RAYON. See *Rayon*.

VISE or VICE. An archaic term for a spiral staircase around a column called a newel. The staircase was usually constructed of stone.

VISE

VITRAIL. A French term for glass set into windows. A stained-glass window. Illustrated is the rose window of the north transept of Chartres Cathedral.

VITRAIL

VITREOUS ENAMEL. A shiny porcelain enamel fused upon metal.

VITRIFIED. Describes clay products (tiles, etc.) which have been sufficiently fired so that all the grains are fused and the pores are closed. The end product is impervious to water.

VITRINE. A curio cabinet with a glass front. It was used for the display of china, glass, or objets d'art. A verrier.

VITRINE

VITRUVIAN SCROLL

VITRUVIAN SCROLL. A series of undulating, wavelike scrolls. A continuous band of horizontal scrolls. It was named after Vitruvius, the classic Roman architect. See the following.

VITRUVIUS. The Roman authority on architecture in the time of Augustus. He considered three things vital in every construction: "utility, durability, and beauty. . . . Beauty will result from the form and correspondence of the whole with respect to the several parts, of the parts with regard to each other, and of these again to the whole." Palladio, in 1570, published his *Five Orders of Architecture* in Venice. It was based on Vitruvius' work. This book became the textbook of Renaissance architecture in Europe. See *Palladio, Andrea,* and *Vignola, Giacomo Barozzi da.*

V–MATCH

V-MATCH. Two slices of wood or veneer butted together like facing pages in a book. The graining resembles a series of *V*'s set one over the other.

VOIDER. A tray used for carrying dishes and utensils to and from the table. An 18th-century English term.

VOILE. A light transparent fabric of plain weave. It is usually piece-dyed, and then striped or figured. Voile can be made of cotton, wool, silk, and some synthetic fibers. See *Sheer.*

VOLUTE. A scroll line or spiral form such as that used on Ionic and Corinthian capitals. A flat or rising spiral in furniture decoration, at the end of furniture legs, etc. See *Earpiece* and *Scroll.*

VOLUTE

VOUET, SIMON (1590–1649). A French painter who was appointed first painter to Louis XIII. He created many tapestry designs, and he was the teacher of Charles Le Brun and Nicolas Mignard. Vouet was a great promoter of the Renaissance in France.

VOUSSOIR. In architecture, a wedge-shaped block used in arch construction. The central voussoir is the keystone, and it is marked "clef" in the diagram. The lintel in the diagram is marked "linteau."

VOUSSURE. French word for the curve of a vault or arch.

VOYELLE. A cockfight chair of the Louis XVI period. One straddles the chair, facing the chair back, and rests one's arms on the upholstered shelflike top rail. See *Cockfight Chair.*

VOYEUSE. See *Cockfight Chair* and *Voyelle.*

VOUSSOIR

VOUSSURE

VOYSEY, CHARLES FRANCIS ANNESLEY. One of the most important links between the ornamentation of Morris at the end of the 19th century and the 20th century modern movement. Voysey believed in "discarding the mass of useless ornament." See *Morris, William.*

VYCRON. A dacron-like fiber produced from Goodyear's "vitrel" polyester resin by Beaunits Fiber Division. It is produced as a polyester and the name Vycron is used on only those fabrics which meet the specific requirements established by Goodyear.

WACHSTUCH-TAPETE. An 18th-century German variation on gilded leather tapestries. A heavy linen or canvas fabric was used as the base, and the artwork was done on it in durable, brilliant color. Chinoiserie was a popular motif for Wachstuch-Tapete. It was actually a forerunner of modern plastic- or vinyl-ground wall coverings. At the end of the 18th century, this technique was imitated in England.

WAGGON VAULT. A semicylindrical vault or barrel vault.

WAGNER, OTTO (1841–1918). An Austrian architect. One of the first in the late 19th century to admire the machine and to understand its essential character and its relation to design and ornamentation as well as its effect on architecture. He was impressed with the comfort and clean lines of English industrial art. "All modern forms must be in harmony with the new requirements of our time. . . . Nothing that is not practical can be beautiful."

WAGON HEAD CEILING

WAGON HEAD CEILING. A semicylindrical ceiling.

WAG-ON-WALL. A weight-driven clock with exposed weights and pendulum.

WAINSCOT. A wooden lining applied as paneling to interior walls. The paneling or lining may or may not continue up to the ceiling, and the wainscot is made up of stiles and rails which form frames for large or small panels. The name "wainscot" refers to a superior grade of oak, close-grained and without knotholes, which was originally used before the Tudor period in England.

WAINSCOT

W

WAGGON VAULT

WAINSCOT CHAIR

WAINSCOT CHAIR

WAINSCOT CHAIR. An early-17th-century English and American chair which was also called a "panel-back" chair because of its similarity to a wainscot wall. The panel splat was often carved or inlaid, and the seat was usually high and required a footstool. The chair was a sort of "chair of state" in the Tudor and Jacobean periods.

WALL FURNITURE

WALL FURNITURE. Architectural furniture, cabinets, cupboards, seats, etc., which are built as stationary units, and are an integral built-in part of the room. This is in contrast to portable chairs, small tables, and such. In the Pre-Renaissance period, seats and beds were often stationary units. Illustrated is a mid-19th-century bookcase.

WALL LIGHTS. See *Sconce*.

WALL LIGHTS

WALL MIRROR. See *Pier Glasses*.

WALL PLATE. A timber laid on a wall to receive the ends of rafters and joists, and help distribute the load of these elements down the wall to the ground.

WALL RIB. See *Formeret*.

WALL TREATMENT. The decoration applied to a wall, rather than its actual surface. It may consist of a grouping of paintings, graphics, medallions, tiles, bracket clocks, mirrors, lavabos, etc., in various arrangements (symmetrical or asymmetrical). The wall arrangement can also be as simple as a large painting or a mural papered or painted on a wall. In small foyers or entries, the treatment might include a mirror and console shelf with several accessory plaques, objets d'art, and such, depending upon the wall space.

WALL RIB

WALLBOARD. See *Building Board*.

WALLIS, N. An 18th-century English designer. In 1771, he published *A Book of Ornaments in the Palmyrene Taste* with designs for ceilings, panels, paterae, and moldings. In *A Carpenter's Treasure* he combined Chinese and Gothic motifs. In 1772, Wallis published *A Complete Modern Joiner* with designs for chimneypieces and doorcases, their moldings and decorations.

N. WALLIS

WALLPAPER. Paper printed by hand or machine methods in a variety of patterns, textures, and colors, and applied to walls as a decorative and utilitarian covering. The earliest papers were oriental imports in the 17th century. See *Chinese Wallpaper* and *Domino Papers*. Wallpaper today is also printed on various vinyl and fabric grounds. See *Flocking*.

WALNUT. A light-brown wood grown throughout Asia, Africa, Europe, and America. American walnut has coarser grain than the European varieties. It presents a tremendous range of figures, depending upon the method of slicing. Illustrated is a walnut bureau of the early-18th-century Queen Anne period. It is typical of the "Age of Walnut." See *Age of Walnut*.

WALNUT

WALNUT, BLACK. A richly colored wood whose fine-grained quality makes it easy to carve. The wood takes a high polish, and it is fairly expensive because in limited supply. Black walnut is also called "English walnut."

WALNUT, CIRCASSIAN. A beautiful curly-grained brown wood from the Black Sea area. It is relatively expensive, and it is used for furniture and interior paneling.

WALNUT, OILED. Walnut treated with a linseed oil finish. It is used instead of varnish or lacquer on furniture. The oil finish gives the wood a smooth, dull satin feel, and it is usually more resistant to stains, heat, and alcohol than a varnish or lacquer finish.

WALNUT, ORIENTAL. Eucalyptus wood. A pale reddish-yellow figured wood.

WALNUT, WHITE. See *Butternut*.

WALNUT PERIOD. A period in English furniture dating from approximately 1660 to 1720. Walnut was the favored wood at this time for furniture and cabinetwork. Walnut was, of course, used before and after this period. Illustrated is an upholstered walnut stool of the William and Mary period (late 17th century).

WALNUT PERIOD

WARDROBE. As known today, this is basically the Sheraton design for a clothes press and hanging cupboard in one unit. The wardrobe evolved from the medieval ward room (a place for hanging garments) to the 17th-century hanging cupboards and closets, to the 18th century tallboys and clothes presses. See *Armoire, Garde-robe,* and *Kas*.

WARDROBE

WARE, ISAAC

ISAAC WARE

WARE, ISAAC. An 18th-century English architect-designer of buildings and furnishings. In about 1749, he published *Complete Body of Architecture,* and collaborated with William Kent on the interior decoration at Holkham in Norfolk. See *Trim* for illustration.

WARIN, JEAN (1595–1672). A French decorative and figure sculptor of the Louis XIV period.

WARP. The threads that run lengthwise on a loom. The vertical threads of a fabric. See *Weave.* In furniture or woodworking, the twisting or bulging of a piece of wood, which can be caused by a certain change in the moisture content of the wood.

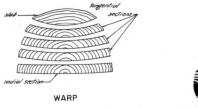

WARP

WARP

WASHSTANDS

WASHSTAND. A stand for a washbasin. Prior to the 18th century, the basin was often placed on a small table or lowboy. Chippendale designed special stands, often corner units with hinged covers and with a drawer to hold a minute basin. Hepplewhite (here illustrated) and Sheraton also designed special stands for small 18th-century washbasins.

WATER BENCH. See *Dry Sink.*

WATER LEAF. An ornamental motif which resembles an elongated laurel leaf, and is often used to enrich a cyma reversa molding. In the 18th century, the water leaf was usually represented in low-relief carving on moldings. Illustrated is a chair splat designed by Sheraton.

← WATER LEAF

WATER TABLE. In masonry, a slight projection on the outside wall of the lower masonry just above the ground.

WATERCOLOR. A painting technique which uses colored pigment ground up with water-soluble gums. When the color is moistened with water, a transparent stain is obtained which is applied in washes to paper. The ground or paper is usually left unpainted to provide white highlights, and gradations of color and tone are accomplished by adding washes. In the 18th and early 19th centuries, Joseph Turner and Alexander Cozens were the masters of the watercolor.

WATERED SILK. See *Moiré*.

WATERFORD GLASS. Fine Irish glassware and crystal.

WATTEAU, JEAN-ANTOINE (1684–1721). A great painter and stylist of the French Régence period. His art was light, coquettish, and graceful, full of idyllic shepherdesses and attenuated decorative borders. Watteau painted musical parties, balls, masquerades, and pastoral scenes. He was trained by Claude Gillot and he was much influenced by Peter Paul Rubens' system of color.

JEAN-ANTOINE WATTEAU

WATTLE AND DAUB. A primitive roof-covering technique used in the early 17th century on American structures and provincial European homes. It consisted of woven, plaited, or entwined twigs covered with clay and mud.

WAVE PATTERN. A continuous horizontal band made up of conventionalized wave crests. It is also called a wave scroll. See *Vitruvian Scroll*.

WAVE PATTERN

WEATHER BOARDING. Horizontal boards, which overlap one another, placed over the framework of a building. It is an exterior wall-facing technique.

WEATHER SLATING. Slate is applied vertically to an exterior wall to form a weatherproof surface. This is similar to weather boarding.

WEATHER TILING. Tile set vertically on an exterior surface. A weatherproofing technique.

WEATHERING. A sloping surface on a buttress, cornice, etc., which helps shed or throw off rain and snow.

WEAVE. The process of making fabrics by interlacing warp threads (the lengthwise threads) with the filler threads (horizontal or across the fabric threads) at right angles. Different patterns and textures are possible depending upon the type of loom, the weaving pattern, yarns used, etc.

WEB FOOT. A heavy, clumsy foot similar to the cloven, hoof, and club foot. It was sometimes used as an ending to a Queen Anne cabriole leg.

WEBB, JOHN (1611–1672). An English architect and designer. He was a student of Inigo Jones and executed some of Jones's designs.

WEATHER BOARDING

WEATHERING

WEAVING

WEBB, PHILIP SPEAKMAN (1831–1915). An English architect, who, with Shaw and Nesfield, brought about a revival of residential architecture based on Queen Anne and Georgian styles. Their aim was to create the artistic effects by means of the intrinsic values of the materials used. Webb was a friend of William Morris, and designed the Red House at Bexley Heath (1859) for him. The planning and furnishing of this historic structure led to the establishment of the firm of Morris, Marshall, Faulkner and Company, in 1861. This group was important in the formation of the arts and crafts movement. Webb was a member of this firm, and he designed furniture, tiles, and stained glass. See *Morris, William.*

WEBBING

WEBBING. Strips of tightly woven burlap used in upholstery construction. The webbing is employed as a reinforcement and support for springs and cushions. The strips can also be made of linen, plastic, or nylon. In some skeletal-type seats, the webbing forms the finished seat or back rest (lawn or beach furniture).

WEDGE. A shaped piece of metal, stone, or wood which tapers down to a fine edge on one side. It is triangular in form.

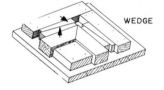

WEDGE

JOSIAH WEDGWOOD

WEDGWOOD, JOSIAH (1730–1795). A distinguished English potter. He produced plaques, medallions, and rondels to adorn the classic designs of the Adam brothers. Wedgwood established his factory at Stoke-on-Trent in 1769. It was called the "Etruria" works. He also produced jasper ware and other fine pottery pieces. Illustrated is an Adam commode which has been enhanced with Wedgwood plaques.

WEFT. The threads that run across the loom from selvage to selvage. These are woven in and out from among the warp threads. The warp threads are also called the "fillers." See *Filling.*

WEISWEILER, ADAM. A great cabinetmaker of the late Louis XVI period. He was strongly influenced by Egyptian as well as classic designs; in a console table which he executed for Marie Antoinette, he used caryatid figures for the leg supports. Weisweiler favored Sèvres plaques as embellishments on his furniture designs.

WELDWOOD FLEXWOOD. A trademark of the United States Plywood Corporation for a wide selection of wood veneers on cloth backing used for wall covering installations. ·This material is adaptable to curved and straight surfaces, and is applied in the same manner as wallpaper. When installed it resembles fine wood paneling.

WELSH DRESSER. A side table with cupboards and drawers with a pot board below and shelves above. It was popular in England in the 17th century, and it was based on the 16th-century French "dressoir de salle à manger" and the English "tri-darn." See *Dutch Dresser* and *Tri-Darn*.

WELTING. A strip of fabric which is sewn between two pieces of upholstery fabric to give a more finished appearance to the seam. The welting is usually made by covering a cord with a tube of fabric with end flaps which are sewn onto the joining sections of the upholstery fabric. The stuffed tube appears above the surface of the seam.

WEST WORK or WESTWERK. The most original and typical innovation of the architecture of the Carolingian period (roughly from the 7th to the 10th century). It was usually a large and almost self-contained church at the western end of a basilican church. This antechurch structure often had a tall central tower with smaller towers on either side, and was several stories high. The west work often opened in arcades toward the nave, and gave emphasis to the entrance façade. It later influenced the towered west fronts of Romanesque cathedrals.

WESTMINSTER ABBEY. Designed by the French architect, Henri de Rheims, and built in London, England, in the 13th century. The French influence is seen in the lofty interior, the lancet arches, the tall clerestory, and the north transept façade. The plan is that of a Latin cross with chapels radiating from the ambulatory. The nave is 100' high, and the traceried windows are in the Early English, Decorated, and Perpendicular styles. The fan tracery of the ceiling is considered the richest vaulting in Europe. The abbey reflects the architecture of almost all of the Gothic periods, as well as the Early Renaissance, Queen Anne, and Georgian in later additions. Kings of England are crowned here.

WESTMINSTER ABBEY

WESTMINSTER ABBEY

WHATNOT

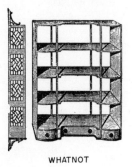

WHATNOT

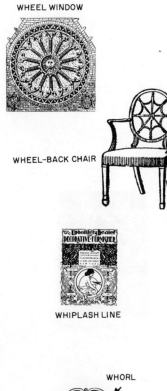

WHEEL WINDOW

WHEEL-BACK CHAIR

WHIPLASH LINE

WHORL

WHATNOT. An ornamental shelf unit which is used to show and hold bric-a-brac, objets d'art, etc. It was usually designed to fit into the corner of a room. Chippendale designed some of these pieces, but it is best known as a Victorian piece. See *Encoignure*.

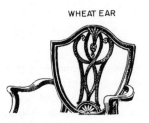

WHEAT EAR

WHEAT EAR. A decorative, carved, painted or inlaid motif on Hepplewhite designs which resembles an ear of wheat. Note the design on the top rail of the Hepplewhite chair back illustrated.

WHEEL WINDOW. A large circular window with tracery radiating from the center. It is similar to a rose window, but the spokes are not as pronounced. A Gothic design.

WHEEL-BACK CHAIR. Chair whose back resembles a wheel with spokes radiating from a central boss, patera, or plaque. It is characteristic of the Adam, 18th-century school, and Hepplewhite also used the wheel-like feature to decorate Windsor chairs. Sometimes the circle was replaced by an oval.

WHIPLASH LINE. The typical curved line of the Art Nouveau period. It is a slow, lazy *S* which sinuously curves back on itself, and resembles the snap curve of a whip which has been flicked. Illustrated is a magazine decoration in the Art Nouveau style.

WHITE LEAD. A heavy, non-water-soluble substance used as a base in house paints when mixed with linseed oil.

WHITEWOOD. A trademark name for yellow poplar and cottonwood. It has a uniform, uninteresting grain, and it is used for the interior parts of furniture and as the core for veneer work. Whitewood is soft, easy to work, and excellent for painted or lacquered finishes.

WHORL. A scroll or spiral effect on the feet or top rails of furniture. Illustrated is an early-17th-century Jacobean English chair.

WICKER. See *Rattan*. Small twigs or flexible strips of wood which are woven into chairs, tables, screens, baskets, etc.

WIG STAND. A 17th- and 18th-century tripod stand fitted with a small basin and drawers to hold wig powder, etc., and a form to hold a headdress or wig. It was also called a "demoiselle."

WILLARD, SIMON (1753–1848). American clockmaker of Roxbury, Massachusetts. In 1802, he designed the banjo clock, which was meant to be hung on the wall. The case was shaped like an inverted banjo, and it was usually made of gilt metal. An eagle or finial usually was set over the dial. Painted decorations rarely appeared on the rectangular glass panel below the dial. Other clockmakers made similarly shaped clocks, and the panel was invariably painted. Simon Willard's younger brother Adam, who had his business in Boston, used the painted panel to decorate his hanging clocks.

WILLIAM AND MARY (1689–1702). King and Queen of England. William III was a Dutch prince. This period in furnishings is sometimes referred to as "Early Queen Anne." They introduced into English design Dutch, Spanish, and Oriental motifs, and made welcome French refugee artisans. See *Marot, Daniel.* This conglomeration gave rise to a distinctly English school of furniture. Illustrated is a walnut tallboy with early cabriole legs and canted corners.

WILLIAM AND MARY

WILLIAMSBURG, VIRGINIA. Established in 1699, the town was originally laid out by Governor Nicholson in a plan delineating the letters "W" and "M" for William and Mary. The houses are mainly symmetrical in shape, with flankers (office and kitchen buildings). It has been said that Sir Christopher Wren designed the brick building of the College of William and Mary on Duke of Gloucester Street, and that he was also involved in the plans for the Capitol. The Capitol was built of pink brick with semicircular bays on the south side, and a white cupola caps the building. The governor's palace has a five-bay façade and a five-dormered hipped roof. The entrance is a magnificent wrought-iron gate which is also credited to Wren. Much of Williamsburg was restored by the Rockefeller Foundation from 1928 to 1934.

WILLIAMSBURG, VIRGINIA

WILLIAMSBURG, VIRGINIA

WILLOW BRASSES. Furniture hardware with plates that have scrolled outlines. An 18th-century decorative motif.

WILLOW BRASSES

WILTON. A pile carpet fabric woven on a Wilton loom which is controlled by a jacquard pattern device. The loom draws up all yarns of a single color at a time, while the pile and the other

WIND BEAM

WINDING STAIRCASE

WINDOW FRAME

WINDOW SEAT

colors remain hidden beneath the surface. The pile may be cut or uncut, or a combination of the two, and thus can accommodate a variety of textures. Wool Wiltons wear well under severe conditions, and have a sturdy foundation construction. A worsted Wilton weave is a luxury fabric, and fine details and delicacy of design are possible in this carpet. See *Wires*.

WIND BEAM or BRACE. A diagonal strut in a roof which extends from the main rafter to a horizontal longitudinal beam or purlin to prevent the roof from swaying longitudinally.

WINDER. In stair construction, a tapered step used at the angle where a stairway makes a turn but has no landing.

WINDING STAIRCASE. A staircase which spirals around a central shaft as it rises from one level to the next. It is also called a spiral staircase. Illustrated is the famous spiral staircase of the Château de Blois, built during the reign of François I of France in the early 16th century.

WINDOW BREAST. Particularly in Gothic architecture, the term refers to a thin screen wall below a window. The mullions of the clerestory window may be carried by this screen which may, itself, be decorated with a blind arcade. See *Blind Arcade* and *Clerestory*.

WINDOW FRAME. A frame around a window opening. A mid-18th-century English design by William Joseph Halfpenny is illustrated.

WINDOW MANTEL

WINDOW MANTEL. A cornice of wood and fabric trim set over a window as a finishing piece for draperies or curtains. Illustrated is a Robert Adam mid-18th-century design. See *Cornice* and *Lambrequin*.

WINDOW SEAT. A small upholstered stool or bench made to fit into a window recess or alcove. Adam and Chippendale designed units of this type in the mid-18th century. In current usage, often an architectural addition in a bay, bow, or window alcove. The unit is usually covered with pillows, and the top is sometimes made to open so that the window seat can be used for storage.

WINDOW SHADE. A window covering, usually made of fabric, which is placed between the glass and the curtain or drapery treatment. The shade fabric is attached to a roller which has an internal spring mechanism. The roller is fixed to the upper inner surface of the window frame. The shade is made to unroll and cover all or part of the window by a pull on the ring or cord attached to the lower hem of the fabric. A quick tug at the ring or cord will cause the fabric to roll back on the roller. See *Austrian Shade Cloth* and *Holland Shade Cloth* for two types of shade cloth fabrics. See *Roman Shade* for an accordion-type folding fabric shade.

WINDOW STOOL. A Hepplewhite term for a upholstered settee or bench made to fit in a window recess. See *Window Seat.*

WINDSOR CHAIR. A domestic or kitchen-type chair introduced in the early 18th century in England. The chair back was filled with vertical rods which created a fiddle-string back or a stick-back appearance. The legs were originally cabriole in shape, and later they were made of turnings. The arms and rails were sometimes continued around the back in a hooped-back effect. Chippendale introduced a pierced splat between the rods of the back. Hepplewhite added a wheel-like feature in the center splat. The withes and bowed shapes that formed the spindles and back were turned and cut originally near Windsor, England, hence the name. See *Comb Back, Fiddle-String Back or Stick-Back,* and *Stick-Back.*

WINDSOR CHAIRS, AMERICAN. These were produced in the 18th and 19th centuries in America, and reproductions are still being made today. The New England variations were lighter, more graceful, and without the wide splat in the back that some of the English forms had. Some of the Pennsylvania designs had ball feet. There are many designs and they are usually designated by the chair-back type: bow- or loop-back, fan-back, low-back, and comb-back. Some had a writing arm. Many 19th-century chairs were characterized by "bamboo" turnings. The nine-spindle, hoop-back chair with spindles and turned balusters supporting the bent armrests was typical of the New England designs.

WINE COOLER. A small, metal-lined stand designed to keep wine bottles chilled during a dinner. An 18th-century Hepplewhite design is illustrated. See *Cellaret* and *Sarcophagus.*

WINE TABLE. A horseshoe-shaped table designed to stand in front of a fireplace, with a curtain across the open end which faced the fire. Persons sat around the convex end of the table.

WINDOW STOOL

WINDSOR CHAIR

AMERICAN WINDSOR CHAIR

WINE COOLER

WING-AND-CLAW FOOT

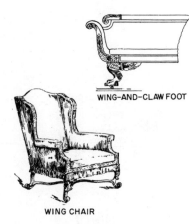

WING-AND-CLAW FOOT

WING CHAIR

A small decanter holder on a pivoting arm was often attached to the curtain support so that the wine bottle could be easily reached from all parts of the horseshoe. See *Horseshoe Table*.

WING-AND-CLAW FOOT. A massive carved foot used on Empire couches and other large pieces of that period. The motif was used in England and America in the early 19th century, and it was also called a "winged paw foot."

WING BOOKCASE. See *Blockfront* and *Broken Front*.

WING CHAIR. A high-backed, upholstered easy chair with side wings or earpieces on either side of the chair back. It was originally a mid-17th-century design, and a forerunner of the 18th-century grandfather chair. This type of chair is also known as forty-wink chair, saddle-back chair, and grandfather chair.

WIRED GLASS. See *Fire-retardant Wire Glass*.

WIRES. In carpet construction, metal rods that are inserted across the loom at the same time the weft yarn is shuttled across the warp threads. When the wires are withdrawn, a series of loops remain which are the pile of the carpet. In Wilton carpets, the wires have a knife edge which cuts the loops into tufts as the wires are withdrawn. Wiltons usually have 13 wires per inch.

WITHE. A separating wall between two flues in a stack of a chimney. A withe is also a twig of a willow or a band of twisted or braided twigs. See *Wythe*.

WOLFE, ELSIE DE. A leading interior designer of the early 20th century. She had a great influence in both America and Europe.

WOMB CHAIR. A curved, enveloping, plastic chair with upholstery covering designed by architect-designer Eero Saarinen for Knoll Associates, Inc., in 1946. Actually it is a very modern version of a wing-type chair. See *Saarinen, Eero*.

WOOD, JOHN, the Elder (1704–1754). An English architect, designer, builder, and artist who created some of the finest architectural features of the city of Bath in England. It was a small town where people went "to take the waters." The town was designed to accommodate a bourgeois society. Wood completed the Circus, and John Wood the Younger built the Royal Crescent development in Bath.

WOOD ENGRAVING. A method of printing in which a design is cut with a graver or burin (a sharp, pointed tool) on a block of wood (like boxwood) which has been cut across the grain. The furrowed lines are filled with ink, the block is set against the paper to be printed, and pressure is applied. The ink records the design of engraved lines on the paper. This technique was popularized by Thomas Berwick in the mid-18th century in England.

WOOD WOOL SLABS. Wood fibers mixed with cement and formed into slabs or blocks which are used in building construction as insulators.

WOODCUT. A method of printing and the printed design obtained thereby. From the surface of a block of wood are gouged out all parts of the design but those which are to be reproduced in ink. The untouched parts are covered with printing ink and the block is pressed onto a sheet of paper or fabric. The ink prints only the level, ungouged, top surface of the wood block. Whatever has been cut away does not print. It is possible to make thousands of impressions from a woodcut block. This technique was used to print the earliest wallpapers, fabrics, and gilded leather tapestries. It is possible to create a multicolored design if a separate printing block is made for each color. This multiplate technique is like silk screening.

WOOF. See *Weave* and *Weft*.

WOOL. A natural crumped fiber from sheep and goats. The scaly surface of the fibers makes it possible to felt wool. Wool is warm, resilient, and it can be processed and felted. It is used for upholstery, drapery, casement fabrics, and also as carpeting material.

WOOL SUEDE. A trademark for an all-wool, nonwoven fabric which is produced by the Felters Company. It can be used for drapery or upholstery or as a wall-covering material. Wool suede is soil- and flame-resistant and has excellent acoustical and insulating properties.

WOOLEN YARN. In carpets, woolen yarn is spun from short fibers which are interlocked, as much as possible, and tightly twisted.

WORKING DRAWING. A carefully detailed scale drawing used in the construction of the object drawn.

WORKTABLE. See *Pouch Table*. Illustrated is an 18th-century design.

WORMHOLES. Tiny, pinhead-sized, crooked holes often found in old pieces of furniture which are made of soft woods. Usually the holes are the result of beetles, or the worms of beetles, eating into the wood. In "faked" antiques, the wormholes are artificially created and go straight through the wood rather than being crooked or squiggly. These holes are made with buckshot or fine dental drills.

WORKING DRAWING

WORKTABLE

WORMY CHESTNUT. Chestnut wood which is holey and pitted as though affected by the chestnut blight. The rough, irregular texture and pleasing light-brown color make it popular for paneling and provincial tabletops and cabinet panels. It is too weak for actual structural woodwork.

WORSTED YARN. In carpets, worsted yarn is spun from the longer types of staple, and then carded to lay the fibers as nearly parallel as possible, and finally combed to extract the shortest fibers as noil.

WOVEN WOOD. A trademark name for thin slats of wood which are woven with various fibers (wool, linen, cotton, nylon, Lurex, etc.) into window shades, draperies, and roll-up shades. The wood can be left its natural color, or lacquered with other colors. The vertical woven yarns can create exciting patterns.

WREATH. A closed or partially closed ring of foliage, fruit and/or flowers. A classic Roman motif, it was adopted in the Renaissance and Classic Revival periods. In the Empire period it became an important ornamental feature, often enclosing the initial "N," Napoleon's personal badge, or an eagle.

WREATHED COLUMN

WREATH

WREATH

SIR CHRISTOPHER WREN

WREATHED COLUMN. See *Twisted Column.*

WREN, SIR CHRISTOPHER (1632–1723). The noted classic architect of St. Paul's Cathedral in London. He was an architect-designer of interior decorations rather than movable furniture: mantels, fireplaces, wall treatments, pews, stalls, etc. Grinling Gibbons was the foremost wood carver of Wren's "school." Wren designed and supervised the execution of the state apartments at Hampton Court Palace, and he was responsible for fifty-three colleges, churches, and town halls, as well as credited with being the overall designer of the architecture of Williamsburg, Virginia. He was influenced by the Louis XIV baroque and Renaissance forms and his contact with Giovanni Bernini in France, as well as the Dutch craftsmen in England. Illustrated is the interior of St. Stephen Walbrook, in London, England. See *Williamsburg, Virginia.*

WRIGHT, FRANK LLOYD (1869–1959). A great midwestern American designer, architect, historian, and critic. He believed that a building should be part of a site, not just set on it, and he expressed a great love and respect for nature and natural materials. In his youth, in Chicago, he worked for and with Louis Sullivan. In domestic architecture, he endeavored to break down the cubicles in which people confined themselves, and bring the outside inside and vice versa. Wright employed continuous casement windows, lowered ceilings, and projecting, streamlined, horizontal overhangs to produce a "prairie"-type house. Early examples of this type of design were the Coonley House, 1908, and the Robie House, 1909. With the Larkin Building, Buffalo, in 1904, he started a new trend toward functional yet comfortable, light, and beautiful commercial buildings. Other noteworthy structures by Wright are: Unity Temple, Oak Park, Illinois, 1906; Midway Gardens, 1914; the Imperial Hotel, Tokyo, 1922; Wright's home, Taliesin, 1925; a regional planning development, Broadacre City, Falling Water at Bear Run, Pennsylvania; the Johnson Administration Building, Racine, Wisconsin; Florida Southern College; and the Guggenheim Museum in New York City.

WRITING ARMCHAIR. See *Roundabout Chair* and *Tablet Chair*.

WRITING ARMCHAIR

WRITING TABLE

WRITING TABLE. See *Desk*. Illustrated is a late-18th-century kidney-shaped writing table designed by Sheraton.

WROUGHT IRON. Iron which has been worked, bent, twisted, and formed. Iron contains a low percentage of carbon, and is malleable (can be drawn out and extended by beating). The material can be used for decoration as well as the functional parts of furniture. Illustrated is a mid-17th-century German Renaissance candlestick. See *Lanthorn* illustration.

WROUGHT IRON

WYTHE or WITHE. In masonry, each four inches or greater thickness of masonry, vertically measured. It is also called a "tier."

X

X-SHAPED CHAIR

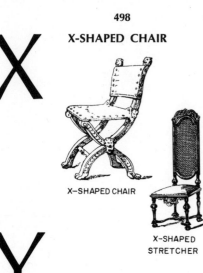

X-SHAPED CHAIR

X-SHAPED
STRETCHER

Y

X-SHAPED CHAIR. A folding chair similar to the current camp stool or yacht chair made with or without a back. This design is found in antiquity, also in Italian medieval furniture of the 14th century. High-backed, armed, and heavily sculptured X-shaped chairs were used in the 17th century. See *Curule Chair, Dante Chair,* and *Savonarola Chair.*

X-SHAPED STRETCHERS. Cross stretchers or "saltires" made flat or curved upward in serpentine form, with knobs or other ornamentation at the intersection. They were used to connect the four supports of a chair or piece of furniture, and to reinforce them. See *Saltire* and *Stretcher.* Illustrated is a Louis XIV chair.

YARN-DYED. Dyed before the yarn is woven into fabric.

YESERIA. Small, colored, lacelike patterns of plaster relief used in Moorish interiors. See *Composition Ornament.*

YOKE BACK

YESERIA

YEW, ENGLISH. A hard, durable, pale reddish-brown wood with a fine, even, lustrous grain. It was used for furniture in England from the Tudor period on. In the late 17th century, yew was used for veneering as well as for long case clocks.

YOKE BACK. A crossbar with two S-shaped curves used as the top rail of chair backs in the Georgian period. The silhouette is that of an ox-yoke.

YOKE-FRONT CHEST

YOKE-FRONT CHEST. An 18th-century chest of drawers with a reverse serpentine front. The sides swell out, and the center area is concave. It is also referred to as "oxbow" or "U-shaped."

YORK STONE. A sandstone used mainly for paving stones.

YORKSHIRE CHAIR

Z

YORKSHIRE CHAIR. A small Jacobean chair with knob-turned legs and straight uprights ending in inward scrolls. The broad carved top rail and seat below were arched above and crescent cut below.

YORKSHIRE LADDER-BACK CHAIR. An 18th-century domestic or provincial chair with a rush seat and a high ladder back usually composed of five slats, plain or slightly shaped and curved to fit the back.

VYART, BAUDREN. A 17th-century French painter in charge of models and designs at the Gobelins during the reign of Louis XIV. He designed many tapestry cartoons.

VYART, JOSEPH. The son of Baudren Vyart and his successor at the Gobelins.

ZEBRAWOOD or ZEBRANO. An African wood with a vigorous brown stripe on a light brown ground. It is used for ornamental cabinetwork and banding. The striped figure is most pronounced, and it is heavy, hard, and has a rather coarse texture.

ZEFRAN. An acrylic staple fiber produced by the Dow Chemical Company. It is a light, bulky fiber, and it has a soft, woolly hand. Zefran is much like Acrilan and Orlon, and it is stronger and more stable than many acrylics, but it does present some dyeing problems.

ZIGGURAT. A feature of Assyrian and Babylonian architecture. A tower made up of a series of setbacks with ramps connecting one level to the next. Each stage was set back, and usually terraced. The stages were also differentiated by color (the exterior surface was often finished in colored glazed tiles). The lowest stage was the black platform for the underworld, the red was the earth, the blue was the sky, and the gold was the heavens.

ZIGZAG. A chevron pattern, a Norman motif.

ZIGZAG

ZOOPHORUS

ZOOPHORUS. A sculptured frieze that combines animals with human figures. Illustrated is the frieze of the Erechtheum in Athens, which was decorated in the Ionic order.

ZOPFSTIL

ZOPFSTIL. German for the mid-18th-century rococo style. Illustrated is a German rococo armchair.

ZUCCHI, ANTONIO PIETRO (1726–1795). A Venetian painter who did decorative paintings for interiors, as well as panels, plaques, and medallions for furniture designed by Adam. He was married to Angelica Kauffmann, who did similar work. See *Kauffmann, Angelica.*